MCTS 70-640 Cert Guide: Windows Server 2008 Active Directory, Configuring

Don Poulton

Pearson
800 East 96th Street
Indianapolis, Indiana 46240 USA

MCTS 70-640 Cert Guide: Windows Server 2008 Active Directory, Configuring

Copyright © 2011 by Pearson Education, Inc.

ISBN-13: 978-0-7897-4708-2

ISBN-10: 0-7897-4708-1

Library of Congress Cataloging-in-Publication Data:

Poulton, Don.

  MCTS 70-640 cert guide : Windows server 2008 Active directory, configuring / Don Poulton.

      p. cm.

  ISBN 978-0-7897-4708-2 (hardcover w/CD)

 1. Microsoft Windows server--Examinations--Study guides. 2. Operating systems (Computers)--Examinations--Study guides. 3. Directory services (Computer network technology)--Examinations--Study guides. 4. Local area networks (Computer networks)--Management--Examinations--Study guides. 5. Telecommunications engineers--Certification. 6. Electronic data processing personnel--Certification. I. Title. II. Title: Windows server 2008 Active directory, configuring.

  QA76.76.O63P6685 2011

  005.4'476--dc22

                         2010043593

Printed in the United States of America

Second Printing: February 2013

Bulk Sales

Que Publishing offers excellent discounts on this book when ordered in quantity for bulk purchases or special sales. For more information, please contact

U.S. Corporate and Government Sales

1-800-382-3419   corpsales@pearsontechgroup.com

For sales outside of the U.S., please contact

International Sales   international@pearson.com

Trademarks

All terms mentioned in this book that are known to be trademarks or service marks have been appropriately capitalized. Pearson IT Certification cannot attest to the accuracy of this information. Use of a term in this book should not be regarded as affecting the validity of any trademark or service mark.

Warning and Disclaimer

Associate Publisher
Dave Dusthimer

Acquisitions Editor
Betsy Brown

Development Editor
Box Twelve Communications, Inc.

Managing Editor
Sandra Schroeder

Project Editor
Mandie Frank

Copy Editor
Mike Henry

Indexer
Erika Millen

Proofreader
Megan Wade

Technical Editor
Chris Crayton

Publishing Coordinator
Vanessa Evans

Multimedia Developer
Dan Scherf

Designer
Gary Adair

Page Layout
Mark Shirar

Contents at a Glance

Table of Contents

v

About the Author

Don Poulton (A+, Network+, Security+, MCSA, MCSE) is an independent consultant who has been involved with computers since the days of 80-column punch cards. After a career of more than 20 years in environmental science, Don switched careers and trained as a Windows NT 4.0 MCSE. He has been involved in consulting with a couple of small training providers as a technical writer, during which time he wrote training and exam prep materials for Windows NT 4.0, Windows 2000, and Windows XP. Don has written or contributed to several titles, including *Security+ Lab Manual* (Que, 2004); *MCSA/MCSE 70-299 Exam Cram 2: Implementing and Administering Security in a Windows 2003 Network (Exam Cram 2)* (Que, 2004); *MCSE 70-294 Exam Prep: Planning, Implementing, and Maintaining a Microsoft Windows Server 2003 Active Directory Infrastructure* (Que, 2006); *MCTS 70-620 Exam Prep: Microsoft Windows Vista, Configuring* (Que, 2008); and *MCTS 70-680 Cert Guide: Microsoft Windows 7, Configuring* (Que, 2011).

In addition, he has worked on programming projects, both in his days as an environmental scientist and more recently with Visual Basic to update an older statistical package used for multivariate analysis of sediment contaminants.

When not working on computers, Don is an avid amateur photographer who has had his photos displayed in international competitions and published in magazines such as *Michigan Natural Resources Magazine* and *National Geographic Traveler*. Don also enjoys traveling and keeping fit.

Don lives in Burlington, Ontario, with his wife, Terry.

Dedication

I would like to dedicate this book to my wife Terry, who has stood by my side and supported me throughout the days spent writing this book. This project would not have been possible without her love and support.

Acknowledgments

I would like to thank all the staff at Pearson and in particular Betsy Brown for making this project possible. My sincere thanks goes out to Chris Crayton for his helpful technical suggestions, as well as Jeff Riley, development editor, and Mike Henry, copy editor, for their improvements to the manuscript.

—Don Poulton

About the Technical Reviewer

Christopher A. Crayton is an author, technical editor, technical consultant, security consultant, trainer, and SkillsUSA state-level technology competition judge. Formerly, he worked as a computer and networking instructor at Keiser College (2001 Teacher of the Year); as network administrator for Protocol, a global electronic customer relationship management (eCRM) company; and at Eastman Kodak Headquarters as a computer and network specialist. Chris has authored several print and online books, including The *A+ Exams Guide, Second Edition* (Cengage Learning, 2008); *Microsoft Windows Vista 70-620 Exam Guide Short Cut* (O'Reilly, 2007); *CompTIA A+ Essentials 220-601 Exam Guide Short Cut* (O'Reilly, 2007); *The A+ Exams Guide* (Charles River Media, 2008); *The A+ Certification and PC Repair Handbook* (Charles River Media, 2005); *The Security+ Exam Guide* (Charles River Media, 2003); and *A+ Adaptive Exams* (Charles River Media, 2002). He is also coauthor of the *How to Cheat at Securing Your Network* (Syngress, 2007). As an experienced technical editor, Chris has provided many technical edits/reviews for several major publishing companies, including Pearson Education, McGraw-Hill, Cengage Learning, Wiley, O'Reilly, Syngress, and Apress. He holds MCSE, A+, and Network+ certifications.

We Want to Hear from You!

As the reader of this book, *you* are our most important critic and commentator. We value your opinion and want to know what we're doing right, what we could do better, what areas you'd like to see us publish in, and any other words of wisdom you're willing to pass our way.

As an associate publisher for Pearson Publishing, I welcome your comments. You can email or write me directly to let me know what you did or didn't like about this book—as well as what we can do to make our books better.

Please note that I cannot help you with technical problems related to the topic of this book. We do have a User Services group, however, where I will forward specific technical questions related to the book.

When you write, please be sure to include this book's title and author as well as your name, email address, and phone number. I will carefully review your comments and share them with the author and editors who worked on the book.

Email: feedback@pearsonitcertification.com

Mail: Dave Dusthimer
         Associate Publisher
         Pearson Education
         800 East 96th Street
         Indianapolis, IN 46240 USA

Reader Services

Visit our website and register this book at www.pearsonITcertification.com/register for convenient access to any updates, downloads, or errata that might be available for this book.

Introduction

MCTS Windows Server 2008 Active Directory, Configuring Cert Guide (Exam 70-640) is designed for network administrators, network engineers, and consultants who are pursuing the Microsoft Certified Technology Specialist (MCTS) or Microsoft Certified IT Professional (MCITP) certifications for Windows Server 2008. This book covers the "TS: Microsoft Windows Server 2008 Active Directory, Configuring" exam (70-640), which earns you the Microsoft Certified Technology Specialist: Windows Server 2008 Active Directory, Configuration certification. The exam is designed to measure your skill and ability to implement, administer, and troubleshoot Active Directory running on Windows Server 2008. Microsoft not only tests you on your knowledge of Active Directory, but it has purposefully developed questions on the exam to force you to problem-solve in the same way that you would when presented with a real-life error. Passing this exam demonstrates your competency in administration.

This book covers all the objectives that Microsoft has established for exam 70-640. It doesn't offer end-to-end coverage of Active Directory in Windows Server 2008; rather, it helps you develop the specific core competencies that you need to master as an Active Directory administrator. You should be able to pass the exam by learning the material in this book, without taking a class.

Goals and Methods

The number-one goal of this book is a simple one: to help you get ready to take—and pass—Microsoft Certification Exam 70-640, "TS: Windows Server 2008 Active Directory, Configuring." You will find information within this book that will help ensure your success as you pursue this Microsoft exam and the Technology Specialist or IT Professional certification.

Because Microsoft certification exams stress problem-solving abilities and reasoning more than memorization of terms and facts, our goal is to help you master and understand the required objectives for the 70-640 exam.

To aid you in mastering and understanding the MCTS certification objectives, this book uses the following methods:

- **Opening topics list:** This defines the topics to be covered in the chapter; it also lists the corresponding 70-640 exam objectives.

- **Do I Know This Already Quizzes:** At the beginning of each chapter is a quiz. The quizzes, and answers/explanations (found in Appendix A), are meant to gauge your knowledge of the subjects. If the answers to the questions don't come readily to you, be sure to read the entire chapter.

- **Foundation Topics:** The heart of the chapter. Explains the topics from a hands-on and a theory-based standpoint. This includes in-depth descriptions, tables, and figures that are geared to build your knowledge so that you can pass the exam. The chapters are broken down into several topics each.

- **Key Topics:** The key topics indicate important figures, tables, and lists of information that you should know for the exam. They are interspersed throughout the chapter and are listed in table form at the end of the chapter.

- **Memory Tables:** These can be found on the DVD within Appendix C, "Memory Tables." Use them to help memorize important information.

- **Key Terms:** Key terms without definitions are listed at the end of each chapter. Write down the definition of each term and check your work against the complete key terms in the glossary.

How This Book Is Organized

Although this book could be read cover-to-cover, it is designed to be flexible and enable you to easily move between chapters and sections of chapters to cover just the material that you need more work with. If you do intend to read all the chapters, the order in the book is an excellent sequence to use.

Chapter 1, "Getting Started with Active Directory," is an introductory chapter that presents the concepts around which Active Directory is built. It serves as a reference to the material that follows and eases users who are new to Active Directory into the book. If you have worked with Active Directory in Windows 2000 or Windows Server 2003, you might want to start with Chapter 2; however, you should take a look at the overview presented here of new capabilities of Active Directory in Windows Server 2008 and its R2 update.

The core chapters, Chapters 2 through 17, cover the following topics:

- **Chapter 2, "Installing and Configuring DNS for Active Directory":** This chapter focuses on the concepts of Domain Name System (DNS) required for setting up an Active Directory domain. You learn about how to install DNS on your server and how to set up and configure DNS zones.

- **Chapter 3, "Installing Active Directory Domain Services":** This chapter shows you how to set up your first domain. It then continues to discuss creating additional domain controllers in this domain and child domain controllers. It also discusses the requirements that must be met when upgrading domains based on older Windows server versions to allow them to operate in Windows Server 2008 with complete functionality.

- **Chapter 4, "Configuring DNS Server Settings and Replication":** This chapter builds on Chapter 2 to delve into additional items that you must configure in server settings, zone transfers, and DNS replication.

- **Chapter 5, "Global Catalogs and Operations Masters":** Proper operation of global catalog servers and operations masters is vital to the day-to-day functioning of your domain and forest. This chapter focuses on the configuration and troubleshooting steps necessary with these specialized domain controllers.

- **Chapter 6, "Configuring Active Directory Sites and Replication":** Active Directory divides forests and domains on a geographical basis by using sites. To function properly, Active Directory depends on data replication among all its domain controllers. This chapter shows you how to set up sites and ensure that all directory objects are located in the site corresponding to their locations. It then continues with configuring replication, both on an intrasite and intersite basis.

- **Chapter 7, "Additional Active Directory Roles":** This chapter takes care of other Active Directory roles including Active Directory Lightweight Directory Services (AD LDS), Active Directory Federation Services (AD FS), and Active Directory Rights Management Service (AD RMS). AD LDS is designed to provide additional directory services where an additional domain and its domain controllers are not required. AD RMS enhances security in your domain by enabling the creation of rights-protected files and folders that can be accessed only by authorized users. AD FS provides a single sign-on capability for authenticating users to multiple web-based applications.

- **Chapter 8, "Read-Only Domain Controllers":** This chapter discusses how to set up a read-only domain controller (RODC) and configure its interaction with other (writable) domain controllers in your forest. An RODC is useful in a situation such as a branch office where physical security of the domain controller might be of concern.

- **Chapter 9, "Active Directory User and Group Accounts":** This chapter shows you how to create user and group accounts in Active Directory, including methods for bulk creation of large numbers of accounts. It introduces the various types and scopes of groups available in Active Directory and the recommended methods of nesting these groups to facilitate the provision of access to resources in your forest. It also looks at account properties, creation of organizational units (OUs), and delegation of control.

- **Chapter 10, "Trust Relationships in Active Directory":** By default, all domains in a forest trust each other. However, you might need to access objects located in another forest, and this chapter talks about methods you might use to provide and troubleshoot such access. Windows Server 2008 provides several types of trust relationships that can be used for meeting different requirements.

- **Chapter 11, "Creating and Applying Group Policy Objects":** Group Policy is at the heart and soul of resource management in Active Directory. This chapter shows you how to set up Group Policy objects and configure them to apply to users, groups, and OUs as required. The hierarchy of GPO application and the methods to modify this hierarchy are also discussed.

- **Chapter 12, "Group Policy Software Deployment":** This chapter shows you how to use Group Policy for deploying software to large numbers of users so that they have the applications they need to perform their jobs. You also learn how to upgrade software when new editions and features become available and how to remove software when it is no longer required by users.

- **Chapter 13, "Account Policies and Audit Policies":** This chapter expands the coverage of Group Policy to include policies that govern the safety and security of accounts in your domain and audit access to Active Directory objects and components so that you can meet the increasingly complex regulatory requirements.

- **Chapter 14, "Monitoring Active Directory":** This chapter focuses on the tools you can use to monitor the functionality of Active Directory. You also learn about the tools and methods used for monitoring Active Directory replication as well as the tools and techniques you can use to monitor and troubleshoot the application of Group Policy.

- **Chapter 15, "Maintaining Active Directory":** This chapter shows you how to back up, recover, restart, and troubleshoot Active Directory and its components.

You learn how to perform nonauthoritative and authoritative restore of Active Directory and how to use the new Windows Server 2008 R2 Active Directory Recycle Bin.

- **Chapter 16, "Installing and Configuring Certificate Services":** A system of certificates is vital to carrying out secure business, especially when an Internet presence is required. This chapter shows you how to set up a hierarchy of certificate servers within Active Directory and back up, restore, and archive your certificates and keys.

- **Chapter 17, "Managing Certificate Templates, Enrollments, and Certificate Revocation":** Certificates issued by your servers require management to ensure that users requiring certificates can obtain them, and that compromised certificates are revoked and cannot be used by unauthorized parties. This chapter looks at these topics and helps you to ensure the security of your certificate hierarchy.

In addition to the 17 main chapters, this book includes tools to help you verify that you are prepared to take the exam. The CD includes the glossary, practice test, and memory tables that you can work through to verify your knowledge of the subject matter.

Study and Exam Preparation Tips

It's a rush of adrenaline during the final day before an exam. If you've scheduled the exam on a workday, or following a workday, you will find yourself cursing the tasks you normally cheerfully perform because the back of your mind is telling you to read just a bit more, study another scenario, practice another skill so that you will be able to get this exam out of the way successfully.

The way that Microsoft has designed its tests lately does not help. I remember taking Microsoft exams many years ago and thoroughly understanding the term *paper certified*. Nowadays, you can't get through a Microsoft exam without knowing the material so well that when confronted with a problem, whether a scenario or real-life situation, you can handle the challenge. Instead of trying to show the world how many MCSEs are out there, Microsoft is trying to prove how difficult it is to achieve a certification, including the newly created MCTS and MCITP as well as the MCSE and MCSA, thereby making those who are certified more valuable to their organizations.

Learning Styles

To best understand the nature of preparation for the test, it is important to understand learning as a process. You are probably aware of how you best learn new material. You might find that outlining works best for you, or, as a visual learner, you might need to "see" things. Or, as a person who studies kinesthetically, the hands-on approach serves you best. Whether you need models or examples, or you just like exploring the interface, or whatever your learning style, solid test preparation works best when it takes place over time. Obviously, you shouldn't start studying for a certification exam the night before you take it; it is very important to understand that learning is a developmental process. Understanding learning as a process helps you focus on what you know and what you have yet to learn.

People study in a combination of different ways: by doing, by seeing, and by hearing and writing. This book's design fulfills all three of these study methods. For the kinesthetic, there are key topics scattered throughout each chapter. You will also discover step-by-step procedural instructions that walk you through the skills you need to master Active Directory in Windows Server 2008. The visual learner can find plenty of screen shots explaining the concepts described in the text. The auditory learner can reinforce skills by reading out loud and copying down key concepts and exam tips scattered throughout the book. You can also practice writing down the meaning of the key terms defined in each chapter, and in completing the memory tables for most chapters found on the accompanying DVD. While reading this book, you will realize that it stands the test of time. You will be able to turn to it over and over again.

Thinking about how you learn should help you recognize that learning takes place when you are able to match new information to old. You have some previous experience with computers and networking. Now you are preparing for this certification exam. Using this book, software, and supplementary materials will not just add incrementally to what you know; as you study, the organization of your knowledge actually restructures as you integrate new information into your existing knowledge base. This leads you to a more comprehensive understanding of the tasks and concepts outlined in the objectives and of computing in general. Again, this happens as a result of a repetitive process rather than a singular event. If you keep this model of learning in mind as you prepare for the exam, you will make better decisions concerning what to study and how much more studying you need to do.

Study Tips

There are many ways to approach studying, just as there are many different types of material to study. However, the tips that follow should work well for the type of material covered on Microsoft certification exams.

Study Strategies

Although individuals vary in the ways they learn information, some basic principles of learning apply to everyone. You should adopt some study strategies that take advantage of these principles. One of these principles is that learning can be broken into various depths. Recognition (of terms, for example) exemplifies a rather surface level of learning in which you rely on a prompt of some sort to elicit recall. Comprehension or understanding (of the concepts behind the terms, for example) represents a deeper level of learning than recognition. The ability to analyze a concept and apply your understanding of it in a new way represents further depth of learning.

Your learning strategy should enable you to know the material at a level or two deeper than mere recognition. This will help you perform well on the exams. You will know the material so thoroughly that you can go beyond the recognition-level types of questions commonly used in fact-based multiple-choice testing. You will be able to apply your knowledge to solve new problems.

Macro and Micro Study Strategies

One strategy that can lead to deep learning includes preparing an outline that covers all the objectives and subobjectives for the particular exam you are planning to take. You should delve a bit further into the material and include a level or two of detail beyond the stated objectives and subobjectives for the exam. Then you should expand the outline by coming up with a statement of definition or a summary for each point in the outline.

An outline provides two approaches to studying. First, you can study the outline by focusing on the organization of the material. You can work your way through the points and subpoints of your outline, with the goal of learning how they relate to one another. For example, you should be sure you understand how each of the main objective areas for Exam 70-640 is similar to and different from another. Then you should do the same thing with the subobjectives; you should be sure you know which subobjectives pertain to each objective area and how they relate to one another.

Next, you can work through the outline, focusing on learning the details. You should memorize and understand terms and their definitions, facts, rules and tactics, advantages and disadvantages, and so on. In this pass through the outline, you should attempt to learn detail rather than the big picture (the organizational information that you worked on in the first pass through the outline).

Research has shown that attempting to assimilate both types of information at the same time interferes with the overall learning process. If you separate your studying into these two approaches, you will perform better on the exam.

Active Study Strategies

The process of writing down and defining objectives, subobjectives, terms, facts, and definitions promotes a more active learning strategy than merely reading the material does. In human information-processing terms, writing forces you to engage in more active encoding of the information. Simply reading over the information leads to more passive processing. Using this study strategy, you should focus on writing down the items that are highlighted in the book—bulleted or numbered lists, key topics, notes, cautions, and review sections, for example.

You need to determine whether you can apply the information you have learned by attempting to create examples and scenarios on your own. You should think about how or where you could apply the concepts you are learning. Again, you should write down this information to process the facts and concepts in an active fashion.

Common-Sense Strategies

You should follow common-sense practices when studying: You should study when you are alert, reduce or eliminate distractions, and take breaks when you become fatigued.

Pretesting Yourself

Pretesting allows you to assess how well you are learning. One of the most important aspects of learning is what has been called *meta-learning*. Meta-learning has to do with realizing when you know something well or when you need to study some more. In other words, you recognize how well or how poorly you have learned the material you are studying.

For most people, this can be difficult to assess. Memory tables, practice questions, and practice tests are useful in that they reveal objectively what you have learned and what you have not learned. You should use this information to guide review and further studying. Developmental learning takes place as you cycle through studying, assessing how well you have learned, reviewing, and assessing again until you feel you are ready to take the exam.

You might have noticed the practice exam included in this book. You should use it as part of the learning process. The Exam Gear test-simulation software included on this book's CD-ROM also provides you with an excellent opportunity to assess your knowledge.

You should set a goal for your pretesting. A reasonable goal would be to score consistently in the 90% range.

Exam Prep Tips

After you have mastered the subject matter, the final preparatory step is to understand how the exam will be presented. Make no mistake: An MCTS exam challenges both your knowledge and your test-taking skills. Preparing for the 70-640 exam is a bit different from preparing for those old Microsoft exams. The following is a list of things that you should consider doing:

- **Combine your skill sets into solutions:** In the past, exams would test whether you knew to select the right letter of a multiple choice answer. Today, you need to know how to resolve a problem that may involve different aspects of the material covered. For example, on exam 70-640 you could be presented with a problem that requires you to understand how to configure Group Policy to apply to a specific set of users and not to other users, and to troubleshoot this policy if it is not properly applied. The skills themselves are simple. Being able to zero in on what caused the problem and then to resolve it for a specific situation is what you need to demonstrate. In fact, you should not only be able to select one answer, but also multiple parts of a total solution.

- **Delve into excruciating details:** The exam questions incorporate a great deal of information in the scenarios. Some of the information is ancillary: It will help you rule out possible issues, but not necessarily resolve the answer. Some of the information simply provides you with a greater picture, as you would have in real life. Some information is key to your solution. For example, you might be presented with a question that lists the components of an Active Directory domain such as the number of server and client computers, the organizational unit (OU) structure, and so on. When you delve further into the question, you realize that the OU structure is the problem. Other times, you will find that the OU structure simply eliminates one or more of the answers that you could select. If you don't pay attention to what you can eliminate, the answer can elude you completely. And other times, the hardware configuration simply lets you know that the hardware is adequate.

- **Microsoft likes to quiz exam takers on the latest modifications of its technology:** From time to time, Microsoft seeds new questions into its exam database and beta tests these questions on exam takers. During the beta period for each question, its answer is not taken into account in computing the final score. However, when Microsoft is satisfied with the question's performance, it becomes live and is scored appropriately. You can expect to see questions that test your knowledge of the latest changes in Active Directory technology, including the enhancements introduced in 2009 with Windows Server 2008 R2.

- **It's a GUI test:** Microsoft has expanded its testing criteria into interface recognition. You should be able to recognize each dialog box, properties sheet, options, and defaults. You will be tested on how to perform typical configuration actions in Active Directory. In fact, Microsoft has begun to include performance-based questions on its exams that instruct you to perform a given task and presents you with a live version of some Active Directory tool. You must complete the required actions and no others; otherwise, your response will be scored as incorrect.

■ **Practice with a time limit:** The tests have always been time restricted, but it takes more time to read and understand the scenarios now and time is a whole lot tighter. To get used to the time limits, test yourself with a timer. Know how long it takes you to read scenarios and select answers.

Microsoft 70-640 Exam Topics

Table I-1 lists the exam topics for the Microsoft 70-640 exam. This table also lists the book parts in which each exam topic is covered.

Table I-1   Microsoft 70-640 Exam Topics

Chapter	Topics	70-640 Exam Objectives Covered
1	The Foundation of Active Directory The Building Blocks of Active Directory New Features of Active Directory in Windows Server 2008	(n/a)
2	The Hierarchical Nature of DNS Installing DNS on Windows Server 2008 Configuring DNS Zones	Configuring Domain Name System (DNS) for Active Directory ■ Configure Zones
3	Planning the Active Directory Namespace Creating Forests and Domains Upgrading Older Versions of Active Directory Additional Forest and Domain Configuration Tasks	Configuring the Active Directory Infrastructure ■ Configure a forest or a domain
4	Configuring DNS Server Settings Configuring Zone Transfers and Replication	Configuring Domain Name System (DNS) for Active Directory ■ Configure DNS Server Settings ■ Configure DNS Zone Transfers and Replication

Table I-1   Microsoft 70-640 Exam Topics

Chapter	Topics	70-640 Exam Objectives Covered
5	Configuring Global Catalog Servers Configuring Operations Masters	Configuring the Active Directory Infrastructure ■ Configure the global catalog ■ Configure operations masters
6	The Need for Active Directory Sites Configuring Sites and Subnets Site Links, Site Link Bridges, and Bridgehead Servers Configuring Active Directory Replication	Configuring the Active Directory Infrastructure ■ Configure sites ■ Configure Active Directory replication
7	New Server Roles and Features Active Directory Lightweight Directory Services (AD LDS) Active Directory Rights Management Services (AD RMS) Active Directory Federation Services (AD FS) Windows Server 2008 R2 Virtualization	Configuring Additional Active Directory Server Roles ■ Configure Active Directory Lightweight Directory Services (AD LDS) ■ Configure Active Directory Rights Management Service (AD RMS) ■ Configure Active Directory Federation Services (AD FS)
8	Installing a Read-Only Domain Controller Managing a Read-Only Domain Controller	Configuring Additional Active Directory Server Roles ■ Configure the read-only domain controller (RODC)
9	Creating User and Group Accounts Managing and Maintaining Accounts	Creating and Maintaining Active Directory Objects ■ Automate creation of Active Directory accounts ■ Maintain Active Directory accounts
10	Types of Trust Relationships Creating and Configuring Trust Relationships Managing Trust Relationships	Configuring the Active Directory Infrastructure ■ Configure trusts

Table I-1   Microsoft 70-640 Exam Topics

Chapter	Topics	70-640 Exam Objectives Covered
11	Overview of Group Policy Creating and Applying GPOs Configuring GPO Templates	Creating and Maintaining Active Directory Objects ■ Create and apply Group Policy objects (GPOs) ■ Configure GPO templates
12	Types of Software Deployment Deploying Software Using Group Policy Upgrading Software Removal of Software	Creating and Maintaining Active Directory Objects ■ Configure software deployment GPOs
13	Use of Group Policy to Configure Security Auditing of Active Directory Services	Creating and Maintaining Active Directory Objects ■ Configure account policies ■ Configure audit policy by using GPOs
14	Tools Used to Monitor Active Directory Monitoring and Troubleshooting Active Directory Replication Troubleshooting the Application of Group Policy Objects	Maintaining the Active Directory Environment ■ Monitor Active Directory
15	Backing Up and Recovering Active Directory Offline Maintenance of Active Directory	Maintaining the Active Directory Environment ■ Configure backup and recovery ■ Perform offline maintenance
16	What's New with Certificate Services in Windows Server 2008? Installing Active Directory Certificate Services Configuring Certificate Authority Server Settings	Configuring Active Directory Certificate Services ■ Install Active Directory Certificate Services ■ Configure CA server settings

Table I-1   Microsoft 70-640 Exam Topics

Chapter	Topics	70-640 Exam Objectives Covered
17	Managing Certificate Templates Managing Certificate Enrollments Managing Certificate Revocation	Configuring Active Directory Certificate Services ■ Manage certificate templates ■ Manage enrollments ■ Manage certificate revocation

This chapter covers the following subjects:

- **The Foundation of Active Directory:** This section describes the X.500 and Lightweight Directory Access Protocol (LDAP) protocols, which are the foundations used by Microsoft when it first designed Active Directory.

- **The Building Blocks of Active Directory:** This section describes the components that Microsoft took from X.500 and LDAP to build the hierarchical structure that is Active Directory.

- **The Logical Components of Active Directory:** This section describes the logical building blocks that Microsoft assembled in creating the structure of Active Directory.

- **The New Features of Active Directory in Windows Server 2008:** This section presents a brief overview of new features added by Microsoft when they created Windows Server 2008 and its new enhancement, Release 2 (R2).

CHAPTER 1

Getting Started with Active Directory

Beginning with Windows 2000, Microsoft completely revolutionized its concept of Windows domains. Gone was the limited size and flat namespace of Windows NT domains, and in its place was the hierarchical Active Directory domain structure built on the concepts of X.500 and Lightweight Directory Access Protocol (LDAP). Active Directory has matured since its beginnings with Windows Server 2003 and now includes Windows Server 2008's new features, improved functionality, and ease of configuration and management. Those of you who have worked with Active Directory in Windows 2000 or Windows Server 2003 will be familiar with much of the contents of this chapter. You might want to skip through to the section that describes what is new with Active Directory in Windows Server 2008, toward the end of this chapter. For those of you who are new to server and network management, or those who have worked with only Windows NT networks, this book begins with a brief introduction to the concepts that Microsoft used to put Active Directory together.

The Foundation of Active Directory

Before studying the structure of Active Directory itself, we will take a little time to introduce the concepts of the X.500 and Lightweight Directory Access Protocol (LDAP) protocols because these are central to the understanding of Active Directory and its structure.

X.500

X.500 was originally developed to assist users on a network to locate users elsewhere for sending email messages. It used an inverted tree concept to identify and describe all objects contained in a hierarchical database. First appearing in 1988, it relied on an inverted tree hierarchical structure in which countries formed the top level (next to the root) and organizations and their organizational roots formed branches beneath these roots. It was also used to provide information on applications that need to access resources elsewhere on the network, or management systems that need to know the name and location of objects on the network. The complete hierarchical X.500 system was known as the *directory*.

Three types of information were used by X.500 to locate resources:

- Name services located specific names.

- Electronic address books identified addresses on the network.

- Directory services of centrally managed electronic address books that helped users search across networks.

The complete directory database, called the Directory Information Base (DIB), provides a total information-locating resource. Entries in the database are known as objects. These include items such as user accounts, files and folders, and resources such as printers.

The problem with X.500 was that it proved to be more complex than what was needed by most organizations. As originally created, it was also much too open for the entire world to see. In addition, it was expensive and, in its original implementation, was slower than other resource-locating methods.

LDAP

LDAP is a protocol originally designed by the Internet Engineering Task Force (IETF) to work as a front-end client service to X.500-compatible directory services. Alternatively, it can function as a directory service on its own. It is a subset of X.500 that operates on TCP/IP networks and uses a lower level of system resources compared to X.500.

LDAP is used as an Internet directory standard that is capable of providing open access to directory services over the Internet or corporate intranet. Using a text-based query system, it enables users to quickly and easily query directories containing information such as usernames, email addresses, telephone numbers, and other user attributes. It has gone through several versions that are defined in Requests for Comments (RFCs) for use as Internet standards. Active Directory supports versions 2 and 3 of LDAP. The most recent implementations of LDAP go beyond the X.500 standards in providing a solution needed to provide a global directory service. Included are such features as the support for extended character sets as used by various global languages and an easier referral mechanism to hand queries from one server to another. There is also an extension mechanism that will facilitate future development of the LDAP standard.

LDAP uses the inverted tree concept originated by X.500 to identify and describe all objects contained in its database. Entries within LDAP's inverted tree can include containers that hold other objects and leaf objects that represent entities such as people, computers, printers, and so on. Introduced with X.500 and further refined by LDAP is a series of definitions that have carried over into the Active Directory naming scheme. The hierarchical naming scheme is illustrated in Figure 1-1 and is explained in the next section.

Figure 1-1 The LDAP hierarchical naming scheme.

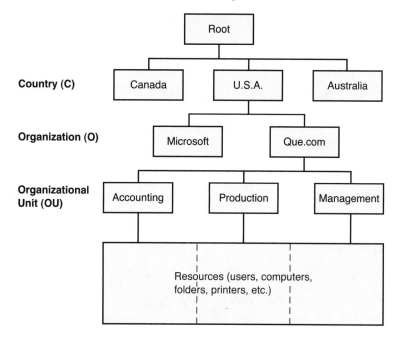

Naming Standards of X.500 and LDAP

Originating with X.500 and expanded on by LDAP is a series of naming standards that define the path to any object that has been defined in the directory. Because Active Directory uses LDAP as the protocol of choice for accessing objects in the directory, these naming paths and their components are important items that you should know to fully understand the capabilities of Active Directory. The naming paths include the distinguished names and relative distinguished names. Additional identifiers that you should be familiar with include the User Principal Names (UPNs) and Globally Unique Identifiers (GUIDs).

Distinguished Names

Each object in the LDAP inverted tree is uniquely identified by a distinguished name (DN) that defines the complete path from the top of the tree to the object.

The concept of distinguished names, which originated in the X.500 specifications, is a global one that was laid out with specific goals in mind:

- To provide an unambiguous representation of the name of any resource
- To provide a readily understood format for the majority of names
- To achieve an attractive representation of information within several different layouts
- To clearly represent the contents of the object being defined

To achieve these goals, a series of X.500-based delimiters was developed with standard abbreviation names, some of which are seen in Figure 1-1. The complete specification of distinguished names, including its complete syntax and full list of delimiters, is given in RFC 1779. The most common delimiters are as follows:

- CN = Common Name
- OU = Organizational Unit
- DC = Domain Component
- O = Organization Name
- C = Country Name

For any given object, the DN is a unique and unambiguous identification of the object and its location within the directory structure. In other words, two different objects can never have exactly the same DN. To specify a DN, include the name of the object itself, followed by the containers and parent containers holding the name in order. Note that a distinguished name may contain more than one instance of a given delimiter. The following is an example of a distinguished name:

```
CN=Tim Brown,OU=Inventory,DC=Que,DC=com.
```

NOTE   Active Directory snap-in tools generally do not display the DN as shown in the previous paragraph. This is shown here to illustrate how LDAP recognizes the components of the DN. However, it is helpful to know the concept of the distinguished name and how objects fit together into the Active Directory hierarchy. You will see more of how this fits together as you progress through this training guide; for example, when you need to restore Active Directory objects.

Relative Distinguished Names

The relative distinguished name (RDN) is the most granular part of the distinguished name that identifies a specific attribute of the object itself. For example, in the distinguished name given previously, the RDN is the first part: CN = Tim Brown. Within any given parent container, no two objects can have the same

RDN. There can, however, be two objects within different containers that have the same RDN.

An analogy could be the fact that more than one city with the same name can exist, as long as the cities are located in different states, such as Springfield, Illinois, and Springfield, Massachusetts. The DNs for these cities could be as follows:

```
CN=Springfield,OU=IL,C=US
```

and

```
CN=Springfield,OU=MA,C=US
```

The CN in these examples defines the exact city as opposed to a different city such as Chicago or Boston; therefore, the CN is also the RDN here.

User Principal Names

In addition to the DN and RDN described previously, Active Directory uses the concept of a UPN, which is introduced here because it is intimately related to these other names. The UPN is a shortcut name for the user that can be the same as a logon name or email address. For example, referring to the DN described previously, the UPN could be TimB@inventory.que.com.

Globally Unique Identifiers

Every object stored in Active Directory also has a unique identifier called the GUID, which is a 128-bit hexadecimal number assigned when the object is created in Active Directory. The GUID is stored in an attribute called `objectGUID`, which exists for every object in Active Directory. Unlike the DN or RDN, this identifier never changes even if you move or rename the object. For example, an employee leaves the company and is replaced. You want the new employee to have the same rights and privileges as the old one, so you rename the user account; this account retains the GUID of the old account. However, if you were to delete an object and then later re-create another object with the same DN, the GUID would not be the same; this is the reason that if you have deleted an object like a user or group account and then must re-create it, you must re-create all properties and attributes associated with the object.

Security Identifiers

The security identifier (SID) is a value that uniquely identifies a security principal such as a user, group, service, or computer account within the Active Directory forest. When created, every account is issued a SID. These are used to identify security principals in Windows Server 2008 for access control purposes. No two objects in the forest may have the same SID. A SID can change under certain circumstances, such as if a user is moved from one domain to another. Like the GUID, if you delete an object and later re-create an object with the same name, the SID would not be the same.

Windows Server 2008 uses the SID, rather than the GUID, in determining object access, for reasons of backward compatibility. Windows NT 4.0 used the SID for this purpose, and these SIDs are maintained when a Windows NT domain is upgraded to Active Directory.

> **NOTE** It is not possible to upgrade a Windows NT domain to Windows Server 2008. If you are still operating such an old domain, you must upgrade to either Windows 2000 or Windows Server 2003 first. You can then upgrade to Windows Server 2008. Upgrading of older Active Directory domains is discussed in Appendix B, "Installing Windows Server 2008 R2."

Active Directory Canonical Names

This is a version of the DN that Active Directory displays. The canonical name lists the RDNs from the root downward (that is, in reverse sequence to the DN); it also does not use the RFC 1779 naming attribute descriptors. However, it does use the DNS domain name. For the DN given previously, the Active Directory canonical name would be as follows:

```
Que.com/incentory/TimB
```

The Building Blocks of Active Directory

Active Directory can support an almost unlimited scope of functions and capabilities in an enterprise network, from small-scale operations to a global-scale multi-domain enterprise. Microsoft took the concepts of X.500 and LDAP, as already discussed, and molded them with a series of new components to come up with Active Directory's structure. To this end, Active Directory embraces the following concepts:

- Namespace
- Object
- Container
- Schema
- Global Catalog
- Partition

Each of these concepts is briefly discussed in the following sections.

Namespaces

The concept of a *namespace* originated with early incarnations of the Internet. This term refers to a bounded area within which a name is resolved or translated into information that is encompassed by the name. For an analogy, you can think of a telephone directory as a type of namespace in which names are resolved to phone numbers; its area is bounded within the city, county, or other geographic area that is served by the directory. An example in the computer world is that of a hostname that represents an IP address. Microsoft took this concept and expanded on it until it encompassed any type of information that anyone might have a need to locate. Further, Microsoft made this concept dynamic so that when items were added, moved, or removed, the directory would reflect these actions. The result was Active Directory.

Namespaces can be either *flat* or *hierarchical*. Flat namespaces have only one level at which they store information, such as the NetBIOS naming concepts used in Windows NT 4. Hierarchical namespaces, as the name suggests, use several levels of name definition, such as those found in an Internet name such as `www.sales.company.com`. Here, `com` represents the top level, `company` represents a second-level domain, `sales` is a subdomain, and `www` is a web server name. As you are undoubtedly aware, DNS uses this type of namespace. The DNS naming scheme is used to create the structure of the Active Directory namespace, permitting interoperability with Internet technologies; therefore, the concept of namespaces is central to Active Directory. By integrating this concept with the system's directory services, Active Directory facilitates the management of multiple namespaces that are often found in the heterogeneous software and hardware environments of corporate networks.

The two types of namespaces are contiguous and disjointed. They are defined as follows:

- **Contiguous:** The name of child objects in the hierarchy contains the name of the parent object; for example, the relationship between domains within the same tree.

- **Disjointed:** The name of a child object in the hierarchy does not contain the name of the parent object; for example, the relationship between different trees in the same forest.

Objects

An *object* is any specific item that can be cataloged in Active Directory. Examples of objects include users, computers, printers, folders, and files. These items are classified by a distinct set of characteristics, known as *attributes*. For example, a user can be characterized by the username, full name, telephone number, email address, and so on. Note that, in general, objects in the same container have the same types of attributes but are characterized by different values of these attributes. The Active Directory schema defines the extent of attributes that can be specified for any object.

The Active Directory service, in turn, classifies objects into *classes*. These classes are logical groupings of similar objects, such as users. Each class is a series of attributes that define the characteristics of the object.

Containers

A *container* is an object designed to hold other objects within the directory. A folder could be considered as a container because it holds files and subfolders that are located beneath it. Like other objects, containers have their own attributes. Forests, trees, domains, and OUs are all different types of containers because they all are designed to contain other objects.

Schemas

The *schema* is a set of rules that define the classes of objects and their attributes that can be created in Active Directory. It defines what attributes can be held by objects of various types, which of the various classes can exist, and what object class can be a parent of the current object class. For example, the User class can contain user account objects and possess attributes such as password, group membership, home folder, and so on.

You can mark attributes as indexed, which means that instances of the attribute are added to a searchable index and are more easily located by a user searching by the container in which the attributes are located. This feature improves search time but increases the size (and replication time) of the Active Directory database.

When you first install Active Directory on a server, a default schema is created, containing definitions of commonly used objects and properties such as users, computers, and groups. This default schema also contains definitions of objects and properties needed for the functioning of Active Directory.

The Active Directory: schema is extensible; that is, you can define new types and attributes of directory objects, as well as new attributes for existing objects. In doing so, you can adapt the schema to a given type of business; for example, a wholesaler might want to add a warehouse object to the directory, including information specific to that business. Additions to the schema are implemented automatically and stored within the Active Directory database. Applications can be built to extend the schema and can use such extensions immediately.

> **WARNING**   Schema modification—As discussed in Chapter 5, "Global Catalogs and Operations Masters," modifying the schema is a serious business. Improper modifications to the schema can harm or disable the domain controllers or even the entire network. For this reason, Microsoft has included a group called Schema Admins. Only members of this group have the right to modify the schema.

Global Catalogs

The *global catalog* is a central information database that can hold data describing objects throughout the Active Directory forest namespace. Active Directory builds up the global catalog by replicating information between all domain controllers in the forest. In this way, a comprehensive and complete database of all available objects is automatically built up. To extend the telephone directory analogy mentioned earlier in the chapter, you can think of the global catalog as a *Yellow Pages* directory that facilitates your locating a specific type of resource, such as a color printer on the seventeenth floor of your building.

As well as providing a physical location that contains a subset of all information in each domain's Active Directory database, the global catalog is a service that permits the resolution of many common queries that originate from anywhere in the forest. It holds and organizes the common attributes used in search operations, such as usernames and group names, filenames, and so on. All information pertaining to universal groups, including their membership, is found here. Usernames are stored in the UPN format; in doing so, a user can log on to any computer in the forest by employing the UPN.

By default, Active Directory stores the global catalog on the first domain controller in a new forest. It is possible to either move or copy the global catalog to another domain controller.

Partitions

Active Directory is divided into several *partitions*—not to be confused with disk partitions—that allow the enterprise-level network to be scaled to enormous proportions while remaining manageable. A schema partition and a configuration partition are stored on all domain controllers within an Active Directory forest, and application and domain partitions are common to domain controllers within a domain. The roles of these partitions are as follows:

- **Domain partition:** This partition contains information about all objects such as users, groups, computers, and OUs in a domain. It is replicated to all domain controllers within the domain, and a subset of this information is replicated to global catalog servers in the forest.

- **Schema partition:** This partition contains definitions of all objects and their attributes. Rules for creating and working with them are also located here. This partition is replicated to all domain controllers in the forest.

- **Configuration partition:** This partition contains information about the structure of Active Directory in the forest, including domains, sites, and services. It is also replicated to all domain controllers in the forest.

- **Application partition:** First introduced in Windows Server 2003, this partition contains application-specific data that needs to be replicated throughout specified portions of the forest. It can be replicated to a specific domain controller or to any set of domain controllers anywhere in the forest. In this way, it differs from the domain partition in which Active Directory replicates data to all domain controllers in that domain. It also contains DNS information for Active Directory–integrated DNS zones.

Logical Components of Active Directory

In creating the hierarchical database structure of Active Directory, Microsoft facilitated locating resources such as folders and printers by name rather than by physical location. These logical building blocks include domains, trees, forests, and OUs. The physical location of objects within Active Directory is represented by including all objects in a given location in its own site.

Because a domain is the basic unit on which Active Directory is built, the domain is introduced first; followed by trees and forests (in which domains are located); and then OUs, which are containers located within a domain.

Domains

Similar to the case in Windows NT, the domain represents the core unit of the network structure. As in Windows NT, the domain is a logical grouping of computers that shares a common directory database and security. However, whereas in Windows NT, each domain was a unit unto itself with no default trust relationship with other domains, in Active Directory, you can have a series of domains organized into larger units called *trees* and *forests*, with inherent trust relationships already built into them. Individuals can be designated with administrative powers over a single domain or across an entire forest, and you can even configure trust relationships to external forests. Furthermore, Active Directory domains can hold millions of objects, as opposed to the Windows NT domain structure, which was limited to approximately 40,000 objects.

As in previous versions of Active Directory, the Active Directory database file (`ntds.dit`) defines the domain. Each domain has its own `ntds.dit` file, which is stored on (and replicated among) all domain controllers by a process called *multimaster replication*. The domain controllers manage the configuration of domain security and store the directory services database. This arrangement permits central administration of domain account privileges, security, and network resources. Networked devices and users belonging to a domain validate with a domain controller at startup. All computers that refer to a specific set of domain controllers make up the domain. In addition, group accounts such as global groups and domain local groups are defined on a domain-wide basis. Some benefits of using multiple domains are as follows:

- Domains can be considered as security boundaries. In other words, domain administrators can define access control lists (ACLs) that determine users' access rights and permissions to objects within the domain at the domain level. Also, each administrator has the authority to set security policy only within his domain.

- You can specify how resources in each domain can be accessed using Group Policy, which can be configured on a domain-wide basis. Group Policies have full control over all objects in the domain but do not have any authority over objects in other domains.

- You can configure domains along geographical lines; for example, a multi-national company might organize its network with a domain for every country. In this manner, the company can deal with legal and other country-specific issues.

- You can configure domains along business lines, such as a parent company with a series of subsidiaries. This configuration simplifies reorganization should a subsidiary be sold or a new one acquired.

Trees

A *tree* is a group of domains that shares a contiguous namespace. In other words, a tree consists of a parent domain plus one or more sets of child domains whose name reflects that of a parent. For example, a parent domain named `examcram.com` can include child domains with names such as `products.examcram.com`, `sales.examcram.com`, and `manufacturing.examcram.com`. Furthermore, the tree structure can contain grandchild domains such as `america.sales.examcram.com` or `europe.sales.examcram.com`, and so on, as shown in Figure 1-2. A domain called `que.com` would not belong to the same tree. Following the inverted tree concept originated by X.500, the tree is structured with the parent domain at the top and child domains beneath it.

All domains in a tree are linked with two-way, transitive trust relationships; in other words, accounts in any one domain can access resources in another domain and vice versa. See Chapter 10, "Trust Relationships in Active Directory," for more information on trust relationships.

Forests

A *forest* consists of a group of domain trees that do not share a contiguous name-space. For example, you can have two trees with parent domains named `examcram.com` and `que.com`, as shown in Figure 1-3. Each tree can contain its own child domains within its namespace. Again, two-way, transitive trust relationships exist between domains in the trees of a single forest. When you first create a new Active Directory structure, the first domain created is the forest root domain. Re-calling the definition of namespace as a bounded area in which the directory can resolve names, the forest itself is also a namespace; in this case, it is a disjointed namespace. In other words, the two portions of the namespace do not share a name in common. By default, two-way, transitive trust relationships exist between the parent domains in each tree throughout the forest. Again, these trust relation-ships do not need to be explicitly configured. In addition, all domains in the forest share a common schema, configuration, and global catalog.

In a forest, one domain has to be the forest root domain. The forest root domain is always the first domain created when a new forest is created.

Figure 1-2 A tree consists of a group of domains that share a contiguous namespace, with the parent domain at the top.

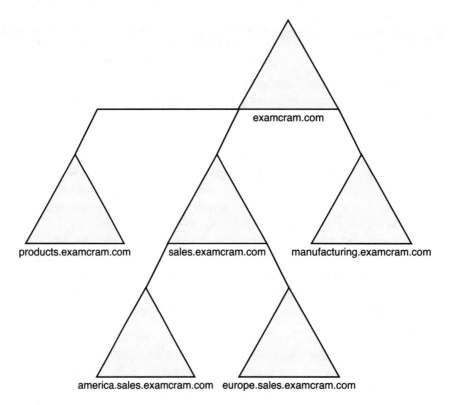

Figure 1-3 A forest is a group of trees that form a disjointed namespace.

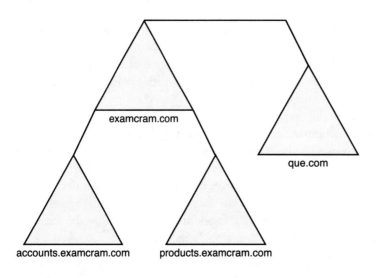

Organizational Units

An *organizational unit (OU)* is a logical subgroup within a domain. It is convenient for locating resources used by a single workgroup, section, or department in a company and applying policies that apply to only these resources (see Figure 1-4). You can create a hierarchy of OUs and child OUs organized in much the same way as that of a hierarchy of folders, subfolders, and sub-subfolders on a disk. You can also delegate control of administrative activities to users within a single OU, such as creating and working with user accounts, groups, printers, and so on. Further, you can control users and computers within an OU by means of Group Policy; this is the smallest unit to which you can deploy Group Policy.

Figure 1-4 You can create hierarchies of OUs within your domain structure.

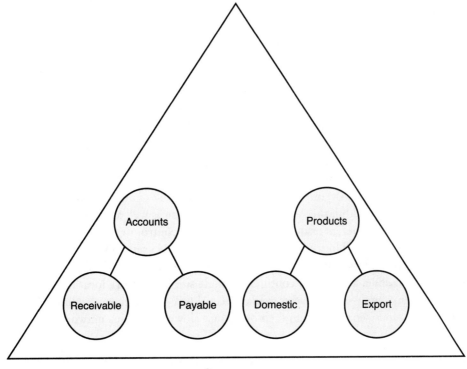

Company.com

Each OU can contain any type of noncontainer object such as users, groups, and computers. In addition, it can contain additional OUs within it. Therefore, you can build an OU hierarchy to any depth within the domain. You can also modify or remove a series of OUs. Within each OU, you can perform actions such as creating, moving, deleting, or modifying objects within the OU, as easily as the OUs themselves.

Some uses of OUs are as follows:

- Apply different sets of policies to users with different requirements. For example, you might want to have a different desktop applied to accountants as compared to engineers. You can do this by specifying Group Policy Objects (GPOs) that apply to the respective OUs.

- Delegate control of certain user and/or computer accounts to a subset of assistant administrators so that they can be responsible for accounts located within only a portion of the company and can perform activities such as resetting passwords and so on.

- Separate various types of objects. For example, you can use one OU to hold just client computers, another for member servers, another for domain controllers, and yet another for user and group accounts. In fact, Microsoft creates a default Domain Controllers OU when you install Active Directory.

Sites

By contrast to the logical grouping of Active Directory into forests, trees, domains, and OUs, Microsoft includes the concept of sites to group together resources within a forest according to their physical location and/or subnet. A *site* is a set of one or more IP subnets, which are connected by a high-speed, always available local area network (LAN) link. Figure 1-5 shows an example with two sites, one located in Chicago and the other in New York. A site can contain objects from more than one tree or domain within a single forest, and individual trees and domains can encompass more than one site. The use of sites enables you to control the replication of data within the Active Directory database as well as to apply policies to all users and computers or delegate administrative control to these objects within a single physical location. In addition, sites enable users to be authenticated by domain controllers in the same physical location rather than a distant location as often as possible. You should configure a single site for all work locations connected within a high-speed, always available LAN link and designate additional sites for locations separated from each other by a slower wide area network (WAN) link.

Using sites permits you to configure Active Directory replication to take advantage of the high-speed connection. It also enables users to connect to a domain controller using a reliable, high-speed connection.

NOTE   The site topology of a network is different from the domain topology. Consequently, you can have one domain across more than one site, and you can have one site that contains multiple domains. You can even have multiple domains, each with portions thereof, on the same multiple sites.

Figure 1-5 A site is a grouping of resources in one physical location and is distinct from any domain grouping.

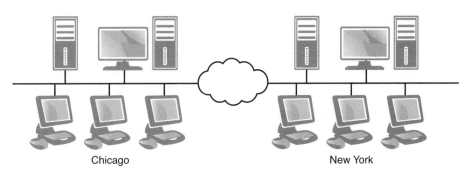

Chicago   New York

Domain Controllers

Any server on which you have installed Active Directory is a *domain controller*. These servers authenticate all users logging on to the domain in which they are located, and they also serve as centers from which you can administer Active Directory in Windows Server 2008. A domain controller stores a complete copy of all objects contained within the domain, plus the schema and configuration information relevant to the forest in which the domain is located. Unlike Windows NT, there are no primary or backup domain controllers. Similar to Windows 2000 and Windows Server 2003, all domain controllers hold a master, editable copy of the Active Directory database.

Every domain must have at least one DC. A domain may have more than one DC; having more than one DC provides the following benefits:

- **Fault tolerance:** If one domain controller goes down, another one is available to authenticate logon requests and locate resources through the directory.

- **Load balancing:** All domain controllers within a site participate equally in domain activities, thus spreading out the load over several servers. This configuration optimizes the speed at which requests are serviced.

Global Catalog Servers

The *global catalog* is a subset of domain information created for enabling domain controllers in other domains in the same forest to locate resources in any domain. By default, the first domain controller installed in a new domain becomes a global catalog server. You can also designate additional domain controllers in the domain as global catalog servers. Doing so spreads out the task of locating resources between servers, thus facilitating response to user queries.

The global catalog server performs the following directory roles:

- **Locates objects within the forest:** When a user searches for objects such as people, folders, or printers, the global catalog enables her to locate objects in other domains within the forest. Active Directory automatically directs any search for the entire directory to the global catalog server.

■ **Authenticates users by their UPNs:** When a user logs on to a domain other than his home domain using the UPN (for example, user1@accounts.examcram.com logging on to the products.examcram.com domain), the domain controller in the products.examcram.com domain contacts the global catalog server to obtain authentication information for this user.

■ **Provides universal group membership information:** A universal group can include members from any domain in the forest, and its membership information, including permissions for resources assigned to it, is stored at the global catalog server. It supplies this information to a DC when a user who belongs to a universal group logs on. First introduced in Windows Server 2003, a DC can then cache this information to facilitate future logons by the same user.

Operations Masters

Microsoft designed Active Directory in such a fashion that you can perform most configuration activities from any domain controller. However, certain functions within the directory are restricted to specific domain controllers, which are known as *flexible single-master operations (FSMO) servers*, or simply as *operations masters*. These functions include the following:

■ **Schema master:** Holds the only writable copy of the Active Directory schema. This is a configuration database that describes all available object and function types in the Active Directory forest. Only one domain controller in the forest holds this role.

■ **Domain naming master:** Ensures that any newly created domains are uniquely identified by names that adhere to the proper naming conventions for new trees or child domains in existing trees. Only one domain controller in the forest holds this role.

■ **PDC emulator:** Serves as a primary domain controller (PDC) for Windows NT 4.0 client computers authenticating to the domain and processes any changes to user properties on these clients, such as password changes. This server also acts as a time synchronization master to synchronize the time on the remaining domain controllers in the domain. One domain controller in each domain holds this role.

■ **Infrastructure master:** Updates references in its domain from objects such as domain group memberships, to objects in other domains. This server processes any changes in objects in the forest received from global catalog servers and replicates these changes to other domain controllers in its domain. One domain controller in each domain holds this role.

- **RID master:** Assigns SIDs to objects created in its domain. A SID consists of a domain identifier common to all objects in its domain and a relative identifier (RID) that is unique to each object. This server ensures that no two objects have the same RID and hands out pools of RIDs to every domain controller in its domain. One domain controller in each domain holds this role.

New Features of Active Directory in Windows Server 2008

As with each previous version of Windows Server, Microsoft has introduced many new components that improve the functionality and manageability of Active Directory and of Windows Server 2008 as a whole. This section briefly summarizes these components, most of which you will learn about later in this book:

- **Server roles and features:** Microsoft has organized the capabilities of a computer into various roles and features. Simply put, a *role* is a specific function that a server can perform on the network, including file services, terminal services, and certificate services. Active Directory Domain Services (AD DS) is the server role that encompasses all domain control functions. A *feature* is an optional component that adds a specific function such as the .NET Framework 3.0, BitLocker Drive Encryption, Network Load Balancing, and so on. Certain roles require that specific features be installed, and these are automatically installed when you add this role. You can add roles and features from the Initial Configuration Tasks window, Server Manager, or the command line. These are discussed later in this chapter.

- **Read-only domain controller:** A *read-only domain controller (RODC)* is a domain controller that contains a read-only copy of the directory database. It can perform all client-based actions such as authenticating users and distributing group policies to clients, but administrators cannot make changes to the database directly from the RODC. It is particularly useful for branch office deployment where security might not be as high as in the central office and no administrative personnel are present for day-to-day operations.

- **Server Core:** A *Server Core* is a stripped-down version of Windows Server 2008 that does not contain any GUI, taskbar, or Start menu. After logging on, you are presented with a command prompt window from which you perform all administrative actions. A Server Core computer uses less hardware and memory resources than a normal server but is able to perform most (but not all) of the roles that a normal server performs. Furthermore, a Server Core computer is more secure because it presents a smaller attack footprint than a normal server.

- **Restartable Active Directory Domain Services:** You can now perform many actions, such as offline defragmentation of the database, simply by stopping Active Directory. This reduces the number of instances in which you must restart the server in Directory Services Restore Mode and thereby reduces the length of time the domain controller is unavailable to serve requests from client computers.

- **Active Directory Certificate Services (AD CS):** Certificate Services has been enhanced considerably from Windows Server 2003. For example, you can enroll network devices such as routers for certificates, you can use new certificate templates that support new cryptographic algorithms, you can designate several limited roles for delegating administrative tasks to different individuals, and you can use the online responder service as an alternative to traditional certificate revocation lists.

- **Active Directory Lightweight Domain Services (AD LDS):** Microsoft has enhanced and modified the previous Active Directory Application Mode (ADAM) feature first introduced in Windows Server 2003 Release 2 (R2).

- **Active Directory Rights Management Service (AD RMS):** Microsoft has added numerous features such as a new interface, delegation of administration, and integration with Active Directory Federation Service (AD FS).

- **Enhancements to Group Policy:** Microsoft has added many new policy settings. In particular, these settings enhance the management of Windows Vista client computers. All policy management is now handled by means of the Group Policy Management Console (GPMC), which was an optional feature first added to Windows Server 2003 R2. In addition, Microsoft has added new auditing capabilities to Group Policy and added a searchable database for locating policy settings from within GPMC. In Windows Server 2008 R2, GPMC enables you to use a series of PowerShell cmdlets to automate many of the tasks (such as maintenance and linking of GPOs) that you would otherwise perform in the GUI. In addition, R2 adds new policy settings that enhance the management of Windows 7 computers.

- **Fine-grained password policies:** Microsoft has added the capability to apply granular password and account lockout policy settings to different sets of users within the same domain.

- **Security enhancements:** Microsoft has hardened Windows Server 2008 to provide the most secure server operating system to date. The most significant security enhancements include the RODC already introduced; network access protection (NAP), which enables you to isolate computers that are noncompliant with security policies; improved clustering features; an improved version of Internet Information Services (IIS); expanded Group Policy settings; and User Account Control (UAC).

Server Manager

Is Server Manager a throwback to Windows NT 4.0? Not at all. It is true in name only. Server Manager is a new Microsoft Management Console (MMC) console that replaces the Computer Management console found in previous Windows Server versions and adds considerable new management functionality. In particular, it includes the management tools formerly part of the Manage Your Server, Configure Your Server, and Add or Remove Windows Components applications in Windows Server 2003. Because this book deals with Server Manager considerably throughout, a brief introduction of its capabilities is provided here.

When you first log on to a Windows Server 2008 computer, Server Manager opens by default. If Server Manager is not open, you can open it by using any of the following methods:

- Click **Start**, right-click **Computer**, and select **Manage**.

- Click **Start > Administrative Tools > Server Manager**.

- Click **Start > Run**, type `compmgmtlauncher`, and then press **Enter.**

Any of these methods opens the Server Manager console shown in Figure 1-6.

Figure 1-6   Server Manager, showing the default options in a new Windows Server 2008 R2 installation.

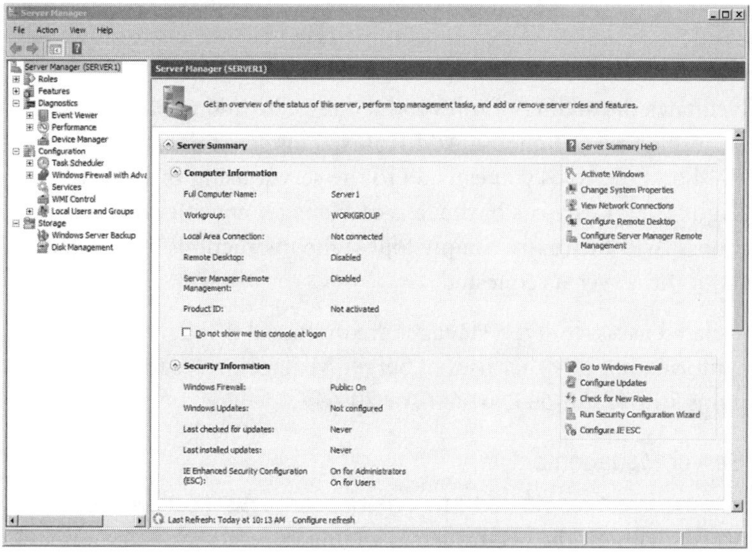

Several of the more significant administrative actions you can perform from Server Manager are as follows:

- Add or remove roles, role service, and server features

- View, manage, and modify the configuration of installed roles and features

- Perform general management tasks such as configuring local user accounts and groups, disk management, and service management

- In Windows Server 2008 R2, connect to remote servers to perform management tasks

- Verify server status, identify critical errors and other events, and troubleshoot configuration problems or server failures

NOTE   The Computer Management snap-in is still available in Windows Server 2008 and contains a subset of the controls available in Server Manager. You can open Computer Management from the Tools tab of the System Configuration dialog box or by typing `compmgmt.msc` at the Run dialog box.

TIP   If you do not want Server Manger to open when you start your domain controller, select the check box labeled **Do not show me this console at logon**, found on the Server Summary page of Server Manager.

Adding Roles and Features

Server Manager facilitates the adding of roles and features. To add a role, right-click **Roles** in the console tree and choose **Add Roles**. This starts the Add Roles Wizard. Figure 1-7 shows the roles you can add to the server using this wizard. To add a feature, right-click **Features** in the Server Manager console (refer to Figure 1-6) and choose **Add Features**. Simply follow the instructions provided by the wizard and reboot the server if requested.

Active Directory–related uses of Server Manager are discussed throughout this book. For further information on other uses of Server Manager, refer to *Exam Cram* books for exams 70-642, 70-643, 70-646, or 70-647.

Command-Line Server Management

Server Manager also provides a command-line version, `ServerManagerCmd.exe`. You can perform many tasks without the GUI, such as adding or removing roles, role services, and features. You can use the command-line version from either the full version of Windows Server 2008 or from Sever Core. To obtain information on the available commands, open a command prompt and type **ServerManagerCmd /?.**

Figure 1-7   The Add Roles Wizard enables you to select from a series of roles that you can add to your server.

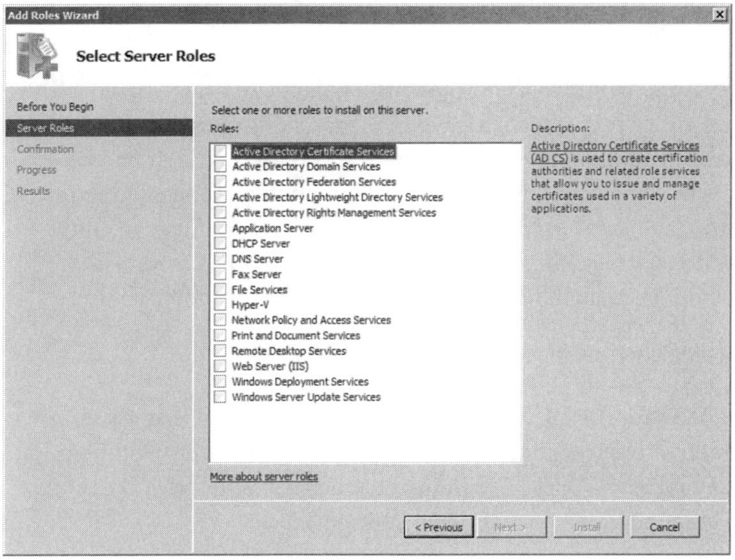

Windows Server 2008 R2

Concurrent to the release of the Windows 7 desktop computer operating system, Microsoft released Release 2 of Windows Server 2008 (Windows Server 2008 R2) on October 22, 2009. Although not a total upgrade of the Windows Server operating system, the R2 release introduces a number of new and enhanced features for Active Directory management. In addition, R2 has several new features that were added specifically to work with Windows 7 client computers. The following are some of the most significant new features:

■ **Active Directory Recycle Bin:** Recovery of accidentally deleted objects in Active Directory has always been a difficult procedure that has resulted in significant domain controller downtime. In Windows Server 2008 R2, objects deleted from AD DS or AD LDS are moved into a recycle bin that works in much the same way as the desktop recycle bin. The deleted object even retains its attributes. You can simply restore the accidentally deleted object from the recycle bin, and all its attributes come with it. This is even true for a container such as an OU; all objects contained within an accidentally deleted OU are restored when you restore the OU from the recycle bin.

■ **Windows PowerShell 2.0:** Included by default in Windows 7 and Windows Server 2008 R2, this is a task-based command-line scripting interface that enables you to perform a large number of remote management tasks. PowerShell includes the Integrated Scripting Environment (ISE), which assists you in the task of writing, testing, and executing scripts. You can also perform automated troubleshooting of remote computers. Included also is an Active Directory module that provides cmdlets for administrative, configuration, and diagnostic tasks.

- **Active Directory Administrative Center (ADAC):** This is a new task-based administrative tool built on PowerShell 2.0 that centralizes a number of object management tasks within a single graphical user interface (GUI). It harnesses the functionality of Active Directory Users and Computers, Active Directory Sites and Services, and Active Directory Domains and Trusts. You can administer objects such as user, group, or computer accounts or OUs from within multiple trusted domains including ones in remote locations. You can also install ADAC on a Windows 7 computer as part of the Remote Server Administration Tools (RSAT).

- **Best Practices Analyzer (BPA):** This is a new management tool that assists you in implementation of best practices in configuring the AD DS environment. You can use this tool to troubleshoot unexpected behavior in Active Directory and obtain recommendations for improved configuration.

- **Offline domain join:** Enables administrators to pre-stage domain accounts in AD DS so that these accounts can be imported into any type of automated computer deployment process such as Sysprep. The newly deployed machines are automatically joined to the domain when they first connect to the network.

- **Active Directory health check:** Microsoft has enhanced the functionality of the `replsum.exe` command to provide additional information on outbound and inbound replication and error diagnostics for failed replications.

- **Active Directory Web Services:** This feature provides a web service–based interface to AD DS domains and AD LDS instances.

- **Active Directory Management Pack:** This feature assists you in monitoring AD DS performance. You can discover and detect problems with computers and software, as well as health state violations.

- **Remote Desktop Services (RDS):** This is an enhancement to Terminal Services, which enables users on the local network or remotely via the Internet to access desktop sessions based on virtual machines or applications in the data center. Any client that supports Remote Desktop Protocol (RDP) can enable user communication with virtual desktops hosted on the RDS server.

- **HyperV:** Available as a server role in Windows Server 2008 R2, this is a hypervisor-based server virtualization technology. It enables you to consolidate multiple servers on a single physical machine, thereby optimizing hardware usage and reducing overall costs. The Live Migration feature enables you to move running virtual servers from one physical machine to another without loss of user connections and consequent user downtime. This facilitates host server management in cases where you need to reboot the host server; simply move all virtual servers to a different physical machine. Virtual server hard disks are configured as VHD files, which can be configured with the native boot function for booting without a virtual machine or hypervisor. In Windows Server 2008 R2, you can use dynamically expanding VHD files with optimized performance.

■ **DirectAccess:** This is a new feature of Windows 7 and Windows Server 2008 R2 that enables users to directly connect to corporate networks from any Internet connection. When enabled, a user is able to access network resources as though he were actually at the office. DirectAccess uses IPv6 over IPSec to create a seamless, bidirectional, secured tunnel between the user's computer and the office network without the need for a virtual private network (VPN) connection. You can configure and monitor this feature from the DirectAccess Management Console.

■ **BranchCache:** This feature provides a local file-caching service that enables users in branch office locations to cache files on a local computer, thereby reducing access time for these files. You can configure this feature through Group Policy. BranchCache uses a hashing mechanism to identify files that have been cached on a local Windows 7 computer so that other users in the same office can access the locally cached version of the file. Changes to the file are saved to both the locally cached version and to the version on the remote server.

■ **Windows Server Migration Tools:** This is a new feature that assists you in migrating server roles, features, operating system settings, and shares from one server to another one.

■ **Managed Service Accounts:** Assists administrators in isolating service accounts and their passwords used by directory-enabled applications for authentication purposes. This helps to protect applications from failing due to authentication failure resulting from accidental lockout, disabling, or other reasons.

The discussion of these new Windows Server 2008 R2 components and features is integrated into the various chapters of this book as appropriate. For comprehensive information on the various editions of Windows Server 2008 R2 as well as their capabilities and enhancements over older Windows Server versions, refer to "Windows Server 2008 R2 Operating System" at http://www.microsoft.com/windowsserver2008/en/us/default.aspx.

TIP   Even though Microsoft has not updated its 70-640 exam objectives following the release of Windows Server 2008 R2, you might find questions that test your knowledge of the new features in R2. Microsoft seeds new items into the question database from time to time, and after a beta testing period in which responses to the questions are not counted toward the final score, incorporates these items into the live exams and expects you to answer them correctly.

Summary

This chapter provided you with an overview of the basic features of Active Directory as included with Windows Server 2008 and Windows Server 2008 R2. The material provided in this introductory chapter will help guide you as you explore the concepts and features of Active Directory in detail in the chapters to come.

This chapter covers the following subjects:

■ **The Hierarchical Nature of DNS:** This section provides a quick introduction to the hierarchical structure on which DNS is built.

■ **Installing DNS on Windows Server 2008 R2:** This section shows you how to install DNS as a server role on a computer running Windows Server 2008 R2.

■ **Configuring DNS Zones:** This section introduces you to the various types of zones into which the DNS namespace is divided. It then shows you how to set up and configure these zones on a Windows Server 2008 R2 computer.

CHAPTER 2

Installing and Configuring DNS for Active Directory

Since Active Directory was first introduced in Windows 2000, the Domain Name System (DNS) has served as the premier name resolution service for all Windows computers and has been fully integrated with Active Directory Domain Services (AD DS). As you learned in Chapter 1, "Getting Started with Active Directory," you must have DNS to install a domain controller, and the Active Directory Installation Wizard automatically installs it for you if it is not present. If DNS is not working properly, client computers will be unable to resolve domain controller names to IP addresses and users will be unable to log on unless cached credentials are available. In the latter case, they still will be unable to access network resources by computer names. So, you can see how vital DNS is to the proper functioning of your network. The DNS naming scheme is used to create the structure of the Active Directory namespace, permitting interoperability with Internet technologies; therefore, the concept of namespaces is central to Active Directory.

"Do I Know This Already?" Quiz

The "Do I Know This Already?" quiz enables you to assess whether you should read this entire chapter or simply jump to the "Exam Preparation Tasks" section for review. If you are in doubt, read the entire chapter. Table 2-1 outlines the major headings in this chapter and the corresponding "Do I Know This Already?" quiz questions. You can find the answers in Appendix A, "Answers to the 'Do I Know This Already?' Quizzes."

Table 2-1 "Do I Know This Already?" Foundation Topics Section-to-Question Mapping

Foundations Topics Section	Questions Covered in This Section
The Hierarchical Nature of DNS	1
Installing DNS on Windows Server 2008 R2	2–3
Configuring DNS Zones	4–13

1. Which of the following are components of the DNS namespace? (Choose all that apply.)

   a. Root domains

   b. Top-level domains

   c. Second-level domains

   d. Hostnames

   e. NetBIOS names

2. Which of the following is most likely to cause a problem when installing a DNS server?

   a. The server is not configured as a domain controller.

   b. The server has only a single network adapter.

   c. The server is not configured with a static IP address.

   d. The server is not configured with the Application Server role.

3. What tool do you use to install DNS on a Windows Server 2008 R2 computer?

   a. Add Roles Wizard

   b. Add Features Wizard

   c. DNS Manager

   d. Control Panel Add or Remove Programs

4. What DNS zone type contains source information about authoritative name servers for its zone only?

   a. Primary zone

   b. Secondary zone

   c. Forwarding zone

   d. Stub zone

   e. Active Directory–integrated zone

5. You have set up two Windows Server 2008 R2 servers as domain controllers and configured them with Active Directory–integrated DNS zones. You have configured another Windows Server 2008 R2 computer as a DNS server. You do not intend to promote this server to domain controller, but you want it to include a backup copy of the DNS zone data for your domain. What DNS zone type should you configure?

   a. Primary zone

   b. Secondary zone

   c. Forwarding zone

   d. Stub zone

   e. Active Directory–integrated zone

6. Your network has several older servers that have static records with single-label names. Historically, you have used WINS for name resolution with these servers, but the WINS server is being removed as your network is being converted to IPv6. What zone type should you configure to support these servers?

   a. Primary zone

   b. Secondary zone

   c. GlobalNames zone

   d. Stub zone

7. You are configuring a reverse lookup zone for your network, which uses the Class C network address range of 192.168.5.0/24. Which of the following addresses should you use for the reverse lookup zone?

   a. `5.168.192.in-addr.arpa`

   b. `0.5.168.192.in-addr.arpa`

   c. `192.168.5.in-addr.arpa`

   d. `192.168.5.0.in-addr.arpa`

8. Which type of resource record would you use to specify a host name to IPv6 address mapping for a computer in your domain?

   a. A

   b. AAAA

   c. NS

   d. PTR

9. Your AD DS network contains a Windows Server 2008 R2 machine that hosts both a web server and an FTP server, which are configured with two different FQDNs. You want to ensure that clients are directed properly to this machine. What type of resource record should you specify?

   a. A

   b. NS

   c. PTR

   d. CNAME

   e. MX

10. You are configuring DNS on your AD DS network and want to ensure that only computers with existing domain accounts can update DNS records. What option should you specify?

   a. Ensure that the **Store the zone in Active Directory** option is selected and that the Dynamic Updates option is set to **Secure only**.

   b. Ensure that the **Store the zone in Active Directory** option is selected and that the Dynamic Updates option is set to **Nonsecure and secure**.

   c. Ensure that the **Primary Zone** option is selected and that the Dynamic Updates option is set to **Secure only**.

   d. Ensure that the **Primary Zone** option is selected and that the Dynamic Updates option is set to **Nonsecure and secure**.

11. Your network is experiencing heavy traffic to and from the DNS server because of large numbers of client requests. On examining DNS server logs and talking to users on the network, you discover that many users are repeatedly accessing the same FQDNs. What should you do to reduce the DNS network traffic in this situation?

   a. Reduce the refresh interval

   b. Increase the refresh interval

   c. Reduce the minimum default TTL value

   d. Increase the minimum default TTL value

12. You are configuring the properties of a secondary DNS server on your network. You want to ensure that the secondary DNS server is kept up-to-date with respect to changes in resource records at the primary DNS server, so you access the Start of Authority (SOA) tab of your server's Properties dialog box. What should you do?

   a. Increase the refresh interval

   b. Reduce the refresh interval

   c. Increase the retry interval

   d. Reduce the retry interval

13. You are responsible for administering DNS on your company's AD DS domain. All domain controllers are configured as DNS servers with an Active Directory–integrated zone. When checking the configuration of a DNS server, you notice that the zone includes resource records for computers that were removed from the network several weeks ago. What should you do to ensure that these records are removed immediately?

    a. In DNS Manager, right-click the DNS server and choose **Scavenge Stale Resource Records**.

    b. From the Zone Aging/Scavenging Properties dialog box, select the **Scavenge stale resource records** check box.

    c. From the Advanced tab of the DNS server's Properties dialog box, select **Enable automatic scavenging of stale records**.

    d. In DNS Manager, select the DNS zone and then delete the stale resource records from the list that appears in the details pane.

Foundation Topics

The Hierarchical Nature of DNS

When you want to go to a website, for example, http://www.microsoft.com, you enter this name into your browser and a DNS query is sent to your local server. This query works its way up the hierarchy of DNS servers, as you will see shortly, and returns an IP address of 207.46.131.99 and makes the connection. Likewise, when you need to access some resource such as a folder or printer located on another computer in your network, you use a program such as the Network and Sharing Center or type a UNC path such as \\server1\document, and a DNS query is used to resolve the computer name to its IP address. Furthermore, when you first log on to your computer on an Active Directory Domain Services (AD DS) network, the Netlogon service must access a domain controller to verify your credentials. Again, DNS is used for this purpose.

Chapter 1 introduced you to the hierarchical Active Directory namespace and showed you what this meant along with its advantages over the flat namespace model that was used in Windows NT. DNS also uses a hierarchical namespace that is called the *domain namespace* (see Figure 2-1). Within this namespace, every computer is identified by its fully qualified domain name (FQDN). Name servers themselves are grouped into different levels of domains and subdomains, just as we can have parent and child domains in the Active Directory namespace. Domains define the different levels of authority in the hierarchical structure of DNS.

Figure 2-1   The hierarchical structure of DNS.

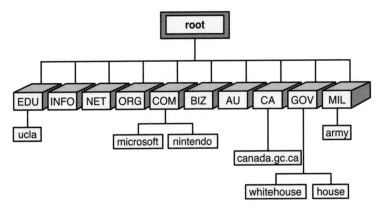

The following are the typical levels of the hierarchical DNS namespace:

- **Root-level domains:** This is the top of the DNS hierarchy. Specified by a period or dot, it is not included in domain names. DNS servers at this level enable you to access servers for the top-level domains.

- **Top-level domains:** This is a standard set of domains that have been assigned by the Internet Society (ISOC). Expanded somewhat in recent years, it includes the domains shown in Figure 2-1 plus several others. In addition, two-letter ISO standard country name abbreviations are used as top-level domain names, for example .ca for Canada and .au for Australia.

- **Second-level domains:** This represents additional groupings; for example, Microsoft or UCLA. Second-level domains can be further subdivided. In fact, you can have up to a limit of 127 levels.

- **Hostnames:** These are the individual names assigned to individual computers within domains. The combination of a hostname, an organization's domain name, and the Internet top-level domain name creates a name (FQDN) that is unique across the Internet. Hostnames used inside domains are added at the beginning of the domain name and are also referred to by their FQDNs. For example, a computer called search in the Microsoft domain has an FQDN of search.Microsoft.com. The www is actually a hostname (or one of the names) used by a particular computer.

DNS is essential to the proper functioning of AD DS—you cannot have AD DS without DNS. For this reason, Microsoft expects you to know how to install, configure, and work with DNS for the 70-640 exam. Whereas Windows NT networks used Windows Internet Naming Service (WINS) as a primary name resolution service, all versions of Active Directory use DNS for this purpose. The purpose of WINS was to resolve the older NetBIOS names to IP addresses. NetBIOS names are flat, single-level computer names unlike the hierarchical names used by AD DS. You might encounter WINS servers on mixed networks, and WINS can work with DNS for dynamic name resolution on these networks.

Installing DNS on Windows Server 2008 R2

In Windows Server 2008 R2, DNS is present as a server role. You can install DNS on any server, including one that you do not want to add the Domain Controller role to, by using the Add Roles Wizard. DNS now provides complete support for IP version 6 (IPv6). After you have installed DNS (whether as part of Active Directory installation or separately on a member server), the DNS Manager MMC snap-in is available in the Administrative Tools folder, from which you can perform all configuration activities associated with DNS.

Before installing DNS on your server, ensure that your server is configured to use a static IP address. You can do this from the Properties dialog box for your network adapter, accessible from the Network and Sharing Center:

Step 1.   From the left panel, select **Change adapter settings**.

Step 2.   Right-click your network connection and choose **Properties**.

Step 3.   From the Local Area Connection Properties dialog box that appears, select either **Internet Protocol Version 4 (TCP/IPv4)** or **Internet Protocol Version 6 (TCP/IPv6)** as required and then click **Properties**.

Step 4.   In the dialog box that appears, select the **Use the following IP address** option and then type the IP address, subnet mask or subnet prefix length, and default gateway.

Use the following procedure to install DNS on a Windows Server 2008 R2 computer:

Step 1.   Open Server Manager and expand the Roles node.

Step 2.   Click **Add Roles** to start the Add Roles Wizard.

Step 3.   If you receive the Before You Begin page, click **Next**. Note that you can disable the appearance of this page by selecting the check box labeled **Skip this page by default**.

Step 4.   The Select Server Roles page shown in Figure 2-2 enables you to select the roles you want to install on your server. Select **DNS Server** and then click **Next**.

Figure 2-2   Selecting the DNS server role.

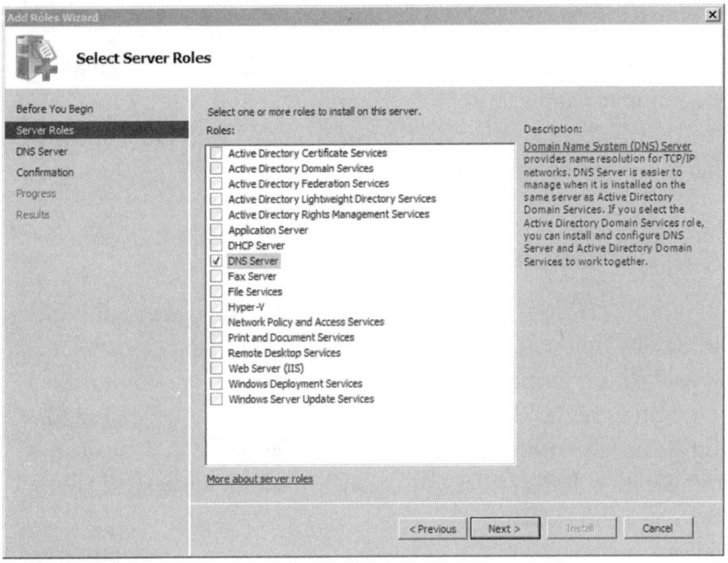

Step 5.   You receive the Introduction to DNS Server page shown in Figure 2-3. To learn more about DNS, click the links provided. When you're ready to proceed, click **Next**.

Figure 2-3   The Introduction to DNS Server page enables you to obtain more information about DNS.

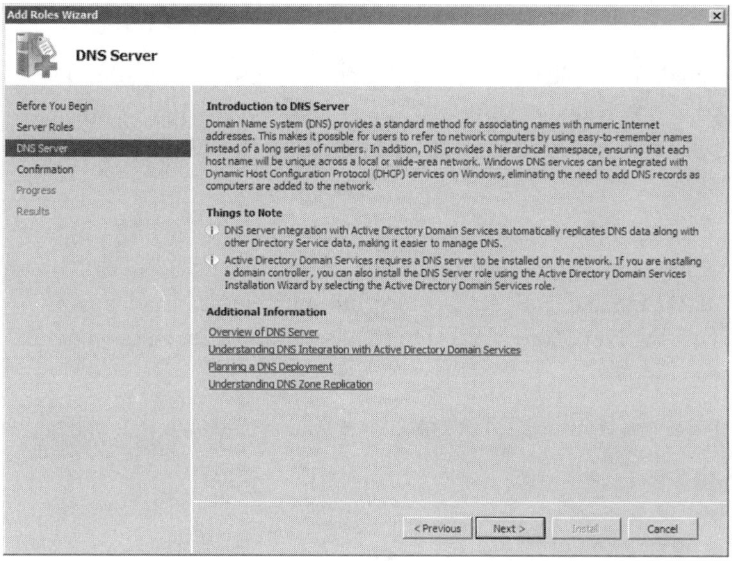

Step 6.   On the Confirm Installation Selections page, click **Install**.

Step 7.   The Installation Progress page tracks the progress of installing DNS. When informed that the installation is complete, click **Close**.

NOTE   For additional information on installing DNS and preinstallation considerations, refer to "Install a DNS Server" at http://technet.microsoft.com/en-us/library/cc725925.aspx.

Configuring DNS Zones

Each DNS name server stores information about a discrete portion of the Internet namespace. Such a portion is known as a *zone* and the DNS server that is primarily responsible for each zone is considered to be *authoritative* for that zone. In other words, the DNS server is the main source of information regarding the Internet addresses contained within the zone. A zone can be considered a part of the big database that is DNS and can contain information on one or more AD DS domains. Zones are defined by who looks after maintaining the records that they contain. In Windows Server 2008, DNS stores its zone data in one or more application directory partitions, each of which is an AD DS partition that contains application-specific data (in this case, DNS) that needs to be replicated throughout specified portions of the forest. This replication takes place by a process called *zone transfers*, which take place among all DNS servers in the forest. You will learn about zone transfers and replication in Chapter 4, "Configuring DNS Server Settings and Replication."

NOTE   A read-only domain controller (RODC) can host the DNS service, but its zones are all configured as read-only. In other words, it cannot process client updates. A client attempting to update its DNS records is returned a referral to a DNS server that is capable of processing the updates.

As you will learn in Chapter 3, "Installing Active Directory Domain Services," when you first install AD DS, a default set of zones and subzones is installed (see Figure 2-4). You can use the New Zone Wizard to create additional zones, as required.

Figure 2-4   A default set of zones is included in DNS Manager when you create your domain.

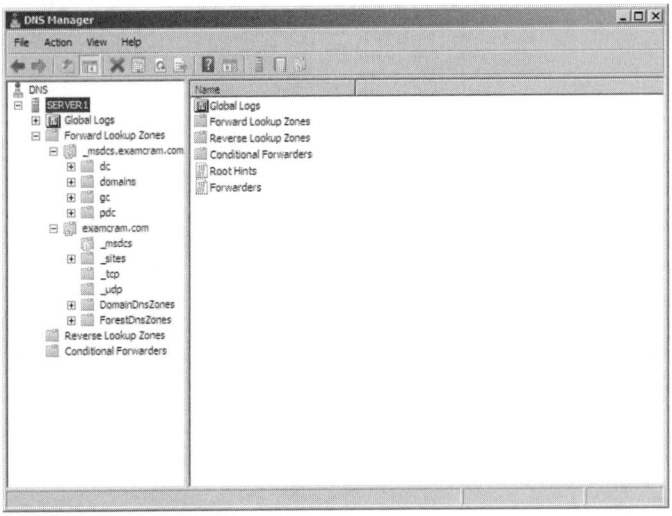

DNS Zone Types

Each DNS server provides for several different types of zones, including primary, secondary, stub, and Active Directory–integrated. You can have forward and reverse lookup zones in each of these zone types. A *forward lookup zone* resolves a computer's fully qualified domain name (FQDN) to its IP address, whereas a *reverse lookup zone* resolves an IP address to the corresponding FQDN.

NOTE   For more information on how zones function, refer to "Understanding Zones" at http://technet.microsoft.com/en-us/library/cc725590.aspx.

Primary Zones

A *primary zone* is a master copy of zone data hosted on a DNS server that is the primary source of information for records found in this zone. This server is considered to be authoritative for this zone, and you can update zone data directly on this server. It is also known as a *master server*. If the zone data is not integrated with AD DS, the server holds this data in a local file named `<zone_name.dns>` that is located in the `%systemroot%\system32\DNS` folder.

Secondary Zones

A *secondary zone* is an additional copy of DNS zone data hosted on a DNS server that is a secondary source for this zone information. This server obtains the zone information from the server hosting the corresponding primary zone. Using secondary zones improves name resolution services on the network by providing redundancy and load balancing. The server that hosts a secondary zone is frequently called the *secondary server*.

Stub Zones

A *stub zone* contains source information about authoritative name servers for its zone only. The DNS server hosting the stub zone obtains its information from another server that hosts a primary or secondary copy of the same zone data. The following are several purposes of stub zones:

- Maintain a current list of delegated zone information within a hierarchy of DNS zones. A DNS server can host a parent zone at the primary or secondary level together with stub zones for its child zones and thereby have a list of authoritative DNS servers for the child zones.

- Enable improved name resolution by enabling a DNS server to rapidly locate the stub zone's list of name servers without the need for querying other servers to locate the appropriate DNS server.

- Simplify the administration of DNS by enabling the distribution of the list of authoritative DNS servers throughout a large enterprise network without the need for hosting a large number of secondary zones.

Active Directory–Integrated Zones

An *Active Directory–integrated zone* stores its data in one or more application directory partitions that are replicated along with other AD DS directory partitions. This helps to ensure that zone data remains up-to-date on all domain controllers hosting DNS in the domain. Using Active Directory–integrated zones also provides the following benefits:

- It promotes fault tolerance because data is always available and can always be updated even if one of the servers fails. If a DNS server hosting a primary zone outside of AD DS fails, it is not possible to update its data because no mechanism exists for promoting a secondary DNS zone to primary.

- Each writable domain controller on which DNS is installed acts as a master server and allows updates to the zones in which they are authoritative; no separate DNS zone transfer topology is needed.

- Security is enhanced because you can configure dynamic updates to be secured; by contrast, zone data not integrated with AD DS is stored in plain-text files that unauthorized users could access, modify, or delete.

Either primary or stub zones can be integrated with AD DS. It is not possible to create an Active Directory–integrated secondary zone.

TIP   Keep in mind the properties of the various zone types. In particular, remember that you must have an Active Directory–integrated zone if you want to enable secure dynamic updates. Also remember that you can configure a secondary server with a copy of an Active Directory–integrated zone, but that this secondary zone copy is stored locally on that server and is not integrated with Active Directory. An exam question might ask which type of DNS zone is appropriate in a given scenario.

GlobalNames Zones

A *GlobalNames* zone is a special type of Active Directory–integrated zone that enables you to resolve static, global records with single-label names without the need for a WINS server. You can use this zone to manage older servers that are assigned static IP addresses and have been managed using WINS. However, the GlobalNames zone is not designed to completely replace WINS. You should not use this zone type to support the name resolution of records that are dynamically registered in WINS.

The following are several situations in which it is useful to deploy a GlobalNames zone:

- You are retiring WINS or planning to convert your network to using only IPv6 (WINS will not work in an IPv6 network).

- You require single-label name resolution only for important servers or websites that can be statically registered in DNS. Note that the GlobalNames zone cannot register hostnames using dynamic updates.

- You are unable to rely on the suffix search lists on client computers for providing single-label name resolution, perhaps because there is a large number of target domains where the possibility of duplicated hostnames exists.

- All the DNS servers that are authoritative for your zones run Windows Server 2008. This is needed so that names registered in the GlobalNames zone can be resolved properly.

A GlobalNames zone is not a unique zone type in the sense of the other zone types mentioned in this section; it is simply an Active Directory–integrated zone that is called GlobalNames.

> **NOTE**   For more information on GlobalNames zones, refer to "Deploying a GlobalNames Zone" at http://technet.microsoft.com/en-us/library/cc731744.aspx.

DNS Name Server Roles

DNS servers can store and maintain the database of names in several different ways and are referred to as *name servers*. The servers need to be specifically configured to perform these roles. Keep in mind that name servers can store the data for one or more zones. This depends, of course, on the way they are configured. The name server roles are described in the following paragraphs.

Primary Name Server

When you are running an Active Directory–integrated zone, all domain controllers on which DNS is installed are considered to be primary name servers because they contain the read/write database for the DNS zone. All domain controllers running DNS are considered to be authoritative for the zone and never have to issue iterative queries to other servers to resolve a hostname for a machine located in its zone.

In the traditional implementation of DNS, there is only a single primary name server for each zone. Additional name servers must be configured as secondary name servers and contain a read-only copy of the primary server's database files.

Secondary Name Server

A *secondary name server* gets a read-only copy of the data for its zone information from another name server across the network that is authoritative for that zone. It uses the process of zone transfer to obtain this copy of the zone information from a primary name server. Changes to zone information cannot be made to a zone file stored on a secondary name server.

You can have secondary name servers on Active Directory–integrated zones as well as standard DNS zones. On an Active Directory–integrated zone, a secondary name server is valuable in situations such as a small remote office that is connected by means of a WAN link that lacks sufficient bandwidth to support the full Active

Directory replication process. This enables DNS clients to obtain name resolution results without having to communicate across the slow link. The zone transfer can be configured to take place at a time of light traffic such as at night. Secondary name servers for an Active Directory–integrated zone also can be used for load-balancing purposes on any part of the network. When used in this manner, the secondary servers take some of the load that is otherwise sent to the domain controllers.

Secondary name servers are also authoritative to a certain degree for their zones. They are designed to answer queries with some authority, just not as much as primary name server that stores the master copy of the zone file. Secondary DNS server records are updated only by means of the zone transfer or replication of zone data from the primary DNS server, whether in a standard or Active Directory–integrated zone. This zone transfer is one of the aspects of DNS that the administrator must configure to happen.

Caching-Only Server

DNS servers don't rely solely on the information in their zone files. All DNS name servers cache queries that they have resolved. By contrast, caching-only servers are DNS name servers whose only job is to perform queries, cache the answers, and return the results. A *caching-only server* can only provide information based on the results of queries that it has already performed; it does not provide any type of zone file. It is not authoritative for any zone.

Caching-only servers are often used in situations where you need to reduce the amount of network traffic—for example, across a slow link. Because they are not involved with zone transfers, the traffic involved in the zone transfer process is not generated. In addition, because they cache the results of previous name queries directed at them, they reduce the network traffic that would otherwise be generated from repeat queries arising from the same network. For this reason, a caching-only server is useful at the far end of a WAN link such as at a small branch office. In addition, caching-only servers are excellent candidates for a forwarder role, discussed next.

Forwarders

A *forwarder* is a special DNS server that accepts requests for name resolution from another DNS server. It is especially useful for protecting internal DNS servers from access by Internet users. It works in the following manner:

Step 1.   A client issues a request for an FQDN on a zone for which its preferred DNS server is not authoritative.

Step 2.   This DNS server forwards the request to another server, which is the forwarder. In other words, the client's preferred DNS server is acting as a forwarding server in relaying the request to the forwarder.

Step 3.   The forwarder attempts to resolve the required FQDN and returns the result to the client's preferred (forwarding) server, which then returns the result to the requesting client. If the forwarder cannot resolve the FQDN, the forwarding server issues an iterative query to resolve the name.

The major factor here is that the client's preferred DNS server first uses the forwarder to resolve the query and issues an iterative request only if the forwarder cannot complete the resolution. As mentioned earlier, caching-only servers make ideal candidates for forwarders.

Creating DNS Zones

One of the first activities you perform when configuring a new DNS server is to specify forward and reverse lookup zones.

The following two types of DNS lookup zones exist:

- **Forward lookup:** This is the usual action in which a client requires the IP address of a remote computer as found in the DNS server's A or AAAA (host) resource record.

- **Reverse lookup:** This occurs when a client computer knows the IP address of another computer and requires its hostname, which can be found in the DNS server's PTR (pointer) resource record.

By creating primary forward and reverse lookup zones, you create a primary name server that is authoritative for the zone that you have created. Or you can create a secondary name server for any zone that you have already created on another DNS server. Note that you can create any number of zones on a single DNS server and that one DNS server can contain any combination of primary and secondary zones.

Forward Lookup Zones

As you already have seen, DNS creates forward lookup zones when you install it as part of creating a new domain. When you install DNS by itself, it does not create any lookup zones. DNS provides the New Zone Wizard to facilitate the creation of all types of zones. It is simple to create a new forward lookup zone, as the following procedure shows:

Step 1.   In the DNS Manager snap-in, right-click **Forward Lookup Zones** and choose **New Zone**. This starts the New Zone Wizard with a Welcome page.

Step 2.   Click **Next**, and on the Zone Type page, select the zone type from the options described earlier in this chapter, and then click **Next** again.

Step 3.   If you select the option to create an Active Directory–integrated zone, you receive the Active Directory Zone Replication Scope page shown in Figure 2-5, which asks you how you want the data in the zone replicated. (The available options are discussed later in this chapter; the default is **To all DNS servers in this domain**.) Make an appropriate choice and then click **Next**.

Figure 2-5   You receive several choices of zone replication scope when creating an Active Directory–integrated zone.

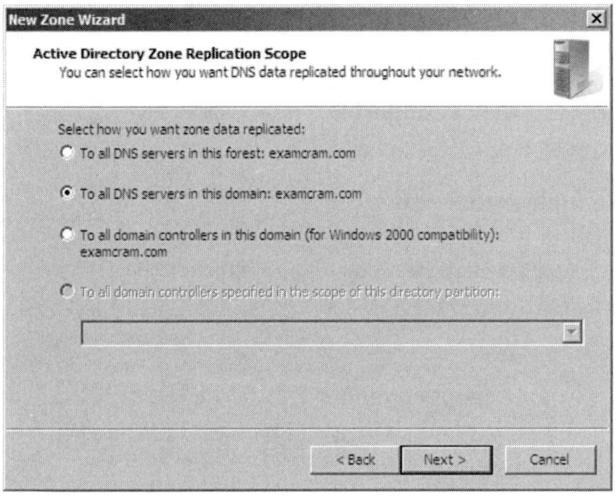

Step 4.   On the Zone Name page, type the name of the zone to be created and then click **Next**.

Step 5.   If you have selected the Secondary zone type, you receive the Master DNS Servers page. On this page, provide the IP addresses of one or more DNS servers from which the zone information will be copied to create the secondary zone, and then click **Next**.

Step 6.   The Zone File page provides a default filename consisting of the zone name with a `.dns` extension. You can modify this if you need to or choose the option of using an existing file that has been saved to the `%systemroot%\system32\dns` folder. Make your choice and then click **Next**.

Step 7.   The Dynamic Update page shown in Figure 2-6 provides a choice of dynamic update types as discussed earlier in this section. Make your selection and then click **Next**.

Step 8.   Review the information provided on the Completing the New Zone Wizard page. When you are done, click **Finish**. If you need to make any modifications, click **Back**. The zone is created and added to the list in the console tree of the DNS Manager snap-in.

Figure 2-6   The New Zone Wizard enables you to specify the type of dynamic update desired.

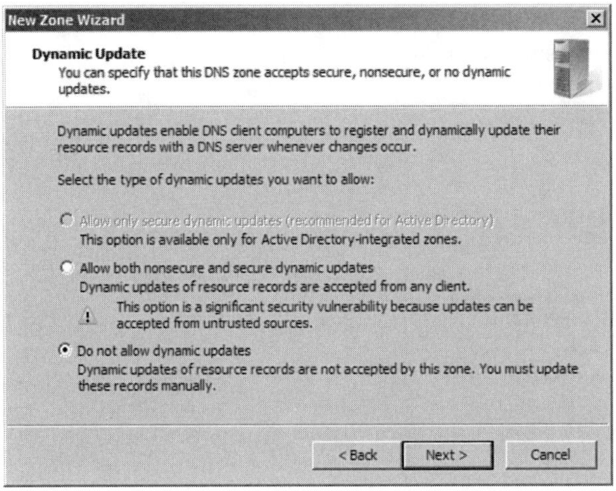

Reverse Lookup Zones

The reverse lookup file maps IP addresses to hostnames by using a special domain name that ends in in-addr.arpa and contains the octets of the network portion of the IP address in reverse sequence (for example, 0.168.192.in-addr.arpa for the Class C network address range of 192.168.0.0/24). It is a database file that is used for reverse lookups; in other words, a client can provide an IP address and request a matching hostname. Pointer (PTR) records, mentioned previously, are used to provide a static mapping of IP addresses to hostnames within a reverse lookup zone. They can be created either manually or automatically when A or AAAA records are added to the forward lookup zone file.

You can use the New Zone Wizard to create a reverse lookup zone, as the following procedure shows:

Step 1.   In the DNS Manager snap-in, right-click **Reverse Lookup Zones** and choose **New Zone**. This again starts the New Zone Wizard.

Step 2.   Click **Next**, and on the Zone Type page, select the zone type from the options described earlier in this chapter, and then click **Next** again.

Step 3.   If creating an Active Directory–integrated zone, select your choice of replication scope as described earlier and shown in Figure 2-5, and then click **Next**.

Step 4.   Choose whether you want to create an IPv4 or IPv6 reverse lookup zone, and then click **Next**.

Step 5. In the Reverse Lookup Zone name page, type the network ID portion of the IP addresses that will belong to the zone in normal sequence. As you can see in Figure 2-7, this creates a reverse lookup zone name as described earlier in this section. Then click **Next**.

Figure 2-7 Specifying the name of the reverse lookup zone.

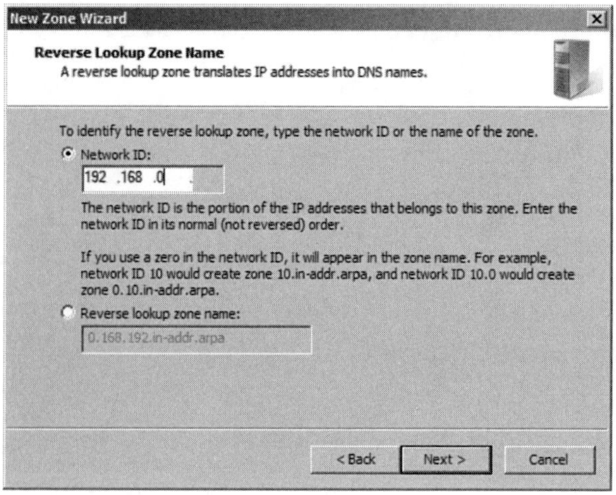

Step 6. The Zone File page gives you a choice of creating a new zone file with the name you just created or using an existing file. In most cases, you will create the file with the name specified. If you have another zone file, ensure that it is copied to the location specified and then select the **Use this existing file** option. Then click **Next**.

Step 7. Select the appropriate option on the Dynamic Update page as previously described and then click **Next**.

Step 8. Review the summary information and click **Finish** to create the zone. The new zone appears under the Reverse Lookup Zones node of the DNS Manager snap-in.

After you have created either type of DNS zone, you can specify additional zone properties. The various zone properties are discussed in the sections to follow.

TIP You can create a pair of forward and reverse lookup zones at the same time from the Configure a DNS Server Wizard. To access this wizard, right-click your server at the top of the DNS Manager console tree and choose **Configure a DNS Server**; then select the **Create forward and reverse lookup zones (recommended for large networks)** option.

DNS Resource Records

Each zone file contains a series of entries known as *resource records* for a DNS domain. If your zone is examcram.com, your database file is called examcram.com.dns. A copy of this database is stored at %systemroot%\System32\dns\backup. Windows Server 2008 supplies a sample database file called place.dns, located in the %systemroot%\System32\dns\Samples folder, as a template. This file is duplicated and renamed whenever you create a new zone using the New Zone Wizard.

Table 2-2 contains descriptions of the most common resource records found in the zone file.

Table 2-2 Common DNS Resource Records

Resource Record	Description
SOA (start of authority)	The first record in any zone file, it identifies the primary name server within the domain. It also includes other properties such as an administrator email address and caching properties for the zone.
A and AAAA (host)	Contains the computer name to IPv4 (A) or IPv6 (AAAA) address mappings for all hosts found in the domain, thereby identifying these hostnames.
NS (name server)	Contains the DNS servers that are authoritative in the domain. This includes both the primary DNS servers and any secondary DNS servers.
SRV (service)	Stores information about where computers that provide a specific service are located on the network. Information in these records includes the name of the service and the DNS name of the host that is providing the service. A computer would still need to access the A or AAAA record for a service provider to resolve the name to an IP address. Examples could include web services associated with a web server or logon services associated with a domain controller on an AD DS domain.
CNAME (alias)	Provides aliases (canonical names), which are additional names that point to a single host. Machines will respond to either the original name or the alias. This facilitates doing such things as hosting both an FTP server and a web server on the same machine, or for server migrations.
PTR (pointer)	Allows for reverse lookups by containing IP address-to-name mappings.
MX (mail exchanger)	Identifies preferred mail servers on the network. When there is more than one mail server, they are listed in order of precedence.

You can create new DNS resource records if required. Right-click your DNS zone and choose the appropriate option from those shown in Figure 2-8. Provide the requested information in the dialog box that appears and then click **OK**. The Other New Records option enables you to select from a complete list of available resource record types and provides a description of each of the available record types.

Figure 2-8 You can create new resource records in DNS by right-clicking your zone name and choosing the appropriate option.

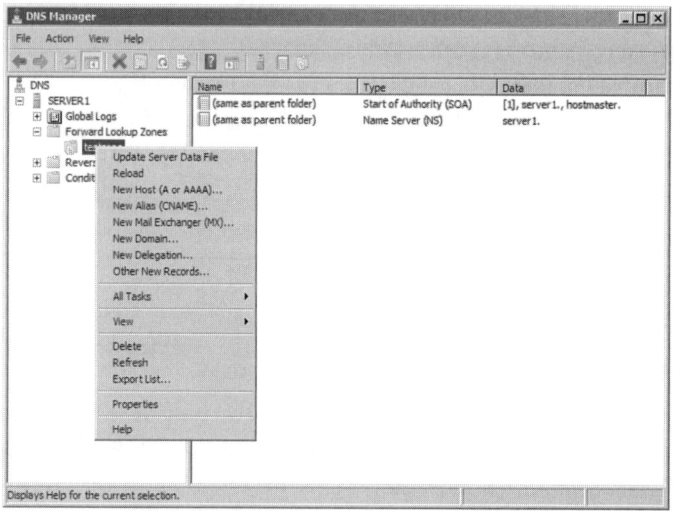

TIP The SRV resource records for a domain controller are important in enabling clients to locate the domain controller. The Netlogon service on domain controllers registers this resource record whenever a domain controller is restarted. You can also re-register a domain controller's SRV resource records by restarting this service from the Services branch of Server Manager or by typing **net start netlogon.** An exam question might ask you how to troubleshoot the nonregistration of SRV resource records.

Configuring DNS Zone Properties

The Properties dialog box for each DNS zone enables you to configure a large number of zone-related properties, including the following:

- Zone types
- Authoritative secondary servers
- Dynamic and secure dynamic updating
- Scavenging and time to live
- Integration with WINS

Right-click the zone in the console tree of DNS Manager and choose **Properties** to display the dialog box shown in Figure 2-9. The sections to follow outline the configuration of the more important properties that you should be aware of.

Figure 2-9 The General tab of a zone's Properties dialog box provides several important details on the zone and enables you to configure zone types, replication, dynamic updates, and scavenging properties.

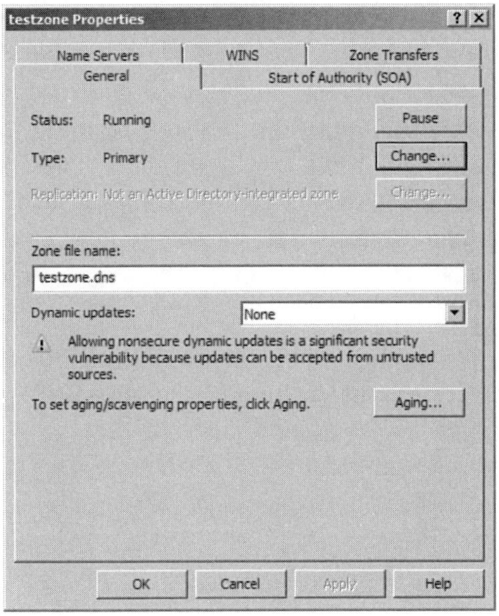

Configuring Zone Types

The Properties dialog box for a DNS zone enables you to change the zone type and determine whether the zone files are stored in Active Directory. In DNS Manager, right-click the zone and choose **Properties**. On the General tab of the zone's Properties dialog box shown in Figure 2-9, click the **Change** button opposite the Type entry. This brings up the Change Zone Type dialog box shown in Figure 2-10, which displays the current zone type and enables you to select the zone type and determine whether the zone data is stored in Active Directory. Click **OK** when finished.

Adding Authoritative DNS Servers to a Zone

When you use secondary DNS servers, you need to add these servers to the NS records to specify them as authoritative for the zone. To do this, proceed as follows:

Step 1. Access the Name Servers tab of the zone's Properties dialog box.

Step 2. Click **Add** to display the New Name Server Record dialog box shown in Figure 2-11.

Step 3. Specify the name and IP address of a DNS server that is to be authoritative for the zone and then click **OK**.

Repeat this procedure as required to add additional authoritative DNS servers. If you need to remove a DNS server, select it on the Name Servers tab and click **Remove**.

Figure 2-10   The Change Zone Type dialog box enables you to configure zone types.

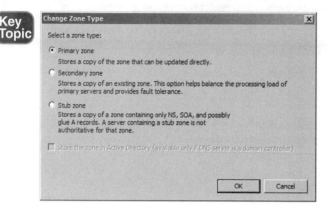

Figure 2-11   The New Name Server Record dialog box enables you to add authoritative DNS servers to your zone.

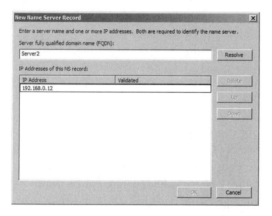

Dynamic, Nondynamic, and Secure Dynamic DNS

Dynamic DNS (DDNS) enables DNS zone files to be updated on the fly, so to speak, whenever DNS client computers update their TCP/IP configuration information. In other words, DNS clients can dynamically update their A and PTR records in the master zone file on startup or whenever their configuration changes. First introduced in Windows 2000, client computers automatically report their TCP/IP information to the DNS server. If your network is using Dynamic Host Configuration Protocol (DHCP), the DHCP server can update the DDNS server with each client computer's current IP address whenever it renews client IP address leases.

Nondynamic DNS (NDDNS) was the default prior to Windows 2000. At that time, the administrator was required to enter A records manually to keep the DNS database up-to-date, although it was possible to integrate DNS with WINS to provide a pseudo-dynamic version of DNS.

Secure dynamic DNS (SDDNS) is an enhancement that enables you to permit dynamic updates only from authorized client computers in an Active Directory–integrated zone. Secure dynamic updates are defined by Request for Comment (RFC) 2137 and offer the following benefits:

- Only computers with existing domain accounts can update DNS records.

- Only computers that create (and therefore own) a DNS record can update the record.

- Only authorized users can modify zones and resource records, thereby protecting them from unauthorized modification.

- You can specify which users and groups are authorized to modify zones and resource records.

You can configure the type of update being used from the General tab of the zone's Properties dialog box, previously shown in Figure 2-9. From the Dynamic updates drop-down list, select **None** for NDDNS, **Nonsecure and secure** for DDNS, or **Secure only** for SDDNS. The default for Active Directory–integrated zones is Secure only.

WARNING   You cannot have secure dynamic updates on a zone that is not integrated with Active Directory. Microsoft recommends that you not allow dynamic updates when creating such a zone because dynamic updates can be accepted from untrusted sources. The New Zone Wizard cautions you to this fact when creating such a zone.

TIP   Know the purpose of the various dynamic update options available here. An exam question might present a scenario in which your DNS server's primary zone contains entries for unknown computers. You must select the **Secure only** option to prevent this problem from occurring. Also remember that the zone must be Active Directory–integrated to enable this option.

NOTE   For more information on dynamic updates and their use, refer to "Understanding Dynamic Update" at http://technet.microsoft.com/en-us/library/cc771255.aspx.

Zone Scavenging

Strange situations can occur in which resource records are not automatically removed from the DNS database. This can happen if a client, such as a remote access client, disconnects improperly from the network. In this case, the A resource record left behind is known as a *stale* resource record. These records take up space on a DNS server and might be used in attempts to resolve queries, resulting in errors and reduced DNS server performance.

For locating and removing these stale resource records, a process known as *scavenging* is employed. In this process, the DNS server searches for and deletes aged resource records. You can control the scavenging process by specifying which servers can scavenge the records, which zones are to be checked, and which records are to be scavenged if they become stale. By default, scavenging is disabled. To enable scavenging, access the General tab of the zone's Properties dialog box and click the **Aging** command button. This brings up the Zone Aging/Scavenging Properties dialog box shown in Figure 2-12. To enable scavenging, select the **Scavenge stale resource records** check box and then specify values for the no-refresh and refresh intervals as described in the figure.

Figure 2-12   You can configure scavenging properties from the Zone Aging/Scavenging Properties dialog box.

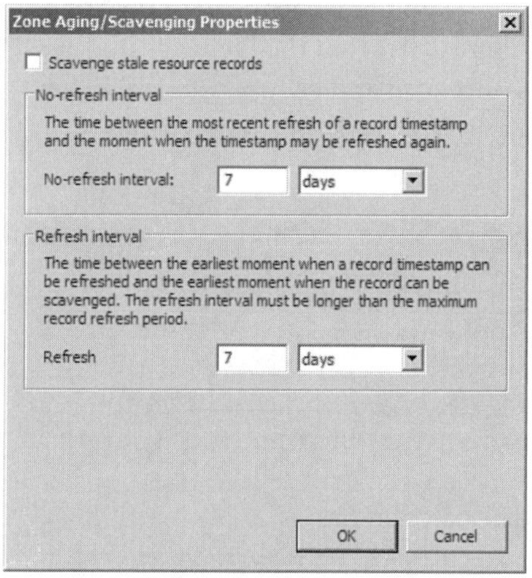

TIP   You can also perform an immediate scavenging of all stale resource records on a DNS server without first configuring scavenging properties. To do so, right-click the DNS server in the console tree of DNS Manager and choose **Scavenge Stale Resource Records**. Then click **Yes** in the message box that appears.

Time to Live

Client computers often request the same FQDNs. Upon receipt of a successful resolution of an iterative query with another DNS server, the server places the query results in its cache. This information is stored in memory and is available to the client (or any other client on the network requesting the same FQDN) without the need for sending an external query. It is retained for the time known as the *time to live* (*TTL*), which is a configurable retention time interval that specifies the length of time that the server will retain cached information for a zone. This value and the next one are both specified as days:hours:minutes:seconds. Increase this value if zone information does not change frequently. A longer TTL reduces the amount of network traffic but consumes more memory utilization on the DNS server.

You can configure a DNS zone's TTL property from the Start of Authority (SOA) tab of the zone's Properties dialog box, as shown in Figure 2-13. In the list box labeled Minimum (default) TTL, type a number and select a unit (days, hours, minutes, or seconds). By default, this TTL is one hour. Note that the TTL for this Record entry immediately beneath specifies the TTL for the SOA record.

Figure 2-13   The Start of Authority (SOA) tab enables you to configure several zone properties, including the TTL for caching externally resolved queries.

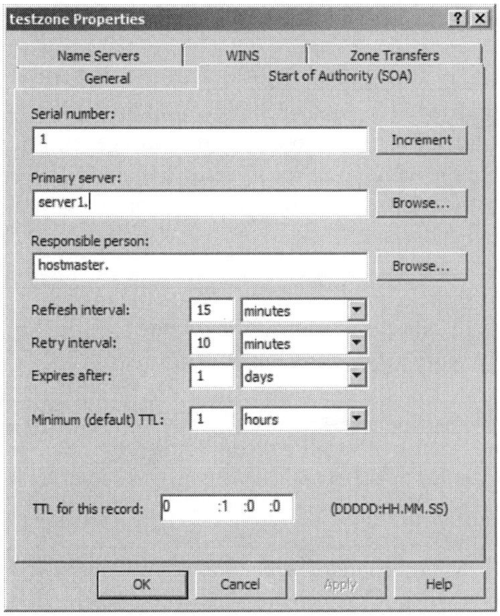

NOTE   DNS cache information is also lost whenever the server is rebooted. For this reason, it is best to avoid rebooting the DNS server unless absolutely necessary.

The Start of Authority (SOA) tab contains the additional settings described in Table 2-3 that you should be aware of; all of these are related to the information contained in the server's SOA resource record.

Key Topic

Table 2-3   SOA Tab Settings

Setting	Description
Serial Number	Starts at one and is incremented every time that a change to some property of the zone occurs. You normally do not change this number. A secondary server that is querying the primary server for updates used this number to determine whether changes to the zone file have occurred. If so, the data is replicated to the secondary server using the zone transfer process.
Primary Server	Designates the primary server for the domain by its FQDN. If you need to change the primary server for any reason, you can either browse to locate a suitable server or type its name here. If zone transfers are failing, check this name for accuracy because if it is incorrect, zone transfers cannot take place.
Responsible Person	Names the designated administrator by his/her Simple Mail Transfer Protocol (SMTP) email address. Even though email addresses generally use the @ symbol to separate the name from the domain, you need to use a period in this address. If zone transfers are not working properly, a message can be sent to this email address.
Refresh Interval	Specifies the interval at which the secondary server queries the master server to see whether the zone data has changed. A low value enables the secondary DNS server to be more up-to-date, but at the expense of increased network traffic.
Retry Interval	Specifies how much time will elapse before the secondary server tries again to contact the master server in the event that the master server does not respond to the initial refresh attempt.
Expires After	Specifies the length of time that a secondary server will resolve queries using the current information when it has been unable to contact the master server for an update. When this interval has been reached, the secondary server will stop resolving queries until it is again able to contact the master server.

WARNING   Try not to confuse the refresh and retry intervals. The refresh interval determines how often other DNS servers hosting the zone will attempt to renew the zone data. It is 15 minutes by default. The retry interval determines how often other DNS servers retry a request for updating the zone every time the refresh interval occurs. It is 10 minutes by default.

Integrating DNS with WINS

If your network is still using WINS servers to resolve computer names not found within the DNS namespace, you can enable WINS lookup integration on your

DNS server. This uses two special resource records called WINS and WINS-R. If the DNS server is unable to resolve a name resolution query, it forwards the query to the WINS servers configured in these resource records. The WINS resource resolves forward lookup queries, whereas the WINS-R resource record handles reverse lookup queries.

To enable WINS integration, access the WINS tab of the zone's Properties dialog box and select the **Use WINS forward lookup** check box. Then type the IP address of the WINS server to be used for name resolution and click **Add**, as shown in Figure 2-14. To enable WINS integration for reverse lookup, select the **Use WINS-R lookup** check box. Then type the required domain name on the **Domain to append to returned name** field.

Figure 2-14   The WINS tab of the zone's Properties dialog box enables you to specify a WINS server.

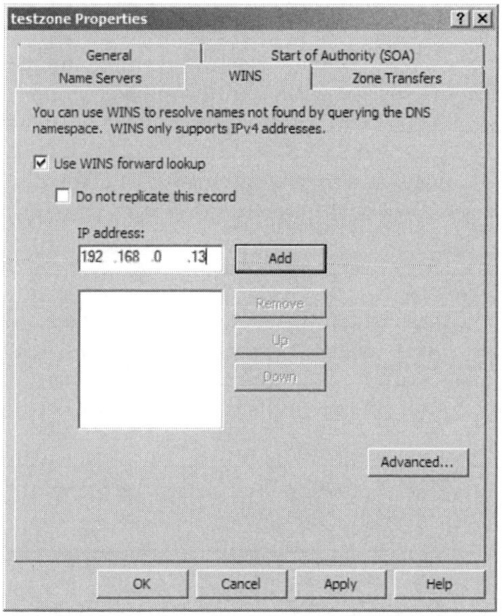

Command-Line DNS Server Administration

You can perform most of the DNS administrative tasks outlined here from the command line by using the Dnscmd.exe utility provided with Windows Server 2008 DNS. This is especially useful for scripting repetitive tasks and is the only method available for configuring DNS locally on a Server Core computer (you can also connect to a Server Core computer from a remote computer running the DNS Manager snap-in). Using this command, you can display and modify the properties of DNS servers, zones, and resource records. You can also force replication between DNS server physical memory and DNS databases or data files.

To use this utility, open a command prompt and type the following:

```
dnscmd server_name command {parameters}
```

In this command, *server_name* is the name or IP address of the DNS server against which the command is to be executed (if omitted, the local server is used), **command** represents the **dnscmd** subcommand to be executed, and **parameters** represents additional parameters required by the subcommand being executed. Table 2-4 summarizes many of the more useful **dnscmd** subcommands.

Table 2-4   Useful **dnscmd** Subcommands

Subcommand	Description
clearcache	Clears resource records from the DNS cache memory.
config	Enables the user to modify a range of configuration values stored in the Registry and individual zones.
enumzones	Displays a complete list of zones configured for the server.
info	Displays DNS server configuration information as stored in the server's Registry. You can specify which setting for which information will be returned.
statistics	Displays or clears statistical data for the specified server. You can specify which statistics are to be displayed according to ID numbers.
zoneadd zone_name	Adds a zone to the DNS server.
zonedelete zone_name	Deletes the specified zone from the DNS server.
zoneexport zone_name	Exports all resource records in the specified DNS zone to a text file.
zoneinfo zone_name	Displays Registry-based configuration information for the specified DNS zone.

You need to use dnscmd when enabling support for a GlobalNames zone on your network. At every authoritative DNS server in the forest, run the following command:

```
dnscmd ServerName /config /enableglobalnamessupport 1
```

In this command, *ServerName* is the name of the DNS server hosting the GlobalNames zone.

NOTE   For a complete list and description of available **dnscmd** commands, including parameters used with the **dnscmd config** command, refer to **"Dnscmd"** at http://technet.microsoft.com/en-us/library/cc772069(WS.10).aspx.

Exam Preparation Tasks

Review All the Key Topics

Key Topic

Review the most important topics in the chapter, noted with the key topics icon in the outer margin of the page. Table 2-5 lists a reference of these key topics and the page numbers on which each is found.

Table 2-5 Key Topics for Chapter 2

Key Topic Element	Description	Page Number
List	Shows you how to install DNS on your server	50
List	Shows you how to create a new DNS zone	57
Table 2-2	Describes common DNS resource records	61
Figure 2-9	Setting properties of a DNS zone	63
Figure 2-10	Configuring zone types	64
Figure 2-12	Configuring zone scavenging properties	66
Table 2-3	Describes important SOA tab settings	68

Complete the Tables and Lists from Memory

Print a copy of Appendix C, "Memory Tables" (found on the CD), or at least the section for this chapter, and complete the tables and lists from memory. Appendix D, "Memory Tables Answer Key," also on the CD, includes completed tables and lists to check your work.

Definitions of Key Terms

Define the following key terms from this chapter, and check your answers in the glossary.

Active Directory–integrated zone, dnscmd, Domain Name System (DNS), dynamic DNS (DDNS), Dynamic Host Configuration Protocol (DHCP), flat namespace, forward lookup query, forwarding, fully qualified domain name (FQDN), non-dynamic DNS (NDDNS), primary zone, resource records, reverse lookup query, scavenging, secondary zone, secure dynamic DNS (SDDNS), stub zone, time to live (TTL), zone

This chapter covers the following subjects:

■ **Planning the Active Directory Namespace:** This section provides a basic introduction to best practices you should follow in planning and designing an Active Directory namespace that will serve your company properly both now and in the years to come.

■ **Creating Forests and Domains:** In this section, you learn how to create your first domain controller in a new Active Directory forest. You then learn how to add additional domain controllers to your forest and create child domains.

■ **Interoperability with Previous Versions of Active Directory:** Many organizations are using Active Directory domains based on Windows 2000 and Windows Server 2003. This section takes you through the preparatory tasks you must perform before you can add a Windows Server 2008 R2 domain controller as well as the actual upgrading of older domain controllers. In addition, it introduces you to the concept of forest and domain functional levels, as well as the benefits of the newest Windows Server 2008 R2 functional levels.

■ **Additional Forest and Domain Configuration Tasks:** After you have installed and configured your first domain, you should perform several additional tasks. This section discusses verifying your Active Directory installation, using the Active Directory Migration tool (ADMT), and creating alternative user principal name (UPN) suffixes.

CHAPTER 3

Installing Active Directory Domain Services

In Chapter 1, "Getting Started with Active Directory," you were introduced to the basic building blocks of the logical Active Directory structure: forests, trees, domain, and organizational units (OUs). You were also introduced to the concept of sites for distinguishing portions of the network separated physically by slow WAN links. Now you begin to create an actual Active Directory forest and domain structure.

The act of installing Active Directory on a server is conceptually very simple. You need only run the Active Directory Domain Services (AD DS) Installation Wizard from the Add Roles Wizard of Server Manager and provide answers to the questions the wizard asks. The actual act of installing AD DS, however, can be thought of as the tip of the iceberg. Before you install AD DS, you need to plan how Active Directory will fit into your company's corporate and geographical structure as well as your expectations for future growth and the potential for acquiring other companies. This chapter serves only as a basic introduction to the topic of planning.

"Do I Know This Already?" Quiz

The "Do I Know This Already?" quiz enables you to assess whether you should read this entire chapter or simply jump to the "Exam Preparation Tasks" section for review. If you are in doubt, read the entire chapter. Table 3-1 outlines the major headings in this chapter and the corresponding "Do I Know This Already?" quiz questions. You can find the answers in Appendix A, "Answers to the 'Do I Know This Already?' Quizzes."

Table 3-1 "Do I Know This Already?" Foundation Topics Section-to-Question Mapping

Foundations Topics Section	Questions Covered in This Section
Planning the Active Directory Namespace	1
Creating Forests and Domains	2–7
Interoperability with Previous Versions of Active Directory	8–9
Additional Forest and Domain Configuration Tasks	10–11

1. Which of the following are best practices that you should follow when planning an AD DS domain structure? (Choose all that apply.)

   a.   Employ a test lab

   b.   Prepare thorough documentation

   c.   Keep everyone, including top managers, informed

   d.   Understand thoroughly the network's TCP/IP infrastructure

   e.   Develop and adhere to an adequate security policy

   f.   Know the capabilities of your WAN links

2. On which of the following editions of Windows Server 2008 R2 can you install the AD DS role? (Choose all that apply.)

   a.   Web

   b.   Foundation

   c.   Standard

   d.   Enterprise

   e.   Datacenter

3. Which of the following tools can you use to install AD DS on a server running Windows Server 2008 R2? (Choose two.)

   a.   The dcpromo.exe command

   b.   The Manage Your Server tool

   c.   The Configure Your Server tool

   d.   The Add Roles Wizard

   e.   The Add Features Wizard

4. Which of the following conditions would represent a problem when you are attempting to install the first domain controller in your domain?

   a.   A DHCP server is not present.

   b.   A DNS server is not present.

   c.   The server's hard disk is formatted with the FAT32 file system.

   d.   The server's hard disk has only 10 GB free space available.

5. Which of the following is a new AD DS administrative tool included with Windows Server 2008 R2 and was not present in older versions of Windows Server?

   a.   Active Directory Users and Computers

   b.   Active Directory Administrative Center

   c.   Active Directory Sites and Services

    d. Active Directory Domains and Trusts

    e. User Manager for Domains

6. Your computer is running the Server Core edition of Windows Server 2008 R2. You want to promote this server to domain controller. What should you do?

    a. Use Server Manager to run the Add Roles Wizard.

    b. Use the Initial Configuration Tasks window to run the Add Roles Wizard.

    c. Use dcpromo.exe and specify the required parameters when prompted.

    d. Use dcpromo.exe together with an answer file that provides the required parameters.

    e. You cannot promote this server to domain controller without reinstalling Windows Server 2008 as a full edition server.

7. You are the administrator of DC1, which is a Windows Server 2008 R2 domain controller in your company's domain. You are experiencing problems with DC1 and decide to run the Active Directory Installation Wizard again on this machine. What happens?

    a. A new copy of the AD DS software is installed.

    b. Two copies of the AD DS software will exist side-by-side.

    c. The domain controller is demoted to a member server.

    d. You receive an error message informing you that the wizard cannot be run again.

8. Which of the following is not a valid domain or forest functional level for a domain controller running Windows Server 2008 R2?

    a. Windows 2000 mixed

    b. Windows 2000 native

    c. Windows Server 2003 native

    d. Windows Server 2008 native

    e. Windows Server 2008 R2 native

9. You have installed Windows Server 2008 R2 on a brand-new server and want to promote this server to domain controller in your domain, which has domain controllers running Windows Server 2003 and operates at the Windows Server 2003 native domain functional level. What should you do first?

    a. Run adprep /forestprep and then run adprep /domainprep.

    b. Run adprep /domainprep and then run adprep /forestprep.

    c. Raise the domain functional level to Windows Server 2008 R2.

    d. Raise the forest functional level to Windows Server 2008 R2.

10. Your company has acquired another company, and both companies operate an AD DS forest with a single domain. The CIO has decided that all users of the acquired company are to be moved into your company's domain so that the other company's forest and domain can be decommissioned. What tool should you use to assist you in this action?

   a. Active Directory Users and Computers

   b. Active Directory Administrative Center

   c. Active Directory Migration Tool (ADMT)

   d. User State Migration Tool (USMT)

11. You are the administrator for the `sales.que.com` domain. You are configuring an implicit user principal name (UPN) suffix user named Sharon. Which of the following is a valid implicit UPN?

   a. `Sharon@sales.que.com`

   b. `Sharon@sales`

   c. `Sales.que.com\Sharon`

   d. `Sales\Sharon`

Foundation Topics

Planning the Active Directory Namespace

As discussed in Chapter 1, "Getting Started with Active Directory," the domain is the primary administrative unit within an Active Directory namespace. Windows Server 2008 uses the concept of domains to separate available resources among registered users. It is also the basic security unit, as you will see throughout this book, because many of the security requirements in Active Directory are focused at the domain level. Therefore, it is important to begin the process of planning any company's Active Directory Domain Services (AD DS) namespace from the viewpoint of the domain structure.

All planning starts from the name of your company's root domain. Recall in Chapter 1 that each tree has a root domain that is located at the top of the inverted tree structure. All subdomains contain this root domain name in their own domain names. In addition, the first domain in the entire forest is not only a root domain, it is also the forest root. Also, the top-level domain names used on the Internet and defined in the DNS hierarchy are included. The latter is not an absolute requirement if you are planning a domain that has no Internet representation whatsoever, but what company these days does not have a presence on the Internet?

Therefore, it makes sense that your root domain can take the same name as your Internet domain name as registered with InterNIC (Internet Network Information Center). Consider a fictional company with an Internet domain name of mycompany.biz. Although you can use this name as your AD DS root domain name, it creates a risk of revealing your company's AD DS structure to the public Internet. Consequently, you might want to keep the internal name separate and use something like mycompany.local for the AD DS root domain name of the same fictional company.

Subdividing the Active Directory Namespace

You can subdivide your namespace within Active Directory in two ways:

- Separate domains

- Organizational units (OUs)

In many instances, the use of separate domains or OUs would serve just as well as the other. In larger companies, the use of separate domains often arose from the limitations of the Security Accounts Manager (SAM) database in Windows NT. Because the AD DS database can hold millions of objects, this limitation is seldom of importance in AD DS design. For this reason, and because a single domain structure is the easiest type of structure to administer, this method is the best means of organizing your company's namespace if possible. There is no specific need to create separate domains for administrative functions, geographical sites, or departments in the company. Logically, you can handle this function by setting up a system of OUs. An internal system of OUs provides the following additional advantages:

■ It can be administered either centrally or locally. The concept of delegation of control in AD DS facilitates the assignment of individuals as local administrators.

■ User authentication is simpler and faster within a single domain environment, regardless of where a user is located.

■ It is far simpler to modify when needed—for example, if your company is reorganized.

■ It is flexible and can include an internal hierarchy of departments, sections, work units, and so on.

There are, however, reasons for using separate domains for discrete divisions of your company:

■ This approach can facilitate decentralized administration of network resources.

■ In the case of multiple Internet domain names, the domain can be built to mirror the Internet functionality.

■ Multiple domains representing different geographical locations might reduce the amount of replication traffic across low wide area network (WAN) links.

■ User account requirements that vary among departments or locations, such as password complexity, are more easily handled with separate domains.

■ International legal and language needs might be handled more easily by using separate domains.

■ Very massive organizations can be broken down into a domain structure.

Administrative or Geographical Organization of Domains

You can organize a series of domains along either administrative or geographical means. For example, Figure 3-1 shows mycompany.biz organized along three administrative divisions—Accounting, Products, and Advertising—all reporting to a Management group, contrasted with the company's main offices located in San Francisco, Dallas, Toronto, and Atlanta.

You need to take into account conditions that favor either the administrative or geographical model. This can include the following factors:

■ Plans for future offices in additional cities

■ Projected growth of each of the company's divisions

■ Potential for reorganization of the company along new departmental lines

■ Requirements for centralized or decentralized administration of the company

Figure 3-1 Administrative and geographical divisions of **mycompany.biz**.

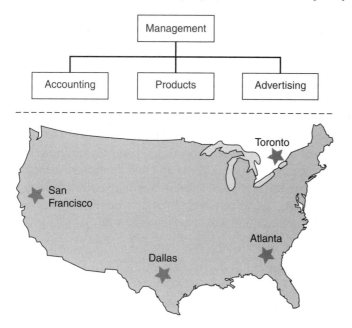

- Needs for different security levels in either certain departments or certain offices

- Current or future use of one or more Internet DNS namespaces

Such factors suggest the best domain organization for your company's AD DS namespace.

Use of Multiple Trees

Within the AD DS forest, you can have one or more trees. As outlined in Chapter 1, the main difference between trees and forests is that domains within a tree share a contiguous namespace, whereas domains located in different trees in the same forest have a disjointed namespace. Thus, que.com and examcram.com are root domains in two separate trees of the same forest.

In almost all multiple domain enterprises, it makes sense to employ a single tree. The major exception occurs when two companies merge and want to maintain their separate identities. Their identities, and indeed their Internet namespaces, are best served by having more than one tree in the forest.

NOTE Another way of designing a multidomain forest is to employ an empty forest root domain with a series of child domains representing administrative or geographical divisions of the company. The root domain contains only a small number of objects, and you can readily control membership in the Enterprise Admins and Schema Admins groups. The impact of business decisions, such as the spin-off or renaming of subsidiary companies, can be handled more readily. On the other hand, you must ensure that the forest root domain controllers are carefully secured and protected against disaster because their loss effectively destroys the entire forest structure.

Best Practices

Planning the AD DS domain structure is an act that has far-reaching implications. This process is something that cannot simply be decided by a few network administrators sitting down with a few diagrams of the network and company business structures. Rather, it must involve the company's senior and middle management as well as business strategy specialists and representatives from remote offices. If you use internally developed applications, representatives of the development team should be involved. The following guidelines will help you make your AD DS implementation proceed smoothly:

- **Know everything there is to know about the network:** Although this guideline might sound intuitive for senior administrators who have built the network from the ground up, those who have come on the scene more recently need to gather information about everything that must be accounted for in an AD DS plan.

- **Employ a test lab:** The lab should contain representative domain controllers, member servers, and client computers. Set up a mini version of your complete network and engage the assistance of a representative set of users to test all facets of the implementation thoroughly.

- **Prepare thorough documentation:** This point can never be understated. Use tools such as Microsoft Visio to prepare diagrams of different levels of company detail, from the major administrative units down to the smallest workgroups. Visio is a tool that is specifically designed for preparing administrative diagrams such as those required in this scenario. This exercise also helps in optimizing communication between technical individuals and top management.

- **Use an email distribution list to keep everyone informed:** When all concerned individuals have full access to the latest developments, unpleasant surprises are minimized.

- **Keep all employees informed:** Although the regular workers might not understand the details of what is happening, they should be informed of the summary points of any planned changes. They will then be much more able to cope with the changes. In addition, they could provide valuable feedback.

- **Ensure that all top managers know what's happening:** This point also can never be understated. This helps prevent unpleasant surprises and the need to redo portions of the planning process.

- **Understand thoroughly the network's TCP/IP infrastructure:** Your understanding helps in designing the network and DNS configuration that is the foundation of the AD DS infrastructure. It is especially true in developing the proper site structure, as will be discussed in Chapter 6, "Configuring Active Directory Sites and Replication."

- **Develop and adhere to an adequate security policy:** Thoroughly review any security policy that your company already has in place. Apply the policy's constraints to the proper design of your company's domain structure. Make any appropriate changes as you develop the AD DS infrastructure.

- **Know the capabilities of your WAN links:** If your network includes slow WAN links, test and monitor the use of these links before and during the AD DS implementation to ensure that you have the optimum configuration.

Creating Forests and Domains

After you have created a comprehensive plan for your organization's AD DS structure, you are almost ready to begin the installation. The first task that you must perform is to install the first domain controller for the forest root domain.

Requirements for Installing Active Directory Domain Services

Before you can install AD DS, you must have at least one server that meets the following requirements:

- **Operating system:** The server must be running the Foundation, Standard, Enterprise, or Datacenter edition of Windows Server 2008 R2. Note that a server running the Web edition cannot act as a domain controller.

- **Adequate hard disk space:** Beyond the space used for installing Windows Server 2008 R2, the server must have a minimum of 500 MB of disk space for the Active Directory database and SYSVOL folder, plus at least 100 MB for the transaction log files. The larger the proposed network, the more disk space is necessary. And in practical terms, you should have several gigabytes of available space at a minimum. In Windows Server 2008 R2, you should have additional disk space for the following reasons:
  —The online defragmentation process is changed in Windows Server 2008 R2.
  —Windows Server 2008 R2 domain controllers have additional indices on the large link table.
  —The Active Directory Recycle Bin in Windows Server 2008 R2 holds deleted objects and their attributes until cleared.

- **A disk volume formatted with the NTFS file system:** This ensures security of the database; furthermore, it is required for the SYSVOL folder. Windows Server 2008 R2 creates an NTFS partition by default when installed.

TIP It is strongly recommend that you use a fault-tolerant disk volume such as RAID-1 (disk mirroring) or RAID-5 (disk striping with parity) for the Active Directory files. This enables the domain controller to function in the event of a disk failure, until the failed disk can be replaced. However, fault-tolerant disks are no substitute for regular backups of Active Directory. Backups are discussed in Chapter 15, "Maintaining Active Directory."

- **A DNS server:** Active Directory requires that a DNS server that supports service (SRV) resource records be present. This can be any server running Windows 2000 or later or a UNIX server running Berkeley Internet Name Domain (BIND) 4.9.7 or later. If you want to integrate the DNS database with Active Directory, you should install DNS on the same server that you install AD DS. If the Active Directory Installation Wizard cannot find a suitable DNS server, you will be prompted to install one. DNS is discussed in Chapter 2, "Installing and Configuring DNS for Active Directory," and Chapter 4, "Configuring DNS Server Settings and Replication."

- **Administrative privileges:** You must be logged on with an account that has the appropriate administrative privileges. For the first domain controller, this is a local administrator. To add a domain to an existing forest, you must be a member of the Enterprise Admins group in this forest; to add a domain controller to an exiting domain, you must be a member of the Domain Admins or Enterprise Admins group in this domain. Group memberships are discussed in Chapter 9, "Active Directory User and Group Accounts."

Installing Active Directory Domain Services

As in Windows 2000 and Windows Server 2003, Active Directory provides the Active Directory Installation Wizard (dcpromo.exe) that handles all aspects of installing or removing Active Directory. Windows Server 2008 is different from previous Windows Servers in that you install AD DS first and then install a domain controller. You can install AD DS without installing a domain controller if you are configuring your server for a directory-related application such as Exchange Server. This section looks at the use of this wizard for installing different types of domain controllers.

You can start the Active Directory Installation Wizard from the Add Roles Wizard in Server Manager or directly from the dcpromo.exe command. The following sections describe the use of the Add Roles Wizard for installing AD DS.

NOTE If you run dcpromo.exe without having first installed AD DS, Windows installs this service before starting the Active Directory Installation Wizard.

New Forests

As already noted, the first domain installed is the root domain in its forest. You must be a local administrator on the server on which you install Active Directory to proceed. The following procedure describes the installation of the first domain:

Step 1.   In the Add Roles Wizard, select **Active Directory Domain Services** and then click **Next**.

Step 2.   If you receive a message box labeled Add features required for Active Directory Domain Services and asking you to install .NET Framework 3.5.1, click **Add Required Features**.

Step 3.   The wizard displays the Introduction to Active Directory Domain Services page shown in Figure 3-2. Make note of the points displayed by this page. If you want additional details regarding installation of Active Directory, click any of the links provided. When finished, click **Next**.

Figure 3-2   You can use the Add Roles Wizard to begin the installation of AD DS.

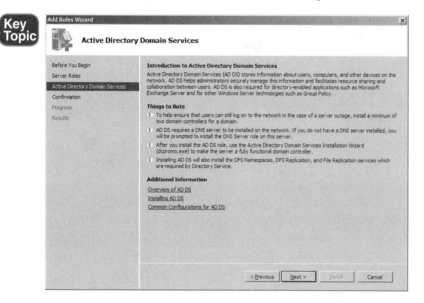

Step 4.   Note the information provided on the Confirm Installation Selections page and then click **Install** to begin installing Active Directory.

Step 5.   The wizard displays an Installation Progress page that charts the progress of installation. After a few minutes, it informs you that the AD DS role has been installed successfully and that you need to launch the Active Directory Domain Services Installation Wizard (`dcpromo.exe`). Click **Close** to exit the wizard and return to Server Manager.

Step 6. Scroll down to the Roles Summary section of Server Manager. Note that Active Directory Domain Services is shown as having been installed. A message marked with a red X indicates the number of system services that are not running.

Step 7. Click this message. You are informed that the server is not yet running as a domain controller. Click the link provided to start the AD DS Installation Wizard.

Step 8. This wizard opens with a Welcome page. Click **Next**.

Step 9. The Operating System Compatibility page shown in Figure 3-3 informs you that Windows Server 2008 R2 security settings affect how older versions of Windows communicate with the domain controller. Access the Knowledge Base article quoted for more information. Click **Next** to proceed with AD DS installation.

Figure 3-3   You are informed about security settings that prevent some older Windows clients or non-Windows systems from logging on to the Windows Server 2008 R2 domain controller.

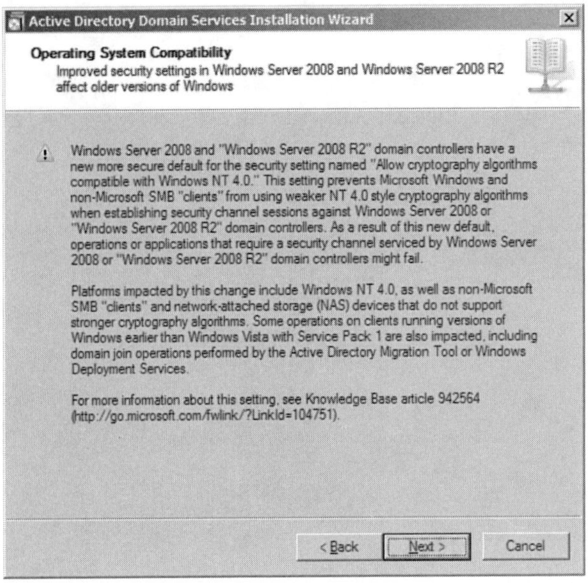

Step 10. On the Choose a Deployment Configuration page shown in Figure 3-4, select **Create a new domain in a new forest** and then click **Next**. On this page, you would select the **Existing forest** option when creating a new domain in an existing forest or adding a domain controller to an existing domain. These options are discussed later in this chapter.

Step 11. Type the full DNS name of the forest root domain and then click **Next**.

Figure 3-4 The wizard provides options for installing a domain controller in an existing forest or a new one.

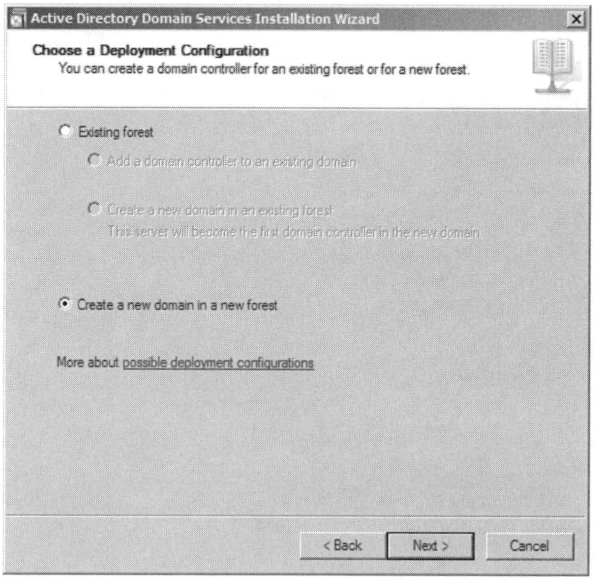

NOTE Windows Server 2008 R2 no longer supports the creation of single-label domain names; however, you can still upgrade existing single-label domains to Windows Server 2008 R2. For more information, refer to "Information about configuring Active Directory domains by using single-label DNS names" at http://support.microsoft.com/kb/300684.

Step 12. The wizard verifies the forest and NetBIOS names and then displays the Set Forest Functional Level page shown in Figure 3-5. Select the appropriate forest functional level and then click **Next**. The available domain and forest functional levels are discussed later in this chapter.

Step 13. Select a domain functional level and then click **Next**.

Step 14. The Additional Domain Controller Options page provides the following additional options that you can install for the domain controller. Ensure that **DNS Server** is selected and then click **Next**.

—**DNS Server:** Installs DNS on this server. This option is selected by default when first installing AD DS because DNS is required for Active Directory.

—**Global Catalog:** Installs a Global Catalog server. This option is not available but selected when installing the first domain controller in any domain because this server must be a global catalog server.

Figure 3-5   The wizard enables you to select from four forest functional levels.

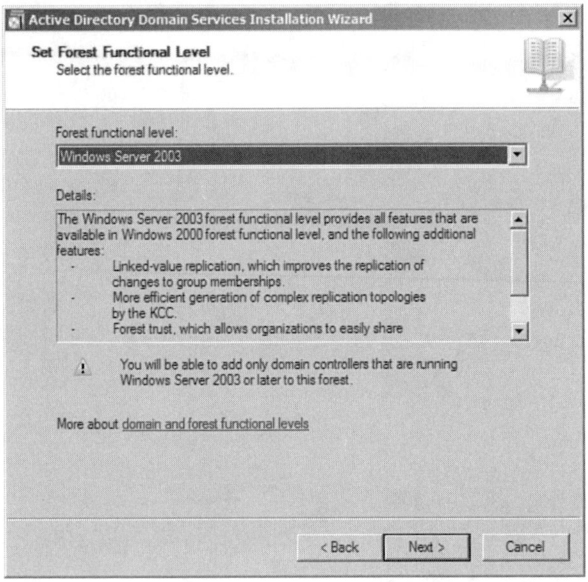

—**Read-Only Domain Controller (RODC):** Installs an RODC. This option is not available because the first domain controller cannot be an RODC. Installing an RODC is discussed in Chapter 8, "Read-Only Domain Controllers."

Step 15.   If the server does not have a statically assigned IP address, you are informed of this fact. A domain controller (and in particular, one that is configured as a DNS server) should always have a statically assigned IP address to ensure that client computers can always reach it. Select **Yes, open the IP properties so that I can assign a static IP address to the network adapter**, and then configure an appropriate IP address, subnet mask, default gateway, and default DNS server address.

Step 16.   If you receive a message informing you that a delegation for the DNS server will not be created, click **Yes** to continue. You might receive this message if you are installing DNS on this server. If so, you should manually create this delegation later.

Step 17.   Confirm the locations provided for the database, log files, and SYSVOL folders. If you want to change any of these locations, type the desired path or click **Browse**. When finished, click **Next**.

TIP   When setting up a domain controller on a production network, it is advisable to place the database and log folders on a separate drive from the SYSVOL folder.

The reason for doing so is to improve only I/O performance; this does not improve security or fault tolerance, as an exam question might lead you to believe.

Step 18. On the Directory Services Restore Mode Administrator Password page, type and confirm a secure password. Make a careful note of the password you typed in case you need to use it later and then click **Next**.

Step 19. The wizard provides a Summary page as shown in Figure 3-6. Review the information provided on the Summary page. If you want to change any settings, click **Back** and make the appropriate changes. If you want to export information to an answer file, click **Export settings** and provide an appropriate path and filename. Then click **Next** to configure AD DS. This process takes several minutes.

Figure 3-6   The wizard provides a summary page that enables you to review the settings you've specified.

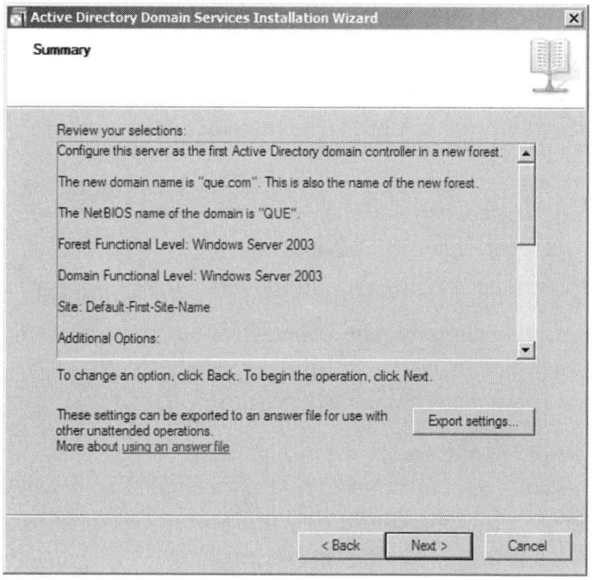

Step 20. When the completion page appears, click **Finish** and then click **Restart Now** to reboot your server. To reboot the server automatically, select the **Reboot on Completion** check box.

NOTE   The Welcome page of the Active Directory Installation Wizard also contains an Advanced mode option. Select the check box provided to perform any of the following actions:

■ Installing a domain controller from backup media created on an existing domain controller

■ Modifying the NetBIOS name generated by default

■ Selecting a source domain controller when installing an additional domain controller in the domain

■ Defining a password replication policy that specifies the passwords cached on a read-only domain controller (RODC)

You can also invoke the Advanced mode directly from the dcpromo command by including the /adv parameter with this command.

New Domains in Existing Forests

After you have installed the forest root domain, you can add additional child domains or domain trees to the forest. Either procedure is similar to the procedure already outlined for creating a forest root domain, as follows:

Step 1.   Follow the procedure to install AD DS and start the Active Directory Installation Wizard as described in the previous section until you receive the Choose a Deployment Configuration page previously shown in Figure 3-4.

Step 2.   On this page, select **Existing forest**, and then select **Create a new domain in an existing forest**. Then click **Next**.

Step 3.   On the Network Credentials page, type the name of the parent domain in which you want to install a child domain. Then click **Set** and specify the username and password of an account with the appropriate privileges described earlier in this chapter and click **Next**.

Step 4.   On the Name the New Domain page shown in Figure 3-7, type the name of the parent and child domains in the spaces provided. The new domain will be created as a child domain or new tree automatically depending on the name you provide. Then click **Next**.

Step 5.   On the Set Domain Functional Level page, select the required functional level and then click **Next**. Domain functional levels are discussed later in this chapter.

Step 6.   On the Select a Site page, select an appropriate site and then click **Next**. Sites are discussed in Chapter 6.

Step 7.   Complete the installation of the domain controller according to steps 14–20 of the previous procedure.

Figure 3-7   You create a child domain name from the name of the parent domain and the new top-level name on the Name the New Domain page.

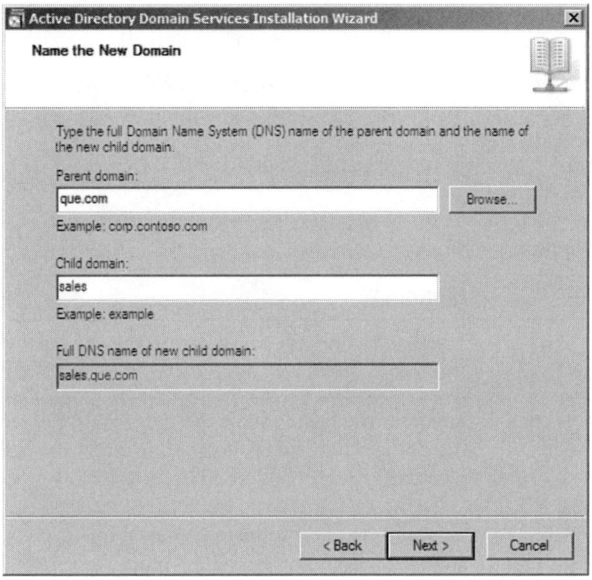

Existing Domains

Installing additional domain controllers in an existing domain is important for the following reasons:

- Doing so adds fault tolerance and load balancing to the domain. In other words, additional domain controllers help share the load and improve performance.

- Users logging on to the domain can connect to any available domain controller for authentication.

- Users at a remote location can connect to a domain controller at their site rather than making a slow connection across a WAN link.

- If a domain controller should become unavailable because of a network or hardware failure, users can still log on to the domain.

To install an additional domain controller in an existing domain, follow the same procedure as in the previous section, except select the **Add a domain controller to an existing domain** option shown in Figure 3-4. Then select the proper domain from the Select a Domain page (this page will display all available domains in the forest). The remainder of the procedure is the same as that for creating a new domain in an existing forest, except that the Set Domain Functional Level page does not appear.

Performing Unattended Installations of Active Directory

Windows Server 2008 R2 enables you to specify parameters for Active Directory installation in an answer file that you can use to facilitate the installation of multiple domain controllers. This file is formatted as a simple text file containing the statement [DCINSTALL] on the first line followed by statements in the form *option=value*. Table 3-2 describes several of the more common options you can use in this file:

Table 3-2   Several Options Used for Unattended Domain Controller Installation

Option	Value	Meaning
UserName	Username of administrative user	Installs the domain controller in the context of this user.
Password	User's password | *	Specifies the password of the user installing the domain controller. Use * to prompt for the password.
ReplicaOrNewDomain	Domain | Replica | ReadOnlyReplica	Specifies whether to install a new domain, an additional domain controller (replica) in an existing domain, or an RODC in an existing domain.
ReplicaDomainDNSName	Existing domain name	Specifies the fully qualified domain name (FQDN) of the domain in which you are installing an additional domain controller.
NewDomain	Forest | Tree | Child	Specifies whether to install a new forest, a new tree in an existing forest, or a child domain.
NewDomainDNSName	Domain name to be created	Specifies the FQDN for a new domain.
ParentDomainDNSName	Parent domain name	Specifies the FQDN of the parent domain when creating a child domain.
ChildName	Child domain name	Specifies the top-level DNS name of the child domain. This name is prefixed to the parent name to create the FQDN of the child domain.

Table 3-2 Several Options Used for Unattended Domain Controller Installation

Option	Value	Meaning
ForestLevel	`0	2	3	4`	Specifies the forest functional level of a new forest: 0 = Windows 2000 2 = Windows Server 2003 3 = Windows Server 2008 4 = Windows Server 2008 R2
DomainLevel	`0	2	3	4`	Specifies the domain functional level of a new domain. Parameters have the same meaning as just described.
InstallDNS	`Yes	No`	Specifies whether a DNS server is installed.
ConfirmGC	`Yes	No`	Specifies whether the domain controller is installed as a global catalog server.
DatabasePath	Path to database folder	Default is `%systemroot%\NTDS`.
LogPath	Path to log folder	Default is `%systemroot%\NTDS`.
SysvolPath	Path to SYSVOL folder	Default is `%systemroot%\SYSVOL`.
RebootOnCompletion	Yes	No	Specifies whether to restart the computer on completion, regardless of success.

Many additional options are available, including options specific to the demotion of domain controllers. For additional information, consult "Appendix of Unattended Installation Parameters" at http://technet.microsoft.com/en-us/library/cc732086(WS.10).aspx.

To perform an unattended installation of a domain controller, open a command prompt and type the following command:

```
dcpromo /answer:path_to_answer_file
```

where `path_to_answer_file` specifies the complete path to the unattended answer file containing the parameters specified in Table 3-2. You can also include any of these parameters in the command line by prefixing each of them with the "/" character. The output to the command prompt will track the progress of the promotion, and then the server will automatically reboot if the `RebootOnCompletion` parameter has been specified.

Server Core Domain Controllers

You cannot use Server Manager or a simple execution of `dcpromo` to promote a Server Core machine to a domain controller. You must use an unattended installation answer file in a similar manner to that described in the previous section. This file must include the information required to identify the domain being joined, including the username and password for a domain administrator account.

> **NOTE** For further information on the use of Server Core, including its use as a domain controller, refer to "Server Core Installation Option of Windows Server 2008 Step-by-Step Guide" at http://technet.microsoft.com/en-us/library/cc753802(WS.10).aspx.

Removing Active Directory

The Active Directory Installation Wizard also enables you to remove Active Directory from a domain controller, thereby demoting it to a member server. Proceed as follows:

Step 1.   Click **Start > Run**, type **dcpromo,** and then press **Enter.**

Step 2.   Windows checks whether Active Directory Domain Services is installed and then displays the Welcome page. Click **Next**.

Step 3.   If you receive a message warning you of the effects of removing a global catalog server, click **OK**.

Step 4.   You receive the Delete the Domain page shown in Figure 3-8. Note all the warnings displayed about the effects of removing a domain. Select the check box only if you are removing the last domain controller from its domain and then click **Next**.

Step 5.   You receive the Application Directory Partitions page if the server holds the last replica of any application directory partitions. Click **Next**, select the check box labeled **Delete all application directory partitions on this Active Directory domain controller**, and then click **Next** again to remove the application directory partitions.

Step 6.   Type and confirm a password for the local Administrator account on the server, and then click **Next**.

Step 7.   Read the information provided on the Summary page. If you need to make any changes, click **Back**. When ready, click **Next** to demote the server.

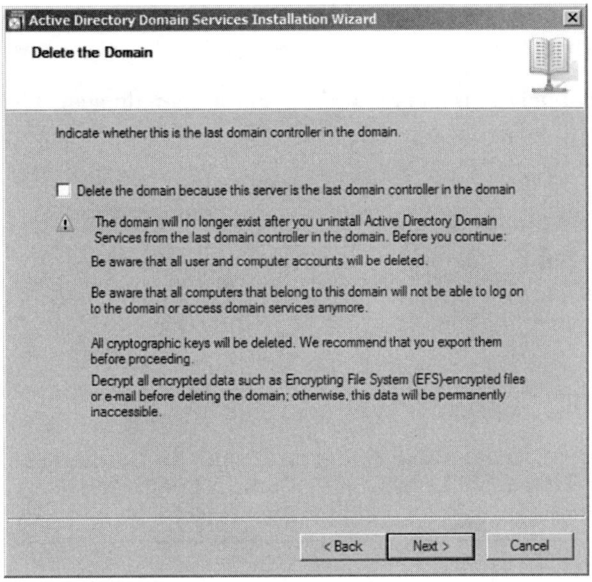

Figure 3-8   When you demote a domain controller, you are warned of the effects of deleting the domain.

Step 8.   When the demotion is finished, click **Finish** and then click **Restart now** to restart the server. To reboot the server automatically, select the **Reboot on Completion** check box.

NOTE   Although this procedure demotes the computer to a member server, it does not remove AD DS. If you want to remove AD DS after demoting the server, use the Remove Roles Wizard available from Server Manager after restarting the server.

Interoperability with Previous Versions of Active Directory

Many organizations have created Active Directory domains based on Windows 2000 or Windows Server 2003 domain controllers and are now in a position to take advantage of the new features of Windows Server 2008 and Windows Server 2008 R2 Active Directory. You can add new Windows Server 2008 domain controllers to an existing older Active Directory forest or upgrade all domain controllers in the forest to Windows Server 2008.

As summarized in Chapter 1, Active Directory in Windows Server 2008 and Windows Server 2008 R2 introduces numerous additional features not supported by previous versions of Windows Server. Many of these features limit the interoperability of Windows Server 2008 with previous versions, and Microsoft has extended the concept of domain and forest functional levels to define the actions that can be done on a network that includes older domain controllers.

This section looks at these functional levels and the tools used for upgrading an older Active Directory network to Windows Server 2008.

Forest and Domain Functional Levels

As you noticed when installing your first domain controller (refer to Figure 3-5), Table 3-3 summarizes the forest and domain functional levels supported by Active Directory in Windows Server 2008.

Table 3-3   Forest and Domain Functional Levels in Windows Server 2008 R2 Active Directory

Forest Functional Level	Domain Functional Levels Supported	Domain Controllers Supported
Windows 2000 native	Windows 2000 native	Windows 2000
	Windows Server 2003 native	Windows Server 2003
	Windows Server 2008 native	Windows Server 2008
	Windows Server 2008 R2 native	Windows Server 2008 R2
Windows Server 2003 native	Windows Server 2003 native	Windows Server 2003
	Windows Server 2008 native	Windows Server 2008
	Windows Server 2008 R2 native	Windows Server 2008 R2
Windows Server 2008 native	Windows Server 2008 native	Windows Server 2008
	Windows Server 2008 R2 native	Windows Server 2008 R2
Windows Server 2008 R2 native	Windows Server 2008 R2 native	Windows Server 2008 R2

To make use of the functionality provided by Windows Server 2008 Active Directory, you must upgrade all domain controllers to Windows Server 2008 and upgrade the functional levels accordingly. A domain running at the Windows Server 2008 domain functional level located in a forest running at a lower functional level supports domain-based Windows Server 2008 Active Directory features but not forest-based ones.

Furthermore, to make use of the newest Active Directory features in Windows Server 2008 R2, you must upgrade all domain controllers to Windows Server 2008 R2 and upgrade the domain and forest functional levels accordingly.

NOTE   You can deploy an RODC to a domain in which the domain and forest functional levels are set to Windows Server 2003, Windows Server 2008, or Windows Server 2008 R2.

Windows Server 2008 does not support the Windows 2000 mixed functional level previously found in older Active Directory networks. If you still have any domain controllers running Windows NT 4.0, you must upgrade or remove these domain controllers before introducing a Windows Server 2008 or Windows Server 2008 R2 domain controller on your network.

Upgrading Domain and Forest Functional Levels

To raise the forest functional level, you must first raise the functional level of all domains in the forest to the same or higher domain functional level. To raise the domain functional level, perform any of the following three actions:

- Open the Active Directory Administrative Center snap-in, right-click your domain, and then choose **Raise the domain functional level**.

- Open the Active Directory Users and Computers snap-in. Right-click **Active Directory Users and Computers** and choose **All Tasks > Raise domain functional level**.

- Open the Active Directory Domains and Trusts snap-in, right-click your domain, and choose **Raise domain functional level**.

In the dialog box shown in Figure 3-9, select the appropriate functional level and click **Raise**. Then click **OK** to accept the warning that is displayed.

Figure 3-9   Raising the domain functional level.

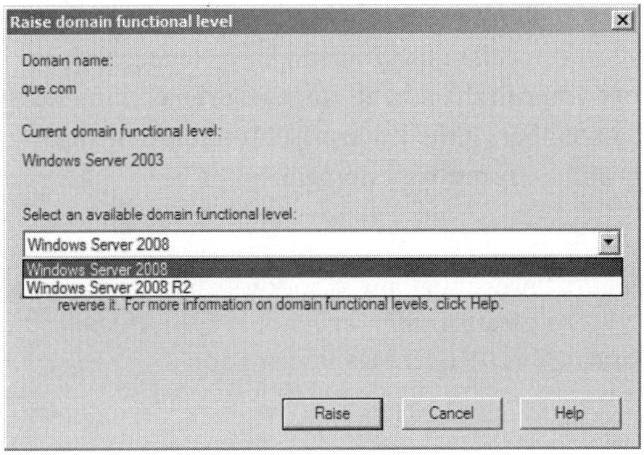

To raise the forest functional level, access the Active Directory Domains and Trusts snap-in. Right-click **Active Directory Domains and Trusts** and select **Raise forest functional level**. Select the appropriate functional level, click **Raise**, and then click **OK** to accept the warning that is displayed. You can also right-click your domain name in the Active Directory Administrative Center and choose **Raise the forest functional level** and then follow the same procedure described here.

WARNING   It is important to remember that raising forest and domain functional levels is a one-way operation. You cannot go back to a lower functional level. In addition, you cannot introduce an older domain controller after you have raised the domain functional level.

NOTE   For additional information on domain and forest functional level upgrades, refer to "Identifying Your Functional Level Upgrade" at http://technet.microsoft.com/en-us/library/cc754209(WS.10).aspx.

The **Adprep** Utility

Microsoft provides the Adprep utility to prepare a down-level Active Directory domain for receiving Windows Server 2008 and Windows Server 2008 R2 domain controllers. Found in the \sources\adprep folder of the installation DVD-ROM, this tool prepares the forest and domain by extending the Active Directory schema and updating several required permissions.

Running the **Adprep /forestprep** Command

You must run the Adprep /forestprep command on the schema master of the forest first. It extends the schema to receive the new Windows Server 2008 enhancements, including the addition of directory descriptors for certain objects including granular password policies. You have to run this command and let its changes replicate throughout the forest before you run the Adprep /domainprep command. To run this command, you must be a member of the Enterprise Admins, Schema Admins, and Domain Admins groups in the forest root domain.

WARNING   Before running this command, ensure that any Windows 2000 domain controllers are upgraded to SP2 or later, or at least to SP1 with hotfix QFE265089. Refer to Microsoft Knowledge Base article 331161 for more information.

Running the **Adprep /domainprep** Command

Run the `Adprep /domainprep` command on the infrastructure master of each domain in which you plan to introduce Windows Server 2008 domain controllers. It adjusts access control lists (ACLs) on Active Directory objects and on the SYSVOL shared folder for proper access by Windows Server 2008 domain controllers. To run this command, you must be a member of the Domain Admins group in the respective domain and the domain must be operating at the Windows 2000 Server native mode or higher.

You can also run the `Adprep /domainprep /prep` command to include updates required for enabling Resultant Set of Policy (RSoP) planning mode functionality.

TIP   Remember that you must run adprep /forestprep on the schema master and that you must run this command before you run adprep /domainprep. Also remember that you must run adprep /domainprep on the infrastructure master of each domain in which you want to introduce a Windows Server 2008 domain controller and that you must complete these commands before promoting or upgrading an existing domain controller.

Upgrading a Windows Server 2003 Domain Controller

You can also upgrade an existing Windows Server 2003 domain controller to Windows Server 2008. See Appendix B, "Installing Windows Server 2008 R2," for information on upgrading Windows Server 2003 computers; the procedure outlined in this chapter automatically upgrades AD DS to Windows Server 2008. However, you cannot upgrade a Windows 2000 domain controller to Windows Server 2008 directly; you must first upgrade to Windows Server 2003 and then to Windows Server 2008.

Note that to upgrade a Windows Server 2003 domain controller to Windows Server 2008, you must first run the Adprep utility as already discussed to upgrade the schema for accepting Windows Server 2008 domain controllers.

You can upgrade a Windows Server 2003 domain controller to Windows Server 2008 R2, provided the server meets the hardware requirements discussed in Appendix B.

Before upgrading the first Windows Server 2003 domain controller, ensure that you have run the Adprep /forestprep and Adprep /domainprep commands and that these commands have completed without error. Then select the **Install now** command from the Welcome screen displayed by the Windows Server 2008 R2 DVD-ROM, and follow the instructions provided by the Installation Wizard and summarized in Appendix B, "Memory Tables".

Additional Forest and Domain Configuration Tasks

This section introduces two additional configuration tasks specified in the Exam 70-640 objectives for configuring a forest or domain: use of the Active Directory Migration Tool (ADMT) v.3.1 and the alternative user principal name (UPN) suffix. Before introducing these tasks, we take a quick look at some procedures that verify that AD DS has been properly installed and, in doing so, introduce some to the administrative tools included with AD DS.

Verifying the Proper Installation of Active Directory

After you have installed Active Directory, there are several steps you should perform to verify that the proper components have been installed. Click **Start > Administrative Tools**. On a Windows Server 2008 R2 computer, you should see links to five Active Directory management tools: Active Directory Administrative Center, Active Directory Domains and Trusts, Active Directory Module for Windows PowerShell, Active Directory Sites and Services, and Active Directory Users and Computers. You should also see a link to the DNS snap-in unless you have specified another server as the DNS server for your domain.

Open Active Directory Users and Computers. You should see the default containers Builtin, Computers, ForeignSecurityPrincipals, Managed Service Accounts, and Users under the domain you have created. You should also see a default Domain Controllers OU. Select this OU and verify that computer accounts for all domain controllers in the domain are present, as shown in Figure 3-10.

On a Windows Server 2008 R2 computer, open Active Directory Administrative Center. As shown in Figure 3-11, this new MMC snap-in enables you to perform a large range of administrative tasks on your domain, including the following:

■ Creating and managing user, group, and computer accounts

■ Creating and managing OUs and other Active Directory containers

■ Managing other trusted AD DS domains

■ Using query-building searches to filter AD DS data

Uses of this tool will be discussed throughout this *Cert Guide* as appropriate, together with references to tools used on Windows Server 2008 computers that are not running R2.

Figure 3-10   After installing Active Directory, you should see a default set of containers in the Active Directory Users and Computers, together with domain controller computer accounts in the Domain Controllers OU.

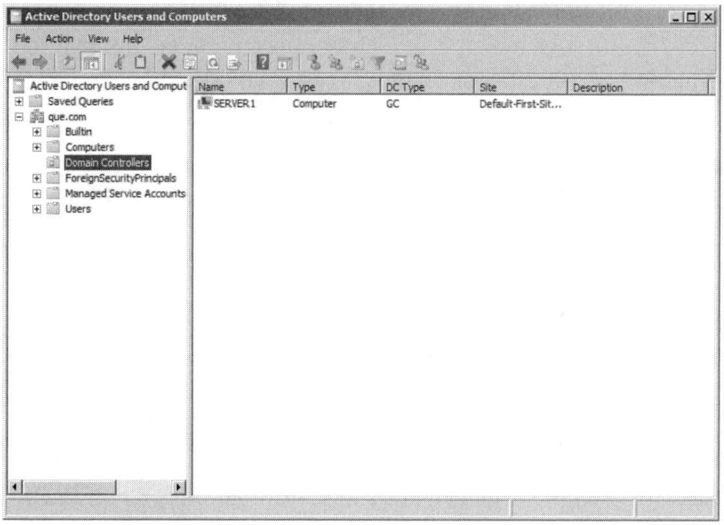

Figure 3-11   Windows Server 2008 R2 adds the Active Directory Administrative Center to the suite of tools provided for administering AD DS.

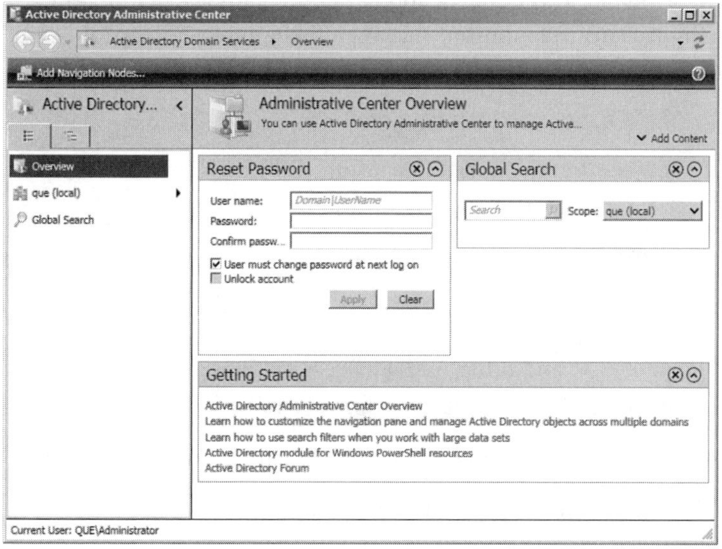

NOTE   In this discussion and elsewhere in this book, the term *Windows Server 2008* is taken to include both the original and R2 versions unless otherwise noted. The term *Windows Server 2008 R2* is used when referring to new features added with this version of the server software.

The Active Directory Administrative Center is installed automatically when you install the AD DS server role in Windows Server 2008 R2. You can also install this tool on a Windows Server 2008 R2 member server or a Windows 7 computer by installing the Remote Server Administration Tools (RSAT) feature. You cannot, however, install Active Directory Administrative Center on a computer running the original version of Windows Server 2008 or on older versions of Windows Server.

NOTE   For an overview of the capabilities of the Active Directory Administrative Center, refer to "What's New in AD DS: Active Directory Administrative Center" at http://technet.microsoft.com/en-us/library/dd378856(WS.10).aspx.

Active Directory Migration Tool v.3.1

ADMT v.3.1 is the most recent version of a utility, available for download from the Microsoft website, which assists you in migrating objects such as users, groups, and computers between Active Directory domains in the same forest or in different forests. This tool assists you in the potentially difficult task of restructuring your AD DS forest structure; for example, when changes in your organization's business structure occur because of mergers, acquisitions, or divestitures. You can migrate these objects from a source domain running at any functional level of Windows 2000 native or higher to a target domain running at any functional level of Windows 2000 native or higher. If the source and target domains are in different forests, you must configure trust relationships between the domains in use to ensure data security during the migration process.

Actions performed by ADMT include the following:

- Ensures security of objects being migrated by using 128-bit encryption with the Passport Export Server (PES) service

- Preserves the SID history of objects being migrated

- Enables migration of user profiles

- Migrates computer accounts including domain controllers

- Enables the restructuring of Active Directory domains between forests

- Enables you to use a preconfigured SQL database to hold migration information

- Enables you to perform test migrations so that you can ensure the actual migration will run properly

- Provides a log file that you can check for migration errors and other problems

- Provides for rollback options in the event that the migration does not proceed properly

- Facilitates the decommissioning of old domains in forests to be removed

NOTE   If you are migrating from or restructuring Windows NT 4.0 domains to Active Directory, you should use the 3.0 version of ADMT. You can use version 3.0 when restructuring a series of Windows NT 4.0 domains (such as account and resource domains structured into a multiple trust model) into a single Active Directory domain. Version 3.0 runs on Windows 2000 and Windows Server 2003 computers only; it does not run on Windows Server 2008 computers.

ADMT 3.1 runs on a server running the original edition of Windows Server 2008 only; it does not run on Windows Server 2008 R2. To use ADMT 3.1, navigate to http://www.microsoft.com/downloads/details.aspx?familyid=AE279D01-7DCA-413C-A9D2-B42DFB746059&displaylang=en and click the **Download** button. Then follow the instructions provided to download and save the `admtsetup31.exe` file to an appropriate location on your computer. Double-click the file, click **Run**, and then follow the instructions provided to install ADMT 3.1.

NOTE   For more information on ADMT 3.1, refer to "ADMT v3.1 Guide: Migrating and Restructuring Active Directory Domains" at http://www.microsoft.com/downloads/en/confirmation.aspx?familyId=6d710919-1ba5-41ca-b2f3-c11bcb4857af&displayLang=en. For information on use of ADMT 3.1 in domains with Windows Server 2008 R2 domain controllers, refer to "Known issues that may occur when you use ADMT 3.1 to migrate to a domain that contains Windows Server 2008 R2 domain controllers" at http://support.microsoft.com/kb/976659.

Alternative User Principal Name Suffixes

As mentioned earlier in this chapter, a UPN is a logon name specified in the format of an email address such as user@examcram.com. It is a convenient means of logging on to a domain from a computer located in another domain in the forest or a trusted forest. Two types of UPNs are available:

- **Implicit UPN:** This UPN is always in the form *user@domain*, such as peter@sales.que.com. It is defined on the Account tab of a user's Properties dialog box in Active Directory Users and Computers.

- **Explicit UPN:** This UPN is in the form *string1@string2*, where an administrator can define values for each string. For example, a user named Peter in the sales.que.com domain could have an explicit UPN in the form peter@sales. Using explicit UPNs is practical when an organization does not want to reveal its internal domain structure.

Windows Server 2008 supports the principle of the UPN suffix, first introduced in Windows Server 2003. This is the portion of the UPN to the right of the at (@) character. By default, the UPN suffix is the DNS domain name of the domain in which the user account is located.

Adding an alternative UPN suffix provides several advantages:

- You can use a common UPN suffix across all users in a forest. This is especially useful if some users have long domain names.

- The UPN suffix enables you to conceal the actual domain structure of the forest from external users.

- You can use separate UPN suffixes in situations where different divisions of a company have separate email domain names, thereby enabling users to log on with a name that matches their email address.

To define an alternative UPN suffix, access Active Directory Domains and Trusts from the Administrative Tools folder. Right-click **Active Directory Domains and Trusts** and click **Properties**. From the Properties dialog box shown in Figure 3-12, type the name of the alternative UPN suffix desired, click **Add**, and then click **OK**. After you have done this, the alternative UPN suffix is available when you are configuring new or existing user accounts. For more information on configuring user accounts, see Chapter 9.

Figure 3-12   You can configure alternative UPN suffixes from the Active Directory Domains and Trusts Properties dialog box.

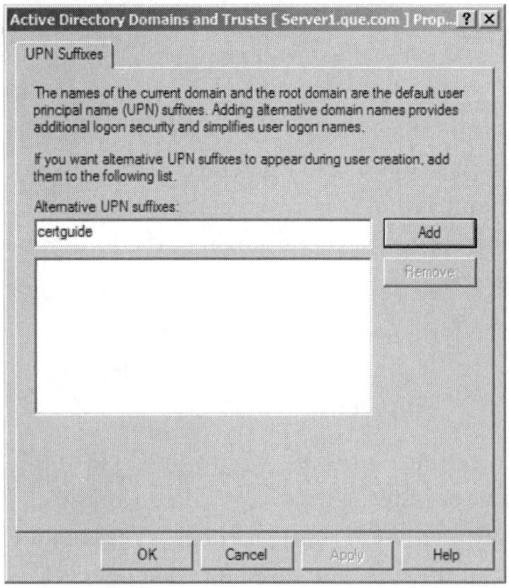

Exam Preparation Tasks

Review All the Key Topics

Review the most important topics in the chapter, noted with the key topics icon in the outer margin of the page. Table 3-4 lists a reference of these key topics and the page numbers on which each is found.

Table 3-4 Key Topics for Chapter 3

Key Topic Element	Description	Page Number
List	Lists important guidelines you should follow in preparing to install AD DS	80
List	Summarizes requirements for installing AD DS	81
Figure 3-2	You use the Add Roles Wizard to begin the installation of AD DS	83
Figure 3-3	Displays important security considerations when installing AD DS	84
Figure 3-5	Selecting a forest functional level	86
List	Summarizes important reasons for installing multiple domain controllers in a domain	89
Paragraph	Describes the methods of performing unattended installations of AD DS	90
Table 3-3	Summarizes available forest and domain functional levels in Windows Server 2008 R2	94
Paragraph	Describes the adprep utility used for preparing forests and domains for upgrade	96
Figure 3-12	Specifying additional UPN suffixes	102

Complete the Tables and Lists from Memory

Print a copy of Appendix C, "Memory Tables" (found on the CD), or at least the section for this chapter, and complete the tables and lists from memory. Appendix D, "Memory Tables Answer Key," also on the CD, includes completed tables and lists to check your work.

Definitions of Key Terms

Define the following key terms from this chapter, and check your answers in the glossary.

Active Directory Migration Tool (ADMT), Active Directory Administrative Center, Adprep, dcpromo, domain controller (DC), domain functional level, forest functional level, forest root, read-only domain controller (RODC), Server Core, universal principal name (UPN), universal principal name (UPN) suffix

This chapter covers the following subjects:

- **Configuring DNS Server Settings:** Each DNS server has a Properties dialog box associated with it from which you can configure a large number of server-specific properties. This section describes the more important settings in detail.

- **Configuring Zone Transfers and Replication:** For DNS to function properly in your domain, the various DNS servers must communicate with each other and synchronize their zone data; changes made at one server must appear in a timely fashion at other servers. This section shows you how to ensure that these transfers take place properly and troubleshoot common problems as they happen.

CHAPTER 4

Configuring DNS Server Settings and Replication

Chapter 2, "Installing and Configuring DNS for Active Directory," introduced you to the Domain Name System (DNS) and its importance with regard to the functionality of Active Directory Domain Services (AD DS). You learned how to configure the various types of DNS zones and their usage with respect to AD DS functionality. This chapter continues the discussion of DNS by showing you how to configure various DNS server settings and then follows up with a discussion of the various types of zone transfers and replication.

"Do I Know This Already?" Quiz

The "Do I Know This Already?" quiz enables you to assess whether you should read this entire chapter or simply jump to the "Exam Preparation Tasks" section for review. If you are in doubt, read the entire chapter. Table 4-1 outlines the major headings in this chapter and the corresponding "Do I Know This Already?" quiz questions. You can find the answers in Appendix A, "Answers to the 'Do I Know This Already?' Quizzes."

Table 4-1   "Do I Know This Already?" Foundation Topics Section-to-Question Mapping

Foundations Topics Section	Questions Covered in This Section
Configuring DNS Server Settings	1–8
Configuring Zone Transfers and Replication	9–13

1. You are responsible for a DNS server named DNS1 on your company's AD DS network. Your company has entered into a partnership agreement with another company that operates its own AD DS forest and DNS servers. Clients on your company's network need access to resources on the partner company's network. Network engineers have installed a T3 line for direct communication between the two companies without using the Internet. How should you configure DNS1 so that requests for the other company go directly to that company's DNS servers without accessing the Internet?

a. Specify the other company's DNS servers as forwarders.

b. Specify DNS1 as a forwarder.

c. Configure DNS1 as a conditional forwarder and include the IP address of the partner company's DNS server for handling name resolution requests for that company's network.

d. Configure the partner company's DNS server as a conditional forwarder and include the IP address of DNS1 for handling name resolution requests for the partner company's network.

2. You are responsible for configuring the DNS server on your network. Users at your company report that they are unable to access external websites. You check network connectivity and find that you can access external websites by IP address but not by name. Which of the following should you check at the DNS server?

a. Conditional forwarders

b. Root hints

c. Zone delegation

d. Round robin

3. You run the New Delegation Wizard to create a zone delegation. When finished, you look at the resource records displayed in the details pane of the DNS Manager snap-in. Which of the following resource records should you find for the delegated zone? (Choose two.)

a. A

b. SOA

c. NS

d. PTR

e. DNSKEY

4. You are working from a computer running the Server Core version of Windows Server 2008 R2 and want to create a zone delegation. What command should you use?

a. `dnscmd/recordadd`

b. `dnscmd/config`

c. `dnscmd/zoneresetsecondaries`

d. `dnscmd/zoneadd`

5. You want to create a record of packets sent to and from your DNS server and store this information in a text file for later analysis. What feature should you enable?

   a. DNS monitoring

   b. Event logging

   c. Debug logging

   d. DNS notify

6. You want to ensure that your DNS server is using digital signatures to validate responses from other DNS servers and responders to reduce the probability of several types of intrusions. On which tab of the DNS server's Properties dialog box should you look for this information?

   a. Event Logging

   b. Debug Logging

   c. Advanced

   d. Security

   e. Trust Anchors

7. You want to ensure that requests for a hostname that is mapped to multiple IP addresses on different subnets always returns an IP address located on the same subnet as the requesting client. Which option should you select?

   a. **Disable recursion**

   b. **Enable round robin**

   c. **Enable netmask ordering**

   d. **Secure cache against pollution**

8. You want to check that your DNS server is able to forward a name resolution query to another DNS server for resolution. What should you do?

   a. Access the server's Monitoring tab and select a simple query.

   b. Access the server's Monitoring tab and select a recursive query.

   c. Access the server's Advanced tab and ensure that the **Disable recursion** option is not selected.

   d. Access the zone's Zone Transfers tab and ensure that the **Automatically notify** option is selected.

9. You are responsible for maintaining the DNS servers on your company's AD DS forest, which contains five domains and 12 DNS servers. One of these servers is still running Windows 2000, and it is also hosting an application that still has not been updated for use with newer Windows versions. You have installed a new DNS server and need to ensure that it can replicate its zone data to all servers including the Windows 2000 server. Which replication scope option should you choose?

   a. **To all DNS servers running on domain controllers in this forest**

   b. **To all DNS servers running on domain controllers in this domain**

   c. **To all domain controllers in this domain**

   d. **To all domain controllers in the scope of this directory partition**

10. Under which of the following conditions does a primary DNS server perform a full zone transfer to its zone's secondary servers?

    a. The secondary server's history file has been deleted.

    b. The secondary server's serial number is less than the primary server's serial number.

    c. The secondary server's serial number is greater than the primary server's serial number.

    d. The secondary server's IP address is not listed on the Name Servers tab of the Zone Transfers tab at the primary server.

11. You are responsible for three DNS servers on your AD DS network, which is configured as a single domain. The servers host an Active Directory–integrated zone that encompasses the entire domain. You want to ensure that other DNS servers are notified of changes to the zone data so that proper replication is maintained. What should you do?

    a. From the Zone Transfers tab of the zone's Properties dialog box, click **Allow Zone Transfers** and select the **Only to the following servers** option. Then ensure that the other DNS servers are listed in the space provided.

    b. From the Zone Transfers tab of the zone's Properties dialog box, click **Allow Zone Transfers** and select the **Only to servers listed on the Name Servers tab** option.

    c. From the Zone Transfers tab of the zone's Properties dialog box, click **Notify** and select the **Servers listed on the Name Servers tab** option.

    d. You do not need to do anything. This notification happens automatically when DNS is configured with Active Directory–integrated zones.

12. You have configured DNS to use Active Directory–integrated zones in your AD DS forest, which includes a forest root domain plus three child domains. Which Active Directory partitions will be used to store the zone data in this scenario?

    a. One ForestDnsZones application directory partition and four DomainDnsZones application directory partitions.

    b. One ForestDnsZones application directory partition and one DomainDnsZones application directory partition.

    c. Four ForestDnsZones application directory partition and four DomainDnsZones application directory partitions.

    d. All data will be stored in the Configuration directory partition.

13. You have created an application directory partition named APP1 on a domain controller in the que.com domain to store data from a custom engineering package and replicate it to domain controllers named DC2 and DC3. DC3 is located in a child domain named design.que.com. What should you do to enable the partition to replicate to these domain controllers?

    a. Specify design.que.com as the application directory partition reference domain.

    b. Create new application directory partitions on both DC2 and DC3.

    c. Create application directory partition replicas on both DC2 and DC3.

    d. You do not need to do anything. AD DS replication will automatically replicate the partition to these domain controllers.

Foundation Topics

Configuring DNS Server Settings

As you learned in Chapter 2, when you install the DNS server role on a Windows Server 2008 or Windows Server 2008 R2 computer, the DNS Manager Microsoft Management Console (MMC) snap-in is automatically installed, providing you with all the tools required to manage and administer DNS. When you install AD DS as described in Chapter 3, "Installing Active Directory Domain Services," the DNS zones needed for administering DNS in the AD DS domain are added to your DNS installation. This section introduces you to server-specific settings that you can configure from the DNS server's Properties dialog box.

From the DNS Manager snap-in, right-click the DNS server and choose **Properties** to display the dialog box shown in Figure 4-1. This dialog box enables you to configure a comprehensive range of server-specific properties. The more important properties are discussed in this section.

Figure 4-1   The DNS server's Properties dialog box enables you to configure many DNS server properties.

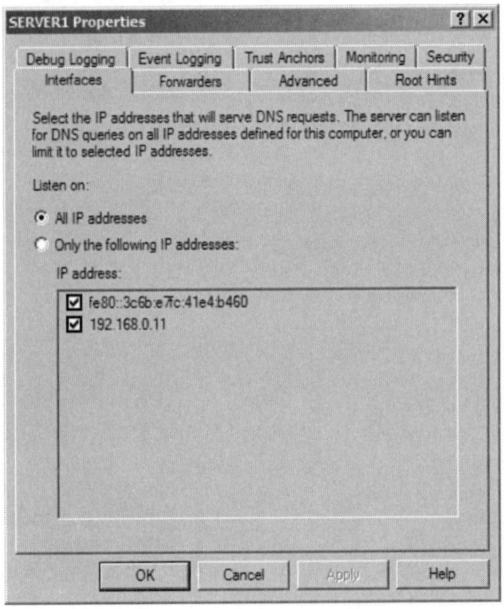

Forwarding

The act of *forwarding* refers to the relaying of a DNS request from one server to another one when the first server is unable to process the request. This is especially useful in resolving Internet names to their associated IP addresses. By using a forwarder, the internal DNS server passes off the act of locating an external resource, thereby reducing its processing load and network bandwidth. The use of forwarding is also helpful for protecting internal DNS servers from access by unauthorized Internet users. It works in the following manner:

Step 1.   A client issues a request for a fully qualified domain name (FQDN) on a zone for which its preferred DNS) server is not authoritative (for example, an Internet domain such as www.google.com).

Step 2.   The local DNS server receives this request but has zone information only for the internal local domain and checks its list of forwarders.

Step 3.   Finding the IP address of an external DNS server (such as one hosted by the company's ISP), it forwards the request to the external server (forwarder).

Step 4.   The forwarder attempts to resolve the required FQDN. Should it not be able to resolve this FQDN, it forwards the request to another forwarder.

Step 5.   When the forwarder is able to resolve the FQDN, it returns the result to the internal DNS server by way of any intermediate forwarders, which then returns the result to the requesting client.

You can specify forwarders from the Forwarders tab of the DNS server's Properties dialog box, as shown in Figure 4-2. Click **Edit** to open the Edit Forwarders dialog box shown in Figure 4-3. In the space provided, specify the IP address of a forwarder and click **OK** or press **Enter**. The server will resolve this IP address to its FQDN and display these in the Forwarders tab. You can also modify the sequence in which the forwarding servers are contacted by using the Up and Down command buttons, or you can remove a forwarding server by selecting it and clicking **Delete**.

You can also specify forwarders from the command line by using the dnscmd command. This command was introduced for command-line administration of DNS in Chapter 2; further uses of this command are included throughout this chapter. Open an administrative command prompt and use the following command syntax:

```
dnscmd ServerName /ResetForwarders MasterIPaddress ... [/TimeOut Time]
  [/Slave]
```

The parameters of this command are as follows:

■ *ServerName:* Specifies the DNS hostname of the DNS server. You must include this parameter; use a period to specify the local computer.

■ **/ResetForwarders:** Indicates that you are configuring a forwarder.

■ *MasterIPaddress ...:* Specifies a space-separated list of one or more IP addresses of DNS servers to which queries are forwarded.

■ **/TimeOut:** Specifies a timeout setting in seconds.

■   **/Slave**: Determines whether the DNS server uses recursion when querying for the domain name specified by *ZoneName*.

Figure 4-2   The Forwarders tab of the DNS server's Properties dialog box enables you to specify forwarders used by the current DNS server.

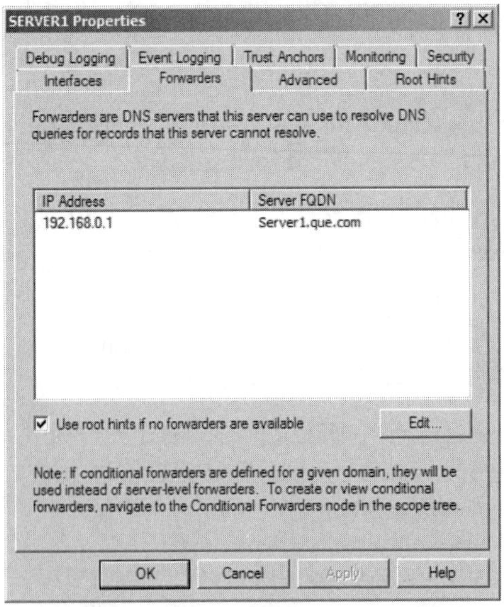

Figure 4-3   The Edit Forwarders dialog box enables you to add or remove forwarding servers or to modify the sequence in which they are contacted.

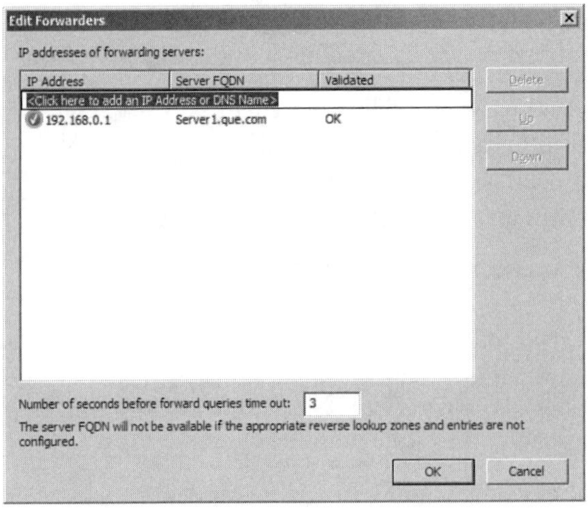

Conditional Forwarders

You can configure a DNS server as a conditional forwarder. This is a DNS server that handles name resolution for specified domains only. In other words, the local

DNS server will forward all the queries that it receives for names ending with a specific domain name to the conditional forwarder. This is especially useful in situations where users in your company need access to resources in another company with a separate AD DS forest and DNS zones, such as a partner company. In such a case, specify a conditional forwarder that directs such queries to the DNS server in the partner company while other queries are forwarded to the Internet. Doing so reduces the need for adding secondary zones for partner companies on your DNS servers.

The DNS snap-in provides a Conditional Forwarders node where you can specify forwarding information. Use the following procedure to specify conditional forwarders:

Step 1.   Right-click the Conditional Forwarders node and choose **New Conditional Forwarder** to display the dialog box shown in Figure 4-4.

Figure 4-4   Creating a new conditional forwarder.

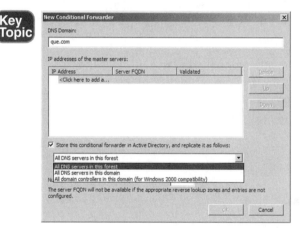

Step 2.   Type the DNS domain that the conditional forwarder will resolve and the IP address of the server that will handle queries for the specified domain.

Step 3.   If you want to store the conditional forwarder information in AD DS, select the check box provided and choose an option in the drop-down list as shown in Figure 4-4 that specifies the DNS servers in your domain or forest that will receive the conditional forwarder information. Then click **OK**.

Information for the conditional forwarder you have configured is added beneath the Conditional Forwarders node in the DNS Manager snap-in. Name queries for the specified DNS domain will now be forwarded directly to this server.

NOTE   For more information on forwarders and conditional forwarders, refer to "Understanding Forwarders" at http://technet.microsoft.com/en-us/library/cc730756.aspx.

> **TIP** The **All DNS servers in this forest** and **All DNS servers in this domain** options will replicate conditional forwarder information to DNS servers running Windows Server 2003 or 2008 only. If you have any DNS servers running Windows 2000 that are to receive the conditional forwarder information, you must select the **All domain controllers in this domain** option. An exam question might test your knowledge of this fact.

Root Hints

Whenever a DNS server is unable to resolve a name directly from its own database or with the aid of a forwarder, it sends the query to a server that is authoritative for the DNS root zone. Recall from Chapter 2 that the root is the topmost level in the DNS hierarchy. The server must have the names and addresses of these servers stored in its database to perform such a query. These names and addresses are known as *root hints*, and they are stored in the cache.dns file, which is found at %systemroot%\system32\dns. This is a text file that contains NS and A records for every available root server.

When you first install DNS on a server connected to the Internet, it should download the latest set of root hints automatically. You can verify that this has occurred by checking the Root Hints tab of the server's Properties dialog box. You should see a series of FQDNs with their corresponding IP addresses, as shown in Figure 4-5.

Figure 4-5 The Root Hints tab of the DNS server's Properties dialog box displays the names and IP addresses of the Internet root zones.

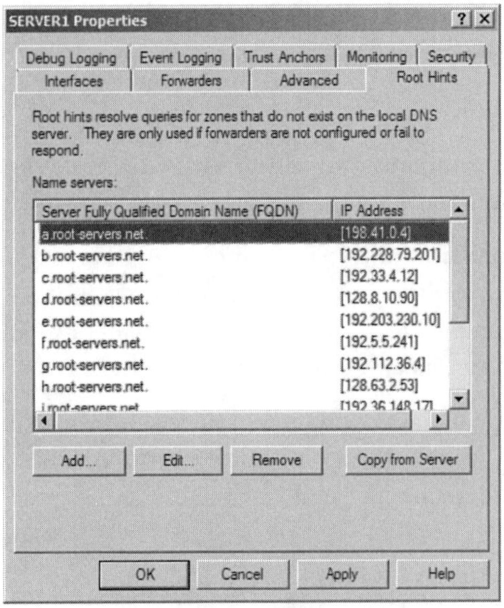

If your internal DNS server does not provide access to Internet name resolution, you can improve network security by configuring the root hints of the internal

DNS servers to point to the DNS servers that host your root domain and not to Internet root domain DNS servers. To modify the configuration on this tab, perform one or more of the following actions:

- Click **Add** to display the New Name Server Record dialog box, from which you can manually type the FQDNs and IP addresses of one or more authoritative name servers.

- Select an entry and click **Edit** to display the Edit Name Server Record dialog box, which enables you to modify it or add an additional IP address to an existing record.

- Select an entry and click **Remove** to remove a record.

- Click **Copy from Server** to copy a list of root hints from another DNS server. Type the DNS name or IP address in the dialog box that appears. This action is useful if your server was not connected to the Internet at the time DNS was installed.

- Although this is not a recommended action, you can also edit the cache.dns file using a text editor such as Notepad.

TIP   You can also use the Configure a DNS Server Wizard to configure root hints for your server. Right-click your server in the console tree of the DNS Manager snap-in and choose **Configure a DNS Server**. Then select the **Configure root hints only (recommended for advanced users only)** option from the Select Configuration Action page of the wizard.

Configuring Zone Delegation

As you have seen, you can divide your DNS namespace into a series of zones. You can delegate management of these zones to another location or workgroup within your company by delegating the management of the respective zone. Configuring zone delegation involves creating delegation records in other zones that point to the authoritative DNS servers for the zone being delegated. Doing so enables you to transfer authority as well as providing correct referral to other DNS servers and clients utilizing these servers for name resolution.

Zone delegation offers the following benefits:

- You can delegate the administration of a portion of your DNS namespace to another office or department in your company.

- You can subdivide your zone into smaller zones for load balancing of DNS traffic among multiple servers. This also enables improved DNS name resolution performance and fault tolerance.

- You can extend the namespace by adding additional subdomains for purposes such as adding new branch offices or sites.

You can use the New Delegation Wizard to create a zone delegation. The wizard uses the information you supplied to create name server (NS) and host (A or AAAA) resource records for the delegated subdomain. Perform the following procedure:

Step 1. Right-click the parent zone in the console tree of DNS Manager and choose **New Delegation**. This starts the New Delegation Wizard.

Step 2. Click **Next** and then enter the name of the delegated subdomain.

Step 3. As shown in Figure 4-6, the wizard appends the parent zone name to form the FQDN of the domain being delegated. Click **Next** and then click **Add**.

Figure 4-6   Creating a zone delegation.

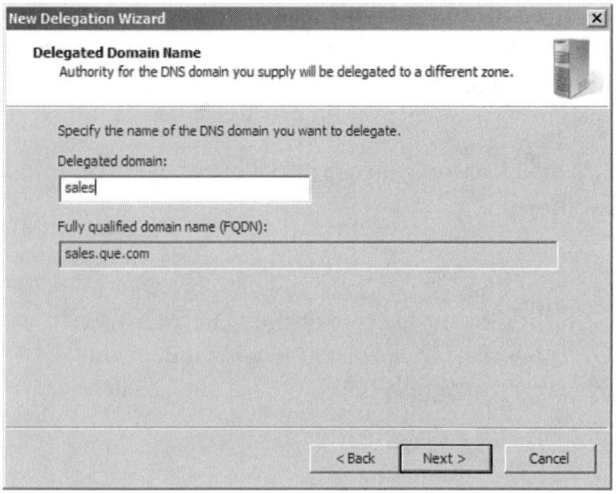

Step 4. In the New Name Server Record dialog box, type the FQDN and IP address of the DNS server that is authoritative for the subdomain and then click **OK**. Repeat if necessary to add additional authoritative DNS servers.

Step 5. The servers you've added are displayed on the Name Servers page of the wizard, as shown in Figure 4-7. When finished, click **Next** and then click **Finish**.

NOTE   When you use `dcpromo.exe` to create a new domain and install DNS at the same time, the AD DS Installation Wizard automatically creates the zone delegation for the new domain.

You can also use the `dnscmd` utility to perform zone delegation from the command line. Open an administrative command prompt and use the following command:

```
dnscmd ServerName /RecordAdd ZoneName NodeName
  [/Aging] [/OpenAcl] [Ttl] NS {HostName¦FQDN}
```

Figure 4-7   Specifying a name server that hosts the zone delegation.

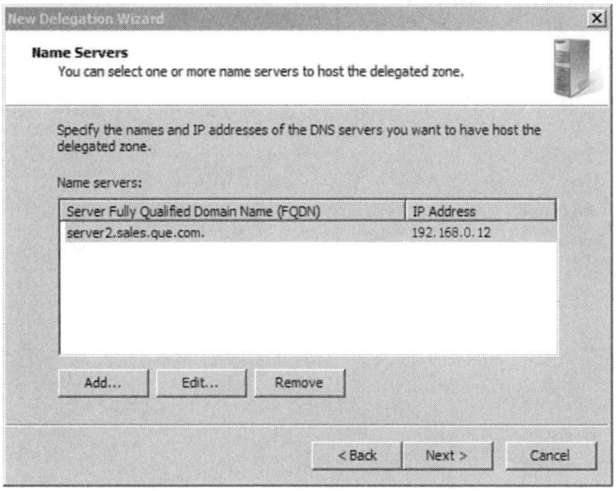

The parameters of this command are as follows:

- *ServerName*: Specifies the DNS hostname of the DNS server. You must include this parameter; use a period to specify the local computer.

- **/RecordAdd**: Required; indicates that you are adding a resource record.

- *ZoneName*: Required; specifies the FQDN of the zone being delegated.

- *NodeName*: Required; specifies the FQDN of the node in the DNS namespace for which the start of authority (SOA) record is added.

- **/Aging**: Enables the resource record to be aged and scavenged.

- **/OpenAcl**: Specifies that any user is permitted to modify the new records (otherwise only administrators can modify them).

- *Ttl*: Specifies the time to live (TTL) setting for the resource record, if different from the TTL defined in the SOA resource record.

- **NS**: Required; specifies that you are adding an NS resource record for the delegated zone.

- *HostName¦FQDN*: Required; specifies the hostname or FQDN of the new authoritative server.

> **NOTE**   For more information on zone delegation, refer to "Create a Zone Delegation" at http://technet.microsoft.com/en-us/library/cc753500.aspx.

Debug Logging

The DNS server also supports debug logging of packets sent to and from the DNS server to a text file named dns.log. This file is stored in the

`%systemroot%\system32\dns` folder. To configure logging, right-click the server in the DNS Manager snap-in and choose **Properties**. Click the **Debug Logging** tab to receive the dialog box shown in Figure 4-8.

Figure 4-8   Configuring debug logging.

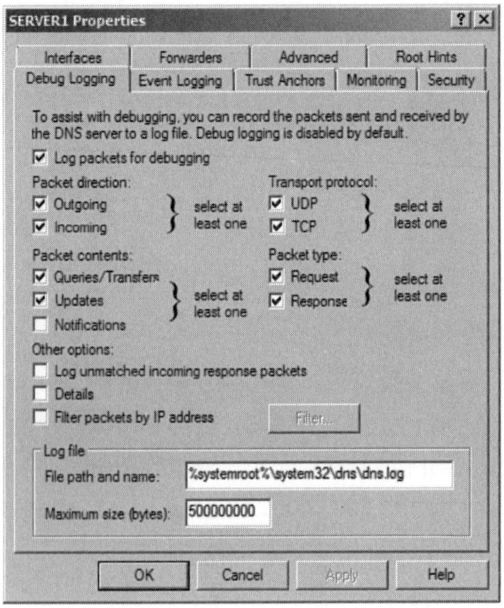

By default, no logging is configured. Select the **Log packets for debugging** check box, which makes all other check boxes available. Table 4-2 describes the available logging options.

Table 4-2   DNS Debug Logging Options

Option	Description
Packet direction	Determines the direction of packets logged, incoming or outgoing or both.
Transport protocol	Select **UDP** to log the number of DNS requests received over a UDP port, and select **TCP** to log the number of DNS requests received over a TCP port.
Packet contents	Select at least one of the available options to determine the types of packets logged by the server: ■ **Queries/Transfers**: Logs packets containing standard queries, according to RFC 1034. ■ **Updates**: Logs packets containing dynamic updates, according to RFC 2136. ■ **Notifications**: Logs packets containing notifications, according to RFC 1996.

Table 4-2 DNS Debug Logging Options

Option	Description
Packet type	Determines whether the request or response (or both) packets are logged.
Other options	Select **Details** to enable logging of detailed information.
	Select **Filter** to limit the packets that are logged according to IP address. This logs packets sent from specific IP addresses to the DNS server or from the DNS server to these specific IP addresses (according to the incoming or outgoing choice).
Log file	Enables you to change the default file path, name, and maximum size. If the maximum size is exceeded, the DNS server overwrites the oldest logged data.

WARNING Configure debug logging only when absolutely necessary, only on required DNS servers, and only on a temporary basis. Its use is highly resource intensive. It is for this reason that debug logging is disabled by default.

To view the DNS log, first stop the DNS service by right-clicking the DNS server in DNS Manager and choosing **All Tasks > Stop**. Then open the log in either Notepad or WordPad. When you are finished, restart the DNS service by right-clicking the DNS server and choosing **All Tasks > Start**.

Event Logging

The Event Logging tab of the DNS server's Properties dialog box enables you to control how much information is logged to the DNS log, which appears in Event Viewer. You can choose from one of the following options:

- **No events:** Suppresses all event logging (not recommended).

- **Errors only:** Logs error events only.

- **Errors and warnings:** Logs errors and warnings only.

- **All events:** Logs informational events, errors, and warnings. This is the default.

Choosing either the **Errors only** or **Errors and warnings** option might be useful to reduce the amount of information recorded to the DNS event log.

DNS Security Extensions

DNS in itself is vulnerable to certain types of intrusions such as spoofing, man-in-the-middle, and cache-poisoning attacks. Because of this, DNS Security Extensions (DNSSEC) was developed to add additional security to the DNS protocol. Outlined in Requests for Comments (RFCs) 4033, 4034, and 4035,

DNSSEC is a suite of DNS extensions that adds security to the DNS protocol by providing origin authority, data integrity, and authenticated denial of existence. Although an older form of DNSSEC was used in Windows Server 2003 and the first iteration of Windows Server 2008, DNSSEC has been updated completely according to the specifications in the just-mentioned RFCs. The newest form of DNSSEC is available for Windows Server 2008 R2 and Windows 7 only.

DNSSEC enables DNS servers to use digital signatures to validate responses from other servers and resolvers. Signatures are stored in a new type of resource record called DNSKEY within the DNS zone. On resolving a name query, the DNS server includes the appropriate digital signature with the response, and the signature is validated by means of a preconfigured trust anchor. A *trust anchor* is a preconfigured public key associated with a specific zone. The validating server is configured with one or more trust anchors. Besides DNSKEY, DNSSEC adds RRSIG, NSEC, and DS resource records to DNS.

You can view zones that are signed with DNSSEC in the DNS Manager tool, and you can view the trust anchors from the Trust Anchors tab of the DNS server's Properties dialog box, as shown in Figure 4-9.

Figure 4-9   The Trust Anchors tab of the DNS server's Properties dialog box enables you to view and specify trust anchors configured on your DNS server.

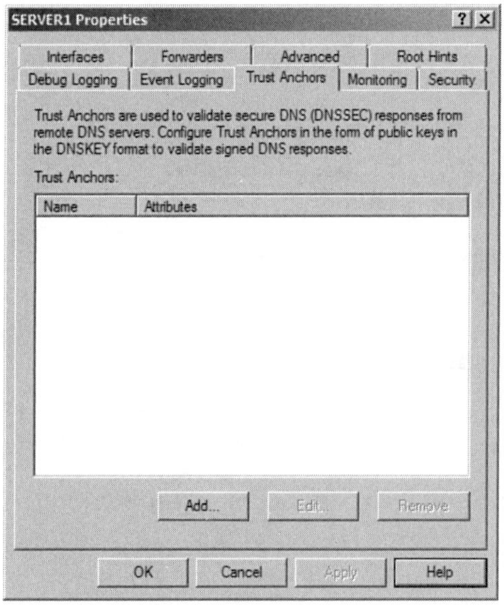

To specify a trust anchor, click **Add**. Provide the information requested in the New Trust Anchor dialog box, including its name and public key value, and then click **OK**. The public key value must be formatted as a Base64 encoding value; for more information on the public key, refer to http://www.rfc-archive.org/getrfc.php?rfc=4034. Doing so adds the trust anchor to the Trust Anchors tab and enables its use for signing DNS query responses.

> **NOTE** For more information on how DNSSEC works, refer to "DNSSEC Security Extensions (DNSSEC)" at http://technet.microsoft.com/en-us/library/ee683904(WS.10).aspx, "Introduction to DNSSEC" at http://technet.microsoft.com/en-us/library/ee649205(WS.10).aspx, and "Understanding DNSSEC in Windows" at http://technet.microsoft.com/en-us/library/ee649277(WS.10).aspx.

Advanced Server Options

The Advanced tab of the DNS server's Properties dialog box shown in Figure 4-10 contains a series of options that you should be familiar with.

Figure 4-10 The Advanced tab of the DNS server's Properties dialog box enables you to configure several additional server options.

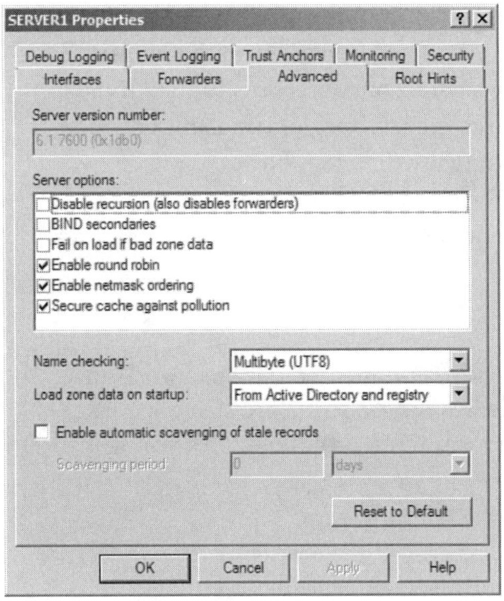

Server Options

The Server options section of this dialog box contains the following six options, the last three of which are selected by default:

- **Disable recursion:** Prevents the DNS server from forwarding queries to other DNS servers, as described later in this section. Select this check box on a DNS server that provides resolution services only to other DNS servers because unauthorized users can use recursion to overload a DNS server's resources and thereby deny the DNS Server service to legitimate users.

- **BIND secondaries:** During zone transfer, DNS servers normally utilize a fast transfer method that involves compression. If UNIX servers running a version of Berkeley Internet Name Domain (BIND) prior to 4.9.4 are present, zone transfers will not work. These servers use a slower uncompressed data transfer method. To enable zone transfer to these servers, select this check box.

- **Fail on load if bad zone data:** When selected, DNS servers will not load zone data that contains certain types of errors. The DNS service checks name data using the method selected in the Name Checking drop-down list on this tab.

- **Enable round robin:** Enables round robin, as described later in this section.

- **Enable netmask ordering:** Prioritizes local subnets so that when a client queries for a hostname mapped to multiple IP addresses, the DNS server preferentially returns an IP address located on the same subnet as the requesting client.

- **Secure cache against pollution:** Cache pollution takes place when DNS query responses contain malicious items received from nonauthoritative servers. This option prevents attackers from adding such resource records to the DNS cache. The DNS servers ignore resource records for domain names outside the domain to which the query was originally directed. For example, if you sent a query for que.com and a referral provided a name such as quepublishing.com, the latter name would not be cached when this option is enabled.

> **TIP**   Remember that if you have a UNIX server running an older version of BIND, you should select the **BIND secondaries** option to ensure that zone transfer takes place properly with such a server. An exam question might ask you why a UNIX server is not staying up-to-date.

Round Robin

Round robin is a load-balancing mechanism used by DNS servers to distribute name resolution activity among all available DNS servers. If multiple A or AAAA resource records are found in a DNS query (for example, on a multihomed computer), round robin sequences these resource records randomly in repeated queries for the same computer. An example in which round robin is useful is a situation where you have multiple terminal servers in a server farm that users access for running applications. DNS uses round robin to randomize the sequence in which users accessing the terminal servers reach given servers.

NOTE For more information on using round robin in a terminal server environment, refer to "TS Session Broker Load Balancing Step-by-Step Guide" at http://technet.microsoft.com/en-us/library/cc772418(WS.10).aspx.

By default, round robin is enabled on Windows Server 2008 R2 DNS servers. You can verify or modify this setting from the Advanced tab of the DNS server's Properties dialog box already shown in Figure 4-10. Select or clear the check box labeled **Enable round robin** as required.

Disable Recursion

The act of recursion refers to the name-resolution technique where a DNS server queries other DNS servers on behalf of the requesting client to obtain the required FQDN, which it returns to the client. Unauthorized individuals can use recursion to overload a DNS server's resources, thereby causing a denial of service (DoS) attack on the DNS server and preventing its servicing of legitimate name resolution requests.

To reduce the possibility of a DoS attack on an internal network DNS server that does not need to process recursive queries, you should disable recursion on the DNS server. To do so, select the check box labeled **Disable recursion (also disables forwarders)** from the Advanced tab of the server's Properties dialog box previously shown in Figure 4-10.

You can also disable recursion from the command line. Open an administrative command prompt, and type the following command:

```
dnscmd ServerName> /Config /NoRecursion {1¦0}
```

In this command, the /Config parameter specifies that the server indicated by *ServerName* is being configured, and the /NoRecursion parameter together with the numeral 1 disables recursion. To reenable recursion, reissue the same command with the numeral 0.

NOTE For more information on disabling recursion, refer to "Disable Recursion on the DNS Server" at http://technet.microsoft.com/en-us/library/cc771738.aspx.

Name Checking

The Name Checking setting enables you to configure the DNS server to permit names that contain characters that are not allowed by the normal DNS standards outlined in RFC 1123. You can select the following options:

- **Strict RFC (ANSI):** Uses strict name checking according to RFC 1123 host naming specifications. Noncompliant DNS names generate error messages.

- **Non RFC (ANSI):** Permits nonstandard names that do not conform to RFC 1123 host naming specifications. ASCII characters that are not compliant to RFC 1123 specifications are accepted.

- **Multibyte (UTFB):** The default setting, enables the transformation and recoding of multibyte non-ASCII characters according to Unicode Transformation Format (UTF-8) specifications.

- **All names:** Permits names containing any types of characters.

If you receive an error with ID 4006, indicating that the DNS server was unable to load the records in the specified name found in the Active Directory–integrated zone, this means that the DNS name contains unsupported characters. You can resolve this problem by selecting the **All names** option and restarting the DNS service. This enables the DNS names to be loaded. If the names are improper, you can delete them and then reset the Name Checking setting.

Loading Zone Data

When a DNS server containing an Active Directory–integrated zone starts up, it normally uses information stored in this zone and in the Registry to initialize the service and load its zone data. This option enables you to specify that the DNS server starts from the Registry only or from a file named Boot and located in the %systemroot%\System32\Dns folder. This optional file is similar in format to that used by BIND servers.

Server Scavenging

When DHCP registers A and PTR resource records automatically, these records remain in the DNS zone data indefinitely. If computers are frequently added to or removed from the network (for example, when many portable computers are in use), many stale resource records can accumulate. As mentioned in Chapter 2, these records can degrade the DNS server's performance. By selecting the **Enable automatic scavenging of stale records** check box, the DNS server checks the age of each dynamically assigned record and removes records that are older than the scavenging period that you specify in this option (7 days by default). Note that Windows computers send a request to the DNS server to update their records every 24 hours; consequently, DNS records from active computers never become stale even if their TCP/IP configuration does not change.

Scavenging is disabled by default. You should enable scavenging if computers are frequently added to or removed from the network to ensure continued optimum performance of DNS servers.

> **NOTE**   You can also set server scavenging properties by right-clicking the server in the console tree of DNS Manager and choosing **Set Aging/Scavenging for All Zones**, as was discussed in Chapter 2. The Server Aging/Scavenging Properties

dialog box that displays offers the same options previously shown in Figure 2-12 for zone scavenging; however, these settings are applied to all zones hosted by this server.

TIP   If you have improperly configured options on this tab and want to return to the default options, click the **Reset to Default** command button at the bottom of this tab and then click **Apply** to apply this change without closing the dialog box (or **OK** to apply the changes and close the dialog box).

Monitoring DNS

DNS Manager includes a testing capability that enables you to perform test queries that verify the proper installation and operation of the DNS server. In the console tree of the DNS snap-in, right-click the DNS server name and choose **Properties** to open the server's Properties dialog box. Shown in Figure 4-11, the Monitoring tab enables you to perform two types of test queries:

- **Simple query:** The DNS client software performs a local query to a zone stored in the DNS server (including Active Directory–integrated zones).

- **Recursive query:** A recursive query is forwarded to another DNS server for resolution.

Figure 4-11   The Monitoring tab enables you to perform simple and recursive test queries against the DNS server.

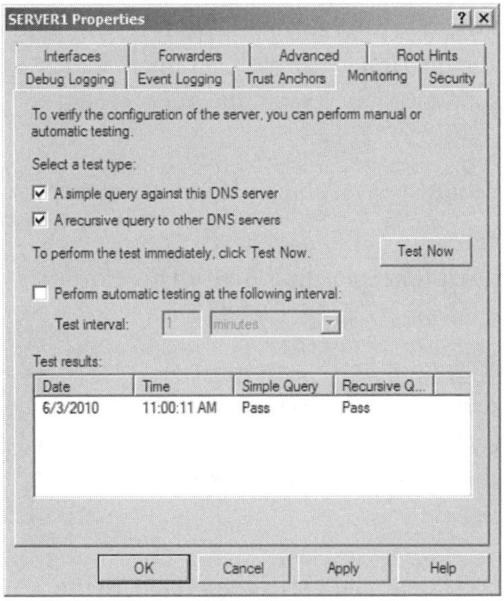

To perform these queries, select the appropriate check boxes as illustrated in Figure 4-11 and click the **Test Now** command button. The result is displayed in the Test results field directly below. You can also schedule the test to occur automatically at preconfigured intervals.

A `Pass` result for the simple test confirms that DNS has been correctly installed on this server. If the simple test fails, you should ensure that the local server contains the zone `1.0.0.127.in-addr.arpa`. If the recursive test fails, check the connectivity to the remote server as well as the presence and correctness of the root hints file (`cache.dns`).

> **NOTE**   Refer to "Monitor Your DNS Servers on Windows Server 2008 R2" at http://technet.microsoft.com/en-us/magazine/ff521760.aspx for more information on using the Monitoring tab.

DNS also adds a log to the Event Viewer and several objects and counters to the Performance Monitor. In addition, you can use the `Nslookup` utility to verify the accuracy of resource records.

> **NOTE**   Refer to "`Nslookup`" at http://technet.microsoft.com/en-us/library/cc725991(WS.10).aspx and "DNS Tools" at http://technet.microsoft.com/en-us/library/cc753579.aspx for additional details on these monitoring tools.

Configuring Zone Transfers and Replication

When changes are made to zone data on the master DNS server, these must be replicated to all DNS servers that are authoritative for the zone. This is essential in order that the data be available for answering queries. Otherwise, if only a single DNS server is available and if it fails to respond for any reason, the query would fail.

The following two methods of DNS replication are available in Windows Server 2008 DNS:

- Active Directory replication, which is used for replicating Active Directory–integrated zones.

- Zone transfer, which can be used by all types of DNS zones. Active Directory–integrated zones also use zone transfer to replicate data to a standard secondary zone located on another DNS server operated for purposes of fault tolerance, load balancing, and reduction of DNS network traffic.

Replication Scope

The replication scope of an Active Directory–integrated DNS zone refers to the subset of DNS servers or domain controllers that actively participate in replication of the specific zone. DNS in Windows Server 2008 makes available the replication scopes described in Table 4-3.

Table 4-3 Available DNS Replication Scopes

Replication Scope	Description
All DNS servers in the forest hosted on domain controllers running Windows Server 2003 or 2008	Replicates zone data to all Windows Server 2003 or 2008 domain controllers running DNS in the AD DS forest. By replicating zone data to the ForestDNSZones application directory partition, it provides the broadest replication scope.
All DNS servers in the domain hosted on domain controllers running Windows Server 2003 or 2008	Replicates zone data to all Windows Server 2003 or 2008 domain controllers running DNS in the AD DS domain, by replicating zone data to the DomainDNSZones application directory partition. This is the default replication scope.
All domain controllers in the AD DS domain	Replicates zone data to all domain controllers in the AD DS domain. This scope is required if you want Windows 2000 DNS servers to be included in the scope of an Active Directory–integrated zone. When this scope is used, zone data is stored in the domain directory partition.
All domain controllers hosting a specified application directory partition	Replicates zone data according to the replication scope of the specified application directory scope. Enables the replication of zone data to domain controllers in multiple domains without replicating the data to the entire AD DS forest.

You can change the replication scope of an Active Directory–integrated primary or stub forward lookup zone, but not that of a secondary forward lookup zone. To change the replication scope of a zone, right-click the zone in DNS Manager and choose **Properties**. On the General tab of the zone's Properties dialog box, click **Change** next to **Replication**. From the dialog box shown in Figure 4-12, select the desired option and then click **OK**.

Note that replication scope is not available for DNS zones that are not integrated with Active Directory. These zones use the zone transfer method only for replication.

Figure 4-12   The Change Zone Replication Scope dialog box offers options for configuring a zone's replication scope.

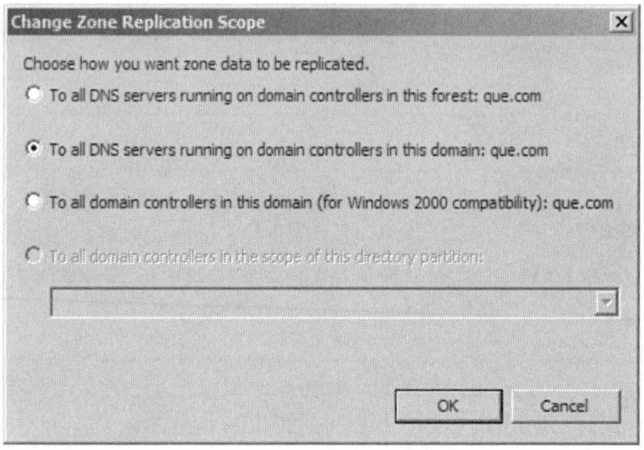

NOTE   For more information on DNS zone replication scopes, refer to "Understanding DNS Zone Replication in Active Directory Domain Services" at http://technet.microsoft.com/en-us/library/cc772101.aspx.

You can also specify an application directory partition within which a zone will be stored from the command line. Open an administrative command prompt and type the following command:

```
dnscmd ServerName /ZoneChangeDirectoryPartition ZoneName
  NewPartitionName
```

In this command, the /ZoneChangeDirectoryPartition parameter directs that the zone specified by *ZoneName* will be stored in the application directory partition whose FQDN is specified as *NewPartitionName*.

TIP   If you have any Windows 2000 DNS servers, you must select the **To all domain controllers in this domain** option in Figure 4-12. If you upgrade all Windows 2000 DNS servers to Windows Server 2003 or 2008, you can change the replication scope to any of the other available options.

Types of Zone Transfers

Every version of DNS since Windows 2000 has supported two types of zone transfer: *full zone transfer (AXFR)* and *incremental zone transfer (IXFR)*.

Full Zone Transfer

The original specifications for DNS supported only the full zone transfer process, in which the master server transmits the entire zone database to that zone's secondary servers. When a new secondary DNS server is added to the network, it uses AXFR to obtain a full copy of the zone's resource records. AXFR was the only zone transfer process supported by Windows NT 4.0 DNS.

Incremental Zone Transfer

The process of incremental zone transfer, as specified in RFC 1995, replicates only the modified portion of each zone file. It is therefore more efficient and uses less bandwidth than the full zone transfer process.

The DNS servers involved in the IXFR process use the following sequential procedure:

Step 1.   The secondary DNS server sends an IXFR request to the primary server. This request contains a serial number for the secondary server's current zone database, which is found in its SOA resource record. This serial number is incremented each time the zone information changes. The SOA record also contains a number called the *refresh interval*, which is 15 minutes by default and determines how often the server sends the IXFR request.

Step 2.   The master server checks the secondary server's serial number against the current one.

Step 3.   If the two serial numbers are equal, the master server determines that no zone transfer is needed at the current time and the process ends.

Step 4.   If the primary server's serial number is higher, it determines that a zone transfer is required.

Step 5.   This server checks its history file that indicates which portions of the zone have been modified at what time. It uses this file to determine the updates that must be sent in response to the IXFR request.

Step 6.   When the secondary server receives the incremental zone transfer, it creates a new version of the zone file and replaces the updated records with the new ones, beginning with the oldest one.

Step 7.   When the secondary server has updated all the records, it replaces the old version of the zone with the newest version of the zone.

A full zone transfer might still take place rather than an incremental zone transfer under the following conditions:

- If the master DNS server does not support incremental zone transfers

- If the bandwidth required for sending an incremental zone transfer is greater than that required for sending a full zone transfer

- If the master DNS server does not possess all the data required for the incremental zone transfer, such as an accurate history file

DNS servers that load zone data from Active Directory use a similar process, in which they poll the directory at an interval determined by the refresh interval in the SOA record for updating and refreshing their zone.

Configuring Zone Transfers

The Zone Transfers tab of a zone's Properties dialog box enables you to configure the scope of zone transfers. Right-click the zone in DNS Manager, choose **Properties**, and then select the **Zone Transfers** tab. You can select any of the options displayed in Figure 4-13 to specify the scope of zone transfers.

Figure 4-13   Specifying the scope of zone transfers.

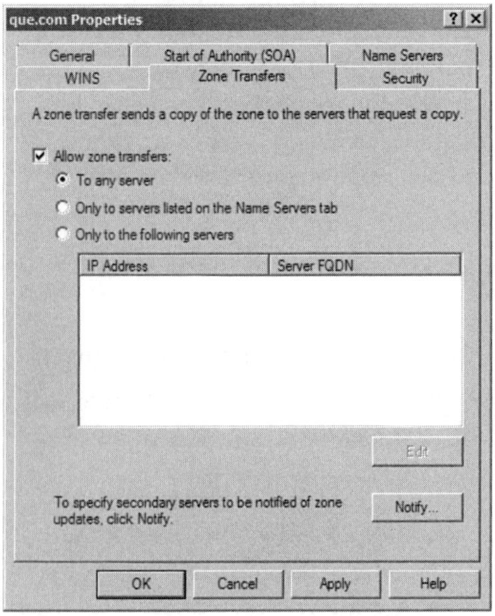

By selecting **Only to servers listed on the Name Servers tab**, you enable zone transfers to all DNS servers for which NS records are specified in the zone data. The Name Servers tab and its configuration are discussed later in this section. By specifying the **Only to the following servers** option, you can specify DNS servers that are to receive zone transfers according to IP address or FQDN.

You can also specify the scope of a zone transfer from the command line. Open an administrative command prompt and type the following:

```
dnscmd ServerName /ZoneResetSecondaries ZoneName {/NoXfr ¦ /NonSecure ¦
    /SecureNs ¦ /SecureList [SecondaryIPAddress...]}
```

The parameters of this command are as follows:

- *ServerName*: Specifies the DNS hostname of the DNS server. You must include this parameter; use a period to specify the local computer.

- **/ZoneResetSecondaries**: Required; indicates that you're modifying the scope of the zone transfer.

- *ZoneName*: Required; specifies the FQDN of the zone being configured.

- **/NoXfr**: Disables zone transfers for the specified zone.

- **/NonSecure**: Permits zone transfers to any DNS server.

- **/SecureNs**: Permits zone transfers to only those DNS servers specified by the /SecureList parameter.

- *SecondaryIPAddress*: Required if /SecureList is used; specifies the IP addresses of DNS servers to which zone transfers are permitted.

Additional parameters are available for this command. For more information, open a command prompt and type **dnscmd /ZoneResetSecondaries /?.**

NOTE If you are using Active Directory–integrated zones, zone data is automatically replicated to all other domain controllers in the domain. Consequently, you cannot limit zone transfers for Active Directory–integrated zones.

Configuring DNS Notify

DNS notify is a process in which the master DNS server for a zone notifies secondary servers of changes to the zone so that the secondary servers can check to determine whether they need to initiate a zone transfer. You can configure the DNS server for DNS notify by specifying the list of IP addresses to which notifications are to be sent. Configuring the notify list also helps you to prevent attempts by unknown DNS servers to request zone updates from your server.

To configure the notify list, proceed as follows:

Step 1. Access the Zone Transfers tab of the zone's Properties dialog box previously shown in Figure 4-13, and click the **Notify** command button.

Step 2. On the Notify dialog box shown in Figure 4-14, ensure that **Automatically notify** is selected.

Figure 4-14 Specifying a DNS notify list.

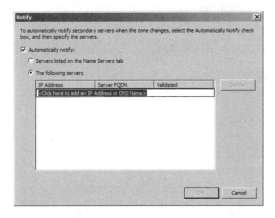

Step 3. Select **Servers listed on the Name Servers tab** to use the list of DNS servers for which NS records are configured (as discussed later in this section), or select **The following servers** to specify the desired servers by IP address.

Step 4. When finished, click **OK** to close the Notify dialog box and click **OK** again to close the zone's Properties dialog box.

> **NOTE**   The notify list is required only for servers that operate as secondary DNS servers for zones that are not integrated with AD DS. You do not need to configure DNS notify for Active Directory–integrated zones.

Secure Zone Transfers

If you are using DNS servers running BIND 9 or higher, you can specify that zone transfers be digitally signed. This feature enables secondary DNS servers to verify that zone transfers are being received from a trusted source.

As already discussed, you cannot limit the scope of zone transfer when using Active Directory–integrated zones. If you are concerned about zone data passing through an unsecured network segment, you can use a security mechanism such as IP Security (IPSec) to specify rules that secure the zone transfer process. When used, only zone transfers between servers whose IP addresses are specified on the Zone Transfers tab and that meet the conditions specified in the IPSec rule are permitted.

To specify an IPSec secure zone transfer policy, use the following procedure:

Step 1. At the DNS server, click **Start** and type `gpedit.msc` in the Start menu Search field. Then select **gpedit.msc** to open the Local Group Policy Editor.

Step 2. Navigate to the **Computer Configuration\Windows Settings\ Security Settings\Windows Firewall with Advanced Security\ Windows Firewall with Advanced Security–Local Group Policy Object** node.

Step 3. Right-click **Connection Security Rules** and choose **New Rule**.

Step 4. On the Rule type page of the New Connection Security Rule Wizard, select **Custom** and then click **Next**.

Step 5. On the Endpoints page, specify the IP address ranges of the computers between which secure zone transfers are to be permitted. To do so, select **These IP addresses** under the appropriate endpoint and click **Add**. As shown in Figure 4-15, you can specify IP address ranges as single addresses, subnets, ranges of addresses, or predefined sets of computers (which includes a DNS Servers option). Perform this task for both endpoints, and then click **Next**.

Figure 4-15   The New Connection Security Rule Wizard provides several means of identifying the range of computers to which the rule applies.

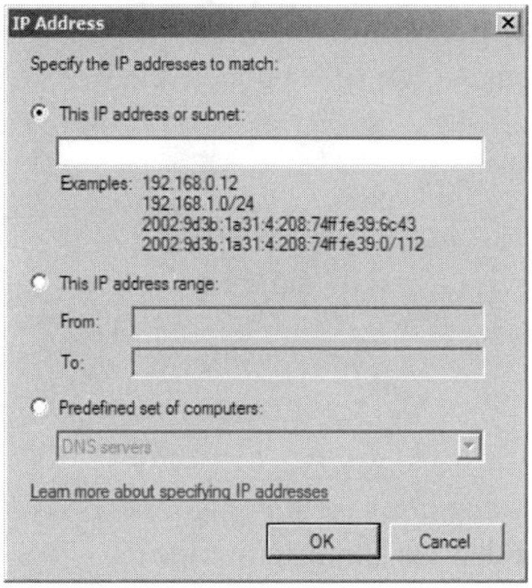

Step 6.   On the Requirements page shown in Figure 4-16, select the **Require authentication for inbound and outbound connections** option and then click **Next**.

Figure 4-16   The New Connection Security Rule Wizard provides four authentication requirement options.

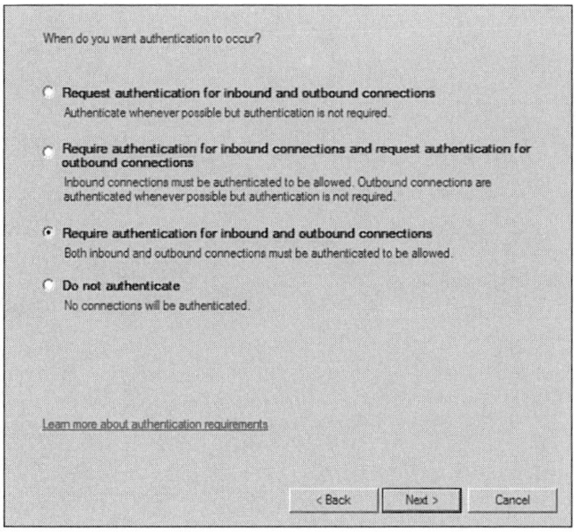

Step 7.   On the Authentication Method page, select **Computer (Kerberos V5)** and then click **Next**.

Step 8.   On the Protocol and Ports page, ensure that **Any** is selected next to Protocol Type and then click **Next**.

Step 9.   On the Profile page, ensure that all three check boxes are selected and then click **Next**.

Step 10.   On the Name page, type a name and optional description for the rule and then click **Finish**. You have now enabled an IPSec policy rule for secured zone transfers.

> **NOTE**   For more information on configuring secured zone transfers, refer to "Secure Zone Transfers with IPSec" at http://technet.microsoft.com/en-us/ library/ee649192(WS.10).aspx.

Configuring Name Servers

The Name Servers tab of the zone's Properties dialog box shown in Figure 4-17 enables you to configure secondary name servers that are authoritative for the zone, which are DNS servers that receive zone updates for zones that are not integrated with AD DS. To add a name server to this list, click **Add** and in the New Name Server Record dialog box shown in Figure 4-18, type the server FQDN and IP address. Click **Resolve** to validate the name and IP address combination and then click **OK**. The FQDN and IP address are added to the list in the Name Servers tab. By selecting the zone name in the console tree of the DNS Manager snap-in, you can see the NS record that has been added to the list.

Figure 4-17   The Name Servers tab lists all DNS servers for which NS resource records are available.

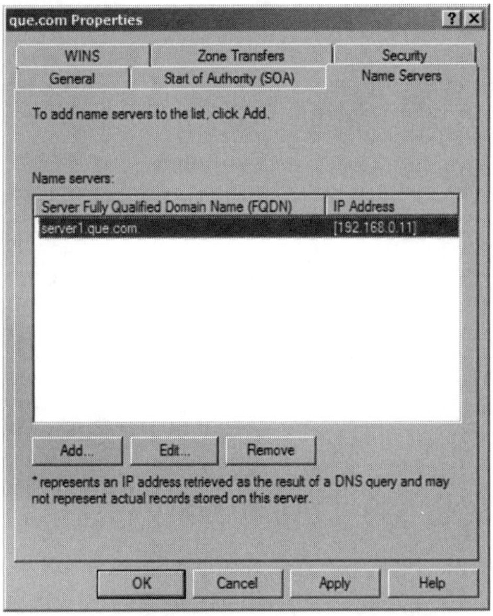

Figure 4-18 The New Name Server Record dialog box enables you to add a new name server to the list in the Name Servers tab of the zone's Properties dialog box.

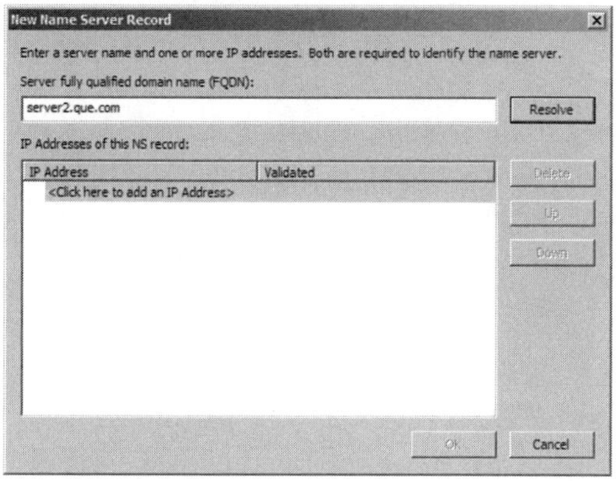

To edit an entry in the Name Servers tab, select it and click **Edit**. The **Edit Name Server Record** dialog box, which is similar to the New Name Server Record dialog box, enables you to add additional IP addresses or modify the name of the server. You can prioritize the IP addresses on the IP address list by using the **Up** and **Down** buttons or delete an IP address by selecting it and using the **Delete** button. You can also delete an entry from the Name Servers tab by selecting it and clicking **Remove**.

You can also specify name servers from the command line by using the dnscmd tool. Open an administrative command prompt and type the following:

```
dnscmd ServerName /RecordAdd ZoneName NodeName [/Aging] [/OpenAcl]
   [Ttl] NS {HostName ¦ DomainName}
```

The parameters of this command are as follows:

- *ServerName*: Specifies the DNS hostname of the DNS server. You must include this parameter; use a period to specify the local computer.

- **/RecordAdd**: Required; adds a resource record.

- *ZoneName*: Required; specifies the FQDN of the zone being configured.

- *NodeName*: Required; specifies the FQDN of the node in the DNS namespace for which you are adding a SOA record.

- **/Aging**: Enables aging and scavenging of the resource record. If not used, the resource record stays in the DNS database until manually deleted or updated.

- **/OpenAcl**: Specifies that any user is permitted to modify the new records. If not used, only administrators have permission to modify the new record.

- *Ttl*: Specifies the TTL setting for the resource record. If not used, the default TTL in the SOA resource record is used.

- **NS**: Required; specifies that you are adding a NS resource record to the specified zone.

Application Directory Partitions

First introduced in Windows Server 2003, an *application directory partition* (also simply called an *application partition*) contains application-specific data that needs to be replicated only to specific domain controllers in one or more domains of the Active Directory forest. DNS stores its Active Directory–integrated zone data in the following application directory partitions, which are automatically created when you install DNS during creation of your domain:

- **ForestDnsZones**: Contains forestwide DNS zone data, one partition per forest.

- **DomainDnsZones**: Contains domainwide DNS zone data, one partition for each domain in the forest.

By utilizing application directory partitions, Active Directory replicates its DNS data to other domain controllers in the forest. A benefit of application directory partitions is that their data can be replicated to only specific domain controllers, as opposed to domain partitions, which are replicated to all domain controllers in the domain. Consequently, replication traffic is reduced. For example, DNS application directory partitions are replicated only to those domain controllers that are running DNS. The same application directory partition can replicate to domain controllers in more than one domain in the forest.

Installing and Configuring Application Directory Partitions

An application directory partition is identified by its LDAP distinguished name (DN). For example, you could create an application partition named app on the que.com domain by using the DN dc=app,dc=que,dc=com. You can use the ntdsutil tool for creating an application directory partition. This is a command-line utility that provides a number of management capabilities for managing AD DS and Active Directory Lightweight Directory Services (AD LDS). It is installed automatically when you add either of these roles to your Windows Server 2008 R2 computer. Use the following procedure:

Key Topic

Step 1.   Log on to a domain controller or member server as a member of the Domain Admins or Enterprise Admins group.

Step 2.   Open a command prompt and type **ntdsutil.**

Step 3.   At the ntdsutil prompt, type **domain management.**

Step 4.   At the domain management prompt, type **connection.**

Step 5.   At the connection prompt, type **connect to server** *server*, **where** *server* is the name of the domain controller to which you want to connect.

Step 6.   Type **quit** to return to the **domain management** prompt.

Step 7. At this prompt, type **create nc** *application_directory_partition*
domain_controller, where *application_directory_partition* is the
DN of the application directory partition you want to create and
domain_controller is the name of the domain controller on which you
want to create the partition. Type **null** to create the application directory partition on the current domain controller. For example, to create
an application directory partition named App1 on Server1, type **create**
nc App1 Server1.

Step 8. You receive a prompt informing you that the object was added to the
directory. Type **quit twice to exit the ntdsutil** utility.

You can also use ntdsutil to delete application directory partitions that
are no longer required. At step 7 of this procedure, type **delete**
nc *application_directory_partition domain_controller.*

Creating Application Directory Partition Replicas

The previous procedure creates an application partition on the indicated domain controller only. To replicate the partition to other domain controllers in the domain or
forest, you need to create an *application directory partition replica*. In this manner, you
can control the set of domain controllers among which the partition is replicated.

The procedure for creating a replica is the same as that for creating the application
directory partition as outlined in the previous section, except that at step 7, type
add nc replica *application_directory_partition domain_controller.* The
DN you specify should be the same as that of the partition you have created, and
domain_controller is the name of the domain controller on which the replica is to
be placed. For example, to add a replica of the App1 application directory partition
to server Server2, type **add nc replica App1 Server2.**

Should you no longer require a replica on a given domain controller, you can follow this procedure using the remove nc replica command in place of the add nc
replica command.

Application Directory Partition Reference Domains

The *application directory partition reference domain* is the parent domain of the application directory partition; in other words, it is the domain name as included in the
partition's DN. It is also known as the *security descriptor reference domain*.

You can change an application directory partition's reference domain by using the
ntdsutil utility. Follow the procedure previously described for installing an
application directory partition, and in step 7, type **set nc reference**
domain *application_directory_partition reference_domain,* where
reference_domain is the DN of the desired reference domain.

Exam Preparation Tasks

Review All the Key Topics

Review the most important topics in the chapter, noted with the key topics icon in the outer margin of the page. Table 4-4 lists a reference of these key topics and the page numbers on which each is found.

Table 4-4   Key Topics for Chapter 4

Key Topic Element	Description	Page Number
Figure 4-2	Shows how to specify DNS forwarders	114
Figure 4-4	Displays replication options available when configuring DNS conditional forwarders	115
Figure 4-6	Shows how to specify a zone delegation	118
Table 4-2	Describes debug logging options	120
Figure 4-10	Displays advanced DNS server configuration options	123
Table 4-3	Describes DNS replication scope options	129
Paragraph	Describes types of zone transfers	130
Figure 4-13	Shows how to specify the scope of zone transfers	132
Figure 4-17	Specifying DNS servers to act as name servers	136
List	Describes how to create an application directory partition	138

Complete the Tables and Lists from Memory

Print a copy of Appendix C, "Memory Tables" (found on the CD), or at least the section for this chapter, and complete the tables and lists from memory. Appendix D, "Memory Tables Answer Key," also on the CD, includes completed tables and lists to check your work.

Definitions of Key Terms

Define the following key terms from this chapter, and check your answers in the glossary.

application directory partition, conditional forwarding, DNS notify, dnscmd, DNSSEC (Domain Name System Security Extensions), forwarding, full zone transfer (AXFR), incremental zone transfer (IXFR), recursion, replication scope, root hints, round robin, secure zone transfer, zone delegation

This chapter covers the following subjects:

■ **Configuring Global Catalog Servers:** A global catalog server holds a subset of Active Directory information for each domain in the forest as well as information on universal group membership. In this section, you learn how to configure domain controllers as global catalog servers.

■ **Configuring Operations Masters:** Each Active Directory forest has five important roles that are held by single domain controllers. This section shows you how to configure these roles. You also learn the important characteristics of the Active Directory schema and why the schema is so important to the proper functioning of Active Directory.

CHAPTER 5

Global Catalogs and Operations Masters

For users to achieve the maximum benefit of Active Directory, they must be able to locate resources on the network, whether they are in the local domain, another domain in the forest, or a trusting forest. Chapter 1, "Getting Started with Active Directory," introduced the various components of Active Directory. Included was the concept of the global catalog, which is a central information database that can hold data describing objects throughout the Active Directory forest namespace. Chapter 1 also introduced several directory roles performed by the global catalog, including providing universal group information. This chapter takes you further into the strategy of placing global catalog servers and universal group information and shows you how you can configure these aspects of the directory.

Chapter 1 also introduced you to the five operations masters roles, which are initially held on the first domain controller in each domain. Recall that these are specialized roles that can be held on only a single domain controller in your domain. This chapter also discusses configuring these roles as well as several problems that might arise if these roles become unavailable.

"Do I Know This Already?" Quiz

The "Do I Know This Already?" quiz enables you to assess whether you should read this entire chapter or simply jump to the "Exam Preparation Tasks" section for review. If you are in doubt, read the entire chapter. Table 5-1 outlines the major headings in this chapter and the corresponding "Do I Know This Already?" quiz questions. You can find the answers in Appendix A, "Answers to the 'Do I Know This Already?' Quizzes."

Table 5-1 "Do I Know This Already?" Foundation Topics Section-to-Question Mapping

Foundations Topics Section	Questions Covered in This Section
Configuring Global Catalog Servers	1–4
Configuring Operations Masters	5–13

1. In which of the following situations does the global catalog server play a minor role, such that it is not important for you to designate additional global catalog servers?

    a. Your AD DS forest consists of a single domain.

    b. Your AD DS forest consists of three domains but only a single site.

    c. Your AD DS forest contains an empty forest root domain plus a single child domain holding all user and computer accounts.

    d. Your AD DS forest consists of two domains and eight sites, and at least one domain controller is located at every site in the forest.

2. What tool do you use to designate a domain controller as a global catalog server?

    a. Active Directory Administrative Center

    b. Active Directory Users and Computers

    c. Active Directory Domains and Trusts

    d. Active Directory Sites and Services

3. On which of these servers does it make the greatest sense to enable universal group membership caching?

    a. On domain controllers at the head office of a multiple domain enterprise that are not designated as global catalog servers

    b. At a small branch office of a multiple domain enterprise that has a single domain controller that is also designated as a global catalog server

    c. On a domain controller in a small branch office of a multiple domain enterprise where no global catalog server is located and which is connected to the head office by a low-bandwidth WAN

    d. On a member server in a small branch office of a multiple domain enterprise where no global catalog server is located and which is connected to the head office by a low-bandwidth WAN

    e. On a domain controller in a small branch office of a company with a single domain forest where no global catalog server is located and which is connected to the head office by a low-bandwidth WAN

4. You are the network administrator for a company that operates an AD DS forest consisting of three domains. There are five branch offices with slow WAN links to the head office. Users at one of the branch offices, which has a domain controller running Windows Server 2008 R2, report that logon times are often slow. Further, attempts at accessing resources across domain boundaries are also slow. What should you do?

    a. Ensure that at least two domain controllers in the head office are designated as global catalog servers.

    b. Designate the branch office domain controller as a global catalog server.

    c. Configure all head office domain controllers that are not global catalog servers for universal group membership caching.

    d. Configure the branch office domain controller for universal group membership caching.

5. Your company is operating an AD DS forest containing an empty root domain and three child domains that represent operational divisions. You are responsible for maintaining the operations masters in the forest. In total, how many operations masters are you responsible for?

    a. One schema master, one domain naming master, one RID master, one PDC emulator, and one infrastructure master

    b. Four schema masters, four domain naming masters, four RID masters, four PDC emulators, and four infrastructure masters

    c. One schema master, one domain naming master, four RID masters, four PDC emulators, and four infrastructure masters

    d. One schema master, one domain naming master, three RID masters, three PDC emulators, and three infrastructure masters

6. You are responsible for configuring the schema and need to add new classes, so you log on to the schema master, which runs Windows Server 2008 R2, as a member of the Schema Admins group. You cannot find the Active Directory Schema snap-in, so you open an empty MMC console and attempt to add this snap-in. However, the snap-in does not appear in the Add or Remove Snap-ins dialog box. What do you need to do first?

    a. Use Control Panel Add or Remove Programs to locate the Active Directory Schema snap-in.

    b. Open a command prompt and type `regsvr32 schmmgmt.dll.`

    c. Access the Microsoft website and download the Remote Server Administration Tools (RSAT).

    d. You do not need the Active Directory Schema snap-in with Windows Server 2008 R2. Use the Active Directory Management Center instead.

7. You have added several new attributes and classes to the schema in your company's AD DS forest. However, one of the attributes is causing problems and you want to remove it. What do you need to do?

    a. Deactivate the attribute.

    b. Delete the attribute.

    c. Move the attribute to a different class.

    d. Change the Unique X.500 Object ID property of the attribute to a null value.

8. The day after completing a three-week vacation, you come to the office and discover that users have complained that one of the domain controllers is not accepting logons. On checking Event Viewer, you notice several W32Time errors. You connect to the problematic domain controller and discover that its time is 15 minutes slow. Which of the following operations masters should you check for problems?

   a. Infrastructure master

   b. Schema master

   c. RID master

   d. PDC emulator

9. You are planning to move several of the operations master roles to new domain controllers that have been recently added to your company's AD DS network, which consists of four domains. Two domain controllers in each domain are designated as global catalog servers. Which of the following operations master roles should you not place on a server that is designated as a global catalog server?

   a. Infrastructure master

   b. Schema master

   c. RID master

   d. PDC emulator

10. You are the network administrator for a small company that operates an AD DS network consisting of a single domain. The company is expected to grow at only a very slow rate for the next decade or so, and it is not anticipated that any additional domains will be added. As long as the network consists of a single domain, which of the following operations masters will not perform any significant specific functions during this time? (Choose two.)

   a. Infrastructure master

   b. Schema master

   c. RID master

   d. Domain naming master

   e. PDC emulator

11. The day after your network was down because of a power failure that lasted for several hours, several users report that they are unable to access shared resources in other domains of your company's AD DS forest, which consists of four domains in two domain trees. Which of the following operations masters should you check for problems?

    a. Infrastructure master

    b. Schema master

    c. RID master

    d. PDC emulator

12. You have installed Windows Server 2008 R2 on a powerful new server and promoted this computer to domain controller. You now want to transfer operations master roles to this server, so you open Active Directory Users and Computers and connect to this server. Which of the following operations master roles can you transfer to this server using this tool? (Choose all that apply.)

    a. Infrastructure master

    b. Schema master

    c. RID master

    d. PDC emulator

    e. Domain naming master

13. The motherboard and processor on the domain controller hosting the infrastructure master role has failed; it will be several weeks before parts will be available to repair it and you need to get this role up and running as soon as possible. What should you do?

    a. Use the `ntdsutil` tool to transfer this role to another domain controller.

    b. Use the `ntdsutil` tool to seize this role to another domain controller.

    c. Use Active Directory Administrative Center to transfer this role to another domain controller.

    d. Use Active Directory Administrative Center to seize this role to another domain controller.

Foundation Topics

Configuring Global Catalog Servers

Global catalog (GC) servers maintain a subset of information pertaining to all objects located in its domain, plus summary information pertaining to objects in other domains of its forest. In doing so, a GC server enables the following features:

- It validates universal group memberships at logon.

- It enables users to search the entire forest for resources they might need to access.

- It validates references to objects located in other domains in the forest.

- It validates user principal names (UPNs) across the entire forest, thereby enabling user logon in other domains.

> **NOTE**   For more information on the purposes of GC servers, refer to "Understanding the Global Catalog" at http://technet.microsoft.com/en-us/library/cc730749.aspx.

Planning the Placement of Global Catalog Servers

It is important to understand the need for global catalog servers and their functions, particularly on a multidomain network, when you are setting up your Active Directory Domain Services (AD DS) forest. In particular, you should have at least two GC servers in each domain for fault tolerance purposes. If you have just a single domain in your forest, the global catalog server plays a minor role, and it is unlikely that you would need to designate additional global catalog servers.

You should be concerned with the following two opposing issues when deciding how many global catalog servers to deploy and where to deploy them:

- As your forest increases in size, the size of the global catalog, and hence the amount of replication traffic among GC servers, increases. The GC servers replicate with each other in a loop that is separate from other AD DS replication. The more global catalog servers you deploy, the greater the amount of replication traffic generated.

- On the other hand, with increasing forest size, the forest will have more users with cross-domain queries. Consequently, the time required for users to reach resources in other domains will increase unless you add global catalog servers that users can easily reach. Adding such global catalog servers is especially important in multisite networks.

When a user logs on to a given domain controller for the first time in a large enterprise, it is important for this domain controller to connect to a GC server to obtain information about any universal groups to which the user might belong. This information includes access permissions assigned to these groups. If the user is located in a branch office that does not have a GC server locally present, the domain controller must cross the slow link to the location in which the GC server resides. This results in slow logon performance, particularly when several users are logging on at the same time.

Consider Figure 5-1, in which users in the head office and in Branch Office 1 have access to a GC server in their own sites; consequently, the logon and object search times are fast. However, users in Branch Office 2 must access a GC server in the head office across the slow intersite link. This can result in unacceptably slow logon and object search times, particularly if there is a lot of other intersite traffic. Furthermore, should the slow link go down and the GC server become unavailable as a result, users would be unable to log on at all.

Figure 5-1   Logon and search times are much faster when a global catalog server is located onsite.

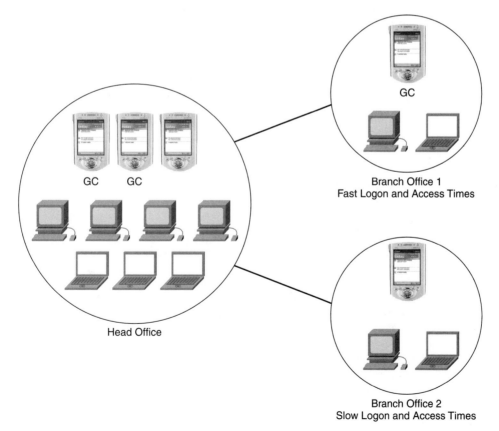

If sufficiently high bandwidth exists between two sites, locating a GC server at the remote site might not be necessary. You should monitor the growth in network traffic and check with users to see whether performance suffers.

You should balance the need for additional GC servers against users' need for additional disk space and AD DS replication bandwidth. Windows Server 2008 supports the feature of *universal group membership caching*, which enables users to log on without access to a GC server after they have logged on once to a given domain controller. This topic is discussed later in this section.

Promoting Domain Controllers to Global Catalog Servers

By default, the first domain controller in each domain is automatically designated as a GC server. You can designate additional GCs from the Active Directory Sites and Services snap-in by performing the following steps:

Step 1. Expand the Sites container, and expand the site in which the domain controller is located.

Step 2. Expand the Servers container, and expand the entry for the domain controller to be designated as a GC.

Step 3. Right-click **NTDS Settings** and choose **Properties**.

Step 4. In the General tab of the NTDS Settings Properties dialog box, select the **Global Catalog** check box and click **OK** or **Apply**, as shown in Figure 5-2.

Figure 5-2   Designating an additional global catalog server.

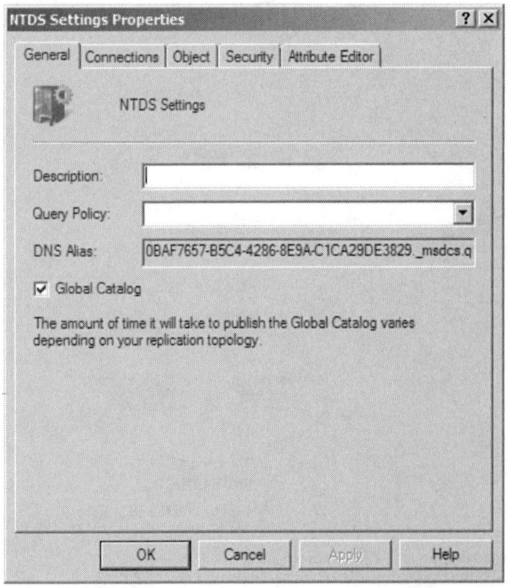

You can also remove a GC server; simply clear the **Global Catalog** check box shown in Figure 5-2.

Using Universal Group Membership Caching

A *universal group* is one that can contain users or global groups from any domain in the forest. You can use this group scope to grant permissions for accessing resources in any domain in the forest, either directly or by adding the group to domain local groups in other domains. More information on the various types and scopes of groups available in AD DS is provided in Chapter 9, "Active Directory User and Group Accounts."

As already mentioned, GC servers store universal group membership information. It is important that this information be available so that a user receives a complete access token at logon. The logon will fail if a GC server is unavailable for any reason. Microsoft provides another mechanism for obtaining universal group information in the absence of a GC server: universal group membership caching (UGMC). When you configure UGMC, any domain controller that services a user's logon will store the user's universal group information when he logs on to that domain controller for the first time. At subsequent logons, the domain controller can verify the user's universal group membership information without contacting a GC server. This speeds up the logon process and ensures that it will complete successfully even if a GC server is unavailable.

WARNING   You should be aware that the GC server still must be available if the user has never logged on to this particular domain controller previously. UGMC will then cache this user's universal group membership information.

It is most practical to employ UGMC in a small branch office connected to the head office with a low-bandwidth WAN connection and low-end servers, where the replication load might place an undesirable load on either the server or the connection. You can enable UGMC by performing the following steps:

Step 1.   In the Active Directory Sites and Services snap-in, select the site at which you want to enable UGMC.

Step 2.   Right-click the **NTDS Site Settings** object in the details pane of this snap-in and choose **Properties**.

Step 3.   On the Site Settings tab of the NTDS Site Settings Properties dialog box shown in Figure 5-3, select the **Enable Universal Group Membership Caching** check box and click **OK** or **Apply**.

Step 4.   If you want to select a specific site from which UGMC data is replicated, select the site from the Refresh cache from drop-down list.

Figure 5-3   Enabling universal group membership caching.

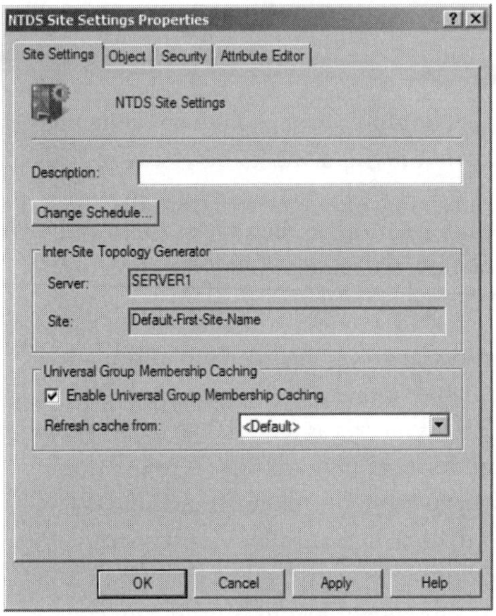

TIP An exam question might offer the choice between designating additional global GC servers or enabling UGMC. If the question informs you that logons are slow and does not mention slow resource access, the most likely answer is to enable UGMC. If the question informs you that resource access across a WAN is slow, you should configure a GC server. Also remember that you do not need to enable both a GC and UGMC at the same site. Furthermore, in a single-domain forest, neither additional GC servers nor UGMC provides any benefit.

Using Partial Attribute Sets

The *partial attribute set* is a schema attribute that tracks the internal replication status of partial replicas, such as those found on GC servers. Attributes included in the partial attribute set are those required by the schema plus the attributes most commonly utilized during user search activities. These include information on objects of the domain directory partitions of other domains of the forest. Storing these attributes in the global catalog improves the efficiency of user searches by reducing the amount of network activity required.

Using the Active Directory Schema snap-in, you can designate additional attributes to be included in the partial attribute set. From this snap-in, select the check box labeled **Replicate this attribute to the global catalog**; doing so denotes an `attributeSchema` object as a member of the partial attribute set.

NOTE For more information on partial attribute sets, refer to "How the Global Catalog Works" at http://technet.microsoft.com/en-us/library/how-global-catalog-servers-work(WS.10).aspx.

The Active Directory schema and its configuration are discussed later in this chapter.

Configuring Operations Masters

Recall that the five operations masters roles are initially held on the first domain controller in each domain. Also recall that these operations masters perform single-master roles in the forest that can be held by only specific controllers. The number of domain controllers in a multiple-domain forest that hold these roles is as follows:

- The domain naming master and schema master roles are held by only one domain controller in the forest.

- The RID master, infrastructure master, and PDC emulator roles are held by one domain controller in each domain of the forest.

This section looks at configuring these roles as well as several problems that might arise if these roles become unavailable.

NOTE   A read-only domain controller (RODC) cannot host any of the operations masters roles because the nature of these roles requires the capability to write to the AD DS database.

Schema Master

The schema master holds the only writable copy of the Active Directory schema. Briefly stated, the schema is a set of rules that define the classes of objects and their attributes that can be created in the directory. All domains in the forest share a common schema, which is replicated to all domain controllers in the forest. Only one schema master is present in the forest.

Table 5-2 summarizes several important definitions as they relate to the schema.

Table 5-2   Schema Definitions

Term	Definition
Object	A specific item that can be cataloged in Active Directory. Some types of objects include OUs, users, computers, folders, files, and printers. When you first install Active Directory, the default schema contains definitions of commonly used objects and their properties.
Container	A type of object that can hold other objects. The schema contains the Classes and Attributes containers. Default containers are also created when you first install Active Directory.

Table 5-2   Schema Definitions

Term	Definition
Attribute	A distinct characteristic held by a specific object. For example, a user object holds attributes such as the username, full name, email address, and so on. In general, objects in the same container have the same type of attributes but are characterized by different values of these attributes. The extent of attributes that can be specified for any object is defined by an `attributeSchema` object in the schema.
Class	A series of attributes associated with each object. The attributes associated with each class are defined by a `classSchema` object in the schema.

NOTE   For comprehensive information on the workings of the schema, including descriptions of available object classes and attributes, refer to "How the Active Directory Schema Works" at http://technet.microsoft.com/en-us/library/cc773309(WS.10).aspx.

NOTE   A dependency exists between the schema master and the global catalog. It is possible to list every schema attribute in the global catalog by selecting the Replicate this attribute to the Global Catalog option, located on the Properties dialog box for the attribute. Selecting this option adds information pertaining to that attribute to the global catalog, requiring a fast connection to the nearest global catalog server. This includes the installation of programs such as Exchange Server that add attributes to the schema. But note that if there are any Windows 2000 global catalog servers on the network, this option causes these servers to completely rebuild their global catalogs, resulting in a large amount of network traffic. This is not a problem if all the global catalog servers run Windows Server 2003 or later.

WARNING   Improper modifications of the schema can cause irreparable harm to Active Directory. For this reason, Microsoft created a global group called Schema Admins, and only members of this group can perform such modifications. As a best practice to avoid unauthorized modifications, you should remove all users from this group and add a user only when it is necessary to modify the schema. In addition, it is strongly advisable to create a test forest in a lab environment and test schema modifications here before deploying them to a production forest.

Configuring the Schema

You use the Active Directory schema snap-in to configure the schema. This snap-in is not present on domain controllers by default, and you must register and install it before you can perform any modifications to the schema.

To register the Active Directory schema snap-in, open a command prompt and type **regsvr32 schmmgmt.dll.** You will receive a message box informing you that DllRegisterServer in schmmgmt.dll succeeded.

After registering the snap-in, perform the following steps to install it:

Step 1.   Click **Start > Run**, type **mmc**, and press **Enter.** This opens a blank MMC console.

Step 2.   Click **File > Add or Remove Snap-in** to display the Add or Remove Snap-ins dialog box.

Step 3.   Select **Active Directory Schema** from the Available Snap-ins field and click **Add** to display this snap-in in the Selected snap-ins field as shown in Figure 5-4. Then click **OK**.

Figure 5-4   Installing the Active Directory Schema snap-in.

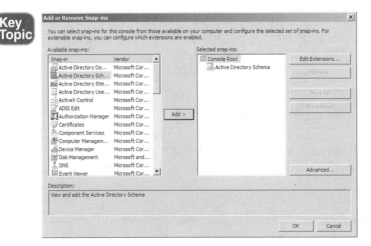

Step 4.   Save the console with a descriptive name, such as **Active Directory Schema**. By default, it is stored in the Administrative Tools folder.

> **TIP** An exam question might ask you why you are unable to locate this snap-in. Remember that you must be a member of the Schema Admins group and that you must first register the snap-in so that it appears in the Add or Remove Snap-ins dialog box.

Extending the Schema

After you have installed the Active Directory schema snap-in, you can extend the schema to include any classes or attributes not defined by default. To extend the schema, proceed as follows:

Step 1.   Open the Active Directory schema snap-in.

Step 2.   If necessary, expand Active Directory Schema in the console tree to reveal the **Classes** and **Attributes** containers.

Step 3.   Select the **Attributes** container. As you can see in Figure 5-5, a long list
of attributes is available.

Figure 5-5   By default, the Active Directory Schema snap-in contains a large number of
attributes.

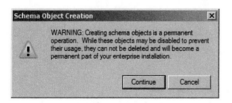

Step 4.   Right-click **Attributes** and select **Create Attribute**. You will receive
the warning shown in Figure 5-6 informing you of the seriousness of
this action.

Figure 5-6   You are warned that creating schema objects is a permanent operation.

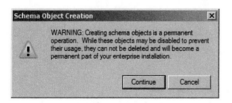

Step 5.   Click **Continue** and, in the **Create New Attribute** dialog box shown
in Figure 5-7, supply the following information that describes the attribute you are creating:

—**Common Name:** A unique name related to the LDAP display name.

—**LDAP Display Name:** A unique display name that programmers and
system administrators can use to programmatically reference the
object.

Figure 5-7   You can use the Create New Attribute dialog box to create attributes.

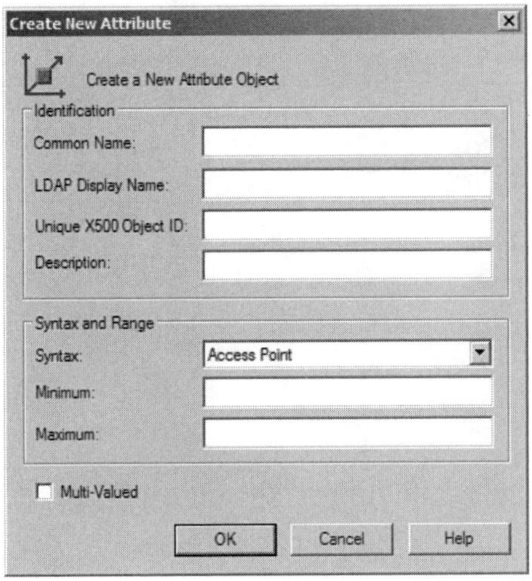

—**Unique X.500 Object ID:** A required, unique identifier associated with all object classes or attributes defined in the schema.

—**Description:** An optional description for the class or attribute.

—**Syntax:** Type of information stored by this attribute, such as a case-insensitive string, distinguished name, integer, numerical string, and so on.

—**Minimum** and **Maximum:** Depending on the syntax, can be an optional string length, minimum and maximum values of integers, and so on.

Step 6.   Click **OK**. The attribute is created and displayed in the attributes list. If you have difficulty finding it, click the **Name** header to arrange the attributes in alphabetical order.

You can also create new classes by right-clicking the **Classes** container and choosing **Create Class**. The procedure is similar to that for creating attributes as already described. After you have created new attributes and classes, you can easily add attributes to classes by using the following steps:

Step 1.   In the console tree of the Active Directory Schema snap-in, double-click **Classes** to expand it. This action displays a long list of available classes, as shown in Figure 5-8.

Step 2.   Right-click the class to which you want to add an attribute and select **Properties**. This action displays the Properties dialog box for the selected class, as shown in Figure 5-9.

Step 3.   Select the **Attributes** tab and then click **Add** to display the Select Schema Object dialog box, as shown in Figure 5-10.

Figure 5-8   By default, the Active Directory Schema snap-in contains a large number of classes.

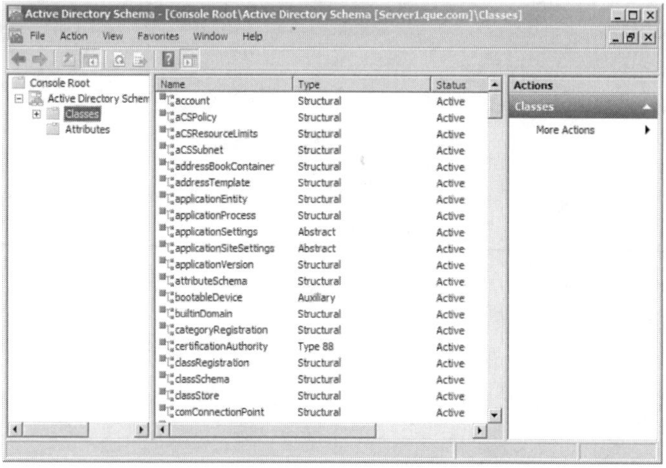

Figure 5-9   In the Properties dialog box for a schema class, you make all modifications to the class.

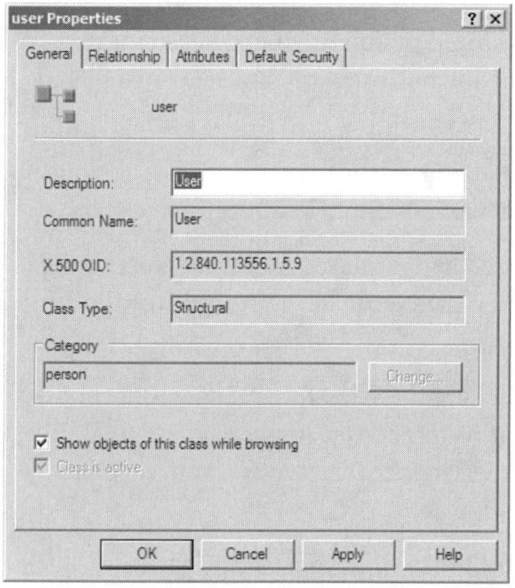

Step 4.   Scroll down to locate the attribute and then click **OK**. You return to the Attributes tab of the class's Properties dialog box, with the new attribute highlighted.

Step 5.   Click **OK** to close the class's Properties dialog box.

Figure 5-10   You use the Select Schema Object dialog box to select the desired attribute.

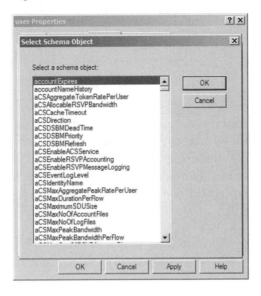

Deactivating Schema Objects

After you have added an object (class or attribute) to the schema, you cannot simply delete it. However, you can deactivate an unneeded schema object by using the following procedure:

Step 1.   In the console tree of the Active Directory Schema snap-in, select either **Classes** or **Attributes**, depending on the type of object you want to deactivate.

Step 2.   In the details pane, scroll to locate the class or attribute you want to deactivate, right-click it, and then choose **Properties**.

Step 3.   On the General tab of the Properties dialog box that appears, clear the check box labeled **Attribute is active** or **Class is active**. If this check box is unavailable (grayed out; see Figure 5-9), it means that the class or attribute is essential for Active Directory functionality and cannot be disabled.

Step 4.   You receive a message box, as shown in Figure 5-11, warning you that if you make the schema object defunct, you will be unable to make further changes to it.

Step 5.   Click **Yes** to deactivate the object.

WARNING   After you have added a class or attribute to the schema, it is permanently added. You cannot delete a class or attribute; you can only deactivate it.

Figure 5-11   You receive a warning when you attempt to deactivate a schema object.

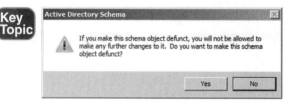

The procedures given here provide you with a small example of the possible schema modifications. Other procedures are available to perform such tasks as adding values to a series of attributes, adding attribute display names, conducting searches based on the new attributes, and so on. Many of these procedures involve the use of scripts created using Windows PowerShell and are beyond the scope of the 70-640 exam.

NOTE   For additional details, refer to "Active Directory Administration with Windows PowerShell" at http://technet.microsoft.com/en-us/library/ dd378937(WS.10).aspx.

Domain Naming Master

The domain naming master comes into play whenever an administrator creates a new domain anywhere in the forest or renames or removes an existing domain. Failure of the domain naming master is not ordinarily a problem and comes into play only if an administrator wants to perform any of these activities. There is only one domain naming master in the entire forest, and by default it is located on the first domain controller installed in the forest. Microsoft recommends that you keep the domain naming master and schema master roles on the same computer.

NOTE   Refer to "AD DS: The schema master role and the domain naming master role should be owned by the same domain controller in the forest" at http://technet.microsoft.com/en-us/library/dd378868(WS.10).aspx

PDC Emulator

In Windows 2000 and Windows Server 2003 Active Directory, the PDC Emulator served as a primary domain controller (PDC) for any Windows NT 4.0 backup domain controllers (BDCs) in the domain. This role is no longer significant in Windows Server 2008 because Windows NT BDCs can no longer be supported on the network. However, pre–Windows 2000 computers such as Windows 98 and Windows NT 4.0 can still exist on the network and the PDC emulator handles account management activities such as password changes for users at these computers. It also processes error messages and lockout actions for users entering incorrect passwords at these computers. The PDC emulator also acts as a time synchronization master for all computers in the domain. This role is discussed further in the next section. There is one PDC emulator in each domain in the forest.

TIP   Microsoft recommends that you leave the PDC emulator role in the forest root domain on a Windows Server 2008 domain controller.

Should the PDC emulator become unavailable, users of pre–Windows 2000 computers will be unable to change their passwords. If their passwords expire, they will be unable to log on until the PDC emulator is brought back online.

Time Service

On a network in which all member servers and client computers are running Windows 2000 or higher, the sole function of the PDC emulator is that of the time synchronization master. It uses the Windows Time Service (W32time) to perform this activity.

By default, the Windows Time Service uses the PDC emulator's local clock for providing time to client computers. You should utilize one of the following best practices for ensuring accurate time on the PDC emulator:

- Install a hardware clock such as a radio or global positioning service (GPS) device on the PDC emulator.

- Configure the Windows Time Service to synchronize with an external time source such as the Microsoft time server at `time.windows.com`. You can use the `w32tm` utility to perform this task. Type `w32tm /?` at a command prompt to obtain information on using this command.

NOTE   For further information, refer to "Configure the Windows Time Service" at http://technet.microsoft.com/en-us/library/cc731191(WS.10).aspx.

If you have deployed an RODC at a branch office, the PDC emulator for the domain must be running Windows Server 2008. Otherwise, the RODC will be unable to act as a time source for client computers in the branch office. Client computers will be unable to synchronize their time with the RODC, and a time difference (clock skew) between their time and that of the RODC might develop. Should the clock skew exceed five minutes, client computers will be unable to receive new Kerberos tickets, which can prevent users from accessing resources.

Another solution to this problem is available. You can configure a writable Windows Server 2008 domain controller in the domain to act as GTIMESERV for the domain. A GTIMESERV is a domain controller or member server running Windows Server 2008 that acts as an authoritative time server within the domain, and client computers can use this server as a time synchronization master.

A server acting as GTIMESERV in the forest root domain acts as the authoritative time source for the entire forest. You should configure this server to receive time from an external time server and configure the PDC emulator in this domain to synchronize time with this server. In domains that are not the forest root domain, the GTIMESERV server can synchronize time from the PDC emulator or a GTIMESERV server higher up in the domain hierarchy. You can also configure this server to receive time from an external time server.

Infrastructure Master

The infrastructure master performs two critical actions in multidomain forests:

- It updates references to objects in other domains in the forest. In doing so, it ensures that changes made by different administrators from different locations are not in conflict. Such changes include adding users or groups or modifying group memberships. For example, if two administrators in two different cities were to create a user named Mary at the same time, a problem would occur. In this case, the infrastructure master would generate a uniqueness error. Further, if you were to create a user account in one domain from a domain controller in another domain, you would need to contact the infrastructure master in the domain where the account will be created.

- It tracks group membership changes that cross domain boundaries within the forest. For example, domain local groups can contain users and global groups in other domains, and global groups can be made members of domain local groups in other domains. In addition, these groups can be members of universal groups and vice versa. The infrastructure master ensures that these changes occur properly and without conflict.

If the infrastructure master were to fail, an administrator would notice a problem if she attempts to perform either of these actions. She would be unable to move or rename a large number of accounts. Users might be unable to access objects in other domains because their references would not be updated.

> **WARNING** You should not place the infrastructure master role on a domain controller that is configured as a global catalog server unless all domain controllers are configured as global catalog servers. Otherwise, the infrastructure master would be unable to update its references to objects in other domains properly. New to Windows Server 2008, when you create an additional domain controller in a child domain, dcpromo checks whether the infrastructure master is on a global catalog server. If so, it prompts you to transfer this role to the new domain controller.

RID Master

All objects such as user or group accounts defined in a forest must have a security identifier (SID), which uniquely identifies the object to Active Directory and contains a domain identifier plus a domain-specific RID. The RID master keeps track of all RIDs assigned within its domain and issues blocks of 500 RIDs to all other domain controllers in the domain so that administrators can create accounts. The RID master issues a new block of RIDs after the existing block is down to 20% of its original value. You can modify Registry keys to allow larger pools if desired in a large environment. If the RID master were to fail, administrators at other domain controllers would be able to create accounts until the existing pool of RIDs at that domain controller was exhausted, after which account creation would fail.

TIP   Remember that an RODC cannot be either a global catalog server or an operations master. An exam question might trick you into believing that you can install a GC server or transfer an operations master role to an RODC.

Placement of Operations Masters

Recall that the first domain controller installed in a new forest holds all five operations master roles and that the first domain controller installed in a new child domain or tree in an existing forest holds all three domainwide operations master roles. The placement of operations masters affects the performance of your network, both in single-domain and multiple-domain situations. Moving one or more FSMO roles to different domain controllers has the obvious benefit of load balancing; in other words, the tasks associated with each role are distributed among different domain controllers. At the same time, you need to be aware of the need for availability of the FSMO servers and what can happen should any of the FSMO servers be unavailable for any reason. Some examples follow:

■ When you create a new tree or child domain in an existing forest, the server you are promoting must be able to contact the domain naming master to ensure that the domain name you are providing is unique. If the domain naming master is unavailable, you cannot create a new child domain.

■ If you need to modify the schema, the server you are working from must be able to contact the schema master. This includes the installation or configuration of server applications such as Exchange Server that add classes or attributes to the schema. Such an installation will fail if the schema master is unavailable.

■ Client computers running pre–Windows 2000 operating systems must be able to contact the PDC emulator if users on these computers want to perform account modifications such as password changes.

■ The PDC emulator also ensures that clocks on all computers in the domain remain synchronized. Should the PDC emulator be unavailable and the clocks on other domain controllers go out of sync, certain operations could fail or generate errors. You can also configure another domain controller with GTIMESERV to ensure clock synchronization.

■ When creating new users or groups, you must be able to contact the infrastructure master to ensure that conflicting changes are not occurring elsewhere in the domain.

■ Remember that the infrastructure master also tracks changes in group membership that can cross domains. This capability is important because domain local groups can contain users and global groups in other domains, and global groups can be made members of domain local groups in other domains. In addition, these groups can be members of universal groups and vice versa. In the absence of the infrastructure master, these changes will fail.

■ When creating new user, group, or computer accounts, the server on which you are performing these tasks must have RIDs available so that these objects can be assigned a unique SID. So that SIDs never become duplicated in the domain, the RID master assigns a pool of 500 relative identifiers to each domain controller in the domain. The RID master sends a new pool to each domain controller when it has fewer than 50 remaining. In the absence of a RID master, domain controllers can continue to create accounts until the pool of identifiers on that server is exhausted, after which account creation will fail.

It is evident from these examples that some operations masters must be more continuously available on the network than others. All operations masters should be located on domain controllers that are accessible to as much of the network as possible over a fast link.

Transferring and Seizing of Operations Master Roles

When you first create a new domain or forest, all the operations master roles are located on the first domain controller by default. You might want to transfer these roles to other domain controllers for any of several reasons, or if an operations master role holder becomes unavailable, you might want to seize this role. We look at these actions here.

TIP It is recommended that you back up the system state on your domain controllers before performing a transfer of operations master roles. We discuss backup of servers including operations master roles in Chapter 15, "Maintaining Active Directory."

Because each of these roles is held by only a single domain controller at any given time, failure of the domain controller holding one or more of the roles results in that role becoming unavailable. The consequences of such a failure depend on which operation master has failed and on the types of operations users or administrators are attempting to perform. You might have to seize operations masters should the role holder be unavailable for a period of time when its use is required. Table 5-3 summarizes the most frequent consequences of failure of each operations master.

Table 5-3   Operations Master Failures

Operations Master	Failure Symptoms
Schema Master	Unable to add classes or attributes to the schema.
	Unable to install applications (such as Exchange Server) that make modifications to the schema.
Domain Naming Master	Unable to create new child domains or domain trees.
	Unable to rename domains.
RID Master	No symptoms until another domain controller runs out of relative IDs. At that point, an error informs you that the domain controller was unable to allocate a relative identifier.
PDC Emulator	Users with pre–Windows 2000 computers are unable to change their passwords. If passwords have expired, these users are unable to log on.
	Time settings on domain controllers become out of sync.
Infrastructure Master	References to objects in other domains are not updated.
	Unable to move or rename a large number of accounts.

Transferring Operations Master Roles

You can transfer operations master roles to another domain controller when the original role holder is still available and functioning. The following are several reasons why you might want to do this:

■   You might want to perform load balancing; in other words, you might want to distribute the processing load among more than one server to avoid overloading a single machine.

■   You might need to perform scheduled maintenance on the computer holding one or more of these roles.

■   A role holder located on a WAN might be creating excessive replication traffic that hinders other network traffic.

- You might want to move role holders to locations near the administrators responsible for them.

- You need to ensure that the infrastructure master is not held on a computer that hosts the global catalog.

- In general, you should host the schema master and domain naming master roles on the same server, and this server should be close to another server that you can use as a backup if required.

You can transfer the three domainwide operations masters roles from the Active Directory Users and Computers console. You should be logged on as a member of the Domain Admins group. Then perform the following steps:

Step 1.   Open the Active Directory Users and Computers snap-in.

Step 2.   Right-click **Active Directory Users and Computers** at the top of the console tree and select **Change Domain Controller**.

Step 3.   In the Change Domain Controller dialog box, select the server to which you want to transfer one or more roles, and then click **OK**.

Step 4.   Right-click your domain and choose **All Tasks > Operations Masters**.

Step 5.   In the Operations Masters dialog box shown in Figure 5-12, select the tab corresponding to the role you want to transfer, click **Change**, and then click **Yes** on the confirmation message box that appears.

Figure 5-12   You can transfer domainwide operations masters roles from the Operations Masters dialog box.

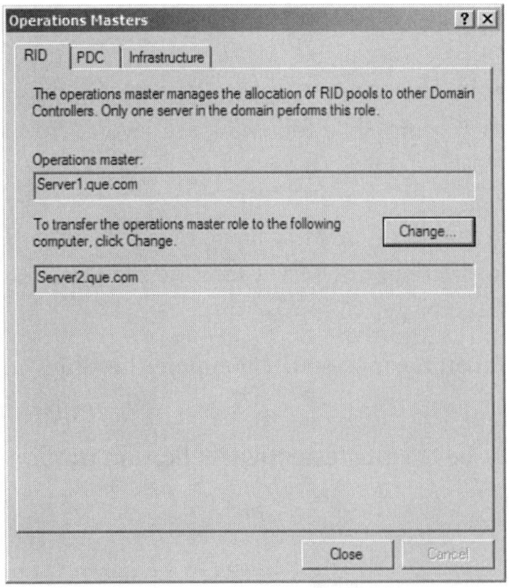

To transfer the domain naming master role, access the Active Directory Domains and Trusts console on the server to which you want to transfer this role. Right-click **Active Directory Domains and Trusts** and select **Operations Master**. Then follow a procedure similar to that described earlier. To transfer this role, you must be logged on as a member of the Enterprise Admins group.

> **NOTE**   You can also perform this procedure from a different domain controller in any domain of your forest. To do so, simply right-click **Active Directory Domains and Trusts** and select **Change Active Directory Domain Controller**. Then browse to the proper domain and select the domain controller to which you want to transfer the role.

To transfer the schema master role, perform this task in a similar manner from the Active Directory Schema console. To transfer this role, you must be logged on as a member of the Schema Admins group.

Seizing Operations Masters Roles

Should an operations master role become unavailable due to a network or computer crash, you cannot use the procedures just described to transfer its roles to an operational server. You can use the `ntdsutil` command-line utility to seize the role at another domain controller. Use the following procedure:

Step 1.   Open a command prompt and type **ntdsutil.**

Step 2.   At the `ntdsutil` command prompt, type **roles.**

Step 3.   At the `FSMO maintenance` command prompt, type **connection.**

Step 4.   At the `server connections` command prompt, type **connect to server** *server*, where *server* is the name of the server to which you want to seize the role.

Step 5.   At the `server connections` command prompt, type **quit.**

Step 6.   At the `FSMO maintenance` command prompt, type **seize *role***, where *role* is the operations master role you want to seize.

Step 7.   Click **Yes** on the confirmation message box that appears.

Step 8.   `ntdsutil` first attempts to connect to the server and confirms that it is unavailable. After receiving an error message, it seizes the role, displaying the output shown in Figure 5-13.

Step 9.   Type **quit** twice to exit `ntdsutil`.

> **NOTE**   You can also use `ntdsutil` to transfer an operations master role, using a similar procedure to that described here. In step 6, type **transfer <role>**, where

<role> is the operations master role you want to transfer. Further, if you type **seize** *<role>* and **ntdsutil** finds that the server holding the role you are seizing is online, it transfers the role rather than seizing it.

Figure 5-13 Seizing an operations master role.

In general, after you have seized an operations master role, the server originally holding this role should never be brought back online. You should reformat this server's hard disk and reinstall Windows Server 2008 R2. However, it is possible to transfer the infrastructure master or PDC emulator role back to the original holder after you have restored it and brought it back online without having to rebuild its operating system completely.

NOTE Many additional options are available with the ntdsutil utility. Some of the more important ones include creating application directory partitions, restoring AD DS, performing an online compaction of the AD DS database, and cleanup of metadata left behind by decommissioned domain controllers. For more information, type **ntdsutil /?** at a command prompt. You can also type **help** or **?** as a subcommand to see a description of the available options.

Exam Preparation Tasks

Review All the Key Topics

Review the most important topics in the chapter, noted with the key topics icon in the outer margin of the page. Table 5-4 lists a reference of these key topics and the page numbers on which each is found.

Table 5-4   Key Topics for Chapter 5

Key Topic Element	Description	Page Number
List	Summarizes important functions of global catalog servers	148
Figure 5-2	Shows how to designate an additional global catalog server	150
Figure 5-3	Shows how to configure universal group membership caching	152
List	Defines the number of operations masters present in an Active Directory forest	153
Table 5-2	Defines important terms with regard to the Active Directory schema	153
Figure 5-4	Installing the Active Directory Schema snap-in	155
Figure 5-8	Shows the large number of classes present by default in the Active Directory schema	158
Figure 5-11	Deactivating a schema object is a serious matter	160
Table 5-3	Summarizes principal causes of operations master failures	165
List	Shows how to seize an operations master role	167

Complete the Tables and Lists from Memory

Print a copy of Appendix C, "Memory Tables" (found on the CD), or at least the section for this chapter, and complete the tables and lists from memory. Appendix D, "Memory Tables Answer Key," also on the CD, includes completed tables and lists to check your work.

Definitions of Key Terms

Define the following key terms from this chapter, and check your answers in the glossary.

attribute, class, container, domain naming master, flexible single-master operations (FSMO) servers, global catalog (GC), global catalog server, infrastructure master, Ntdsutil, object, operations master, partial attribute set, primary domain controller (PDC) emulator, relative identifier (RID), relative identifier (RID) master, schema, schema master, seizing a role, transferring a role

This chapter covers the following subjects:

■ **The Need for Active Directory Sites:** This section presents several benefits that arise from configuring sites on your network, as well as considerations you should plan for when setting up sites.

■ **Configuring Sites and Subnets:** This section shows you how to create sites and perform the necessary actions that must be performed to ensure that the sites are functional.

■ **Site Links, Site Link Bridges, and Bridgehead Servers:** Domain controllers at different sites must be able to communicate with each other properly and in a timely fashion. Active Directory uses site links and site link bridges as components of the network topology that links the sites in a fashion that mirrors the physical connectivity between the sites on the network.

■ **Configuring Active Directory Replication:** This section defines and describes many terms and concepts you must be familiar with in understanding the process of Active Directory replication. It then goes on to show you how you can modify the default schedules associated with both intersite and intrasite replication. This is important in ensuring that users have up-to-date information without overburdening low-bandwidth WAN links.

CHAPTER 6

Configuring Active Directory Sites and Replication

You have learned how to install Active Directory forests, trees, and domains and perform the basic configuration actions related to these components. You have also learned how to configure the Domain Name System (DNS) to work properly with Active Directory installations of various sizes. Now you will turn your attention to configuring Active Directory to work properly in today's large organizations that are spread across multiple geographic locations, both local and around the world.

"Do I Know This Already?" Quiz

The "Do I Know This Already?" quiz enables you to assess whether you should read this entire chapter or simply jump to the "Exam Preparation Tasks" section for review. If you are in doubt, read the entire chapter. Table 6-1 outlines the major headings in this chapter and the corresponding "Do I Know This Already?" quiz questions. You can find the answers in Appendix A, "Answers to the 'Do I Know This Already?' Quizzes."

Table 6-1 "Do I Know This Already?" Foundation Topics Section-to-Question Mapping

Foundations Topics Section	Questions Covered in This Section
The Need for Active Directory Sites	1
Configuring Sites and Subnets	2–3
Site Links, Site Link Bridges, and Bridgehead Servers	4–7
Configuring Active Directory Replication	8–12

1. Which of the following are benefits you can achieve by configuring your AD DS topology to include separate sites for branch offices connected to your head office network using dial-up WAN links? (Choose all that apply.)

   a. The ability to schedule replication at times when the network is not busy such as at night

   b. The ability to configure branch offices for universal group membership caching

   c. The ability to specify group policies that apply to only the branch offices

   d. The ability to isolate segments with poor network connectivity

2. You have created a new site for your company's branch office that is being opened in a neighboring city. Which of the following tasks does Microsoft recommend that you do to complete configuring this site? (Choose three.)

   a. Ensure that the site is linked to other sites as needed.

   b. Add subnets for the new sites to the Subnets container.

   c. Configure a licensing server for the new site.

   d. Specify a site link bridge for the new site.

   e. Install one or more domain controllers at the new site.

3. Your company, which has an office in Indianapolis, has just taken over a smaller company located in Louisville. You have set up a dedicated ISDN line to connect the two offices and added all users and computers in the Louisville office to your company's domain. You have created sites for both locations and assigned the domain controllers to their respective sites while working from the Indianapolis location.

A few days later, users in Louisville start complaining about slow logon and resource access. What should you do to speed up access?

   a. Assign the subnet containing computers located in Louisville to the Louisville site.

   b. Add an explicit3e UPN suffix for the users in the Louisville site.

   c. Specify universal group membership caching for users in the Louisville site.

   d. Obtain approval from management to upgrade the ISDN line to a T1 line.

4. Your company operates an AD DS forest consisting of two domains, one of which is located in Anchorage and the other in Fairbanks. The two offices are connected by a dial-up link that often experiences outages, especially during the long Alaskan winter. You install the SMTP protocol on domain controllers at both locations and configure the site link to use SMTP for replication. However, you discover that no replication is taking place. Which of the following additional actions do you need to perform?

   a. Create an additional site link that is dedicated to SMTP replication.

   b. Create a site link bridge.

   c. Reduce the cost of the site link.

   d. Install an enterprise certification authority (CA).

5. Your company has a head office in Austin and a branch office in San Antonio, which are connected by a T1 line. Having experienced occasional downtime at the T1 line, you set up a dial-up link that uses regular phone lines as a backup. A month later, on receiving your phone bill, you notice that the dial-up link has been used several times a day even though you have not experienced outages at the T1 line. What should you do?

   a.   Set the cost of the dial-up link to 50.

   b.   Set the cost of the dial-up link to 200.

   c.   Create a site link bridge that encompasses both links.

   d.   Configure the dial-up line to use SMTP replication.

6. Your company's AD DS forest consists of five domains and 10 sites, each of which represents an office in a different city. Some of these offices are not directly connected to each other, and it is not anticipated that connections will be installed in the foreseeable future. You discover that domain controllers in certain offices are not always up-to-date. What should you do to improve this situation?

   a.   Increase the cost of unreliable site links.

   b.   Create additional site links for the available direct connections.

   c.   Create site link bridges that connect the offices according to the available direct connections.

   d.   Use SMTP replication between offices that are not connected.

7. Which of the following best describes the role of the intersite topology generator (ISTG) in a multiple domain AD DS forest?

   a.   It is a process that runs automatically on every domain controller in the forest and builds intersite and intrasite replication topologies.

   b.   It is a process that builds site link bridges for crossing unreliable connections between sites that are not well connected.

   c.   It is a single domain controller in the forest that is used by the Knowledge Consistency Checker (KCC) to build the network's intersite replication topology.

   d.   It is a single domain controller at each site that is used by the KCC to build the network's intersite replication topology.

8. Which of the following statements are *not* true about intersite replication, as opposed to intrasite replication? (Choose all that apply.)

   a.   Intersite replication is compressed, whereas intrasite replication is not compressed.

    b. Intersite replication occurs automatically at frequent intervals, whereas intrasite replication can be configured and scheduled.

    c. Intersite replication takes place across site links according to their configured site link cost, whereas intrasite replication takes place between all domain controllers at the site according to a ring topology.

    d. Both intersite and intrasite replication can be configured to use either RPC over IP or SMTP transport protocols.

9. Which of the following is true about AD DS replication in Windows Server 2008 R2?

    a. Windows Server 2008 R2 uses DFS replication for replicating all AD DS database components, except for replicating the SYSVOL folder on domain controllers in domains that are still using the Windows 2000 or Windows Server 2003 domain functional levels.

    b. Windows Server 2008 R2 uses DFS replication for replicating all AD DS database components to all domain controllers, regardless of the domain functional level in use.

    c. Windows Server 2008 R2 uses DFS replication for replicating the SYSVOL folder to other domain controllers, provided that the domain is operating at the Windows Server 2008 or Windows Server 2008 R2 functional levels. FRS is used for replicating the other AD DS components to all other domain controllers.

    d. Windows Server 2008 R2 uses FRS replication for replicating all AD DS database components to all domain controllers, regardless of the domain functional level in use.

10. Which of the following statements are *not* true about SMTP replication, as opposed to RPC over IP replication? (Choose all that apply.)

    a. SMTP replication replicates only the domain and configuration partitions, whereas RPC over IP replication replicates all AD DS partitions.

    b. SMTP replication can be used for intersite replication only, whereas RPC over IP replication can be used for either intersite or intrasite replication.

    c. SMTP replication requires the use of a certification authority (CA), whereas RPC over IP replication does not require a CA.

    d. Both SMTP and RPC over IP replication can be used for replicating AD DS data within and between domains in the same forest.

    e. You can use Active Directory Sites and Services to modify the schedule for both SMTP and RPC over IP replication.

11. You want to ensure that AD DS replication between the two sites on your network does not occur during times when the WAN link is busy, but also ensure that changes in the morning are replicated to the other site during lunch hour. What should you do to accomplish this task with the least amount of effort?

    a. Configure replication to take place once every four hours.

    b. Retain the default replication interval and schedule replication to not take place between 8 AM and 12 noon, and again from 1 PM to 5 PM.

    c. Configure replication to take place once every eight hours, and manually force replication to take place during lunch hour each day.

    d. Configure replication to take place once every 30 minutes, and schedule replication to not take place between 8 AM and 12 noon, and again from 1 PM to 5 PM.

12. You want to ensure that intrasite replication takes place once every 15 minutes. What should you do?

    a. In Active Directory Sites and Services, right-click your site and choose **Properties**. Then click **Change Schedule** and specify the desired schedule in the dialog box that appears.

    b. In Active Directory Sites and Services, right-click the **NTDS Settings** folder for one of the servers in your site and choose **Properties**. Then click **Change Schedule** and specify the desired schedule in the dialog box that appears.

    c. In Active Directory Sites and Services, expand the Inter-Site Transports folder. Click the desired transport to display all site links, right-click the intrasite site link, and then choose **Properties**. Then click **Change Schedule** and specify the desired schedule in the dialog box that appears.

    d. You do not need to do anything. Intrasite replication takes place every 15 minutes by default.

Foundation Topics

The Need for Active Directory Sites

Nowadays, most companies do business from multiple office locations, which might be spread across a single metropolitan area or encompass an entire state, country, or even multiple international locations. Active Directory includes the concept of *sites*, which are groupings of computers and other objects that are connected by a high-speed local area network (LAN) connection.

An individual site includes computers that are on one or more Internet Protocol (IP) subnets. It can encompass one building or several adjacent buildings in a campus setting. Figure 6-1 shows an example with two sites, one located in Los Angeles and the other in Dallas. Sites are connected with each other by slower wide area network (WAN) connections that might not always be available and are always configured with separate IP subnets. It is important to configure diverse locations connected by WAN links as separate sites to optimize the use of the WAN link, especially if your company needs to pay for the link according to the length of time it is active or the amount of data sent across it.

Figure 6-1   A site is a group of resources in one physical location.

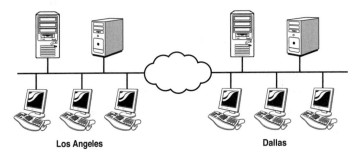

Los Angeles   Dallas

The following are several benefits that you achieve by creating sites:

- **Configurable replication:** You can configure replication between sites to take place at specified intervals and only during specified times of the day. Doing so enables you to optimize bandwidth usage so that other network traffic between sites can proceed without delay.

- **Isolation of poorly connected network segments:** You can place network segments connected by less reliable connections such as dial-up links in their own site and bridge these sites according to network connectivity.

- **Site-based policies:** If certain locations such as branch offices need policies that should not be applied elsewhere on the network, you can configure site-based

Group Policy to apply these policies. Chapter 11, "Creating and Applying Group Policy Objects," discusses this use of sites.

The following are several factors you should take into account when planning the site structure of your organization:

- **Physical environment:** You should assess the geographic locations of your company's business operations, together with the nature of their internal and external links. It might be possible to include multiple locations (for example, on a campus) in a single site if they are connected by reliable high-speed links (such as a T3 line).

- **Data replication versus available bandwidth:** A location that needs the most up-to-date Active Directory information and is connected with a high-speed link can be on the same site as the head office location. When properly configured, the network's site structure should optimize the process of Active Directory Domain Services (AD DS) replication.

- **Types of physical links between sites:** You should assess the type, speed, availability, and utilization of each physical link. AD DS includes site link objects that you can use to determine the replication schedule between sites that it links. A cost value can also be associated with it; this value determines when and how often replication can occur.

- **Site links and site link bridges:** Active Directory provides for site links and site link bridges so that you can group sites together for optimized intersite replication. These concepts are discussed later in this chapter.

NOTE You must be aware that the site and domain structures are totally independent. Sites represent the physical structure of the network, whereas domains represent its logical structure. A single site can include portions of several domains, and each domain can be spread out over multiple sites.

Configuring Sites and Subnets

Active Directory provides the Active Directory Sites and Services snap-in, which enables you to perform all configuration activities pertinent to sites. When you first open this snap-in, you will notice folders named Subnets and Inter-Site Transports as well as a site named Default-First-Site-Name. By default, the new domain controller is placed in this site when you first install Active Directory. You can rename this site to whatever you want, just as you can rename a file or folder. This section shows you how to create sites, add domain controllers to sites, and associate IP subnets with specific sites.

> **NOTE**   You can also use Active Directory Sites and Services to manage Active Directory Lightweight Directory Services (AD LDS) instances. AD LDS is discussed in more detail in Chapter 7, "Additional Active Directory Roles."

> **TIP**   You can use the Find command in Active Directory Sites and Services (the rightmost icon in the toolbar) to determine the site in which an object such as a domain controller is located.

Creating Sites

You can create additional sites by using the Active Directory Sites and Services snap-in, as described by the following procedure:

Step 1.   Click **Start** > **Administrative Tools** > **Active Directory Sites and Services**.

Step 2.   Right-click **Sites** and choose **New Site**.

Step 3.   In the New Object - Site dialog box shown in Figure 6-2, type the name of the site. Select a site link object from the list provided and then click **OK**.

Figure 6-2   Creating a new site.

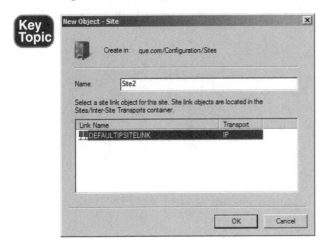

Step 4.   Windows informs you that the site has been created and reminds you of several other tasks that you should perform, as shown in Figure 6-3. Click **OK**.

Figure 6-3   Windows reminds you of several tasks to be completed after creating a site.

After you have created the new site, it appears in the console tree of Active Directory Sites and Services. The new site includes a default Servers folder that includes all domain controllers assigned to the site, as well as a NTDS Site Settings container that is described in a later section.

Adding Domain Controllers

The first task you should undertake is to add one or more domain controllers to your new site. To do this, proceed as follows:

Step 1.   Open Active Directory Sites and Services and expand the site that currently holds the domain controller that you want to move to the new site.

Step 2.   Select the **Servers** folder to display the domain controllers currently located in this site in the details pane.

Step 3.   Right-click the server you want to move and choose **Move**.

Step 4.   In the Move Server dialog box shown in Figure 6-4, select the site to which you want to move the server and then click **OK**.

Figure 6-4   Moving a domain controller to the new site.

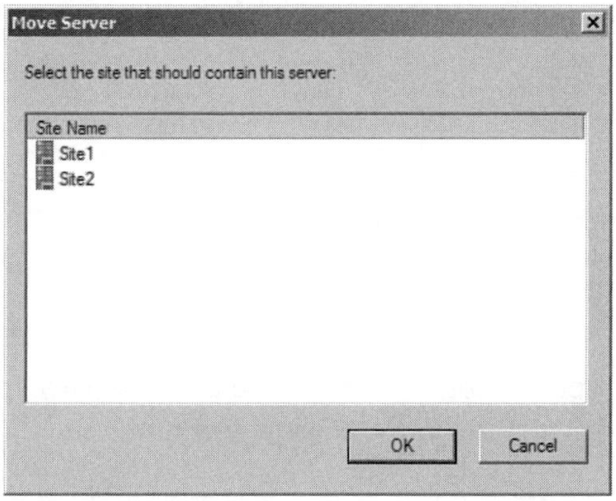

> **NOTE**   You can also use the Move-ADDirectoryServer Windows PowerShell
> cmdlet to move a domain controller to a new site. For more information on using
> PowerShell cmdlets for administering AD DS, refer to "What's New in AD DS:
> Active Directory Module for Windows PowerShell" at
> http://technet.microsoft.com/en-us/library/dd378783(WS.10).aspx.

Creating and Using Subnets

Recall that the purpose of using sites is to control Active Directory replication
across slow links between different physical locations. Bydefault, Active Directory
does not know anything about the physical topology of its network. You must configure Active Directory according to this topology by specifying the IP subnets
that belong to each site you have created. Use the following procedure to assign
subnets to each site:

Step 1.   In the console tree of Active Directory Sites and Services, right-click the
Subnets folder and choose **New Subnet**.

Step 2.   In the New Object - Subnet dialog box shown in Figure 6-5, enter the
IPv4 or IPv6 subnet address prefix being configured.

Figure 6-5   Creating a subnet.

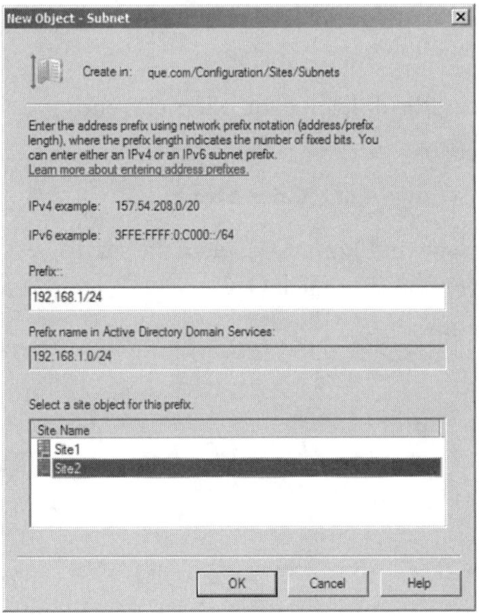

Step 3.   Select the site for this network prefix from the sites listed and then click
OK. The subnet you have added appears in the console tree under the
Subnets folder.

You can view and edit a limited number of properties for each subnet in Active Directory Sites and Services. Right-click the subnet and choose **Properties**. The various tabs of the Properties dialog box shown in Figure 6-6 enable you to do the following:

- **General:** Provide a description of the site. You can also change the site to which the subnet is assigned. The description is for information purposes and helps you document the purpose of the site for others who might be administering the site later.

- **Location:** Provide a description of the location of the site. This is also for information purposes.

- **Object:** View the site's Active Directory canonical name (CN) and its update sequence number (USN), and protect it from accidental deletion.

- **Security:** Modify security permissions assigned to the object.

- **Attribute Editor:** View and edit attributes set by Active Directory for the site.

Figure 6-6   You can configure a subnet's properties from its Properties dialog box.

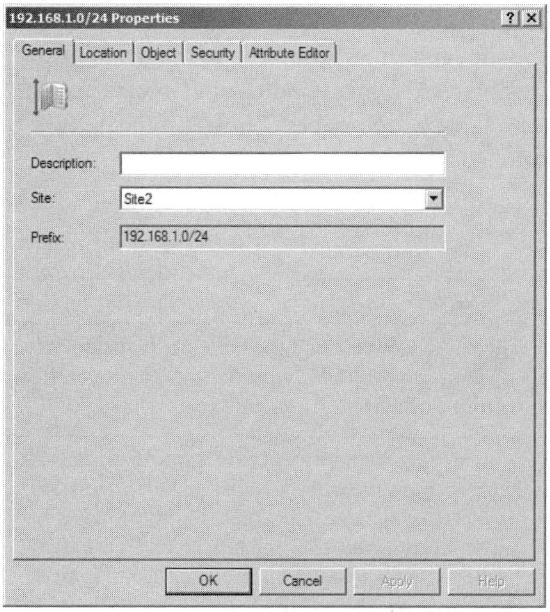

TIP   After you have configured your sites and their associated subnets, you can install a new domain controller directly to its desired site. The Active Directory Installation Wizard offers a Select a Site page that lists all sites you have configured for the domain to which you are installing a new domain controller. Refer to Chapter 3, "Installing Active Directory Domain Services," for more information.

> **TIP** Microsoft expects you to be familiar with IPv6 for the new generation of exams, including those for Windows Vista, Windows 7, and Windows Server 2008. You might see questions that assume you know about IPv6 networks or subnets on this or another Microsoft exam. For more information, refer to "IPv6" at http://technet.microsoft.com/en-us/network/bb530961.aspx or to *Exam Cram* books on exams 70-680 and 70-642.

Site Links, Site Link Bridges, and Bridgehead Servers

As already stated, one of the prime purposes of sites is to control Active Directory replication across slow links. Microsoft has created several additional types of objects in Active Directory that enable you to manage your network's physical topology and replication processes. In this section, you will learn about site links, site link bridges, and bridgehead servers.

The Need for Site Links and Site Link Bridges

A *site link* is an object used by Active Directory to replicate information between sites. This includes Active Directory information and other data such as shared folders. Each site link represents a WAN connection between two or more sites. You can use site links to optimize intersite replication according to the reliability, availability, and bandwidth of the available WAN links. Configuring intersite replication is discussed later in this chapter. Table 6-2 describes the two protocols used by site links for intersite data replication:

Table 6-2 Intersite Replication Protocols

Protocol	Description
Remote Procedure Call (RPC) over IP	This is the default replication protocol and the only one that supports replication within a domain. It enables low-speed, synchronous replication of all AD DS partitions using remote procedure calls.
Simple Mail Transfer Protocol (SMTP)	This is an asynchronous email-based protocol that can be used to replicate the schema and configuration partitions of the AD DS forest structure and the global catalog between domains. This protocol is useful for interdomain replication across unreliable links. To use this protocol, you must install an enterprise certification authority (CA) to sign the SMTP messages sent across the link. You also need to install SMTP on the domain controllers using this site link.

A *site link bridge* is a grouping of one or more site links that enable any two domain controllers to communicate directly with each other, whether or not they are directly linked by means of a site link. By default, Active Directory bridges all site links. You will see how you can modify the default configuration of site links and site link bridges in this section.

Configuring Site Links

By default, Active Directory creates a default site link object named DEFAULTIPSITELINK (refer to Figure 6-2) when you first install it. You can create additional site links by completing the following procedure:

Step 1.   In the console tree of Active Directory Sites and Services, expand the Inter-Site Transports folder to reveal the IP and SMTP subfolders.

Step 2.   Right-click the folder corresponding to the desired transport protocol and choose **New Site Link**.

Step 3.   In the New Object - Site Link dialog box shown in Figure 6-7, type a name for the site link. Ensure that at least two sites are included in the site link and then click **OK**.

Figure 6-7   Creating a site link.

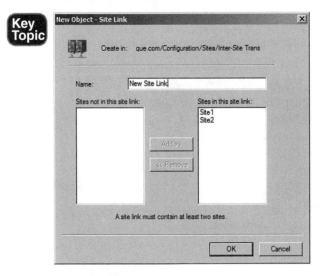

Site Link Bridges

By default, Active Directory creates site link bridges for all site links you have configured. Each site link bridge is a chain of site links that enables any two domain controllers to communicate directly with each other, whether or not they are directly connected with a site link. To begin with, all site links for a single transport protocol (IP or SMTP) are included in one site link bridge for that protocol. This is known as *automatic site link bridging* or *transitive site links*.

In some cases such as the following, you might need to disable automatic site link bridging and create your own site link bridges:

- Your network is not completely routed. In other words, not all domain controllers can directly communicate with each other.

- A security policy prevents direct communication between all domain controllers.

- A large enterprise might contain many sites that are not well connected.

To disable automatic site link bridging and create your own site link bridges, proceed as follows:

Step 1.   In the console tree of Active Directory Sites and Services, expand the Inter-Site Transports folder to reveal the IP and SMTP subfolders.

Step 2.   Right-click the appropriate protocol (**IP** or **SMTP**) and choose **Properties**.

Step 3.   In the General tab of the protocol's Properties dialog box, clear the **Bridge all site links** check box, and then click **OK**. This disables automatic site link bridging.

Step 4.   Right-click the protocol again and choose **New Site Link Bridge**.

Step 5.   In the New Object - Site Link Bridge dialog box shown in Figure 6-8, type a name for the site link bridge you are creating. (Figure 6-8 shows New Bridge as an example.) Ensure that at least two site links are in the bridge, and then click **OK**.

> **TIP**   You might encounter a question containing a scenario in which multiple sites are linked by different bandwidth links and considerable intersite traffic is clogging a slow link when faster links crossing three or more sites are available. In such a case, you should create a site link bridge that encompasses the faster links. Such a bridge will direct intersite replication traffic across the fast links.

Site Link Costs

Some networks might consist of multiple sites with more than one physical link. For example, you might have a head office and branch office that are connected by a dedicated T1 link. Having experienced occasional downtime with the T1 link, you decide to install a dial-up link that uses regular phone lines as a backup connection between the two offices. In such a case, you want replication to always utilize the T1 link when it is available. Active Directory enables you to handle such a scenario by means of a parameter called the *site link cost*.

Figure 6-8   Creating a site link bridge.

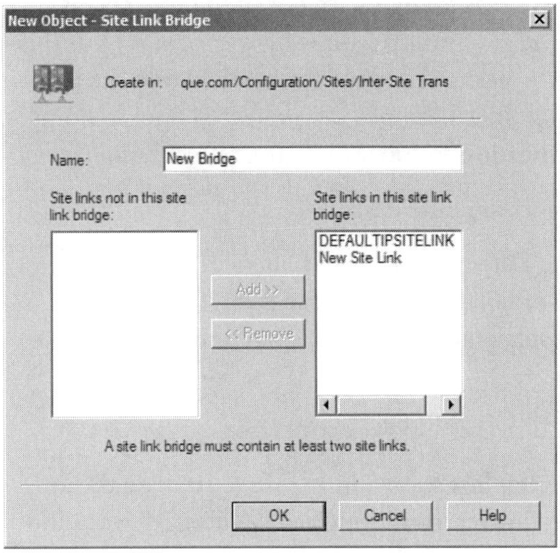

New Object - Site Link Bridge   ✕

      🖳   Create in: que.com/Configuration/Sites/Inter-Site Trans
      ───

      Name: │New Bridge   │

      Site links not in this site   Site links in this site link
      link bridge: bridge:
      ┌──────────────────┐   ┌──────────────────┐
      │   │   │DEFAULTIPSITELINK │
      │   │   │New Site Link   │
      │   │   │   │
      │   │   Add >>   │   │
      │   │   │   │
      │   │   << Remove   │   │
      │   │   │   │
      │   │   │◀ ▭▭▭▭▭▭▭▭▭ ▶│
      └──────────────────┘

          A site link bridge must contain at least two site links.
      ───

                     ┌────────┐   ┌────────┐   ┌────────┐
                     │   OK   │   │ Cancel │   │ Help │
                     └────────┘   └────────┘   └────────┘

By default, Active Directory sets the cost of each site link to 100. You should set the costs of various site links so that the cost of a faster, more reliable link is lower than that of a slower, less reliable link. In the example outlined here, you might set the cost of the dial-up link to 200 while leaving the T1 link at its default of 100.

You can extend this example to cover more complicated networks. Consider the network shown in Figure 6-9. In this example, domain controllers in each site are linked with two replication paths. As shown in the figure, you should configure site link costs according to bandwidth, availability, and reliability.

Figure 6-9   An example of site links and site link costs.

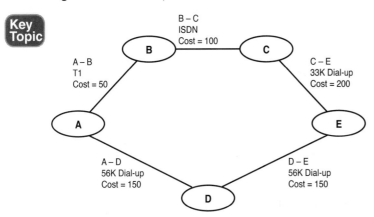

The total site link cost between two sites that are not directly linked is always the sum of the costs of all links crossed in making the connection. For example, in

Figure 6-9, there are two paths between sites A and E. Going by way of sites B and C, the cost is (50 + 100 + 200) = 350, whereas going by way of site D, the cost is (150 + 150) = 300. Therefore the desired replication path is by way of site D. If this is not the appropriate replication path, you should adjust the costs so that the path that uses two dedicated plus one dial-up links becomes the preferred one. In doing so, you can adjust the costs so that replication traffic utilizes the fastest link.

Use the following procedure to configure site link costs:

Step 1.   In the console tree of Active Directory Sites and Services, select the folder (**IP** or **SMTP**) that contains the link whose cost you want to modify. The details pane displays all site links and site link bridges associated with this protocol.

Step 2.   Right-click the desired site link and choose **Properties**.

Step 3.   In the General tab of the dialog box shown in Figure 6-10, type the appropriate cost or use the up/down arrows to select the desired value and then click **OK**.

Figure 6-10   The Site Link Properties dialog box enables you to configure site link costs and replication schedules.

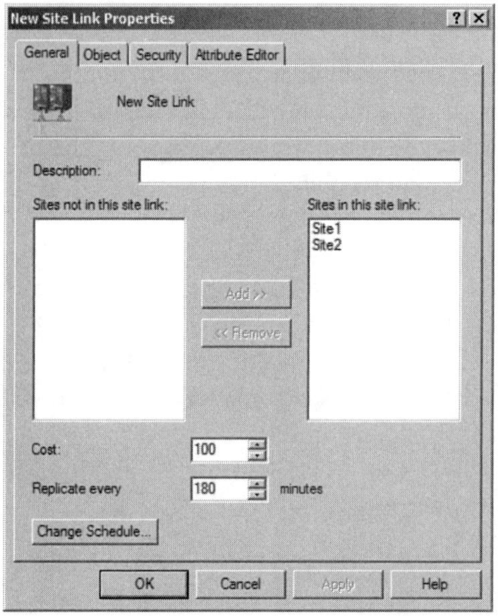

NOTE   The cost of a site link bridge is the sum of the costs of all links contained within the site link bridge. However, you must ensure that each site link in the bridge has at least one site in common with another site link in the bridge;

otherwise, you cannot compute costs for the site link bridge and such a bridge serves no real purpose.

Sites Infrastructure

Active Directory includes several sites infrastructure components that you must understand to manage your network's sites properly. This includes the Knowledge Consistency Checker (KCC) and the Intersite Topology Generator (ISTG).

Knowledge Consistency Checker

The KCC is a process that runs automatically on every domain controller and creates intrasite and intersite Active Directory replication topologies. It creates optimum topologies every 15 minutes that take into account the currently existing conditions, including the addition of new sites and domain controllers. The KCC generates a bidirectional ring topology that provides for fault tolerance of replication paths, with at least two paths with no more than three hops between any two domain controllers on the network.

The KCC normally runs in the background without requiring configuration. If you need to force the KCC to run at any time, you can use one of the Active Directory replication monitoring tools, `replmon` or `repadmin`. These tools are discussed in Chapter 14, "Monitoring Active Directory." `repadmin` is installed by default in Windows Server 2008, and you can install `replmon` from the Active Directory management tools.

Intersite Topology Generator

The ISTG is a single domain controller in each site that the KCC uses to build its intersite replication topology. It considers the cost of intersite connections and checks whether any domain controllers have been added to or removed from each site. Using this information, the KCC then adds or removes connection objects to optimize replication as needed. If the forest is operating at the Windows Server 2003, Windows Server 2008, or Windows Server 2008 R2 native forest functional level, the KCC uses an improved randomized process to determine the bridgehead servers used by each site for intersite replication.

The `dcdiag` tool, installed by default in Windows Server 2008, enables you to identify the ISTG computer in each site. We discuss `dcdiag` in Chapter 14.

Configuring Active Directory Replication

You have learned that all domain controllers act as peers and that most changes to AD DS can be made at any domain controller. AD DS uses the process of multimaster replication to propagate these changes to other domain controllers in the domain. In addition, the global catalog is replicated to other global catalog servers in the forest. Application directory partitions are replicated to a subset of domain controllers in the forest, and the schema and configuration partitions are also replicated to all domain controllers in the forest. You can see that replication is an important process that must take place in a timely manner so that updates to AD DS are synchronized properly among all domain controllers in the forest. The amount of replication necessary to maintain AD DS could easily overwhelm network bandwidth, especially on slow-speed WAN links.

Concepts of Active Directory Replication

In general, the process of replication refers to the copying of data from one server to another. This can include both the AD DS database and other data such as files and folders. In particular, Active Directory replicates the following components or partitions of the database to other domain controllers:

- **Domain partition:** Contains all domain-specific information such as user, computer, and group accounts. This partition is replicated to all domain controllers in its domain but is not replicated to other domains in the forest.

- **Configuration partition:** Contains forestwide configuration information. This partition is replicated to all domain controllers in the forest.

- **Schema partition:** Contains all schema objects and attributes. This partition is replicated from the schema master to all other domain controllers in the forest.

- **Application directory partitions:** As introduced in Chapter 1, "Getting Started with Active Directory," these partitions contain application-specific (such as DNS) information that is replicated to specific domain controllers in the forest.

- **Global catalog:** As introduced in Chapter 1, the global catalog contains partial information on all objects in each domain that is replicated to all global catalog servers in the forest.

Active Directory replicates all data in these partitions to the specified domain controllers in the domain so that every domain controller has an up-to-date copy of this information. By default, any domain controller can replicate data to any other domain controller; this process is known as *multi-master replication*. A read-only domain controller (RODC) can receive updated information from another domain controller (inbound replication), but it cannot replicate any information to other servers. If your domain that is spread across more than one site, a single domain controller in each site known as a *bridgehead server* replicates information to bridgehead servers in other sites; other domain controllers in each site replicate information to domain controllers in their own site only.

NOTE An RODC can receive updates to the schema, configuration, and application directory partitions and the global catalog from any Windows Server 2003 or 2008 domain controller in its domain; however, it can receive updates to the domain partition from domain controllers running Windows Server 2008 only.

The process of replication is vital to the proper performance of Active Directory. If replication fails, the domain will not function properly. For this reason, Microsoft expects you to understand how replication works and how to configure and troubleshoot it for the 70-640 exam.

NOTE For a further introduction to Active Directory replication, along with several example scenarios, refer to "Active Directory Replication Considerations" at http://technet.microsoft.com/en-us/library/cc772065(WS.10).aspx and "Active Directory Replication Topology Technical Reference" at http://technet.microsoft.com/en-us/library/cc755326(WS.10).aspx.

Intersite and Intrasite Replication

Most of the discussion in this chapter centers around the topic of intersite replication because this is the type of replication that you will need to configure and troubleshoot. However, you should keep in mind that replication also occurs between domain controllers on the same site, in other words, *intrasite replication*. The KCC automatically configures intrasite replication so that each domain controller replicates with at least two others. In this way, should one replication partner become temporarily unavailable, no domain controller will miss an update. The KCC uses a default bidirectional ring topology, with additional connections as required to limit the number of hops between replication partners to three or less.

Table 6-3 compares several characteristics of intrasite and intersite replication.

Key Topic

Table 6-3   Comparison of Intrasite and Intersite Replication

Characteristic	Intrasite	Intersite
Compression	Uncompressed	Compressed
Interval	Frequent, automatic	Scheduled, configured
Connection type	Between all domain controllers in ring topology	According to site link cost
Transport protocol	RPC over IP	SMTP, RPC over IP

Intrasite replication is totally automatic and requires no additional configuration after you have established your site topology. It is possible to modify intrasite replication if required; configuration of replication intervals, both intersite and intrasite, is discussed later in this chapter.

Key Topic

Distributed File System

First introduced in Windows Server 2003 R2, Distributed File System (DFS) replication improves upon the File Replication Service (FRS) replication previously used in Windows 2000 and the initial version of Windows Server 2003. New to Windows Server 2008, Active Directory uses DFS replication to replicate the SYSVOL shared folder, provided that the domain is operating at the Windows Server 2008 domain functional level or higher. DFS replication uses an improved compression algorithm to improve the efficiency of transmitting data across limited bandwidth links; in addition, it replicates only the changes to updated data. The original version of Windows Server 2008 continued to use FRS replication to replicate other components of the AD DS database; however, Windows Server 2008 R2 uses DFS replication for replicating all AD DS database components, provided that the domain functional level is set to Windows Server 2008 or higher. FRS is used in Windows Server 2008 R2 only for replicating the SYSVOL folder on domain controllers in domains that are still using the Windows 2000 or Windows Server 2003 domain functional levels.

> **NOTE**   For more information on these replication technologies, refer to "SYSVOL Replication Migration Guide: FRS to DFS Replication" at http://technet.microsoft.com/en-us/library/dd640019(WS.10).aspx.

DFS facilitates access to information across the network, including files, load sharing, and the AD DS database. DFS includes the following two components:

- **DFS Namespaces:** Enables you to create logical groupings of shared folders on different servers that facilitate the access to data by users on the network. It is optimized to connect users to data within the same site wherever possible.

- **DFS Replication:** An efficient multi-master replication component that synchronizes data between servers with limited bandwidth network links. It is used for replicating AD DS including the SYSVOL folder in domains operating at the Windows Server 2008 or higher domain functional level.

To use DFS replication, you must first install DFS on all domain controllers that will use DFS for replication. Proceed as follows:

Step 1.   Open Server Manager and select **Roles** from the console tree.

Step 2.   In the details pane, scroll to **Role Services** under **File Services**, and then click **Add Role Services.**

Step 3.   In the Select Role Services page of the Add Role Services wizard that appears, select **DFS Namespaces** and **DFS Replication** and then click **Next.**

Step 4.   Select **Create a namespace later using the DFS Management snap-in in Server Manager**, click **Next**, and then click **Install.**

Step 5. Wait while the services are being installed, and then click **Close** when you are informed that installation was successfully completed.

After you have installed DFS, you can access the DFS Management snap-in from the Administrative Tools folder. This snap-in enables you to configure and manage DFS namespaces and replication groups.

> **NOTE** For further information on configuring and using DFS replication, refer to "DFS Step-by-Step Guide for Windows Server 2008" at http://technet.microsoft.com/en-us/library/cc732863(WS.10).aspx or to the *Exam Cram* book on exam 70-642.

> **NOTE** You can use DFS replication and DFS namespaces either separately or together; each does not require the presence of the other. You can also use DFS replication to replicate standalone DFS namespaces.

One-Way Replication

An RODC supports inbound replication of Active Directory including the SYSVOL folder only. This type of replication is referred to as *one-way replication*. It is what makes an RODC suitable for a location such as a branch office where physical security can become an issue. In one-way replication, changes to the AD DS database are replicated to the RODC but outbound replication does not occur; consequently, any changes to the database configured at the RODC are not saved in the database. Note that you can prevent certain attributes from replicating to the RODC.

It is also possible to configure one-way replication connections between other domain controllers. However, this is not recommended because several problems can occur, such as health check topology errors, staging issues, and problems with the DFS replication database. Microsoft recommends that administrators make changes only at servers designated as primary servers. You can also configure share permissions on the destination servers so that normal users have only Read permissions. Then it is not possible to replicate changes backward from the destination servers and you have, in effect, a one-way replication scheme.

Bridgehead Servers

A *bridgehead server* is the domain controller designated by each site's KCC to take control of intersite replication. The bridgehead server receives information replicated from other sites and replicates it to its site's other domain controllers. It ensures that the greatest portion of replication occurs within sites rather than between them.

In most cases, the KCC automatically decides which domain controller acts as the bridgehead server. However, you can use Active Directory Sites and Services to specify which domain controller will be the preferred bridgehead server by using the following steps:

Step 1.   In Active Directory Sites and Services, expand the site in which you want to specify the preferred bridgehead server.

Step 2.   Expand the Servers folder to locate the desired server, right-click it, and then choose **Properties**.

Step 3.   From the list labeled Transports available for inter-site data transfer, select the protocol(s) for which you want to designate this server as a preferred bridgehead server and then click **Add**.

As shown for the IP transport protocol in Figure 6-11, the protocol you have configured appears in the list on the bottom-right of the dialog box.

Figure 6-11   Designating a preferred bridgehead server.

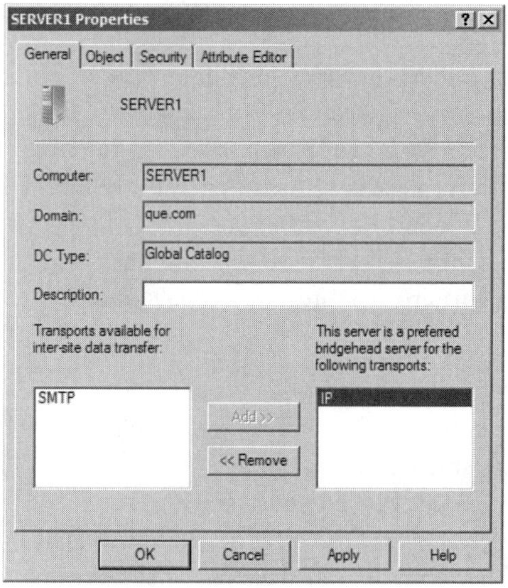

Replication Protocols

The IP and SMTP replication protocols used by Active Directory to replicate the AD DS database between sites were introduced earlier in this chapter. Table 6-4 provides additional comparative details on the two replication protocols.

Key Topic

Table 6-4 Comparison of Replication Protocols

Characteristic	RPC over IP	SMTP
Data replicated	All AD DS partitions	Configuration and schema partitions only
Where used	Intersite and intrasite	Intersite only
Certification authority required	No	Yes
Scheduling	Can be scheduled (synchronous)	Cannot be scheduled (asynchronous)

If you use SMTP replication, the data is replicated according to times you have configured for transmitting email messages. You must install and configure an enterprise certification authority (CA) and SMTP on all domain controllers that use the SMTP site link for data replication. The CA signs the SMTP messages exchanged between domain controllers, verifying the authenticity of AD DS updates. SMTP replication utilizes 56-bit encryption.

TIP   Remember the difference between the IP and SMTP intersite transport protocols. SMTP replicates only the schema and configuration partitions of AD DS between domains and requires a certification authority and SMTP installed on the replicating domain controllers. It is useful for interdomain replication across unreliable links. An exam question might ask you to select an appropriate transport protocol for a given scenario.

Ports Used for Intersite Replication

The default ports used by ISTG for RPC-based intersite replication are the TCP and UDP ports 135. LDAP over Secure Sockets Layer (SSL) employs TCP and UDP ports 636, Kerberos employs TCP and UDP port 88, Server Message Block (SMB) over IP uses TCP and UDP ports 445, and DNS uses TCP and UDP ports 53. Global catalog servers also utilize TCP ports 3268 and 3269. You can modify the default ports for RPC-based replication by editing the following Registry key:

`HKEY_LOCAL_MACHINE\SYSTEM\CurrentControlSet\Services\NTDS\Parameters`

Add a REG_DWORD value named TCP/IP Port and specify the desired port number. In addition, edit the following Registry key:

`HKEY_LOCAL_MACHINE\SYSTEM\CurrentControlSet\Services\NTFRS\Parameters`

Add a REG_DWORD value named RPC TCP/IP Port Assignment and specify the same port number. Configure these changes at every domain controller, and make sure that you have configured all firewalls to pass traffic on the chosen port.

NOTE   For additional information on port numbers that you should open, refer to "Active Directory Replication over Firewalls" at http://technet.microsoft.com/

en-us/library/bb727063.aspx. Note that you can also secure RPC-based replication by using IP Security (IPSec) and configuring the firewalls to pass IPSec traffic. Refer to the same reference for more details.

Replication Scheduling

Active Directory permits you to schedule replication so that you can control the amount of bandwidth consumed. This is important because bandwidth affects the efficiency of replication. The frequency of replication is a trade-off between bandwidth consumption and maintaining the AD DS database in an up-to-date condition.

Although you will be mainly concerned with modifying the schedule of intersite replication, we also take a brief look at scheduling intrasite replication in this section.

Intersite Replication Scheduling

By default, intersite replication takes place every three hours (180 minutes) and occurs 24 hours a day, seven days a week. You can modify both the interval and frequency of replication, as described here.

To configure intersite replication scheduling, proceed as follows:

Step 1. In Active Directory Sites and Services, expand the Inter-Site Transports folder.

Step 2. Click the transport (normally IP) containing the site link whose schedule you want to modify. The details pane displays all site links and site link bridges you have configured, as shown in Figure 6-12.

Figure 6-12   You can configure site link properties from the IP or SMTP folder of Inter-Site Transports in Active Directory Sites and Services.

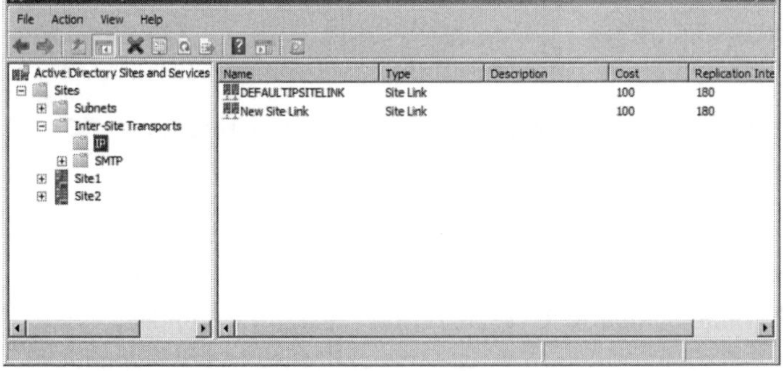

Step 3. Right-click the appropriate site link and choose **Properties** to display the General tab of the properties dialog box for the site link (see Figure 6-13).

Figure 6-13   You can modify the intersite replication schedule in the Properties dialog box for the site link of concern.

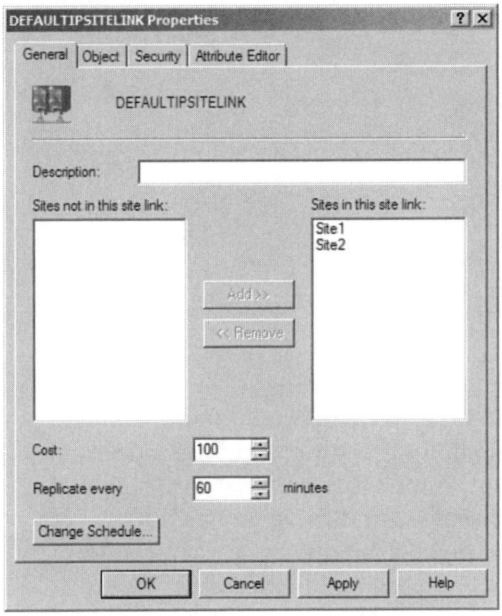

Step 4.   In the text box labeled Replicate every, type the number of minutes between replications and then click **OK**.

Active Directory processes the interval you enter as the nearest multiple of 15 minutes, up to a maximum of 10,080 minutes (one week).

If you need to specify that replication not take place during certain times of the day (such as business hours when other WAN traffic must be able to proceed without delay), you can restrict the times that replication takes place. To do so, use the following procedure:

Step 1.   Access the Properties dialog box for the site link whose replication times you want to specify, as already described and shown in Figure 6-13.

Step 2.   To limit the time intervals in which replication can take place, click **Change Schedule**.

Step 3.   In the Schedule for (*site link name*) dialog box, select the time block for which you want to deny replication (as shown in Figure 6-14) and then click **OK**.

Step 4.   In the text box labeled Replicate every, use the up/down arrows to specify the desired replication interval or type the replication interval. Then click **OK**.

Figure 6-14   Configuring a time block in which intersite replication is unavailable.

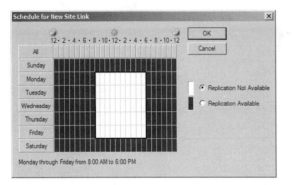

TIP   If you were dealing with a limited-bandwidth link, you would want to sched-ule replication to take place only during times of low bandwidth utilization, such as at night (for example, replication not available on weekdays between 8 AM and 6 PM as shown in Figure 6-14). On the other hand, if you were using a link that is available only at certain times of the day, you would schedule replication to take place only when the link is available.

You might have to ignore the replication schedule so that replication can occur at any time of day or night. This is useful if you want to ensure that new changes are replicated in a timely manner. To do so, right-click the transport protocol in the console tree of Active Directory Sites and Services, and choose **Properties**. On the General tab of the protocol's Properties dialog box, select the **Ignore schedules** check box (as shown in Figure 6-15) and then click **OK**.

Performing this procedure causes Active Directory to ignore availability schedules and replicate changes to AD DS at the configured interval. Site links are always available for replication. Clear the **Ignore schedules** check box to reenable the replication schedules.

Notice that this is the same dialog box from which you can choose whether to bridge all site links, as discussed earlier in this chapter.

Intrasite Replication Scheduling

By default, intrasite replication takes place once per hour. You can change this schedule to twice or four times per hour according to specific time blocks and spe-cific connection objects. To configure intersite replication scheduling, proceed as follows:

Step 1.   In Active Directory Sites and Services, expand the site in which the con-nection you want to schedule is located.

Figure 6-15   You can choose to ignore replication schedules from the IP or SMTP Properties dialog box.

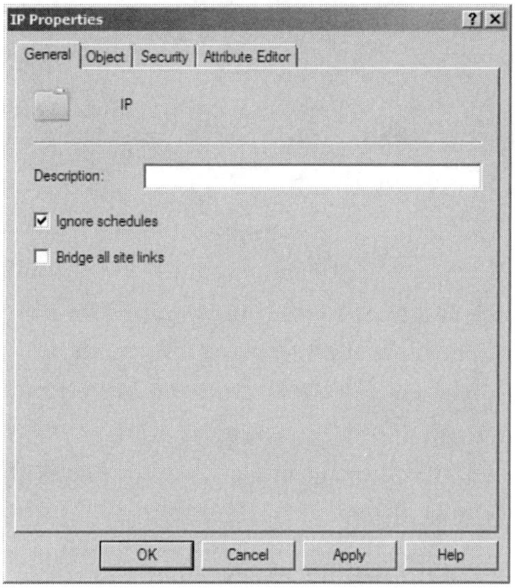

Step 2.   Expand one of the servers included in the intersite replication to reveal the NTDS Settings folder.

Step 3.   Right-click this folder and choose **Properties**.

Step 4.   On the General tab of the connection's Properties dialog box, click **Change schedule**.

Step 5.   On the Schedule for dialog box shown in Figure 6-16, select the desired time block and replication interval (once, twice, or four times per hour) and then click **OK**.

Figure 6-16   Modifying intrasite replication schedules.

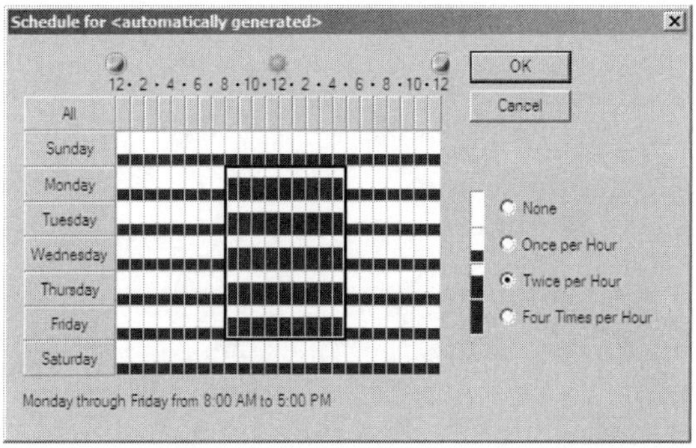

TIP   Remember the available options for scheduling replication. An exam question might ask you how to configure a replication schedule according to a given scenario. Know that you should not set the intersite replication interval to less than the 15-minute minimum intrasite replication interval. If you do not want replication to occur at certain times of the day, specify the appropriate replication schedule. If you want replication to occur when it is not scheduled, select **Ignore schedules**.

Forcing Intersite Replication

If you have performed necessary actions such as adding new users or groups for a branch office, you might want Active Directory replication to occur immediately. In such a case, you can force replication from Active Directory Sites and Services by using the following procedure:

Step 1.   In the console tree of Active Directory Sites and Services, expand the server to which you want to force replication.

Step 2.   Select the **NTDS Settings** folder to display the connection objects in the details pane.

Step 3.   Right-click the desired connection object and choose **Replicate Now**, as shown in Figure 6-17.

Figure 6-17   Active Directory Sites and Services enables you to force immediate replication.

NOTE   When you force replication using this procedure, the replication is one way only, toward the selected domain controller. To ensure immediate replication, you should perform this action on both sides of the link. Use the **Connect to** option to connect to the other domain controller and manually force replication in the other direction.

TIP   You can also use the **Connect To** option to connect to the branch office domain controller and perform actions such as creating users or groups directly at this server. Doing so makes these objects immediately available at its site without waiting for intersite replication to occur.

Exam Preparation Tasks

Review All the Key Topics

Review the most important topics in the chapter, noted with the key topics icon in the outer margin of the page. Table 6-5 lists a reference of these key topics and the page numbers on which each is found.

Table 6-5   Key Topics for Chapter 6

Key Topic Element	Description	Page Number
Figure 6-2	Shows how to create a new site	180
Figure 6-5	Shows how to assign a subnet to your site	182
Table 6-2	Compares and describes the two intersite transport protocols	184
Figure 6-7	Shows how to configure a site link	185
Figure 6-9	Provides an example of calculating site link costs	187
Figure 6-10	Shows how to specify site link costs	188
List	Describes the components of Active Directory that are replicated among domain controllers in the forest and domain	190
Table 6-3	Compares several important characteristics of intersite and intrasite replication	191
Paragraph	Describes the Distributed File System (DFS) and its use in AD DS replication	192
Figure 6-11	Shows how to designate a preferred bridgehead server	194
Table 6-4	Compares several important characteristics of IP and SMTP-based replication	195

Table 6-5   Key Topics for Chapter 6

Key Topic Element	Description	Page Number
Figure 6-13	Shows how to modify the intersite replication interval	197
Figure 6-17	Shows you how to force immediate intersite replication	200

Complete the Tables and Lists from Memory

Print a copy of Appendix C, "Memory Tables" (found on the CD), or at least the section for this chapter, and complete the tables and lists from memory. Appendix D, "Memory Tables Answer Key," also on the CD, includes completed tables and lists to check your work.

Definitions of Key Terms

Define the following key terms from this chapter, and check your answers in the glossary.

bridgehead server, connection object, Distributed File System (DFS), Event Viewer, Intersite Topology Generator (ISTG), Knowledge Consistency Checker (KCC), replication, repadmin, replmon, site, site link, site link bridge, site link cost

This chapter covers the following subjects:

- **New Server Roles and Features:** This introductory section outlines the server roles to be discussed in this chapter and shows you how to install server roles and features.

- **Active Directory Lightweight Directory Services (AD LDS):** In this section, you learn about AD LDS, which enables you to provide additional directory services without the need for additional domains or domain controllers.

- **Active Directory Rights Management Services (AD RMS):** In this section, you learn how AD RMS enhances security by enabling you to create and work with rights-protected files and folders. You can ensure that only authorized users have access to these items and monitor user access to them.

- **Active Directory Federation Services (AD FS):** In this section, you learn how AD FS provides a single sign-on capability for authenticating users to multiple web-based applications.

- **Windows Server 2008 R2 Virtualization:** You can run multiple instances of Windows Server 2008 R2 on a single physical machine that can also run older Windows Server or client operating systems, as well as non-Windows operating systems such as Linux. In this section, you learn how you can use Hyper-V to create a virtualized environment that can run any or all of AD LDS, AD RMS, or AD FS.

CHAPTER 7

Additional Active Directory Roles

Now that you have learned how to configure Active Directory sites and replication, you'll learn about new roles and features included with Windows Server 2008 that are important to working with Active Directory. Several of these were first introduced with Windows Server 2003 R2, and others are new to Windows Server 2008.

"Do I Know This Already?" Quiz

The "Do I Know This Already?" quiz enables you to assess whether you should read this entire chapter or simply jump to the "Exam Preparation Tasks" section for review. If you are in doubt, read the entire chapter. Table 7-1 outlines the major headings in this chapter and the corresponding "Do I Know This Already?" quiz questions. You can find the answers in Appendix A, "Answers to the 'Do I Know This Already?' Quizzes."

Table 7-1   "Do I Know This Already?" Foundation Topics Section-to-Question Mapping

Foundations Topics Section	Questions Covered in This Section
New Server Roles and Features	1
Active Directory Lightweight Directory Services (AD LDS)	2–7
Active Directory Rights Management Services (AD RMS)	8–10
Active Directory Federation Services (AD FS)	11–14
Windows Server 2008 R2 Virtualization	15

1. An additional component to a Windows Server 2008 role that provides supporting functionality is known by which term?

   a. Feature

   b. Role service

   c.   Extension

   d.   Add-on

2. You are installing AD LDS on a Windows Server 2008 R2 member server that you plan to promote to a domain controller in the near future. Which of the following actions should you take to ensure that domain controller installation occurs properly?

   a.   Install DNS on the server before installing AD LDS.

   b.   Ensure that you select the option to create an application directory partition.

   c.   Install the AD DS server role before installing AD LDS.

   d.   Specify ports 50000 and 50001 rather than the default ports of 389 and 636.

3. You have installed AD LDS on a Windows Server 2008 R2 computer and created an instance that is to be used for data storage with two directory-enabled applications. Which of the following tools can you use to manage this AD LDS instance? (Choose all that apply.)

   a.   Active Directory Users and Computers

   b.   Active Directory Sites and Services

   c.   Active Directory Domains and Trusts

   d.   Active Directory Schema

   e.   Active Directory Administrative Center

   f.   Active Directory Services Interface (ADSI)

   g.   `Ldp.exe`

4. You have created an AD LDS instance and used `Ldp.exe` to connect to this instance. Which of the following actions do you need to do before you can obtain information about LDAP objects contained within the instance?

   a.   Bind a user account to the `Ldp.exe` interface.

   b.   Ensure that you have an appropriate certificate.

   c.   Specify an authentication server.

   d.   You do not need to do anything else.

5. You have several X.500 directory-based applications that were formerly used on a UNIX server and are now to be used with a new instance of AD LDS that you have created on a Windows Server 2008 R2 member server. What tool should you use to migrate this data to AD LDS?

   a.   `Ntdsutil`

   b.   `Csvde`

c. Ldifde

d. Xcopy

6. Your company's AD DS network includes several AD LDS instances that enable connections to directory-enabled applications. A contractor named Ryan requires access to one of these applications from his laptop computer running Windows 7 Professional, but he should not have access to shared resources in AD DS. What should you do to enable this access?

   a. Configure an AD LDS security principal for Ryan.

   b. Configure a domain user account for Ryan.

   c. Add Ryan's local user account to the Domain Guests group in AD DS.

   d. You do not need to do anything. Ryan can access the applications simply by plugging his laptop into the network and using his local user account.

7. You are planning to install AD RMS on a member server running Windows Server 2008 R2 in your company's domain. You are uncertain that your server has met all the requirements for installing AD RMS, so you review a checklist. Which of the following do you *not* need to do before installing AD RMS?

   a. Obtain a Secure Sockets Layer (SSL) certificate for the server.

   b. Reserve a URL for the AD RMS cluster that is different from the name of the AD RMS server.

   c. Create a user account that is a member of the Domain Admins group in the domain.

   d. Ensure that the domain and forest functional levels are set to Windows Server 2003 or higher.

8. You are administering an AD RMS server in your domain that enables user access to rights-protected content on your network. A user named Jennifer needs access to this content. What certificate should you ensure that Jennifer has received?

   a. Client Licensor certificate (CLC)

   b. Machine certificate

   c. Rights account certificate (RAC)

   d. Use license

9. You want to grant a junior administrator named Paul the right to manage your AD RMS server's policies and settings. You want to ensure that Paul can perform this task but not any other administrative tasks. What role should you delegate to him?

   a. AD RMS Auditors

   b. AD RMS Enterprise Administrators

   c. AD RMS Template Administrators

   d. AD RMS Server Operators

10. You have been charged with the responsibility of implementing AD FS on your company's Active Directory domain. Users from several partner companies need to authenticate to a web application on a server located in your company's perimeter network. What role service should you install on this server?

   a. Federation Service

   b. Federation Service Proxy

   c. Claims-aware agent

   d. Windows token-based agent

11. You are installing AD FS on a Windows Server 2008 R2 Standard Edition computer that is configured as a standalone server in a workgroup setting within your company's network. You want to make this server a federation server so that external users can authenticate to web-based applications in your company. On the Select Role Services page of the Add Roles Wizard, you notice that the Federation Service role service is not available. What should you do to complete the installation of a federation service server?

   a. Join the server to your company's AD DS domain.

   b. Install IIS on the server.

   c. Install ASP .NET 2.0 and Microsoft .NET Framework 2.0.

   d. Upgrade the server to Windows Server 2008 R2 Enterprise Edition.

12. You are the network administrator for a company that operates an AD DS network with servers that are configured for both AD FS and AD RMS. You have set up a federation trust with a partner company so that users can share documents protected in AD RMS across the boundary between the companies' forests. Which of the following do you need to configure to enable users to share these protected documents?

   a. A group claim

   b. A custom claim

   c. An account store

   d. A trust policy

13. Which of the following best describes the process of claim mapping in AD FS?

   a. Incoming claims are passed from the account partner to the resource partner, which in turn maps these claims into organization claims sent to the resource application by the resource federation service.

   b. Incoming claims are passed from the resource partner to the account partner, which in turn maps these claims into organization claims sent to the resource application by the account partner federation service.

   c. Incoming claims are sequenced according to the claim types, with UPN claims processed first, and then email claims, and finally common name claims.

   d. Incoming claims are passed into account stores according to the resource application to which they refer.

14. Which of the following claim types are collectively known as identity claims? (Choose three.)

   a. UPN claims

   b. Email claims

   c. Common name claims

   d. Group claims

   e. Custom claims

15. You are attempting to install Hyper-V on your server, which runs Windows Server 2008 R2 Standard Edition. After selecting Hyper-V from the Add Roles Wizard, the wizard informs you that you are unable to install Hyper-V on this computer. Which of the following are most likely reasons for receiving this error? (Choose two.)

   a. The server is not running the Enterprise or Datacenter edition of Windows Server 2008 R2.

   b. The server is not joined to an AD DS domain.

   c. The server does not have a processor that includes a hardware-assisted virtualization option.

   d. The server is not equipped with hardware-enforced Data Execution Prevention (DEP).

   e. The server is running a 32-bit version of Windows Server 2008.

Foundation Topics

New Server Roles and Features

Chapter 1, "Getting Started with Active Directory," introduced the concept of *server roles*, which are specific functions that a server can perform on the network, including Active Directory Domain Services (AD DS). Active Directory in Windows Server 2008 includes the following additional server roles, which we introduce here and provide additional details for later in this chapter:

- **Active Directory Lightweight Directory Service (AD LDS):** Provides a storage location for directory-enabled application data. AD LDS is an upgrade to the Active Directory Application Mode (ADAM) introduced in Windows Server 2003. Essentially, it is a stripped-down version of AD DS without the overhead of domains and forests.

- **Active Directory Rights Management Service (AD RMS):** Uses a certification base to confirm the identity of users or information on the network, thereby protecting the information from unauthorized access. AD RMS also provides a licensing service that confirms the privileges of users accessing information and a logging service for monitoring and troubleshooting purposes.

- **Active Directory Federation Service (AD FS):** Provides a single sign-on capability for authenticating users to multiple web-based applications. AD FS security shares credentials across enterprise boundaries. Consequently, users needing access to these applications are not required to have additional user accounts.

- **Active Directory Certificate Services (AD CS):** Provides a centralized certification authority (CA) for creating, managing, revoking, and working with digital certificates that verify the identity of individuals and applications within and beyond the domain environment. Active Directory Certificate Services are discussed in Chapter 16, "Installing and Configuring Certificate Services," and Chapter 17, "Managing Certificate Templates, Enrollments, and Certificate Revocation."

In addition to these Active Directory-related server roles, Windows Server 2008 provides many additional server roles that are beyond the scope of this book. For information on these services, refer to *Exam Cram* books for exams 70-642, 70-643, 70-646, and 70-647.

Many server roles also include *role services*, which are components that provide additional functionality to its role. The Active Directory domain controller is considered a role service in support of the AD DS role.

Furthermore, Windows Server 2008 includes components known as *features*, which provide additional functionality to roles or the server itself. Although most features are optional, certain roles automatically install required features when you install the role. For example, AD DS automatically installs the Group Policy Management Console and a subset of the remote server administration tools.

You can install roles and features from either the GUI-based or command-line versions of Server Manager. From the GUI, right-click the **Roles** or **Features** node in the console tree and select **Add Roles** or **Add Features**, as required. Either of these starts a wizard that enables you to select the desired roles or features, similar to that previously shown Figure 1-7 in Chapter 1. You can also remove roles and features from the same location by selecting **Remove Roles** or **Remove Features**. From the command-line version, type the following command to add a role:

```
Servermanagercmd -install role
```

In this command, *role* is the role you want to install (for example, `adlds` for installing AD LDS). To remove a role, type the following:

```
Servermanagercmd -remove role
```

In either case, you are informed of the success or failure after the installation or removal has finished.

Note that you can obtain help for the command-line version of Server Manager by typing `servermanagercmd /?.`

> **NOTE**   You cannot remove the AD DS role from a domain controller using the Remove Roles Wizard. You must first run `dcpromo.exe` to demote the domain controller (as discussed in Chapter 3, "Installing Active Directory Domain Services") and then use the wizard to remove AD DS.

Key Topic | Active Directory Lightweight Directory Services

Built upon the Lightweight Directory Access Protocol (LDAP) also used by AD DS, AD LDS provides additional directory services for Windows networks and applications without deploying additional domains or domain controllers. These include multi-master replication, support for application directory partitions and the Active Directory Service Interfaces (ADSI) application-programming interface (API), and Lightweight Directory Application Protocol (LDAP) over Secure Sockets Layer (SSL). As already mentioned, AD LDS is an upgrade to ADAM and provides data storage for directory-enabled applications that do not require the features of AD DS. You can configure multiple instances of AD LDS on one server, and each instance can have its own schema. Furthermore, you can run AD LDS without the need for a domain controller or DNS server.

Directory-based applications managed by AD LDS store their data in a directory in addition to or in place of ordinary flies or databases. Examples of directory-based applications include global address book, consumer relationship management (CRM), and human resources (HR) applications.

Common uses of AD LDS include the following:

- **Enterprise directory stores:** You can use AD LDS to store data used by directory-enabled enterprise applications within a localized directory service without the need for AD DS. This enables you to store and replicate the data as required by the application only, without the need to replicate the data to other domain controllers, thereby reducing the amount of network replication traffic and enhancing security by limiting the visibility of the data used by the application.

- **Development of applications for AD DS:** Developers who are testing applications intended to work with AD DS can test them in an AD LDS environment because both AD LDS and AD DS use the same LDAP-based model. Among other advantages, use of AD LDS for this purpose enables developers to test possible schema modifications without risking compromise of the AD DS forest's schema.

- **Extranet authentication stores:** You can use AD LDS in conjunction with applications on a web-based portal that provides extranet access to your organization's partners and clients. Servers used with these applications require an authentication store that saves information related to users and others that must access these portal applications. You can even use AD FS in conjunction with AD LDS to provide web-based single sign-on technologies as described in more detail later in this chapter.

- **Migrating legacy applications:** If your company uses an older X.500-based naming system that supports legacy applications that are to be migrated to AD DS, you can use AD LDS as an interim solution for testing and porting these applications. As explained later in this chapter, you can use a metadirectory service such as Microsoft Identity Information Service to synchronize the data across AD LDS and AD DS to enhance the migration occurrence.

Similar to AD DS, each AD LDS instance includes a configuration partition and a schema partition. Each instance also includes one or more application directory partitions (in which application data is stored), but AD LDS instances do not include domain partitions.

NOTE   If you have deployed applications on your network that use ADAM in Windows Server 2003, these applications will work with AD LDS without the need for additional modification or configuration.

> **NOTE**   For more introductory information on AD LDS, including descriptions of additional uses of AD LDS and a summary of included features, refer to "Active Directory Lightweight Directory Services Overview" at http://technet.microsoft.com/en-us/library/cc754361(WS.10).aspx.

Installing AD LDS

Installing AD LDS involves completion of the following two steps:

- Installing the AD LDS role

- Installing one or more AD LDS instances

This section looks at these two actions in more detail.

Installing the AD LDS Role

When you install AD LDS using the Add Roles Wizard, you receive the page shown in Figure 7-1 that provides links to additional information on this role. Review the information from the Help and Support Center referenced here for additional details.

Figure 7-1   When you install AD LDS, you can access further information on this role.

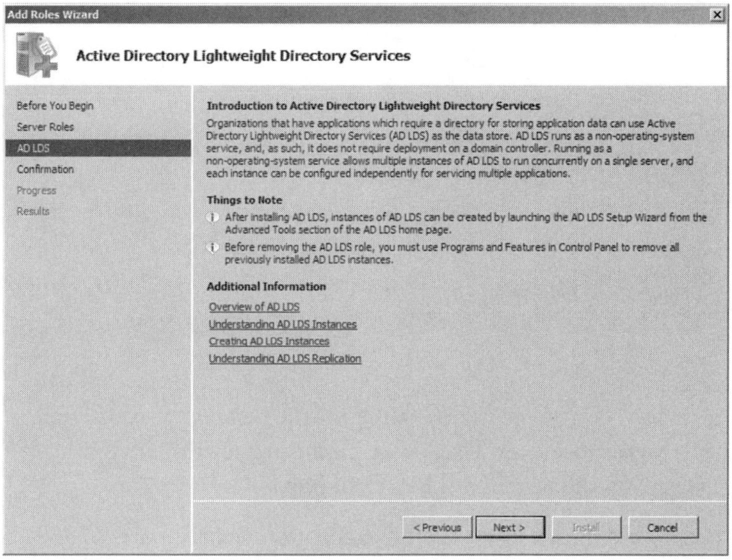

To complete installing AD LDS, click **Next**, read the informational messages provided, and then click **Install**. You might be asked to install .NET Framework 3.5.1 if this is not already installed on your computer. You might need to reboot the server to complete the installation.

Installing AD LDS Instances

After you have installed AD LDS, you must create a new AD LDS instance, which simply represents a single running copy of the AD LDS directory service. Each instance includes a separate directory data store, a unique service name, and a unique service description. AD LDS provides the Active Directory Lightweight Directory Services Setup Wizard that guides you through this process. Proceed as follows to create a new AD LDS instance:

Step 1.   Click **Start > Administrative Tools > Lightweight Directory Services Setup Wizard**.

Step 2.   Click **Next** to bypass the welcome page.

Step 3.   On the Setup Options page shown in Figure 7-2, select **A unique instance** for the first AD LDS instance and then click **Next**.

Figure 7-2   AD LDS enables you to create a new (unique) instance or use a replica of an existing instance.

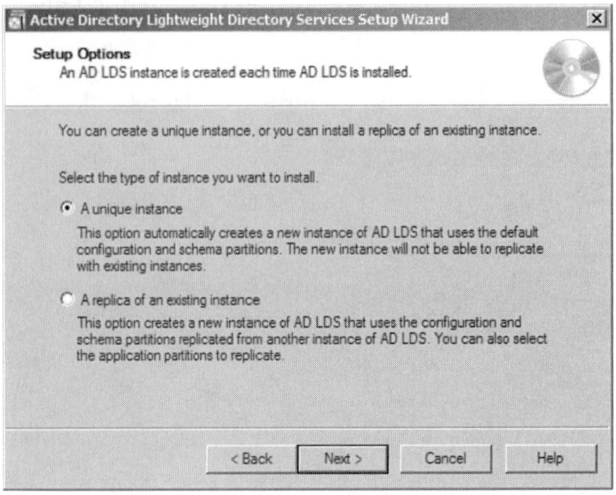

Step 4.   On the Instance Name page, type a name for the instance that will help you identify its purpose later. Users will see this name at their computers when accessing the instance. Then click **Next**.

Step 5.   On the Ports page shown in Figure 7-3, accept the default ports of 389 and 636 used by AD LDS for communicating by means of LDAP and Secure Sockets Layer (SSL) from a server that is not a domain controller or 50000 and 50001 from a domain controller. If you want to use alternative port numbers, type these instead. Then click **Next**.

Figure 7-3   You can specify which ports are used by client computers in connecting to AD LDS.

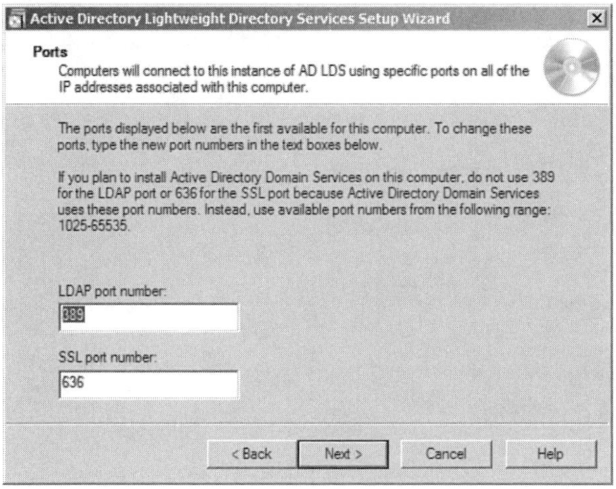

WARNING   If you are installing AD LDS on a server on which you intend to install AD DS at a later time, you should not use the default ports as noted in Figure 7-3. Use ports 50000 and 50001 instead.

Step 6.   On the Application Directory Partition page, select **Yes, create an application directory partition** to create an application partition now or select **No, do not create an application directory partition** if the application you are using creates its own application partition. If you select the **Yes** option, type an X.500- or DNS-style name for the application partition. Then click **Next**.

Step 7.   On the File Locations page, accept the file locations provided or type or browse to a different location is desired and then click **Next**.

Step 8.   On the Service Account Selection page, select **Network service account** to configure AD LDS to perform its operations with the permissions of the default Windows service account or select **This account** and then type or browse to the user account under which the AD LDS service is to be run. Then click **Next**.

Step 9.   On the AD LDS Administrators page, select the required user or group that is to have administrative permissions for this AD LDS instance and then click **Next**.

Step 10.   On the Importing LDIF Files page shown in Figure 7-4, select one or more of the provided types of LDIF files to be imported into the AD LDS application directory partition and then click **Next**.

Figure 7-4   The wizard enables you to select from several types of LDIF files to be imported into the AD LDS application directory partition.

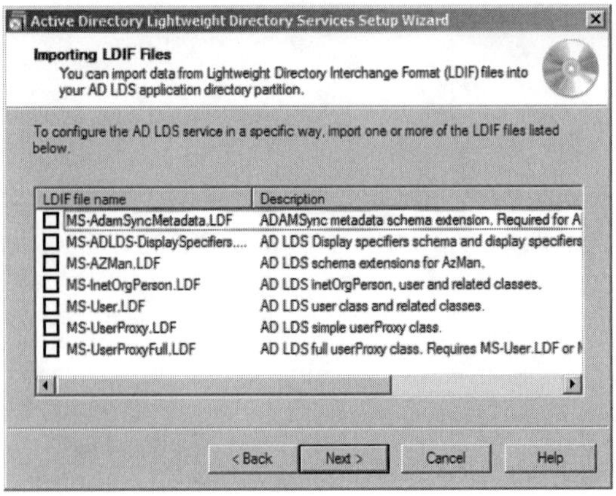

Step 11.   The Ready to Install page shown in Figure 7-5 provides a summary of the parameters you have specified for the instance you are creating. Review this information and then click **Next** to continue or **Back** to change any of these parameters.

Figure 7-5   The wizard provides a summary of the installation configuration and enables you to make changes if required.

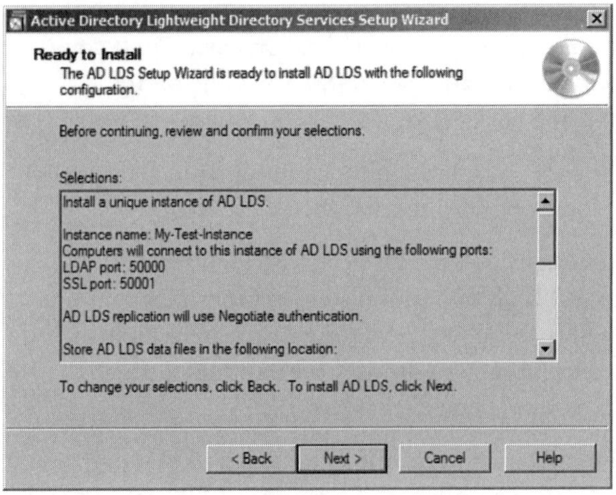

Step 12.   The Installing AD LDS page tracks the progress of installing the instance you have configured. When you receive the completion page, click **Finish**.

> **TIP**   You can also use an answer file to perform an unattended installation of a new AD LDS instance. For information on how to perform an unattended installation refer to "AD LDS Getting Started Step-by-Step Guide" at http://technet.microsoft.com/en-us/library/cc770639(WS.10).aspx, and select the link labeled Step 2: Practice Working with AD LDS Instances.

Configuring Data Within AD LDS

After you have installed an AD LDS instance using the procedure described in the previous section, you can manage it by means of any of the following tools:

- The Active Directory Services Interface (ADSI) Edit snap-in

- The Ldp.exe administrative tool

- The Active Directory Schema snap-in

- The Active Directory Sites and Services snap-in

It should be noted that you cannot use the new Active Directory Administrative Center to administer any components of AD LDS.

Using the ADSI Edit Snap-in

You can use ADSI Edit for general administration of an AD LDS instance, including viewing, creating, modifying, and deleting any AD LDS object. It is installed automatically to the Administrative Tools folder when you install either AD LDS or AD DS.

To use this tool for managing an AD LDS instance, ensure that you are logged on as an administrator, and then use the following procedure:

Step 1.   Click **Start > Administrative Tools > ADSI Edit**.

Step 2.   Right-click the root node and choose **Connect to**.

Step 3.   You receive the Connection Settings dialog box shown in Figure 7-6. In the Name field, type an identifying label that identifies the connection from within the console tree of ADSI Edit.

Step 4.   Under Connection Point, do one of the following:

—Choose **Select or type a Distinguished Name or Naming Context**, and then type the distinguished name of the AD LDS instance you created.

—Choose **Select a well known Naming Context** and then select an option in the drop-down list, including **Configuration**, **RootDSE**, or **Schema**.

Step 5.   If you need to administer an AD LDS instance on another server, choose the option labeled **Select or Type a domain or server (Server**

| **Domain [:port])**, and then type the name or IP address of the desired server, followed by a colon and the LDAP communication port that you assigned when you created the AD LDS instance. Otherwise, leave the **Default** option selected. Then click **OK**.

Figure 7-6   You can use ADSI Edit to connect to and manage the AD LDS instance you just installed.

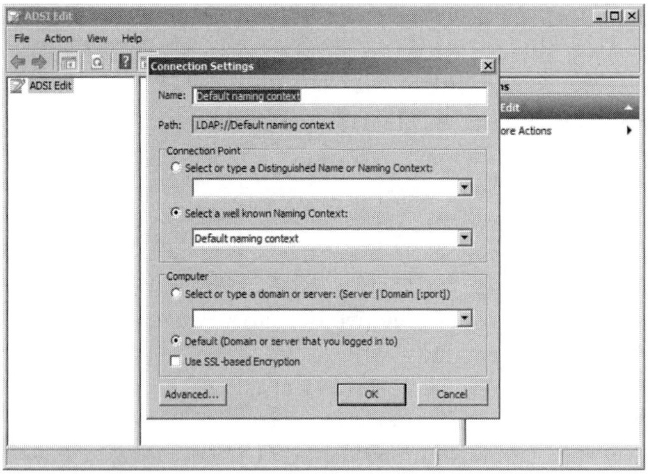

Completing this procedure displays links in the console tree that enable you to view information on the AD LDS instance's connections and top-level containers. You can expand a top-level container to view the next level of objects in the container, and so on.

Using `Ldp.exe`

This utility enables you to perform general administrative actions on any LDAP directory service, including AD DS and AD LDS. Its use involves connecting and binding to the instance to be managed and then displaying the hierarchy (tree) of a distinguished name of the instance to be managed.

Use the following procedure to use `Ldp.exe`:

Step 1.   Open Server Manager and expand the Roles node in the console tree.

Step 2.   Select **Active Directory Lightweight Directory Services** to display information about AD LDS in the details pane (see Figure 7-7).

Step 3.   Under Advanced Tools (you might need to scroll the information to locate this section), select **Ldp.exe**.

Step 4.   From the Connection menu, click **Connect** and type the name or IP address of the computer on which the AD LDS instance is installed (you can type **localhost** if the AD LDS instance is on the local computer).

Figure 7-7   When you access AD LDS in Server Manager, you receive information about this role and its instances that are running on your computer.

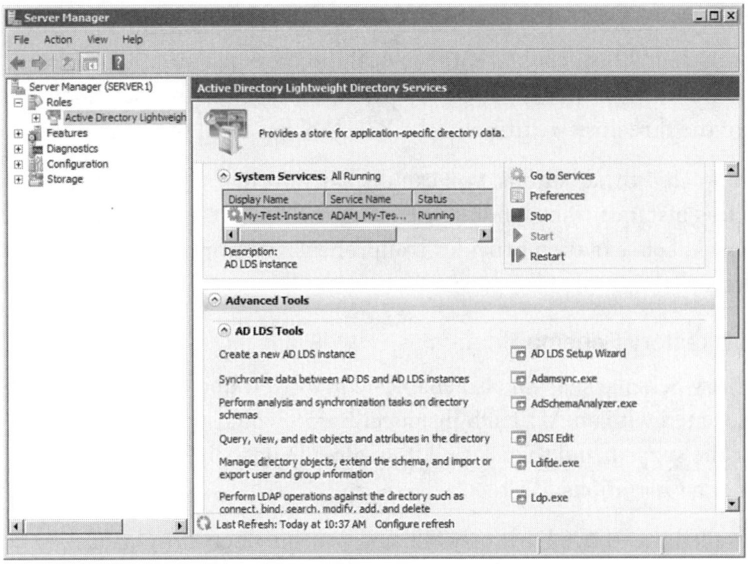

Step 5.   Ensure that the port number is correct and then click **OK**.

Step 6.   Return to the Connection menu and click **Bind** to select the user account to be used for administering the AD LDS instance.

Step 7.   Select one of the options shown in Figure 7-8 and supply the required credentials, and then click **OK**.

Figure 7-8   You have several options for binding a user account to the **ldp.exe** interface.

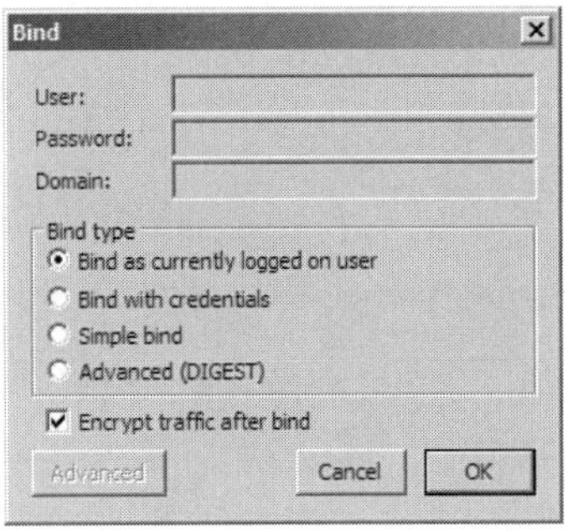

Step 8.   From the View menu, click **Tree** to display the Tree View dialog box. This enables you to select the directory partitions of the AD LDS instance.

Step 9.   From this dialog box, click **OK** to view all directory partitions. If you want to view only a specific directory partition, type the distinguished name of the directory partition in the BaseDN field and then click **OK**.

After you have completed these actions, you can display information about any LDAP objects in this instance by expanding the list in the console tree and selecting the desired object. Ldp.exe then provides comprehensive information about the selected object in its right (details) pane.

Using the Active Directory Schema Snap-in

The Active Directory Schema snap-in also enables you to view and manage objects in the schema associated with an AD LDS instance. Before you use this tool, you must first register the snap-in and then install it, as already described in Chapter 5, "Global Catalogs and Operations Masters."

After you have installed the Active Directory Schema snap-in, open it, right-click **Active Directory Schema** in the console tree, and then click **Change Active Directory Domain Controller**. In the Change Directory Server dialog box shown in Figure 7-9, type the name or IP address of the server with the port specified when you created the AD LDS instance in the format *servername:port,* click **OK,** and then click **Yes** to confirm this connection. For the local server, type `localhost:389`.

Figure 7-9   The Change Directory Server dialog box enables you to connect to the server hosting the AD LDS instance you are interested in.

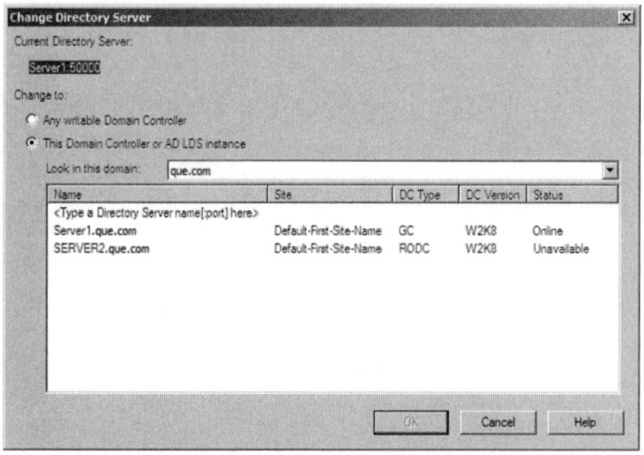

Using the Active Directory Sites and Services Snap-in

The Active Directory Sites and Services snap-in enables you to connect to an AD LDS instance and administer directory data replication among all sites in an AD LDS configuration set. Open this snap-in from the Administrative Tools folder, right-click **Active Directory Sites and Services** at the top of the console tree, and then select **Change Active Directory Domain Controller**. Perform the same action in the Change Directory Server dialog box already shown in Figure 7-9 to connect to and manage replication within your AD LDS instance.

> **NOTE**   For more information on managing data replication among AD LDS instances, refer to "AD LDS Replication Step-by-Step Guide" at http://technet.microsoft.com/en-us/library/cc731246(WS.10).aspx.

Migrating to AD LDS

AD LDS enables you to import legacy X.500 directory-based applications and their data or migrate them directly to AD DS. Further, you can use a metadirectory server such as Microsoft Identity Integration Server (MIIS) to automatically synchronize the data during the migration procedure.

You can use the ldifde command from an administrative command prompt to import data from a legacy application or file. Open a command prompt and type the following:

```
Ldifde -I -f filename -s servername:port -a username domain password
```

The parameters are as described in Table 7-2.

Table 7-2   Ldifde Parameters Used for Importing Data to AD LDS

Parameter	Meaning
-i	Imports the specified file. Use -e to export data to the specified file.
-f filename	Specifies the file to be imported.
-s servername port	Specifies the name and port number used to connect to the AD LDS instance. If omitted, the current server is assumed.
-a username domain password	Specifies the username, its domain, and its password of the account used for binding to the specified directory service. If omitted, the currently logged on user is used.

You can also use ldifde to export data from an AD LDS instance. Simply use this command with the parmaeter -e in place of -i. This utility has additional parameters used with other situations. For a complete list of parameters, type **ldifde /?** at a command prompt, or refer to "Step 2: Practice Working with AD LDS Instances" at http://technet.microsoft.com/en-us/library/cc725619(WS.10).aspx.

Configuring an Authentication Server

Users requesting directory data from AD LDS instances must be authenticated before they can receive access. In general, these users run a directory-enabled application that makes an LDAP request to AD LDS. AD LDS must successfully authenticate users to the directory, a process also known as *binding*.

Users can bind to the AD LDS instance in several ways:

- Through a user account that resides directly in AD LDS (an AD LDS security principal)

- Through a local or domain user account

- Through an AD LDS proxy object

Creating AD LDS User Accounts and Groups

You can use ADSI Edit to create user accounts, groups, and organizational units (OUs) that reside directly in AD LDS. To do so, proceed as follows:

Step 1.   Open ADSI Edit and connect to the instance in which you want to create the object, as previously described and shown in Figure 7-6.

Step 2.   Right-click the desired instance and choose **New > Object** to display the Create Object dialog box shown in Figure 7-10.

Figure 7-10   You can create objects such as users, groups, and OUs in an AD LDS instance by means of the Create Object dialog box.

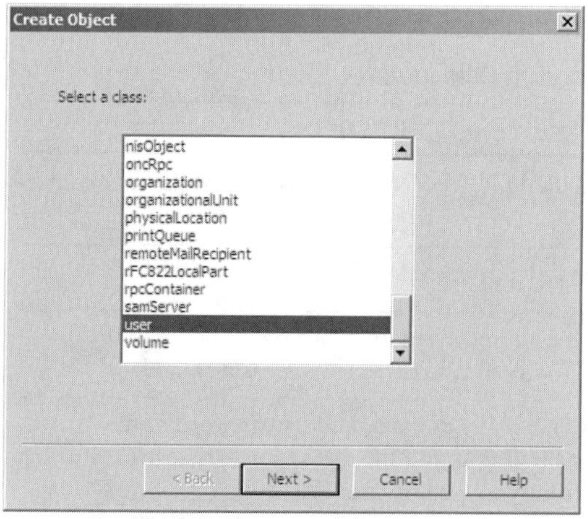

Step 3.   Select the appropriate class (for example, **group**, **organizationalUnit**, or **user**) and then click **Next**.

Step 4.   Provide values for the common name and SAM-Account Name attributes of the object to be created and then click **Finish**. If you want to specify additional attributes, such as group membership for a user, click **More Attributes**.

You can add users to groups from the Properties dialog box of the appropriate group using the following procedure.

Step 1.   In ADSI Edit, right-click the group and choose **Properties**.

Step 2.   In the Attribute Editor tab of the group's Properties dialog box, scroll to select the **Member** attribute and then click **Edit**.

Step 3.   In the dialog box that appears, click **Add DN** and type the distinguished name for the user to be added (see Figure 7-11), and then click **OK** three times.

Figure 7-11   Adding an AD LDS user to a group.

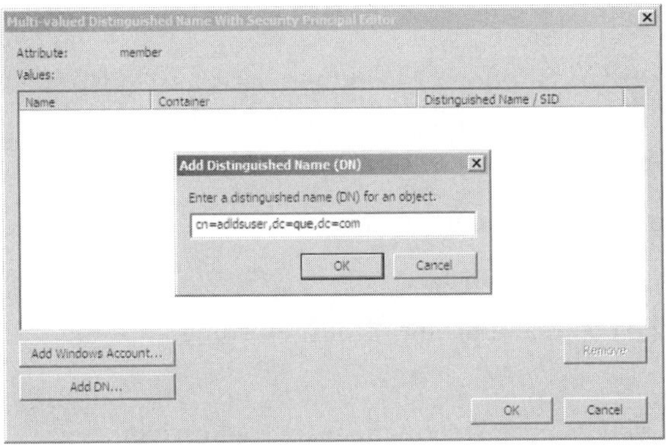

You can also add a user account or group from AD DS to the AD LDS group. In the Multi-valued Distinguished Name With Security Principal Editor dialog box shown in Figure 7-11, select **Add Windows Account** and then type or browse to the appropriate account in the Select Users, Computers, or Groups dialog box that displays.

NOTE   You can also use the dsadd.exe utility to create users, groups, and OUs in AD LDS. We discuss this utility in Chapter 9, "Active Directory User and Group Accounts."

TIP   If a user requires access to applications or data stored in AD LDS but not to the network in general, it is a good practice to provide him with an AD LDS user account, also known as an *AD LDS security principal*. An exam question might give you choices of creating other types of user accounts.

Binding to an AD LDS Instance with an AD LDS User

You can use an AD LDS user (security principal) you have already created to bind to an AD LDS instance from the Ldp.exe routine. Proceed as follows:

Step 1.   From Server Manager, click **Ldp.exe** (refer to Figure 7-7).

Step 2.   From the Connection menu, click **Connect** and specify the server and port associated with the required AD LDS instance.

Step 3.   Return to the Connection menu and click **Bind**. In the Bind dialog box previously shown in Figure 7-8, select **Simple bind**.

Step 4.   Type the distinguished name of the user in the User field and its password in the Password field and then click **OK**.

You can also use an Active Directory user account to bind to the AD LDS instance. From the Bind dialog box, select **Bind with credentials**. Specify the username, password, and domain of the Active Directory user account and then click **OK**.

Using AD LDS on Server Core

As discussed in Chapter 1, the Server Core option of Windows Server 2008 R2 does not display a GUI; it displays only a command prompt window. You must use command syntax to perform administrative activities on a Server Core computer.

To install the AD LDS role, type the following command:

```
start /w ocsetup DirectoryServices-ADAM-ServerCore
```

Note that the /w option prevents the command prompt from returning until the installation is completed.

New to Windows Server 2008 R2, you can use Deployment Image Servicing and Management (DISM) for adding or removing server roles and features. To install the AD LDS role, type the following command:

```
Dism /online /enable-feature /featurename:DirectoryServices-ADAM-ServerCore
```

To install an AD LDS instance, you must have a text-based answer file that you can create in Notepad. Figure 7-12 shows a sample answer file. Type the following command:

```
%systemroot%\ADAM\adaminstall.exe /answer:path_to_answer_file
```

In this command, *path_to_answer_file* represents the complete path to the text-based answer file. You receive a series of informative messages that track the progress of creating the AD LDS instance and its directory partitions and objects, followed by a message that informs you that the setup wizard has completed successfully.

NOTE   For information on the available parameters that you can use in your answer file, refer to "Perform an Unattended Install of an AD LDS Instance" at http://technet.microsoft.com/en-us/library/cc816774(WS.10).aspx. For more information on Server Core, refer to "Server Core Installation Option" at http://technet.microsoft.com/en-us/library/cc771345(WS.10).aspx.

Figure 7-12 A sample answer file used for installing AD LDS on Server Core.

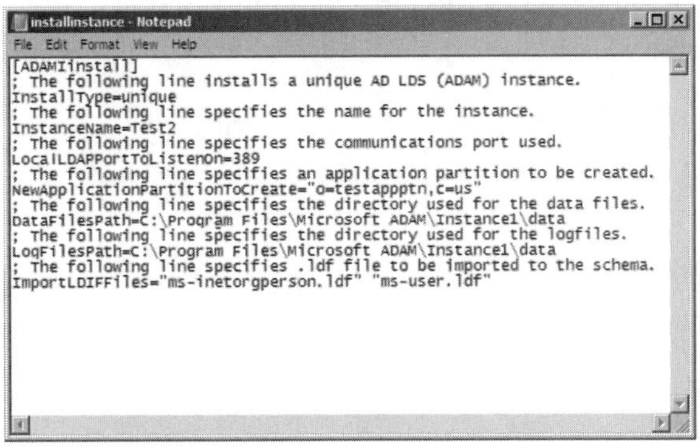

installinstance - Notepad

```
[ADAMInstall]
; The following line installs a unique AD LDS (ADAM) instance.
InstallType=unique
; The following line specifies the name for the instance.
InstanceName=Test2
; The following line specifies the communications port used.
LocalLDAPPortToListenOn=389
; The following line specifies an application partition to be created.
NewApplicationPartitionToCreate="o=testappptn,c=us"
; The following line specifies the directory used for the data files.
DataFilesPath=C:\Program Files\Microsoft ADAM\Instance1\data
; The following line specifies the directory used for the logfiles.
LogFilesPath=C:\Program Files\Microsoft ADAM\Instance1\data
; The following line specifies .ldf file to be imported to the schema.
ImportLDIFFiles="ms-inetorgperson.ldf" "ms-user.ldf"
```

You can use the same `ldifde` command described earlier in this section to import data into your AD LDS instance running on a Server Core computer.

Active Directory Rights Management Services

First introduced in Windows Server 2003 as Windows Rights Management Services, AD RMS enables you to create and work with rights-protected files and folders and ensure that only authorized users have access to these types of data. AD RMS includes a certification service that identifies authorized users, a licensing service that provides these users with access to protected documents, and a logging service that assists administrators in monitoring and troubleshooting AD RMS. The following are several benefits of AD RMS:

- **Protection of sensitive data:** You can enable AD RMS for applications such as word processors, email clients, and line-of-business applications to help protect sensitive information. AD RMS enables users to define who can perform actions on protected files such as opening, editing, and printing them.
- **Enhanced protection:** AD RMS works together with current security actions such as firewalls and access control lists (ACLs) to embed usage rights directly within each document. Its protection remains with the file even after its recipient has opened it.

■ **Flexibility and customizability:** You can enable any application or server to work with AD RMS for safeguarding sensitive data. Information protection can be integrated into server-based solutions including automated workflows, email gateways and information archival, document and records management, and content inspection.

The following are several enhancements to AD RMS introduced in Windows Server 2008:

■ You can create an information protection solution that works with any AD RMS–enabled application to enforce usage access policies that protect sensitive data.

■ AD RMS is integrated with Active Directory Federation Services (AD FS). AD FS is discussed later in this chapter.

■ You can create right-protected files and templates and license right-protected data to trusted entities.

■ Self-enrollment of AD RMS servers is supported.

■ You can delegate administration using new AD RMS administrative roles.

■ In Windows Server 2008 R2, new Windows PowerShell cmdlets enable you to administer AD RMS from the command line. This includes both deployment and administrative functionality.

> **NOTE** For more information on AD RMS, refer to "Active Directory Rights Management Services Overview" at http://technet.microsoft.com/en-us/library/cc771627.aspx.

> **WARNING** You must have a rights-enabled application such as Microsoft Office 2007 or 2010 to create content that AD RMS can protect.

Installing AD RMS

You can install AD RMS on any member server running Windows Server 2008 R2 in the domain where the users will be accessing the rights-protected content. You must meet the following requirements before installing AD RMS. For additional information, refer to "Pre-installation Information for Active Directory Rights Management Servers" in Windows Server 2008 Help and Support:

■ Ensure that the domain and forest functional levels are set to Windows Server 2003 or higher.

- Create a user account that is a member of the Domain Users group only. This will be used as the AD RMS service account. If AD RMS is installed on a domain controller, this account must be a member of the Domain Admins group.

- Reserve a URL for the AD RMS cluster that will be used by the AD RMS installation. This URL must be different from the name of the AD RMS server.

- If you are installing a database server, use a separate server for this installation to optimize performance. Also ensure that the user account that will install AD RMS has the right to create new databases on this server. The database server should run Microsoft SQL Server 2005 or later.

- It is recommended that you use a Secure Sockets Layer (SSL) certificate from a trusted root certification authority when installing the AD RMS cluster. Use self-signed certificates for testing purposes only.

- Create a DNS host (A or AAAA) resource record or a DNS alias (CNAME) for the AD RMS cluster URL. If the AD RMS servers suffer hardware problems or need to be reinstalled or renamed, you can update these records without the need to republish the rights-protected files.

- Install the AD RMS client software on all Windows 2000 or XP client computers that will be accessing rights-protected client. Windows 2000 computers must have Service Pack 4 or later installed, and Windows XP computers must have Service Pack 2 or later installed. Windows Vista and Windows 7 computers have this software installed by default.

To install AD RMS, use an account with Domain Admin privileges that is different from the AD RMS service account already mentioned. You can use the Add Roles Wizard from Server Manager to install the AD RMS role. The wizard will ask you to install the following additional role services and features required by AD RMS:

- Internet Information Services (IIS): Web Server and Management Tools

- Windows Process Activation Service

- Message Queuing Services

Click **Add Required Role Services** and then click **Next**. You should read the information provided on the Introduction to Active Directory Rights Management Services page, including the links provided. Click **Next** and follow the remaining steps provided by the wizard to complete the installation of AD RMS. Ensure that you specify a strong password and keep a careful record of this password when prompted to specify the AD RMS cluster key password. This password is used to add additional AD RMS servers to the cluster that is automatically created and to restore the cluster from backup. You should also read the information provided on the Introduction to Web Server (IIS) page. When presented with the Confirm Installation Selections page, read the information provided and then click **Install** to perform the installation. When the installation completes, review the Installation Results page for errors and warnings.

After you have completed this procedure, you must log off and log back on or reboot the server. After you have done this, you can access AD RMS from the Administrative Tools folder. It opens to the MMC snap-in shown in Figure 7-13.

Figure 7-13   You can manage AD RMS from the AD RMS MMC snap-in.

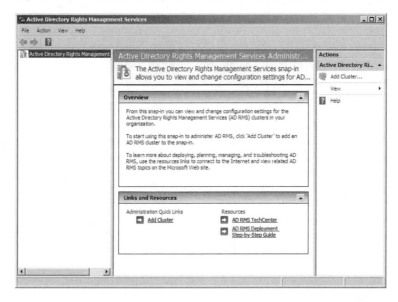

TIP   Similar to AD RMS, many roles and features require the presence of certain additional roles and role services to function properly. The Add Roles Wizard asks you to install these components if they are not present. Refer to "Role, Role Service, and Feature Dependencies in Server Manager" in the Windows Server 2008 Help and Support Center for more information.

NOTE   For additional information on installing and working with AD RMS, refer to "AD RMS Prerequisites" at http://technet.microsoft.com/en-us/library/dd772659(WS.10).aspx and "AD RMS Step-by-Step Guide" at http://technet.microsoft.com/en-us/library/cc753531(WS.10).aspx.

Certificate Request and Installation

AD RMS uses a system of rights account certificates to identify users that are empowered to access and work with protected information from an AD RMS–enabled application. A user with such a certificate can assign usage rights and conditions to any data files she creates with a rights-enabled application. Another user attempting to access such a data file causes a request to be sent to the AD RMS licensing service within the AD RMS cluster. (Note that the AD RMS cluster can be a single server or a group of servers in a load-balancing configuration.) The service then issues a usage license that provides access according to the permitted uses assigned by the creator of the file. Usage rights remain with the document and stay with it regardless of its distribution within and outside the organization.

Users wanting to view right-protected documents must have a rights account certificate. When these users attempt to access the documents, their RMS-enabled application sends a request to the AD RMS server for access to the material. The server then issues a certificate that includes the usage license that interprets the conditions applied to the document and grants the permitted level of access.

AD RMS uses a series of certificates and licenses arranged in a hierarchy that enables the AD RMS client to follow a chain from a given certificate through trusted certificates, up to a trusted key pair. Certificates and licenses used by AD RMS include the following:

- **Server Licensor certificate (SLC):** Created when you install AD RMS and validates the identity of the AD RMS server cluster. This SLC contains the public key issued to the server.

- **Client Licensor certificate (CLC):** Issued by the AD RMS cluster as requested by the client application. This CLC is sent to the client when connected to the network and enables the client to publish rights-protected content. It is tied to the rights account certificate (RAC) issued to each user and required for the user to be able to access the RMS cluster. It contains the client licensor public and private key pair, as well as the public key of the cluster that issued the certificate, which is signed by the private key of the AD RMS cluster that issued the certificate.

- **Machine certificate:** Created on the client computer running Windows Vista/7 when an AD RMS–enabled application is used for the first time. It includes the public key of this computer. Also included is a lockbox on a computer or device that holds the corresponding private key.

- **Rights account certificate (RAC):** Establishes a user's identity when she first attempts to open rights-protected content. This certificate contains the public key of the user, as well as the corresponding private key, which is encrypted with the public key of the activated computer.

- **Publishing license:** Created by the client when the user saves rights-protected content. This license specifies users who can open the protected content, the conditions under which the content can be opened, and the rights granted to each user with access to this content.

■ **Use license:** Specifies the rights granted to the authenticated user for the rights-protected content. This license is associated with the RAC; without a valid RAC, the use license cannot be used to access the protected content.

> **NOTE**   For more information on certificates and licenses, refer to "Understanding AD RMS Certificates" at http://technet.microsoft.com/en-us/library/cc753886.aspx.

Self-Enrollments

An AD RMS cluster is automatically enrolled without the need to connect to the Microsoft Enrollment Service. The enrollment process takes place by means of a server self-enrollment certificate. Previous Rights Management Server versions required that a server licensor certificate be signed by the Microsoft Enrollment Service by means of an Internet connection to this service.

Windows Server 2008 AD RMS includes a server self-enrollment certificate. This certificate signs the server's server licensor certificate. Consequently, you can run AD RMS on a network that is completely isolated from the Internet.

Delegation

AD RMS in Windows Server 2008 includes the ability to delegate responsibility using new AD RMS administrative roles. Table 7-3 outlines the administrative roles that are included with AD RMS.

Key Topic

Table 7-3   AD RMS Administrative Roles

Administrative Role	Description
AD RMS Enterprise Administrators	Members of this group can manage all AD RMS policies and settings. When you install AD RMS, the user account used for installation and the local Administrators group are added to this group. Best practices stipulate that you should limit membership in this group to those users that need full AD RMS administrative control only.
AD RMS Template Administrators	Members of this group can manage rights policy templates. This includes reading cluster information, listing rights policy templates, creating new templates or modifying existing ones, and exporting templates.
AD RMS Auditors	Members of this group can manage audit logs and reports. They have read-only access to cluster information, logging settings, and available reports on the AD RMS cluster.

Use of these roles enables you to delegate management tasks without granting complete administrative control over the entire AD RMS cluster.

Active Directory Metadirectory Services

First introduced in Windows Server 2003 as Identity Integration Feature Pack (IIFP), Active Directory Metadirectory Services provides a consistent, enterprisewide view of user information in the AD DS directory database with application directories. AD MDS coordinates user information across AD DS along with other components including AD LDS and Microsoft Exchange Server. AD MDS enables you to combine identity information for users and resources into a single, logical view. AD MDS also automates the processing of new and updated identity information, thereby reducing the time spent in manually processing these types of data.

Active Directory Federation Services

First introduced with Windows Server 2003 R2, AD FS 2.0 provides a single sign-on capability for authentication of users to multiple web-based applications within a single session. It enables companies and business partners to collaborate with each other without the need to establish trust relationships and without the need for users in these companies to remember multiple usernames and passwords. Windows Server 2008 enhances AD FS with improved installation and administration capabilities as well as integration with AD RMS and Microsoft Office SharePoint Services 2007.

To provide a simple example, refer to Figure 7-14. Let's assume that Que.com is hosting a web application to which users in its own company and partner company Certguide.com need access. Each company operates its own Active Directory forest, but IT directors in both companies do not want to set up a trust relationship similar to those that will be covered in Chapter 10, "Trust Relationships in Active Directory." So, both companies set up a server running Windows Server 2008 with AD FS that enables users in Certguide.com to authenticate to the web server operated by Que.com with their regular usernames and passwords. The Que.com AD FS server authenticates a user from Certguide.com and grants access to the web application. The company hosting the web application is known as the *resource partner*, and the company being trusted for access is known as the *account partner*. Web applications involved are known as *federated applications*. As you can see from Figure 7-14, this constitutes a type of trust between the AD FS servers without an external or forest trust between the two forests.

The following are several key features included with AD FS in Windows Server 2008 R2:

- **Federation and web-based single sign-on:** AD FS integrates with AD DS to extend domain-based single sign-on functionality to Internet-based applications, thereby enhancing the user experience when users such as business partners, suppliers, and customers access web-based applications on a company's website.

Figure 7-14 AD FS enables users from one company to authenticate to a federated application in a second company without the need for a separate username and password.

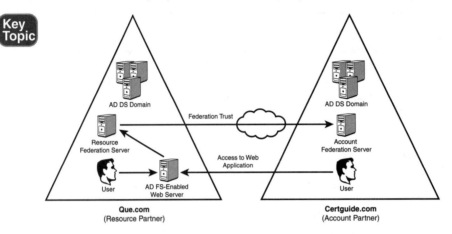

- **Web services interoperability:** The federated identity management solution provided by AD FS interoperates with other security products that support Web Services architecture.

- **Extensible architecture:** Included is an extensible AD FS architecture that supports the Security Assertion Markup Language (SAML) 1.1 token type and Kerberos authentication.

Table 7-4 describes the role services included with AD FS that can be configured for enabling web-based single sign-on, federation of web-based resources, access customization, and authorization of users.

Table 7-4 AD FS Role Services

Role Service	Description
Federation Service	Comprises one or more federation servers sharing a common trust policy. These servers handle authentication requests from external or Internet-based user accounts. The servers running this service in the resource and account partners are known as the *resource federation server* and *account federation server*, respectively.

Table 7-4 AD FS Role Services

Role Service	Description
Federation Service Proxy	Serves as a proxy to the Federation Service on a perimeter network or demilitarized zone. This service uses WS-Federation Passive Requestor Profile (WS-FPRP) protocols to obtain user credentials from browser clients, and it forwards this information to the Federation Service on their behalf. The servers running this service in the resource and account partners are known as the *resource federation proxy* and *account federation proxy*, respectively. This service cannot be installed on the same server that runs the Federation Service.
Claims-aware agent	Uses a claims-aware application to enable the querying of AD FS security token claims. This is a Microsoft ASP .NET application that uses claims that are present in an AD FS security token to perform authorization decisions and personalize applications. It includes the `default.aspx`, `web.config`, and `default.aspx.cs` files.
Windows token-based agent	Used on a web server that hosts a Windows NT token-based application to support conversion from an AD FS security token to a Windows NT access token by means of Windows-based authorization mechanisms.

NOTE A server running the Federation Service role can also act as a proxy to another server running Federation Service; for example, a server in the AD DS forest of a partner company. You do not need to install a separate federation proxy server.

The claims-aware agent and token-based agent are also known as AD FS *Web agents*.

NOTE For more information on AD FS role services, see "Understanding AD FS Role Services" in Windows Server 2008 R2 Help and Support or "Active Directory Federation Services Role" at http://technet.microsoft.com/en-us/library/cc772313(WS.10).aspx.

Installing the AD FS Server Role

Similar to other server roles discussed in this chapter, you can install AD FS from the Add Roles Wizard in Server Manager. The server must be running IIS together with the Microsoft ASP .NET 2.0 and Microsoft .NET Framework 2.0 add-ons; the wizard will ask you to install these if they are not present. Perform the following steps to install the AD FS server role:

Step 1. From the Roles node of Server Manager, select **Add Roles** and bypass the Initial Configuration Steps page (if this is presented).

Step 2. On the Select Server Roles page, select **Active Directory Federation Services** and then click **Next**.

Step 3. The Introduction to AD FS page provides links to additional information from the Help and Support Center. Select these links to view additional information. You can return to the Add Roles Wizard at any time to continue the installation procedure.

Step 4. On the Select Role Services page shown in Figure 7-15, select the role services you want to install on this computer and then click **Next**.

Figure 7-15 The Add Roles Wizard enables you to install any of or all the role services used by AD FS.

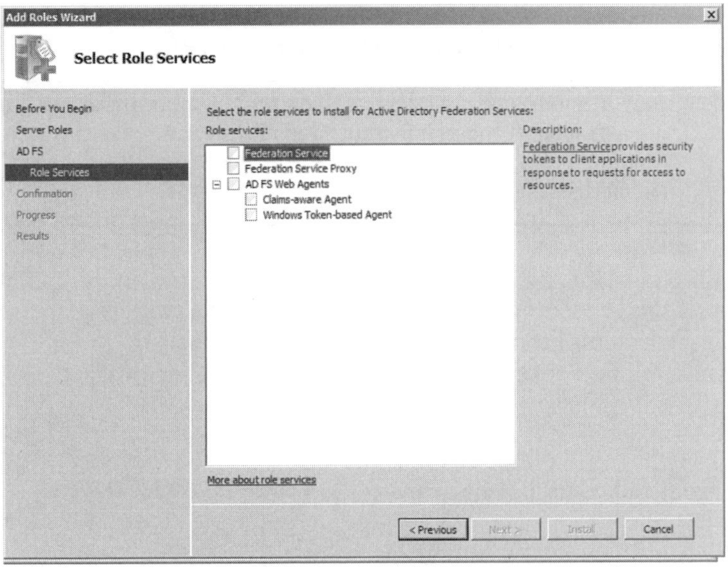

Step 5. If IIS and the Windows Process Activation Service are not installed on the server, the wizard displays a dialog box that asks you to install these services. Click **Add Required Role Services** to proceed.

Step 6. On the Choose a Server Authentication Certificate for SSL Encryption page shown in Figure 7-16, select an existing certificate if you have one (this is the most secure option). For learning purposes, it is sufficient to select the **Create a self-signed certificate for SSL encryption** option and then click **Next**.

Step 7. If you are installing the Federation Service role service, you receive the Choose a Token-Signing Certificate page, which enables you to choose an existing certificate or create a self-signed certificate similar to the options shown in Figure 7-16. Make your selection and then click **Next**.

Figure 7-16   You can choose to use an existing certificate or create a self-signed certificate for SSL encryption.

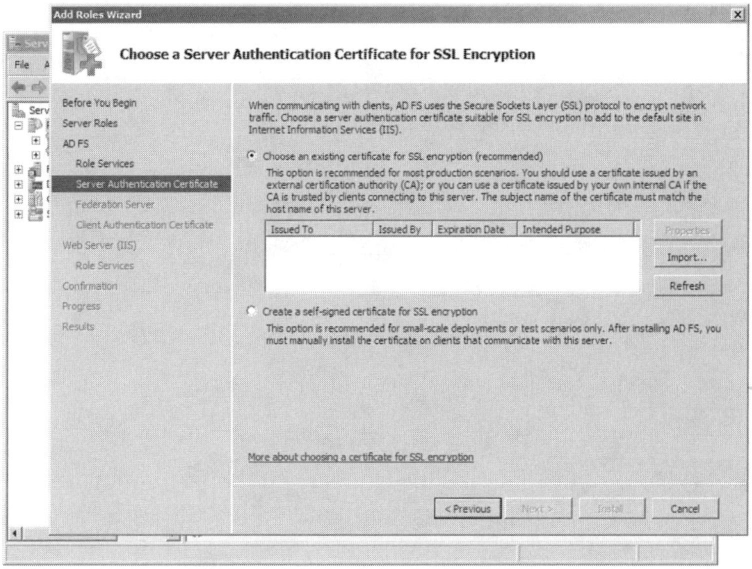

Step 8.   On the Specify Federation Server page, type the fully qualified domain name (FQDN) of your server and then click **Next**. If installing the Federation Service role service, this is the name of the server you are working on; if installing the Federation Proxy role service or one of the Web Agent role services, this is the name of the Federation Service server.

Step 9.   If you are installing the Federation Server Proxy role, you receive the Choose a Client Authentication Certificate page, which presents the same options as shown in Figure 7-16. Make your selection and then click **Next**.

Step 10.   On the Select Trust Policy page shown in Figure 7-17, accept the default of **Create a new trust policy** (unless you have an existing trust policy that you want to use) and then click **Next**.

Step 11.   If you are also installing the Web Server (IIS) role, you receive the Introduction to Web Server (IIS) page. Click links on this page to obtain additional information about this role and then click **Next**.

Step 12.   Leave the default IIS role services selected and then click **Next**.

Step 13.   On the Confirm Installation Selections page, review the information to ensure that you've made the correct selections. If you need to make any changes, click **Previous**. When ready, click **Install**.

Figure 7-17   The Select Trust Policy page enables you to create a new trust policy or use an existing one.

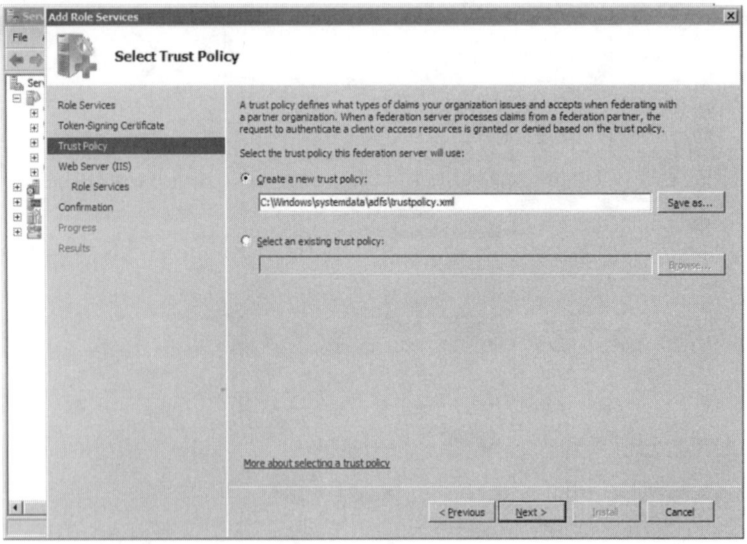

Step 14.   The wizard charts the progress of installation and displays a Results page when finished. Click **Close**.

NOTE   Your server must be joined to a domain to install Federation Service or the Windows Token-based Agent. A standalone server can only act as a Federation Service Proxy or Claims-aware Agent and must be able to connect to a server running the Federation Service.

After installing AD FS, you can access the AD FS snap-in from the Administrative Tools folder. This snap-in enables you to perform configuration activities for the Federation Service or federation server farm and to manage other AD FS activities such as trust policies.

Configuring Trust Policies

Trust policies enable users to share documents protected in AD RMS across internal or external AD DS forests. You use the AD FS snap-in to configure trust policies, including the following tasks:

■   Administer account stores in AD DS or AD LDS.

■   Manage partners that will trust your company, including account partners and resource partners.

- Manage claims and certificates used by federation servers, as well as web applications protected by AD FS.

To configure an AD FS trust policy, open the AD FS snap-in and expand the node in the console tree to display the Trust Policy subnode. Right-click **Trust Policy** and choose **Properties**. In the General tab of the Trust Policy Properties dialog box shown in Figure 7-18, type the appropriate Federation Service uniform resource identifier (URI) (points to the federation server at the account partner organization). Then select the **Display Name** tab, type the name of the partner organization in the Display Name for this Trust Policy field, and then click **OK**.

Figure 7-18   Configuring a trust policy.

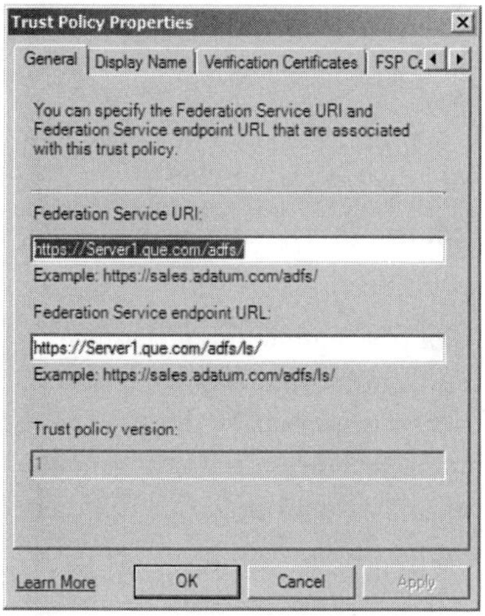

NOTE   For more information on using AD FS and AD RMS together, refer to "Using Identity Federation with Active Directory Rights Management Services Step-by-Step Guide" at http://www.microsoft.com/downloads/details.aspx?FamilyID=518d870c-fa3e-4f6a-97f5-acaf31de6dce&displaylang=en.

User and Group Claim Mapping

A *claim* is a statement made by a server about a client, such as its name, identity, key, group, privilege, or capability that is understood by both partners in the AD FS federation. Web applications use these claims to perform authorization decisions. The AD FS Federation Service negotiates trusts among disparate entities. It allows exchange of claims containing specified values, thereby allowing parties such as resource partners to use these claims in deciding whether to authorize access to its federated applications.

The following are several types of claims that you can enable when configuring the account partner:

- **UPN:** Specify a list of user principal name (UPN) domains and suffixes to be accepted from the account partner. Unknown UPN identities will be rejected.

- **Email:** Specify a list of email domains and suffixes to be accepted. Unknown email identities will be rejected.

- **Common name:** Specify whether common name claims can be accepted. This type of claim cannot be mapped; it is simply passed through if enabled.

- **Group:** Specify a set of incoming group claims to be accepted from the account partner. These incoming groups are associated with an organizational group claim, thereby creating a group mapping. Incoming groups that have no mapping are rejected.

- **Custom:** Specify custom information about users such as ID numbers.

The first three types of claims are also collectively known as *organization* or *identity claims*.

The process of claim mapping refers to the process of passing incoming claims to the federation partner, which in turn maps these claims into organization claims sent to the resource application by the resource federation service. In this process, claims proceed through the Federation Service from the account store to the account Federation Service to the resource partner or application or from the account partner to the resource Federation Service to the resource application. This process is shown schematically in Figure 7-19.

This process can be different for each federation partner. Defining this process is important for the configuration of the federation.

> **NOTE**   For more information on claims and claim mapping, refer to "Understanding Claims" at http://technet.microsoft.com/en-us/library/cc730612.aspx.

Configuring Federation Trusts

The AD FS snap-in enables you to perform the activities associated with configuring federation trusts. The console tree of this snap-in includes nodes for the Federation Service and trust policies between the organization in which the AD FS server is located ("My Organization") and partner organizations. We look at the activities here in terms of a resource partner that has one or more federated applications to be accessed by users in one or more account partners:

Figure 7-19   The exchange of claims between federation partners is known as claim mapping

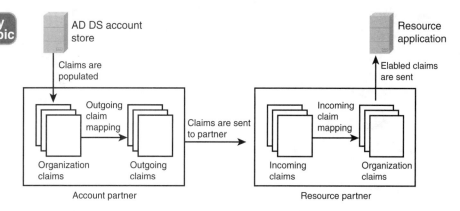

- Creating claims

- Creating account stores

- Enabling federated applications

- Creating federation trusts

Creating Claims

As already mentioned, a claim is a statement made by a server about a client. Perform the following procedure to create a new claim:

Step 1.   In the console tree of the AD FS snap-in, expand the **Trust Policy** node to reveal nodes for My Organization and Partner Organizations.

Step 2.   Expand **My Organization**, right-click **Organization claims**, and then select **New > Organization claim**.

Step 3.   In the Create a New Organization Claim dialog box shown in Figure 7-20, type the desired claim name (note that this name is case-sensitive), select the claim type (**Group claim** or **Custom claim**, as previously defined), and then click **OK**.

Figure 7-20   Creating an organization claim.

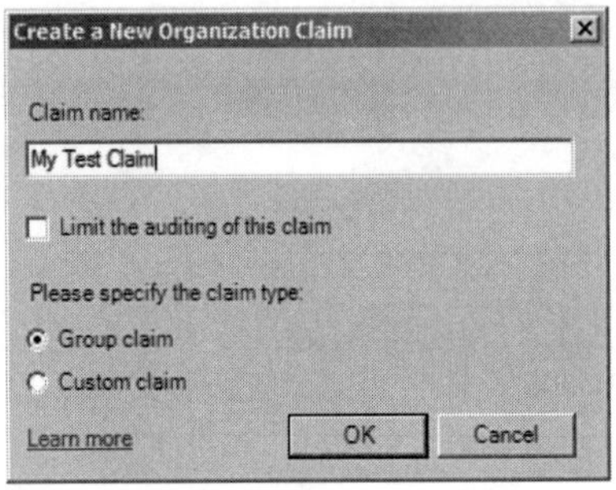

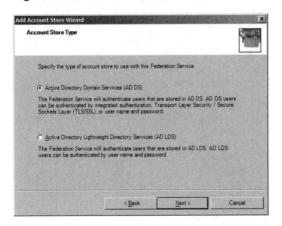

Creating Account Stores

An account store stores user accounts that AD FS must authenticate for using your organization's federated applications. To enable users from the account partner to authenticate, you must add an account store:

Step 1.   In the console tree of the AD FS snap-in, right-click the **Account Stores** subnode and choose **New > Account Store**.

Step 2.   Click **Next** to bypass the introductory page of the Add Account Store Wizard.

Step 3.   On the Account Store Type page shown in Figure 7-21, select the type of account store (**AD DS** or **AD LDS**) and then click **Next**. If you choose the **AD DS** option, skip to step 7 of this procedure.

Figure 7-21   You can create an account store based on either AD DS or AD LDS.

Step 4. On the AD LDS Store Details page, type a display name and URI for the account store and then click **Next**.

Step 5. On the AD LDS Server Settings page, specify the server's name or IP address, the port number, LDAP search base distinguished name, and username LDAP attribute, and then click **Next**.

Step 6. On the Identity Claims page, select one or more identity claim types (**UPN, email**, or **common name**), specify their LDAP attributes, and then click **Next**.

Step 7. On the Enable this Account Store page, ensure that the check box is selected, click **Next**, and then click **Finish**.

Enabling Applications

Applications that you want to make available to users in the account partner must be enabled (federated). AD FS provides the Add Applications Wizard to assist you in performing this task. To enable your federated application, perform the following steps:

Step 1. In the console tree of the AD FS snap-in, right-click the **Applications** subnode and choose **New > Application**.

Step 2. Click **Next** to bypass the welcome page of this wizard.

Step 3. On the Application Type page shown in Figure 7-22, select the application type (in most cases, this will be **Claims-aware application**) and then click **Next**.

Figure 7-22 You have two choices of application type when enabling applications for AD FS.

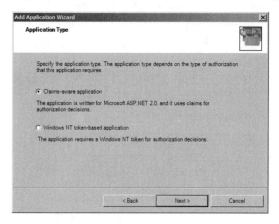

Step 4. On the Application Details page, provide a display name and the URL that points to the application and then click **Next**.

Step 5.   On the Accepted Identity Claims page shown in Figure 7-23, select the type(s) of identity claims to be accepted by the application and then click **Next**.

Figure 7-23   You have three choices of identity claims supported by your application.

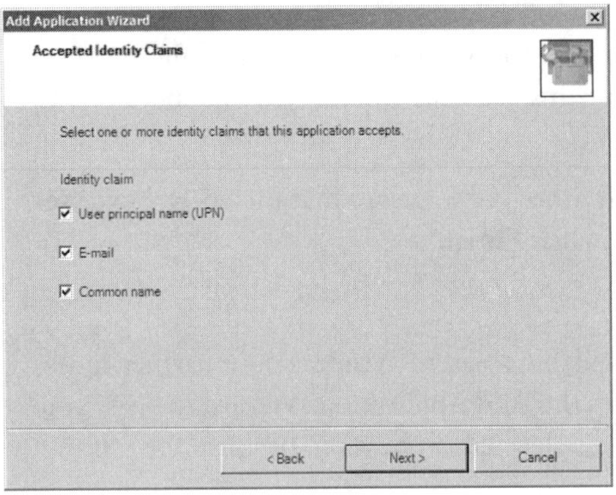

Step 6.   On the Enable this Application page, ensure that the application is enabled and then click **Next**.

Step 7.   Click **Finish**.

Creating Federation Trusts

The federation trust is the relationship between your organization to the account partner. This relationship must be enabled in both directions so that their users in the account partner can access your applications. AD FS provides the Add Account Partner Wizard to facilitate this action, as follows:

Step 1.   Under the Partner Organizations node, right-click **Account Partners** and choose **New > Account Partner**.

Step 2.   Click **Next** to bypass the welcome page of this wizard.

Step 3.   If the account partner has provided a policy file, select **Yes** and provide the path to the policy file. Otherwise, click **No** and then click **Next**.

Step 4.   Provide the required information about the account partner on the Account Partner Details page shown in Figure 7-24 and then click **Next**.

Step 5.   Type or browse to the location of the verification certificate and then click **Next**.

Figure 7-24   Establishing a federation trust relationship using the Add Account Partner Wizard.

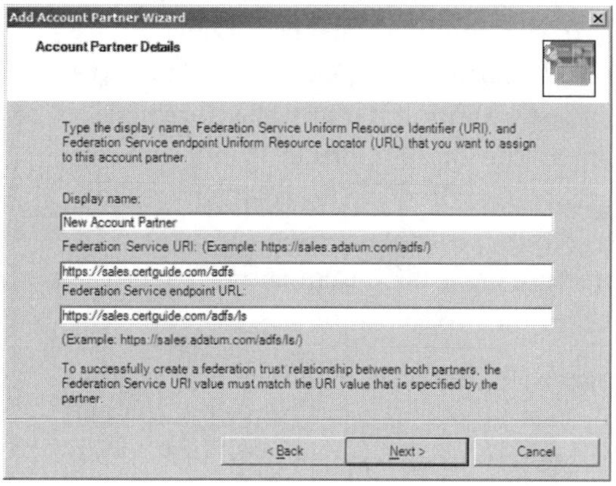

Step 6.   On the Federation Scenario page, if you do not have a forest trust relationship with the other company, select the **Federated Web SSO** option and then click **Next**.

Step 7.   On the Account Partner Identity Claims page, select the appropriate claim types to be accepted and then click **Next**.

Step 8.   Type the UPN suffixes to be accepted from the account partner, click **Add** after each one, and then click **Next**.

Step 9.   Type the email suffixes to be accepted from the account partner, click **Add** after each one, and then click **Next**.

Step 10.   Ensure that the **Enable this account partner** check box is selected, click **Next**, and then click **Finish**.

The account partner must complete the other side of this trust relationship from his server running AD FS. He should right-click **Resource Partners** and choose **New > Resource Partner**. The Add Resource Partner Wizard contains steps similar to those outlined here for adding an account partner.

NOTE   For additional practice with configuring AD FS, refer to "AD FS in Windows Server 2008 R2 Step-by-Step Guide" at http://technet.microsoft.com/en-us/library/dd378921(WS.10).aspx.

Windows Server 2008 R2 Virtualization

New to the 64-bit editions of Windows Server 2008 is built-in virtualization (also known as Hyper-V), which enables you to run multiple instances of operating systems on a single server. It presents a robust, scalable virtualization platform with capabilities to run both 32- and 64-bit guest operating systems as well as non-Windows operating systems such as Linux. Previous editions of Windows Server required that you use an add-on product such as Microsoft Virtual Server 2005. Unlike such add-on products, Hyper-V acts as a true hypervisor, sitting directly above the hardware in the server architecture design. Consequently, Hyper-V machines should run much faster than previous virtualization designs.

The following are some of the advantages of Hyper-V in Windows Server 2008:

- It simplifies the procedures involved in setting up test labs. A test lab is useful for procedures such as validating patches, testing new software applications, and so on. You can set up a complete test lab including several servers and client computers on one or two machines.

- You can reduce the number of physical servers that must be deployed in the server room, thereby saving space and power requirements. Consequently, operational costs are reduced and utilization of server hardware is improved.

- If a single virtual server crashes, it does not affect other virtual servers running on the same machine. Consequently, server availability is improved.

- Hyper-V also leverages other server components such as failover clustering to improve server availability.

- Security is improved because server virtualization reduces exposure of virtual servers that contain sensitive information. The host operating system is also protected from compromise by guest operating systems running on the host.

- Network-based security features such as Windows Firewall, Network Address Translation (NAT), and Network Access Protection (NAP) further enhance the security of virtual servers.

Your server must meet the following requirements for running Hyper-V:

- The server must be running Windows Server 2008 R2 or a 64-bit edition of the original Windows Server 2008. If your server runs a 32-bit operating system, you cannot use Hyper-V; you must run an add-on product such as Virtual Server 2005 or Virtual PC 2007 on these computers.

- The server must have a processor that includes a hardware-assisted virtualization option, such as Intel Virtualization Technology or AMD Virtualization, and you must enable this option in the BIOS.

- The server must be equipped with hardware-enforced Data Execution Prevention (DEP). Ensure that this feature is enabled.

- Also ensure that the server has enough hardware resources (such as RAM, hard disk space, and processing power) to enable all virtual machines to run properly.

To install Hyper-V, start the Add Server Roles Wizard from Server Manager and select **Hyper-V** from the Select Server Roles page. On the Create Virtual Networks page, select any network adapters whose connections you want to make available to virtual machines. Then confirm your selections and click **Install**. When installation is completed, click **Close** and then restart your computer. When the computer has restarted, the Hyper-V Manager utility is available from the Administrative Tools folder. This utility includes a New Virtual Machine Wizard that enables you to create a default virtual machine that includes a series of default settings that include a dynamically expanding hard disk but no operating system. The wizard also enables you to create a customized virtual machine, enabling you to specify configuration parameters, including specifying the name and location of virtual hard disk (VHD) files, memory usage, networking, and several other parameters. You can then install an operating system on the virtual machine from a CD-ROM, a DVD-ROM, a network location, or an image (.iso) file.

The Hyper-V Manager utility also provides a wizard that enables you to create and customize new virtual hard disks. You can create any of the three types of virtual hard disks described in Table 7-5.

Key Topic

Table 7-5   Types of VHDs

Tool	Description
Fixed	Describes a VHD with a fixed size. For example, if you create a fixed VHD of 30 GB size, the file size will always be about 30 GB (some space is used for the internal VHD structure) regardless of how much data is contained in it.
Dynamic	The VHD is only as large as the data contained in it. You can specify the maximum size. For example, if you create a dynamic VHD of 30 GB size, it starts out at around 80 MB but expands as you write data to it. It cannot exceed the specified maximum size. Fixed VHDs are recommended over dynamic because they offer the highest I/O performance; also, as a dynamic disk expands, the host volume could run out of space, causing write operations to fail.

Table 7-5   Types of VHDs

Tool	Description
Differencing	Also known as a *child VHD*, this VHD contains only the modified disk blocks of the parent VHD with which it is associated. The parent VHD is read-only, and all modifications are written to the differencing VHD. The parent VHD can be any of these three VHD types, and multiple differencing VHDs are referred to as a *differencing chain*. A differencing VHD is useful in a test environment; when a developer performs tests, all updates are made on the differencing VHD. To revert to the clean state of the parent VHD, all you need to do is delete the differencing VHD and create a new one.

In the context of this chapter, you can use Hyper-V to create networked environments that include any or all of AD LDS, AD FS, or AD RMS. The environment can include additional servers such as a database server, as well as client computers. You can also include a regular (writable) domain controller together with an RODC and examine how replication works between the various machines. The major limitation is that you need plenty of memory, enough to enable all virtual computers that you will be running concurrently.

WARNING   Microsoft recommends that you should never pause a virtualized domain controller. Doing so can cause its database to become inconsistent because of creating lingering objects that can cause failed replication. For additional potential concerns regarding virtualized domain controllers, refer to "Things to consider when you host Active Directory domain controllers in virtual hosting environments" at http://support.microsoft.com/kb/888794.

NOTE   For additional information on Windows Server 2008 virtualization, refer to the Exam Cram book on exam 70-643. Also refer to "Microsoft ® Hyper-V Server 2008 R2" at http://www.microsoft.com/downloads/details.aspx?familyid=48359DD2-1C3D-4506-AE0A-232D0314CCF6&display-lang=en, "Hyper-V Getting Started Guide" at http://technet.microsoft.com/en-us/library/cc732470(WS.10).aspx, and to "Hyper-V" in Windows Server 2008 R2 Help and Support.

NOTE   Microsoft is planning to introduce new virtualization technologies in Windows Server 2008 R2 Service Pack 1 (SP1). Plans include a new graphics acceleration platform called RemoteFX as well as an addition that will dynamically adjust memory allocated to a virtual server as required by that server.

Exam Preparation Tasks

Review All the Key Topics

Review the most important topics in the chapter, noted with the key topics icon in the outer margin of the page. Table 7-6 lists a reference of these key topics and the page numbers on which each is found.

Table 7-6   Key Topics for Chapter 7

Key Topic Element	Description	Page Number
Paragraph	Describes AD LDS and provides and overview of its capabilities, functions, and uses	211
Figure 7-2	Shows how to create AD LDS instances	214
List	Introduces the tools used in administering AD LDS	217
Figure 7-10	Shows how to use ADSI Edit to create objects within AD LDS	222
Figure 7-11	Shows how to add a user to a group by means of ADSI Edit	223
Table 7-3	Describes the available AD RMS administrative roles	230
Figure 7-14	Illustrates a typical manner in which AD FS can function	232
Table 7-4	Describes the available AD FS role services	232
Figure 7-15	Shows how to install the various AD FS role services	234
Figure 7-18	Shows how to configure an AD FS trust policy	237
List	Describes typical AD FS claims	238
Figure 7-19	Illustrates the process of claims mapping	239
Table 7-5	Describes the types of virtual hard disks you can use with Hyper-V	245

Complete the Tables and Lists from Memory

Print a copy of Appendix C, "Memory Tables" (found on the CD), or at least the section for this chapter, and complete the tables and lists from memory. Appendix D, "Memory Tables Answer Key," also on the CD, includes completed tables and lists to check your work.

Definitions of Key Terms

Define the following key terms from this chapter, and check your answers in the glossary.

account partner, Active Directory Application Mode (ADAM), Active Directory Federation Services (AD FS), Active Directory Lightweight Directory Service (AD LDS), Active Directory Rights Management Services (AD RMS), Active Directory Service Interfaces (ADSI), AD LDS instances, ADSI Edit, claim, claim mapping, federated application, federation trust, Hyper-V, `Ldp.exe`, resource partner, Single Sign-on (SSO), Windows Server virtualization

This chapter covers the following subjects:

- **Installing a Read-Only Domain Controller:** This section introduces you to the advantages of using a read-only domain controller (RODC) in a branch office and then shows you how to install this computer and to prestage its computer account at a writable domain controller.

- **Managing a Read-Only Domain Controller:** This section shows you how to define administrator roles at an RODC and discusses how passwords are stored and replicated on the RODC. Several security measures that help you to protect the RODC are also outlined.

As previously mentioned in Chapter 1, "Getting Started with Active Directory," a read-only domain controller is a domain controller that contains a read-only copy of the AD DS database. It is most useful in situations such as a branch office where physical security of the domain controller might be of concern. The RODC can perform all client-based actions such as authenticating users and distributing group policies to clients, but administrators cannot make changes to the database directly from the RODC.

CHAPTER 8

Read-Only Domain Controllers

"Do I Know This Already?" Quiz

The "Do I Know This Already?" quiz enables you to assess whether you should read this entire chapter or simply jump to the "Exam Preparation Tasks" section for review. If you are in doubt, read the entire chapter. Table 8-1 outlines the major headings in this chapter and the corresponding "Do I Know This Already?" quiz questions. You can find the answers in Appendix A, "Answers to the 'Do I Know This Already?' Quizzes."

Table 8-1 "Do I Know This Already?" Foundation Topics Section-to-Question Mapping

Foundations Topics Section	Questions Covered in This Section
Installing a Read-Only Domain Controller	1–2
Managing a Read-Only Domain Controller	2–7

1. Which of the following tasks should you perform before installing an RODC? (Each answer represents part of the solution. Choose all that apply.)

    a. Ensure that the forest and domain functional levels are set to Windows Server 2008 or higher.

    b. Ensure that the PDC emulator role is hosted on a domain controller running Windows Server 2008 or higher.

    c. Install a domain controller running Windows Server 2008 or higher in the same site as the proposed RODC.

    d. Ensure that a domain controller running Windows Server 2008 or higher is available and has network connectivity to the proposed RODC.

    e. Run the `Adprep /rodcprep` utility.

2. You are running the Active Directory Installation Wizard to install an RODC in a branch office of your organization. Which of the following are valid options when running this wizard? (Choose three.)

    a. Create a new domain in an existing forest

    b. DNS server

    c. Global catalog

    d. BitLocker drive encryption

    e. Delegation of administration

    f. Password replication policy

3. Which tool would you use to add a user or group with administrative access to the RODC after you've completed installing the RODC?

    a. `dsmgmt`

    b. Active Directory Users and Computers

    c. `ntdsutil`

    d. `syskey`

4. You are the network administrator for a company that has a head office in Chicago and a branch office in Milwaukee. You are installing an RODC in the Milwaukee office, which does not have any employees that are highly skilled in network administration. A user named Karen has demonstrated the ability to perform hardware upgrades and minor configuration changes, so you would like her to have the ability to perform these actions on the RODC. What should you do to grant her this capability without giving her excessive administrative privileges?

    a. Add her user account to the Domain Admins group.

    b. Add her user account to the Server Operators group.

    c. Add her user account to the local Administrators group on the RODC.

    d. Add her user account to the Power Users group.

5. You have installed a Windows Server 2008 R2 computer as an RODC. This server will be located behind the receptionist's desk in a small branch office, so you would like to use BitLocker to encrypt the system drive as an added measure of security against possible theft or compromise. The server is not equipped with a Trusted Platform Module (TPM). What do you need to do to enable BitLocker?

    a. Configure a Group Policy setting that enables the use of a USB flash drive to store the encryption keys and password.

    b. Use `syskey` to specify a password that must be entered at server startup.

    c. Add BitLocker as a server feature in the Add Features Wizard.

    d. You cannot use BitLocker in this scenario. You must use the Encrypting File System (EFS) instead.

6. You are responsible for administering an RODC located in a branch office that has only limited WAN connectivity with your company's head office. Users report that they often are unable to log on to the domain. What should you do so that they can log on when the WAN link is unavailable?

a. Specify new passwords for the users from Active Directory Users and Computers at the RODC.

b. Add the user accounts of the users to the Denied list for password replication.

c. Add the user accounts of the users to the Allowed list for password replication.

d. Replace the RODC with a writable domain controller.

7. You would like to determine which users are being authenticated by an RODC in a branch office of your company so that you can remove the user accounts of inactive users. What should you do?

a. Access the Advanced Password Replication Policy dialog box at the RODC and select the **Accounts whose passwords are stored on this Read-only Domain Controller** option.

b. Access the Advanced Password Replication Policy dialog box at the RODC and select the **Accounts that have been authenticated to this Read-only Domain Controller** option.

c. Access the Advanced Password Replication Policy dialog box from the partnered writable domain controller and select the **Accounts whose passwords are stored on this Read-only Domain Controller** option.

d. Access the Advanced Password Replication Policy dialog box from the partnered writable domain controller and select the **Accounts that have been authenticated to this Read-only Domain Controller** option.

Foundation Topics

Installing a Read-Only Domain Controller

Many companies are structured with a large, well-staffed head office plus smaller branch offices located in different cities served by the company. These branch offices often lack the security of the head office—for example, the branch office server might be located under the receptionist's desk or in another location that could be accessed by outsiders. In addition, such offices rarely have an experienced individual onsite who is capable of day-to-day server administration. Such an office is an ideal location for using an RODC and helps to reduce total cost of ownership (TCO). Furthermore, such offices are generally connected to the head office with slow wide area network (WAN) links that might not always be available.

Use of RODCs also provides additional benefits in large, complex AD DS implementations. Unidirectional replication as utilized by RODCs reduces the performance load on bridgehead servers in head office sites, thereby helping to reduce TCO. In addition, RODCs in Windows Server 2008 R2 support the concept of read-only copies of data stored in Distributed File System (DFS) replicas. Branch office users receive read-only access to such data, thereby protecting the data from accidental corruption or deletion at branch office locations.

Planning the Use of RODCs

It is important to plan the use of RODCs before proceeding to install them. The following are a few considerations that you should take into account in the planning process:

- Although the RODC enables branch office employees to be authenticated to Active Directory Domain Services (AD DS) without access to a writable DC, a writable DC must be available the first time users log on so that a complete access token including all group memberships can be built. After a user has logged on for the first time, her password will be stored on the RODC in accordance with the established password replication policy. The password replication policy is discussed later in this chapter.

- Access to a writable DC is also required so that changes in user account properties such as password changes can be completed. A user whose password has expired will be unable to log on if a writable DC is unavailable.

- Should a user account be locked out because of too many attempts to enter a password incorrectly, the account cannot be unlocked if a writable DC is unavailable.

- An RODC depends on access to a writable DC for replication of changes to AD DS. If multiple site links are in use, ensure that the RODC is placed so that it can access the site link with the lowest site link cost. Site links and site link costs were discussed in Chapter 6, "Configuring Active Directory Sites and Replication."

- It is not desirable to have both an RODC and a writable DC in the same AD DS site; otherwise, inconsistent behavior during logons and object access can occur.

- In multiple domain forests, all users in a given branch office should belong to the same domain; users in other domains require access to a domain controller for their own domain and such cross-domain authentication (or resource access) requests will fail if connectivity to the proper DC is unavailable.

- RODCs function very well under conditions where directory-enabled applications read data from application directory partitions in AD DS; however, if these applications require write access to AD DS, you should deploy a writable DC instead.

- In general, an RODC should not host additional roles or role services except for the global catalog and DNS. It is useful for an RODC to host the global catalog in a multiple domain forest; this facilitates any cross-domain authentication or resource access that might be needed.

Before installing an RODC, you should perform the following several preparatory actions:

- Raise the forest functional level to Windows Server 2003 or higher.

- Ensure that the PDC emulator role is hosted on a domain controller running Windows Server 2008 or higher.

- Run the `Adprep /rodcprep` utility. This utility updates the permissions on all the DNS application directory partitions in the forest so that these permissions can be replicated properly. To run this utility, log on to any domain controller in the forest as a member of the Enterprise Admins group and open an administrative command prompt. Have the appropriate Windows Server installation DVD (as mentioned later) available, navigate to the proper folder, and type **Adprep /rodcprep.** Then allow the changes to replicate throughout the forest before attempting to install the RODC.

- Ensure that a writable domain controller that runs Windows Server 2008 or higher is available and has network connectivity to the proposed RODC.

NOTE Adprep.exe comes in different versions according to whether you are using the original or R2 version of Windows Server 2008. In the original version, Adprep.exe is found in the sources\adprep folder of the installation DVD; in Windows Server 2008 R2, Adprep.exe is found in the support\adprep folder of the DVD. If you are running this tool from a 32-bit computer, use the 32-bit version (Adprep32.exe).

> **WARNING** If the infrastructure master for each application directory partition in the forest is unavailable when you run `adprep /rodcprep`, you might receive an error. `Adprep.exe` must be able to locate all application directory partitions (in particular the DNS application partition); otherwise, an error will be logged in the `Adprep.log` file mentioning the application directory partition for which `Adprep.exe` failed.

> **NOTE** For more information on preparing a forest for an RODC, refer to "Prerequisites for Deploying a Read-Only Domain Controller (RODC)" at http://technet.microsoft.com/en-us/library/cc731243(WS.10).aspx.

Installing RODCs

You can install an RODC using the same basic procedure outlined in Chapter 3, "Installing Active Directory Domain Services," for installing additional domain controllers in the same domain. Note that the RODC cannot be the first domain controller in a new domain. When you receive the Additional Domain Controller Options page (see Figure 8-1), simply select the **Read-only domain controller** option and complete the remainder of the installation procedure.

Figure 8-1   Installing an RODC.

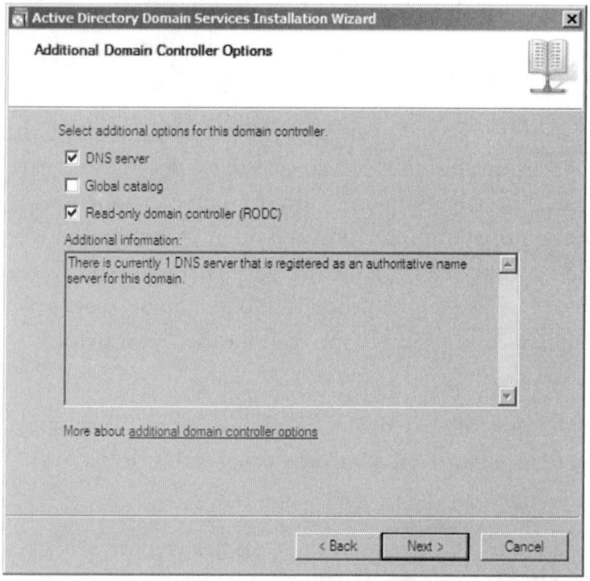

> **WARNING** Microsoft recommends that you install the DNS Server service on an RODC so that clients in the branch office can perform name resolution even if the connection to the head office is unavailable.

The AD DS Installation Wizard also asks you to specify a group that is permitted to administer the RODC (see Figure 8-2). You should specify a group whose users are local to the office in which the RODC is situated.

Figure 8-2   You can delegate administration of the RODC to a group during installation.

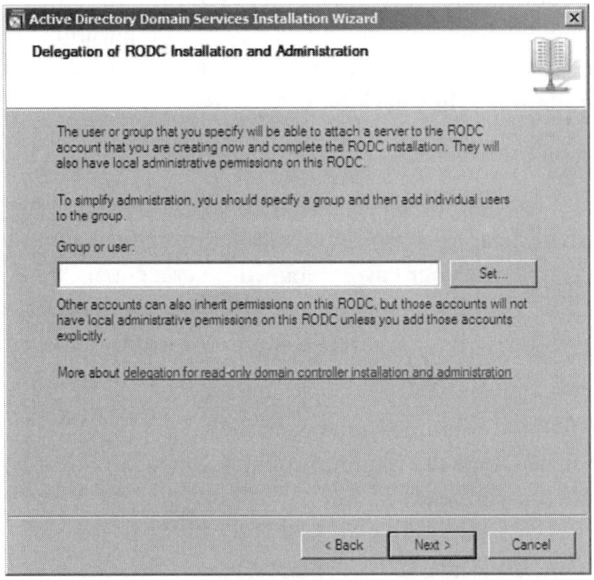

TIP   You can also install an RODC on a Server Core computer by using the appropriate answer file. For a sample answer file and instructions for creating a customized answer file, refer to "Performing a Staged RODC Installation by Using an Answer File" at http://technet.microsoft.com/en-us/library/dd378860(WS.10).aspx.

TIP   Remember that before you install an RODC, you must ensure that the forest functional level is at least Windows Server 2003 and that the PDC emulator is running Windows Server 2008. Also remember that you must run the Adprep /rodcprep utility on the schema master unless all domain controllers in the domain are running Windows Server 2008. An exam question might trick you into other alternatives such as having the forest functional level at Windows Server 2008.

Prestaging an RODC

The Active Directory Installation Wizard also enables you to prestage the installation of an RODC by creating a computer account for the RODC on an existing domain controller in the domain where you want to add an RODC. Doing so enables you to prepare for installation of a server as an RODC at a remote office by a nonadministrative user who has been delegated the ability to perform this task. Use the following steps:

Step 1.   Open **Active Directory Users and Computers**.

Step 2.   In the console tree, expand the domain, right-click the **Domain Controllers** OU, and then choose **Pre-create Read-only Domain Controller account**.

Step 3.   The Active Directory Domain Services Installation Wizard starts with a Welcome page. If you want to modify the default password replication policy (discussed later in this chapter), select the check box labeled **Use advanced mode installation**. Then click **Next**.

Step 4.   Read the information on the Operating System Compatibility page and then click **Next**.

Step 5.   The Network Credentials page asks you to provide appropriate credentials. In most cases, you will use your current logged-on credentials; if you need to specify a different user account, select **Alternate credentials**, click **Set**, and then type the required username and password. When done, click **Next**.

Step 6.   You receive the Specify the Computer Name page shown in Figure 8-3. Read the warning provided, type the required computer name in the space provided, and then click **Next**.

Figure 8-3   Specifying the name of the domain controller being prestaged.

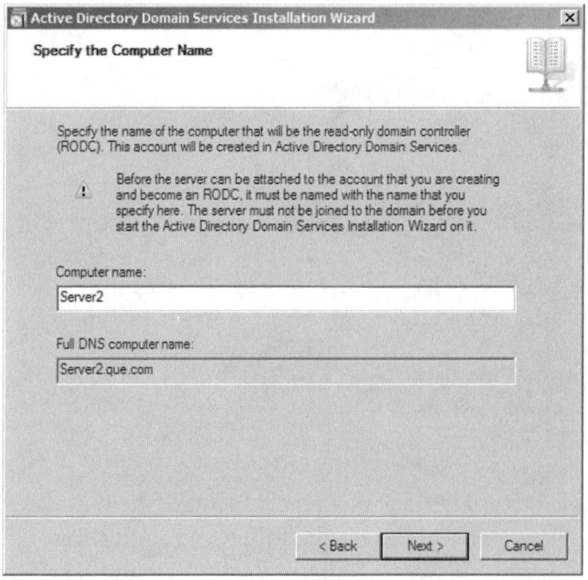

Step 7.   From the Select a Site page, select the site where the RODC will be placed, and then click **Next**.

Step 8.   From the Additional Domain Controller Options page, similar to that already shown in Figure 8-1, specify **DNS server** and/or **Global catalog** as required, and then click **Next**.

Step 9.   If you selected the **Use advanced mode installation option** on the Welcome page, you receive the Specify the Password Replication Policy page. Configure the options on this page according to information provided later in this chapter, and then click **Next**.

Step 10.   You receive the Delegation of RODC Installation and Administration page previously shown in Figure 8-2. Specify a user or group that is local to the office in which the RODC will be created, and then click **Next**.

Step 11.   Review the information provided in the Summary page. If you need to make any changes, click **Back**. Otherwise, click **Next** to proceed.

Step 12.   The RODC account is created and the completion page displays. Click **Finish**.

After you have completed this procedure, the delegated user can install AD DS on the server in the branch office. The server must not be joined to the domain before the procedure is started; the Installation Wizard simply associates the server's name with the prestaged account and proceeds to install AD DS and promote the server to domain controller.

NOTE   For more information on prestaging an RODC account, including information on how you can use an answer file and prestage the installation of the RODC from the command line, refer to "Performing a Staged RODC Installation" at http://technet.microsoft.com/en-us/library/cc770627(WS.10).aspx.

Managing a Read-Only Domain Controller

After you've installed an RODC in a branch office, it can function smoothly to authenticate users in its office and facilitate access to resources within its domain and other domains of the forest. However, there are ongoing administrative tasks you must be aware of, and Microsoft expects you to know how to perform these tasks, both for the 70-640 exam and for the real world.

Unidirectional Replication

By default, an RODC does not perform outbound replication. In other words, all replication is unidirectional, from any writable domain controller to the RODC— this includes any DFS replication, as well as replication of DNS zones, which is discussed later in this section. This provides several benefits, including the following:

■   Because changes to AD DS cannot be written to an RODC, other domain controllers do not need to pull changes from an RODC. Consequently, other domain controllers can ignore RODCs when setting up replication topologies, and the overall replication topology is simplified and WAN bandwidth utilization is improved.

■   Managing and monitoring AD DS replication is also simplified for the same reason.

■   The RODC provides enhanced security, in that even if an unauthorized user were somehow able to make changes to the AD DS database on the RODC, these changes would not be replicated to other domain controllers. Consequently, a compromised RODC has no effect on other domain controllers.

■   Accidental corruption or deletion of database components or the SYSVOL folder by an inexperienced individual in the branch office does not have any impact on network operations.

When an RODC received a request for a change to AD DS from a user or application at its site, several actions can take place:

■   The RODC forwards the write request to a writable domain controller and then receives the change back at the next scheduled replication interval. These write requests can include actions such as password changes, service principal name (SPN) updates, updates to certain client attributes over Netlogon, and the LastLogonTimeStamp attribute.

■   The RODC refers the client directly to a writable domain controller to perform the change. The application requesting the change can then communicate directly with the writable domain controller for changes such as Lightweight Directory Access Protocol (LDAP) updates and DNS record updates.

■   In a few instances, the attempt fails because it is neither referred nor forwarded to a writable domain controller. You should update the application requesting the write operation to directly access the writable domain controller. This can include some remote procedure call (RPC) write attempts.

You should note that there are some issues regarding the replication of changes to the SYSVOL shared folder on an RODC, depending on the type of replication in use. Recall from Chapter 6 that replication of the SYSVOL folder can take place using either of the following two protocols:

■ If the domain functional level is Windows 2000 or Windows Server 2003, File Replication Service (FRS) replication is used.

■ If the domain functional level is Windows Server 2008 or Windows Server 2008 R2, DFS replication is used.

It is possible that changes can be mode to the SYSVOL folder at the RODC. However, when FRS replication is used, any local changes to the SYSVOL folder are not replicated out, but they are not discarded either. This can result in SYSVOL becoming out of sync with other domain controllers. Should an individual who is delegated administrative capability modify the SYSVOL folder at the RODC, client computers that obtain items such as Group Policy objects (GPOs) or logon scripts from the RODC might receive unintended GPOs or logon scripts, or might fail to obtain intended GPOs or logon scripts. It might become necessary to rebuild the SYSVOL shared folder on the RODC to properly synchronize it with the rest of the domain. For more information in this issue, refer to "How to rebuild the SYSVOL tree and its content in a domain" at http://support.microsoft.com/kb/315457.

When DFS replication is used to replicate the contents of the SYSVOL folder, this is no longer an issue. However, it should be noted that Windows Server 2008 R2 enhances the security of SYSVOL by blocking any local changes by a file system filter driver. In the original version of Windows Server 2008, local changes to SYSVOL could still take place, but they were discarded when inbound replication next occurred.

Administrator Role Separation

You can configure a local user with administrative rights to the RODC without designating this user as a member of the Domain Admins group. This user is included in the RODC's local Administrators group stored on the Security Accounts Manager (SAM) on the RODC and has administrative rights to that server only. This is in contrast to writable domain controllers, at which local administrators are automatically members of the Domain Admins group and have administrative rights to all domain controllers in the domain. Consequently, you can designate a junior employee such as a desktop support technician as a local administrator with the authority to perform routine tasks such as administering file and print services, disk reconfiguration, system monitoring and troubleshooting, and so on.

You can use administrative role separation for the following purposes:

■   For completion of RODC installation after you have prestaged the RODC computer account at a writable domain controller, as described earlier in this chapter. As part of this action, you can specify the password replication policy and the user or group granted the right to administer the RODC. This enables the designated user or group to promote the server in the remote office to the RODC role.

■   The delegated user or group is granted the right to log on to the RODC to perform administrative and maintenance activities such as upgrading applications or drivers, adding hotfixes or service packs, installing other server roles, performing offline defragmentation of the AD DS database, and so on. This user or group does not have any rights for administering other RODCs or writable domain controllers.

As you have seen, you define a user or group with administrative access to the RODC during the installation process. You can also add a user or group with administrative access at any time using the dsmgmt utility. Proceed as follows:

Step 1.   Open a command prompt and type **dsmgmt**.

Step 2.   At the dsmgmt prompt, type **local roles.**

Step 3.   At the local roles prompt, type **add *domain\user* administrators,** where *domain* is the domain name and *user* is the username or group name to be added (for example, type **add que\user1 administrators** to add the que domain user named user1 to the administrative access group).

Step 4.   Type **quit** twice to return to the command prompt.

To remove a user or group, perform the same procedure, substituting the keyword remove for add. For further available keywords, type **?** at the **local roles** prompt.

> **TIP**   Keep in mind that this is a simple means of extending administrative access to a local user without granting him the ability to manage other domain controllers in the domain.

Read-Only DNS

As you have seen, Microsoft recommends that you install DNS on the RODC during installation. As discussed in Chapter 2, "Installing and Configuring DNS for Active Directory," DNS in Windows Server 2008 includes all its zone data in application directory partitions, including the ForestDNSZones and DomainDNSZones partitions. If you have configured DNS on another domain controller to host an Active Directory–integrated zone, the zone file on the RODC is always a read-only copy. Active Directory replicates all application directory partitions, including those associated with DNS, in a unidirectional fashion.

A client computer that is updating its TCP/IP configuration must be referred to a writable DNS server that hosts a primary or Active Directory–integrated copy of the zone file. To do so, the RODC refers the client to a writable DNS server by checking the name server (NS) resource records that it has, to locate the NS resource record of an appropriate DNS server. If a new client computer is installed in a site using DNS on an RODC, the RODC attempts to replicate the client's DNS server to the writable DNS server approximately five minutes after the RODC responds to the client's original Find Authoritative Query.

WARNING   If a branch office has only a single DNS server and RODC, you should configure client computers to point to a hub site DNS server, in case the local DNS server becomes unavailable. You can do this by specifying the IP address of the hub site DNS server in the **Alternate DNS Server** field of the client's TCP/IP Properties dialog box, or by configuring the DHCP server to set the primary DNS server to the branch office server and the alternative DNS server to the hub site DNS server. You can also enable the **Next Closest Site** setting in Group Policy that directs Windows Vista and Windows 7 client computers to the next nearest site for any domain controller operations in the event that the RODC is not available. For more information on this setting, refer to "Enable Clients to Locate a Domain Controller in the Next Closest Site" at http://technet.microsoft.com/en-us/library/cc772592(WS.10).aspx.

BitLocker

First introduced with Windows Vista and enhanced in Windows 7, BitLocker is a hardware-enabled data encryption feature that serves to protect data on a computer that might become exposed to unauthorized access or theft. In the typical environment of a branch office hosting an RODC, you can use BitLocker to encrypt all the data on the server's hard disk. By using BitLocker, a thief that manages to steal the RODC will be unable to recover information such as the Active Directory database, Group Policy information, file shares, and other data on local volumes. In Windows 7 and Windows Server 2008 R2, you can also use BitLocker to encrypt data on a portable hard drive or USB thumb drive.

BitLocker utilizes the Trusted Platform Module (TPM) version 1.2 to provide secure protection of encryption keys and checking of key components when Windows is booting. A TPM is a microchip built into a computer that is used to store cryptographic information such as encryption keys. Information stored on the TPM is more secure from external software attacks and physical theft. You can store keys and passwords on a USB flash drive that the user must insert to boot the computer. You can also employ an option that requires the user to supply a PIN code, thereby requiring multifactor authentication before the data becomes available for use. If an unauthorized individual has tampered with or modified system files or data in any way, the computer will not boot up.

On a computer that is equipped with a compatible TPM, BitLocker uses this TPM to lock the encryption keys that protect the contents of the protected drive; this includes the operating system and Registry files when you have used BitLocker to protect the system drive. When starting the computer, TPM must verify the state of the computer before the keys are accessed. Consequently, an attacker cannot access the data by mounting the hard drive in a different computer.

At startup, TPM compares a hash of the operating system configuration with an earlier snapshot, thereby verifying the integrity of the startup process and releasing the keys. If BitLocker detects any security problem such as a disk error, change to the BIOS, or changes to startup files, it locks the drive and enters Recovery mode. You can store encryption keys and restoration password on a USB flash drive or a separate file for additional data security and recovery capability. Should a user need to recover data using BitLocker's recovery mode, she merely needs to enter a recovery password to access data and the Windows operating system.

Your computer does not need to be equipped with the TPM to use BitLocker. If your computer is equipped with TPM, you can use BitLocker in any of the following modes:

- **TPM only:** TPM alone validates the boot files, the operating system files, and encrypted drive volumes during system startup. This mode provides a normal startup and logon experience to the user. However, if the TPM is missing or the integrity of the system has changed, BitLocker enters Recovery mode, in which you will be required to provide a recovery key to access the computer.

- **TPM and PIN:** Uses both TPM and a user-supplied PIN for validation. You must enter this PIN correctly or BitLocker enters Recovery mode.

- **TPM and startup key:** Uses both TPM and a startup key for validation. The user must provide a USB flash drive containing the startup key. If the user does not have this USB flash drive, BitLocker enters Recovery mode.

- **TPM and smart card certificate:** Uses both TPM and a smart card certificate for validation. The user must provide a smart card containing a valid certificate to log on. If the smart card is not available or the certificate is not valid, BitLocker enters Recovery mode.

If the computer does not have a TPM, BitLocker uses either a USB flash drive or smart card containing a startup key. In this case, BitLocker provides encryption, but not the added security of locking keys with the TPM.

NOTE   Many newer computers are equipped with TPM, but TPM is not always activated. You might need to enter your BIOS setup system to enable TPM. The location of this setting depends on the BIOS in use but is typically in the Advanced section.

Preparing Your Computer to Use BitLocker

To use BitLocker on any server including an RODC, you must prepare the computer prior to installing Windows Server 2008. The computer's hard disk must have two partitions: a smaller partition that remains unencrypted and is designated as the system partition and a large partition that will contain the Windows Server 2008 operating system files, applications, and data. After installing Windows Server 2008, you can install BitLocker from the Initial Configuration Tasks window that is displayed at the first logon or from the Add Features Wizard accessed from Server Manager.

You can use a computer that does not have a TPM module if you have a USB flash drive to store the encryption keys and password. On such a computer, you need to enable BitLocker without a TPM from Group Policy, as the following procedure describes:

Step 1.   Click **Start**, type `gpedit.msc` in the Search field, and then press **Enter**. Accept the User Account Control (UAC) prompt if you receive one.

Step 2.   In the Local Group Policy Editor, navigate to **Computer Configuration\ Administrative Templates\Windows Components\BitLocker Drive Encryption\Operating System Drives**.

Step 3.   Double-click **Require Additional Authentication at Startup**, enable this policy, select the **Allow BitLocker Without a Compatible TPM** option, and then click **OK**.

Step 4.   Close the Local Group Policy Editor.

Step 5.   Click **Start**, type `Gpupdate /force` in the Search field, and then press **Enter**. This forces Group Policy to apply immediately.

After you've completed this procedure, you are ready to enable BitLocker as described next.

Enabling BitLocker

If your computer is equipped with a TPM, you can enable BitLocker directly without first accessing Group Policy. Use the following procedure to add the BitLocker server feature:

Step 1.   Open Server Manager and expand the Features node.

Step 2.   From the details pane of Server Manager, click **Add Features** to start the Add Features Wizard.

Step 3.   You receive the Select Features page shown in Figure 8-4. Select **BitLocker Drive Encryption** and then click **Next**.

Figure 8-4   You can install BitLocker from the Add Features Wizard.

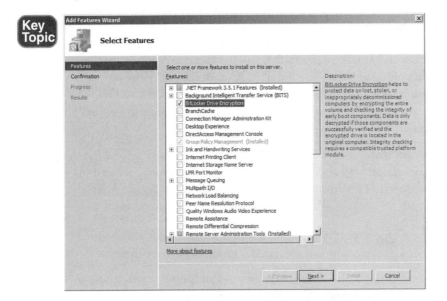

Step 4.   Click **Install** to proceed.

Step 5.   The Installation Results page informs you that you must restart your server. Click **Close** and then click **Yes** to restart the server.

Step 6.   After the server has restarted and you have logged back on, the Resume Configuration Wizard appears and installation of BitLocker completes. When informed that BitLocker Drive Encryption has installed, click **Close**.

Adding the BitLocker server feature in itself does not actually encrypt any of your computer's drives. You need to use the following procedure to enable BitLocker on your operating system drive:

Step 1.   Click **Start > Control Panel > System and Security > BitLocker Drive Encryption**. You receive the Help Protect Your Files and Folders by Encrypting Your Drives dialog box. You can also access this utility by typing **bitlocker** into the Start menu search field and then selecting **BitLocker Drive Encryption** from the Programs list.

NOTE If this dialog box is not available or the BitLocker Drive Encryption link does not appear in the Programs list, it means that the computer does not have a compatible TPM module. You will need to perform the procedure given in the previous subsection before you can enable BitLocker.

Step 2.   Opposite the drive you want to encrypt, select the **Turn On BitLocker** link. You can also right-click the desired drive in an Explorer window and choose **Turn On BitLocker**.

Step 3.   You receive a BitLocker Drive Encryption window, and after a few seconds, this window displays the Set BitLocker startup preferences page shown in Figure 8-5. Select from the following options:

Figure 8-5   The BitLocker Drive Encryption applet in Control Panel enables you to encrypt your drive.

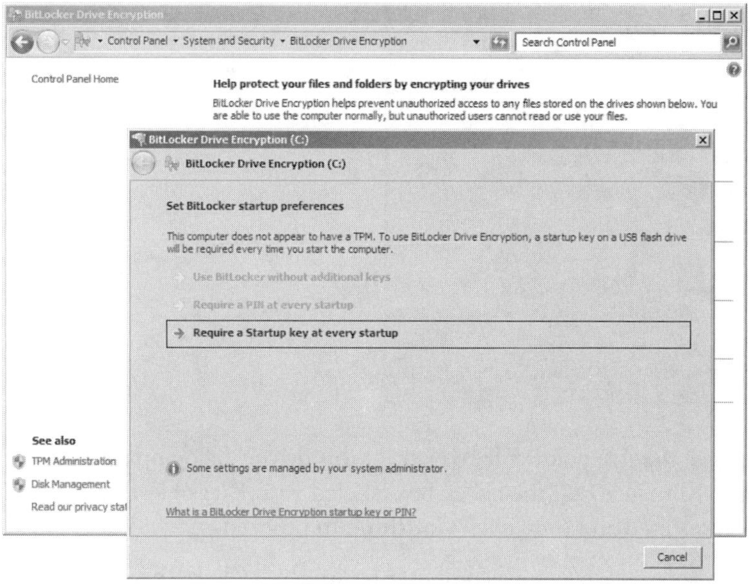

—**Use BitLocker without additional keys:** Uses the TPM Only mode for validation, enabling the computer to start up without user interaction. If any hardware component has changed, BitLocker assumes the computer has been tampered with and locks up.

—**Require a PIN at every startup:** Enables the TPM and PIN option, requiring the user to enter a PIN at startup.

—**Require a Startup key at every startup:** Creates a startup key and writes it onto a USB flash drive. This is the only option available if your computer is not equipped with a TPM.

Step 4.   If you have selected the **Require a Startup key at every startup** option, insert the USB drive when prompted, and then click **Save**. If you have selected the **Require a PIN at every startup** option, enter and confirm the PIN, and then click **Save**.

Step 5.   The How do you want to store your recovery key? page provides the three options shown in Figure 8-6. Use one or more of these options to save the recovery password. If you print it, ensure that you save the printed document in a secure location. If you save it to a USB flash drive, select the removable drive from the list displayed, slick **Save**, and then click **Next**.

Figure 8-6   You are given three options for storing your recovery key.

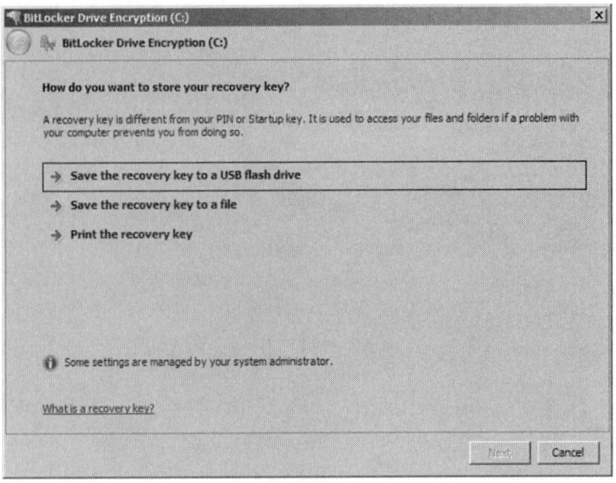

Step 6.   You receive the Are you ready to encrypt this drive? dialog box shown in Figure 8-7. Ensure that the check box labeled **Run BitLocker system check** is selected and then click **Continue** to proceed.

Step 7.   You will need to restart your computer to proceed. Click **Restart Now**.

Step 8.   Encryption takes place and Windows displays an icon in the notification area. This process can take an hour or longer, but you can use your computer while it is occurring. You can track the progress of encryption by hovering your mouse pointer over this icon. You are informed when encryption is complete. Click **Close**.

After you have completed this procedure, you must have the USB drive to start your computer. Alternatively, you can use the recovery mode and type the recovery password that was automatically created while enabling BitLocker. BitLocker provides the BitLocker Drive Encryption Recovery Console to enable you to insert the USB drive that contains the recovery password. Or press **Enter**, type the recovery password, and then press **Enter** again.

Figure 8-7   Select Continue to encrypt your partition.

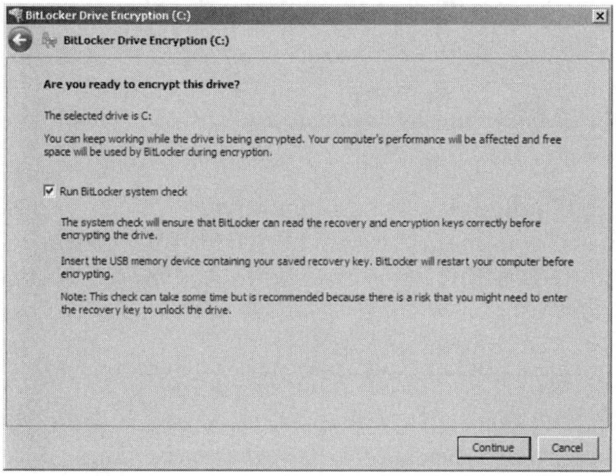

> **WARNING**   Ensure that you do not lose the recovery password. If you lose the recovery password, your Windows installation and all data stored on its partition will be permanently lost. You will need to repartition your hard drive and reinstall Windows. Consequently, you should create at least two copies of the password as described in the previous procedure and store these in a secure location. Do not leave the USB flash drive in any location accessible to outsiders; attach it to your key chain or store it elsewhere on your person.

Managing BitLocker

After you've encrypted your drive using BitLocker, the BitLocker applet shows the following additional options for the protected drive:

- **Manage BitLocker:** Enables you to save or print the recovery key again or to duplicate the startup key, thereby enabling you to recover these items while the system is running.

- **Suspend Protection:** Enables you to temporarily disable BitLocker. Select this option and then click **Yes**. After doing so, this option changes to Resume Protection; click it to reenable BitLocker.

- **Turn Off BitLocker:** Enables you to remove BitLocker protection. To do so, select **Turn Off BitLocker**. On the BitLocker Drive Encryption dialog box that appears, select **Decrypt Drive**. This procedure decrypts your volume and discards all encryption keys; it begins immediately without further prompts. You will be able to monitor the decryption action from an icon in the notification area.

When using BitLocker on an RODC, you should configure Group Policy settings to back up recovery information for BitLocker and the TPM. Use the following steps:

Step 1. Open the Group Policy Management Console focused on the Default Domain Controllers Policy GPO (or other appropriate GPO).

Step 2. Access the **Computer Configuration\Administrative Templates\Windows Components\BitLocker Drive Encryption** node and enable the **Turn on BitLocker backup to Active Directory** option.

Step 3. Ensure that the **Require BitLocker backup to AD DS** check box is selected.

Step 4. To ensure that TPM recovery information is backed up, access the **Computer Configuration\Administrative Templates\System\Trusted Platform Module Services** node and enable the **Turn on TPM backup to Active Directory** setting.

Step 5. Select the **Require TPM backup to AD DS** check box.

Having performed these actions, the recovery information is stored in a child object of the RODC's computer object.

> **NOTE** For more information, refer to "BitLocker Drive Encryption Configuration Guide: Backing Up BitLocker and TPM Recovery Information to Active Directory" at http://technet.microsoft.com/en-us/library/cc766015(WS.10).aspx.

Replication of Passwords

Each RODC is partnered with a writable domain controller for password replication purposes. When you deploy an RODC, you must configure the password replication policy on its replication partner. When an RODC's replication partner sends AD DS database information to the RODC, user account information is replicated without any password information. You can configure which user account passwords are replicated. This reduces the number of passwords that could potentially be compromised should the RODC be breached.

The password replication policy acts as an access control list (ACL), indicating which user accounts can be permitted to store their passwords on the RODC. If a user account's password is stored on the RODC, this user can log on to the domain from the RODC without having to contact the writable domain controller, after the user has logged on for the first time to the RODC. On the first logon, the RODC must contact the writable domain controller to verify the user's password; when the user changes her password, the RODC must contact the writable domain controller again so that the changed password can be recorded in the AD DS database.

TIP   You can configure which users whose passwords can be replicated, either to a single RODC or to all RODCs in the domain. For example, users who work at a single branch office can have their passwords replicated to that office's RODC. Traveling users who need to access the network from any branch office can have their passwords replicated to all RODCs in the domain.

Each RODC holds the following two lists of user accounts:

- **Allowed list:** Lists the user accounts whose passwords are allowed to be cached. By default, no users are included in this list. You can manually configure a different Allowed list for each RODC in the domain. Typically, this list includes those users who work at the branch office where the RODC is located.

- **Denied list:** Lists the user accounts whose passwords cannot be cached. By default, high-security user accounts such as members of the Domain Admins, Enterprise Admins, and Schema Admins groups are included in this list.

When a user attempts to log on to an RODC, the RODC checks its Allowed and Denied list to determine whether the password can be cached. It first checks the Denied list and denies the request if the user account is listed here. Then it checks the Allowed list and allows the request if the account is listed. If the account is not listed in either list, the request is denied. Note that this behavior is similar to the Allowed and Denied security permissions on NTFS files and folders.

Planning a Password Replication Policy

When deciding on a password replication policy to be used for branch office RODCs, you need to take into account the needs for ease of access versus security. The more passwords that are replicated to an RODC, the easier it is for users to log on without accessing a writable domain controller; however, this exposes more passwords to compromise should the RODC be stolen or physically compromised. Microsoft has defined three possible administrative models for defining your password replication policy:

- **No accounts cached:** This represents the most secure option because no passwords are replicated to the RODC except for its computer account and its special krbtgt account. With this model, all users must authenticate across the

WAN to log on. This is the default setting and requires little or no additional configuration actions by the administrator.

■ **Most accounts cached:** This enables the simplest operation by users because the Allowed list contains groups that represent the largest portion of users in the domain, with only users from security-sensitive user groups such as Domain Admins found on the Denied list. Microsoft recommends that this model be used only in situations where the RODC is located in a well-secured location such as a locked closet.

■ **Few accounts (branch-specific accounts) cached:** This represents a balance where the Allowed list for each RODC is populated with groups representing users with the greatest need of access at a given RODC—generally employees whose work location is at the site in which the RODC is located. While limiting the number of passwords that might be compromised, this model allows for ease of access without the need for authentication across the WAN. However, more administrative overhead is associated with this model because there is no automated method of populating each Allowed list other than using specific security groups in AD DS to which the appropriate user accounts have been added.

NOTE For more information on planning a password replication policy and how the Allowed and Denied lists function, refer to "Password Replication Policy" at http://technet.microsoft.com/en-us/library/cc730883(WS.10).aspx.

Configuring a Password Replication Policy

To configure a password replication policy, you must be a member of the Domain Admins group and work from the writable domain controller that is partnered to the RODC. Proceed as follows:

Step 1. Click **Start > Administrative Tools > Active Directory Users and Computers**.

Step 2. In the console tree, select the **Domain Controllers** OU.

Step 3. In the details pane, right-click the required RODC and choose **Properties**.

Step 4. Select the **Password Replication Policy** tab to view the list of accounts included in the Allowed and Denied lists by default, as shown in Figure 8-8.

Step 5. To add a user or group to either list, click **Add** and in the Add Groups, Users and Computers dialog box that appears; choose the appropriate option (see Figure 8-9); and then click **OK**.

Figure 8-8   The Password Replication Policy tab of the RODC's Properties dialog box displays the default users and groups in the Allowed or Denied groups.

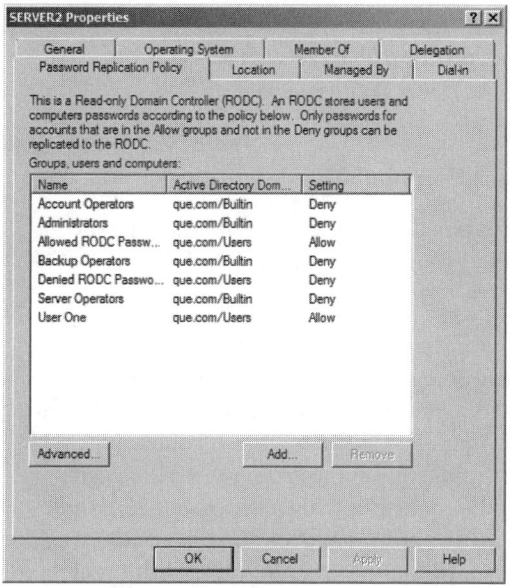

Figure 8-9   You can configure the password replication policy to allow or deny caching of passwords for users or groups.

Step 6.   Type the name of the desired user or group in the Select Users, Computers, or Groups dialog box and then click **OK**. The user or group is added to the list.

Step 7.   Click **OK** to close the server's Properties dialog box.

Credential Caching

The RODC provides a feature known as *configurable credential caching*. In other words, you can specify which users have passwords cached on each RODC. By default, the password cache in the RODC does not include any passwords. Users logging on to the RODC for the first time must authenticate to the partnered writable domain controller across the WAN.

You can prepopulate the password cache so that passwords are available on the RODC to users without the need to cross the WAN, thereby enabling users to log on even if the WAN is unavailable. To do so, proceed as follows:

Step 1.   At the partnered writable domain controller, access the Password Replication Policy tab of the RODC's Properties dialog box, as previously shown in Figure 8-8.

Step 2.   Click **Advanced** and then click **Prepopulate passwords**.

Step 3.   On the Select Users or Computers dialog box that displays, type the usernames whose passwords you want to prepopulate and then click **OK**.

TIP   If you suspect that the RODC's password cache has been compromised, you can reset its password cache. While logged on at the partnered writable domain controller as a member of the Domain Admins group, access the RODC's computer account in Active Directory Users and Computers, right-click the account and choose **Delete**, and then click **Yes** on the confirmation message box that appears. You receive the Deleting Active Directory Domain Controller dialog box shown in Figure 8-10. Select the check box labeled **Reset all passwords for user accounts that were cached on this Read-only Domain Controller**. All users with cached passwords must obtain a new password after you perform this action. If the RODC is stolen, you can perform the same action to ensure the security of the user accounts whose passwords were cached on the RODC.

Figure 8-10   When deleting an RODC, you receive several options for resetting account passwords and exporting lists of accounts.

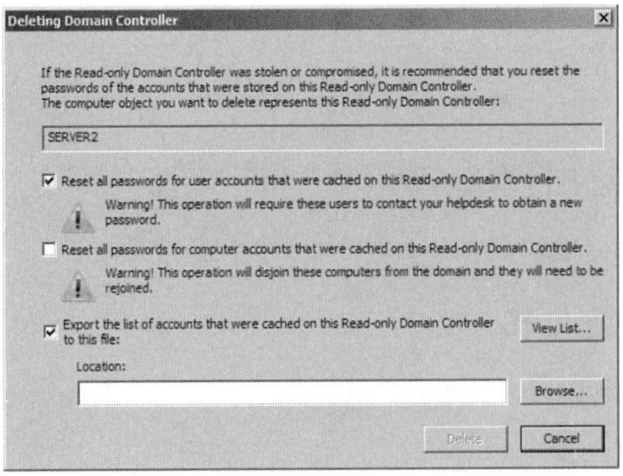

You can also administer the password replication policy from the command line by using the `repadmin /prp` command. At the partnered writable domain controller, open an administrative command prompt and type the following:

```
repadmin /prp OPERATION RODC [ADDITIONAL_ARGS]
```

In this command, OPERATION is the type of operation to be performed, as follows:

- **Add:** Adds the specified security principal (user or group) to the Allowed list on the RODC.

- **Delete:** Deletes one or more specified security principals from the Allowed list or the Authenticated to list on the RODC.

- **Move:** Moves all the security principals from the Authenticated to Account list to the specified group. Specify the name of the group to which you want to move the security principals; if the group does not exist, it is created within the default built-in Users container.

- **View:** Displays the security principals in the specified list. You can also specify a user and this command will display the current allowed or denied password replication policy setting for this user.

In this command, RODC specifies the hostname or the fully qualified domain name (FQDN) of the RODC at which the operation is to be performed, and [ADDITIONAL_ARGS] represents additional parameters available for the various operations, including the names of the security principals involved in these operations.

NOTE   For more information, including the additional parameters and examples of the use of the repadmin /prp command, refer to "Repadmin /prp" at http://technet.microsoft.com/en-us/library/cc835090(WS.10).aspx.

Administering the RODC's Authentication Lists

You should look at the lists of cached credentials and users that have been authenticated by the RODC from time to time in order to keep the lists up-to-date and remove any passwords that are not required. Such steps help to improve security at the RODC. To perform these actions, proceed as follows:

Step 1.   At the partnered writable domain controller, access the Password Replication Policy tab of the RODC's Properties dialog box, as previously shown in Figure 8-8.

Step 2.   Click **Advanced** to display the Advanced Password Replication Policy dialog box shown in Figure 8-11.

Step 3.   On the drop-down list labeled **Display users and computers that meet the following criteria**, select one of the following options:

—**Accounts whose passwords are stored on this Read-only Domain Controller:** Displays user, computer, and group accounts whose passwords have been cached according to the credential caching policy.

—**Accounts that have been authenticated to this Read-only Domain Controller:** Displays user, computer, and group accounts that the RODC has authenticated.

Figure 8-11   The Advanced Password Replication Policy dialog box enables you to perform two additional actions.

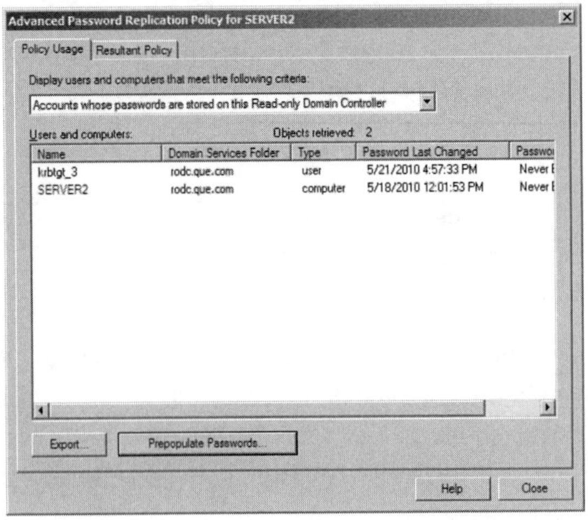

syskey

Windows 2000 and later computers encrypt the SAM database with a locally stored system key. For security purposes, Windows requires that password hashes be encrypted, thereby preventing the usage of stored, unencrypted password hashes. This system key is required for Windows to start.

By default, the system key is stored locally. For additional security, you can configure Windows to store the startup key on a floppy disk or you can specify a password to be entered manually at startup. To do so, open a command prompt and type **syskey.** A dialog box displays and informs you that encryption of the accounts database (SAM) is enabled and that this encryption cannot be disabled. To configure further, click **Update** to display the Startup Key dialog box shown in Figure 8-12. To specify a manually entered password, click **Password Startup** and type and confirm the required password. To store a startup key on a floppy disk, insert a disk and select **Store Startup Key on Floppy Disk**. Then click **OK**.

Figure 8-12   The **syskey** utility enables you to configure options for a system startup key or password.

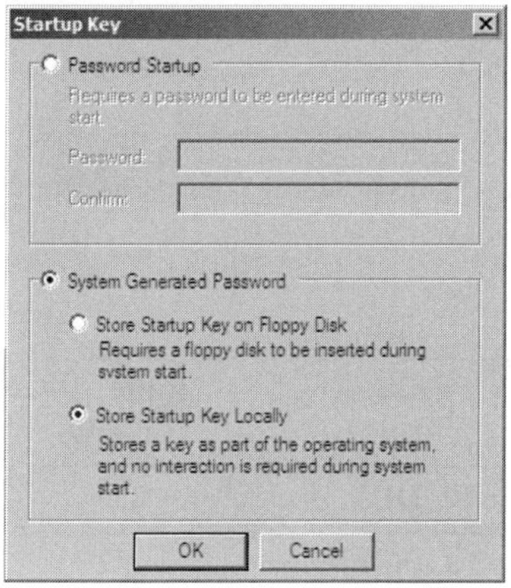

By storing this floppy disk in a secured location away from the server, such as a locked cabinet, you can prevent an intruder who steals your RODC from starting it elsewhere and reading your AD DS database. Because many computers no longer have a floppy disk drive, you might have to specify the manually entered password; store a copy of this password in the locked cabinet to provide the same level of security.

NOTE   You can also specify a system key when installing a new domain controller. Dcpromo.exe has a /syskey option that enables you to do so.

Exam Preparation Tasks

Review all the Key Topics

Review the most important topics in the chapter, noted with the key topics icon in the outer margin of the page. Table 8-2 lists a reference of these key topics and the page numbers on which each is found.

Table 8-2   Key Topics for Chapter 8

Key Topic Element	Description	Page Number
Figure 8-1	Shows the setting that enables installation of an RODC	256
Figure 8-2	Describes how to delegate administration of an RODC to a user or group	257
List	Describes several benefits of unidirectional replication as used by RODCs	260
List	Shows you how to add a group with administrative capabilities on the RODC	262
Paragraph	Describes the benefits of BitLocker	263
Figure 8-4	Installing BitLocker	266
List	Describes the Allowed and Denied lists for password replication	266
Figure 8-9	Adding groups to the password replication policy lists	273
Figure 8-11	Shows how to administer the RODC's authentication lists	276

Definitions of Key Terms

Define the following key terms from this chapter, and check your answers in the glossary.

BitLocker, credential caching, password replication policy, read-only domain controller (RODC), syskey

This chapter covers the following subjects:

- **Creating User and Group Accounts:** All users logging on to the domain must have user accounts, and these are combined into group accounts to facilitate resource access. This section introduces the various concepts of user and group accounts and then shows you how to automate the creation of large numbers of accounts.

- **Managing and Maintaining Accounts:** You need to perform a large range of activities when managing user and group accounts. This section takes you through the various account maintenance tasks that you should know to perform.

CHAPTER 9

Active Directory User and Group Accounts

The heart and soul of any Active Directory implementation is the users who must access the network on a daily basis. A company must be able to ensure that its employees are able to access all the resources on the network that they require so that they can perform the activities associated with their job but not be able to access other resources that might contain confidential information.

This chapter turns its attention to the nuts and bolts of Active Directory that enable all these activities to take place in a controlled manner. It shows you how to create user accounts for all these various employees and manage them in terms of groups. It then takes you through all the account management tasks.

"Do I Know This Already?" Quiz

The "Do I Know This Already?" quiz enables you to assess whether you should read this entire chapter or simply jump to the "Exam Preparation Tasks" section for review. If you are in doubt, read the entire chapter. Table 9-1 outlines the major headings in this chapter and the corresponding "Do I Know This Already?" quiz questions. You can find the answers in Appendix A, "Answers to the 'Do I Know This Already?' Quizzes."

Table 9-1 "Do I Know This Already?" Foundation Topics Section-to-Question Mapping

Foundations Topics Section	Questions Covered in This Section
Creating User and Group Accounts	1–6
Managing and Maintaining Accounts	7–13

1. Sharon works for a company that has an AD DS forest that consists of a forest root domain plus four child domains. She needs to create a group containing 55 users who require access to resources in all five domains. All the user accounts are located in the forest root domain. Which group scope should Sharon use?

   a. Local

   b. Domain local

    c. Global

    d. Universal

2. Which of the following represents the most valid reason why you would want to create a template account in AD DS?

    a. Such an account enables an occasional user to log on to the domain and access a limited amount of resources.

    b. Such an account facilitates the creation of a large number of domain user accounts that have similar properties and need for resource access.

    c. Such an account provides a means of testing other domain user accounts to ensure that they have no more than the required resource access for users to do their jobs.

    d. Such an account enables you to group users with similar resource needs and add the appropriate permissions directly.

3. The Human Resources department of your company has provided you with an Excel spreadsheet containing names and additional information pertaining to 75 student interns who will start work with the company next Monday. You need to create user accounts for these interns as soon as possible. What tool should you sue for this purpose?

    a. Csvde

    b. Ldifde

    c. Dsadd

    d. Active Directory Administrative Center

4. You are a consultant charged with the responsibility of designing the AD DS structure for a company that is decommissioning its UNIX server structure and will be deploying Windows Server 2008 R2 in its place. You have been given a script written in the Microsoft Visual Basic Scripting Edition (VBScript) language that will automate the creation of a large number of user, group, and computer accounts for the new domain. What tool do you need to use with this script to create the required accounts?

    a. Windows PowerShell

    b. JavaScript (Jscript)

    c. Windows Script Host (WSH)

    d. A batch file

5. You would like to create a UPN suffix so that users can log on directly to your company's domain using their email addresses. What tool should you use?

    a. Active Directory Administrative Center

    b. Active Directory Users and Computers

   c. Active Directory Sites and Services

   d. Active Directory Domains and Trusts

6. You are a network administrator working for your state's environmental agency. You have been provided with a list of 50 individuals representing citizen groups and area companies who will be providing input on a proposed water diversion project. You need to ensure that these individuals receive email messages from the assessment committee that is studying this proposal regularly without receiving access to the agency's AD DS domain. What should you do?

   a. Create user accounts for each of these individuals and add these contacts to a distribution group.

   b. Create contacts for each of these individuals and add these contacts to a distribution group.

   c. Create user accounts for each of these individuals and add these contacts to a security group.

   d. Create contacts for each of these individuals and add these contacts to a security group.

7. You are a consultant who has been given the responsibility of defining the OU structure for a new company just setting up its first domain. Which of the following types of information are helpful in designing an appropriate OU structure for this company? (Choose all that apply.)

   a. Corporate organizational charts

   b. Names and addresses of company executives

   c. Geographical distribution of company offices

   d. Requirements for delegation of administrative control

   e. AD DS information on partner companies and their need for resource access

8. You are planning the group structure of your company's AD DS forest, which includes two domains in a single tree. You have created a domain local group in the child domain and want to add other groups to this domain. Which of the following can you add to this group? (Choose all that apply.)

   a. Universal groups from the parent domain

   b. Global groups from the parent domain

   c. Global groups from the child domain

   d. Domain local groups from the parent domain

   e. Domain local groups from the child domain

9. You are planning the group structure of your company's AD DS forest, which includes two domains in a single tree. You have created a global group in the child domain so that you can provide resource access throughout the forest. To which of the following can you add this group as a member?

    a. Universal groups from the parent domain

    b. Global groups from the parent domain

    c. Global groups from the child domain

    d. Domain local groups from the parent domain

    e. Domain local groups from the child domain

10. You are designing a group strategy for an AD DS forest consisting of seven domains in two trees. Twenty users, whose user accounts are located in various domains of the forest, require access to resources in three child domains, so you create a universal group to grant the required access to these users. Which of the following is the recommended strategy you should follow in granting the required access?

    a. Add the user accounts to the universal group, and then grant the universal group the required permissions for these resources.

    b. Add the user accounts to the universal group, and then add the universal group to three domain local groups, one located in each child domain to which the users need access. Then finally grant permissions to the domain local groups.

    c. Add the user accounts to global groups in their respective domain. Then add these global groups to the universal group, and then grant the universal group the required permissions for these resources.

    d. Add the user accounts to global groups in their respective domain. Then add these global groups to the universal group, and finally add the universal group to three domain local groups, one located in each child domain to which the users need access. Then finally grant permissions to the domain local groups.

11. Which of the following best describes the Protected Admin feature of Windows Server 2008 Active Directory?

    a. A network administrator uses the default administrative account created when Windows Server 2008 R2 is installed, and when she needs to perform an administrative task, User Account Control (UAC) asks her to confirm her intentions by clicking **Yes** or **Continue** in a message box.

    b. A network administrator uses an administrative user account that is a member of the Domain Admins group, and when she needs to perform an administrative task, UAC asks her to confirm her intentions by clicking **Yes** or **Continue** in a message box.

c. A network administrator uses an administrative user account that is a member of the Domain Admins group, and when she needs to perform an administrative task, UAC asks her to confirm her intentions by retyping her username and password in a message box.

d. A network administrator uses a standard (nonadministrative) user account that is a member of the Domain Admins group, and when she needs to perform an administrative task, UAC asks her to confirm her intentions by clicking **Yes** or **Continue** in a message box.

12. You are responsible for maintaining the user and group accounts in your company's AD DS domain. A user named Ryan whose job is vital to the company's business resigns to work for a competitor. You are afraid that Ryan might log back on to your network to steal corporate secrets. At the same time, your company must hire a replacement for Ryan to begin work as soon as possible. What should you do with Ryan's user account?

a. Turn Ryan's account into a template that you can later copy to create a user account for the new employee.

b. Remove Ryan's account from the groups that grant him access to the resources he used in performance of his job. After the new employee is hired, rename the account and put it back into the groups for access to these resources.

c. Disable Ryan's account and then rename and reenable it once the new employee is hired.

d. Delete Ryan's account and then re-create a new user account after the new employee is hired.

13. You want to enable the help desk technicians to reset user passwords without permitting them to do other administrative tasks in your domain. The technicians have user accounts that are members of the HelpDesk global group. What should you do?

a. Use the Delegation of Control Wizard to grant members of the HelpDesk global group the **Reset user passwords and force password change at next logon** task.

b. Use the Delegation of Control Wizard to grant each help desk technician the **Reset user passwords and force password change at next logon** task.

c. Add the HelpDesk group to the domain's Account Operators built-in group.

d. Add each help desk technician's user account to the domain's Account Operators built-in group.

Foundation Topics

Creating User and Group Accounts

If a user is unable to log on to an Active Directory Domain Services (AD DS) network, he cannot gain access to the data and resources, such as files, folders, printers, and so on, that are stored on the network. Further, in most organizations numerous employees have similar work functions and requirements. Providing such employees access to resources individually would be a tedious and error-prone job were it not for the ability to group these users together.

Introducing User Accounts

Everyone who requires access to an AD DS network requires a user account. User accounts allow users to log on to computers and domains. They also authorize or deny access to specific resources within the domain. User accounts embody specific information pertinent to a user, such as username, password, and specific logon limitations. User accounts can be either built-in accounts or self-generated. Each user account has a comprehensive set of configurable properties associated with it. Among these are group memberships, logon scripts, logon hours, account expiration, user profile, and dial-in permission.

The following three types of user accounts are present in an AD DS network:

- **Domain user accounts:** This account provides access to an AD DS domain and all its associated resources. It is the most common account type you will encounter on the network. You can give permission to an account from one AD DS domain to access resources in other domains.

- **Local user accounts:** This account exists on a standalone or member server, or on a Windows XP Professional or Vista Business, Enterprise, or Ultimate, or Windows 7 Professional, Enterprise, or Ultimate computer. It enables a user to log on to the computer with which it is associated and gain access to resources on that computer only. A local user account cannot gain access to domain-based resources.

- **Built-in user accounts:** These accounts exist for specific administrative tasks to ease the burdens of administration. Special accounts are defined up front that have permissions to various resources and components of the AD DS forest.

> **NOTE**   For more information on user accounts and built-in accounts, refer to "Understanding User Accounts" at http://technet.microsoft.com/en-us/library/dd861325.aspx.

Introducing Group Accounts

Common networks have hundreds to thousands of users and large numbers of network resources such as files, folders, and printers. Granting access to these resources based solely on user accounts would be time-consuming, error-prone, and highly repetitive. That's why there are groups. Simply put, you can create a group within AD DS and grant or deny access to this single entity. Then you can add user accounts as members of the group. Belonging to the group, the user accounts inherit the permissions assigned to the group. It is much simpler to modify the permissions once on a group object than many times on the users. Further, you can build a hierarchy of groups and assign different permissions to each level, an activity known as *nesting*. This refers to the act of making one group a member of a different group, thereby creating a hierarchy. Nesting groups further simplifies your security model.

Windows Server 2008 provides two group types:

- **Security groups:** You can use these groups for assigning rights and permissions to users. They can also be used for distribution purposes. These group types have security information, such as unique security identifiers (SIDs), assigned to them.

- **Distribution groups:** You can use these groups for distribution purposes such as email lists. These groups do not possess SIDs and cannot be assigned permission to resources.

Within each group type, Windows Server 2008 provides three group scopes:

- **Global:** These groups can include users, computers, and other global groups from the same domain. You can use them to organize users who have similar functions and therefore similar requirements on the network. For example, you might include all sales staff in one global group, all engineering staff in another global group, and so on.

- **Domain local:** These groups can include users, computers, and groups from any domain in the forest. They are most often utilized to grant permissions for resources and can be used to provide access to any resource in the domain in which they are located. It is thus logical for a domain local group to include global groups that contain all users with a common need for a given resource.

- **Universal:** These groups can include users and groups from any domain in the AD DS forest and can be employed to grant permissions to any resource in the forest. A universal group can include users, computers, and global groups from any domain in the forest.

Creating User, Computer, and Group Accounts

Before discussing the automation of AD DS account creation, this chapter takes a quick look at manual creation of accounts. You can perform this basic administrative task through the Active Directory Users and Computers console. New to Windows Server 2008 R2, you can also perform this task from the Active Directory Administrative Center, shown in Figure 9-1. When you open either console, you can navigate through the list of containers in the domain as shown in the console tree. User accounts are typically located in the Users container, although they can be created in other folders as well.

Figure 9-1 Windows Server 2008 R2 introduces the new Active Directory Administrative Center console.

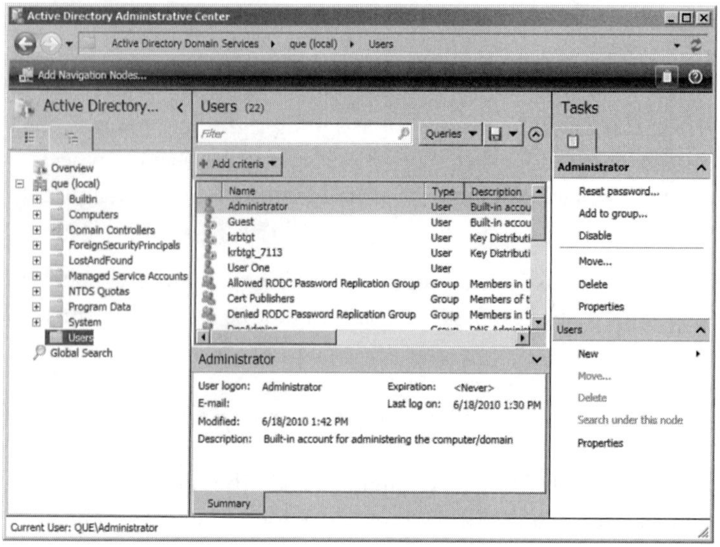

Perform the following procedure to create a new user account:

Step 1. Open either Active Directory Users and Computers or Active Directory Administrative Console and expand the domain node in the console tree to reveal the OUs and other containers found within.

Step 2. Right-click the desired container and choose **New > User**.

Step 3. If you are using Active Directory Users and Computers, the New Object - User dialog box shown in Figure 9-2 appears. Type the user's first and last name and assign a user logon name. When you type the user logon name, a pre-Windows 2000–compatible logon name is automatically created. This creates a NetBIOS-type name of the type used on older Windows NT networks.

Step 4. Click **Next** and enter a password for the user and confirm this password.

Figure 9-2 Using Active Directory Users and Computers to create a new user account.

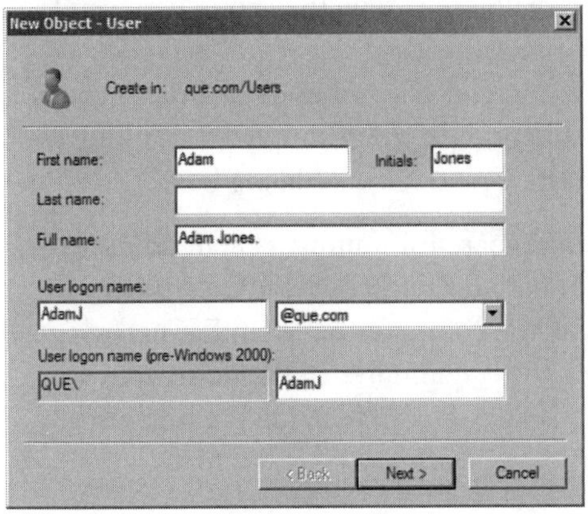

Step 5. Configure additional account settings as required, including requiring the user to change the password at next logon, whether users can change their own passwords, whether the password should never expire, and whether the account should be disabled.

Step 6. Click **Next** and then click **Finish** to finish creating the account.

The Active Directory Administrative Center enables you to specify all these settings and additional ones such as group membership from a single Create User dialog box, as shown in Figure 9-3. Supply all the needed information and then click **OK** to create the new user account.

Figure 9-3 Using Active Directory Administrative Center to create a new user account.

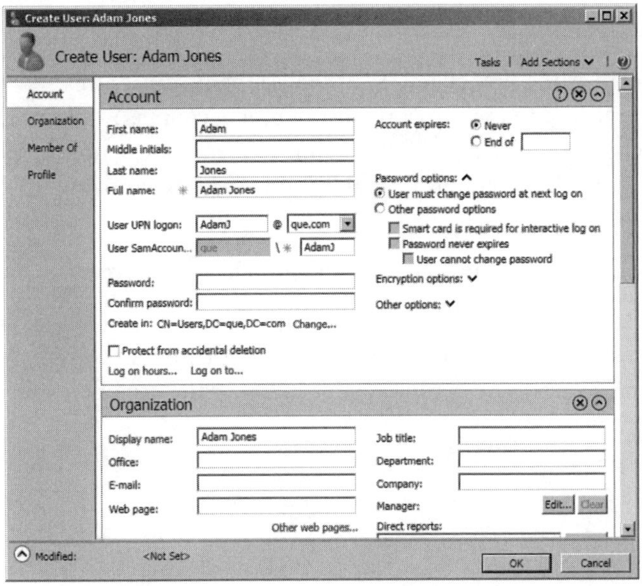

Creating a new group is similar. Right-click the desired container and select **New > Group**. In the New Object - Group dialog box, type the group name and provide a group scope and type from the options already discussed. Then click **OK**. In Active Directory Administrative Center, you can add users or other groups to this group or make the group a member of another group simply by scrolling to the **Member Of** and **Members** sections of the Create Group dialog box.

Creating a computer account enables you to prepare for joining a client computer to the domain. Right-click the desired container and select **New > Computer**. In the New Object - Computer dialog box, type the computer name and, if necessary, click **Change** to assign the privilege of joining the computer to the domain to a different user or group. As for users, a NetBIOS-compatible name is automatically created for both groups and computers.

Use of Template Accounts

A *template account* is a special account that is used only for copying as needed when you have to create a large number of user accounts. You should configure it to hold the various properties that are required for each and every user so that you need enter only individual information such as usernames.

Access the New Object - User dialog box in the appropriate AD DS container and specify the following properties:

- Last name: `template`

- User logon name: `_TEMPLATE`

- Password: (blank)

- Account is disabled: (selected)

Note that using an underscore as the first character of the username causes this account to be listed at or very close to the top of the list of user accounts. You can also use a name that is descriptive of the type of user being created; for example, `_SALESPERSON`. By specifying that the account be disabled, it ensures that no one can log on using this account.

After completing this procedure, right-click the account and select **Properties** to configure common account properties such as the following:

- On the Account tab, specify any additional account options that might be required, such as requiring a smart card for interactive logon or the use of one of several types of encryption.

- On the Profile tab, specify a profile path to a share on a file server that will hold the user's documents and other settings—for example, `\\server1\docs\%username%`. By using the `%username%` variable, a subfolder for each employee is automatically created and given the same name as the employee's username. You can also specify a local path in the same location.

- On the Member Of tab, specify one or more groups that each user should be made a member of.

- Add any additional common properties that apply to all users, such as address and organizational information, and Terminal Services and remote access settings.

NOTE   When using the Active Directory Administrative Center to create the template account, you can add all these account properties at the time you create the account. Expand the Account section of this dialog box previously shown in Figure 9-3 to access smart card logon and encryption options, and scroll this dialog box to access the Member Of and Profile sections.

To use the template account, right-click it in the details pane of Active Directory Users and Computers and choose **Copy**. You receive the Copy Object - User dialog box, which is similar to the New Object - User dialog box shown in Figure 9-2 or the Create User dialog box shown in Figure 9-3. After you have provided name and password information, a user account is created with all the properties you have provided for the template account.

Using Bulk Import to Automate Account Creation

Although use of a template account can expedite the creation of a series of user accounts with similar properties, the creation of a large number of accounts in an enterprise environment can quickly become time-consuming. If you need to create hundreds, or even thousands, or new user or group accounts, you can use one of several tools provided by Microsoft for automating the creation of new accounts, as follows:

- **Csvde**: The Comma Separated Value Data Exchange (`Csvde`) tool enables you to import data to AD DS from files containing information in the comma-separated (CSV) format. You can also export AD DS data to CSV-formatted files.

- **Ldifde**: The LDAP Data Interchange Format Data Exchange (`Ldifde`) tool enables you to create, modify, and delete directory objects. You can also extend the schema, export AD DS user and group information, and add data to AD DS from other directory sources.

- **Dsadd**: The `Dsadd` tool enables you to add object types such as computers, contacts, groups, users, organizational units (OUs), and quotas to AD DS.

- **Scripts:** You can use scripts and batch files with tools such as `Dsadd` to auto-mate the creation of large numbers of accounts. You can also use Windows Script Host to automate account creation.

Csvde

The `Csvde` tool works with comma-separated text files with a `.csv` extension—in other words, values are separated from one another by commas. This is a format supported by many other applications such as Exchange Server and Microsoft Excel. Because Excel supports this format, it is a convenient tool for creating the `.csv` file.

The first line of the `.csv` file is known as the attribute line. It defines the format of the following lines according to attributes defined in the schema. The attributes are separated by commas and define the order in which the attributes will appear on each data line.

Following the attribute line, each line includes one set of user data to be included in the bulk import. The data must conform to the following rules:

- The sequence of the source values must be the same as that specified in the attribute line.

- A value containing commas must be enclosed in quotation marks.

- If a user object does not have entries for all the values included in the attribute line, you can leave the field blank; however, you must include the commas.

The following are examples of code lines conforming to these rules:

```
Dn,cn,objectClass,sAMAccountName,userPrincipalName,telephoneNumber,
    userAccountControl

"cn=Bob Wilson,OU=engineering,dc=que,dc=com", Bob Wilson,user,
    BobW,BobW@que.com,555-678-9876,512
"cn=Clara Perkins,OU=sales,dc=que,dc=com", Clara Perkins,user,
    ClaraP,ClaraP@que.com,555-678-4321,514

"cn=Computer1,OU=engineering,dc=que,dc=com",Computer1,computer,
    Computer1,,,
```

The variable called `userAccountControl` determines the account's enabled status; a value of `512` enables the user account and a value of `514` disables it. The last entry is an example of a computer object (`objectClass=computer`), with no values defined for `userPrincipalName` or `telephoneNumber`. You would normally import this object to the default Computers container; however, you can import it to any desired container.

To import the `.csv` file to AD DS, run the following command from the command prompt:

`Csvde -I -f` *`filename.csv`*

In this command, **`-I`** specifies import mode (the default is export mode) and **`-f` *`filename.csv`*** specifies the name of the file to be imported. After you press **Enter**, the command provides status information including any errors that might occur. When the command has completed, you should check some of the user accounts to confirm its proper completion.

> **TIP**   `Csvde` is a convenient tool for importing user and group account information provided in an Excel spreadsheet file because Excel offers a convenient means for exporting data to a comma-separated text file.

Ldifde

The `Ldifde` tool works in a similar manner to `Csvde` except that it uses the LDIF file format, which is a line-separated format. In other words, each record is separated by a blank line. A record is a distinct collection of data to be added to AD DS or modify existing data; for example, a username or computer name.

Each line describes a single attribute and specifies the name of the attribute (as defined by the schema) followed by its value. A line beginning with # is a comment line. The following example uses the text from one of the comma-separated values used in the previous section. This should facilitate your comparing the two formats:

```
# These are the attributes for Bob Wilson.
DN: cn=Bob Wilson,OU=engineering,dc=que,dc=com
CN: Bob Wilson
DisplayName: Bob Wilson
GivenName: Bob
Sn: Wilson
ObjectClass: user
SAMAccountName: BobW
UserPrincipalName: BobW@que.com
TelephoneNumber: 555-678-4321
PhysicalDeliveryOfficeName: 7th Floor, SE Corner
```

To use `Ldifde`, run the following command from the command prompt:

`Ldifde -I -f` filename.`ldf`

The usage and parameters of `Ldifde` are identical to those used with `Csvde`. Table 9-2 describes several more common parameters used by these commands. You can also use `Ldifde` to modify or delete accounts, extend the schema, export AD DS data to other applications or services, and import information from other directory services to AD DS.

Key Topic

Table 9-2   Common Parameters Used by **Csvde** and **Ldifde**

Parameter	Description
-I	Specifies import mode. If not specified, the default is export mode.
-f *filename*	Specifies the import or export filename.
-s *servername*	Specifies the domain controller to be used during import or export.
-c *string1 string2*	Replaces occurrences of *string1* with *string2*. This is useful if you have to import data from one domain to another and need to modify the distinguished names accordingly.
-j *directory path*	Specifies the path to the log file. By default this is the current directory path.
-b *username domain password*	Allows you to run the command using the credentials of another user account. Specify the username, domain, and password of the required account.

NOTE   For additional parameters used with Csvde and Ldifde, refer to the Windows Server 2008 R2 Help and Support Center, or to "Csvde" at http://technet.microsoft.com/en-us/library/cc732101(WS.10).aspx and "Ldifde" at http://technet.microsoft.com/en-us/library/cc731033(WS.10).aspx.

Dsadd

The Dsadd command-line tool enables you to add objects including users, groups, computers, OUs, contacts, and quotas to the AD DS database. To add a user, execute the following command:

```
Dsadd user UserDN -fn FirstName -ln LastName -display DisplayName
    -pwd {password ¦ *} -samid SAMName -tel PhoneNumber
    -disabled {yes ¦ no}
```

In this command, *userDN* refers to the distinguished name of the user you are adding, *FirstName* and *LastName* are the user's first and last names, *DisplayName* is the display name, *password* is the password (if you specify *, the user is prompted for the password), *SAMName* is the unique SAM account name, *PhoneNumber* is the user's telephone number, and *disabled* is the enabled/disabled status (if you specify **yes**, the account is disabled, and if you specify **no**, the account is enabled). An example follows:

```
Dsadd user "cn=Bob Wilson,OU=accounting,dc=que,dc=com" -fn Bob
    -ln Wilson -display "Bob Wilson" -pwd P@ssw0rd =samid BobW
    -tel 555-678-1234 -disabled yes
```

To add a group, execute the following command:

```
Dsadd group GroupDN -fn FirstName -secgrp {yes ¦ no} -scope {l ¦g ¦u}
    -samid SAMName -memberof Group ... -members member ...
```

In this command, *GroupDN* refers to the distinguished name of the group you are adding, **secgrp** specifies whether the group is a security group (**yes**) or distribution group **(no)**, **scope** refers to the group scope (**l** for domain local, g for global, u for universal), **memberof** specifies the groups to which the new group is to be added, and **members** specifies the members to add to the new group. By default, Windows creates a new group as a global security group.

Many additional parameters are available. For additional information, execute this command followed by /**?** or consult the Windows Server 2008 R2 Help and Support Center.

Additional Command-Line Tools

AD DS provides the following additional command-line tools, the functionality of which is similar in nature to that of dsadd. To obtain information about the parameters associated with each tool, type the command name followed by /**?**.

- **dsmod**: Modifies objects

- **dsrm**: Removes objects

- **dsmove**: Moves objects to another container within the domain

- **dsget**: Provides information about objects

- **dsquery**: Displays objects matching search criteria

NOTE For more information on all the command-line tools discussed in this section, refer to "11 Essential Tools for Managing Active Directory" at http://technet.microsoft.com/en-us/magazine/2007.09.adtools.aspx.

Scripts

By creating scripts, you can fully utilize the power of these commands in automating the creation, modification, or deletion of multiple AD DS objects. You can choose from the following three scripting environments:

- **Batch files:** You can include commands such as `dsadd`, `dsmod`, or `dsrm` in a batch file, which enables the rapid processing of command-line tools for managing multiple AD DS objects.

- **Windows Script Host (WSH):** A powerful scripting environment that enables you to run files containing commands written in the Microsoft Visual Basic Scripting Edition (VBScript) or Java Script (JScript) languages.

- **Windows PowerShell:** A new, powerful, command-line shell and scripting language that works with existing scripting and command-line tools to provide a high level of productivity and system control. Windows PowerShell includes an extensive list of subcommands known as *cmdlets*, together with a comprehensive tutorial and help system to get you started. This is included by default with Windows 7 and Windows Server 2008 and available as an add-on for Windows XP, Vista, and Server 2003.

Configuring the UPN

A user principal name (UPN) is a logon name formatted in a manner similar to that of an email address such as `user1@que.com`. The first part uniquely identifies the user and the second part by default identifies the domain to which she belongs. It is especially convenient when logging on to a domain from a computer located in another domain in the forest or a trusted forest.

UPN Suffixes

First introduced in Windows Server 2003 is the concept of the UPN suffix. This is the portion of the UPN to the right of the at (@) character. By default, the UPN suffix is the DNS name of the domain to which the user belongs. You can provide an additional UPN suffix to simplify administrative and logon procedures. Doing so provides the following advantages:

- Using a common UPN suffix throughout a multidomain forest simplifies logon procedures for all users. This is especially true in the case of long child domain names. For example, a user with a default UPN of `James@east.marketing.que.com` could be provided with a simpler UPN such as `James@que`.

- Using a common UPN suffix also enables you to hide the true domain structure from users in external forests. It also simplifies configuring remote access servers for visitor access.

- You can use the UPN suffix to match the email domain name in cases where the company has more than one division with different email domain names but a common AD DS domain. Using the additional UPN suffix enables users to log on using their email addresses.

- A common UPN suffix is also useful in enabling users to log on to a domain in an existing forest. However, if more than one forest uses the same UPN suffix, you can log on to a domain in the same forest only; furthermore, if you are using explicit UPNs and external trusts, you can use the UPN to log on to a domain in the same forest only.

Adding or Removing UPN Suffixes

You can create alternative UPN suffixes by opening the Active Directory Domains and Trusts console. In the console tree, right-click **Active Directory Domains and Trusts** and choose **Properties** to bring up the dialog box shown in Figure 9-4. Simply type the desired UPN suffix, click **Add**, and then click **OK**.

Figure 9-4   You can easily add or remove alternative UPN suffixes in Active Directory Domains and Trusts.

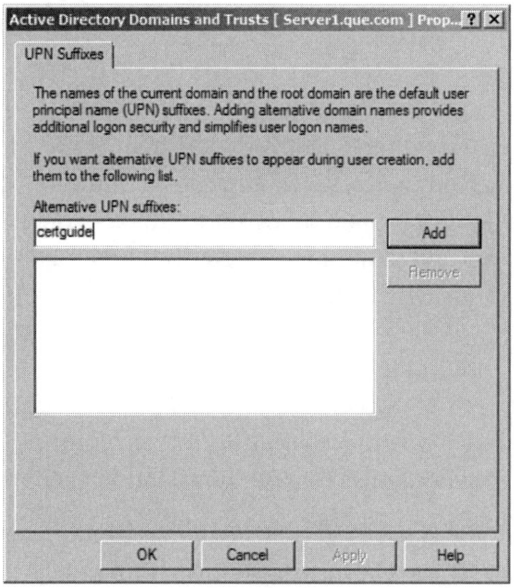

You can use the added UPN suffix in Active Directory Users and Computers to configure new or existing users. When adding a new user, the alternative UPN suffix is available from the drop-down list in the New Object - User dialog box (refer back to Figures 9-2 and 9-3). You can also configure an existing user with the alternative UPN suffix from the Account tab of the user's Properties dialog box. As shown in Figure 9-5, the alternative UPN suffix is available in the drop-down list of the Account tab of the user's Properties dialog box.

Figure 9-5 The Account tab of a user's Properties dialog box enables you to configure an alternative UPN suffix.

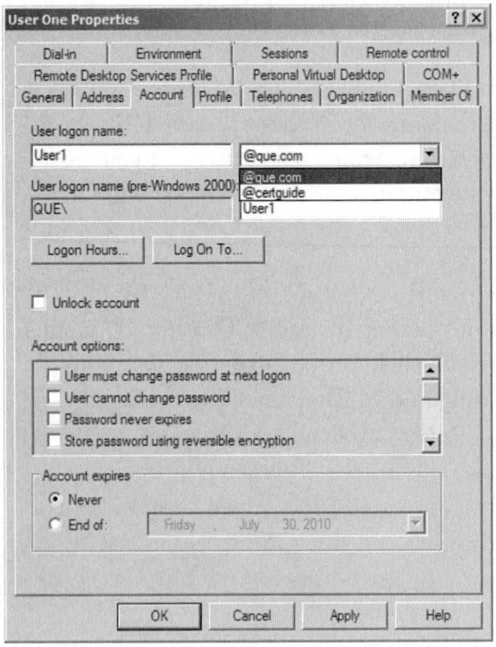

To remove an alternative UPN suffix, access the same dialog box shown in Figure 9-4, select the UPN suffix, and click **Remove**. Then accept the warning that users who use this UPN suffix will no longer be able to log on to the network. You should then open Active Directory Users and Computers or Active Directory Administrative Center, select any user accounts that refer to this suffix, and change them to one that is still in use.

Configuring Contacts

A *contact* is simply a collection of information about an individual or organization. AD DS provides the Contacts folder, which you can use to store information such as the contact's name, email address, street address, and telephone number.

You can create a contact in the Users group or any OU in your domain's hierarchy. Right-click the container and choose **New > Contact**. This displays the dialog box shown in Figure 9-6.

The contact you have created appears in the details pane of Active Directory Users and Computers or Active Directory Administrative Center. Right-click the contact and choose **Properties** to configure a limited set of properties including items such as the address, telephone numbers, organization, and so on. You can also add the contact to groups for purposes such as creating distribution lists, which are discussed next.

Figure 9-6 You can create contacts by using the New Object - Contact dialog box.

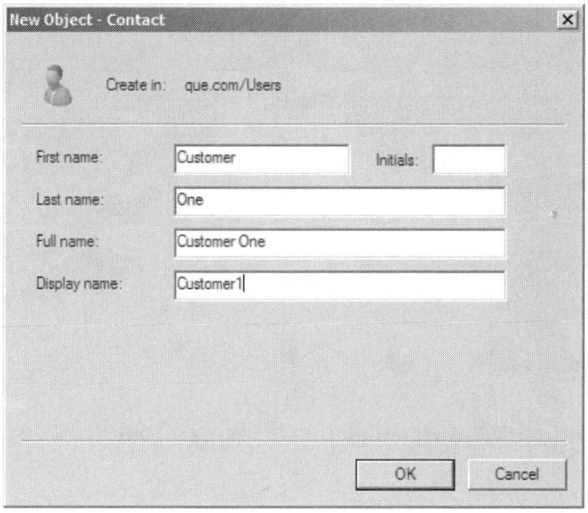

You can also automate the creation of contacts using any of the methods discussed earlier in this chapter and setting the `objectClass` value to `Contact`.

Creating Distribution Lists

Earlier in this chapter, the concept of distribution groups was introduced. The main purpose of a distribution group is to create a distribution list that is used with an email application such as Microsoft Exchange Server to send messages to a collection of users. By sending an email message to the group, it is automatically sent to all members of the group.

> **TIP**   You can also use a security group for distribution purposes. This is useful in cases where you need both the ability to send messages to a group and to provide the same group access to resources in AD DS.

Windows Server 2008 includes the Message Queuing feature, which provides guaranteed message delivery, efficient routing, security, and priority-based messaging between applications, including those that run on different operating systems. You can install Message Queuing from the Add Features Wizard in Server Manager.

Creating a distribution group is similar to creating other AD DS objects. Simply select the **Distribution** group type from the New Object - Group dialog box discussed earlier. Then right-click the new group and choose **Properties**. Select the **Members**; tab; click **Add**; and add the required users and groups from the Select Users, Contacts, Computers, Service Accounts, or Groups dialog box (see Figure 9-7). Use semicolons to separate multiple names from each other.

To add contacts or computers to the list, click **Object Types** to display the Object Types dialog box shown in Figure 9-8 and select either or both of these object types.

Figure 9-7   The Select Users, Contacts, Computers, Service Accounts, or Groups dialog box enables you to add these types of objects to your distribution list.

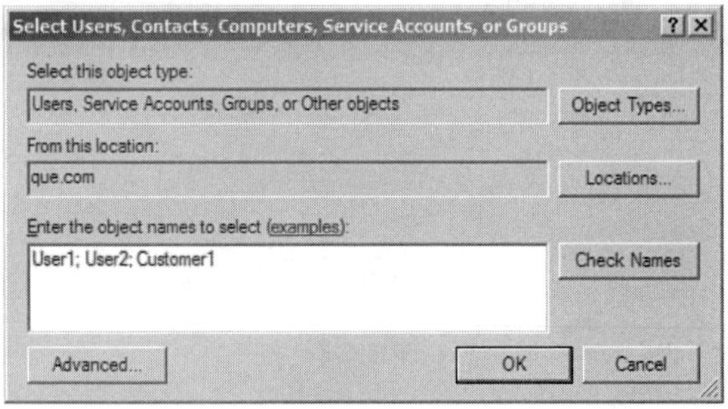

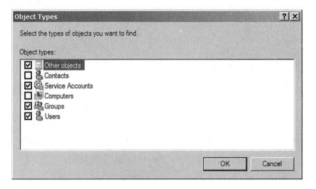

Figure 9-8   Select the appropriate object types from the Object Types dialog box to add these types of objects to your distribution list.

To send an email message to all members of a distribution list, simply right-click the list and choose **Send Mail**. The default email application opens and displays a blank outgoing message with the email addresses of all members automatically filled in. You can do the same thing by selecting **New Message** from your email application and filling in the group name in the To field.

Managing and Maintaining Accounts

After you have created user and group accounts that encompass all the employees in your organization's AD DS structure, you must be able to work with and manage all these accounts. Account management is a large part of an administrator's everyday actions. The following aspects of account management are discussed in this section:

■   Creating and managing OUs

■   Configuring group membership

■   Resetting accounts

- Nesting groups

- Denying privileges

- Local and domain local groups

- Protected Admin

- Disabling and deleting accounts

- Deprovisioning

- Delegating administrative control

The following sections briefly introduce each of these concepts.

Creating Organizational Units

Chapter 1, "Getting Started with Active Directory," introduced the concept of OUs as logical subgroups within Active Directory that you can employ to locate resources used by a single workgroup, section, or department in a company and apply policies that apply to only these resources.

An easily managed OU structure that reflects some aspects of your company's internal organization is highly important to the day-to-day functioning of your AD DS domain. Before you proceed to create new OUs in your domain, you should take some time to plan an appropriate OU structure. Your OUs must be meaningful to administrators for them to be able to navigate through the hierarchy and perform their functions. You can arrange OUs to be intuitive by using a model that combines the network administrative structure with the company's organizational chart. You can design an OU structure that is wide and shallow, as shown in Figure 9-9, or one that is slim and deep, as shown in Figure 9-10. You can have as many OUs as you want at any level, although a wide and shallow structure tends to be easier to manage, easier to navigate, and somewhat faster when performing LDAP queries than a slim and deep structure.

Network designers often use OUs as a way of restructuring domains during an upgrade and migration project to provide an administrative boundary for delegated tasks. When planning an OU structure for an organization, your first task should be to gather the business requirements. The types of information that you should collect include the following:

- **Corporate organizational charts:** Companies generally group persons within the same hierarchical structure when those persons must share the same physical location or production requirements. You can create an OU hierarchy that mirrors the company's organizational layout, including departments, branches, sections, work units, and so on. Such a hierarchy facilitates the administration of the network including assigning permissions, group policies, and so on.

Figure 9-9   An OU structure can be wide and shallow.

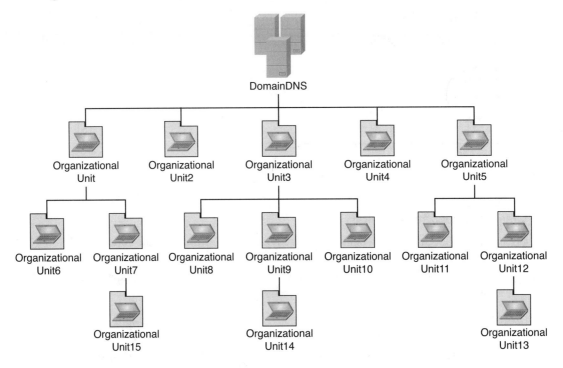

- ■ **Administrative control:** The most useful information that you will gather for planning your OUs to delegate control is the administrative configuration of the organization. You should find or develop a document that describes which administrators are assigned to manage which users, computers, and other network resources. In addition, you should document which powers of control the administrators have. With this information, you can create an OU hierarchy that enables you to assign junior administrators the ability to perform actions on certain parts of the domain only. Delegation of administrative control is discussed later in this chapter.

- ■ **Geographical layout:** Many businesses establish administrative boundaries based on the geographical locations of the users, computers, and resources being managed. Using this model, you can create an OU hierarchy that mirrors the geographical arrangement of your company's operations. This can include multiple levels reflecting countries, states or provinces, counties or cities, and so on. This enables you to design location-specific policies or administrative actions, and so on.

Creating OUs is similar to the creation of other object types in Active Directory. Simply access Active Directory Users and Computers, right-click the domain or other container in which you want to create an OU, and then choose **New >**

Organizational Unit. In the New Object - Organizational Unit dialog box, type a name for the OU and then click **OK**. You can also use the Dsadd command-line tool. In Windows Server 2008 R2, you can perform this task from the Active Directory Administrative Center. You receive the Create Organizational Unit dialog box shown in Figure 9-11. Type the name of the OU and add any additional optional information as desired in the available fields. Then click **OK**.

Figure 9-10   You can design an OU structure to be slim and deep.

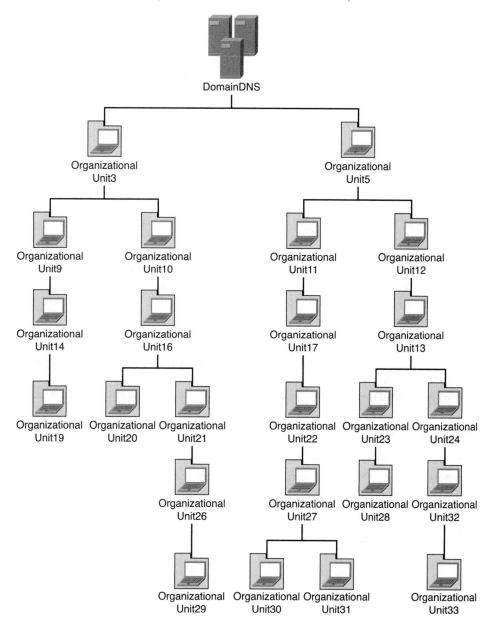

Figure 9-11 Active Directory Administrative Center enables you to specify several properties of a new OU when you create it.

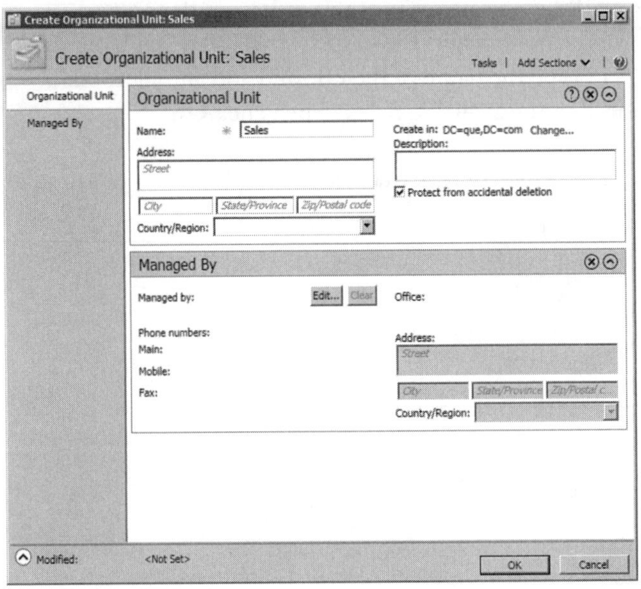

After you have created new OUs, it is easy to move objects such as users, computers, and groups to the new OU. Simply drag the required objects in Active Directory Users and Computers or Active Directory Administrative Center to the appropriate location. You can also right-click an object and choose **Move**. Select the desired destination in the Move dialog box and then click **OK**. Furthermore, you can use the Dsmove utility to move a series of objects at the same time.

TIP Try to keep the OU hierarchy of your organization simple, with no more than two or three levels of OU nesting, if at all possible. Complex structures can result in unexpected application of Group Policy or difficulty in locating and administering objects.

Configuring Group Membership

A group is of no use until you have added members to it. As already stated, groups are used to collect a set of users who need to share a particular set of permissions to a resource such as a file, folder, or printer. However, the available membership depends on the group scope. Table 9-3 outlines group membership and access considerations for the three group scopes.

Key Topic

Table 9-3 Comparison of Groups

	Global	**Domain Local**	**Universal**
Member List	User and group accounts from the same domain	User accounts and domain local groups from the same domain, global groups, and universal groups from any domain in the forest	User accounts, global groups, and other universal groups in any domain in the forest
Nesting	Universal and domain local groups in any domain and global groups in the same domain	Domain local groups in the same domain	Local and universal groups in any domain
Scope	Can be used in its own domain and any trusted domains	Can be used only in its own domain	Can be used in any domain in the forest
Permissions	Resources in all domains in the forest	Resources in the domain in which the group exists only	Resources in any domain in the forest

Using Active Directory Users and Computers or Active Directory Administrative Center, you can configure group membership in any of the following ways:

- **Add a series of users or groups to the group:** Right-click the group and choose **Properties**. On the Members tab, select **Add** and then enter the desired account names in the Select Users, Contacts, Computers, Service Accounts, or Groups dialog box (previously shown in Figure 9-7).

- **Add a user to one or more groups:** Right-click the user and choose **Add to a group**. Then enter the desired groups in the Select Groups dialog box and click **OK**. Alternatively, select **Properties** and then select the **Member Of** tab and click **Add**. You can also use this procedure to add one group to another within the limits described in Table 9-3.

- **Use the Dsadd utility:** This utility enables you to add any allowable combinations of users and groups, and also enables you to script these actions.

You can also remove a user or group from another group if required. From the Members tab of the user or group's Properties dialog box, select the required entry and click **Remove** (or use the dsrm utility).

NOTE Unlike previous versions of Windows, the allowable levels of group nesting are not dependent on domain functional level. This is because Windows Server 2008 no longer supports Windows NT domain controllers and the Windows 2000 mixed functional level, which severely limited the extent of group nesting.

AGDLP/AGUDLP

Microsoft continues to recommend the same strategy for nesting groups that it has supported since Windows NT 4.0. The following list outlines the strategy:

Step 1.   Place accounts (A) into global groups (G).

Step 2.   Add the global groups to domain local groups (DL).

Step 3.   Finally, assign permissions (P) to the domain local groups.

In short, this strategy is known as AGDLP, Accounts to Global groups to Domain Local groups to Permissions.

> **NOTE**   Simple nesting of groups is always best. Minimize levels of nesting as just stated (AGDLP). This strategy simplifies the process of keeping track of permissions and troubleshooting resource access. In addition, it is useful to base your global groups on job functions. When another person takes over a job, you need only change the person's group membership, and not all the associated permissions.

You can use the same strategy in multidomain environments. Add users from each child domain to a global group in the same domain. Then add these global groups to a domain local group in the parent domain and grant permissions to this group. Figure 9-12 shows this strategy in graphical form.

Figure 9-12   You can use the AGDLP strategy in multiple-domain situations.

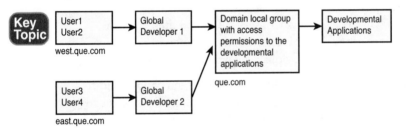

You can extend this strategy by using universal groups, as shown schematically in Figure 9-13. Doing so changes the acronym from AGDLP to AGUDLP. The two child domains `west.que.com` and `east.que.com` both contain users that require access to developmental applications located in the `que.com` domain. By employing a universal group, you can grant access to these applications to users in both domains by employing just a single group (the universal group). Although you can grant access directly to the universal group, Microsoft recommends that you secure access to these resources by creating a domain local group in the domain in which they are located and adding the universal group to this domain local group. Then grant the appropriate permissions to the domain local group. If necessary, you can extend this strategy to domain local groups located in additional domains containing applications to which you must grant access.

Figure 9-13   You can use the AGUDLP strategy to grant access to resources in more than one domain.

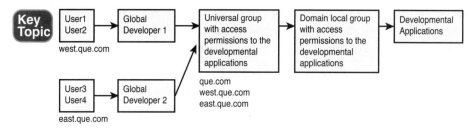

However, the use of universal groups results in a higher level of network traffic between domain controllers at replication time because any membership changes must be propagated to all global catalog servers in the forest.

The following are several suggestions for using universal groups:

- Use universal groups sparingly and use them only when their membership is relatively static. If universal group membership changes frequently, these changes result in a high level of network traffic between domain controllers in different domains because any membership changes must be propagated to all global catalog servers in the forest.

- Use universal groups when you need to assign permissions to resources located in several domains. Simply follow the strategy illustrated in Figure 9-13 and grant the appropriate permissions to the domain local groups. Use of this strategy simplifies the allocation of permissions and reduces the amount of interdomain replication traffic.

- In a single-domain forest, you do not need to use universal groups. Use the AGDLP strategy only.

THINGS CAN EASILY GO WRONG IN GROUP NESTING

A few years ago, I heard of a situation in which student interns at a company where a friend worked were able to access confidential corporate documents and obtain information they could have passed on to a competitor. One network administrator at that company had assigned the interns to one global group. Another administrator then added this group to a second global group, which was included in a domain local group with permissions to confidential corporate documents. As a result, the interns had access to the confidential documents. Several of them used this confidential information in writing term papers at school the following semester.

In such an instance, the administrators should have created a global group specifically for the interns. Then they could have added this group to only the groups containing the required privileges or assigned these privileges directly to the group.

Account Resets

A common task that network administrators and desktop or help desk personnel must perform is the resetting of passwords for users who have forgotten them. Related to this is the task of unlocking user accounts that have been locked out because of too many incorrect attempts at entering a password.

To reset a password, open Active Directory Users and Computers or Active Directory Administrative Center and select the container or OU in which the account is located from the console tree listing. In the details pane, right-click the user account and choose **Reset Password**. In the Reset Password dialog box shown in Figure 9-14, type and confirm a new password. By default, the user is required to change this password at next logon, thereby enabling the user to select a password of his choice. He must select a password that is within the limits of the password complexity policy, which is discussed in Chapter 13, "Account Policies and Audit Policies." If the account is locked out, select the check box labeled **Unlock the user's account**.

Figure 9-14   The Reset Password dialog box enables you to reset the password for a user who has forgotten his password.

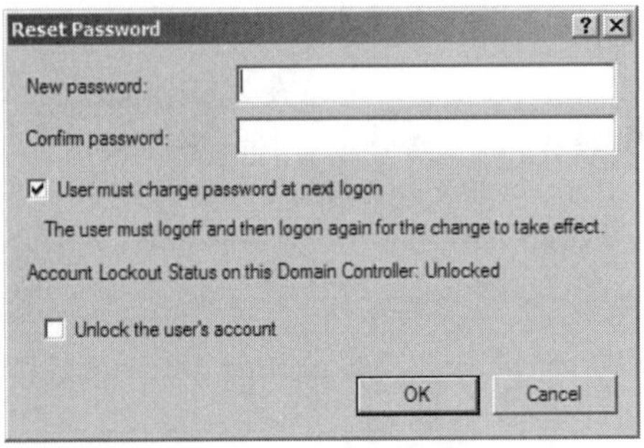

> **NOTE**   A Microsoft Gold Certified Partner, Lieberman Software, has produced an Account Reset Console that enables users to reset forgotten or expired passwords without the help of an administrator. Like other third-party add-on solutions, this product is beyond the scope of the 70-640 exam.

Deny Domain Local Group

You have learned about the assigning of permissions using the AGDLP and AGUDLP strategies. In both cases, you assign permissions to domain local groups for resources in the domain in which the group is located. You can use the same strategy for denying access to domain local groups.

As was the case in all previous Windows versions, when you explicitly deny access to a user or group, members of that group are denied access the resource, regardless of any permissions they might receive directly or by means of membership in other groups. To deny access, proceed as follows:

Step 1. Right-click the resource (file, folder, printer, and so on) and choose **Properties**.

Step 2. Select the **Security** tab of the resource's Properties dialog box and click the **Edit** button.

Step 3. On the Permissions dialog box that appears, click **Add** to add the required group; type the group name in the Select Users, Computers, or Groups dialog box that appears; and then click **OK**.

Step 4. Select the appropriate entry in the **Deny** column (see Figure 9-15) and then click **OK**.

Figure 9-15   You can deny access to a resource from its Permissions dialog box.

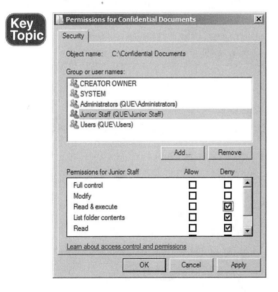

Step 5. You receive a Windows Security message box that warns you that deny entries take precedence over allow entries. Click **Yes** to accept this warning, and then click **OK** to close the resource's Properties dialog box.

Protected Admin

Previous versions of Windows Server have limited the ability to perform tasks when using a nonadministrative user account, with the result that many users would always use an administrative account, whether they needed it or not. This practice often left the servers open to many types of attack by malware programs such as viruses, Trojan horses, spyware, and so on. Starting with Windows Vista and continued in Windows 7 and Windows Server 2008, a new feature called User

Account Control (UAC) requires users performing administrative tasks to confirm that they actually initiated the task. This includes all administrative accounts except the default Administrator account created when you first install Windows Server 2008 or the default account created when you create the first domain controller in a new forest.

Key Topic

Microsoft recommends that you not use this default administrative account and instead create a different administrative account for everyday domain administration activities. In doing so, you are working with what Microsoft calls a *Protected Admin account*. This account works with standard user privileges, thereby preventing many types of attack. When you need to perform an administrative task, Windows displays a UAC prompt as shown in Figure 9-16. Click **Continue** to perform the activity or **Cancel** to quit. (On a Windows 7 computer, click **Yes** to perform the activity or **No** to quit.) If a malicious program attempts to run, Windows will display the UAC prompt that includes the program name, alerting you to what program is asking for your permission. Thereby, you can cancel such an unexpected prompt and be protected from whatever damage could otherwise occur.

Figure 9-16   User Account Control displays this prompt to ask for approval of an administrative task.

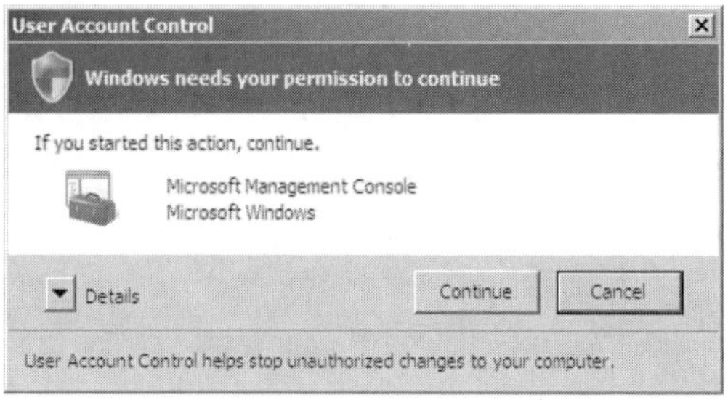

If you are logged on as a user that is not a member of the Domain Admins group, you receive a slightly different UAC prompt, as shown in Figure 9-17. This prompt asks you to specify the username and password of an administrative account to proceed with your desired task.

> **WARNING**   When you receive a UAC prompt, always ensure that the action indicated is the one you want to perform. This is especially true if a UAC prompt appears unexpectedly, which could indicate a malware program attempting to run. Should this happen, click **Cancel** and the program cannot run. You should then scan your computer with one or more malware detection programs.

Local Versus Domain Groups

Similar to previous Windows versions, Windows 7 and Windows Server 2008 R2 enable you to create local groups on any computer not configured as a domain controller. This group is similar in usage and membership capabilities to a domain local group. However, this type of local group does not exist in AD DS and grants users access to resources on its computer only. For access to resources located on more than one computer in the domain, always use domain local groups.

Figure 9-17   User Account Control displays this prompt to ask for approval of an administrative task when logged on as a nonadministrative user.

To create a local group in Windows 7 or Windows Server 2008 R2, proceed as follows:

Step 1.   Open Server Manager and then expand the Configuration node in the console tree to reveal the **Local Users and Groups** folder.

Step 2.   Expand this folder, right-click **Groups**, and choose **New Group**.

Step 3.   In the New Group dialog box shown in Figure 9-18, type a name and optional description for the group and click **Add** to add members to this group.

Step 4.   Type the usernames or group names in the Select Users, Computers, or Groups dialog box and then click **OK**.

Step 5.   If you receive a Windows Security dialog box, type the name and password of an appropriate domain account (member of Domain Admins, Account Operators, or another user that has been delegated this permission).

Step 6.   Click **Create** to create the group.

On a Windows XP, Windows Vista, or Windows 7 computer, click **Start**, right-click **My Computer** or **Computer**, and then choose **Manage**. If you receive a UAC prompt in Vista or Windows 7, click **Continue**. From the Computer Management console, expand the Local Users and Groups node, right-click **Groups**, choose **New Group**, and then proceed from step 3 in the previous list.

Figure 9-18   Creating a local group on a member server.

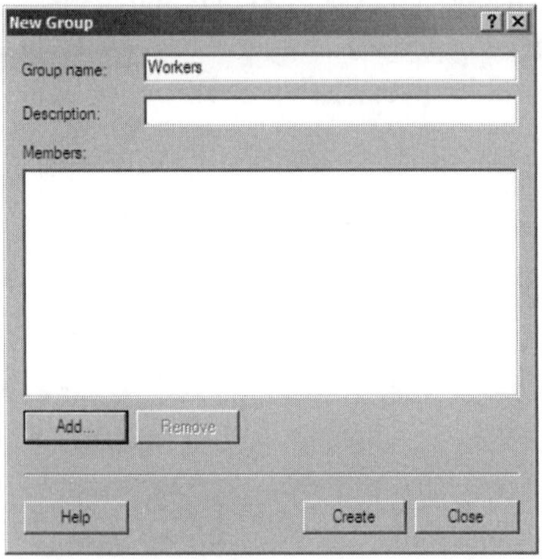

New Group	? X

Group name: Workers

Description:

Members:

Add...   Remove

Help   Create   Close

You can also use the net localgroup command from the command line to create and populate local groups. This command works on any member server or client computer, including Server Core machines. Type this command followed by /? to obtain information about its syntax.

Deprovisioning Accounts

What should you do if a user quits, is fired, or goes on some type of extended leave? You need to deprovision the user's account to prevent unauthorized access— in other words, prevent someone from logging on using this account. The next section looks at two choices for deprovisioning an account: disabling or deleting the account.

When this happens, you have several choices. If a replacement has been hired, you can simply rename the user account for the replacement. Otherwise, you can simply delete it. However, if there is a possibility that a replacement will be hired in the future, you have an additional choice: disabling the account. Disabling an account rather than deleting it provides several advantages:

- When disabled, nobody can log on using this account. In this way, a disgruntled employee who has resigned or been fired cannot log on and delete or steal important data.

- Security is also improved in the case of an employee taking an extended sabbatical or disability leave.

- The disabled account retains all group memberships, rights, and permissions assigned to it. When you hire a replacement, you can reenable and rename the account, and you do not need to go through the procedure of creating everything from scratch.

To disable an account, right-click it in Active Directory Users and Computers or Active Directory Administrative Center and choose **Disable Account**. You receive a message that the object has been disabled. To reenable the account, right-click it and choose **Enable Account**. To delete an account, right-click it and choose **Delete** or simply press the **Delete** key. You are asked whether you are sure you want to delete this account. Click **Yes** to confirm or **No** to cancel.

If you need to deprovision a group account, simply delete it. There is no means of disabling a group.

Delegating Administrative Control of Active Directory Objects

One of the major benefits of Active Directory is that you can split up administrative tasks among different individuals. You can assign different sets of administrative responsibility to different users, and these can include segments of the directory structure such as OUs or sites. The following are several benefits of delegating administrative control:

- You can assign subsets of administrative tasks to users and groups.

- You can assign responsibility of a limited portion of the domain, such as OUs or sites, to users or groups.

- You can use a nested hierarchy of OUs for even more granular control over which users can perform certain administrative tasks.

- You can enhance network security by placing more restrictive limits on the membership of powerful groups such as Domain Admins, Enterprise Admins, and Schema Admins.

When designing your AD DS forest structure, you should keep in mind the administrative requirements of each domain. Each domain has the capability to contain a different OU hierarchy. The forest administrators, who are members of the Enterprise Admins group, are automatically granted the ability to create an OU hierarchy in any domain within the entire forest. Domain administrators, who are members of the Domain Admins group in each separate domain, by default are granted the right to create an OU hierarchy within their own domain.

When you initially create your OU design, you should do so to enable administration. After that, you should create any additional OUs required for the application of Group Policy. You might also need to create OUs to limit the visibility of some objects. For example, if you have a business requirement for security purposes that restricts access to user accounts that are created for use solely with applications, such as a SQL Administrator account, you could create an OU that is outside the main OU hierarchy and limit access to that OU and its contents.

You have the capability to assign a single user or group full control of the entire domain, of a single OU, or limited rights to a set of OUs. When you delegate control, keep in mind that the default behavior of AD DS is to make such permissions inheritable. For example, if your top-level OU is named Corp and it contains OUs named Users and Computers, as shown in Figure 9-19, and if you delegate full control of Corp to a user named Joe, he is able to make changes throughout all the Users and Computers child OUs, as well as the parent OU named Corp. However, if you delegate to another user named Jean the Reset Password right in Users, she will not be able to reset passwords for users in the Corp or Computer OUs.

Figure 9-19   Delegated tasks flow down the tree from the OU where the rights are delegated.

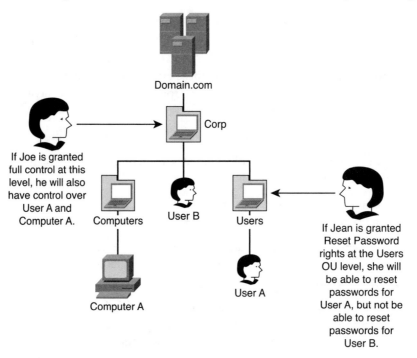

Windows Server 2008 provides the Delegation of Control Wizard to facilitate the task of delegating administrative control. Proceed as follows:

Step 1.   In Active Directory Users and Computers or Active Directory Administrative Center, right-click the desired OU and choose **Delegate Control**. To delegate control over a site, right-click the desired site in Active Directory Sites and Services and choose **Delegate Control**.

Step 2.   Click **Next** to bypass the introductory page of the Delegation of Control Wizard.

Step 3.   On the Users or Groups page, click **Add** and type the name of the required user or group in the Select Users, Computers, or Groups dialog box. Click **OK** and then click **Next**.

Step 4. On the Tasks to Delegate page shown in Figure 9-20, select the task or tasks you want to delegate. If you want to delegate a task that is not shown in the list provided, select the **Create a custom task to delegate** option. Then click **Next**.

Figure 9-20 Using the Delegation of Control Wizard to delegate administrative tasks.

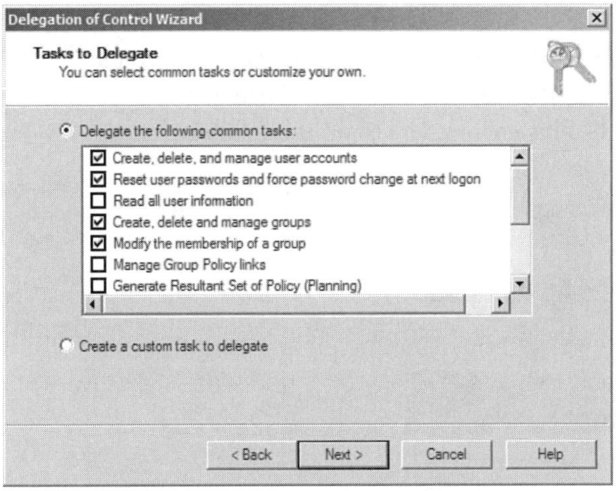

Step 5. If you have chosen the **Create a custom task to delegate** option, the Active Directory Object Type page enables you to delegate control over a large range of subfolders in the AD DS namespace. Click **Next** to choose whether to provide the ability to create or delete selected objects in the folder; you can choose from an extensive range of permissions. When finished, click **Next**.

Step 6. Review the information presented on the completion page. If you need to make any changes, click **Back**. When done, click **Finish**.

NOTE AD DS provides several built-in security groups that enable members to perform limited administrative capabilities within the domain in which they are located. These include Account Operators, Server Operators, Print Operators, and Backup Operators. You can add members to these groups when their defined rights match the administrative capabilities you want to confer to these users. Note that these groups are defined on a domainwide basis. For more information, refer to Windows Server 2008 R2 Help and Support.

TIP You should know when and how to use the Delegation of Control Wizard. The exam might present a scenario requiring a limited set of control over a given list of objects. You should also be aware that if you run the Delegation of Control

Wizard multiple times, permissions granted are cumulative rather than having the wizard replace prior permissions each time you run it.

To view, modify, or delete permissions granted using this wizard, open the Active Directory Administrative Center in Windows Server 2008 R2 or Active Directory Users and Computers in the original version of Windows Server 2008. From the console tree, right-click the OU or site and choose **Properties**. Scroll this dialog box to the Extensions section, select the **Security** tab of the dialog box found here, and then click **Advanced** to display the Advanced Security Settings for (container) dialog box shown in Figure 9-21. This enables you to do the following:

Figure 9-21   The Advanced Security Settings dialog box enables you to view and modify granular permissions.

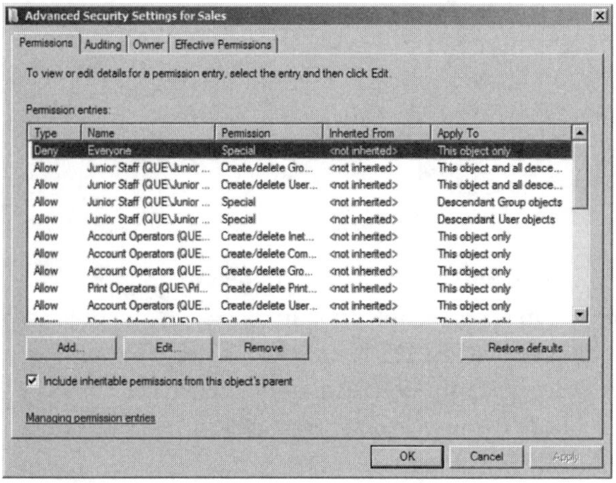

- To add an additional user or group with permission to perform a listed task, select the task and click **Add**. Then type the required user or group in the Select Users, Computers, or Groups dialog box.

- To modify the scope of a permissions entry, select it and click **Edit**. From the Permission Entry dialog box that appears, select the appropriate permissions. You can also explicitly deny permissions from this dialog box.

- To remove a delegated permission, select it and click **Remove**.

- To remove all delegated permissions from the container, click **Restore defaults**.

TIP   To view the effective permissions granted to a user or group, click the **Effective Permissions** tab and then select the required user or group. This tab displays a long list of permissions with check marks beside the granted permissions. This includes all permissions inherited through membership in other groups.

Exam Preparation Tasks

Review All the Key Topics

Review the most important topics in the chapter, noted with the key topics icon in the outer margin of the page. Table 9-4 lists a reference of these key topics and the page numbers on which each is found.

Table 9-4   Key Topics for Chapter 9

Key Topic Element	Description	Page Number
List	Describes types of user accounts in AD DS	286
List	Describes group scopes available in AD DS	287
List	Describes utilities available for automated creation of accounts in AD DS	288
Paragraph	Describes the use and purpose of template accounts	290
Table 9-2	Describes important parameters used with Csvde and Ldifde	294
Figure 9-4	Shows how to create alternative UPN suffixes	297
Figure 9-6	Shows how to create a contact	299
Figure 9-11	Shows how to create an OU in Active Directory Administrative Center	304
Table 9-3	Compares group scopes and their nesting capabilities in AD DS	305
Figure 9-12	Describes the AGDLP strategy	306
Figure 9-13	Describes the AGUDLP strategy	307
Figure 9-15	Shows how to deny access to a resource	309
Paragraph	Describes the Protected Admin capability	310
List	Provides reasons for disabling, rather than deleting, accounts	312
Figure 9-20	Shows how to delegate administrative control	315

Complete the Tables and Lists from Memory

Print a copy of Appendix C, "Memory Tables" (found on the CD), or at least the section for this chapter, and complete the tables and lists from memory. Appendix D, "Memory Tables Answer Key," also on the CD, includes completed tables and lists to check your work.

Definitions of Key Terms

Define the following key terms from this chapter, and check your answers in the glossary.

AGDLP, AGUDLP, built-in account, Csvde, domain local group, domain user account, Dsadd, global group, Ldifde, local user account, nesting, Protected Admin, security identifier (SID), template account, universal group, User Account Control (UAC), user logon name, user principal name (UPN), user principal name (UPN) suffix

This chapter covers the following subjects:

- **Types of Trust Relationships:** Windows Server 2008 permits external trusts, forest trusts, shortcut trusts, and realm trusts. This section introduces and compares these types of trust relationships.

- **Creating and Configuring Trust Relationships:** It is important that you know how to create and configure trust relationships for the 70-640 exam. This section shows you how to create the various types of trust relationships and describes the options available when creating and configuring them.

- **Managing Trust Relationships:** This section introduces several additional trust management tasks that you should know about, including selective and forestwide authentication, SID filtering, and removing trust relationships.

CHAPTER 10

Trust Relationships in Active Directory

Business in the twenty-first century is rapidly becoming more globalized, with a growing number of companies doing business on an international scale with multi-forest network enterprise structures. Such structures demand a level of trust among domains in the same and multiple forests. Active Directory has enabled several types of trust relationships to accommodate these needs.

"Do I Know This Already?" Quiz

The "Do I Know This Already?" quiz allows you to assess whether you should read this entire chapter or simply jump to the "Exam Preparation Tasks" section for review. If you are in doubt, read the entire chapter. Table 10-1 outlines the major headings in this chapter and the corresponding "Do I Know This Already?" quiz questions. You can find the answers in Appendix A, "Answers to the 'Do I Know This Already?' Quizzes."

Table 10-1 "Do I Know This Already?" Foundation Topics Section-to-Question Mapping

Foundations Topics Section	Questions Covered in This Section
Types of Trust Relationships	1–4
Creating and Configuring Trust Relationships	5–6
Managing Trust Relationships	7–9

1. You are the administrator for a large company that operates an AD DS forest containing six domains in two domain trees. Users in one child domain often access the network from a different child domain and report that logon times are frequently slow. What type of trust relationship should you configure?

   a. Forest trust

   b. Realm trust

   c. External trust

   d. Shortcut trust

2. You are the administrator for a company that operates an AD DS forest containing two domains. Your company has entered into a partnership agreement with a second company that operates an AD DS forest that is configured with the Windows 2000 native forest functional level. Users in your company will need to access resources in the second company's forest. What type of trust relationship should you configure?

   a. Forest trust

   b. Realm trust

   c. External trust

   d. Shortcut trust

3. Which of the following trusts can be configured as transitive trusts? (Choose all that apply.)

   a. Forest trust

   b. Realm trust

   c. External trust

   d. Shortcut trust

4. You are the administrator of the que.com domain, which is configured as a single domain in its own Active Directory forest. Users in your domain require access to resources in the certguide.com domain, which is a single domain in a different forest. Users in the certguide.com domain should not have access to resources in the que.com domain. What type of trust should you configure?

   a. A one-way external trust in which the certguide.com domain trusts the que.com domain.

   b. A one-way external trust in which the que.com domain trusts the certguide.com domain.

   c. A one-way shortcut trust in which the certguide.com domain trusts the que.com domain.

   d. A one-way shortcut trust in which the que.com domain trusts the certguide.com domain.

5. You are working at a computer running the Server Core version of Windows Server 2008 R2. You want to create an external trust relationship with another AD DS forest belonging to a partner company. Which tool should you use?

   a. Active Directory Administrative Center

   b. Active Directory Domains and Trusts

   c. The netdom command-line tool

   d. The dsmgmt command-line tool

6. You are using the New Trust Wizard to create a forest trust with the AD DS forest belonging to a company that has entered into a partnership agreement with your company's forest. You want to ensure that you can specify the users and groups from a trusted forest who are permitted to authenticate to servers containing resources in the trusting forest. All resources that users must access are located in one child domain of this forest. What authentication scope should you choose?

   a. Forestwide authentication

   b. Domainwide authentication

   c. Selective authentication

   d. One-way authentication

7. Last Friday, while working from a domain controller in the `que.com` domain, you created a one-way forest trust in which the `certguide.com` domain trusts the `que.com` domain. You are unsure that this trust relationship was properly established, so you decide to verify the relationship. What should you do? (Each answer represents a complete solution to the problem. Choose two.)

   a. In Active Directory Domains and Trusts, right-click the `certguide.com` domain and choose **Properties.** On the Properties dialog box that appears, click **Validate.**

   b. In Active Directory Domains and Trusts, select the Trusts tab of the `que.com` domain's Properties dialog box. From this tab right-click the `certguide.com` domain and choose **Validate.**

   c. In Active Directory Domains and Trusts, select the Trusts tab of the certguide.com domain's Properties dialog box. From this tab right-click the `que.com` domain and choose **Properties.** On the Properties dialog box that appears, click **Validate.**

   d. Use the `netdom trust certguide.com /d:que.com /verify` command

   e. Use the `netdom trust que.com /d:certguide.com /verify` command

8. You are the administrator of the `sales.que.com` domain. You need to change the authentication scope of the external trust relationship that you configured between your domain and `marketing.certguide.com` domain so that you can specify the users and groups that are permitted to access resources in the `marketing.certguide.com` domain. What should you do?

   a. From the Trusts tab of the `sales.que.com` domain Properties dialog box in Active Directory Domains and Trusts, select the `marketing.certguide.com` domain and click **Properties.** From the Authentication tab of the dialog box that appears, click **Domain-wide authentication.**

b. From the Trusts tab of the `sales.que.com` domain Properties dialog box in Active Directory Domains and Trusts, select the **`marketing.certguide.com`** domain and click **Properties.** From the Authentication tab of the dialog box that appears, click **Selective authentication.**

c. From the Trusts tab of the `marketing.certguide.com` domain Properties dialog box in Active Directory Domains and Trusts, select the **`sales.que.com`** domain and click **Properties.** From the Authentication tab of the dialog box that appears, click **Domain-wide authentication.**

d. From the Trusts tab of the `marketing.certguide.com` domain Properties dialog box in Active Directory Domains and Trusts, select the **`sales.que.com`** domain and click **Properties.** From the Authentication tab of the dialog box that appears, click **Selective authentication**.

9. You are the administrator of the `que.com` domain, and have configured an external trust relationship in which the `que.com` domain trusts the `certguide.com` domain. You want to ensure that SID filtering is enabled on this trust relationship. Which of the following commands should you type?

a. `Netdom trust que.com /domain:certguide.com /quarantine:Yes`

b. `Netdom trust certguide.com /domain:que.com /quarantine:Yes`

c. `Netdom trust que.com /domain:certguide.com /quarantine:No`

d. `Netdom trust certguide.com /domain:que.com /quarantine:No`

Foundation Topics

Types of Trust Relationships

Simply stated, a *trust relationship* is a configured link that enables a domain to access resources in another domain, or a forest to access resources in another forest. A trust relationship provides such access to users without the need to create additional user accounts in the other forest or domain. Consequently, administrators do not need to configure multiple user accounts, and users do not need to remember multiple usernames and passwords.

This section introduces the following types of trust relationships:

- Transitive trusts

- Forest trusts

- External trusts

- Realm trusts

- Shortcut trusts

Transitive Trusts

Microsoft introduced the concept of *transitive trusts* in Windows 2000. This represented a considerable improvement over the previous Windows NT trusts that required explicitly defining each and every trust relationship, a requirement that could become unwieldy in a large enterprise network. To understand the principle of transitive trusts, look at Figure 10-1. In a nontransitive trust, as was the case in Windows NT 4.0, if you configured Domain A to trust Domain B and Domain B to trust Domain C, Domain A does not trust Domain C unless you configure a separate trust relationship. Furthermore, the trust relationship worked in one direction only (as shown by the arrows in Figure 10-1); for a two-way trust relationship, you had to create two separate trusts, one in each direction.

Figure 10-1 A transitive trust relationship enables trusts to "flow through" one domain to the next one, whereas in a nontransitive trust relationship, this does not occur.

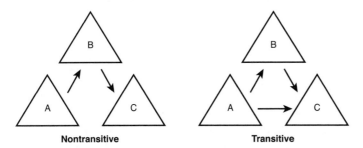

Nontransitive   Transitive

In all versions of Active Directory back to Windows 2000, the default behavior is that all domains in the forest trust each other with two-way transitive trust relationships. Whenever you add a new child domain or a new domain tree to an existing forest, new trust relationships are automatically created with each of the other domains in the forest. These trusts do not require administrative intervention. The other types of trust relationships, which we discuss next, require manual configuration by the administrator.

Forest Trusts

A forest trust is used to share resources between forests. This type of trust relationship consists of transitive trusts between every domain in each forest. The trust relationship is created manually and can be either one-way or two-way. The following are several benefits of a forest trust:

- They provide simple management of resource sharing by reducing the number of external trusts required in multidomain forests.

- They enable a wider scope of user principal name (UPN) authentication across all domains in the trusting forests.

- They provide increased administrative flexibility by allowing administrators to collaborate on task delegation across forest boundaries.

- Each forest remains isolated in certain aspects, such as directory replication, schema modification, and adding domains, all of which affect only the forest to which they apply.

- They improve the trustworthiness of authorization data. You can use both the Kerberos and NTLM authentication protocols when authenticating across forests.

External Trusts and Realm Trusts

External trusts are one-way individual trust relationships that you can set up between two domains in different forests. They are nontransitive, which means you use them explicitly to define a one-to-one relationship between domains. You can use them to create trust relationships with AD DS domains operating at the Windows 2000 domain functional level or with Windows NT 4.0 domains. Furthermore, you can use an external trust if you need to create a trust relationship that involves only specific domains within two different forests.

You can use a realm trust to share information between an AD DS domain and any non-Windows realm that supports Kerberos version 5 (V5), such as UNIX. A realm trust supports UNIX identity management to enable users in UNIX realms to seamlessly access Active Directory resources by means of password synchronization with Windows Server 2008's Server for Network Information Service (NIS) feature. Password synchronization enables users with accounts in UNIX realms in AD DS to synchronize password changes across both the AD DS domain and the UNIX realm. Furthermore, an AD DS domain controller can act as a master NIS server for the UNIX realm.

Shortcut Trusts

Unlike the previously discussed trusts, a shortcut trust relationship exists within a single forest. It is an additional trust relationship between two child domains, which optimizes the authentication process when a large number of users require access to resources in another domain. It is especially useful if the normal authentication path must cross several domains. Figure 10-2 shows an example of such a situation.

Figure 10-2   A shortcut trust is useful if the authentication path to another domain in the forest must cross several domain boundaries.

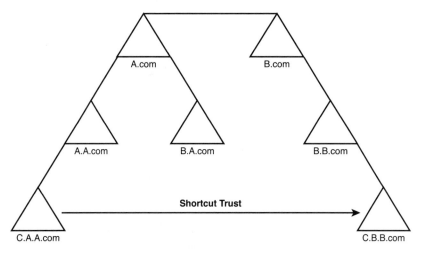

Suppose that users in the C.A.A.com domain require access to the C.B.B.com domain, which is located in another tree of the same forest. The authentication path must cross five domain boundaries to access the C.B.B.com domain. If an administrator sets up a shortcut trust between these two domains, the logon process speeds up considerably. This is also true for other possible authentication paths such as B.A.com to B.B.com or even C.A.A.com to B.A.com.

A SEPARATE RESEARCH FOREST

A major aircraft manufacturer landed a contract with NASA to design one module of a prototype spacecraft for a manned Mars mission. Realizing that the research necessary to complete this project successfully required a high level of security, management asked the senior network administrator to set up a separate forest in the organization's Windows Server 2008 AD DS design.

For the project to succeed, researchers needed access to certain data stored in the organization's existing forest. Their user accounts would be in the new forest. Users in the existing forest did not require access to the research forest. The administrator had to choose a trust model that would enable the appropriate levels of access. With these needs in mind, the administrator decided to set up a one-way external trust relationship in which the existing forest trusted the research forest. This enabled him to place the researchers who needed access into a group with access to the appropriate resources in the existing forest. Because the trust relationship was one-way, no access in the opposite direction was possible.

Table 10-2 summarizes and contrasts the major features of the different trust relationships that you can establish in Windows Server 2008 R2.

Table 10-2   Trust Types

Trust Type	Transitivity	Description
Forest	Transitive	Enables you to share resources between forests operating at the Windows Server 2003 or higher forest functional level. If established as a two-way trust, users in either forest can be authenticated to and access resources in the other forest.
External	Nontransitive	Enables you to provide access to resources located in a Windows NT 4.0 domain or a domain in another forest running at any forest functional level and not connected by a forest trust.
Realm	Transitive or nontransitive	Enables you to provide access to resources in a non-Windows Kerberos realm such as a UNIX realm.
Shortcut	Transitive	Used to improve user logon times and resource access between two child domains in the same forest running at the Windows Server 2008 or Windows Server 2008 R2 forest functional level. This is useful for two child domains located in separate trees.

Note that any of these trusts can be established in either a one-way or two-way fashion.

Creating and Configuring Trust Relationships

This section examines creating the various types of trust relationships already introduced. Before you begin to create trust relationships, you must be aware of several prerequisites:

- You must be a member of the Enterprise Admins group or the Domain Admins group in the forest root domain. In a Windows Server 2003 or newer domain, you can also be a member of the Incoming Forest Trust Builders group in the forest root domain. This group has the rights to create one-way, incoming forest trusts to the forest root domain. If you hold this level of membership in both forests, you can set up both sides of an interforest trust at the same time.

- You must ensure that DNS is properly configured so that the forests can recognize each other. You might have to configure conditional forwarding to enable DNS servers in one forest to forward queries to DNS servers in the other forest so that resources are properly located. Conditional forwarding was discussed in Chapter 4, "Configuring DNS Server Settings and Replication."

- In the case of a forest trust, both forests must be operating at the Windows Server 2003 or higher forest functional level.

> **WARNING**   It is not possible to delegate the creation of trusts to a user who is not a member of the Domain Admins or Enterprise Admins group. Although you can delegate the Create Trusted Domain Object (TDO) or Delete TDO right in the System container of a domain, this does not grant the user the right to create a trust.

Windows Server 2008 R2 provides the New Trust Wizard to create the various types of trust relationships. You can also use the `netdom` command-line tool to create trust relationships.

Creating a Forest Trust Relationship

Perform the following procedure to create a forest trust using the New Trust Wizard:

Step 1.   From one of the domains that will be participating in the trust relationship, open Active Directory Domains and Trusts.

Step 2.   In the console tree, right-click the domain and choose **Properties**.

Step 3.   Select the **Trusts** tab. This tab contains fields listing domains trusted by this domain and domains that trust this domain. Initially these fields are blank, as shown in Figure 10-3.

Step 4.   Click New Trust to start the New Trust Wizard, as shown in Figure 10-4.

Figure 10-3   You can manage all types of trusts from the Trusts tab of the domain's Properties dialog box.

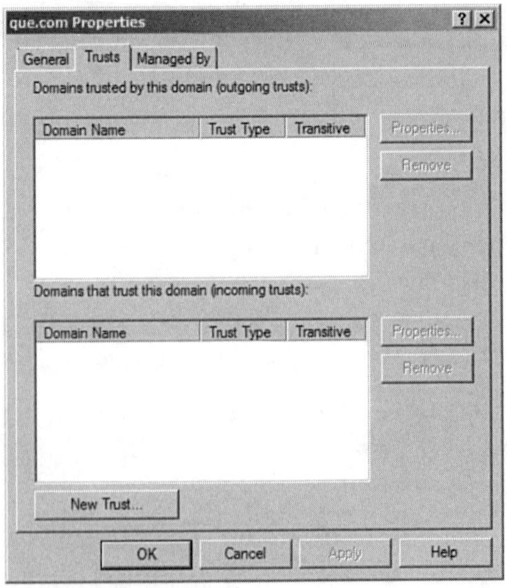

Figure 10-4   You can create new trust relationships by using the New Trust Wizard.

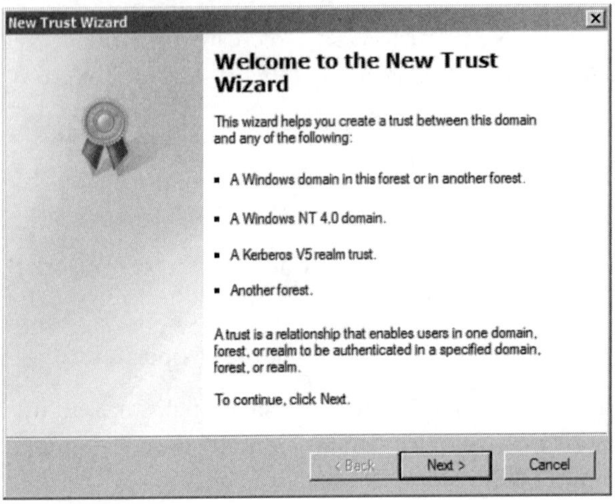

Step 5.   Click **Next**, and on the Trust Name page shown in Figure 10-5, type the name of the forest with which you want to create the trust relationship. Then click **Next** again.

Step 6.   The Trust Type page shown in Figure 10-6 offers you a choice between an external trust and a forest trust. Select **Forest trust** and then click **Next**.

Figure 10-5   Use the Trust Name page to specify the name of the domain or forest with which you are creating the trust.

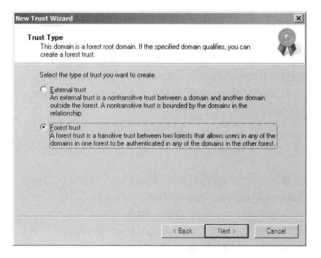

Figure 10-6   Use the Trust Type page to select the type of trust you want to create.

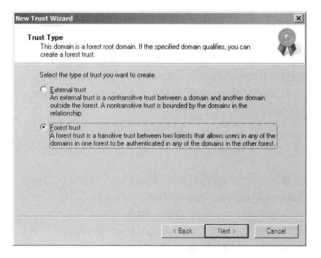

Step 7.   On the Direction of Trust page shown in Figure 10-7, choose between the following types of trusts and then click **Next**.

—**Two-way:** Creates a two-way trust, in which users in both domains can be authenticated in each other's domain.

—**One-way: incoming:** Creates a one-way trust in which users in your (trusted) domain can be authenticated in the other (trusting) domain. Users in the other domain cannot be authenticated in your domain.

—**One-way: outgoing:** Creates a one-way trust in which users in the other (trusting) domain can be authenticated in your (trusted) domain. Users in your domain cannot be authenticated in the other domain.

Figure 10-7 The Direction of Trust page provides choices for creating one-way or two-way trusts.

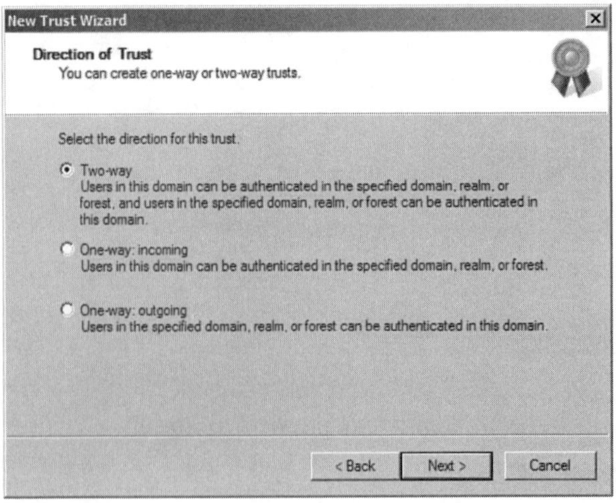

Step 8. The Sides of Trust page enables you to complete both sides of the trust if you have the appropriate permissions in both forests. If this is so, select **Both this domain and the specified domain**. Otherwise, select **This domain only**. Then click **Next**.

Step 9. The next step depends on your answer to the Sides of Trust page, as follows:

—If you selected **This domain only**, the Trust Password page asks you to specify a password that conforms to security guidelines. The administrator in the other forest will be required to type the same password when completing the other side of the trust. Type and confirm a password, and then click **Next**.

—If you selected **Both this domain and the specified domain**, the Outgoing Trust Authentication Level—Local Forest page shown in Figure 10-8 asks you to specify either **Forest-wide authentication**, which authenticates users from the trusted forest for all resources in the local forest, or **Selective authentication**, which does not create default authentication. This choice of authentication scopes is discussed later in this chapter. Make a choice and then click **Next**.

Figure 10-8   The Outgoing Trust Authentication Level—Local Forest page provides two choices of authentication scope for users in the trusted forest.

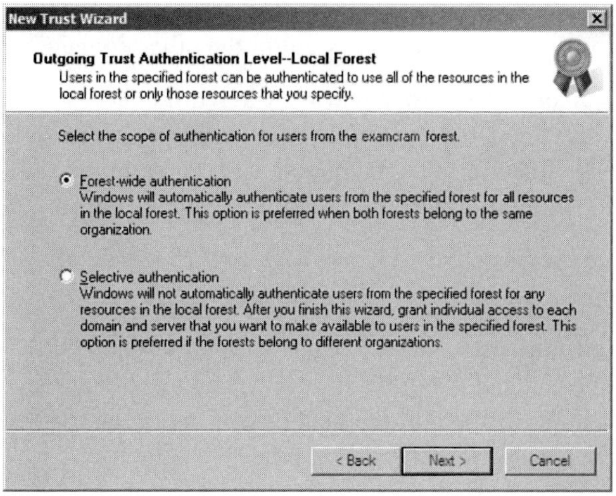

Step 10.   The Trust Selections Complete page shown in Figure 10-9 summarizes the options you have selected. Review these selections and click **Back** (if necessary) to make any required changes. To create the trust relationship, click **Next**.

Figure 10-9   The Trust Selections Complete page displays a review of the trust settings you specified.

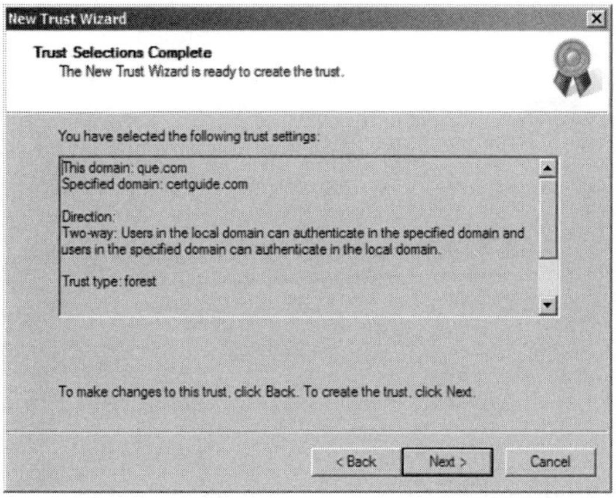

Step 11.   The Trust Creation Complete page informs you that the trust relationship was successfully created. Click **Next** to finish the process.

Step 12.   If you are creating an outgoing or two-way trust, you receive the Confirm Outgoing Trust page. This page asks whether you want to confirm the outgoing trust. To confirm the outgoing trust, enter a username and password for the administrator account in the other domain.

If you are creating an incoming or two-way trust, you receive the Confirm Incoming Trust page. This page asks whether you want to confirm the incoming trust. To confirm the incoming trust, enter a username and password for the administrator account in the other domain.

Step 13.   When the Completing the New Trust Wizard page confirms the creation of the trust from the other side, click **Finish**.

Step 14.   You are returned to the Trusts tab of the domain's Properties dialog box (see Figure 10-10). The name of the domain with which you configured the trust now appears in one or both of the fields according to the trust type you created. Click **OK** to close this dialog box.

Figure 10-10   After you have created the trust relationship, the Trusts tab of the domain's Properties dialog box shows the name of the trusted domain together with the trust type and transitivity.

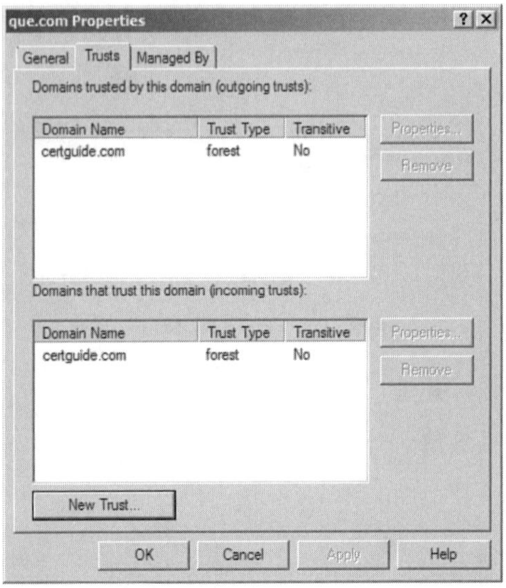

NOTE   If you have selected the **This domain only** option from the Sides of Trust page, the trust will not be fully established until you (or another administrator) run the New Trust Wizard from the other domain involved in the trust.

TIP   Remember the prerequisites for creating a forest trust. All domains involved must be at the Windows Server 2003 or higher domain functional level, and the forests must be at the Windows Server 2003 or higher forest functional level. Also remember that a forest trust is the simplest way to connect forests when access to resources in multiple domains is needed and when Kerberos authentication across the forest boundary is required.

To create a new forest trust from the command line, open an administrative command prompt by clicking **Start > All Programs > Accessories**, right-clicking **Command Prompt**, and then choosing **Run as administrator**. Accept the User Account Control (UAC) prompt if presented and then use the following command syntax:

```
netdom trust TrustingDomainName /d:TrustedDomainName /add /twoway
```

In this command, the **trust** subcommand specifies that you are managing a trust relationship and the /add parameter adds a trust relationship between the domains specified in *TrustingDomainName* and *TrustedDomainName*. The /**twoway** keyword specifies that you are creating a two-way trust relationship (if omitted, this command creates a one-way trust by default).

NOTE   The **netdom trust** command includes a large number of parameters for managing all types of trust relationships. For additional details and other usage scenarios on the **netdom trust** command, type **netdom trust /?** at a command line. Also refer to "Netdom trust" at http://technet.microsoft.com/en-us/library/cc835085(WS.10).aspx.

Creating External Trust Relationships

You can use the New Trust Wizard or the netdom trust command-line utility in much the same way as described in the previous section to create an external trust relationship. Simply select **External trust** on the Trust Type page of the New Trust Wizard (previously shown in Figure 10-6). You receive the same options shown in Figure 10-7 for configuring one-way or two-way trusts. You receive the authentication choices shown in Figure 10-11 that specify the two domains involved. After completing the wizard, the Trusts tab of the domain's Properties dialog box shows the trust type and transitivity of the trusts you have created.

Figure 10-11   The Outgoing Trust Authentication Level—Local Domain page provides two choices of authentication scope for users in the trusted domain.

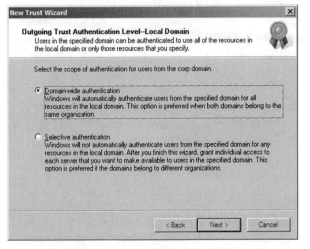

NOTE   For more information on creating external trust relationships, refer to "Creating External Trusts" at http://technet.microsoft.com/en-us/library/cc816837(WS.10).aspx.

Creating Realm Trust Relationships

Use the New Trust Wizard or the `netdom trust` command-line utility in a similar fashion to create a realm trust relationship. When specifying the name of a UNIX realm on the Trust Name page of the New Trust Wizard (previously shown in Figure 10-5), you must use all uppercase characters. After doing so, the Trust Type page offers an option to set up a realm trust, as shown in Figure 10-12. You also receive the choice of transitivity as well as whether to make the trust one-way or two-way.

Figure 10-12   Creating a realm trust.

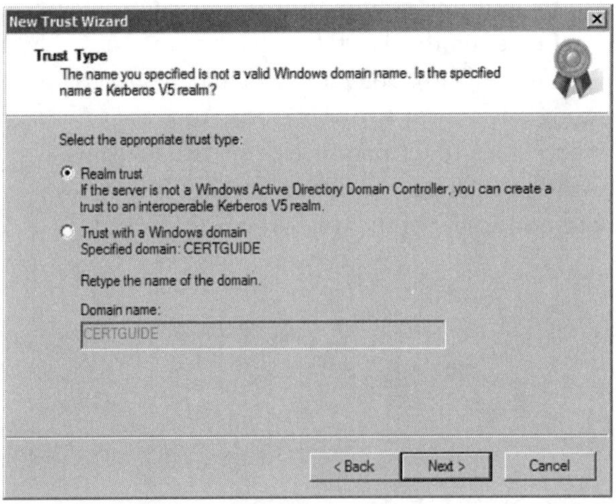

> **NOTE** For more information on creating realm trust relationships, refer to "Creating Realm Trusts" at http://technet.microsoft.com/en-us/library/cc816879(WS.10).aspx.

Creating Shortcut Trust Relationships

As already discussed, a shortcut trust relationship is used to facilitate authentication and access control between two child domains in the same forest. You can use the New Trust Wizard to create a shortcut trust, as the following steps demonstrate:

Step 1. From one of the domains that will be participating in the trust relationship, open Active Directory Domains and Trusts.

Step 2. In the console tree, right-click your domain and choose **Properties**.

Step 3. From the Trusts tab of the domain's Properties dialog box, click **New Trust** to start the New Trust Wizard, as described previously and shown in Figure 10-4.

Step 4. Click **Next**, and on the Trust Name page previously shown in Figure 10-5, type the name of the domain to which you want to establish the shortcut trust. Then click **Next** again.

Step 5. Select the appropriate direction from the Direction of Trust page previously shown in Figure 10-7, and then click **Next**.

Step 6. Follow the remaining steps in the New Trust Wizard. When completed, the trust relationship will be displayed in the Trusts tab of each domain's Properties dialog box, in a similar fashion to that previously shown in Figure 10-10 with the trust type of shortcut.

You can also use the `netdom trust` command for creating a shortcut trust. The syntax is the same as previously described; `netdom` creates the shortcut trust when it recognizes both domains as belonging to the same forest.

> **NOTE** For more information on creating shortcut trust relationships, refer to "Understanding When to Create a Shortcut Trust" at http://technet.microsoft.com/en-us/library/cc754538.aspx.

Managing Trust Relationships

After you have created a cross-forest trust, the following limited set of configuration options is available from the trust's Properties dialog box:

- **Validate trust relationships:** This option enables you to verify that a trust has been properly created and that the forests can communicate with each other.

- **Change the authentication scope:** This option enables you to change the selection of domainwide authentication or selective authentication that you made during creation of the trust, should you need to modify access control to the trusting forest's resources.

- **Configure SID filtering:** Windows Server 2008 provides security identifier (SID) filtering by default on all new, outgoing, external trusts. This helps to prevent malicious administrators from the trusted domain from granting elevated access privileges in the trusting domain. You can enable or disable SID filtering for forest trusts and external trusts.

Validating Trust Relationships

You can validate a trust relationship from the trust's Properties dialog box by performing the following steps:

Step 1. In Active Directory Domains and Trusts, right-click your domain name and choose **Properties**.

Step 2. On the Trusts tab of the domain's Properties dialog box, select the name of the domain or forest whose trust relationship you want to verify and click **Properties**.

Step 3. You receive the trust's Properties dialog box, as shown in Figure 10-13. To validate the trust relationship, click **Validate**.

Step 4. If the trust is in place and active, you receive a confirmation message box; otherwise, you receive an error message informing you of the problem. Click **OK**.

To validate a trust relationship from the command line, type the following:

```
netdom trust TrustingDomainName /d:TrustedDomainName /verify
```

In this command, `TrustingDomainName` and `TrustedDomainName` are the names of the two domains involved in the trust relationship, and the `/verify` keyword indicates that you want to verify the trust.

Authentication Scope

As you have already seen in Figure 10-8, the New Trust Wizard offers a choice between two authentication scopes: selective authentication and domainwide or forestwide authentication.

Figure 10-13   The General tab of the Properties dialog box of the other domain provides information on the trust's properties and enables you to validate the trust.

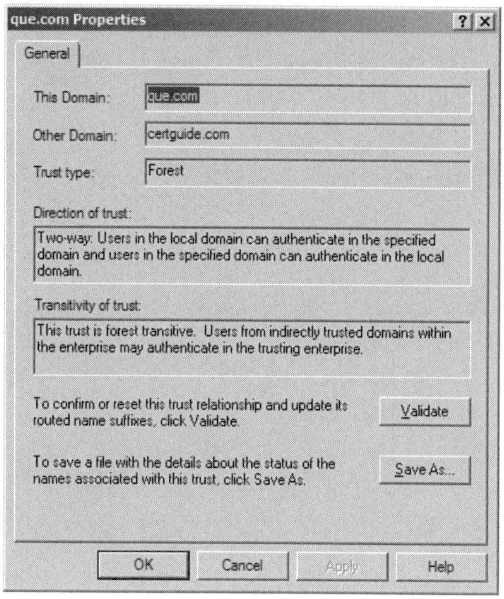

Domain-wide authentication: Available in the case of external trusts, this option permits unrestricted access by any users in the trusted domain to all available shared resources in the trusting domain, according to sharing and security permissions attached to the resources. It is the default option for external trusts.

Forest-wide authentication: Available in the case of forest trusts, this option permits unrestricted access by any users in the trusted forest to all available shared resources in any domain of the trusting forest, according to sharing and security permissions attached to the resources. It is the default option for forest trusts. Microsoft recommends the domain-wide and forest-wide options for trusts within the same organization only.

Selective authentication: This option does not create any default authentication. It enables you to specify the users and groups from a trusted forest who are permitted to authenticate to servers containing resources in the trusting forest. Microsoft recommends this option for trusts that involve separate organizations, such as contractor relationships. It improves security by limiting the quantity of authentication requests that can pass through the trust.

You can change the authentication scope of a trust relationship after creating it from the trust's Properties dialog box by using the following procedure:

Step 1.   In Active Directory Domains and Trusts, right-click your domain name and choose **Properties**.

Step 2.   On the Trusts tab of the domain's Properties dialog box, select the domain name for which you want to configure the authentication scope and then click the **Properties** button.

Step 3.   Select the **Authentication** tab of the trust's Properties dialog box and select from the options shown in Figure 10-14.

Figure 10-14   The Authentication tab of the trust's Properties dialog box enables you to change the trust's authentication scope.

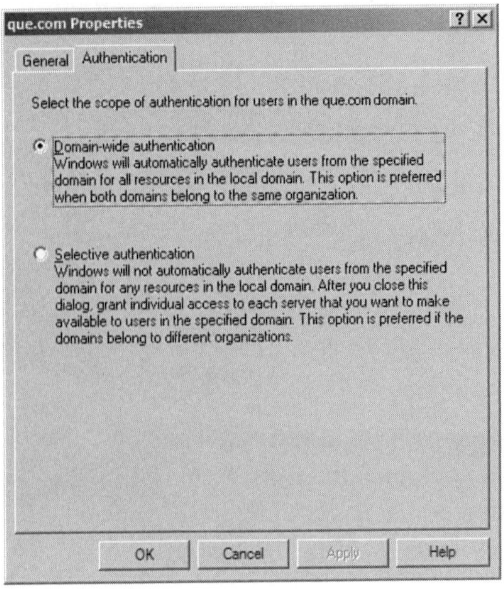

Step 4.   Click **OK**.

> **NOTE**   This procedure displays the authentication settings for only the outgoing trust. To obtain the current authentication settings for the incoming side of a two-way forest trust, connect to the other forest (right-click **Active Directory Domains and Trusts** and choose the **Change forest** option) and then view the authentication settings for this side of the trust.

SID Filtering

SID filtering is another mechanism that enhances the security of communications between forests in a trust relationship. When a user from a trusted domain attempts to authenticate to a trusting domain, SID filtering validates the SIDs within the user's authentication ticket by verifying that the incoming authentication request contains SIDs of security principals in only the trusted domain. If SIDs from domains other than the trusted domain are present, they are filtered out, thereby denying the authentication request.

You can use the `netdom` command line tool to configure SID filtering. By default, SID filtering is enabled on external trusts but not on domain trusts such as short-cut trusts. To disable SID filtering, type the following command:

Netdom trust *trusting_domain* **/domain:***trusted_domain* **/quarantine:No**

In this command, *trusting_domain* and *trusted_domain* are the names of the trusting and trusted domains, respectively. You must be a member of the Domain Admins or Enterprise Admins group, or specify the username and password of an appropriate account according to the following:

- If you are working from the trusted domain, use the **/usero: and /passwordo:** keywords, respectively, to specify the user account and password used to connect to the trusting domain. These keywords can also be specified as **/uo:** and **/po:**, respectively.

- If you are working from the trusting domain, use the **/userD: and /password:** keywords, respectively, to specify the user account and password used to connect to the domain specified in the /domain parameter. These keywords can also be specified as **/ud:** and **/pd:**, respectively.

To reenable SID filtering, type this command with the keyword **/quarantine:Yes.**

NOTE   For more information on SID filtering, refer to "SID Filtering Dialog box-Securing External Trusts" at http://technet.microsoft.com/en-us/library/dd145367.aspx and "Configuring SID Filter Quarantining on External Trusts" at http://technet.microsoft.com/en-us/library/cc794757(WS.10).aspx. For more information on the `Netdom trust` command, including other uses of this command, refer to "Netdom trust" at http://technet.microsoft.com/en-us/library/cc835085(WS.10).aspx.

Removing a Cross-forest Trust Relationship

At times there might be a need to remove a trust relationship between two forests. For example, a contract may have completed or been terminated, an acquisition of one company by another might have fallen through, and so on. You might need to remove and re-create a trust relationship if you have incorrectly specified properties such as an incorrect trust type or direction.

Use the following steps to remove a trust relationship from the Active Directory Domains and Trusts snap-in:

Step 1.   In Active Directory Domains and Trusts, right-click your domain name and choose **Properties**.

Step 2.   On the Trusts tab of the domain's Properties dialog box, select the trust to be removed and click **Remove**.

Step 3.   You are asked whether you want to remove the trust from the local domain only or from the local domain and the other domain (see Figure 10-15). If you want to remove the trust from both domains, select **Yes, remove the trust from both the local domain and the other domain**; type the username and password for an account with administrative privileges in the other domain; and then click **OK**.

Figure 10-15   You are asked whether you want to remove the trust from the local domain only or from the local domain and the other domain.

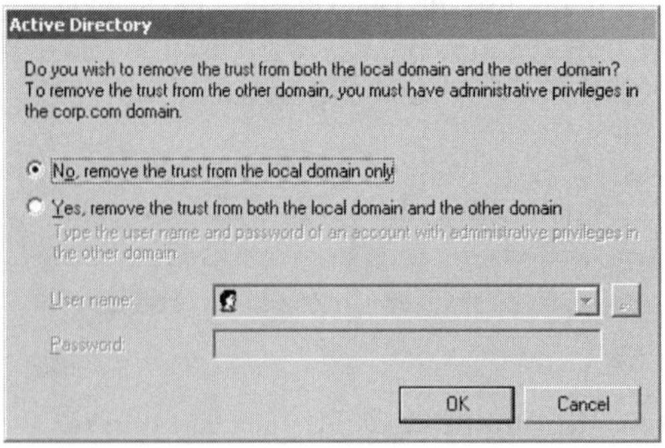

Step 4.   Click **Yes** on the next dialog box to confirm the trust removal.

Step 5.   You are returned to the Trust tab of the domain's Properties dialog box. Notice that the name of the other domain has been removed.

You can also use the `netdom` command to remove a trust. Type the following command:

```
netdom trust TrustingDomainName /d:TrustedDomainName /remove /UserD:User
/PasswordD:*Password
```

In this command, `TrustingDomainName` and `TrustedDomainName` specify the DNS names of the domains in the trust being removed; `User` and `Password` specify the user account and password for an account with administrative credentials in the other domain.

Exam Preparation Tasks

Review All the Key Topics

Review the most important topics in the chapter, noted with the key topics icon in the outer margin of the page. Table 10-3 lists a reference of these key topics and the page numbers on which each is found.

Table 10-3   Key Topics for Chapter 10

Key Topic Element	Description	Page Number
Table 10-2	Summarizes the types of trust relationships available in AD DS	328
List	Requirements you must satisfy to create a trust	329
List	Shows how to create a trust relationship	329
Figure 10-7	Shows the available trust directions	332
List	Describes how to create a shortcut trust relationship	337
List	Describes the available authentication scopes	339
List	Specifying SID filtering	341
Figure 10-15	Shows how to remove a trust relationship	342

Complete the Tables and Lists from Memory

Print a copy of Appendix C, "Memory Tables" (found on the CD), or at least the section for this chapter, and complete the tables and lists from memory. Appendix D, "Memory Tables Answer Key," also on the CD, includes completed tables and lists to check your work.

Definitions of Key Terms

Define the following key terms from this chapter, and check your answers in the glossary.

authentication scope, external trust, forest trust, one-way trust, realm trust, shortcut trust, security identifier (SID), SID filtering, transitive trust, two-way trust

This chapter covers the following subjects:

■ **Overview of Group Policy:** This section provides a foundation for the remainder of your studies on Group Policy by introducing its components and summarizing the major updates to Group Policy included with Windows Server 2008.

■ **Creating and Applying GPOs:** This section shows you how to use the Group Policy Management Console to create and work with Group Policy objects (GPOs). It also discusses the processing hierarchy of GPOs and ways in which you can modify the default hierarchy.

■ **Configuring GPO Templates:** This section discusses the Administrative Templates feature of Group Policy and shows you how to configure the more important settings. It also shows you how to work with Starter GPOs and use them to create customized policies.

CHAPTER 11

Creating and Applying Group Policy Objects

Users are naturally curious beings. It is human nature to explore your computer and see what you can do, what Control Panel is all about, and so on. Invariably, problems result, users make changes and cannot back out of them, and they call the help desk for assistance. For a business network to function properly, it is mandatory that a secure means of limiting what uses can do be in place, and Microsoft has recognized this fact ever since the days of Windows NT and its System Policy.

Beginning with Windows 2000, Group Policy enabled administrators to exert more control over users' environments and reduce the extent of user-originated problems. Each successive iteration of Windows has added additional components to the list of available policies, and Windows Server 2008 and Windows Server 2008 are no exception.

"Do I Know This Already?" Quiz

The "Do I Know This Already?" quiz enables you to assess whether you should read this entire chapter or simply jump to the "Exam Preparation Tasks" section for review. If you are in doubt, read the entire chapter. Table 11-1 outlines the major headings in this chapter and the corresponding "Do I Know This Already?" quiz questions. You can find the answers in Appendix A, "Answers to the 'Do I Know This Already?' Quizzes."

Table 11-1 "Do I Know This Already?" Foundation Topics Section-to-Question Mapping

Foundations Topics Section	Questions Covered in This Section
Overview of Group Policy	1
Creating and Applying GPOs	2–9
Configuring GPO Templates	10–14

1. Which of the following best describes how Active Directory stores the various components of Group Policy?

   a. Group Policy containers (GPCs) are stored in the SYSVOL shared folder, and Group Policy templates (GPTs) are stored in the domain partition of AD DS.

   b. GPCs are stored in the domain partition of AD DS, and GPTs are stored in the SYSVOL shared folder.

   c. Both GPCs and GPTs are stored in the domain partition of AD DS.

   d. Both GPCs and GPTs are stored in the SYSVOL shared folder.

2. Which tool do you use in Windows Server 2008 for creating GPOs and performing various management activities on them?

   a. Group Policy Management Console

   b. Group Policy Management Editor

   c. Active Directory Users and Computers

   d. Active Directory Administrative Center

3. Which of the following components of GPOs enables you to configure the settings that influence the appearance of the desktop environment, including many of the actions users are permitted to perform?

   a. Preferences

   b. Software Settings

   c. Windows Settings

   d. Administrative Templates

4. You have configured a GPO whose settings were needed for a special project and are no longer needed. You expect that the settings in this GPO might be needed for a similar project next year. Which of the following should you *not* do with the GPO?

   a. Delete the links of the GPO to various AD DS containers.

   b. Disable the links of the GPO to various AD DS containers.

   c. Delete the GPO.

   d. Disable the GPO.

   e. Disable the User Configuration and Computer Configuration branches of the GPO.

5. You want to enable a junior administrator named Ted to edit settings in existing GPOs without giving him the capability of creating, linking, or deleting GPOs. What should you do? (Each answer represents a complete solution. Choose two.)

    a. Use the Delegation of Control Wizard to grant Ted the required capabilities.

    b. Make Ted a member of the Group Policy Creator Owners group.

    c. Make Ted a member of the Server Operators group.

    d. From the Delegation tab of the Group Policy Objects node in GPMC, add Ted's user account to the list provided.

6. Which of the following represents the default sequences in which GPOs linked to different AD DS containers are applied?

    a. Site (S), Domain (D), organizational unit (OU), local (L)

    b. D, S, OU, L

    c. L, S, D, OU

    d. L, D, S, OU

7. You have created a GPO that applies desktop settings that must be applied to all computers in your domain. You want to ensure that any GPOs applied to sites or OUs in the domain do not apply settings on top of these desktop settings. What should you do?

    a. Configure the domain with the Enforced setting.

    b. Configure the GPO with the Enforced setting.

    c. Configure the domain with the Block Inheritance setting.

    d. Configure the GPO with the Block Inheritance setting.

    e. You do not need to do anything. By default, domain-based policies override all other policy settings.

8. Your AD DS forest consists of three domains and seven sites. You are responsible for configuring Group Policy that applies to one child domain. An administrator at one of the branch offices has configured a GPO with site-specific settings that are applicable to two of the domains but should not be applied to computers and users in your domain. What should you do?

    a. Configure your domain with the Enforced setting.

    b. Configure your domain's Default Domain Policy GPO with the Enforced setting.

    c. Configure your domain with the Block Inheritance setting.

    d. Configure your domain's Default Domain Policy GPO with the Block Inheritance setting.

9. You have configured a domain-based GPO that locks down the desktop settings of all computers in the domain. You realize that this will limit the actions that administrators can perform, so you want to ensure that members of the Domain

Admins group are not affected by this GPO. Members of this group might need access to users' computers to correct problems from time to time. What should you do?

a. Use a WMI filter that exempts members of the Domain Admins group from applying the GPO.

b. Write a Windows PowerShell script that disables application of the policies in the GPO from applying to computers used by members of the Domain Admins group.

c. Disable the GPO's link for computers used by members of the Domain Admins group.

d. Deny the Apply Group Policy permission to the Domain Admins group from the Delegation tab of the GPO's Properties in the GPMC.

10. You are the network administrator for a municipal library system, which operates a single-domain AD DS network. Each branch library has a series of computers that library patrons use for locating books and other information. All client computer accounts for the domain are located in a single OU, including those in staff offices.

Occasionally, a staff member uses one of these computers to access protected information from his or her domain user account. You must ensure that the computer settings for these computers take precedence over the user settings specified in Group Policy. However, when applying Group Policy, you notice that the user settings override the computer settings. What should you do?

a. Enable the loopback processing mode with the merge option.

b. Enable the loopback processing mode with the replace option.

c. Disable the computer settings for the affected GPO.

d. Disable the user settings for the affected GPO.

11. You are responsible for configuring Group Policy in your domain. Domain client computers run a mix of Windows XP, Vista, and Windows 7. You configure a GPO that contains Administrative Templates settings that are to be applied to all computers in the domain; however, a few days later you realize that the settings are not being applied to Windows XP computers although they are applied properly to Windows Vista and Windows 7 computers. What is the most likely reason for this problem?

a. The Windows XP computers do not process WMI filters; because you used a WMI filter to prevent servers from applying the policy, the policy also did not apply to the Windows XP computers.

b. A loopback setting using the Replace mode replaced the settings in this GPO with another one that applies conflicting user-based settings; you need to change the loopback setting to the Merge mode.

c. The Administrative Templates settings were created using the ADMX format; you should have used the older ADM format instead.

d. The Administrative Templates settings were stored in an incorrect subfolder of the SYSVOL share; you should reconfigure the location of these settings.

12. Which of the following groups of Administrative Template settings apply to users only and not to computers? (Choose all that apply.)

a. Control Panel

b. Desktop

c. Printers

d. Shared Folders

e. Start Menu and Taskbar

f. System

13. You want to ensure that only members of the Domain Admins group can belong to the local Administrators group on all client computers in your company's AD DS domain. What should you do?

a. From the Computer Configuration\Policies\Windows Settings\Security Settings node of a GPO linked to the domain, configure a Restricted Groups setting that limits the membership of the local Administrators group to the Domain Admins group.

b. From the User Configuration\Policies\Windows Settings\Security Settings node of a GPO linked to the domain, configure a Restricted Groups setting that limits the membership of the local Administrators group to the Domain Admins group.

c. From the Delegation tab of the properties for a GPO linked to the domain, delegate control of all client computers to the Domain Admins group.

d. From the Delegation tab of the properties for a GPO linked to the domain, specify a Restricted Groups setting that limits the membership of the local Administrators group to the Domain Admins group.

14. You are responsible for configuring Group Policy in a child domain of your company's AD DS forest. One of your colleagues, who is responsible for the forest root domain, has created a Starter GPO that contains settings that you want to apply to computers in your domain. What should you do?

   a. Link the Starter GPO to the child domain.

   b. Copy the settings in the Starter GPO to the Default Domain Policy GPO in the child domain.

   c. Create a new GPO linked to the child domain and copy the settings in the Starter GPO to this GPO.

   d. Create a new GPO linked to the child domain and specify the name of the Starter GPO in the New GPO dialog box.

Foundation Topics

Overview of Group Policy

Group Policy lies at the heart of every Active Directory implementation. It does far more than just define what users can and cannot do with their computers. It is a series of configuration settings that you can apply to an object or a series of objects in Active Directory to control a user's environment in numerous contexts, including the following:

- **Network access:** Enables you to control access to network devices including terminal servers, wireless access, and so on.

- **Folder redirection:** Enables you to use Group Policy settings to redirect users' local folders to network shares.

- **Logon/logoff/startup/shutdown scripts:** Enables you to assign scripts on a user or computer basis for such events as logon, logoff, startup, or shutdown.

- **Application deployment:** Enables you to administer applications on your network, including their assignment, publication, updating, repair, and removal.

- **Security options of all types:** Enables you to use Group Policy security settings to enforce restrictions and control access on user or computer properties.

Group Policy can be applied to server and client computers running Windows 2000 and up and includes both computer and user settings. As the names suggest, computer policies are computer-specific and are applied when the computer starts up and user policies are user-specific and are applied with the user logs on to the computer.

Components of Group Policy

As its name implies, a group policy is a group of policies that are applied together. It is a set of configuration settings that can be applied to one or more Active Directory Domain Services (AD DS) objects to define the behavior of the object and its child objects.

Group Policy has a structure that provides a high degree of flexibility in managing users and computers. The policies are contained in sets known as *Group Policy objects (GPOs)*. In turn, the content of GPOs is stored in two different locations: *Group Policy containers (GPCs)*, which are Directory Services objects that include subcontainers for machine and user Group Policy information, and *Group Policy templates (GPTs)*, which are folder structures including a GPT folder and its subfolders that together contain all the Group Policy information including the actual policy settings for any particular GPO.

All GPOs are identified by their Globally Unique Identifier (GUID), which is a unique 128-bit number assigned when the GPO is first created. This number is stored as an attribute of the object and is used to identify it within the AD DS hierarchy.

Group Policy Containers

GPCs are objects that are defined within AD DS and are used to store the properties of GPOs, including attributes and version information. They contain subcontainers for user and computer Group Policy data. Information as to whether the GPO is enabled or disabled is also stored here.

Being stored in AD DS, computers can access GPCs to locate GPTs, and domain controllers can access them to obtain version information, which verifies that they have the most recent edition of GPOs. If not, they can use AD DS replication to obtain the latest version of the GPO from another domain controller.

You can view GPCs in Active Directory Users and Computers by using the following procedure:

Step 1.   Click **Start > Administrative Tools > Active Directory Users and Computers**.

Step 2.   In the View menu of Active Directory Users and Computers, select **Advanced Features**.

Step 3.   Expand your domain name and then expand the **System** folder.

Step 4.   Select the **Policies** node. The GUIDs of existing GPCs appear in the details pane, as shown in Figure 11-1.

Group Policy Templates

The GPT is a folder hierarchy composed of the GPT folder at the top and subfolders under it. This structure holds all the information for a given GPO.

Every domain has associated with it a folder hierarchy found in the domain controllers at the shared folder `%systemroot%\SYSVOL\sysvol\<domain_name>\Policies`. For example, the following shared folder:

```
C:\WINDOWS\SYSVOL\Sysvol\Que.com\Policies\{31B2F340-016D-11D2-945F-
00C04FB984F9}
```

Figure 11-1   You can view GPCs in Active Directory Users and Computers.

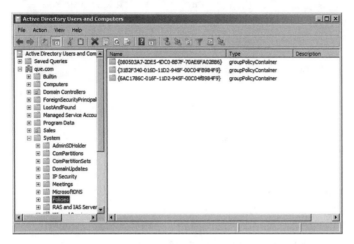

This container object holds policy settings for the various GPOs that have been created for that domain at any level. Subfolders are defined within this shared folder and named by the GUID of the GPO, as mentioned previously. Inside each GPT is a series of subfolders related to user and machine settings and administrative template files, and there are additional subfolders under them. Within the subfolders are text files named Registry.pol; these files are processed by Windows Server 2008 to apply changes to the Registry as a computer is started up and a user logs on. As with other components of SYSVOL, Windows Server 2008 uses Distributed File System (DFS) to replicate changes in the GPT to other domain controllers if the domain functional level is Windows Server 2008 or higher, or File Replication Service (FRS) to replicate SYSVOL if the domain functional level is Windows Server 2003 or lower.

The root of each GPT also contains a file called Gpt.ini. This file contains entries for the following parameters:

- **Version:** The version number is a variable that starts at 0 when the GPO is first created and increments by 1 each time it is modified. This number is used for replication purposes.

- **Disabled:** This parameter indicates whether a local GPO is enabled or disabled. Information for nonlocal GPOs is contained in a GPC within Active Directory.

NOTE   Besides the GPOs stored in AD DS, every computer has its own local GPO, which is stored on the local hard drive in the %systemroot%\system32\GroupPolicy folder on a 32-bit server or the %systemroot%\sysWOW64\GroupPolicy folder on a

64-bit server. Settings in this GPO apply to the computer on which it is configured only and are always overridden by any policy settings applied in AD DS. It is recommended that you not use these settings within a domain environment, except for standalone machines that do not belong to a domain, or specific settings that are required by one or two machines only.

New Features of Group Policy in Windows Server 2008 and Windows Server 2008 R2

Group Policy in Windows Server 2008 provides several new features, including the following:

- **Additional policy settings:** Microsoft has considerably expanded the areas that you can manage in Group Policy. Some categories you can now manage include blocking device installation, managing power settings, and controlling access to external devices. Settings on many additional categories have been enhanced, such as security settings, Internet Explorer settings, and location-based printer assignment. Windows Server 2008 R2 further expands the available Group Policy settings, including settings designed specifically for management of Windows 7 client computers as well as an improved Administrative Templates management interface and improvements to Group Policy preferences for configuration of components such as Internet Explorer 8, Scheduled Tasks, and Power Plans settings.

- **Exclusive use of the Group Policy Management Console (GPMC):** You can no longer access Group Policy from a container's Properties dialog box in Active Directory Users and Computers as was the case in previous Windows versions. GPMC is included by default in Windows Server 2008 and is the sole location of Group Policy management actions.

- **Comments for Group Policy settings:** Large organizations have many individuals responsible for policy administration. This feature enables you to document the purpose of policies and their settings for the benefit of others.

- **Use of ADMX format:** ADMX refers to Extensible Markup Language (XML)–based files. This is a new format that stores all configuration objects. It allows for language-neutral and language-specific resources. For example, you can configure Group Policy in the United States and a colleague in Germany can review your settings in German.

- **Network Location Awareness (NLA):** This improves the ability of Group Policy to respond to changes in network conditions. It provides more efficient startup times while a computer is waiting to access a domain controller and the capability to reapply a policy when a wireless network connection is created after the user has already logged on. It also improves the efficiency of deploying policy changes to mobile users across virtual private networks (VPNs).

In addition, Group Policy in Windows Server 2008 R2 adds additional Group Policy preference items and improvements to Starter GPOs. In Windows Server 2008 R2, you can also manage Group Policy using Windows PowerShell and you can run PowerShell scripts during startup and logon. A powerful new set of 25 cmdlets enables you to perform actions such as automation of policy application, backup, restore, and configuration of GPOs.

> **NOTE**   For additional details on new Group Policy features in Windows Server 2008 R2, refer to "What's New in Group Policy" at http://technet.microsoft.com/en-us/library/dd367853(WS.10).aspx. Further information on Group Policy as a whole and up-to-date team blogs and forums are available from "Group Policy" at http://technet.microsoft.com/en-us/windowsserver/bb310732.aspx.

Creating and Applying GPOs

You perform all Group Policy administrative activities, including creating, editing, and applying GPOs from the GPMC. First available for download with Windows Server 2003 R2, GPMC is included by default with Windows Server 2008 and is the sole location for managing all aspects of Group Policy. GPMC provides a simplified user interface for managing Group Policy in multisite, multidomain environments. It enables an administrator to back up, restore, copy, and import GPOs in these environments. You can create scripts to simplify the various management tasks. Key features of GPMC include the following:

- An advanced GUI that facilitates the use and management of Group Policy

- The ability to back up and restore GPOs

- The ability to copy, paste, import, and export GPOs and Windows Management Instrumentation (WMI) filters

- Enhanced management of security within Group Policy

- Enhanced reporting by means of HTML for policy settings as well as Resultant Set of Policy (RSoP) data

- The ability to script Group Policy–related tasks

Let's take a look at the GPMC and go through a sample procedure showing how you would create and link a new GPO:

Step 1.   Click **Start > Administrative Tools > Group Policy Management**. This opens the GPMC, which shows a node for your forest in the

console tree that you can expand to reveal subnodes for every domain with entries for each OU as well as a Group Policy Objects node.

Step 2. In the console tree, expand the **Group Policy Objects** node. You will notice two default GPOs: the Default Domain Policy and the Default Domain Controllers Policy. These are installed automatically when you create your domain. Policy settings that you define here are automatically applied to the entire domain and to the domain controllers, respectively.

Step 3. Select one of these policies. As shown in Figure 11-2, the details pane displays GPO properties and configuration options. Information includes the following tabs:

Figure 11-2 You perform all Group Policy management activities from the GPMC.

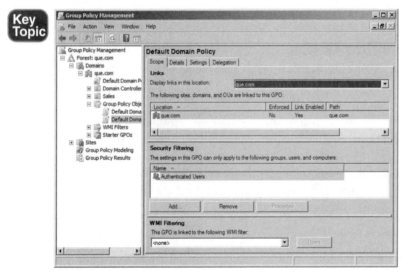

- **Scope:** Enables you to display GPO link information and configure security group filtering and WMI filtering.

- **Details:** Displays information on the owner, dates created and modified, version numbers, GUID value, and enabled status. The enabled status is the only configurable option on this tab.

- **Settings:** Enables you to display policy settings, as shown in Figure 11-3. You can expand and collapse nodes to locate information on any policy setting. Note that the settings shown here are configured for the Default Domain Policy GPO by default when you install AD DS.

Figure 11-3   The Settings tab of a GPO enables you to view configured policy settings.

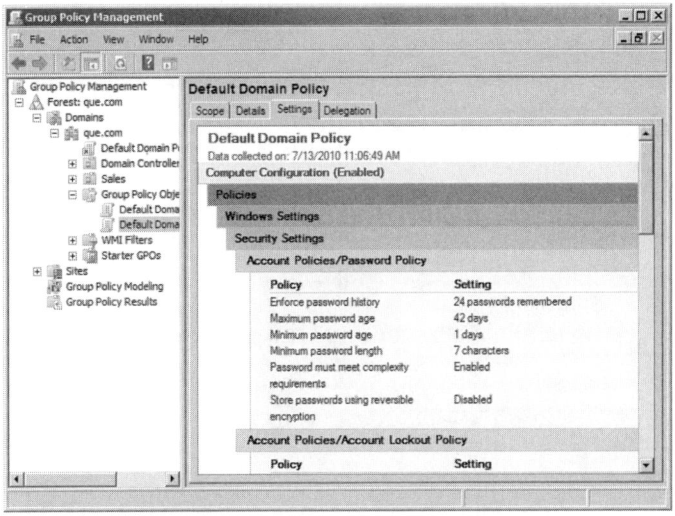

- **Delegation:** Enables you to view and modify GPO permissions.

Step 4.   To create and link a GPO to an OU, right-click the desired OU and select **Create a GPO in this domain, and Link it here**. This displays the New GPO dialog box, as shown in Figure 11-4.

Figure 11-4   The New GPO dialog box enables you to create and name a new GPO.

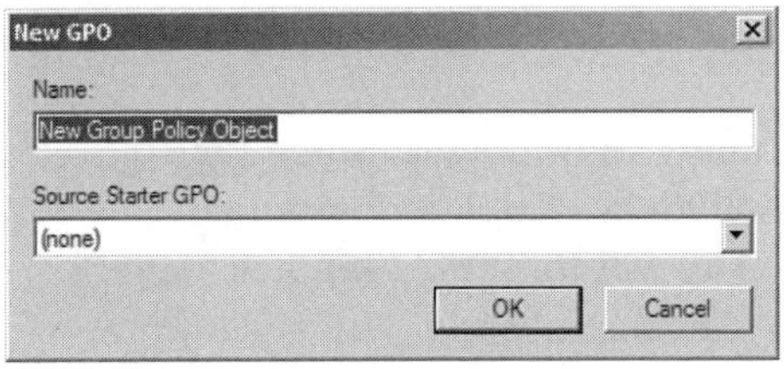

Step 5.   Type a suitable name for the GPO. If you have a Starter GPO that includes settings you want to include in the new GPO, type its name in the Source Starter GPO field and then click **OK**. The new GPO is added to the list in the console tree under the Group Policy Objects node.

Step 6.   To define policy settings for the new GPO, right-click it and choose **Edit**. This brings up the Group Policy Management Editor console, as shown in Figure 11-5. We will discuss the more significant policy settings you should be familiar with in the rest of this chapter and in Chapters 12, "Group Policy Software Deployment," and 13, "Account Policies and Audit Policies."

Figure 11-5   You can configure all policies associated with a GPO from the Group Policy Management Editor snap-in.

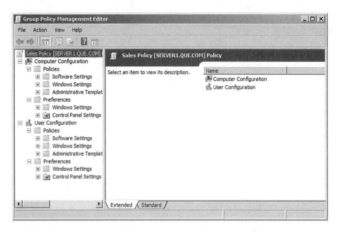

NOTE   The GPMC is installed when you install AD DS. You can also install the GPMC on a member server by accessing the Add Features Wizard in Server Manager. GPMC is also included in the Remote Server Administration Tools package, which you can install on a client computer running Windows 7 Professional or higher.

TIP   You can also access the GPMC directly from Server Manager, where it can be found under the Features node. In this case, it opens as a component snap-in within the Server Manager console.

The Group Policy Management Editor (formerly known as the Group Policy Object Editor) is where you perform all policy configuration actions for your GPO. Let's take a brief look at this tool here; we will cover many of the configuration activities later in this chapter and in Chapters 12 and 13. Table 11-2 describes its container structure.

Table 11-2   Group Policy Management Editor Container Structure

Component	Description
Root container	Defines the focus of the Group Policy Management Editor by showing the GPO being edited plus the fully qualified domain name (FQDN) of the domain controller from which you are working.
Computer Configuration	Contains all computer-specific policy settings. Remember that these settings are processed first when the computer starts up and before the user logs on.
User Configuration	Contains all user-specific policy settings. Remember that these settings are processed after the user logs on.

Table 11-2 Group Policy Management Editor Container Structure

Component	Description
Policies	Includes classic and new Group Policy settings for Software Settings, Windows Settings, and Administrative Templates.
Preferences	Include new Group Policy extensions that expand the range of configurable policy settings. Included are items such as folder options, mapped drives, printers, local users and groups, scheduled tasks, services, and Start menu settings. You can manage these items without using scripts.
Software Settings	A subcontainer found under both the Computer and User Configuration Policies containers that holds software installation settings for computers and users.
Windows Settings	A subcontainer found under both the Computer and User Configuration Policies and Preferences containers that holds script and security settings, plus other policy settings that affect the behavior of the Windows environment.
Administrative Templates	A subcontainer found under both the Computer and User Configuration Policies containers that holds most of the settings that control the appearance of the desktop environment. New to Windows Server 2008 is an All Settings subnode that provides a comprehensive list of all policy settings that you can sort according to name, state, comment, or path, or filter according to several criteria.
Control Panel Settings	A subcontainer found under both the Computer and User Configuration Preferences containers that holds most of the preferences settings related to Control Panel applets.

NOTE When you create a new GPO or edit an existing one, users affected by the GPO must log off and log back on again to receive the new settings in the User Configuration node. If you have configured new settings in the Computer Configuration node, users must reboot their computers to receive the new settings.

Managing GPOs

You have seen how to create a GPO. Now it's time to turn your attention to several additional activities that you should be aware of, including the following:

- Linking GPOs
- Managing GPO links
- Disabling and deleting GPOs

- ■ Delegating control of GPOs

- ■ Specifying a domain controller

In addition, Chapter 15, "Maintaining Active Directory," covers the backing up and restoring of GPOs.

Linking GPOs

The GPMC also enables you to create unlinked GPOs and link any GPO to other Active Directory containers. To create an unlinked GPO, right-click **Group Policy Objects** and choose **New**. You receive the same dialog box previously shown in Figure 11-4. The resulting GPO is not linked to any container.

To link this (or any other) GPO to a domain or OU, use the following steps:

Step 1.   Right-click the domain or OU in the console tree of the GPMC and choose **Link an Existing GPO**.

Step 2.   From the dialog box shown in Figure 11-6, choose the GPO that you want to link in this location, and then click **OK**.

Figure 11-6   Selecting a GPO for linking to a domain.

Linking a GPO to a site is similar. However, the Sites node in the GPMC does not show any sites by default. To include the available sites, right-click **Sites** and choose **Show Sites**. Then select the desired site and click **OK**. After you have done this, you can right-click the desired site and choose **Link an Existing GPO** to display the same dialog box previously shown in Figure 11-6.

Managing GPO Links

When you perform the procedure outlined in the previous section, you can link GPOs to multiple AD DS containers. This is perfectly acceptable; however, you might need to view the existing GPO links to keep track of them. You can do so by selecting the desired GPO under the Group Policy Objects node of the GPMC. As shown in Figure 11-7, the Links section of the GPO's properties shows the available links. In a multiple-domain environment, simply select the required domain from the drop-down list. To view links to sites, select **All Sites** from the drop-down list, and to view links to all sites and domains in the forest, select **Entire forest** from this list.

Figure 11-7   The Links section enables you to locate all sites, domains, and OUs to which a GPO is linked.

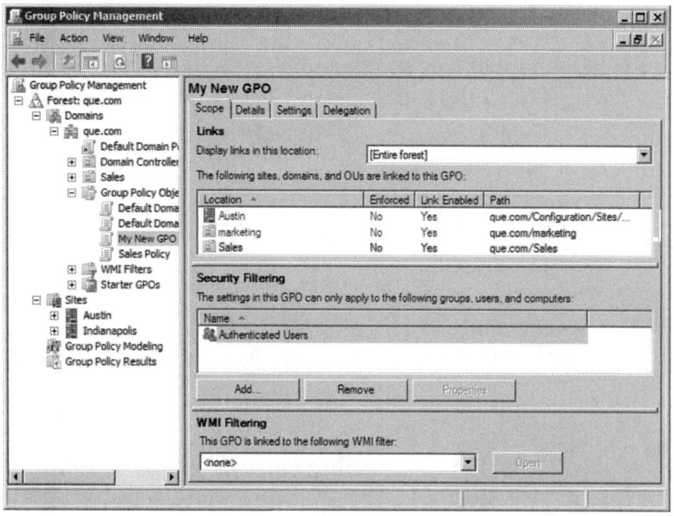

Should you need to delete a GPO link to test its effects or because the GPO is linked to the wrong AD DS container, you can delete the link. Expand the container from which you want to delete the link, right-click the desired GPO, and then choose **Delete** (or press the **Delete** key). Click **OK** in the dialog box shown in Figure 11-8 to confirm its deletion.

You can also disable a GPO link if you want to temporarily stop the GPO from applying to a site, domain, or OU. To do so, expand the site, domain, or OU in Group Policy Management Console to display the linked GPOs. Right-click the desired GPO and choose **Link Enabled**. This removes the check mark against this entry in the pop-up menu to indicate that the link is disabled. In addition, the Link Enabled column in the Scope tab of the GPO's Properties (refer back to Figure 11-7) will indicate No. To reenable the link, simply right-click the GPO and choose **Link Enabled** a second time. You will notice that the check mark is again present and the Link Enabled column will indicate Yes. You can also disable a GPO link from the Scope tab of the GPO's Properties in the details pane of GPMC as previously shown in Figure 11-7; right-click and choose **Link Enabled**. You will see a No entry in the Link Enabled column there.

Figure 11-8 Deleting a GPO link.

Deleting a GPO

You might want to delete a GPO completely if you no longer need its settings. To do so, select it from the Group Policy Objects node and press the **Delete** key. Then click **Yes** in the dialog box shown in Figure 11-9 to confirm its deletion.

Figure 11-9 Deleting a GPO.

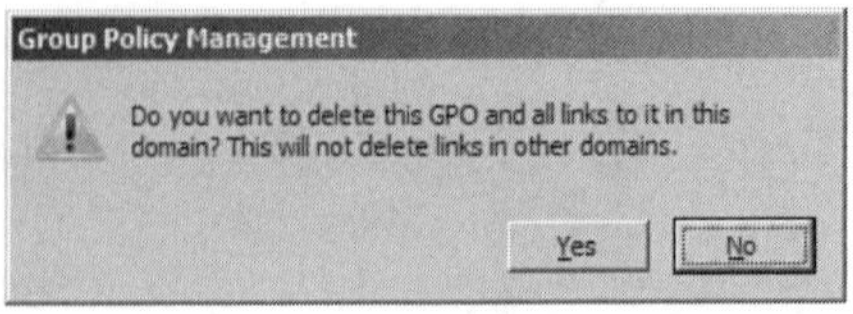

> **WARNING** Be sure you never need the GPO again before you delete it! There is no way to recover a deleted GPO. If you need it back, you must re-create it and all the policy settings contained within it. If you might want the GPO back, it is better to disable it or remove the links.

Delegating Control of GPOs

Chapter 9, "Active Directory User and Group Accounts," showed you how to delegate control of Active Directory objects to users and groups to enable partial administrative control and ease the overall burden of administration. By default, only members of the Domain Admins and Group Policy Creator Owners groups have permissions to create GPOs. You can extend this concept to the administration of GPOs. Several methods for performing this task are available. First, you can add the required user or group to the Group Policy Creator

Owners Group. This group has the right to create GPOs in any container by default.

To delegate the creation of GPOs to additional users or groups, select the **Group Policy Object** node from the console tree of GPMC. As shown in Figure 11-10, this tab displays a list of groups and users with permission to create GPOs in the domain.

Figure 11-10   The Delegation tab shows the users and groups that are granted permission to create GPOs.

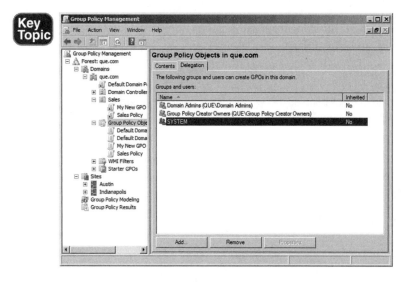

To add a user or group to this list, click **Add** and add the required user or group from the Select User, Computer, or Group dialog box that appears. To remove a user or group, select it and click **Remove**, and then click **OK** in the message box that appears.

You can also delegate control of specific GPOs to users or groups. Use the following procedure:

Step 1.   Expand the **Group Policy Object** node of the console tree in GPMC to reveal the available GPOs.

Step 2.   Select the required GPO to display information about this GPO in the details pane, and then click the **Delegation** tab to display the users and groups to which management of the GPO is delegated.

Step 3.   Click **Add** and add the required user or group from the Select User, Computer, or Group dialog box.

Step 4.   Select the required permissions from the list shown in the dialog box in Figure 11-11, and click **OK**.

Figure 11-11   You have a choice of three permissions when adding a user or group to the administrative delegation list of a GPO.

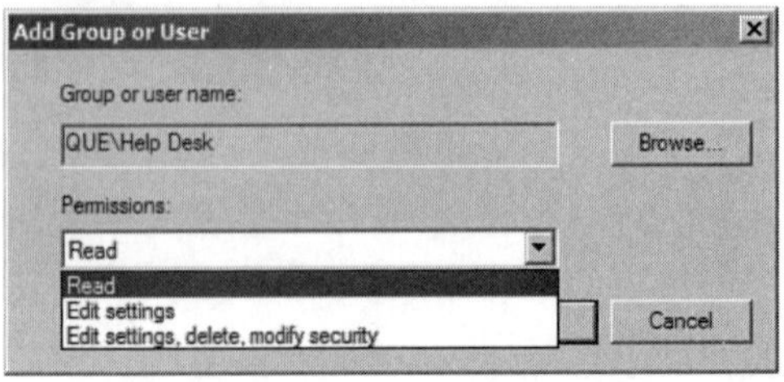

You can then modify the permissions or configure advanced permissions by clicking **Advanced** and specifying the required permissions from the Security Settings dialog box that is displayed.

NOTE   You can also use the Delegation of Control Wizard to delegate the task of managing Group Policy links for a site, domain, or OU. This enables the user to create or delete links to existing GPOs but not to create new GPOs or edit existing ones. You can also delegate the control of Group Policy Container objects from the list of custom tasks. This wizard was introduced in Chapter 9.

Specifying a Domain Controller

It is possible to edit a GPO from any writable domain controller, or even to connect to a writable domain controller from a client computer running Windows XP, Vista, or Windows 7. You might want to specify which domain controller you are working against for any of the following reasons:

- If multiple administrators are working on the same GPO from multiple machines, conflicting changes will be overwritten and lost.

- If you are working against a domain controller at a remote site, you might encounter slow performance, which can become frustrating. You can select a local domain controller to avoid this problem.

- If you are editing a GPO that is to be applied to users or computers at the remote site, it might be advantageous to work against the domain controller in the same site so that changes take effect immediately rather than waiting for replication to occur.

- To ensure that you are working against the PDC emulator. By default, AD DS defaults to this domain controller. However, you might want to change this if the PDC emulator is not readily available.

To select a domain controller, right-click your domain in GPMC and choose **Change Domain Controller**. Select an appropriate option from those provided by the Change Domain Controller dialog box shown in Figure 11-12. The selected domain controller saves your changes and replicates them to other domain controllers in the next AD DS replication.

Configuring GPO Hierarchy and Processing Priority

All GPOs except the local GPO are associated with, or linked to, some AD DS container, such as sites, domains, and OUs. Although it is possible to create an unlinked GPO, it is not applied until you link it to an AD DS container.

As already mentioned, each GPO contains both computer-specific and user-specific settings. Computer-specific settings are applied when the computer starts up and before the user logs on; user-specific settings are applied after the user logs on. Consequently, if any user-specific settings conflict with computer-specific settings, the user-specific settings override the computer-specific settings.

As shown in Figure 11-13, by default all GPOs are applied in the following well-defined order:

- The local (L) GPO is applied first.

Figure 11-12 You can specify which domain controller you are working against when editing a GPO.

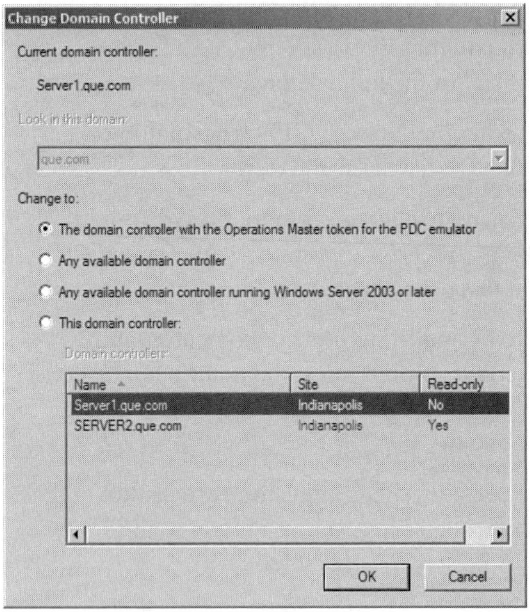

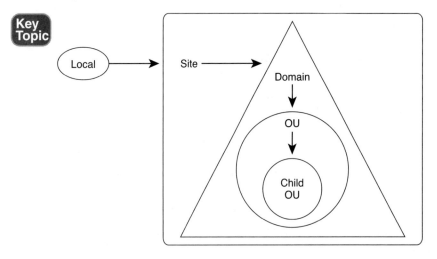

Figure 11-13 Group policies are applied in the local, site, domain, OU, and then child OU sequence.

Key Topic

- Site-based (S) GPOs are applied next, overriding any conflicting local policy settings.
- Domain-based (D) GPOs are applied next, overriding any conflicting local or site-based settings.

■ OU-based (OU) GPOs are applied last, overriding any conflicting local-, site-, or domain-based settings.

This sequence can be abbreviated as LSDOU. It is important to remember this sequence because it determines how GPOs with conflicting policy settings apply to both the user and the computer. Furthermore, because all computer-specific settings are applied before user logon and user-specific setting are applied after logon, any user-specific setting, even a local one, would override a conflicting computer-specific setting applied at any level.

> **TIP**   Keep the Group Policy processing order in mind, both for the 70-640 exam and for the real world. An exam question might present a sequence of conflicting policies and ask you which one is applicable in a given scenario. It is important that you remember the LSDOU sequence as well as the computer, then user, sequence.

OU Hierarchy

As you saw in Chapter 9, you can create a nested hierarchy of OUs. When more than one level of OU is present, policies linked to the parent OU are applied first, followed by child OUs in order. Consequently, the lowest-level OU policy becomes the determining factor should conflicts in the various GPOs arise.

Microsoft provides several controls that you can use to modify the default sequence of GPO application, as described in Table 11-3.

Key Topic

Table 11-3   Group Policy Controls

Policy Control	Description
Enforced	Enforces the application of policy settings, regardless of settings defined in lower-level GPOs.
Block Inheritance	Prevents the application of policy settings from containers higher in the LSDOU hierarchy.
Modifying the sequence of GPO application	Enables you to specify in which sequence multiple GPOs linked to the same AD DS container will be applied.
Enable/Disable	Enables you to selectively disable GPOs or portions of GPOs.

Enforced

Known as No Override prior to use of the GPMC, the Enforced setting is a method of altering the default policy inheritance behavior in Windows Server 2008. This option prevents policies contained in the GPO where it is specified from being overwritten by other GPOs that are processed later. For example, if you want to set up a domain desktop policy that applies to all domain users and do not want conflicting settings at the OU level to apply, you can configure this option from the Scope tab of a policy's properties as displayed in the details pane of the GPMC.

To specify the Enforced option, perform the following steps:

Step 1.   In the console tree of GPMC, expand the container on which you want to enforce a GPO to display all GPOs linked to this container.

Step 2.   Right-click the container where you want to enforce the policy and select **Enforced**.

Step 3.   As shown in Figure 11-14, the word Yes under Enforced informs you that this policy is now enforced.

Figure 11-14   An enforced policy is labeled **Yes** in the Enforced column within the Links section of the Scope tab of the GPO's Properties in the details pane of GPMC.

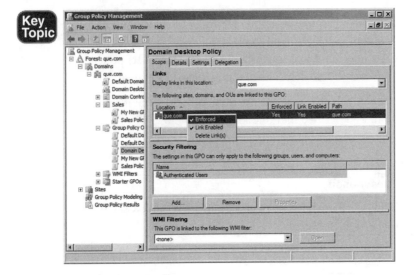

Note that you can specify the Enforced option for individual GPOs. This is useful in situations where you want to include critical corporatewide policies in a domain-based GPO that is to apply to all domain users, regardless of OU-based policies. You should link such a GPO high in the hierarchy, such as at a site or domain.

> **NOTE**   Note that the Enforced option applies to the link and not to the GPO itself. If the same GPO is linked to more than one AD DS container, it is possible for the GPO to be enforced on one link but not on another one.

Block Inheritance

Known as Block Policy Inheritance prior to use of the GPMC, the Block Inheritance setting enables you to prevent GPOs that are linked to parent containers from being applied at the lower level. A situation in which this might be useful is where the administrator of an OU wants to control all GPOs that apply to computers or users in the OU without inheriting settings from the site or parent domain.

To configure the Block Inheritance option, perform the following steps:

Step 1.   In the console tree of GPMC, right-click the domain or OU in the console tree of GPMC where you want to apply this setting and select **Block Inheritance**.

Step 2.   As shown in Figure 11-15, the icon for the container on which inheritance is blocked appears with a blue exclamation point icon. GPOs from containers higher in the application sequence no longer appear in the Group Policy Inheritance tab.

Figure 11-15   Configuring the Block Inheritance option.

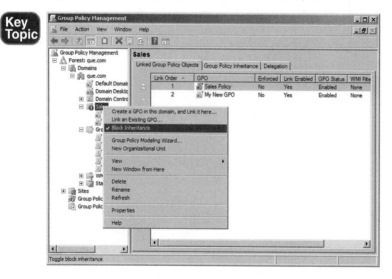

What happens if you have configured both the Block Inheritance and Enforced options at the same time? If a parent GPO is configured with the Enforced option, it overrides the application of Block Inheritance at a lower level. For example, if you have configured the Domain Desktop Policy GPO shown previously in Figure 11-14 with the Enforced option and then configure the Sales OU with Block Inheritance as shown in Figure 11-15, settings in the Domain Desktop Policy GPO still apply to users in the Sales OU.

TIP   Try to use the Enforced and Block Inheritance options sparingly. Their extensive use can make it extremely complex to troubleshoot policy application-related problems, especially as the size of your domain and the number of GPOs grow. We discuss the use of Group Policy Results to determine policy application in Chapter 14.

Modifying the Sequence of GPO Application

You have already seen the default LSDOU sequence that applies when process-ing GPOs linked to different types of Active Directory containers. But what happens if more than one GPO is linked to the same container? Consider the situation for the Sales OU as shown in Figure 11-16. The GPOs are applied in reverse order: bottom to top. Therefore, if settings conflict, those in the GPO highest in the order will prevail. In this example, it would be the Sales Policy. You can modify the sequence of policy application. Simply select the desired GPO and use the **Up** or **Down** buttons as needed.

Figure 11-16   You can use the Up and Down buttons provided to modify the sequence of GPO application.

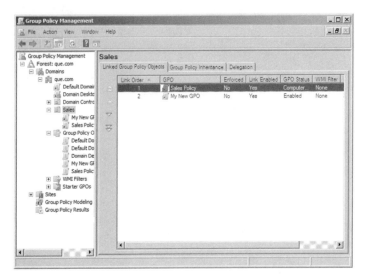

Disabling User Objects

When troubleshooting Group Policy problems, you might want to disable por-tions of a GPO. The Details tab of the GPO's properties in the details pane of the GPMC enables you to disable the entire GPO or the computer or user con-figuration settings. Select the desired option from the GPO Status drop-down list, as shown in Figure 11-17. The option you have applied is then indicated with a check mark. After you have completed policy troubleshooting, you can reenable the GPO from the same location.

Figure 11-17   From the GPO's Details tab, you can disable either the computer or user configuration portion of a GPO or the entire GPO.

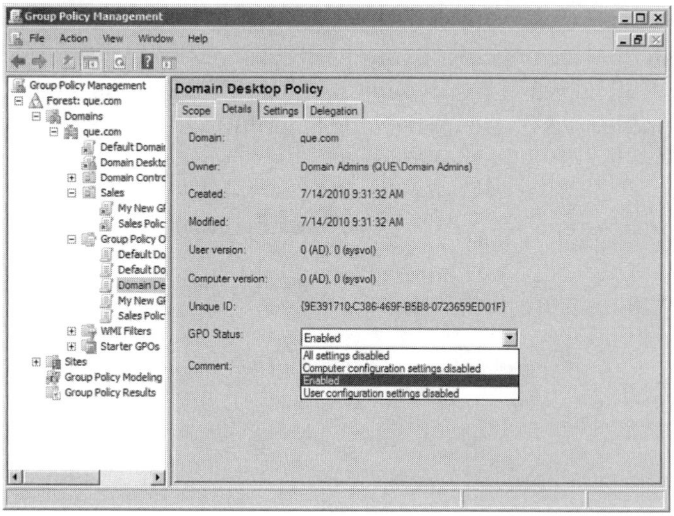

TIP   If a given GPO has no settings configured in one of the Computer Configuration or User Configuration branches, you can speed up policy processing by disabling that branch from this location.

Group Policy Filtering

The settings discussed earlier in this chapter provide you with powerful options for restricting the range of GPO applications according to the logical makeup of your AD DS forest. But what if you wanted to do more—for example, lock down the desktop settings of ordinary workers but at the same time provide the full range of applications and controls to others such as IT workers? Microsoft has provided the following two options for filtering the effect of Group Policy application:

- **Security Filtering:** Enables you to filter the application of a GPO according to a user or computer's membership in a security group

- **Windows Management Instrumentation (WMI):** Enables you to modify the scope of a GPO according to the attributes of destination computers

Security Filtering of GPOs

The Security Filtering section of the Scope tab of a GPO's properties (refer to Figure 11-7) displays the users, groups, and computers to which the GPO settings apply. These users, groups, and computers automatically have the Apply Group Policy permission granted to them. You can add additional users and groups to this list by using the **Add** button provided. To remove a user or group, select it and click **Remove**.

To filter the application of a GPO, select it in the console tree of GPMC and select the **Delegation** tab from its properties in the details pane. As shown in Figure 11-18, this tab lists all users and groups with specified permissions on the GPO. You can add or remove users or groups by using the **Add** and **Remove** buttons in the same way as described for the Scope tab.

Figure 11-18   The Delegation tab lists all users and groups with specified permissions on its GPO.

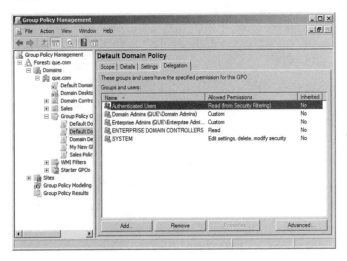

This location enables you to explicitly deny application of a GPO to certain groups. For example, you might want to lock down the desktops of all users except members of the Domain Admins group. To do this, you would deny the Apply Group Policy permission to this group. Use the following procedure:

Step 1.   From the Delegation tab, select the **Domain Admins** group from this tab and click **Advanced.**

Step 2.   On the Security Settings dialog box that appears, select the required group and deny the **Apply group policy** permission as shown in Figure 11-19.

Step 3.   Click **OK**. You are reminded that the Deny entry takes precedence over Allow entries, as shown in Figure 11-20.

Step 4.   Click **Yes** to accept this warning. The entry for this group under Allowed Permissions in the Delegation tab now states Custom to inform you that you have set a customized permission.

Figure 11-19   You can deny the application of a GPO to a given group by selecting the Deny entry for the Apply group policy permission.

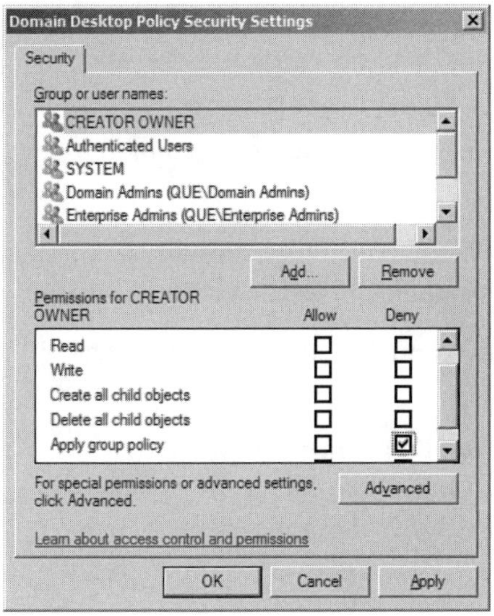

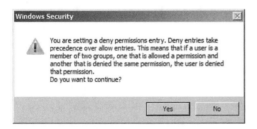

Figure 11-20   You are warned that the Deny entry takes precedence over Allow.

NOTE   The Properties button at the bottom of the Delegation tab previously shown in Figure 11-16 takes you to the same Properties dialog box for the group that we discussed in Chapter 9, enabling you to modify the membership of the group. For a user, you receive the dialog box previously shown in Figure 9-5.

Windows Management Instrumentation

First introduced with Windows XP and Windows Server 2003 and continuing with Windows Vista, Windows 7, and Windows Server 2008/R2, WMI filters enable an administrator to modify the scope of a GPO according to the attributes of destination computers.

WMI in Windows Server 2008/R2 provides several new features including the following:

- **Improved tracing and logging:** WMI uses Event Tracing for Windows, which enables the logging of WMI events available in Event Viewer.

- **Connection with User Account Control:** UAC now affects what WMI data is returned, remote access to WMI, and how WMI runs scripts.

- **Enhanced WMI namespace security and auditing:** You can now secure WMI namespace security in the Managed Object Format file. Further, WMI audits system access control lists (SACLs) and reports events to the Security event log.

The WMI Filters node in GPMC enables you to configure WMI filters. You can create new WMI filters and import filters from external locations at this location. These WMI filters are then available to any GPO in your forest. Use the Scope tab of a GPO's properties in GPMC to apply a WMI filter to the GPO.

TIP   You do not need to know how to write WMI filter queries for the 70-640 exam. However, you do need to know that WMI filters can query destination computers for hardware and other attributes. Also remember that Windows 2000 computers do not support WMI and always apply GPOs to the WMI filters that are linked.

NOTE   For more information on creating and applying WMI filters, refer to "Work with WMI Filters" at http://technet.microsoft.com/en-us/library/cc732796.aspx.

Windows PowerShell

In Windows Server 2008 R2, you can use Windows PowerShell cmdlets to automate many of the tasks already described for managing GPOs from GPMC. These include such tasks as creating GPOs and managing their links, setting permissions on GPOs, and modifying their processing and inheritance hierarchy. You can also back up, restore, and import GPOs using PowerShell. You can also write Windows PowerShell scripts and configure these scripts to run during startup, logon, logoff, or shutdown.

Windows Server 2008 R2 provides more than 20 Group Policy cmdlets to assist you in performing these actions. You must be working from a computer running Windows Server 2008 R2 or a Windows 7 computer on which the Remote Server Administration Tools (RSAT) have been installed. Before working with these cmdlets, you must import the Group Policy module. To do so, click **Start > All Programs > Accessories > Windows PowerShell > Windows PowerShell**. From the PowerShell command prompt, type `Import-Module GroupPolicy -verbose`. As shown in Figure 11-21, you receive a series of messages informing you that the cmdlets have been imported. You can now use them to perform most Group Policy management tasks.

Figure 11-21 Importing Group Policy management cmdlets in Windows PowerShell.

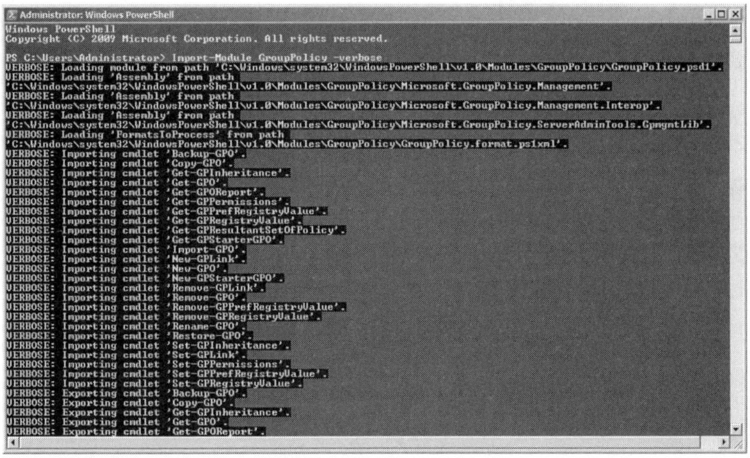

To learn how to use any cmdlet, type `Get-Help <cmdlet>` at the PowerShell command prompt. Use the `-detailed or -full` keywords to obtain additional information on the specified cmdlet.

NOTE For more information on using PowerShell to manage Group Policy, refer to "Use Windows PowerShell to Manage Group Policy" at http://technet.microsoft.com/en-us/library/dd759177.aspx.

To apply PowerShell scripts, open the Group Policy Management Editor focused on the desired GPO. For startup or shutdown scripts, expand the **Computer Configuration\Policies\Windows Settings\Scripts** node, and for logon or logoff scripts, expand the **User Configuration\Policies\Windows Settings\Scripts** node. In the details pane, right-click the desired script type and choose **Properties**. From the dialog box shown in Figure 11-22, you can perform the following actions:

Figure 11-22   Configuring the use of PowerShell scripts.

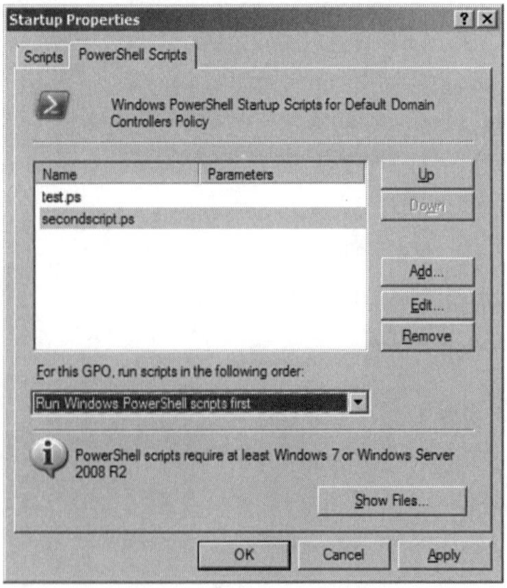

- **Add or remove scripts:** Click **Add** to add a script or select a script, and click **Remove** to remove it.

- **Replace a script:** Select a script and click **Edit**. From the dialog box that appears, you can type the name of a different script to be used.

- **Change the sequence of script processing:** Scripts are processed in the sequence displayed on the dialog box. Select a script and use the **Up** and **Down** buttons to change the sequence.

- **Change the processing order of PowerShell and other scripts:** The drop-down list enables you to run Windows PowerShell scripts either first or last.

Configuring GPO Templates

Microsoft has reworked the Administrative Templates format for Windows Server 2008 completely, replacing the previous ADM format with a new XML-based ADMX format. This format provides several new advantages, including the following:

- You can create a central ADMX store to hold these files; this store is accessible to anyone with the privilege of editing GPOs.

- Because they are stored in this location, they are no longer duplicated in in-dividual GPOs as they were with the old ADM format, thereby reducing the size of the SYSVOL folder.

- The files support multiple languages in the descriptive text associated with a GPO.

- They are backward-compatible with the older ADM files, so organizations with a large number of ADM files do not need to convert them to ADMX.

You can work with either the older ADM files or ADMX in Windows Server 2008 Group Policy. However, ADMX files work with Windows Vista, Windows 7, and Windows Server 2008 only and can be managed from computers running these operating systems only.

Group Policy Loopback Processing

As already stated, the normal behavior of Group Policy is to apply computer settings when the computer starts up, followed by user settings when the user logs on. In certain cases, it might be undesirable for the settings to be applied when the user is logging on to a particular computer. For example, your organi-zation might have kiosk computers located in its lobby for public access. If users occasionally log on to these computers, it would be undesirable for certain user settings to be applied that are used when they log on to their corporate work-stations. Likewise, administrators might receive certain settings such as assigned software that are appropriate to their workstations but not appropriate when they log on to a domain controller.

Microsoft provides the *loopback processing mode* to handle situations of this kind. This setting causes affected computers to apply only the set of computer-based GPOs to any user who logs on to these computers. You have the choice of the following two modes of loopback processing:

- **Merge:** Combines user-specific and computer-specific settings, but allows computer-specific settings to override user-specific ones. For example, if a user in the Sales OU logs on to a computer in the Kiosk OU, the settings for the two OUs are merged. If a conflict occurs, the settings for the computer-specific policy (in this case, the Kiosk OU) prevail.

- **Replace:** Replaces user-specific policy settings with the list already obtained for the computer (for example here, the Kiosk OU policy settings). Here, the user-based settings that would normally apply to the user (in this case, the Sales OU) are disregarded.

To enable loopback processing, open the Group Policy Management Editor fo-cused on the required GPO. Navigate to the **Computer Configuration\Policies\ Administrative Templates\System\Group Policy** node, right-click the

User Group Policy Loopback Processing Mode policy, and choose **Edit**. Select **Enabled** from the Properties dialog box shown in Figure 11-23, select either **Replace** or **Merge** from the drop-down list, and then click **OK**.

Figure 11-23   Configuring Group Policy loopback processing.

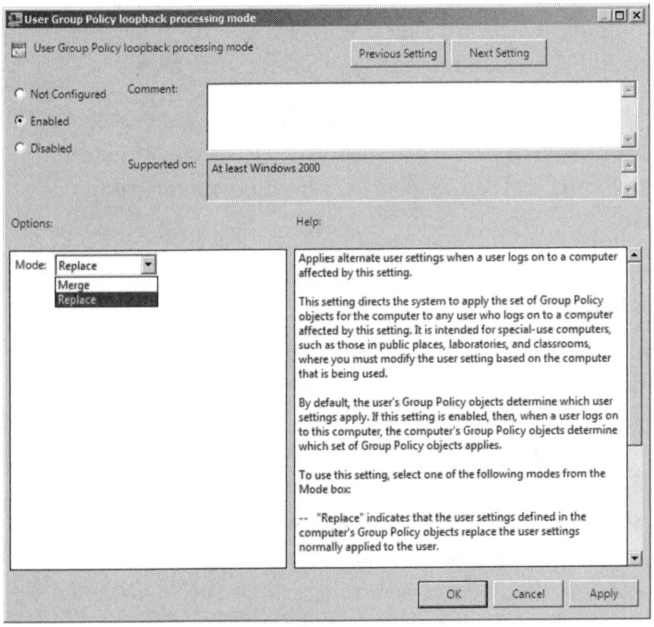

User Rights

User rights are defined as a default set of capabilities assigned to built-in domain local groups that define what members of these groups can and cannot do on the network. They consist of privileges and logon rights.

You can manage these predefined user rights from the Computer Configuration\ Policies\Windows Settings\Security Settings\Local Policies\User Rights Assignment node in the Group Policy Management Editor. When focused on the Default Domain Controllers Policy GPO, you can view the default rights assignments, as shown in Figure 11-24. To modify the assignment of any right, right-click it and choose **Properties**. In the Properties dialog box, click **Add User or Group**, and in the Add User or Group dialog box, type or browse to the required user or group. Then click **OK**.

You can also create a new GPO and configure a series of settings in this node to be applied to a specific group, and then link the GPO to an appropriate OU and grant the required group the Read and Apply Group Policy permissions. This is an easy way to grant user rights over a subset of the domain to a junior group of employees such as help desk technicians.

Figure 11-24   The Default Domain Controllers Policy GPO includes an extensive set of predefined user rights assignments.

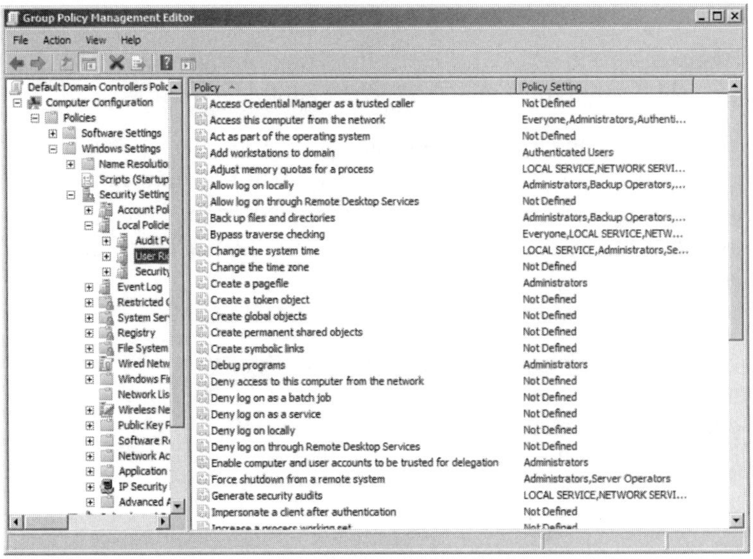

ADMX Central Store

When you are administering domain-based GPOs, you can use the ADMX central store, which is the new storage location that considerably reduces the quantity of storage space required for GPO maintenance, especially in a large domain with many OUs and many linked GPOs.

The central store is not available by default; you must create it in order that the GPOs you are working with can access the same set of ADMX files. It is a folder structure within the SYSVOL folder on the domain controllers in each domain of your forest. It contains a root-level folder with all language-neutral ADMX files plus subfolders that contain the language-specific ADML resource files.

To create the central store and populate it with ADMX files, perform the following steps:

Step 1.   In Windows Explorer, navigate to `%systemroot%\sysvol\domain\Policies` and create a subfolder named `PolicyDefinitions`.

Step 2.   Create a subfolder within `PolicyDefinitions` for each language used in your organization; for example, `EN-US` for U.S.-based English, `FR-CA` for Canadian French, or `ES` for Spanish.

Step 3.   Copy language-neutral ADMX files from `%systemroot%\PolicyDefinitions` to the subfolder you created in step 1.

Step 4.   Copy language-specific ADML files from the appropriate subfolder in the same location to the language-specific subfolder.

After you have performed this procedure, the Group Policy Management Editor will automatically read all ADMX files from the central store of the domain in which the GPO was created. You have to perform this procedure only once for each domain; Active Directory replication will automatically propagate the central store and its contents to all other domain controllers.

> **TIP**   Microsoft provides the downloadable ADMX Migrator Tool that enables you to convert existing ADM files to ADMX or to edit existing ADMX files. This tool is available from http://www.microsoft.com/downloads/details.aspx?FamilyId=0F1EEC3D-10C4-4B5F-9625-97C2F731090C&displaylang=en.

> **NOTE**   For more information on language-neutral ADMX and language-specific ADML files, refer to "ADMX Technology Review" at http://technet.microsoft.com/en-us/library/cc749513(WS.10).aspx. For additional general information on ADMX, refer to "Managing Group Policy ADMX Files Step-by-Step Guide" at http://technet.microsoft.com/en-us/library/cc709647(WS.10).aspx.

Administrative Templates

Administrative templates (both the older ADM files and the newer ADMX files) provide the principal means of administering the user environment and controlling the end-user interface. You can use administrative templates to deny access to certain functions of the operating system (for example, the capability to install or remove software) or to define settings that affect a user's computing experience (for example, desktop wallpaper or screen savers). These become a part of the GPO in which you configure them, and they are automatically applied to all computers and users within the scope of influence of this GPO.

You can configure Administrative Templates sections within either the Computer Configuration or User Configuration sections of the GPO. Some policy settings are available in both sections, and the section you choose when applying them determines whether they apply to the computer regardless of who is logged on or to the user regardless of which computer he/she is logged on to.

Table 11-4 summarizes the types of settings available in the Administrative Templates nodes of Computer Configuration and User Configuration.

Table 11-4   Groups of Administrative Templates Settings

Setting	What You Can Control	Applied To
Control Panel	Part or all of the Control Panel settings. This capability is useful in the corporate environment, where many help desk calls come from users who have experimented with settings in Control Panel. You can restrict or prevent users from installing unauthorized or pirated software and limit the extent to which users can modify the display appearance including wallpaper, screen saver, and so on. You can also show or hide specified applets; control the users' ability to add, delete, and search for printers; and restrict the language selection used for Windows menus and dialog boxes.	Computers and Users
Desktop	What is seen or not seen on the user's desktop. These items include many of the ones that are configurable in Start menu and taskbar, such as Documents and Network Locations. You can also configure options that pertain to the Active Desktop enhancements and options that pertain to the size and refinement of Active Directory searches.	Users
Network	Behavior of offline files, network connections, and several other networking parameters. Network connection settings specify how Windows Firewall functions, including allowed actions in domain and standard profiles. Different settings are available in the Computer Configuration and User Configuration containers.	Computers and Users
Printers	The publication of printers in Active Directory, including web-based printing. You can prevent users from adding or deleting printers. You can also control the directory pruning service, which checks the operational status of printers on the network.	Computers
Shared Folders	Whether users can publish shared folders and Distributed File System (DFS) roots.	Users

Table 11-4   Groups of Administrative Templates Settings

Setting	What You Can Control	Applied To
Start Menu and Taskbar	What is seen or not seen on the user's Start menu and taskbar. You can hide items that you do not want users to have available, such as the Search command, the Run command, the Documents, Pictures, Music, Network icons, and so on. You can also remove sub-menus from the Start menu and gray out un-available Windows Installer Start menu shortcuts.	Users
System	A large range of system functions, including group policy itself. Logon policies determine how scripts are processed, the effect of slow links, and so on. You can control the installa-tion of external devices and their drivers by users and control read and write access to re-movable storage devices. You can control how power management and sleep mode settings are specified on computers. You can restrict access to specified Windows applications and disable users' ability to run Registry editing tools such as Regedit.	Computers and Users
Windows Components	Components such as Internet Explorer, Windows Explorer, Microsoft Management Console, BitLocker Drive Encryption, Task Scheduler, Terminal Services, Windows Installer, Windows Messenger, Windows Media Player, and Windows Update. You can control the behavior of these programs—from what functionality is available to the user to configuring an application's features.	Computers and Users

Although settings in these nodes keep inexperienced users from poking around in places you would rather not have them access, users can access these items by other means. If the users can access a command prompt, they can run many of these components. However, by hiding items such as the Network and Sharing

Center and its associated tasks such as View Computers and Devices, you can make it difficult for users to explore servers just for the fun of seeing what they can find.

To configure a policy in the Administrative Templates folder, right-click it and choose **Edit**. From the policy's Properties dialog box as shown in Figure 11-25, select one of the following three options:

Figure 11-25 The Hide specified Control Panel items Properties dialog box in Windows Server 2008 R2.

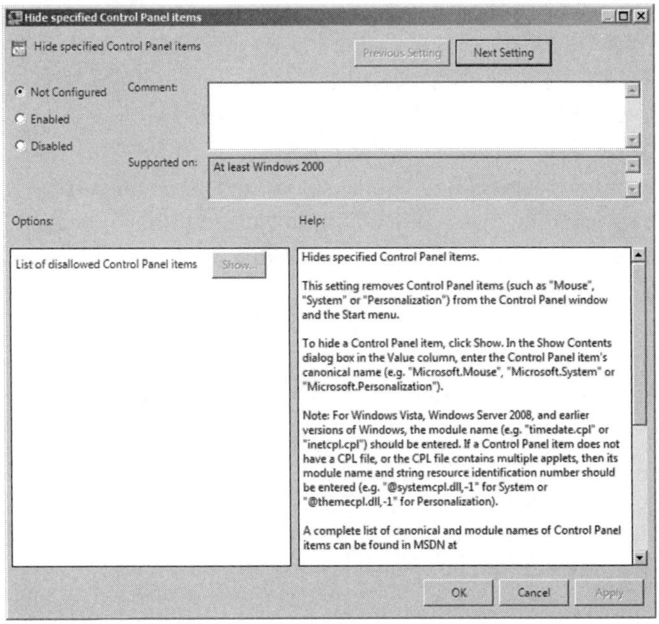

- **Not Configured:** This default setting does not modify the Registry and permits any other setting from a higher-level GPO to remain applied.

- **Enabled:** This setting modifies the Registry to specify that the setting is enabled.

- **Disabled:** This setting modifies the Registry to specify that the setting is disabled.

In Windows Server 2008 R2, each policy setting's Properties dialog box contains two additional fields (these appeared as tabs in the Properties dialog box of the original version of Windows Server 2008):

- **Help:** Provides a description that assists you in selecting the policies to be applied.

- **Comment:** Enables you to type a descriptive comment of your choice. From here you can inform other administrators of facts such as when and why you enabled this policy, and so on.

NOTE For more information on improvements to Administrative Template settings in Windows Server 2008 R2, refer to "Administrative Template Settings" at http://tinyurl.com/2wd5hhs and "Group Policy Settings Reference for Windows and Windows Server" at http://tinyurl.com/nbk7zc.

A TYPICAL POLICY APPLICATION SCENARIO

Let's suppose that you are the network administrator for a large retail department store chain. You are setting up a system of computers that customers can use to search the store's large online catalog and order merchandise. Credit cards are processed and merchandise is shipped directly to the customers.

In such an environment, customers are accessing your network and you would not want them to alter the operating system or the user environment in any fashion. So, you would lock down components such as Start menu and taskbar, desktop, and Control Panel from their User Configuration subnodes to prevent changes from being made. You would disable the Control Panel, remove the Run line from the Start menu, hide all desktop icons, and prevent users from saving changes upon exiting. In addition, you would use settings under the System node in both Computer Configuration and User Configuration to disable Registry editing so that a savvy customer couldn't circumvent your policy settings by disabling them in the Registry; you would also disable the command prompt so that he couldn't execute programs from this location. By configuring all these settings and others, you can essentially lock down the user environment, which is what you would want in this type of scenario.

Restricted Groups

The Restricted Groups node, available under Computer Configuration\Policies\
Windows Settings\Security Settings, enables you to specify who (user or group) can be a member of a group and which groups each group can belong to. Such groups can include local groups on member servers or client computers, such as the local Administrators group. For example, you can specify which users or groups can be members of the local Administrators group on all member servers and client computers affected by the GPO so that local users cannot make themselves administrators of their computers. If any other members have been specified for a restricted group, they are removed when the policy applies. It is reapplied each time Group Policy is refreshed, which is every 5 minutes for domain controllers and every 90 minutes for member servers and client computers.

To specify a restricted group, perform the following steps:

Step 1.   Open the Group Policy Management Editor focused on the appropriate GPO.

Step 2.   Navigate to the **Computer Configuration\Policies\Windows Settings\Security Settings** node, right-click **Restricted Groups**, and then choose **Add Group**.

Step 3.   Specify the group to be restricted and click **OK**.

Step 4.   In the dialog box shown in Figure 11-26, click **Add** under **Members of this group** and specify the members to be added as shown, separating multiple entries with semicolons. Then click **OK**. These members appear in the Members of this group section of the dialog box.

Figure 11-26   Restricting the membership of the local Administrators group.

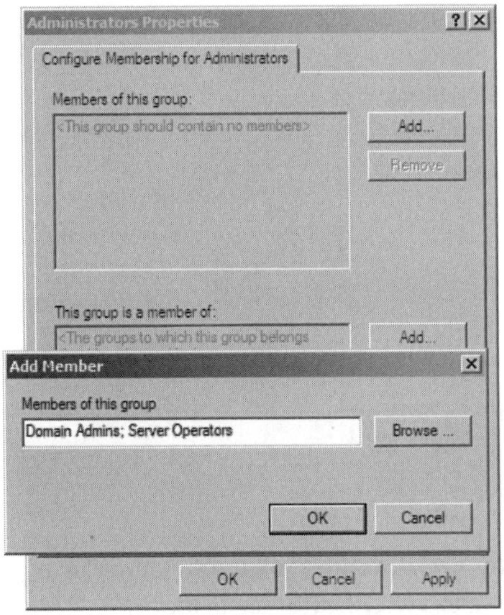

Step 5.   To specify a group that the restricted group can belong to, click **Add** under **This group is a member of** and type the name of the required group.

Step 6.   Click **OK**. The restricted group name and its membership appear in the details pane of the Group Policy Management Editor.

Starter GPOs

Another new feature in Windows Server 2008 Group Policy is the ability to create *Starter GPOs*. These are sets of preconfigured Administrative Templates policy settings, including comments, which you can use for ease of creating new

GPOs. When you use a Starter GPO to create a new GPO, the new GPO includes all settings, their values, comments, and delegation as defined in the Starter GPO. They also enable you to import and export them to other environments such as additional domains in the forest or a trusted forest.

To create a Starter GPO, perform the following steps:

Step 1.   In GPMC, right-click the **Starter GPOs** folder and choose **New**.

Step 2.   In the New Starter GPO dialog box, type a name and optional comment and then click **OK**. This adds the Starter GPO to this folder, as shown in Figure 11-27.

Figure 11-27   Starter GPOs are stored in the Starter GPOs folder and available for use in creating new GPOs.

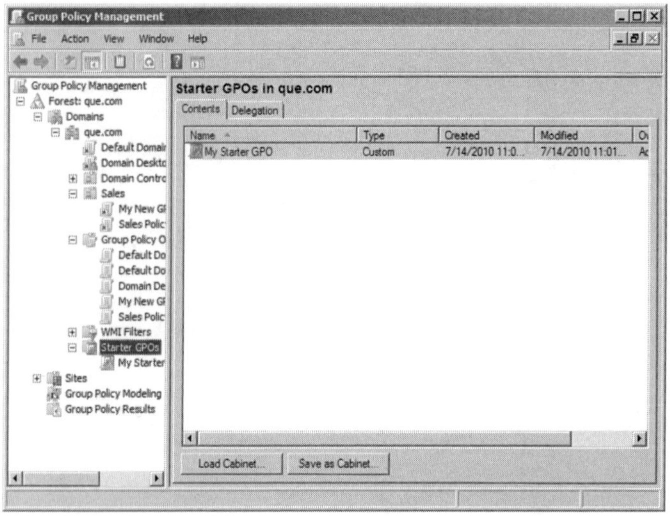

Step 3.   To configure settings in this Starter GPO, right-click it and choose **Edit** to open the Group Policy Starter GPO Editor snap-in.

Step 4.   Configure the required settings. This tool works the same way as the Group Policy Management Editor, except that only the Administrative Templates folder is available under both Computer Configuration and User Configuration.

The settings and their comments that you configure here are incorporated into all GPOs that you create later from this Starter GPO.

You can also perform the following tasks with Starter GPOs:

■   **Delegate the action of creating Starter GPOs:** Select the **Delegation** tab. Then click **Add** to add a user or group with the ability to create additional Starter GPOs in the domain.

- **Export for use elsewhere in the forest or another forest:** Click **Save as Cabinet** and specify a location to save the set of Starter GPOs.

- **Import GPOs from another forest:** Click **Load Cabinet**, and in the Load Starter GPO dialog box that appears, click **Browse for CAB** to locate and import the desired file.

After you have created a Starter GPO, you can use this GPO to create new GPOs. To do so, right-click the required site, domain, or OU and choose **Create a GPO in this domain, and link it here**, or right-click the **Group Policy Objects** container and choose **New**. In the New GPO dialog box previously shown in Figure 11-4, select the Starter GPO from the Source Starter GPO drop-down list and click **OK**. You can now use the Group Policy Management Editor on this GPO to add any additional required settings.

> **TIP**   Remember the proper method of applying a Starter GPO. You can create another GPO that is linked to an AD DS object, but you cannot directly link a Starter GPO to an AD DS object, as an exam answer choice might suggest.

Shell Access Policies

The shell can be thought of as the command interpreter that passes commands to the operating system. It is a separate software program that works from the nongraphical command prompt interface. Using this, a knowledgeable user can often circumvent restrictive policy settings by entering the corresponding command from the command prompt.

To prevent users from accessing the command prompt, open an appropriate GPO in the Group Policy Management Editor and navigate to the **User Configuration\Policies\Administrative Templates\System** node, right-click **Prevent Access to the Command Prompt**, and choose **Edit**. From the dialog box shown in Figure 11-28, enable this setting and select an appropriate option for the **Disable the command prompt script processing also?** setting:

- If you select **Yes**, no scripts can be run. This prevents the user from running batch files but also prevents any logon, logoff, startup, or shutdown scripts from running even if these have been configured in Group Policy to run.

- If you select **No**, logon, logoff, startup, or shutdown scripts can run but the user might be able to execute script files from within a program window.

Figure 11-28   Disabling access to the command prompt.

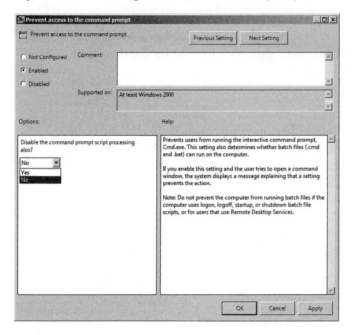

Review All the Key Topics

Review the most important topics in the chapter, noted with the key topics icon in the outer margin of the page. Table 11-5 lists a reference of these key topics and the page numbers on which each is found.

Table 11-5   Key Topics for Chapter 11

Key Topic Element	Description	Page Number
Paragraph	Describes the components of Group Policy	351
List	Describes how to create a GPO	355
Figure 11-2	Introduces the Group Policy Management Console and shows its main features	356
Table 11-2	Describes the components of the Group Policy Management Editor snap-in	358
Figure 11-7	Shows how to manage GPO links	361
Figure 11-10	Shows the process of delegating control of GPOs to users or groups	363
Figure 11-13	Illustrates the default sequence in which GPOs are applied	366
Table 11-3	Summarizes the available controls you can use for modifying the GPO processing sequence	367
Figure 11-14	Shows how to configure the Enforced option	368
Figure 11-15	Shows how to configure the Block Inheritance option	369
Figure 11-19	Shows how to deny processing of a GPO to a security group	373
Figure 11-23	Shows how to configure GPO loopback processing	378
Figure 11-25	Enabling and configuring an Administrative Templates GPO	383
List	Describes how to create and configure a Starter GPO	384

Complete the Tables and Lists from Memory

Print a copy of Appendix C, "Memory Tables" (found on the CD), or at least the section for this chapter, and complete the tables and lists from memory. Appendix D, "Memory Tables Answer Key," also on the CD, includes completed tables and lists to check your work.

Definitions of Key Terms

Define the following key terms from this chapter, and check your answers in the glossary.

ADMX central store, administrative templates, block inheritance, enforced, filtering, Group Policy, Group Policy object (GPO), Group Policy Management Editor, Group Policy Management Console (GPMC), inheritance, linked policy, loopback processing, Starter GPOs, Windows Management Instrumentation (WMI)

This chapter covers the following subjects:

- **Types of Software Deployment:** This section introduces the benefits of using Group Policy to deploy software and describes the methods you can use for software deployment.

- **Deploying Software Using Group Policy:** This section shows you how to use Group Policy to deploy software and explains the various options available that affect software deployment as a whole, as well as those that affect deployment of a specific software package.

- **Upgrading Software:** Software developers introduce upgrades from time to time that provide new functionality or solve problems related to bugs or security issues. This section shows you how to provide these upgrades to software packages that you have already deployed using Group Policy.

- **Removal of Software:** All software packages eventually become out of date, and Group Policy provides two options for removing outdated software. This section shows you how you can allow users to continue using the software or you can immediately remove the software from affected computers without giving the users an option to keep it.

CHAPTER 12

Group Policy Software Deployment

In Chapter 11, "Creating and Applying Group Policy Objects," you learned the nuts and bolts of Group Policy and how you can use Group Policy to control the working environment applied to users and computers in your Active Directory Domain Services (AD DS) network. Now you learn about how you can use Group Policy to ensure that users have the software they need to perform their job tasks efficiently and properly. You also learn how to ensure that users have the most up-to-date versions of their software and that old software no longer required for their job functions is promptly removed from their computers.

Before Windows 2000, the deployment or upgrading of software packages was a heavy burden on the shoulders of network administrators. It used to be that you had to go to each computer with the installation disks and manually install the application or update. Resources were available to assist you, including Microsoft's Systems Management Server (SMS) and third-party packages, but they were difficult to use and often did not accomplish the task properly.

Beginning in Windows 2000 and continuing with the newer Windows Server versions up to and including Windows Server 2008 R2, Microsoft introduced Software Installation and Maintenance, which enables you to manage the installation, configuration, updating, repair, and removal of software on client computers in your organization. In addition to applications, this includes other types of software such as service packs and hotfixes. To manage these tasks, you configure Group Policy settings that specify which applications users can employ and how software updates are managed. This enables users to have the applications they need to do their jobs without visits from support staff for installation and configuration purposes.

"Do I Know This Already?" Quiz

The "Do I Know This Already?" quiz enables you to assess whether you should read this entire chapter or simply jump to the "Exam Preparation Tasks" section for review. If you are in doubt, read the entire chapter. Table 12-1 outlines the major headings in this chapter and the corresponding "Do I Know This Already?" quiz questions. You can find the answers in Appendix A, "Answers to the 'Do I Know This Already?' Quizzes."

Table 12-1   "Do I Know This Already?" Foundation Topics Section-to-Question
Mapping

Foundations Topics Section	Questions Covered in This Section
Types of Software Deployment	1–3
Deploying Software Using Group Policy	4–6
Upgrading Software	7–9
Removal of Software	10

1. Which of the following is *not* a valid means of deploying software by means of Group Policy?

   a. Assigning software to users

   b. Assigning software to computers

   c. Publishing software to users

   d. Publishing software to computers

2. Which of the following are true when you assign a software package to computers by using Group Policy? (Choose all that apply.)

   a. The software is installed when a user selects it from the Start menu or double-clicks an associated document file.

   b. The software package is not advertised on the Start menu; the user must access Control Panel Add or Remove Programs to install it.

   c. The software is installed when a user reboots her computer.

   d. If a component of the software is deleted or becomes corrupted, it is reinstalled automatically.

   e. The software is available at any computer in the domain that the user might access.

3. Which of the following are true when you publish a software package to users by using Group Policy? (Choose all that apply.)

   a. The software is installed when a user selects it from the Start menu or double-clicks an associated document file.

   b. The software package is not advertised on the Start menu; the user must access Control Panel Add or Remove Programs to install it.

   c. The software is installed when a user reboots her computer.

   d. If a component of the software is deleted or becomes corrupted, it is reinstalled automatically.

  e. The software is available at any computer in the domain that the user might access.

4. Your company has hired a private developer to create a new inventory application that will be deployed using Group Policy to users in the AD DS domain. The developer did not provide an `.msi` file when he was creating the application. What type of file should you use to facilitate deployment of this package?

  a. An `.mst` file

  b. An `.msp` file

  c. A `.zap` file

  d. An `.exe` file

5. You have received several complaints from users during software deployment that they receive all sorts of dialog boxes and message boxes during software installation. They report that they need to click **OK** several times to complete software installation. What should you do to prevent this from occurring when you are deploying other software packages via Group Policy?

  a. Select the **General** tab of the Software installation Properties dialog box. From the Installation user interface options section, select the **Basic** option.

  b. Select the **General** tab of the Software installation Properties dialog box. From the Installation user interface options section, select the **Maximum** option.

  c. Select the **Deployment** tab of the Software installation Properties dialog box. From the Installation user interface options section, select the **Basic** option.

  d. Select the **Deployment** tab of the Software installation Properties dialog box. From the Installation user interface options section, select the **Maximum** option.

6. You are responsible for software deployment in your company's AD DS domain. A user named Phil is transferring from the Marketing department to the Design department. Each department is represented by an OU in the domain structure, and each OU has a GPO that assigns specific applications to users in its department. You have transferred Phil's user account from the Marketing OU to the Design OU.

Although Phil has transferred to his new department, he still needs applications from the Marketing department retained on his laptop computer so that he can complete several outstanding tasks from his previous position. Other users in the Design department should not have access to these applications. What should you do to ensure that he still has access to these applications?

  a. Add Phil's user account to a group in the Marketing OU that has privileges for the software packages that he requires.

b. From the Deployment tab of the applications required by Phil, ensure that the **Uninstall the applications when they fall out of the scope of management** option is cleared.

c. From the Security tab of the applications required by Phil, add Phil's user account and allow the **Read** and **Read & Execute** permissions.

d. Link the GPO that deploys the applications required by Phil to the Design OU.

7. Users in your company's Graphics department have been using Adobe Photoshop CS4 for a couple of years. You now want to upgrade to Adobe Photoshop CS5, but you want to ensure that users of Photoshop do not lose their preferences or plug-ins during the upgrade. What should you do?

a. From the Add Upgrade Package dialog box, select the **Uninstall the existing package, then install the upgrade package** option.

b. From the Add Upgrade Package dialog box, select the **Package can upgrade over the existing package** option.

c. From the Upgrades tab of the software's Properties dialog box, clear the **Required upgrade for existing packages** check box.

d. Package each user's preferences and plug-ins into a transformation file with the `.mst` extension, and include this file when performing the upgrade.

8. Your company does business in several foreign countries, and you are in the midst of deploying Microsoft Office 2010 to all users at all locations. You want to ensure that everyone has access to a localized version of Office with the required languages always available. What should you do?

a. Create multiple GPOs linked to the various AD DS sites. Deploy a different version of Microsoft Office 2010 to each site as required.

b. Use a single GPO linked to the domain to deploy Microsoft Office 2010. Use `.zap` files with pointers to the required language packs to apply these packs where they are required.

c. Use a single GPO linked to the domain to deploy Microsoft Office 2010. Use patch files with the `.msp` extension to apply the required language packs in the locations where they are required.

d. Use a single GPO linked to the domain to deploy Microsoft Office 2010. Use transform files with the `.mst` extension to apply the required language packs in the locations where they are required.

9. You have received several patches and hotfixes for an application used by employees of your company's Engineering department. You want to ensure that all users in this department receive these patches and hotfixes the next time they reboot and log on to their computers. What should you do?

   a. From the Group Policy Management Editor focused on the GPO deploying the application, right-click the application and choose **All Tasks > Redeploy application.**

   b. From the Upgrades tab of the application's Properties dialog box, select the **Uninstall the existing package, then install the upgrade package** option.

   c. From the Upgrades tab of the application's Properties dialog box, select the **Package can upgrade over the existing package** option.

   d. From the Upgrades tab of the application's Properties dialog box, select the **Required upgrade for existing packages** check box.

10. Your company has just purchased a volume license to a new computer-assisted design (CAD) package that you will be deploying to all users in the Design department. The package will replace an older CAD package currently in use. You want to remove the older package, but several users in the department are adamant that they must be still able to use the older package. What should you do?

   a. Use Group Policy to remove the software package and select the **Immediately uninstall the software from users and computers** option.

   b. Use Group Policy to remove the software package and select the **Allow users to continue to use the software, but prevent new installations** option.

   c. Deploy the new CAD package over the old one and ensure that the **Required upgrade for existing packages** check box is cleared.

   d. Provide copies of the old CAD package to users who want to continue using it.

Foundation Topics

Types of Software Deployment

As already noted, the Software Installation and Maintenance feature enables administrators to deploy software so that it is always available to users and repairs itself if needed. The software is always available to a user, regardless of what happens. If a user's computer fails, a support person needs only to provide a replacement computer with Windows 7 installed. The user starts the computer and logs on, and the required software packages are automatically installed. Should necessary files become corrupted or deleted, they are automatically reinstalled the next time the user requires the application.

Users benefit from Group Policy software deployment in several additional ways:

■ A user who needs access to the network from multiple computers always has her assigned set of software available.

■ A user who changes job responsibilities within the organization can automatically receive new software required by his new position.

■ Assigned software is *resilient*—that is, if a user deletes files or folders required by the software package, they will be automatically replaced the next time he attempts to run the program. This saves trips to computers by support people to repair problems.

■ You can specify that software that is no longer required is automatically removed, including all required files and Registry entries, while any shared files (such as .dll files used by other programs) are retained.

Software Installation and Maintenance enables you to manage the following steps in the software life cycle:

■ **Software installation:** You can deploy almost any type of software application, including custom in-house applications. This includes options that enable you to assign or publish software to computers or users. You can use Microsoft Software Installer (.msi) files to specify the software installation conditions, including the available components and options. You can also use transform (.mst) files to specify installation options such as languages.

■ **Software upgrades and patches:** You can automate the installation of service packs, hotfixes, and other patches that are designed to correct problems with applications and provide new functionality as released by software manufacturers. You can also use patch (.msp) files to add hotfixes and other patches as required. You can also deploy service packs as they become available and upgrade software to new versions—for example, Office 2007 to Office 2010.

- **Software removal:** When a program is no longer used or supported by the IT department, you can remove it from users' computers. You can specify an option to provide users with an option to retain obsolete software, or you can remove it automatically without a user option.

Assigning and Publishing Software

Software Installation and Maintenance provides three methods of software deployment. The method you choose to employ depends on which users require access to the software package and its urgency. You can either assign the package to users or computers or publish it to users. No option exists for publishing software to computers.

Assigning Software to Users

When you assign a software package to users, the software follows them to whatever computers they log on to. Consequently, it is always available to each user. When a user logs on to the computer after the application has been assigned, the application appears in the Start menu and, if specified, an icon appears on the desktop. When a user invokes the application from either of these points, it is automatically installed.

Assigning Software to Computers

When you assign software to computers, it is available to all authenticated users of the computer, regardless of their group membership or privileges. The software package is installed when the computer is next restarted after the package has been assigned. For example, suppose that you have a design application that should be available on all computers in the Engineering OU but not to computers elsewhere on your network. You would assign this application to computers in a Group Policy object (GPO) linked to the Engineering OU.

Publishing Software to Users

When you publish software to users, it is not advertised in the same manner as when you assign it. It does not appear in the Start > All Programs menu and no icons appear on the desktop. To install it, a user needs to go to the Add or Remove Programs (Windows XP) or Programs and Features (Windows Vista/7) applet in Control Panel. The user can also install it by double-clicking a file whose extension is associated with the application (document activation). For example, if you have published Microsoft Word to users, when a user logs on, Microsoft Word appears in the Start > All Programs folder and is installed when she selects this path; if this user double-clicks a file with the `.doc` or `.docx` extension, Microsoft Word is installed. If the user double-clicks a file of unknown file extension, a query is sent to Active Directory to determine whether an application is available for that file type (and the user has the proper permissions to that application). If so, the application is installed.

NOTE   Software deployed using Group Policy is resilient only if you have assigned it to the users or computers that require the software. Published software is not resilient; a user needs to return to Control Panel Programs and Features to reinstall a damaged published software program.

Table 12-2 summarizes the more important properties of each software deployment method:

Table 12-2   Software Deployment Methods

Deployment Method	Where Available	When Installed	Resilient?
Assigning to users	At any computer accessed by assigned user	When selected from Start menu or desktop icon, or when associated document is selected	Yes
Assigning to computers	At any computer covered by the deployment GPO	When computer is next restarted	Yes
Publishing to users	At any computer accessed by user to whom the software has been published	When associated document is selected, or when selected from Programs and Features applet	No

TIP   Remember the software deployment options. An exam question might give you choices that include publishing software to computers. Remember that you cannot publish software to computers. This is true because users must manually commence the installation of published software.

Deploying Software Using Group Policy

You can use any existing GPO to deploy a software package or create a special GPO according to requirements. Linking the GPO to an OU is often beneficial when the users who need the software package are all grouped within a specific OU. For example, you might create a GPO that is linked to the Financial OU to deploy a financial application that all members of this OU require but that should not be available to users or computers in other OUs.

Before you deploy a new software package, you must copy the installation files to a *distribution point*, which is a shared folder accessible to both the server and all client computers requiring the package. After you have created a shared installation folder and copied the software installation files, including the .msi package files to this folder, you are ready to deploy the package. The following steps outline the general procedure:

Step 1. Open the Group Policy Management Editor focused on the required GPO.

Step 2. Navigate to the appropriate node for software deployment, as follows:

—To assign or publish an application to users, navigate to User Configuration\Policies\Software Settings\Software installation.

—To assign an application to computers, navigate to Computer Configuration\Policies\Software Settings\Software installation.

Step 3. Right-click this node and choose **New > Package**.

Step 4. In the Open dialog box that appears, navigate to the shared folder where the .msi file is located, select it, and then click **Open**.

Step 5. In the Deploy Software dialog box shown in Figure 12-1, select the option with which you want to deploy the software package. As discussed later in this chapter, you would select **Advanced** to include transforms or modifications to the software packages.

Figure 12-1   Selecting the method of software deployment.

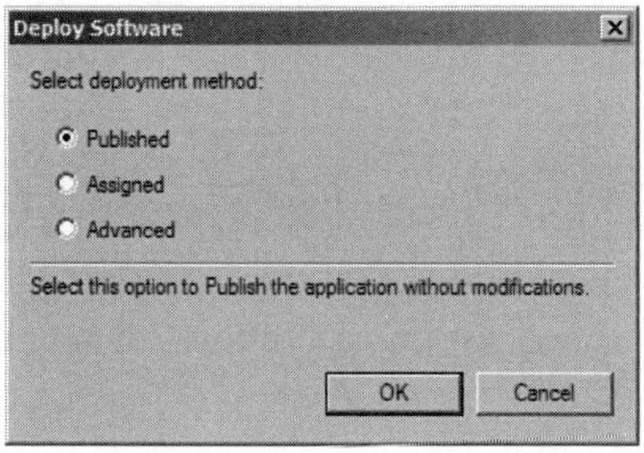

Step 6. Click **OK**. The deployed package (in this example, Mozilla Firefox) appears in the details pane along with information describing its deployment method, as shown in Figure 12-2.

When you finish this procedure, the deployed package appears in the details pane of the Group Policy Management Editor, together with its version, deployment state (published or assigned), and path to source files.

Figure 12-2 The deployed package appears in the details pane of the Group Policy Management Editor.

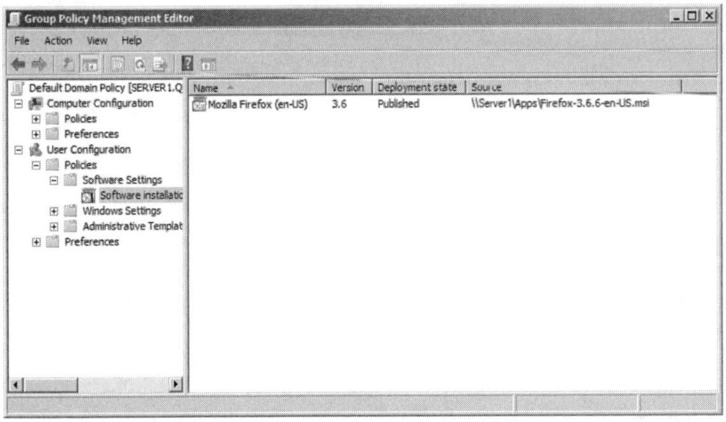

NOTE You should select a network share by means of its Universal Naming Convention (UNC) path in step 4 of this procedure; otherwise, users will be unable to locate the package. If you do not select a UNC path, a warning message will alert you to this fact.

ZAP Files

Another deployment option when no `.msi` file is available is to use a *ZAP (Zero Administration Package)* file. This is a text file with the `.zap` extension that specifies the path to the setup files associated with the application. You can only publish applications to users when using a ZAP file; you cannot assign applications when using this method.

A sample ZAP file looks like the following:

```
[application]
; You may include comments by prefixing the line with a semicolon.
FriendlyName = "Que Financial Version 5.0"
SetupCommand = \\server2\packages\Quefinancial\Setup.exe
DisplayVersion = 5.0
[ext]
qfn =
```

Within the `[application]` section is included the friendly name that will be displayed in the Add or Remove Programs (XP) or Programs and Features (Vista/7) applet and the UNC path to the setup files. `DisplayVersion` indicates the version of the program. You can also include the address of a support website by specifying it on a `URL =` line. The optional `[ext]` section contains any file extensions that are to be associated with the application, so that when the user double-clicks a file with the indicated extension, the application is installed.

To deploy the package, copy the .zap file to the shared location containing the application's setup files and then follow the procedure described in the preceding section to include the installation package in the appropriate GPO.

ZAP files do not benefit from some of the advantages possessed by Windows Installer .msi files. They are not resilient; that is, they do not automatically repair themselves if a required file becomes corrupted or missing. They also do not use elevated permissions for installation, install features on their first use, or roll back unsuccessful installations or modifications. In addition, you cannot use transform files with .zap files.

Software Installation Properties

You can configure global properties of all software installation packages deployed to either users or computers, as well as properties of individual software packages. Use the following procedure:

Step 1. Open the Group Policy Management Editor snap-in for the GPO whose default software installation options you want to configure.

Step 2. Expand the **Software Settings** node under Computer Configuration or User Configuration, as appropriate.

Step 3. Right-click **Software installation** and choose **Properties**. This displays the General tab of the Software installation Properties dialog box, as shown in Figure 12-3.

Figure 12-3 Configuring global software installation properties.

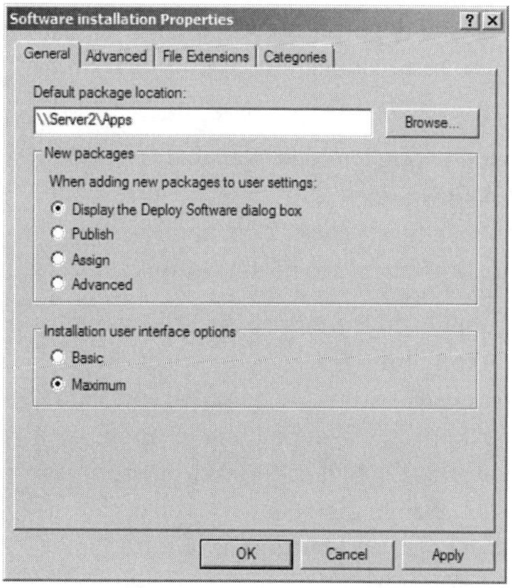

Step 4.   Configure the following options as required. They apply to all software packages deployed from this section of this GPO:

—**Default package location:** The UNC path to the shared folder containing the installation files.

—**New packages:** Specify the deployment type. The default option is **Display the Display Software dialog box**, which displays the dialog box previously shown in Figure 12-1 so that you can select the deployment method individually for each software package.

—**Installation user interface options:** Determines what the user sees during application installation. Select **Basic** to provide only progress bars and error messages. The **Maximum** option provides additional information including all installation messages and dialog boxes displayed during installation.

Step 5.   Select the **Advanced** tab to configure the following additional options:

—**Uninstall the applications when they fall out of the scope of management:** Automatically removes the software should the GPO that installed it no longer be applied to the user or computer. For example, suppose that a user in the Sales OU has a sales application installed from a GPO linked to this OU. His job responsibilities change and he is moved to the Marketing OU; consequently, he no longer needs this application and it is removed from his computer.

—**Include OLE information when deploying applications:** The Object Linking and Embedding (OLE) option enables you to specify whether information about Component Object Model (COM) components included with a package are deployed so that these components can be installed as required in a manner similar to file extension activation.

—**Make 32-bit X86 Windows Installer applications available to Win64 machines** and **Make 32-bit X86 down-level (ZAP) applications available to Win64 machines:** Specify whether 32-bit applications of the indicated type will be made available to 64-bit computers.

Step 6.   If you need to specify preferred applications for opening a file with a given extension, select the **File Extensions** tab. Type or select the file extension from the **Select file extension** drop-down list. All applications associated with the selected file extension will appear in the Application precedence field. The application with the highest precedence appears at the top of the list. If you need to change this sequence, select the application and use the **Up** or **Down** command buttons as required.

Step 7.   To specify categories into which published applications will be grouped, select the **Categories** tab. Click **Add** to specify new categories (see Figure 12-4); in this example, our category is Drafting applications. These categories are displayed to users who access programs from the Control Panel Add or Remove Programs (XP) or Programs and Features (Vista/7) applet and assist them in locating the appropriate applications.

Figure 12-4   You can use the Categories tab of the Software Installation Properties dialog box to specify categories into which published applications will be divided.

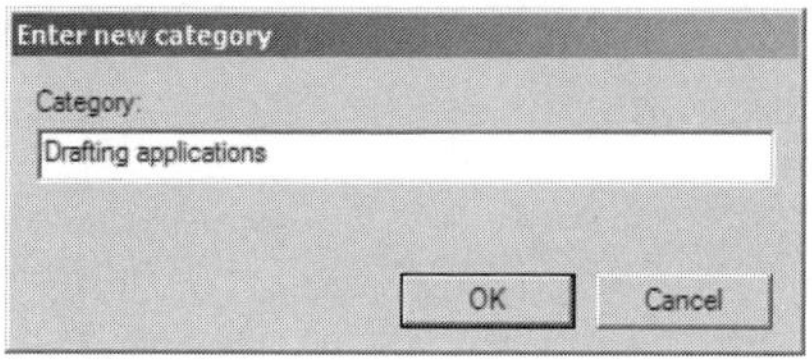

Step 8.   When you are finished, click **OK**.

Software Package Properties

You can configure individual software package properties from its Properties dialog box. Right-click the package in the details pane of the Group Policy Management Editor snap-in and choose **Properties** to display this dialog box, which has the following six tabs:

- **General:** Includes product information, such as the name and version number. You can include a friendly name for users and contact information.

- **Deployment:** As shown in Figure 12-5, you can modify the deployment options that you specified when you originally deployed the package. You can configure the following options:
  —**Deployment type:** You can change the deployment type (published or assigned) if required. You can also select the deployment type from the package's right-click menu in the details pane of the Group Policy Management Editor.
  —**Auto-install this application by file extension activation:** Selected by default, this option enables a published application to be automatically installed when a user opens a file whose extension is associated with the application. Note that you can also select or deselect this option simply by right-clicking the package in the details pane and choosing **Auto-Install**.
  —**Uninstall this application when it falls out of the scope of management:** When this option is selected, the application is automatically uninstalled if the GPO by which it was deployed no longer applies to the user who is logged on.

Figure 12-5   You can configure several advanced settings for an application after you have deployed it.

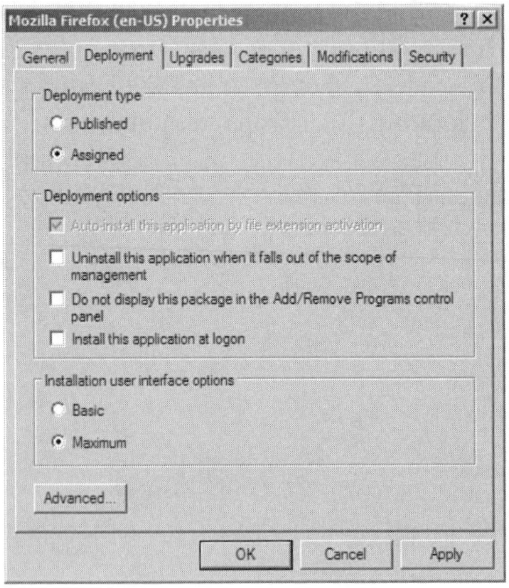

—**Do not display this package in the Add/Remove Programs control panel:** When this option is selected, the program is not advertised in the Add or Remove Programs (XP) or Programs and Features (Vista/7) applet. The user can still install it by opening a file associated with the application.

—**Install this application at logon:** When this option is selected, the application is automatically installed at the next logon without the user having to access it from the Start menu or desktop shortcut. This option is active for assigned software only.

—**Installation user interface options:** This option controls how much the user sees during application installation. It provides the same options as discussed in the previous section for the default software installation properties.

—**Advanced button:** Clicking this button opens the Advanced Deployment Options dialog box. From here, you can choose to ignore language when deploying the package or remove previous versions of the application that were not installed by means of a GPO. Some additional information provided by the package's author is also available in this dialog box.

■ **Upgrades:** Defines the applications to be upgraded by this package as well as packages that can upgrade this package. You can also choose whether to make this package a required upgrade for existing packages.

■ **Categories:** Enables you to specify the category into which a program is displayed in the Control Panel Add or Remove Programs (XP) or Programs and Features (Vista/7) applet. To use this feature, you should first define the categories in the Categories tab of the Software Installation Properties dialog box, as described in the previous section.

■ **Modifications:** Enables you to apply modifications or transforms to the package to customize the deployment. For example, suppose that your company operates in different countries that require localized language dictionaries in Microsoft Word. You can deploy transforms (.mst files) that include the required language files.

■ **Security:** Determines the level of access users have to the package. You can make applications available to specified users, computers, or groups only. Administrators and others who manage software installation should receive the Full Control permission; users installing the software should receive the Read permission.

TIP   An exam question might present a scenario asking whether you would assign or publish an application. If it specifies that it is mandatory that the application should be installed, you should assign it. Assign the application to computers if all computers in the scope of the GPO require it regardless of the user who is logged on, and assign it to users if all users in the scope of the GPO require it regardless of the computer to which they are logged on. If the application is not mandatory but the users will have an option to install it, you should publish it. Again, don't forget that you cannot publish an application to computers.

Upgrading Software

As new versions of applications are released, it might be desirable to upgrade the current packages to take advantage of the new features that are generally offered with the upgraded version.

Group Policy makes it simple for you to deploy an upgraded software package. Simply follow the steps already outlined in this chapter to deploy the upgraded package, usually in the same GPO that holds the package to be upgraded. After you have deployed it, perform the following steps:

Step 1.   Right-click the new package, choose **Properties** to display the dialog box previously shown in Figure 12-5, and then select the **Upgrades** tab.

Step 2.   Click **Add** to display the Add Upgrade Package dialog box shown in Figure 12-6 and configure the following options:

■ **Choose a package from:** If the original software package was deployed from a different GPO, select **A specific GPO** and click **Browse** to locate the appropriate GPO from the Browse for a Group Policy Object dialog box that appears. Otherwise, leave the default option selected.

Figure 12-6   The Add Upgrade Package dialog box.

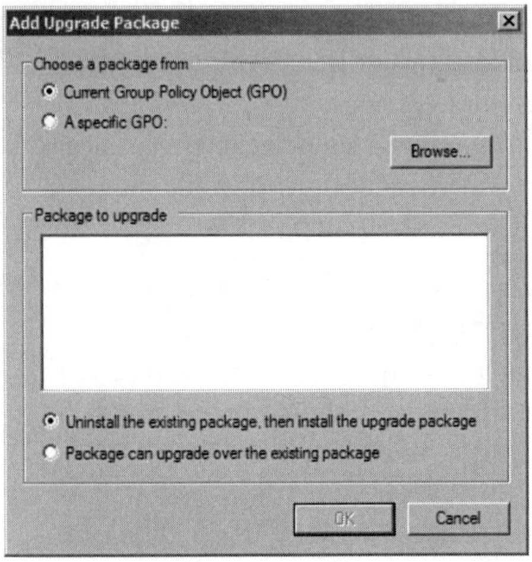

- **Package to upgrade:** Select the package to be upgraded.

- **Uninstall the existing package, then install the upgrade package:** Select this option if you are replacing the application with a completely different one, such as an application from a new vendor. You might have to use this option for some applications that cannot be installed over current installations.

- **Package can upgrade over the existing package:** Use this option when upgrading to a newer version of the same product. It retains the user's application preferences, document type associations, and so on.

Step 3.   Click **OK** to return to the Upgrades tab. The selected package is displayed in the field labeled **Packages that this package will upgrade** (see Figure 12-7).

Step 4.   Select one of the following options to designate the upgrade as either optional or mandatory.

- **Mandatory upgrade:** Automatically upgrades the current version of the software the next time the computer is started or the user logs on. To configure this option, select the **Required upgrade for existing packages** check box.

- **Optional upgrade:** The user can either upgrade the application or continue to use the current version. The user can even have both versions installed and access either one as he chooses. To configure this option, leave the previously mentioned check box cleared.

Step 5.   Close the Group Policy Object Editor console to apply the settings you just configured.

Figure 12-7   The Upgrades tab displays the package that will be upgraded.

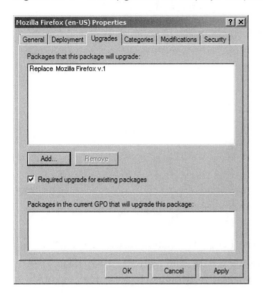

Use of Transform Files to Modify Software Packages

Transform files, which are Windows Installer package files with the `.mst` extension, are used to make changes to an installation database. For example, you can change the language of a user interface by employing a transform file. You can even specify which components of a package such as Microsoft Office will be installed on computers subject to the GPO where the transform is specified.

When using Group Policy to deploy software, you can apply a transform at the time you deploy the software, either by assigning or publishing it. The `.mst` package works in conjunction with the software's `.msi` package to produce the customized deployment.

Use the following procedure to deploy a software package that contains a transform file:

Step 1.   Open the Group Policy Management Editor that is focused on the GPO within which you want to apply the modified software package.

Step 2.   Navigate to the Software Installation folder under **Computer Configuration\Policies\Software Settings** or **User Configuration\ Policies\Software Settings**, depending on whether you are deploying the modification to users or computers.

Step 3.   Right-click **Software installation** and choose **New > Package**.

Step 4.   In the Open dialog box that appears, navigate to the shared folder where the .msi file is located, select it, and then click **Open**.

Step 5.   In the Deploy Software dialog box that appears, select the **Advanced** option, as shown in Figure 12-8.

Figure 12-8   You must select the Advanced deployment option to apply .mst files to the deployment package.

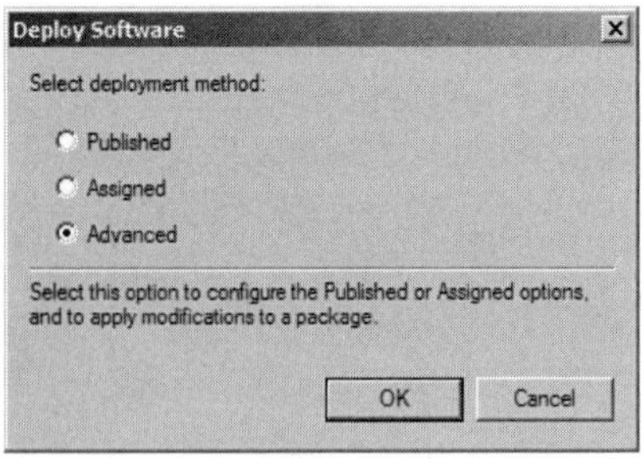

Step 6.   Selecting this option displays the Properties dialog box for the software package. It is a good idea to indicate a specific name for the package on the General tab (for example, Microsoft Office 2010 Premium, Spanish edition).

Step 7.   On the Deployment tab, select the required deployment type (**Published** or **Assigned**). Also, select the required deployment options and installation user interface options, as discussed earlier in this chapter.

Step 8.   Select the **Modifications** tab, as shown in Figure 12-9, and then click **Add**. In the Open dialog box that appears, select the appropriate .mst file and click **Open**.

Step 9.   Repeat step 8 as necessary to add additional .mst files to the list on the Modifications tab. Use the Move Up and Move Down buttons as necessary to sequence the .mst files in the order (top to bottom) in which they are to be applied.

Step 10.   Click **OK** only after you have added and sequenced all the required .mst files. The package appears in the details pane of the Group Policy Management Editor, along with the name you specified in step 6.

Step 11.   Exit the Group Policy Management Editor.

Figure 12-9   Use the Modifications tab to add `.mst` files to the software deployment package.

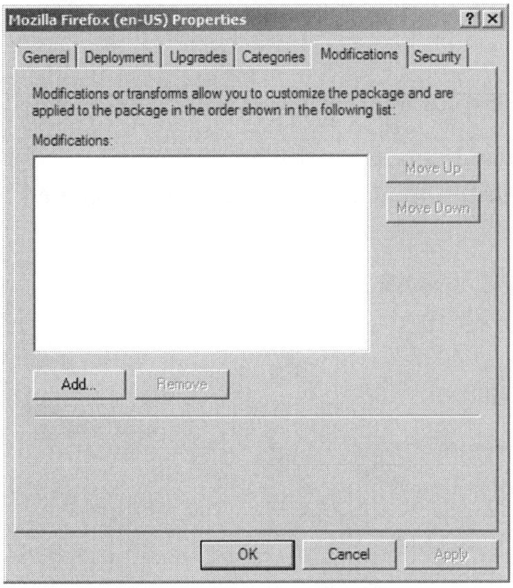

> **TIP**   Know the difference between a transform and a patch and what each can do. Transform files have the `.mst` extension and customize a Windows Installer package at the time of deployment. Patch files have the `.msp` extension and include modifications such as bug fixes and service packs. They are more limited in nature than transforms in that they cannot specify a subset of application features and cannot remove or change the names of shortcuts, files, or Registry keys.

Redeployment of Upgraded Software

In some situations, you might not need to upgrade the package; you might simply want to reinstall it on all computers covered by the GPO. A case in point is the add-ons that software vendors produce from time to time, such as patches, service packs, and hotfixes. These patches are designed to add new features or correct problems with the current application.

You can apply such patches to deployed software by redeploying the software. In doing so, the redeployed software is advertised to everyone to whom the software was originally assigned or published and the update takes place according to the method of original deployment, as follows:

■ Software that was assigned to a computer is automatically redeployed the next time the computer is started.

■ For software that was either published or assigned to a user, modifications are made to the Start menu, desktop shortcuts, and Registry settings when the user logs on. When she starts the program, the patch or service pack is automatically applied.

Use the following steps to redeploy a software package for which you have received a patch, hotfix, or service pack.

Step 1.   Copy the appropriate files to the software package's installation folder.

Step 2.   Navigate to the Software Installation node under **Computer Configuration** or **User Configuration**, depending on the method used to deploy the application.

Step 3.   Right-click the application and choose **All Tasks > Redeploy application**, as shown in Figure 12-10.

Figure 12-10   Redeployment of a software package.

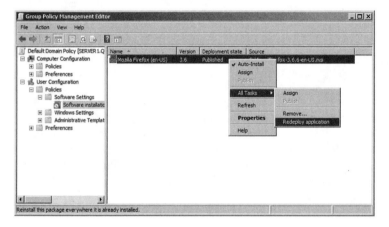

Step 4.   You are warned that redeploying this application will reinstall the application everywhere it is already installed. Click **Yes** to continue.

Step 5.   The next time users log on to their computers, the application will be redeployed, as described in this section.

NOTE   You need a new Windows Installer file to redeploy software. To redeploy the package as described, the patch, hotfix, or service pack must come with a new Windows Installer .msi file. Otherwise, you cannot redeploy the package without preparing a new .msi file. If the supplier has included an .msp file with the patch, it will include instructions for use of this file to update the .msi file.

Removal of Software

When software that was deployed using Group Policy and Windows Installer becomes outdated or is no longer useful to your company, you can use a GPO to remove the software. Software removal can be either mandatory (which automatically removes it from the affected computers) or optional (which allows users to continue to use it, but no longer supports it or makes it available for reinstallation).

Use the following procedure to remove a deployed software package:

Step 1.   Navigate to the Software Installation node under **Computer Configuration** or **User Configuration**, depending on the method used to deploy the application.

Step 2.   Right-click the application and choose **All Tasks > Remove**.

Step 3.   In the Remove Software dialog box (see Figure 12-11), choose one of the following removal methods:

Figure 12-11   Software removal can be either mandatory or optional.

—**Immediately uninstall the software from users and computers:** - Automatically removes the software the next time the affected computer is rebooted or the user logs on. The user does not receive an option to keep the software.

—**Allow users to continue to use the software, but prevent new installations:** The software is not automatically removed, and the user can continue to use it. However, users who remove the software and others who do not have it can no longer install it.

Step 4.   Click **OK**. The software package is no longer listed in the details pane.

Exam Preparation Tasks

Review All the Key Topics

Review the most important topics in the chapter, noted with the key topics icon in the outer margin of the page. Table 12-3 lists a reference of these key topics and the page numbers on which each is found.

Table 12-3 Key Topics for Chapter 12

Key Topic Element	Description	Page Number
Paragraph	Describes available methods of software deployment	399
Table 12-2	Compares the major differences between publishing and assigning software	400
List	Shows you how to use Group Policy to deploy software	401
Figure 12-3	Shows the options available when configuring global software installation properties	403
Figure 12-5	Shows the options available for advanced configuration of a software package	406
Figure 12-6	Shows the process of upgrading deployed software	408
List	Shows how to deploy a software package that contains a transform	409
Figure 12-11	You have two options available when removing a software package	413

Complete the Tables and Lists from Memory

Print a copy of Appendix C, "Memory Tables" (found on the CD), or at least the section for this chapter, and complete the tables and lists from memory. Appendix D, "Memory Tables Answer Key," also on the CD, includes completed tables and lists to check your work.

Definitions of Key Terms

Define the following key terms from this chapter, and check your answers in the glossary.

assigned applications, mandatory upgrade, optional removal, optional upgrade, package, patch files, published applications, redeployment, transform files, Windows Installer

This chapter covers the following subjects:

■ **Use of Group Policy to Configure Security:** Intruders often attempt to crack user accounts and their passwords to gain access to your network. Policies that serve to require strong passwords and lock accounts out when too many incorrect passwords are entered improve your network's security. This section shows you how to use Group Policy to configure policies that improve the security of Active Directory accounts and passwords, including the new fine-grained password policies that enable you to set different policies for portions of a domain.

■ **Auditing of Active Directory Services:** Auditing lets you record actions that take place across your domain, including attempts to access user accounts and resources. This section shows you how to use Group Policy to set up policies that effectively track these types of activities on your network.

CHAPTER 13

Account Policies and Audit Policies

Chapter 11, "Creating and Applying Group Policy Objects," showed you how Group Policy works and how to set up Group Policy objects (GPOs) to configure various aspects of the Windows computing environment. You have also learned about Group Policy succession and how you can modify the sequence in which GPOs are applied and its effect when policy settings conflict with one another. Chapter 12, "Group Policy Software Deployment," then turned your attention to the use of Group Policy to maintain a consistent software environment where users and computers receive a well-regulated set of software applications that can be modified and upgraded as required, as well as the removal of outdated software. This chapter focuses on the use of Group Policy to create and enforce a secure computing environment that protects your computers and data from whatever the bad guys might attempt to throw at you.

"Do I Know This Already?" Quiz

The "Do I Know This Already?" quiz enables you to assess whether you should read this entire chapter or simply jump to the "Exam Preparation Tasks" section for review. If you are in doubt, read the entire chapter. Table 13-1 outlines the major headings in this chapter and the corresponding "Do I Know This Already?" quiz questions. You can find the answers in Appendix A, "Answers to the 'Do I Know This Already?' Quizzes."

Table 13-1 "Do I Know This Already?" Foundation Topics Section-to-Question Mapping

Foundations Topics Section	Questions Covered in This Section
Use of Group Policy to Configure Security	1–7
Auditing of Active Directory Services	8–12

1. You want to ensure that users cannot cycle rapidly through a series of passwords and then reuse their old password immediately. Which password policy should you enable to prevent this action from occurring?

  a.   Enforce password history

  b.   Minimum password age

  c.   Maximum password age

  d.   Password must meet complexity requirements

  e.   Store passwords using reversible encryption

2. What password policy actually reduces password security and is therefore not recommended for use by Microsoft?

  a.   Enforce password history

  b.   Minimum password age

  c.   Maximum password age

  d.   Password must meet complexity requirements

  e.   Store passwords using reversible encryption

3. You want to ensure that a hacker using a brute-force–type of password attack cannot access user accounts in your AD DS domain. At the same time, you want to reduce the instance of help desk calls from users unable to log on because they've entered their password incorrectly too many times. Which policies should you configure to achieve this objective? (Each answer represents part of the solution. Choose three.)

  a.   Account lockout duration

  b.   Account lockout threshold

  c.   Reset account lockout counter after

  d.   Password must meet complexity requirements

4. You have configured a strict password policy for employees in your company's Legal department by configuring the policies contained in a GPO linked to the Legal OU. A few days later, you notice that these policies are not being applied and the Legal employees are able to use passwords according to the policies defined for the rest of the domain. What should you do to ensure that the stricter policies are being applied?

  a.   Specify the **Block Inheritance** setting for the Legal OU.

  b.   Configure the **No Override** option for the GPO containing the Legal department password policies.

  c.   Specify the password policy settings in a Password Settings Object (PSO) that is linked to the Legal OU.

  d.   Specify the password policy settings in a PSO that is linked to a security group in the Legal OU that contains the user accounts of Legal department employees.

5. You want to specify unique account policy settings for users whose accounts are located in the Research group. What tools should you use to accomplish this objective? (Each answer represents part of the solution. Choose two.)

   a. Gpedit.msc

   b. Adsiedit.msc

   c. Windows PowerShell

   d. Active Directory Users and Computers

   e. Group Policy Management Console

6. You have configured several different account policies in PSOs within your company's AD DS domain. Now you need to sort out which policies will actually apply to a user named Linda, whose account is located within the Accountants security group. Which of the following will take precedence?

   a. The settings in a PSO applied directly to Linda's account

   b. The settings in a PSO applied to the Accountants group, with a Password Settings Precedence value of 1

   c. The settings in a PSO applied to the Accountants group, with a Password Settings Precedence value of 2

   d. The settings applied to the Default Domain Policy GPO

7. You are responsible for configuring security policy for all computers on your company's network, which is configured as an AD DS domain. The network also includes a standalone server that is not configured as a domain member. How should you configure security policy settings to apply to this server using the least amount of administrative effort?

   a. Use the Security Configuration and Analysis tool to analyze the security settings on a member server and apply these security settings to the stand-alone server.

   b. Use the Security Templates tool to save a custom security policy template on a member server on the domain, and then use the Security Configuration and Analysis tool to create a database containing settings in the policy template and apply them to the standalone server.

   c. Use the Security Configuration Wizard to copy the required settings from a member server and paste them into the standalone server.

   d. Manually specify all the required settings using the Local Security Policy snap-in at the standalone server.

8. You are responsible for auditing of directory-based actions occurring within your company's AD DS domain. You need to track replication events occurring within the domain including the establishment, removal, or modification of

AD DS replica source naming contexts, replication of attributes for an AD DS object, or removal of lingering objects from a replica. Which of the following audit subcategories should you configure for auditing?

a.   Directory Service Access

b.   Directory Service changes

c.   Directory Service Replication

d.   Detailed Directory Service Replication

9. You are responsible for auditing of activities taking place within your company's AD DS domain. Your boss has requested that you implement auditing of the following:

■ Attempts to log on to any local computer

■ Creation of a user account or group or changing of a user account password

What auditing components should you configure? (Each answer represents part of the solution. Choose two.)

a.   Audit account management, success

b.   Audit account logon events, success and failure

c.   Audit object access, success

d.   Audit logon events, success and failure

10. You have enabled auditing of object access in a GPO linked to the Default Domain Policy GPO in your company's AD DS domain. All departments in your company are represented by OUs within the domain structure. The manager of the Legal department reports that someone has improperly modified many of the legal documents stored on the department's member server, which runs Windows Server 2008 R2. Checking Event Viewer, you cannot find any evidence of who performed these actions. What do you need to do so that future actions of this type are properly documented?

a.   You also need to enable auditing of logon events in the Local Security Policy snap-in at the member server.

b.   You should have enabled auditing of object access in a GPO linked to the Legal OU.

c.   You also need to access Windows Explorer at the member server. From this location, ensure that the appropriate auditing entries have been enabled for the folder in which the legal documents are located.

d.   You should have enabled auditing of directory service access instead.

11. Users in your company's AD DS domain have been complaining about frequent account lockouts at their client computers in recent days. Domain servers run Windows Server 2008 R2 and client computers run Windows 7 Enterprise. You

decide to implement a stronger audit policy that is designed to specifically track account lockouts without generating audit trails for other user account-related events. How should you proceed?

a. From the Group Policy Management Editor focused on the appropriate GPO, navigate to the **Computer Configuration\Policies\Windows Settings\Security Settings\Local Policies\Audit Policy** subnode. Then enable the Audit account logon events policy.

b. From the Group Policy Management Editor focused on the appropriate GPO, navigate to the **Computer Configuration\Policies\Windows Settings\Security Settings\Local Policies\Audit Policy** subnode. Then enable the Audit logon events policy.

c. From the Group Policy Management Editor focused on the appropriate GPO, navigate to the **Computer Configuration\Policies\ Windows Settings\Security Settings\Advanced Audit Policy Configuration\Audit Policies\Account Logon** subnode. Then enable the Audit Account Lockout policy setting.

d. From the Group Policy Management Editor focused on the appropriate GPO, navigate to the **Computer Configuration\Policies\ Windows Settings\Security Settings\Advanced Audit Policy Configuration\Audit Policies\Logon/Logoff** subnode. Then enable the Audit Account Lockout policy setting.

12. You are working from a computer running the Server Core version of Windows Server 2008 R2. You need to enable auditing of object access for computers in your company's AD DS domain. Which tool should you use for this purpose?

a. `Adsiedit.msc`

b. `Auditpol.exe`

c. `Gpedit.msc`

d. `Scwcmd.exe`

Foundation Topics

Use of Group Policy to Configure Security

You can use Group Policy to manage security settings quite effectively on a Windows Server 2008 network. An enhanced range of security options is available, with settings designed for both user and computer configuration. Microsoft continues to expand the available range of security policies, compared to those included with previous versions of Windows Server. The most significant new addition to security settings in the original version of Windows Server 2008 and continued in Windows Server 2008 R2 is that of fine-grained password policies, which enable you to set different password policies for different portions of your Active Directory Domain Services (AD DS) domain.

Group Policy in Windows Server 2008 includes a large range of security options designed for both user and computer configuration. As shown in Figure 13-1, most of these security settings are applied to the Computer Configuration section in the Group Policy Management Editor. This section is mainly concerned with account policies.

Figure 13-1   Group Policy includes both computer- and user-based security settings.

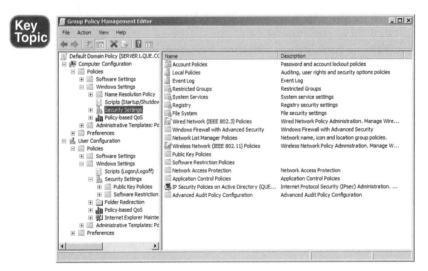

Configuring Account Policies

The Account Policies node contains settings related to user accounts, including the password policy, account lockout policy, and Kerberos policy. Before looking at the new Windows Server 2008 feature of fine-grained password policies, this section examines these policies and how to configure them in general. It briefly introduces each of these concepts in the following sections.

Domain Password Policies

You can use domain-based Group Policy to configure password policy settings that help to protect users of Windows 2000/XP/Vista/7 client computers. The options available in Windows Server 2008 and Windows Server 2008 R2 are similar to those introduced in Windows 2000 and continued in Windows Server 2003.

Password policy controls how passwords are used and created. The more restrictive you make the password policy, the tighter the password security it provides. Common hacker strategies for discovering passwords include continually trying passwords until one works. This approach is not as futile as it might first seem. Hackers employ programs that use dictionaries to run through countless passwords until they discover a working password for a particular user account. In fact, dictionary attacks are only one means of password cracking, and hacker technology continues to improve along with all other technologies. Figure 13-2 shows the available password policies and their default settings.

Figure 13-2   Windows Server 2008 R2 provides default values for the available password policies.

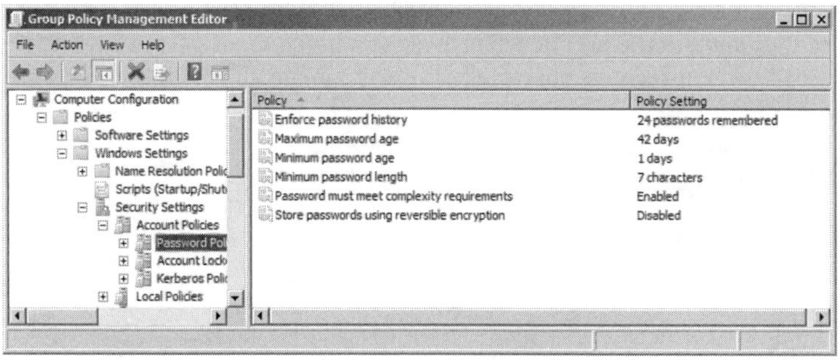

Table 13-2 describes the available password policy settings:

Key Topic

Table 13-2   Password Policy settings

Policy Setting	Description
Enforce password history	Determines the number of passwords remembered by AD DS for each user. Values range from 0 to 24. A user cannot reuse a password retained in the history list. A value of 0 means that no password history is retained and a user is able to reuse passwords at will. Windows Server 2008 continues with the default of 24 established with Windows Server 2003 SP1.
Maximum password age	This value determines the number of days to use a password before a user is required to specify a new password. Again, a value of 0 indicates that a user may manage his password in whatever way he chooses. The default value is 90 days. Values can range from 0 to 999 days.
Minimum password age	Determines the minimum number of days a password must be used before it can be changed. Values range from 0 to 999 days and must be less than the maximum password age. A value of 0 allows the user to immediately change a new password. This value would allow a user to cycle through an entire history list of passwords in a short time; in other words, repeatedly changing a password in order to reuse his old password. This obviously defeats the purpose of enforcing password history. The default is 1 day.
Minimum password length	Determines the minimum number of characters that can make up a password. Values range from 0 to 14. A value of 0 permits a blank password. Use a setting of 10 or higher for increased security. The default is 7 characters.
Password must meet complexity requirements	Stipulates that a password must meet complexity criteria, as follows: The password cannot contain the user account name or full name, or parts of the name that exceed two consecutive characters. It must contain at least three of the following four items: ■ English lowercase letters ■ English uppercase letters ■ Numerals ■ Nonalphanumeric characters such as $; [ ] { } ! .
Store passwords using reversible encryption	Determines the level of encryption used by Windows Server 2008 for storing passwords. Enabling this option reduces security because it stores passwords in a format that is essentially the same as plain text. This option is disabled by default. You should enable this policy only if needed for clients that cannot use normal encryption, such as those using Challenge Handshake Authentication Protocol (CHAP) authentication or Internet Information Services (IIS) Digest Authentication.

You can configure these settings from the Group Policy Management Editor focused on the Default Domain Policy GPO or another domain-based GPO. Use the following steps:

Step 1.   Ensure that you are logged on as an administrator.

Step 2.   Open the Group Policy Management Console. Locate the required GPO, right-click it and choose **Edit** to open the Group Policy Management Editor.

Step 3.   Navigate to **Computer Configuration\Policies\Windows Settings\Security Settings\Account Policies** and then select **Password Policy** to display the available policy settings in the details pane, as previously shown in Figure 13-2.

Step 4.   For each of the available settings, right-click it and choose **Properties**.

Step 5.   In the Properties dialog box for the selected setting, configure the appropriate value and then click **OK**. Each policy setting also has an Explain tab that provides additional information on the policy setting and its purpose. See Figure 13-3 for an example.

Figure 13-3   Configuring the password length policy.

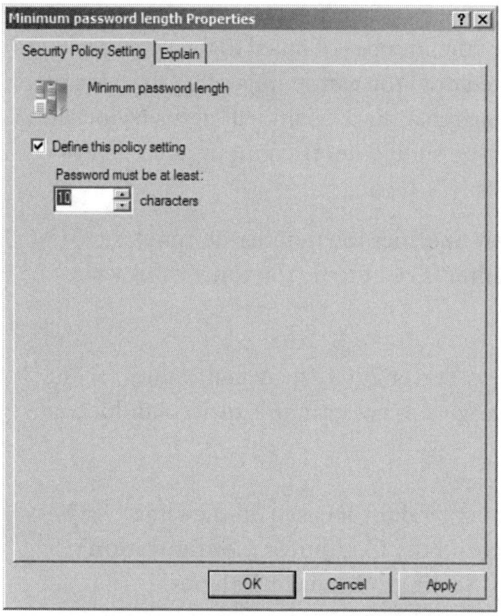

TIP   Password policies are unique in that they apply only when configured in a domain-based GPO. Although they appear in other GPOs, any configuration in GPOs linked to other containers is ignored.

> **WARNING**   Don't require too strong a password policy. If you require overly long and complex passwords, and make users change them too frequently, they will forget their passwords more often, resulting in a lot of help desk calls. Or they will write down the password on a sticky note attached to the monitor or keyboard for anyone else to find and copy. Balance your need for secure passwords against these risks.

Account Lockout

A cracked user account password jeopardizes the security of the entire network. The account lockout policy is designed to lock an account out of the computer if a user (or intruder attempting to crack the network) enters an incorrect password a specified number of times, thereby limiting the effectiveness of dictionary-based password crackers. The account lockout policy contains the following settings:

Key Topic

■ **Account lockout duration:** Specifies the number of minutes that an account remains locked out. Every account except for the default Administrator account can be locked out in this manner. You can set this value from 0 to 99999 minutes, or about 69.4 days. A value of 0 means that accounts that have exceeded the specified number of failed logon attempts are locked out indefinitely until an administrator unlocks the account.

■ **Account lockout threshold:** Specifies the number of failed logon attempts that can occur before the account is locked out. You can set this value from 0 to 999 failed attempts. A value of 0 means that the account will never be locked out. Best practices recommend that you should never configure a setting of 0 here.

■ **Reset account lockout counter after:** Specifies the number of minutes to wait after which the account lockout counter is reset to 0. You can set this value from 1 to 99999.

When you configure this policy, Windows Server 2008 sets default values for the account lockout settings. Use the following steps to configure an account lockout policy:

Step 1.   In the Group Policy Management Editor focused on the same GPO as used for password policies, expand the **Computer Configuration\ Windows Settings\Security Settings\Account Policies\ Account Lockout Policy** node.

Step 2.   In the details pane, right-click the required policy and choose **Properties**.

Step 3.   Specify a value for the policy setting and then click **Apply**.

Step 4.   As shown in Figure 13-4, Windows suggests default values for the other two policy settings. Click **OK** to define the policy settings and set these defaults.

Figure 13-4   When you define an account lockout policy, Windows suggests defaults for the other two lockout policy settings.

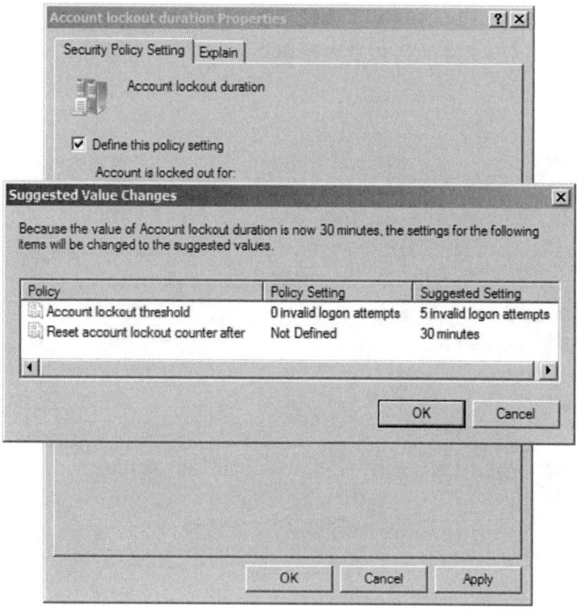

Step 5.   If you want to change an additional policy setting, right-click the appropriate policy, choose **Properties**, and then make the desired modification.

Unlocking an Account

When a user account is locked out because of too many incorrect attempts at entering a password, it is simple for an administrator or user who is delegated the task to unlock it. Right-click the user account in Active Directory Users and Computers and choose **Properties**. On the Account tab of the user's Properties dialog box, the Unlock account check box should display a message stating **This account is currently locked out on this Active Directory Domain Controller**. Select the check box and then click **OK** or **Apply**.

In Windows Server 2008 R2, you can also use Active Directory Administrative Center to unlock the account. Simply right-click the account and choose **Unlock**.

Kerberos Policy

Kerberos v.5 is the default authentication protocol on all Windows domains running Windows Server 2003 SP1 and later. Kerberos also provides the default authorization service required to validate a user's access to resources within the domain. The Kerberos Policy subnode contains settings that enforce user logon restrictions according to validation requests made to the Kerberos Key Distribution Center (KDC) against the user rights policy of the user account. By default, the policies in this section are enabled and define the maximum lifetime for user and service tickets, as well as the maximum tolerance for computer clock synchronization.

WARNING   Kerberos policies generally do not appear on the 70-640 exam. However, you should be aware of the Maximum Tolerance for Computer Clock Synchronization policy setting. This setting specifies the maximum time difference in minutes between the domain controller clock and that on a client computer attempting authentication. If the clocks differ by more than the specified amount (five minutes by default), authentication will fail.

NOTE   For a comprehensive discussion of all account policies and their settings, including password, account lockout, and Kerberos policies, refer to "Account Policies" at http://technet.microsoft.com/en-us/library/dd349793(WS.10).aspx.

Fine-Grained Password Policies

Active Directory domains in Windows 2000 and Windows Server 2003 permitted only a single password and account lockout policy, defined at the domain level. If an organization wanted different password policy settings for a specified group of users, an administrator had to create a new domain or use a third-party custom password filter. Windows Server 2008 introduces the concept of *fine-grained password policies*, which enables you to apply granular password and account lockout policy settings to different sets of users within the same domain. For example, you can apply stricter policy settings to accounts associated with users with access to classified or restricted information such as legal and product research departments. At the same time, you can maintain less strict settings for accounts of other users where these types of information are not available.

To configure a fine-grained password policy, you must be a member of the Domain Admins group and the domain functional level must be set to Windows Server 2008. You can also delegate control of the task to other users if required.

Fine-grained password policies are stored in AD DS by means of two new object classes that are defined in the schema:

- **Password Settings Container:** Created by default under the domain's System container, the Password Settings Container stores the Password Settings Objects (PSOs) for the domain.

- **Password Settings Object:** Holds attributes for all the password policy and account lockout policy settings as defined earlier in this section. It also contains a multivalued link attribute that links the PSO to users and/or groups and an integer precedence value that resolves conflicts if multiple PSOs are applied to the same user or group.

You can link a PSO to a user, global security group, or InetOrgPerson object that is in the same domain. Note that if you link a PSO to a distribution group or a group with different scope, the PSO is ignored. If multiple PSOs are linked to a single user or group because of membership in multiple groups, only one PSO can be applied; settings cannot be merged between PSOs.

TIP   Remember the prerequisites for configuring and applying fine-grained password policies. You must be a member of the Domain Admins group, the domain functional level must be set to Windows Server 2008, and the policies must be applied to the users or global security groups that need them.

Password Settings Precedence

If more than one PSO is linked to a user or group, the PSO that applies is determined by the *precedence* attribute, which is associated with each PSO and has an integer value of 1 or greater. The lower the precedence attribute, the higher the priority of a given PSO; for example, a PSO with a precedence value of 3 overrides another PSO with a precedence value of 5.

The following rules determine the resultant PSO that is applied to a user or group when multiple PSOs are present:

- If a PSO is directly linked to the user object, it prevails. Should more than one PSO be linked directly to the user, the PSO with the lowest precedence value prevails and a warning message is logged to the event log.

- If no PSO is linked directly to the user object, all PSOs applied to the user according to membership in global security groups are evaluated and the PSO with the lowest precedence value prevails. If more than one PSO with the same precedence value is present, the PSO that is obtained first is used.

- If no PSO is linked to either the user object or any global security groups it is a member of, the settings in the Default Domain Policy GPO are applied.

NOTE You cannot apply a PSO directly to an organizational unit (OU). If you want to apply consistent password settings to all users in an OU, you should add these users to a global security group and apply the PSO to that group. If you move a user from one OU to another with different password security needs, you must update that user's group membership to reflect the change.

TIP It is recommended that you specify a unique precedence value for each PSO. This simplifies troubleshooting of password precedence settings problems. But remember if you set a PSO for a user, this PSO takes precedence over PSOs linked to groups, regardless of their precedence setting.

Configuring Fine-Grained Password Policies

As already stated, you must be a member of the Domain Admins group to create and manage PSOs. You can use the ADSI Edit utility to configure a fine-grained password policy. This involves specifying values for all the Password Policy and Account Lockout Policy settings that we described earlier in this chapter. We introduced this tool in Chapter 7, "Additional Active Directory Roles." Perform the following steps:

Step 1.   Click **Start > Run**, type `adsiedit.msc,` and then press **Enter.**

Step 2.   If the domain name is not visible in the console tree, right-click **ADSI Edit** and choose **Connect to**. This displays the Connection Settings dialog box shown in Figure 13-5. If `Default Naming Context` and your domain name are visible, accept these. Otherwise, type the fully qualified domain name (FQDN) of your domain. Then click **OK.**

Figure 13-5   The Connection Settings dialog box ensures that you're connected to the proper domain.

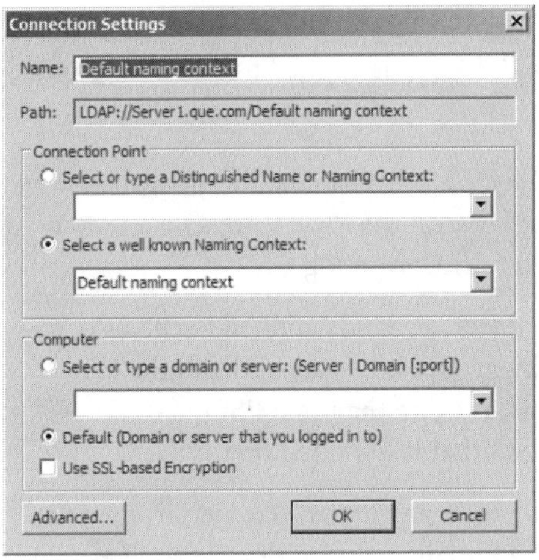

Step 3. Expand your domain name to locate the CN=System container, and then expand this container to locate the CN=Password Settings Container object.

Step 4. Select this container to display any PSOs that are configured in the domain in the details pane. As shown in Figure 13-6, this container is initially empty.

Figure 13-6 Windows provides the Password Settings Container object to store PSOs.

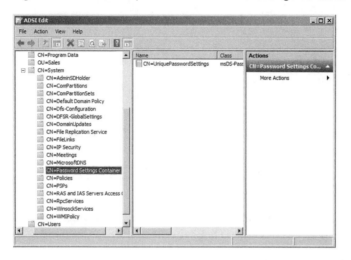

Step 5. Right-click this container and choose **New > Object**. This starts a wizard that enables you to define your PSO.

Step 6. In the Create Object dialog box, the msDS-PasswordSettings object class is the only available class. Ensure that it is selected and then click **Next**.

Step 7. Provide a descriptive value for your PSO (as shown in Figure 13-7) and then click **Next**.

Step 8. Type a value for the Password Settings Precedence and then click **Next**.

Step 9. For Password Reversible Encryption Status for User Accounts, type **False** (unless you need reversible encryption) and then click **Next**.

Step 10. Type a value for the password history length and then click **Next**.

Step 11. To require password complexity, type **True** and then click **Next**.

Step 12. Specify a minimum password length and then click **Next**.

Figure 13-7   Provide a descriptive value that helps you to identify the PSO later.

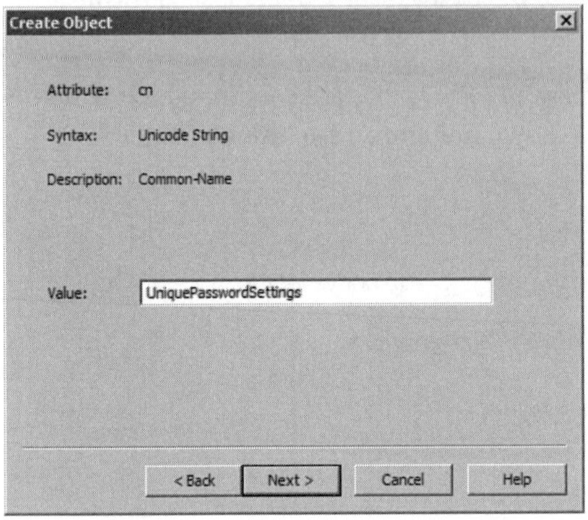

Step 13.   For the Minimum Password Age for User Accounts value, type a value in the format *days:hours:minutes:seconds* (for example, `1:00:00:00` for one day) and then click **Next.**

Step 14.   Type a value for Maximum Password Age for User Accounts in the same format and then click **Next.**

Step 15.   Type a value for the lockout threshold (number of incorrect passwords before account locks out) and then click **Next.**

Step 16.   Type a value for the lockout observation window (time for resetting lockout counter) in the same format as already described (for example, `00:00:30:00` for 30 minutes) and then click Next.

Step 17.   Type a value for the lockout duration in the same format and then click **Next.**

Step 18.   If you want to define additional optional attributes, click **More Attributes**. Otherwise, click **Finish** to complete the creation of the PSO. The PSO is displayed in the details pane of the ADSI Edit snap-in.

To apply the PSO to a user or group, proceed as follows:

Step 1.   Open Active Directory Users and Computers and select **Advanced Features** under the **View** menu. Or open Active Directory Administrative Center on a Windows Server 2008 R2 computer and expand the domain folder hierarchy to locate the System folder.

Step 2.   In the console tree, expand **System** and then select **Password Settings Container**. This displays the PSO in the details pane, as shown for the Active Directory Administrative Center in Figure 13-8.

Step 3.   Right-click the PSO and choose **Properties**.

Figure 13-8 The Active Directory Administrative Center in Windows Server 2008 R2 displays the PSO in the details pane.

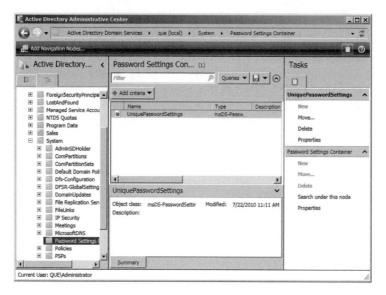

Step 4.   Select the **Attribute Editor** tab. As shown in Figure 13-9, this tab displays the values of all attributes that have been configured for the PSO, including those set when you created the PSO.

Figure 13-9 As shown in Active Directory Administrative Center, the Attribute Editor tab of the PSO's Properties dialog box includes the values of the password and lockout attributes that you configured.

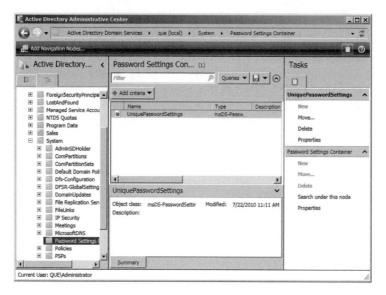

Step 5. Scroll to select the `msDS-PSOAppliesTo` attribute and then click the **Edit** button.

Step 6. On the Multi-valued Distinguished Name With Security Principal Editor dialog box that displays, click **Add Windows Account**, type the user or group name, and then click **OK**. As shown in Figure 13-10, the name you added is displayed in this dialog box. You can also add a user or group with its LDAP distinguished name (DN) by clicking the **Add DN** button.

Figure 13-10 Specifying a user or group that will receive the password policy.

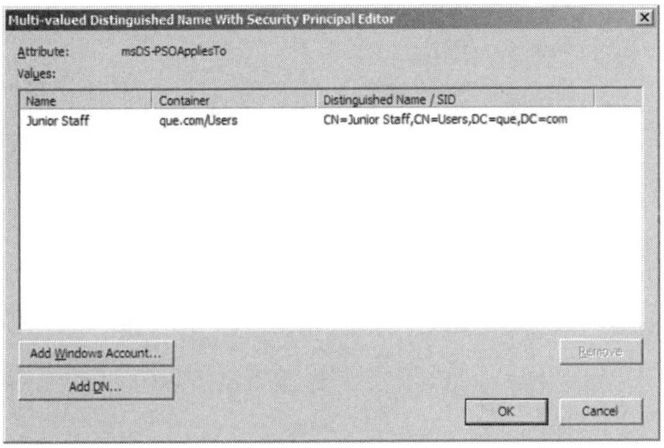

Step 7. Click **OK**. The security identifier (SID) of the user or group appears in the Value column of the Attribute Editor tab. You can repeat this process as many times as needed to link the PSO to additional users or groups.

Step 8. Click **OK** to close the PSO's Properties dialog box.

NOTE You can also use the `ldifde` utility to create a PSO and specify users or groups to which the PSO can apply. This utility was introduced in Chapter 9, "Active Directory User and Group Accounts." Refer to "Step 1: Create a PSO" at http://technet.microsoft.com/en-us/library/cc754461(WS.10).aspx for additional information.

In addition, you can use Windows PowerShell cmdlets in Windows Server 2008 R2 to create and modify fine-grained password policies. Refer to "Changes in Functionality from Windows Server 2008 to Windows Server 2008 R2" at download.microsoft.com/download/0/2/7/027AF805-BF69-4C8D-B827-392E55ED969D/Changes%20in... for details.

Managing Fine-Grained Password Policies

You can perform several additional managerial tasks on your PSO, as follows:

- **Edit policy settings:** As described in the previous section, access the **Attribute Editor** tab of the PSO's Properties dialog box. Select the policy setting to be edited and click **Edit**. Then specify the desired value in the Editor dialog box that appears.

- **Modify the PSO's precedence value:** In the Attribute Editor tab of the PSO's Properties dialog box, select the msDS-PasswordSettingsPrecedence value, click **Edit**, and then specify the desired value in the Integer Attribute Editor dialog box that appears.

- **Delete the PSO:** If you no longer need the PSO, select it in the details pane of Active Directory Users and Computers and press the **Delete** key (or right-click it and choose **Delete**). Click **Yes** in the confirmation message box that appears. The policy settings for any users or groups employing this PSO revert to the settings in a lower-priority PSO or to the Default Domain Policy GPO if no other PSO exists.

Viewing the Resultant PSO

As already stated, a PSO configured for the user takes priority over one that is configured for a group to which the user belongs, and group-based PSOs are applied according to the precedence value. If you have configured a large number of PSOs, troubleshooting their application can become problematic. To facilitate this process, you can view which PSO is applying to a user or group from Active Directory Users and Computers or Active Directory Administrative Center. Proceed as follows:

Step 1. If using Active Directory Users and Computers, ensure that **Advanced Features** is selected.

Step 2. Select the **Users** container or the OU in which the desired user account is located to display the user account in the details pane.

Step 3. Right-click the user account and choose **Properties**.

Step 4. If using Active Directory Administrative Center, scroll to locate the Extensions section of the user account's Properties dialog box.

Step 5. Select the **Attribute Editor** tab and then click **Filter**. In the options list that appears, ensure that **Show attributes/Optional**, **Show read-only attributes/Constructed**, and **Show read-only attributes/ System-only** are checked.

Step 6. Scroll the attribute list to locate msDS-ResultantPSO. The value of this attribute displays the DN of the effective PSO, as shown in Figure 13-11. If it displays <not set>, the password settings in the Default Domain

Policy GPO are in effect for this account. Click **View** to see the complete DN.

Figure 13-11   You can view the effective PSO for a user or group.

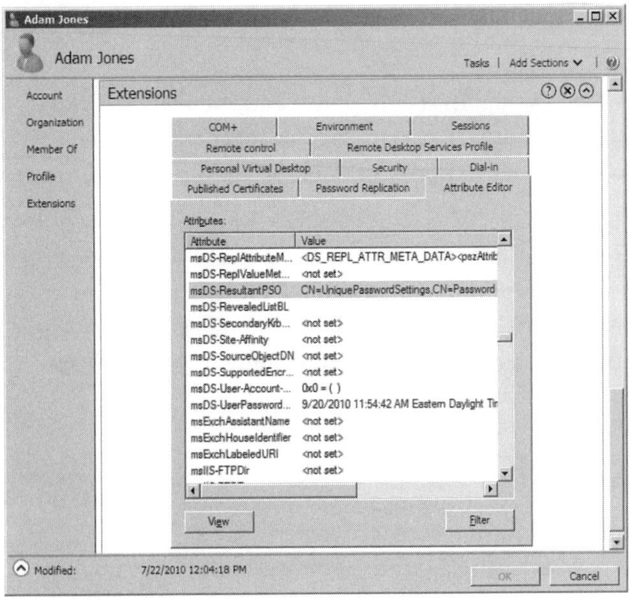

In Windows Server 2008 R2, you can also view the effective PSO for a user or group from the Active Directory Administrative Center. Right-click the desired user or group account and choose **Properties**. In the Properties dialog box, scroll to the Extensions section and select the **Attribute Editor** tab. Then use steps 4 and 5 of the earlier procedure to view the msDS-ResultantPSO attribute.

NOTE   For additional information on fine-grained password policies including some recommended scenarios for applying these policies, refer to "AD DS Fine-Grained Password and Account Lockout Policy Step-by-Step Guide" at http://technet.microsoft.com/en-us/library/cc770842(WS.10).aspx. Links in this reference also provide additional information on the available attributes and their permitted values.

Security Options

Besides account policies, the Security Settings subnode of Computer Configuration includes a large range of additional security-related policy settings. These settings are summarized here:

■ **Local Policies:** Includes audit policies, which are discussed later in this chapter, and user rights assignment, which were discussed in Chapter 11. The

Security Options subnode within this node includes a large set of policy options (as shown in Figure 13-12) that are important in controlling security aspects of the computers to which the GPO applies. Several of the more important options that you should be familiar with are as follows:

Figure 13-12 You can configure numerous local security policy settings with Group Policy in Windows Server 2008 R2.

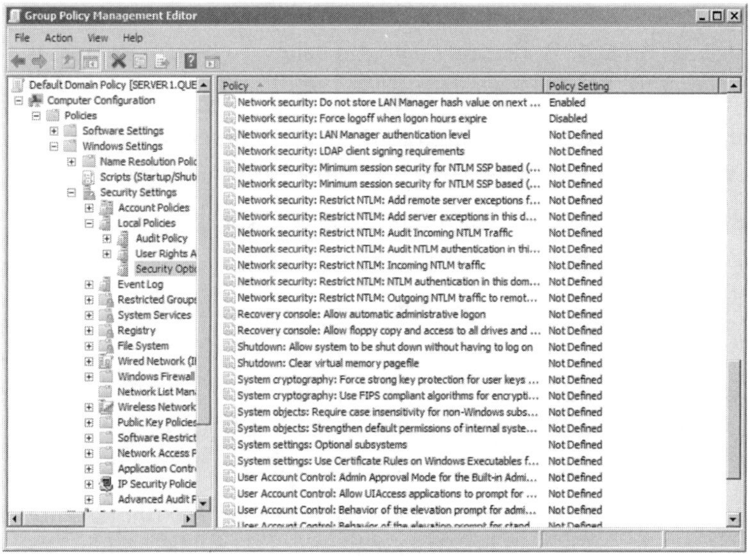

—**Accounts: Rename administrator account:** This option renames the default administrator account to a value you specify. Intruders cannot simply look for "Administrator" when attempting to crack your network.

—**Interactive logon: Do not display last user name:** Enable this option to prevent the username of the last logged-on user from appearing in the logon dialog box, thus preventing another individual from seeing a username. This can also help to reduce lockouts.

—**Interactive logon: Do not require CTRL+ALT+DEL:** When enabled, a user is not required to press **Ctrl+Alt+Delete** to obtain the logon dialog box. Disable this policy in a secure environment to require the use of this key combination. Its use prevents rogue programs such as Trojan horses from capturing usernames and passwords.

—**Interactive logon: Require smart card:** When enabled, users must employ a smart card to log on to the computer.

—**User Account Control:** Several policy settings determine the behavior of the UAC prompt for administrative and nonadministrative users, including behavior by applications that are located in secure locations on the computer such as %ProgramFiles% or %Windir%.

NOTE For more information on the policy settings in the Security Options sub-node, refer to "Domain Controller and Member Server Policy Settings" at http://technet.microsoft.com/en-us/library/cc264462.aspx and "Security Options" at http://technet.microsoft.com/en-us/library/cc749096(WS.10).aspx.

- **Event Log:** Configuration options for the Event Viewer logs, including log sizes and action taken when an event log is full.

- **Restricted Groups:** Determines who can belong to certain groups, as discussed in Chapter 9.

- **System Services:** Enables you to configure system services properties such as startup type and restrict users from modifying these settings.

- **Registry:** Enables you to control the permissions that govern who can access and edit portions of the Registry.

- **File System:** Enables you to configure permissions on folders and files and prevent their modification.

- **Wired Network (IEEE 802.3) Policies:** Enables you to specify the use of IEEE 802.1X authentication for network access by Windows Vista or Windows 7 computers including the protocol to be used for network authentication.

- **Windows Firewall with Advanced Security:** Enables you to configure properties of Windows Firewall for domain, private, and public profiles. You can specify inbound and outbound connection rules as well as monitoring settings.

- **Network List Manager Policies:** Enables you to control the networks that computers can access and their location types such as public and private (which automatically specifies the appropriate firewall settings according to location type). You can also specify which networks a user is allowed to connect to.

- **Wireless Network (IEEE 802.11) Policies:** Enables you to specify wireless settings such as enabling 802.1X authentication and the preferred wireless networks that users can access.

- **Public Key Policies:** Enables you to configure public key infrastructure (PKI) settings. We discuss several of these policies in Chapter 16, "Installing and Configuring Certificate Services."

- **Software Restriction Policies:** Enables you to specify which software programs users can run on network computers, which programs users on multiuser computers can run, and the execution of email attachments. You can also specify whether software restriction policies apply to certain groups such as administrators.

- **Network Access Protection:** Network Access Protection (NAP) is a new Windows Server 2008 feature that enables you to define client health policies that restrict access to your network by computers that lack appropriate security configurations. The NAP policies enable you to specify settings for client user interface items, trusted servers, and servers used for enforcement of client computer security health status.

- **Application Control Policies:** These are a new set of software control policies introduced with Windows 7 and Windows Server 2008 R2 that introduces the AppLocker feature. AppLocker provides new enhancements that enable you to specify exactly what users are permitted to run on their desktops according to unique file identities.

- **IP Security Policies on Active Directory:** Controls the implementation of IP Security (IPSec) as used by the computer for encrypting communications over the network.

- **Advanced Audit Policy Configuration:** New to Windows Server 2008 R2, this node contains 53 new policy settings that enable you to select explicitly the actions that you want to monitor and exclude actions that are of less concern. More information is provided later in this chapter.

You can obtain additional information on many of these policy settings in the Windows Server 2008 R2 Help and Support.

Using Additional Security Configuration Tools

Windows Server 2008 includes the following additional tools that are useful in configuring and maintaining the security of your AD DS network:

- **Security Configuration Wizard:** This wizard assists you in maintaining the security of your servers and checks for vulnerabilities that might appear as server configurations change over time. As shown in Figure 13-13, you can create a new security policy or perform actions on an existing security policy including editing, applying, or rolling back the policy. This wizard is particularly useful in maintaining the security of servers hosting roles that are not installed using Server Manager, such as SQL Server and Exchange Server, as well as servers that host non-Microsoft applications. Microsoft also includes a command-line version, scwcmd.exe, which is useful in configuring Server Core computers.

- **Security Templates snap-in:** From this snap-in, you can save a custom security policy that includes settings from the various subnodes of the Security Settings node of Computer Configuration that we have discussed in the preceding settings. It is most useful in defining a security configuration for standalone servers that are not members of a domain.

- **Security Configuration and Analysis:** This snap-in enables you to analyze and configure local computer security. You can compare security settings on the computer to those in a database created from the Security Templates snap-in and view any differences that are found. You can then use this database to configure the computer's security so that it matches the database settings.

Figure 13-13 The Security Configuration Wizard assists you in working with security policies.

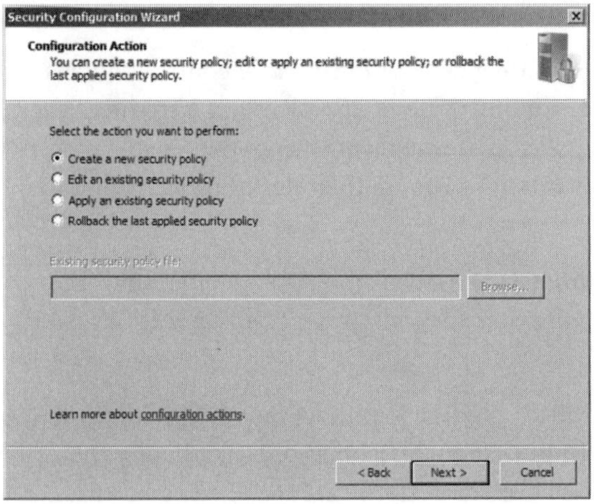

These two snap-ins are not contained in any MMC console by default; to use them you must open a blank console (type `mmc` from the Run dialog box or the Start menu Search field) and add them using the Add or Remove Snap-ins dialog box shown in Figure 13-14.

Figure 13-14 You can use the Add or Remove Snap-ins dialog box to create a Security console containing the Security Templates and Security Configuration and Analysis tools.

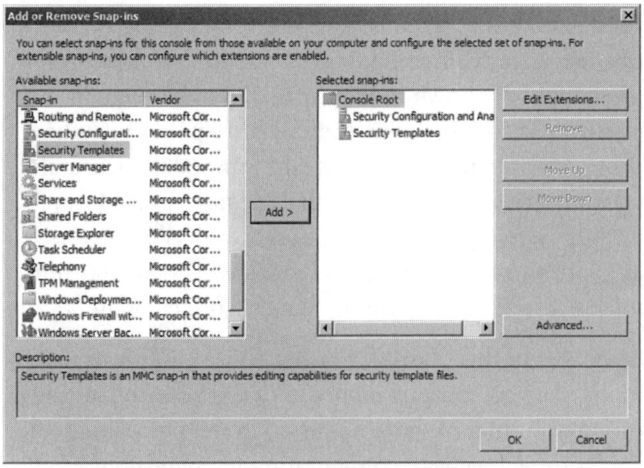

NOTE Unlike previous versions of Windows Server, Windows Server 2008 does not include any predefined security templates, such as the Compatible, Secure

Server, and High Secure Server templates included with Windows Server 2003. However, you can use the Security Templates snap-in to create a custom template that you can use for configuring security settings on standalone servers or servers in another forest.

These security tools are most useful in situations involving standalone computers and servers running custom applications; they are not emphasized on the 70-640 exam. For more information on these tools, refer to "Server Security Policy Management in Windows Server 2008" at http://technet.microsoft.com/en-us/library/cc754373(WS.10).aspx.

Auditing of Active Directory Services

Auditing enables you to track actions performed by users across the domain such as logging on and off or file and folder access. When you create and apply an auditing policy, auditable events are recorded in the security log of the computer at which they happen. You can then use Event Viewer to view any computer's security log by connecting to the required computer.

New Features of Active Directory Auditing

Windows Server 2008 introduces a new command-line tool, `auditpol.exe`, as well as subcategories in the Audit Directory Service Access category. In addition, Windows Server 2008 R2 introduces a new Advanced Audit Policy subnode in the Group Policy Management Editor. In previous versions of Windows Server, a single Directory Service Access category controlled the auditing of all directory service events. In Windows Server 2008, four subcategories of directory service access are available:

- **Directory Service Access:** Tracks all attempts at accessing AD DS objects whose system access control lists (SACLs) have been configured for auditing. This includes deletion of objects.

- **Directory Service Changes:** Tracks modifications to AD DS objects whose SACLs have been configured for auditing. The following actions are included:
  —When an attribute of an object has been modified, the old and new values of the attribute are recorded in the Security log.
  —When a new object is created, values of their attributes—including new attribute values—are recorded in the Security log. This includes objects moved from another domain.
  —When objects are moved from one container to another, the distinguished names of the old and new locations are recorded in the Security log.
  —When objects are undeleted, the location in which they are placed is recorded in the Security log. Any added, modified, or deleted attributes are also recorded.

- **Directory Service Replication:** Tracks the beginning and end of the synchronization of a replica of an Active Directory naming context.

- **Detailed Directory Service Replication:** Tracks additional AD DS replication events, including the establishment, removal, or modification of an Active Directory replica source naming context, replication of attributes for an AD DS object, or removal of a lingering object from a replica.

The `auditpol.exe` tool enables you to configure auditing from the command line. In the original version of Windows Server 2008, you must use this tool to enable the auditing of the new directory service access subcategories outlined here. This tool is discussed later in this section. In Windows Server 2008 R2, you can use the Advanced Audit Policy subnode to configure auditing of these subcategories. This subnode in Windows Server 2008 R2 provides an additional level of granular control over actions that you can audit. For example, instead of the single Audit logon events policy in the Audit Policy subnode, you have eight different policy settings in the Logon/Logoff category, thereby providing you with more detailed control of the aspects of logon and logoff actions you can track.

> **NOTE**   These new auditing categories also apply to auditing of Active Directory Lightweight Directory Services (AD LDS).

Using GPOs to Configure Auditing

Group Policy enables you to configure success or failure for several types of actions. In other words, you can choose to record successful actions, failed attempts at performing these actions, or both. For example, if you are concerned about intruders that might be attempting to access your network, you can log failed logon events. You can also track successful logon events, which is useful in case the intruders succeed in accessing your network.

You can use Group Policy to enable auditing at domain controllers, member servers, and client computers. Be aware that all auditing takes place at the local computer on which the events take place only and that these events are recorded on that computer's Security log. To enable auditing on all domain controllers, configure the auditing settings in the Default Domain Controllers Policy GPO; to enable auditing on other domain computers, configure the auditing settings in the Default Domain Policy GPO or in another GPO as required.

Available Auditing Categories

Windows Server 2008 enables you to audit the following types of events:

- **Account logon:** Logon or logoff by a domain user account at a domain controller. You should track both success and failure.

- **Account management:** Creation, modification, or deletion of computer, user, or group accounts. Also included are enabling and disabling of accounts and changing or resetting passwords. You should track both success and failure.

- **Directory service access:** Access to an AD DS object as specified by the object's SACL. This category includes the four subcategories mentioned earlier in this section; enabling directory service access from the Group Policy Management Editor enables all four subcategories. Enable this category for failures (if you record success, a large number of events will be logged).

- **Logon events:** Logon or logoff by a user at a member server or client computer. You should track both success and failure (success logging can record an unauthorized access that succeeded).

- **Object access:** Access by a user to an object such as a file, folder, or printer. You need to configure auditing in each object's SACL to track access to that object. Track success and failure to access important resources on your network.

- **Policy change:** Modification of policies including user rights assignment, trust, and audit policies. This category is not normally needed unless unusual events are occurring.

- **Privilege use:** Use of a user right, such as changing the system time. Track failure events for this category.

- **Process tracking:** Actions performed by an application. This category is primarily for application developers and does not need to be enabled in most cases.

- **System events:** Events taking place on a computer such as an improper shutdown or a disk with very little free space remaining. Track success and failure events.

NOTE Note the difference between Logon and Account Logon events. *Logon* events refer to authentication of a local user at a workstation or member server, whereas *Account Logon* events refer to the authentication of a domain user account at a domain controller.

TIP Know which types of actions to audit for different scenarios. For example, the exam might present a drag-and-drop interface in which you must select success and failure actions to achieve a given objective.

Configuring Basic Auditing Policies

Use the following procedure to specify basic audit policy settings in either the original or R2 version of Windows Server 2008:

Step 1.   Access the Group Policy Management Editor snap-in for the appropriate GPO linked to a site, domain, or OU.

Step 2.   Navigate to the **Computer Configuration\Policies\Windows Settings\Security Settings\Local Policies\Audit Policy** node.

Step 3.   Click this node to display the available policies in the details pane.

Step 4.   Right-click the appropriate policy and choose **Properties**.

Step 5.   In the Properties dialog box for the policy, select **Define these policy settings** and then choose **Success**, **Failure**, or both, as desired (see Figure 13-15). Then click **OK**. New to Windows Server 2008, the Explain tab of each policy's Properties dialog box provides more information on what the setting does.

Figure 13-15   Enabling auditing of object access.

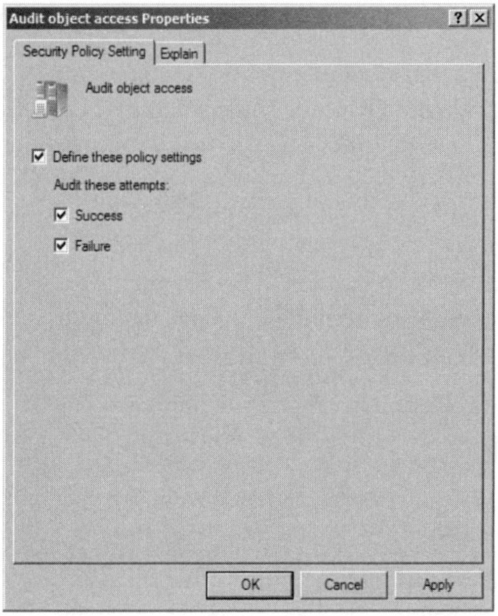

To track object access or directory service access, you must configure the SACL for each required object. Perform the following procedure:

Step 1.   In Windows Explorer, right-click the required file, folder, or printer and choose **Properties**.

Step 2.   Select the **Security** tab of the object's Properties dialog box.

Step 3.   Click **Advanced** to open the Advanced Security Settings dialog box and then select the **Auditing** tab.

Step 4.   To add users or groups to this tab, click **Edit** and then click **Add**.

Step 5. Type the required user or group in the Select User, Computer, or Group dialog box and then click **OK**.

Step 6. On the Auditing Entry dialog box that appears (see Figure 13-16), select the types of actions you want to track and then click **OK**.

Figure 13-16 Configuring the SACL for an AD DS object.

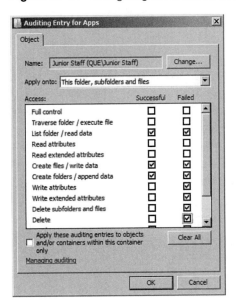

Step 7. The completed auditing entries appear in the Advanced Security Settings dialog box, as shown in Figure 13-17. Click **OK** twice to close these dialog boxes.

After you have configured object access auditing, attempts to access audited objects appear in the Security Log, which you can view from Event Viewer either in Server Manager as shown in Figure 13-18 or in its own snap-in from the Administrative Tools folder. For more information on any audited event, right-click the event and choose **Event Properties**.

TIP Ensure that the security log has adequate space to audit the events that you configure for auditing because the log can fill rapidly. The recommended size is at least 128 MB. You should also periodically save the existing log to a file and clear all past events. If the log becomes full, the default behavior is that the oldest events will be overwritten (and therefore lost). You can also configure the log to archive when full and not to overwrite events, but new events will not be recorded. Loss of recorded events could be serious in the case of high-security installations.

Figure 13-17   The Advanced Security Settings dialog box displays information on the types of object auditing actions that have been specified.

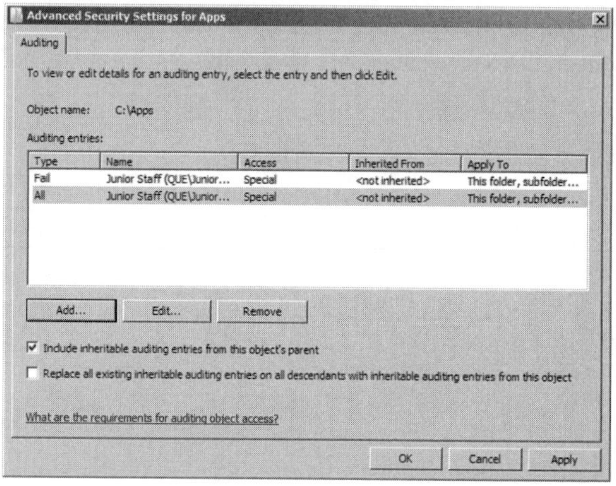

Figure 13-18   Event Viewer displays failed attempts at audited events with a lock icon.

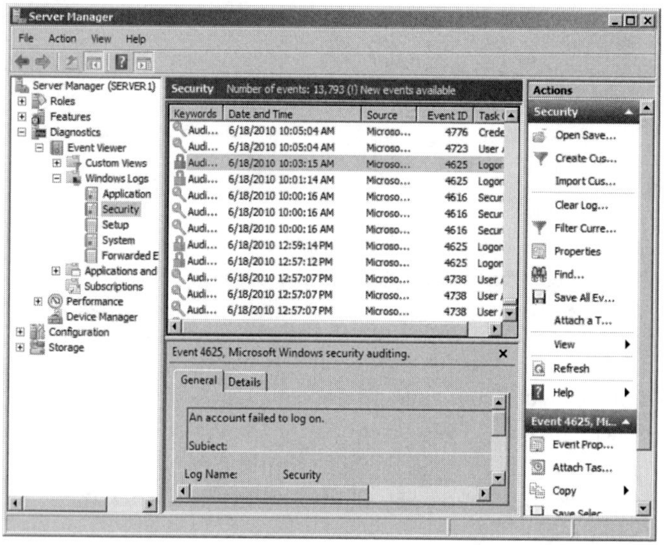

Configuring Advanced Audit Policies

The new Advanced Audit Policy Configuration node in Windows Server 2008 R2 enables you to configure granular auditing policies for the 10 subcategories shown in Figure 13-19. Using these policies, you can even determine which access control entry (ACE) in an object's ACL allowed an access to an audited object. This capability can assist you in modifying an object's ACL to ensure that only the appropriate access is permitted.

Figure 13-19   The Advanced Audit Policy node in Windows Server 2008 R2 enables you to configure auditing policies in 10 different subcategories.

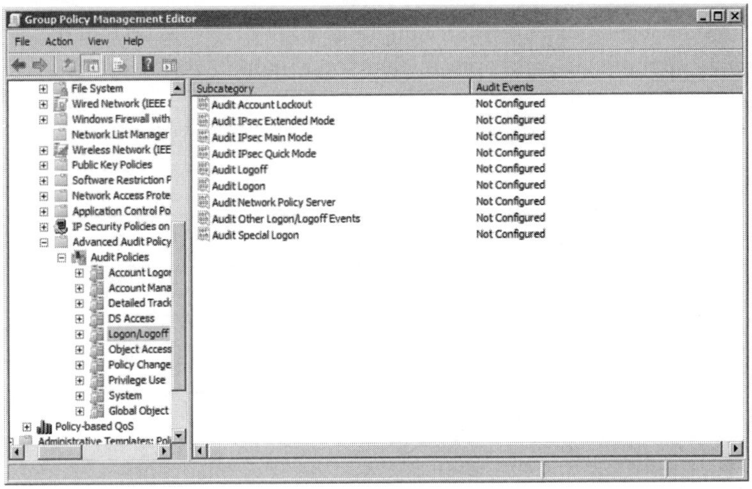

To configure any of these policies, simply right-click the desired policy and choose **Properties**. You can define auditing for success and/or failure of each policy setting in a manner similar to that shown previously in Figure 13-15. Consult the Explain tab of each policy setting's Properties dialog box for further information.

NOTE   For more information on the available advanced policy settings, refer to "Advanced Security Audit Policy Settings" and references cited therein at http://technet.microsoft.com/en-us/library/dd772712(WS.10).aspx. For additional information on configuring audit policies, including a comprehensive guide for setting up a series of policies on a test network, refer to "Advanced Security Audit Policy Step-by-Step Guide" at http://technet.microsoft.com/en-us/library/dd408940(WS.10).aspx.

TIP   You should ensure that advanced audit policy settings are not overwritten by basic audit policy settings. To do so, navigate to the **Computer Configuration\ Policies\Windows Settings\Security Settings\Local Policies\Security Options** node and enable the **Audit: Force audit policy subcategory settings (Windows Vista or later) to override audit policy category settings** policy setting.

Using **Auditpol.exe** to Configure Auditing

The Auditpol.exe tool performs audit policy configuration actions from the command line. This is the only tool you can use to configure auditing on a Server Core computer or to configure directory service auditing subcategories.

To use this tool, type the following at a command line:

```
Auditpol command [sub-command options]
```

Table 13-3 describes the available commands and Table 13-4 describes several of the more important subcommands and options that you should be aware of.

Table 13-3   Auditpol Commands

Command	Meaning
/get	Displays the current auditing policy
/set	Sets the audit policy
/list	Displays audit policy categories and subcategories or lists users for whom a per-user audit policy is defined
/backup	Saves the audit policy to a specified file
/restore	Retrieves the audit policy from a specified file
/clear	Clears the audit policy
/remove	Removes per-user audit policy settings and disables system audit policy settings

Table 13-4   Auditpol Subcommands and Options

Option	Meaning
/user:<username>	Specifies the security principal for a per-user audit. Specify the username by security identifier (SID) or by name. Requires either the /category or /subcategory subcommand when used with the /set command.
/category:<name>	Specifies one or more auditing categories separated by	and specified by name or globally unique identifier (GUID).
/subcategory:<name>	Specifies one or more auditing subcategories separated by	and specified by name or GUID.
/success:enable	Enables success auditing when using the /set command.
/success:disable	Disables success auditing when using the /set command.
/failure:enable	Enables failure auditing when using the /set command.
/failure:disable	Disables failure auditing when using the /set command.
/file	Specifies the file to which an audit policy is to be backed up or from which an audit policy is to be restored.

For example, to configure auditing for directory service changes, you would type the following:

```
Auditpol /set /subcategory:"directory service changes" /success:enable
```

Additional subcommands and options are available with most of the `Auditpol` commands discussed here. For information on the available subcommands and options available for a specified command, type **auditpol /command/?**.

Exam Preparation Tasks

Review All the Key Topics

Review the most important topics in the chapter, noted with the key topics icon in the outer margin of the page. Table 13-5 lists a reference of these key topics and the page numbers on which each is found.

Table 13-5 Key Topics for Chapter 13

Key Topic Element	Description	Page Number
Figure 13-1	Shows the available Group Policy security settings	422
Table 13-2	Describes the available password policy settings in Group Policy	424
List	Describes Group Policy account lockout settings	426
Paragraph	Describes the new fine-grained password policies	428
List	Shows you how to configure fine-grained password policies	430
Figure 13-10	Applying a fine-grained password policy to a group in Active Directory Administrative Center	434
Figure 13-11	Viewing the effective password policy for a user	436
List	Displays policy settings available from the Security Settings node of Group Policy	436
List	Describes the available categories of audit policies	442
Figure 13-15	Shows you how to enable an audit policy	444
Figure 13-18	Audited events are displayed in the Security log in Event Viewer	446
Figure 13-19	Shows you how to configure advanced audit policies in Windows Server 2008 R2	447

Complete the Tables and Lists from Memory

Print a copy of Appendix C, "Memory Tables" (found on the CD), or at least the section for this chapter, and complete the tables and lists from memory. Appendix D, "Memory Tables Answer Key," also on the CD, includes completed tables and lists to check your work.

Definitions of Key Terms

Define the following key terms from this chapter, and check your answers in the glossary.

account lockout, account policies, auditing, `Auditpol.exe`, fine-grained password policies, password settings object (PSO), password complexity, password policy

This chapter covers the following subjects:

■ **Tools Used to Monitor Active Directory:** Many of the tools available for monitoring computers can be used for monitoring and troubleshooting Active Directory. This section introduces these tools and explains their use with Active Directory.

■ **Monitoring and Troubleshooting Active Directory Replication:** It is important that replication take place in an accurate and timely fashion in order that all domain controllers remain up-to-date. Things can and do go wrong with this important function. This section introduces the tools used to track and correct problems with replication.

■ **Troubleshooting the Application of Group Policy Objects:** Group Policy does not always apply in the fashion you might expect it to. This section describes the tools and techniques you can use to monitor and troubleshoot the application of Group Policy.

CHAPTER 14

Monitoring Active Directory

In previous chapters, you learned how Active Directory Domain Services (AD DS) replicates its database across the entire forest. You learned about the structure of AD DS, how to delegate authority to various components of AD DS, and how to use Group Policy to configure and secure the network environment.

Now it's time to turn your attention to monitoring and troubleshooting of AD DS. Things can and do go wrong, often in subtle ways. This chapter looks at tools you can use to monitor AD DS, including replication and Group Policy. If you operate a consistent program of monitoring your domain controllers, this can provide insight toward impending failures and other problems and reduce the need for restorative actions. Monitoring can achieve two goals:

- It can help you to maintain consistent performance over time.

- It can help you in investigating problems such as sudden failures of hardware components.

"Do I Know This Already?" Quiz

The "Do I Know This Already?" quiz enables you to assess whether you should read this entire chapter or simply jump to the "Exam Preparation Tasks" section for review. If you are in doubt, read the entire chapter. Table 14-1 outlines the major headings in this chapter and the corresponding "Do I Know This Already?" quiz questions. You can find the answers in Appendix A, "Answers to the 'Do I Know This Already?' Quizzes."

Table 14-1 "Do I Know This Already?" Foundation Topics Section-to-Question Mapping

Foundations Topics Section	Questions Covered in This Section
Tools Used to Monitor Active Directory	1–8
Monitoring and Troubleshooting Active Directory Replication	9–10
Troubleshooting the Application of Group Policy Objects	11–14

1. You are using Network Monitor to capture and analyze the traffic crossing the network adapter card on your server. Which of the following criteria can you use to filter the traffic to display only selected frames? (Choose all that apply.)

   a. Frames captured using a specified network adapter

   b. Frames using a specified protocol

   c. Frames originating from a specified IP address

   d. Frames originating from a computer running a specific operating system

2. Which of the following actions can you perform from Task Manager? (Choose all that apply.)

   a. Monitor processor and memory usage levels on the local computer

   b. Create alerts when a specified performance counter exceeds a given limit

   c. Terminate a misbehaving application or process

   d. View, start, and stop services running on the computer

   e. Display the users with active or disconnected sessions on the local computer, send them messages, and log them off

   f. Connect to a remote computer and perform monitoring actions on that computer

3. You want to run a processor-intensive application that will perform a financial analysis of a large inventory database. The results are not needed for a few days but in the meantime you have more urgent tasks you want to perform, while allowing the financial analysis program to run only when other tasks are not running. You choose to run the financial analysis program at low priority. What are two ways you can use to set the program's priority? (Each answer represents a complete solution to the problem. Choose two.)

   a. Use Performance Monitor to set the program's priority to **Low**.

   b. From a command prompt, type **Start /low<program_name>**.

   c. In Task Manager, right-click the process associated with the program, choose **Set Priority**, and then select **Low**.

   d. In Windows System Resource Manager, choose the **Resource Monitor** function, right-click the program, and then select **Low Priority**.

   e. In Server Performance Advisor, right-click the process associated with the program, choose **Set Priority**, and then select **Low**.

4. You want to create a custom event log that records only Warning, Error, and Critical events taking place with AD DS on your domain controller. What should you do?

    a. In Event Viewer, right-click the System log and choose **Filter Current Log**. Then select the desired event levels and the Directory Service event source in the Filter Current Log dialog box.

    b. In Event Viewer, right-click the Security log and choose **Filter Current Log**. Then select the desired event levels and the Directory Service event source in the Filter Current Log dialog box.

    c. In Registry Editor, navigate to **HKEY_LOCAL_MACHINE\SYSTEM\ CurrentControlSet\Services\NTDS\Diagnostics**. In this Registry key, select Warning, Error, and Critical from the list of values and set them to 1 while leaving all other values set to 0.

    d. In Event Viewer, right-click the Directory Service log and choose **Filter Current Log**. Then select the desired event levels in the Filter Current Log dialog box.

5. You would like to display a real-time graph of processor and memory usage on your Windows Server 2008 computer so that you can decide whether you might need some type of hardware upgrade. Which of the following tools can you use for this purpose? (Choose all that apply.)

    a. Network Monitor

    b. Task Manager

    c. Event Viewer

    d. Performance Monitor

    e. Windows System Resource Manager

    f. Server Performance Advisor

6. Sharon has configured the Performance Monitor tool to track several NTDS performance objects on her domain controller so that she can have a performance baseline against which she can compare future domain controller performance. After viewing the graph for several minutes, she realizes she needs to save the data logged in the graph for future reference. What should she do to save all monitoring data, including the points that are no longer visible?

    a. She needs to right-click the graph and choose **Save Image As**. In the dialog box that appears, she needs to specify the name of a comma-delimited file to which Performance Monitor will save all data.

    b. She needs to choose the **File > Export** command. In the dialog box that appears, she needs to specify the name of a comma-delimited file to which Performance Monitor will save all data.

    c. She has used the wrong tool. She needs to use the Data Collector Sets tool to configure logging so that she can save the performance data.

    d. She has used the wrong tool. She needs to use the Windows System Resource Manager tool and select Resource Manager logging so that she can save the performance data.

7. You want to view a time trend of your computer's stability since you installed Windows Server 2008 R2, which is now almost a year ago. Which tool should you use?

    a. Reliability Monitor

    b. Resource Monitor

    c. Performance Monitor

    d. Tack Manager

    e. Event Viewer

8. You want to receive a message when your computer's processor time exceeds 85%. What feature of Performance Monitor should you configure?

    a. Event Trace Data Collector Set

    b. Event log

    c. Performance Counter Alert Data Collector Set

    d. System Diagnostics Data Collector Set

9. You are responsible for maintaining and troubleshooting intersite replication on your company's AD DS network, which consists of a single domain, 35 domain controllers, and 10 sites. Having been informed that several offices have not received updates to the AD DS database in a timely fashion, you monitor replication and notice that updates can take as long as 72 hours to reach some branch offices. Which of the following tools should you use to determine the reason for this delay? (Choose all that apply.)

    a. Active Directory Sites and Services

    b. `repadmin`

    c. `replmon`

    d. `netdiag`

    e. Event Viewer

10. You suspect that one of the domain controllers on your company's AD DS network is not replicating properly, so you want to check its replication status and save logged information. What should you do?

    a. In `Replmon`, add the domain controller in concern to the list of monitored servers. Then right-click this server and choose **Show Replication Topologies**.

    b. In `Replmon`, add the domain controller in concern to the list of monitored servers. Then right-click this server and choose **Generate Status Report**.

    c. Use the `dcdiag` tool with the `/c` and `/f:<log>` parameters.

    d. In Event Viewer, filter the Directory Service log to display events related to replication status.

11. From which of the following places can you simulate the application of Group Policy objects (GPOs) in Group Policy to given users and computers before the policies are actually applied? (Choose all that apply.)

    a. Active Directory Users and Computers

    b. Active Directory Sites and Services

    c. Active Directory Domains and Trusts

    d. Active Directory Administrative Center

    e. The `Gpresult` command

    f. The Run dialog box

    g. The Group Policy Management Console

12. You want to simulate the application of policies in a GPO using RSoP planning mode. Which of the following properties can you include in your RSoP query? (Choose all that apply.)

    a. User and computer group memberships

    b. Site where the GPO is applied

    c. Slow network connections

    d. Loopback processing

    e. Application of Windows Management Instrumentation (WMI) filters

13. A user named Fred reports to you that he is unable to access Internet Explorer on his computer, and you wonder if a policy in some GPO is preventing this access. You run RSoP in logging mode from your computer, specifying Fred's user account. You are informed that Fred's user account does not exist. What is the most likely reason for this error?

a. Fred's user account is disabled.

b. Fred's user account is a member of a group that is denied the Apply Group Policy permission on the Default Domain Policy GPO.

c. Another GPO is restricting the application of policies that would enable you to run RSoP in logging mode.

d. Fred has never logged on to your computer.

14. You want to ensure that policy settings in a GPO you have just finished modifying become applied as soon as possible. What command should you execute?

a. Gpupdate /force

b. Gpupdate /apply

c. Gpresult /force

d. Gpresult /apply

Foundation Topics

Tools Used to Monitor Active Directory

Microsoft provides a wealth of support tools to assist you in managing and monitoring AD DS. This section looks at the following tools for monitoring and troubleshooting AD DS:

- Network Monitor

- Task Manager

- Event Viewer

- Reliability and Performance Monitor

- Windows System Resource Manager

- Server Performance Advisor

Many of these tools are accessible from the new Server Manager console, which as you have learned provides a centralized location for accessing many of the server functions. Additional monitoring and troubleshooting tools that are available here and covered on other Windows Server 2008 exams include Device Manager, Windows Firewall with Advanced Security (including IP Security [IPSec] monitoring), and Task Scheduler.

Network Monitor

Network Monitor enables you to capture, view, and analyze frames (packets) as they are transmitted over a network to all network adapter cards on your computer. By analyzing these frames, you can troubleshoot network problems—for example, when users cannot log on because they are unable to communicate with domain controllers, DNS servers, or other servers. It can perform security-related actions, such as the following:

- Detection of intrusion attempts and successes

- Detection of unauthorized users and tracing their activity on the network

- Logs of captures provide information on network actions including source and destination addresses, protocols, and data transferred, thereby maintaining a record of actions that can include unauthorized ones

You can filter Network Monitor to capture or display only frames that meet certain criteria, thereby shortening the long list of frames included in the Frame Summary pane and facilitating the location of a certain frame type. Some of the more common filter criteria are the following:

- Frames captured by a specified network adapter

- Frames using a specified protocol

- Frames with a specified property, such as those originating from a specified IP address

Network Monitor is not included with Windows Server 2008 R2 by default. You need to download the executable file and install it. You will also need to download and install a parser file. This is a tool that queries the captured network traffic and provides customized output formats. The parser can also query other monitoring data such as log files, XML files, and CSV files, as well as data sources such as the Event logs, the Registry, the file system, and AD DS. Use the following steps:

Step 1. Access http://www.microsoft.com/downloads/ details.aspx?familyid=983b941d-06cb-4658-b7f6-3088333d062f&displaylang=en to download Network Monitor 3.4 (or the most recent version) as an executable (.exe) file. Also access http://www.microsoft.com/downloads/details.aspx?FamilyID=890cd06b-abf8-4c25-91b2-f8d975cf8c07&displaylang=en to download the Log Parser 2.2 file. Save these files to a convenient location on your computer.

Step 2. Double-click the Network Monitor installer file and click **Run** on the Internet Explorer - Security Warning dialog box that appears.

Step 3. You are informed that Microsoft Network Monitor Capture and Parser engine will be installed, followed by the Microsoft Network Monitor Parsers. Click **Yes** to continue.

Step 4. The Microsoft Network Monitor 3.4 (Capture and Parser Engine) Setup Wizard starts with a Welcome page. Click **Next**.

Step 5. Accept the end user license agreement and then click **Next**.

Step 6. You might be asked whether you want to use Microsoft Update to keep your computer secure and up-to-date. Select an option as desired and then click **Next**.

Step 7. The Choose Setup Type page provides a choice of three setup types as shown in Figure 14-1. Choose the most appropriate setup type for your needs (for learning purposes, it is adequate to select **Typical**).

Step 8. The Ready to Install page informs you that the wizard is ready to install Network Monitor. If desired, select the option to create a shortcut on the desktop. Click **Install**.

Step 9. The Installing Network Monitor page tracks installation progress, and then the Completing the Setup Wizard page informs you when installation is complete. Click **Finish**. You might be asked to log off and log back on before performing a capture.

Figure 14-1   You receive a choice of three setup types when installing Network Monitor.

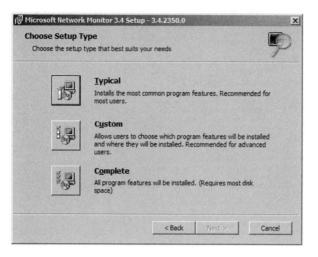

Step 10.   The Log Parser installation runs automatically. Accept the UAC prompt if you receive one.

Step 11.   When informed that the Log Parser 2.2 has been installed, click **Finish**.

After installation has completed, use the following steps to run Network Monitor:

Step 1.   Click **Start > All Programs > Microsoft Network Monitor 3.4** or double-click the desktop icon to start the program. Network Monitor starts and displays the interface shown in Figure 14-2 that includes a summary of new features as well as several "how-to" tips.

Step 2.   To capture network traffic, click **New capture tab** in the Recent Captures section. A tab named Capture1 by default is added at the top of the window that displays a multipane arrangement within which captured data will be displayed.

Step 3.   Click **Start** from the toolbar or the Capture menu to capture network traffic across the network adapter card of your server.

Step 4.   As shown in Figure 14-3, each frame captured creates one line within the Frame Summary pane including such details as source and destination computers (name or IP address), protocol name, and description. The time offset is the number of seconds elapsed since the capture was started.

Step 5.   To display information about a particular frame, select it. The Frame Details pane provides information on the selected frame, and the Hex Details pane provides a hexadecimal rendering of the bits contained within the frame.

Figure 14-2   When you first start Network Monitor, you see a summary of new features.

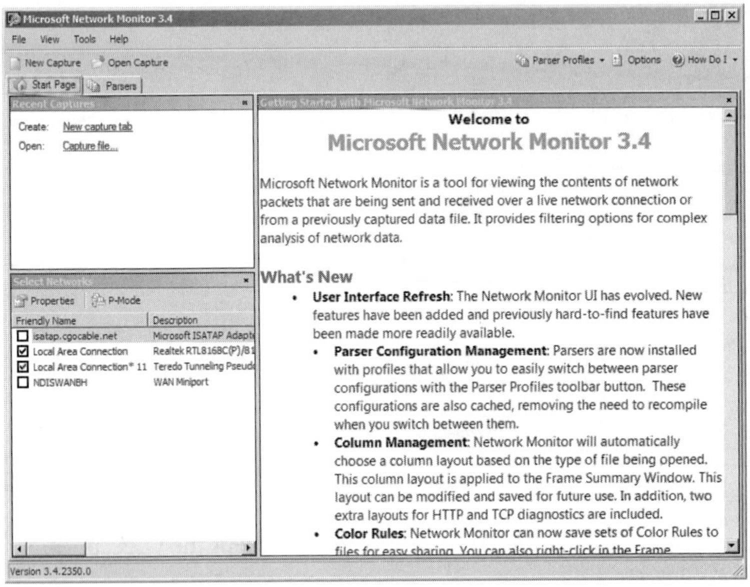

Figure 14-3   Network Monitor provides information on all frames that it captures.

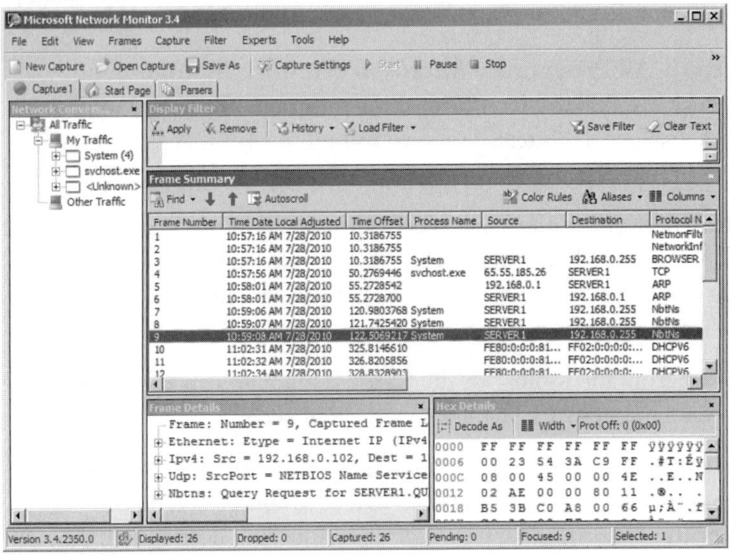

Step 6.   To view additional information about the selected frame in the Frame Details panel, click any of the **+** icons visible at the beginning of lines.

Step 7.   You can also view this information in its own window by using Ctrl or Shift to select multiple frames from the Frame Summary panel, right-clicking, and choosing **View Selected Frame(s) in a New Window**. The

Frame Display View dialog box that opens provides Frame Details and Hex Details panels similar to those in the main Network Monitor window.

Step 8.   To stop capturing frames, click **Stop** from the Capture menu.

NOTE   Details of using Network Monitor are beyond the scope of the 70-640 exam and will not be elaborated on here. For additional information on Network Monitor, consult *MCTS 70-642 Exam Cram: Windows Server 2008 Network Infrastructure, Configuring* (ISBN: 078973818X) and the Help files that are installed on your computer when you install Network Monitor.

TIP   Rather than asking you how to configure Network Monitor, the 70-640 exam is more likely to ask you which tool you should use in a given scenario. Tools suggested might include Network Monitor, and this choice is often used as an incorrect option.

NOTE   Network Monitor also includes a command-line tool, `nmcap.exe`, that you can use to script execution of this product. You can also specify options for starting and stopping captures according to time or specific network traffic types. For information on usage of this tool and its extensive list of options, open a command prompt and type `nmcap /?`. The Network Monitor Help files also includes a description of the available commands and options associated with this tool.

Task Manager

Task Manager provides information about currently running processes, including their CPU and memory usage, and enables you to modify their property or terminate misbehaving applications.

You can use any of the following methods to start Task Manager:

- Press **Ctrl+Shift+Esc**.
- Press **Ctrl+Alt+Delete** and select **Start Task Manager** from the list that appears.
- Right-click a blank area of the taskbar and select **Start Task Manager**.
- Click **Start** and type `taskmgr` in the Start menu Search field. Then click `taskmgr.exe` in the Programs list.

As shown in Figure 14-4, Task Manager has six tabs that perform the following actions:

Figure 14-4 Task Manager enables you to troubleshoot currently running applications, including closing nonresponsive ones.

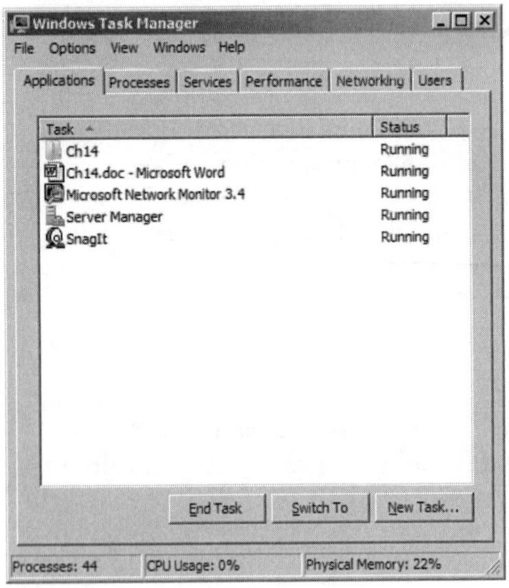

- **Applications:** Displays all applications running on the computer. To terminate an ill-behaved program, select it and click **End Task**.

- **Processes:** Provides information on all processes running on the computer. New to Windows Vista and Windows Server 2008 and continued in Windows 7 and Windows Server 2008 R2 is the Description column, which provides a detailed description of each process. You can modify the property of a running process or terminate an ill-behaved one. You can also display additional information by clicking **View > Select Columns**. The Select Process Page Columns dialog box that appears enables you to choose from a large number of variables associated with each process. To display all processes running on the computer, click the **Show processes from all users** button.

- **Services:** New to Windows Vista and Windows Server 2008 and continued in Windows 7 and Windows Server 2008 R2, this tab provides information on services installed on the computer, including their status, the service group to which they belong, and descriptive information. You can start a stopped service or stop a started one by right-clicking it and choosing the appropriate command. You can access the Services snap-in by clicking the **Services** command button, which enables you to configure more properties such as startup type and recovery options should a service fail.

- **Performance:** Provides a limited performance monitoring function that includes processor and physical memory usage statistics. The memory graph now displays actual memory usage rather than the page file usage displayed in

Windows Server 2003. If your server is equipped with multiple processors or a multi-core processor, the CPU usage history graph is split to show the activity of all processors or cores.

- **Networking:** Provides information on network utilization across the local network adaptors.

- **Users:** Displays the users that have sessions, active or disconnected, running on the local server. You can disconnect or log users off or you can send them messages.

The menu bar of Task Manager enables you to access additional options. From the File menu, you can start a new process. This action is equivalent to using the Run dialog box and is useful should the Explorer process become terminated or misbehave. From the Options menu, you can keep the Task Manager window always visible on the desktop. From the View menu, you can adjust the refresh rate of the graphs on the Performance and Networking tabs.

Configuring Application Priority

You can modify application behavior by adjusting its priority in Task Manager or by starting the application at a different priority. Windows 7 offers the following application priorities, arranged in decreasing order:

- **Realtime:** The highest priority level. Use extreme caution when selecting this priority because it can hang the computer.

- **High:** The highest useful priority level. Devotes a high level of priority to the application without disrupting essential services.

- **AboveNormal:** Runs the application at a priority slightly higher than default.

- **Normal:** The default priority. All processes run at this priority unless configured otherwise.

- **BelowNormal:** Runs the application at a priority slightly lower than default.

- **Low:** The lowest priority.

You can modify an application's priority in either of the following ways:

- **From Task Manager:** From the Processes tab, right-click the required process and choose **Set Priority**. Then select one of the priorities shown here. If you are unsure of the process associated with a given application, right-click the application in the Applications tab and select **Go To Process**. This switches you to the Processes tab, with the required process selected.

- **From a command prompt:** Type `Start /option executable_name`, where `option` refers to one of the priorities shown in the preceding list and `executable_name` refers to the program's name.

Event Viewer

Event Viewer, found both as a component of Server Manager and as a separate MMC console in the Administrative Tools folder, enables you to view logs of events generated by Windows and its applications.

Event Viewer was introduced in Chapter 13, "Account Policies and Audit Policies," with regard to viewing audited events. Event Viewer contains two folders of logs: Windows Logs, which contains five logs common to all servers, and Applications and Services Logs, which contains a series of logs dependent on the roles and role services installed on the server. To access the Event Viewer logs from Server Manager, expand **Diagnostics** and then **Event Viewer**. To access Event Viewer in its own console, type **event** from the Start menu Search field and then select **Event Viewer**. A series of logs is available when you expand the Windows Logs node. Select the desired log to view event information in the central pane and select an event to view information as shown in Figure 14-5. You can also double-click an event to obtain additional details on the event selected.

Figure 14-5 Event Viewer enables you to obtain information on several types of events occurring on your domain controller.

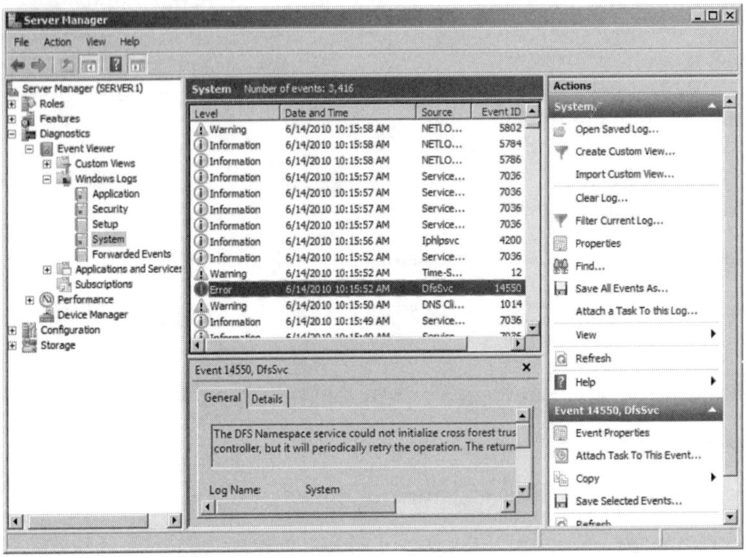

The following Windows Logs are present on all servers:

- **Application:** Displays events recorded by system applications, as well as applications written to Microsoft standards such as many antivirus programs.

- **Security:** Displays results of audited actions as configured in Group Policy. Auditing was discussed in Chapter 13.

- **Setup:** Records information related to the installation of applications and features on the server.

- **System:** Displays events logged by Windows kernel and device drivers, including reasons for the failure of services to start and the cause of stop (blue screen) errors. This log also records errors related to directory access problems.

- **Forwarded Events:** Saves events collected from remote computers. To enable this log, you must create an event subscription, which describes the events that will be collected and where they will be collected from.

Logs included in the Applications and Services node record events related to the particular application or service included as a subnode. Included here are several found on all servers, such as Hardware Events, Internet Explorer, and Key Management Service. The AD DS server role adds additional logs such as Directory Service (see Figure 14-6), File Replication Service, and DNS Server (if DNS is installed). You will also find a log related to each instance of Active Directory Lightweight Directory Service (AD LDS) here. The Microsoft subnode includes a very large number of subfolders, too numerous to mention here; two items of interest to Active Directory administrators here are Group Policy and Backup.

Figure 14-6 The Directory Service log records events related to AD DS.

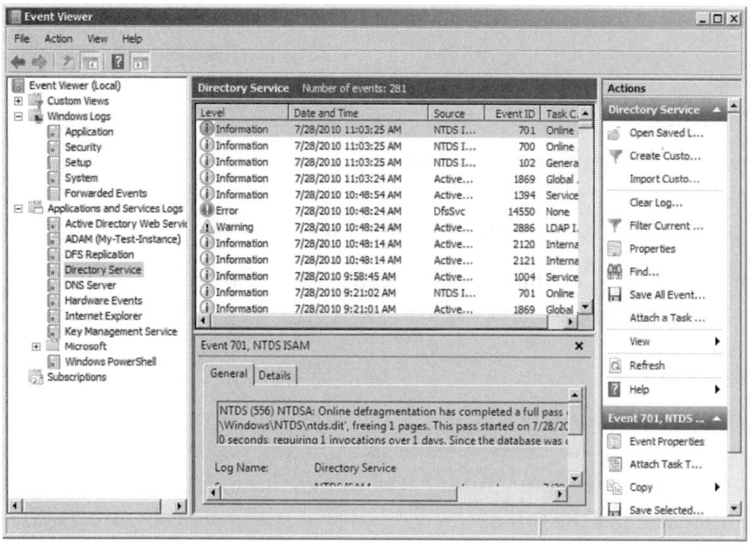

Obtaining information about directory service events from Event Viewer is simple. Use the following steps:

Step 1.   Open Event Viewer as already described.

Step 2.   In the console tree, select **Directory Service** to display Directory Service log information in the details pane. As shown in Figure 14-6, events displayed fall into four categories: information, warning, error, and critical. (Figure 14-6 does not include a critical event because they seldom occur.)

Step 3.   Double-click an event to open its Properties dialog box. This dialog box displays detailed information about the event, as shown in Figure 14-7.

Figure 14-7   Double-clicking an event provides detailed information about it.

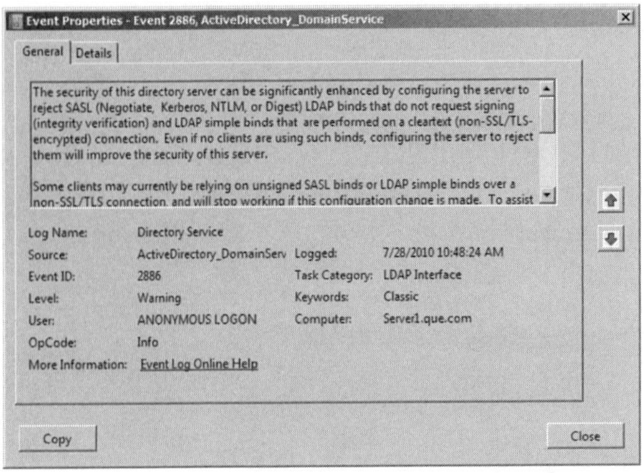

Step 4.   Use the up and down arrows in the event's Properties dialog box to view the properties of other events. These arrows are useful in tracking the progress of an incident that has recorded multiple events.

Step 5.   Repeat steps 2–4, selecting the appropriate log, to view events related to the other Event Viewer logs.

Customizing Event Viewer

With the large number of logs present in Windows Server 2008, you might think that keeping track of these logs would be a major undertaking. Microsoft has added the Custom Views folder at the top of Event Viewer to gather logs from various locations together. Appearing at the top of the console tree as shown in Figure 14-6, this folder includes an Administrative Events node as well as nodes for each of the server roles installed on the computer. The Administrative Events node includes critical, error, and warning events from all logs gathered in a single location, which facilitates your finding events that require your attention. Each log under

Server Roles gathers together events at all levels from the various Windows Logs and Applications and Services Logs that relate to that particular server role, again facilitating your locating these events rapidly. You can also create your own custom views in this area, as the following steps demonstrate:

Step 1.   Right-click **Custom Views** and choose **Create Custom View** to create a new custom view or **Import Custom View** to import one created on another computer.

Step 2.   This displays the Create Custom View dialog box shown in Figure 14-8. Select from the following options to create your customized log:

Figure 14-8   The Create Custom View dialog box enables you to create your own customized event log.

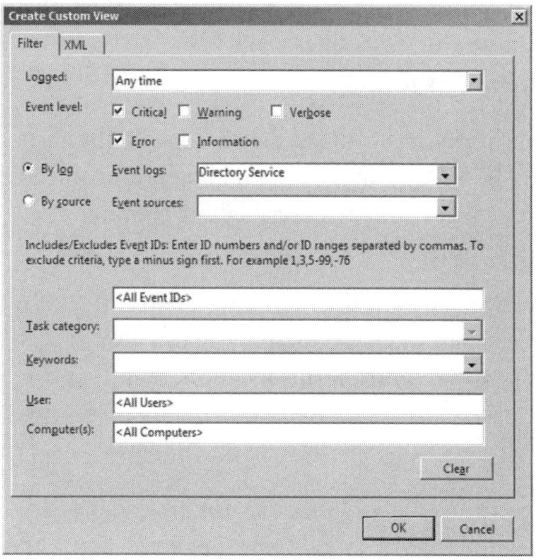

—**Logged:** Supply a time interval ranging from **Last hour** to **Last 30 days**, or choose **Any time** or a customized range of dates and times.

—**Event Level:** Choose one or more of the event levels: **Critical**, **Error**, **Warning**, and/or **Information**. Choose **Verbose** to provide additional detail on the logged events. (In previous Windows versions, you had to perform a Registry edit to obtain additional detail.)

—**By Log:** Enables you to select the logs from which you want to display events.

—**By Source:** Enables you to select from the service, program, or driver that logged the event. You can select only one of these options: **By log** or **By source**.

—**Event IDs:** These are numbers that uniquely define each type of event. You can select the event ID numbers to be displayed (or leave the default of **All Event IDs** selected).

—**Task Category:** Enables you to select task categories to be displayed

—**Keywords:** Enables you to select keywords such as **Audit Success**, **Audit Failure**, and so on.

—**User:** Enables you to select the user account(s) associated with an event. Separate multiple usernames with commas.

—**Computer(s):** Enables you to select the computer(s) associated with an event. Separate multiple computer names with commas.

Step 3. Click **OK**. In the Save Filter to Custom View dialog box that appears, type a name and optional description for the custom view and select the folder in which you want to store the view. Then click **OK**. Your custom filter is added to the console tree in the location you have selected.

You can also customize the level of detail shown by any of the default logs. Right-click a log and choose **Filter Current Log**. The Filter Current Log dialog box enables you to choose from most of the same categories already described for creating a custom log. The By Log and By Source options are not available.

For additional information on Event Viewer, consult the Windows Help and Support Center by choosing Help Topics from the Help menu. You can also go online by selecting the TechCenter website option from this location.

Customizing Event Viewer Detail

You can increase the level of detail that various Active Directory processes record in the Directory Service log. This procedure involves modifying Registry values, as described in the following procedure:

Step 1. Click **Start** and type `regedit` in the Start menu Search field. Then click **regedit.exe** from the Programs list.

Step 2. In the Registry Editor, navigate to **HKEY_LOCAL_MACHINE\SYSTEM\CurrentControlSet\ Services\NTDS\Diagnostics**.

Step 3. As shown in Figure 14-9, this Registry key contains a series of values related to the types of events logged in the Directory Service log. By default, they are all set to zero.

Step 4. To increase the level of detail for a particular type of event, double-click the associated value to display the Edit DWORD Value dialog box (see Figure 14-10). Enter a number between 1 and 5 for the value data (the higher the number, the more information is recorded) and then click **OK**.

Figure 14-9   You can customize the extent of logging of a series of events by editing the Registry.

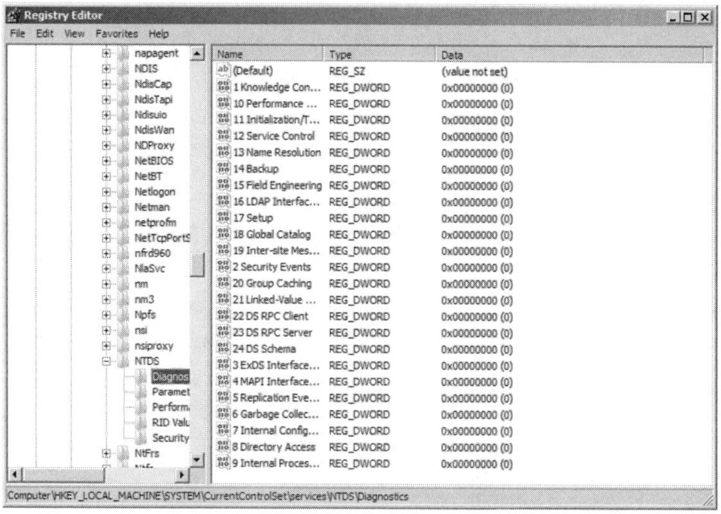

Figure 14-10   Specifying the level of logging detail for an event in the Registry Editor.

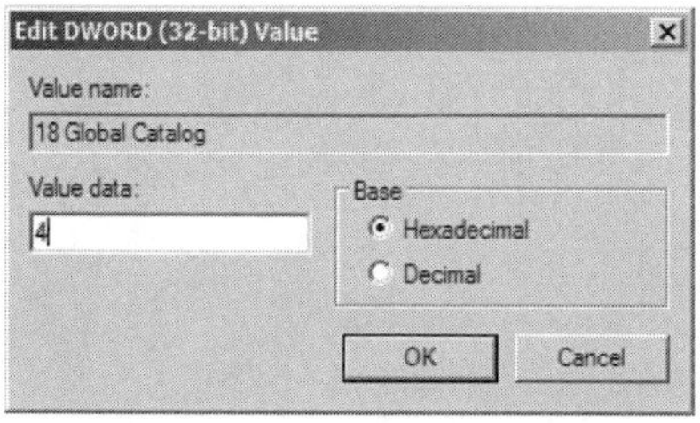

NOTE   Understand the problem you are looking for before raising the logging level. You should check the event logs first and not raise the logging level until you are fully aware of the problem and the information you are seeking.

WARNING   Be careful when editing the Registry! You can do serious harm to your computer if you are careless when editing the Registry. You should back up the Registry before editing it and then perform only the edits you are certain will not cause harm.

Reliability and Performance Monitor

The Windows Server 2008 R2 Performance Monitor snap-in replaces and updates the Performance Console tool used with Windows 2000 and Windows Server

2003. It is included as a component of the Diagnostics section of Server Monitor and also is accessible as a standalone MMC console from the Administrative Tools folder. As shown in Figure 14-11, it includes the following monitoring tools:

- **Performance Monitor:** Provides a real-time graph of server performance, either in the present time or as logged historical data.

- **Data Collector Sets:** Records server performance data into log files. Data collectors are separated into groups that you can use for monitoring performance under different conditions. This feature was previously known as Performance Logs and Alerts.

- **Reports:** Produces performance report data. This feature was included as the Report function of the System Monitor console in previous Windows versions.

Figure 14-11   You can monitor and log your server's performance from the Performance Monitor snap-in, here shown as a component of the Server Manager console.

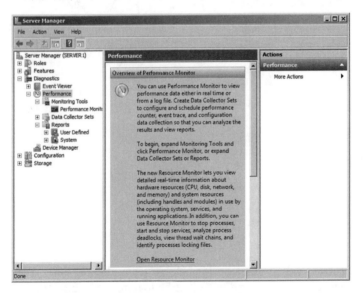

In the original version of Windows Server 2008, this tool is known as the Reliability and Performance Monitor console and includes a Resource Overview section that performs an overall reliability analysis of computer stability with time. This component has been replaced by the Resource Monitor tool mentioned in the next section.

NOTE   For additional information on Reliability and Performance Monitor and its various components, refer to "Performance and Reliability Monitoring Step-by-Step Guide for Windows Server 2008" at http://technet.microsoft.com/en-us/library/cc771692(WS.10).aspx.

Resource Monitor

Resource Monitor is a new tool in Windows 7 and Windows Server 2008 R2 that appears as its own panel and provides a summary of processor, disk, network, and memory performance statistics including mini-graphs of recent performance for these components, as shown in Figure 14-12. Click the triangle at the right side of each of these components to display additional information. This information includes the application whose resource usage is being monitored (referred to as the *image*) and the process identifier number (PID) of the application instance, as well as several statistical measures that pertain to each of the components. Included in the Memory section is a valuable graph that breaks down memory usage according to several interesting categories (see Figure 14-13). In the original version of Windows Server 2008, this tool was called Resource Overview and appeared as a default window when you first started Reliability and Performance Monitor.

Figure 14-12   Resource Monitor provides a performance summary for important CPU, disk, network, and memory counters.

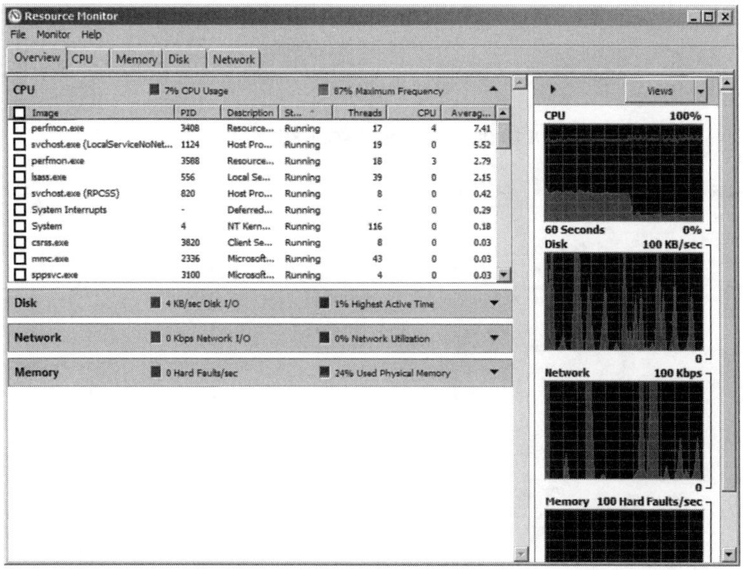

Reliability Monitor

Reliability Monitor is a new tool that utilizes the built-in Reliability Analysis Component (RAC) to provide a trend analysis of your server's stability over time. It provides the System Stability Chart shown in Figure 14-14, which correlates the trend of your computer's stability against events that might destabilize the computer. It tracks several types of events that affect your computer's stability.

Figure 14-13 The Memory section of Resource Monitor provides a graphical summary of memory usage.

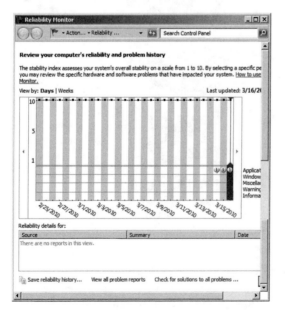

Figure 14-14 Reliability Monitor provides a trend analysis of your server's stability.

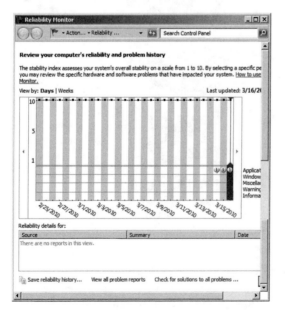

Use the following steps to run Reliability Monitor:

Step 1.   Ensure that you are logged on as an administrator, or have administrator credentials available.

Step 2.   Click **Start** and type `reliability` in the Start Search text box. Then click **View reliability history** in the Programs list.

Step 3.   As shown previously in Figure 14-14, events that cause the performance index to drop are marked in one of the event rows. Click a date containing one of these marks and then expand the appropriate section to obtain more information for the following categories:

—**Application failures:** Software programs that hang or crash. Information provided includes the name of the program, its version number, the type of failure, and the date.

—**Windows failures:** Problems such as operating system crashes, boot failures, and sleep failures. Information provided includes the type of failure, the operating system and service pack version, the Stop code or detected problem, and the failure date.

—**Miscellaneous failures:** Other types of failures such as improper shutdowns. Information includes the failure type, details, and date.

—**Warnings:** Other problems such as unsuccessful application reconfiguration or update installation. Information includes the type of reconfiguration attempted.

—**Information:** Includes the successful installation of various updates and definition packs, as well as successful installation or uninstallation of software programs.

Step 4.   To view a comprehensive list of problems, click the **View all problem reports** link at the bottom of the dialog box. The list displayed includes the various types of failures noted here.

Step 5.   To export an XML-based reliability report, click **Save reliability history**, specify a path and filename, and then click **Save**.

Step 6.   To check for solutions to problems, click **Check for solutions to all problems**. Reliability Monitor displays a Checking for Solutions message box as it goes to the Internet and attempts to locate solutions to your problems. You might have to click **Send information** to send additional information to the Microsoft Error Reporting Service.

NOTE   To display data in the System Stability Chart, you must run your computer for at least 24 hours after first installation of Windows Server 2008 R2. For the first 28 days, Reliability Monitor uses a dotted line on the Stability Chart graph, indicating that the data is insufficient to establish a valid baseline for this index.

Performance Monitor

As shown in Figure 14-15, Performance Monitor provides a configurable real-time graph of computer performance and enables you to perform tasks such as the following:

Figure 14-15   Performance Monitor displays a real-time graph of activity for selected objects and counters.

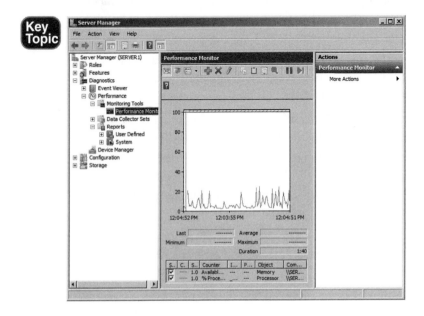

- Identify performance problems such as bottlenecks

- Monitor resource usage

- Establish trends of server performance with time

- Monitor the effects of changes in server configuration

- Generate alerts when unusual conditions occur

Before you learn more about the Performance Monitor tool, you need to be familiar with the terms defined in Table 14-2, which are used in a specific manner when referring to performance metrics.

Table 14-2   Performance Monitor Terms

Term	Description
Object	A specific hardware or software component that Performance Monitor is capable of monitoring. It can be any component that possesses a series of measurable properties. Windows Server 2008 R2 comes with a defined set of objects; applications such as Internet Information Services (IIS) installed on Windows Server 2008 R2 may add more objects to the available set.
Counter	One of a series of statistical measurements associated with each object.
Instance	Refers to multiple occurrences of a given object. For example, if your computer has two hard disks, two instances of the PhysicalDisk object will be present. These instances are numbered sequentially, starting with 0 for the first occurrence. On a multiple processor server, the performance of each processor is recorded as an instance. An instance labeled "_Total" is also present, yielding the sum of performance data for each counter. Note that not all objects have multiple instances.

Information on objects and counters is displayed in the following format: *Object (_instance)\Counter*. For example, Processor (_0)\%Processor Time measures the %Processor time on the first processor. The instance does not appear if only a single instance is present.

Performance Monitor enables you to obtain a real-time graph of computer performance statistics. Use the following procedure:

Step 1.   Click **Start**, type `performance` in the Start Search text box, and then click **Performance Monitor**. You can also start Performance Monitor from the Server Manager console, accessed by right-clicking **Computer** and choosing **Manage**. Expand **Diagnostics** and select **Performance**. You can also open Performance Monitor from the System Configuration dialog box. Click **Start**, type `msconfig` in the Start Menu Search Field, select **Performance Monitor** from the Tools tab of System Configuration, and then click **Launch**.

Step 2.   If you receive a User Account Control (UAC) prompt, click **Yes** or supply administrative credentials.

Step 3.   In the Performance console, click **Performance Monitor**. As shown in Figure 14-16, Performance Monitor displays the Processor\%Processor Time counter.

Step 4.   To add objects and counters, click the **+** icon on the toolbar.

Step 5.   In the Add Counters dialog box that appears (see Figure 14-17), select the server to be monitored from the Select Counters from Computer drop-down list. To monitor local computer performance, you can select

<Local Computer>. Then select the desired object and instance from the lists directly below the Select Counters list.

Figure 14-16 When Performance Monitor first starts, it displays a graph of Processor\% Processor Time.

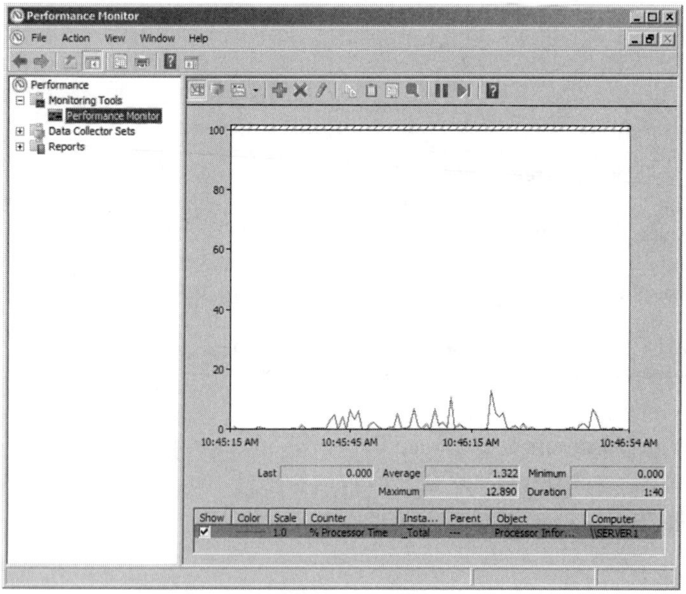

Figure 14-17 You can select from a large number of objects from the Performance Object drop-down list in the Add Counters dialog box.

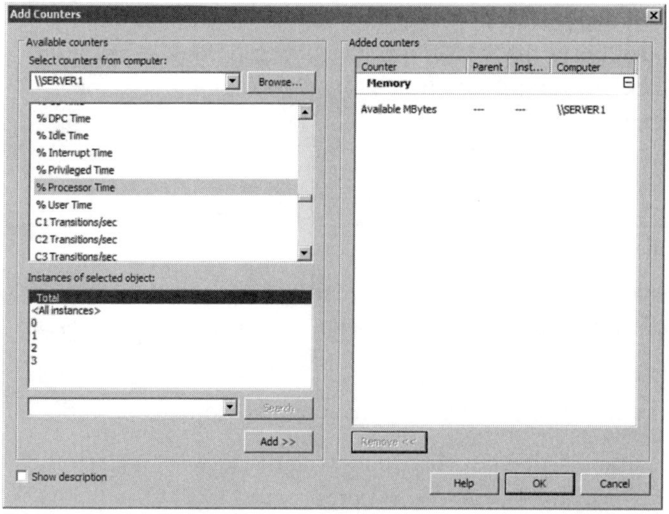

Step 6.   Expand the desired object to display a list of available counters from which you can select one or more counters. To add counters to the graph, select the counter and click **Add**.

Step 7.   Repeat steps 5 and 6 to add more counters. You learn about suitable counters in the following sections.

Step 8.   When you are finished, click **OK**.

TIP   You can highlight individual counters in Performance Monitor. To highlight an individual counter in the Performance Monitor display, select it from the list at the bottom of the details pane and click the highlight icon (looks like a highlighter pen) in the taskbar. You can also press the **Backspace** key to highlight the counter. The highlighted counter appears in a heavy line. You can use the up or down arrow keys to toggle through the list of counters and highlight each one in turn. This feature helps you to find the desired counter from a graph that includes a large number of counters.

NOTE   For more information on Performance Monitor, refer to "Performance Monitor Getting Started Guide" at http://technet.microsoft.com/en-ca/library/dd744567(WS.10).aspx.

Data Collector Sets

Data collector sets are series of performance objects and counters that enable you to log server performance over time for later viewing and analysis in the Performance Monitor snap-in. Previously known as Performance Logs and Alerts, this feature enables you to do the following:

- Establish a performance baseline for each server, which is a log of server performance that you can save for later comparison with future performance and tracking any changes that might have occurred over time.

- Identify potential bottlenecks in server performance so that you can take corrective action.

- Monitor the effectiveness of any changes you make to the server's configuration.

- Alert you to events of unusual server performance, such as a consistently high percentage of processor utilization or low available memory. These might indicate hardware or software problems or the need to upgrade some system component. These alerts are displayed in the Application log in Event Viewer.

Data collector sets are binary files that save performance statistics for later viewing and analysis in the Performance Monitor snap-in; you can also export them to spreadsheet or database programs for later analysis. Windows Server 2008 and Windows Server 2008 R2 create a series of data collector sets by default. The default data collector sets enable you to log default sets of performance counters for various purposes, including system diagnostics, LAN diagnostics, system performance, wireless diagnostics, event trace sessions, and startup event trace sessions. To view these sets, expand the branches under the Data Collector Sets node of the Performance Monitor snap-in. Right-click any available data collector set and choose **Properties** to view information on the selected data collector set.

You can also create your own user-defined data collector set. Use the following procedure to create a data collector set.

Step 1.   In the console tree of the Performance Monitor snap-in previously shown in Figure 14-16, select and expand **Data Collector Sets**.

Step 2.   Select **User Defined**.

Step 3.   To create a new data collector set, right-click a blank area of the details pane and select **New > Data Collector Set**. The Create New Data Collector Set Wizard starts.

Step 4.   You receive the page shown in Figure 14-18. Provide a name for the new data collector set. Select either **Create from a template (Recommended)** or **Create manually (Advanced)**, and then click **Next**. If you select the **Create manually (Advanced)** option, refer to the next procedure for the remainder of the steps you should perform.

Figure 14-18   This page of the Create New Data Collector Set Wizard enables you to name your data collector set and choose whether to use a template.

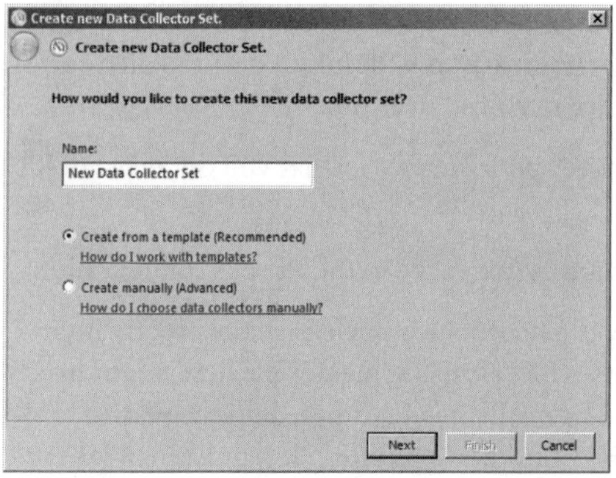

Step 5. If you select the **Create from a Template** option, you receive the dialog box shown in Figure 14-19, which enables you to use one of the following templates:

Figure 14-19 The Create New Data Collector Set Wizard enables you to use several different templates.

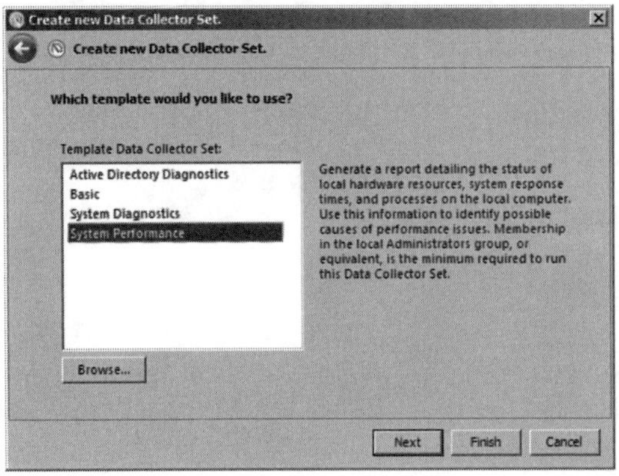

—**Active Directory Diagnostics:** Analyzes performance of AD DS–related counters on a domain controller.

—**Basic:** Enables you to use performance counters to create a basic data collector set, which you can edit later if necessary.

—**System Diagnostics:** Enables you to create a report that contains details of local hardware resources, system response times, and local computer processes. System information and configuration data are also included.

—**System Performance:** Enables you to create a report that provides details on local hardware resources, system response times, and local computer processes.

Step 6. Select the desired template and click **Browse** to locate a template file (XML format) if one exists. Then click **Next**.

Step 7. You receive the Where would you like the data to be saved? page shown in Figure 14-20. Select a location to which you would like the data to be saved (or accept the default location provided), and then click **Next**.

Step 8. The Create the data collector set? page shown in Figure 14-21 enables you to select the user under whom the data collector set will be run. If you want to run it under a different user, click **Change** and supply the requested credentials. To start logging now or configure additional properties, select the option provided. Then click **Finish**.

Figure 14-20   The Where would you like the data to be saved? page enables you to chose the folder to which you want to save the data collector set.

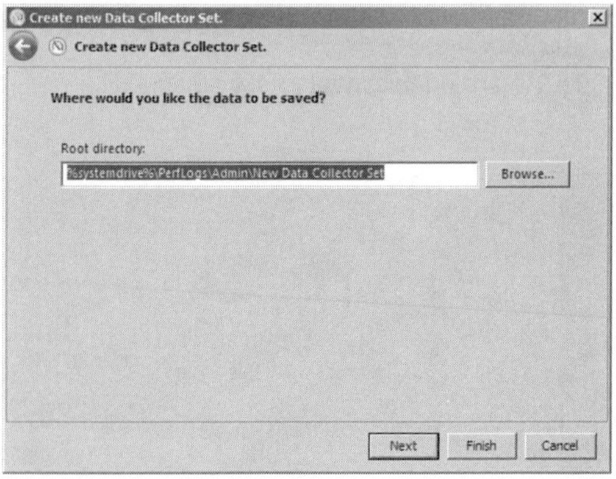

Figure 14-21   The Create the data collector set? page enables you to run the set as another user or open the properties of the data collector set.

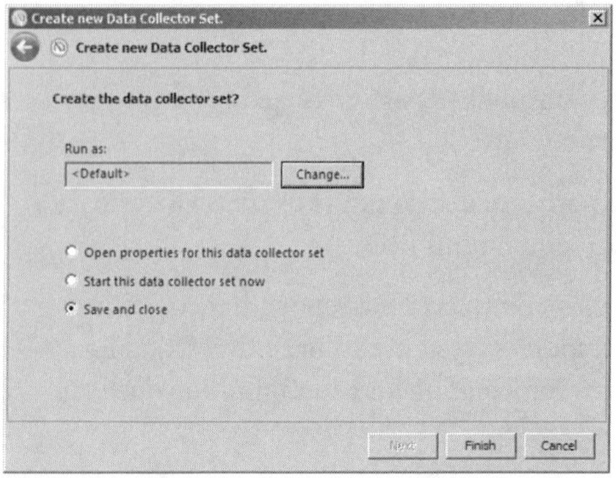

TIP   After you've selected the desired template, you can click **Finish** on any of the remaining pages of the wizard if you want to accept the remaining defaults.

To create a custom data collector set, use the **Create manually (Advanced)** option in step 4 of the previous procedure and then use the following steps to complete the procedure:

Step 1.   After selecting the **Create manually (Advanced)** option and clicking **Next**, you receive the screen shown in Figure 14-22, which enables you to specify the following options:

—**Performance counter:** Enables you to select performance objects and counters to be logged over time. Click **Next** to specify the perform- ance counters to be logged and the desired sampling interval.

Figure 14-22   You can create several types of logs or alerts from the Create manually option in the Create New Data Collector Set Wizard.

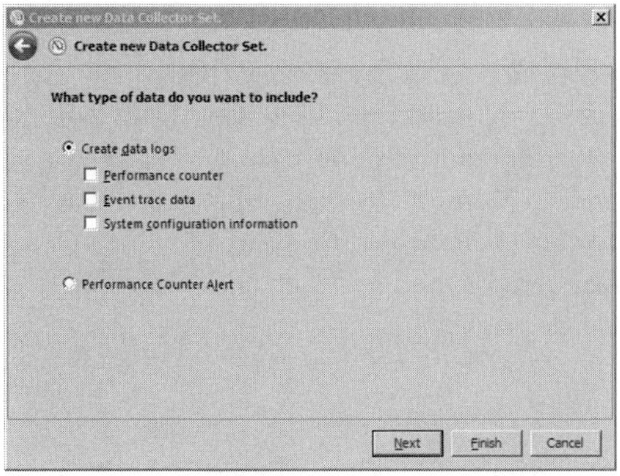

—**Event trace data:** Enables you to create trace logs, which are similar to counter logs, but they log data only when a specific activity takes place, whereas counter logs track data continuously for a specified interval.

—**System configuration information:** Enables you to track changes in Registry keys. Click **Next** to specify the desired keys.

—**Performance Counter Alert:** Enables you to display an alert when a selected counter exceeds or drops beneath a specified value. Click **Next** to specify the counters you would like to alert and the limiting value (see Figure 14-23 for an example).

Figure 14-23   You can create an alert that informs you when the Processor\% Processor Time value exceeds 80%.

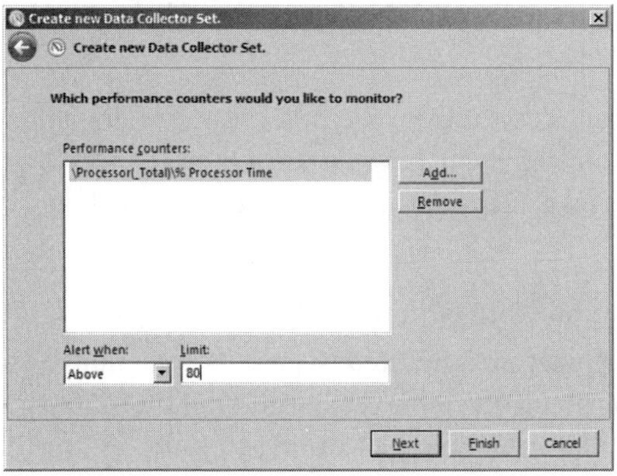

Step 2.   After clicking **Next**, you receive the same dialog box shown previously in Figure 14-21. Make any changes needed and then click **Finish**.

The data collector set is created and placed in the User Defined section. If you se-lect the option to start the data collector set now, logging begins immediately and continues until you right-click the data collector set and choose **Stop**.

You can view data collected by the data collector set in Performance Monitor. From the view previously shown in Figure 14-16, select the **View Log Data** icon (the second icon from the left in the toolbar immediately above the performance graph). In the Source tab of the Performance Monitor Properties dialog box that appears, select the **Log Files** option and click **Add**. Select the desired log file in the Select Log File dialog box that appears, click **Open** and then click **OK**. This displays the selected log in the performance graph.

> **NOTE** For more information on all aspects of Reliability and Performance Monitor covering both the original and R2 versions of Windows Server 2008, refer to "Performance and Reliability Monitoring Step-by-Step Guide for Windows Server 2008" at http://technet.microsoft.com/en-us/library/cc771692(WS.10).aspx.

Windows System Resource Manager

Windows System Resource Manager (WSRM) is an administrative feature that en-ables you to control how processor and memory resources are allocated to applica-tions, services, and processes running on the server. Managing resource allocation reduces the risk of these items competing for processor and memory resources, thereby improving the efficiency and performance of the computer. It is especially useful on servers that are running Terminal Services.

To install WSRM, access the Features node of Server Manager and click **Add Features**. In the Select Features page of the Add Features Wizard, scroll down to select **Windows System Resource Manager**. The wizard will ask you to install Windows Internal Database. Accept this request, click **Next**, and then click **Install**.

After you have installed WSRM, you can access it from the Administrative Tools folder. You can monitor the computer on which you have installed it or connect to another computer. WSRM opens in its own snap-in, which has nodes for the fol-lowing items in the console tree:

- **Resource Allocation Policies:** Used by WSRM to determine how computer resources such as processor and memory are allocated to processes running on the server. WSRM provides four built-in resource allocation policies, or you can create a custom resource allocation policy according to your net-work's need.

- **Process Matching Criteria:** Used by WSRM to match processes running on the server and aggregate the matched processes into groups, which can then be managed in resource allocation policies. Two built-in process-matching criteria are included for your use, or you can create your own custom criteria.

■ **Conditions:** You can have up to six preconfigured events, which represent conditions under which WSRM can automatically switch to a different matching policy.

■ **Calendar:** Enables you to schedule resource management. You can create one-time event or recurring events with which you can associate a resource allocation policy. You can also schedule the times at which a resource allocation policy will take effect or end. Multiple schedules are supported.

■ **Resource Monitor:** Uses Performance Monitor to display a custom set of counters that assist you in understanding how resource management works and how often your policies change the usage of server resources. See Figure 14-24.

Figure 14-24 The Resource Monitor component of WSRM provides a snapshot of your server's performance.

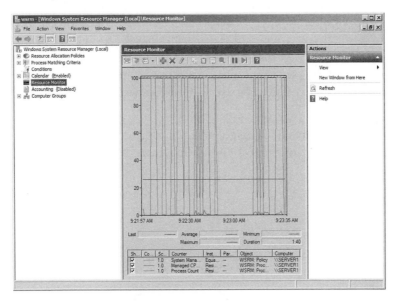

■ **Accounting:** You can log accounting data about applications. This includes information about applications that exceeded their allocated resources and changes made by the management policy. This data is stored in an accounting database on the local computer, another computer running WSRM, or on an SQL Server database.

NOTE For additional information on WSRM, consult *MCTS 70-643 Exam Cram: Windows Server 2008 Applications Infrastructure, Configuring* (ISBN 078978198) or links contained within "Windows System Resource Manager" at http://technet.microsoft.com/en-us/library/cc755056.aspx.

Server Performance Advisor

Server Performance Advisor was introduced in Windows Server 2003 as a tool that gathers information from a series of sources, including performance counters, Registry keys, and Event Tracing for Windows. It provides an in-depth view of current server performance and provides suggestions for making improvements. You can configure Server Performance Advisor to repeat the process of gathering information on a regular basis to obtain trend information that assists in identifying trouble spots.

Server Performance Advisor automatically detects the server roles you have configured, and installs data collector groups that are pertinent to these roles. You can also create custom data collector groups. Each data collector group is defined in an XML-based configuration template that includes the appropriate performance counters, event traces, and Registry keys for the server role in question. It also provides reports that enable you to present the data in formats appropriate for different individuals or groups.

In Windows Server 2008, the functionality of Server Performance Advisor is integrated into Reliability and Performance Monitor. The Reports feature of this tool includes four predefined server diagnostics:

- Active Directory Diagnostics

- LAN Diagnostics

- System Diagnostics

- System Performance

Each of these includes a specific set of performance objects and counters suited for monitoring these aspects of server performance. Also included is a User Defined subnode that you can use to configure your own custom report.

Monitoring and Troubleshooting Active Directory Replication

Proper replication of Active Directory is essential to its proper operation, and many things can and do go wrong. Besides Event Viewer, which was discussed earlier in this chapter, Microsoft provides the following tools that assist you in troubleshooting Active Directory replication problems:

- Active Directory Replication Monitor (`replmon`)
- Active Directory Replication Administrator (`repadmin`)
- Domain Controller Diagnostics (`dcdiag`)

replmon

`replmon` is a GUI-based tool available from the Windows Server 2003 Service Pack 2 Support Tools web page. Although this tool was written for Windows Server 2003, it is still functional on both the original and R2 versions of Windows Server 2008. Navigate to http://www.microsoft.com/downloads/details.aspx?FamilyID=96a35011-fd83-419d-939b-9a772ea2df90&DisplayLang=en, select **suptools.msi**, and then click **Download**. Also select **suptools.cab** and click **Download**. Ensure that both these files are saved to the same folder on your hard drive. When the download is complete, double-click **suptools.msi**, click **Run,** and then follow the instructions provided by the Support Tools Setup Wizard. You will receive a compatibility warning, but proceed to install the tools anyway. Follow the steps in the Windows Support Tools Setup Wizard that displays.

Use the following steps to start Replication Monitor, monitor the status of AD DS replication, and create a log file that records a server's replication events.

Step 1.   Click **Start > Run**, type `replmon`, and then press **Enter** to start the Replication Monitor GUI tool.

Step 2.   Right-click **Monitored Servers** and choose **Add Monitored Server**. This action starts the Add Monitored Server Wizard.

Step 3.   To add a server by name, ensure that the **Add the server explicitly by name** option is selected and then click **Next**.

Step 4.   On the Add Server to Monitor page, ensure that **Enter the name of the server to monitor explicitly** is selected. Type the name of the server you want to monitor and then click **Finish** (see Figure 14-25).

Step 5.   The domain controller you added appears in the left pane along with the Active Directory partitions it hosts. Repeat steps 3 and 4 to add additional domain controllers as needed. Additional domain controllers

appear listed under the sites in which they are located, as shown in
Figure 14-26.

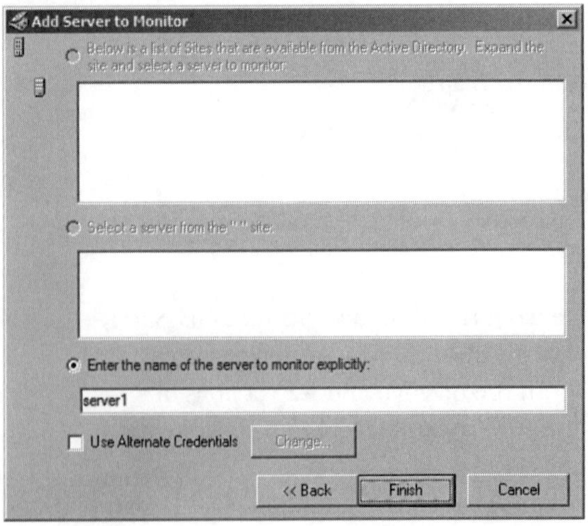

Figure 14-25   You can enter the name of the server to be monitored from the Add Server to
Monitor page.

![Add Server to Monitor dialog box]

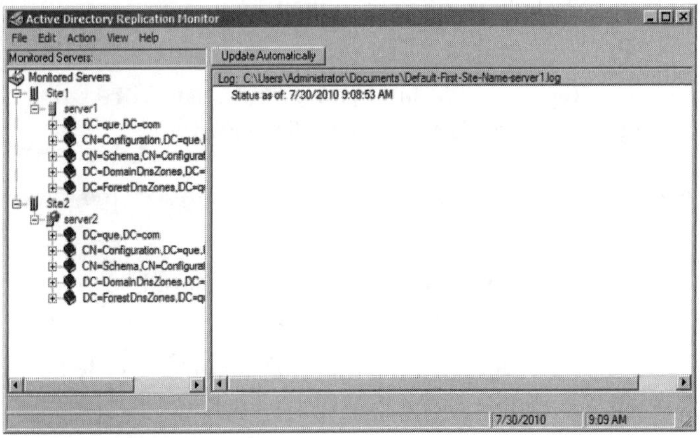

Figure 14-26   replmon lists domain controllers according to the sites in which they are
located.

![Active Directory Replication Monitor window showing Monitored Servers with Site1, server1 and Site2, server2]

Step 6.   To configure replmon to automatically update its information, click the
Update Automatically button and then type the number of minutes to
wait between monitoring intervals. After you do this, the **Update
Automatically** button changes to **Cancel Auto Update**.

Step 7.   Right-click the server for which you want to create a status report and choose **Generate Status Report**, as shown in Figure 14-27.

Figure 14-27   The Generate Status Report option enables you to create a replication status report for a monitored server.

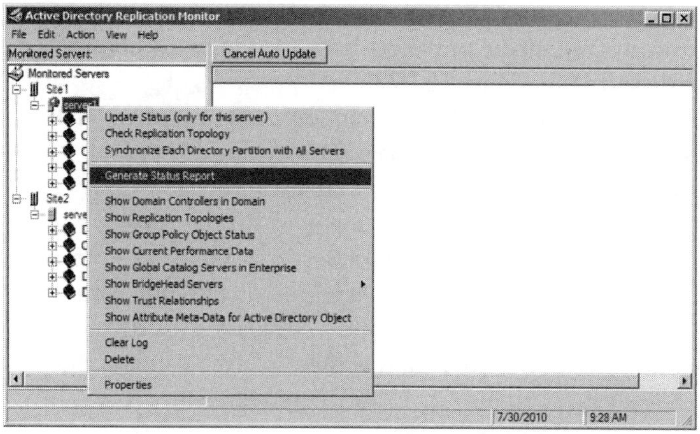

Step 8.   In the Save As dialog box that appears, type a name for the log file you want to create and click **Save**.

Step 9.   In the Report Options dialog box, select the type of information you want to have logged, as shown in Figure 14-28. Then click **OK**.

Figure 14-28   The Report Options dialog box enables you to specify which information **replmon** will save in its log files.

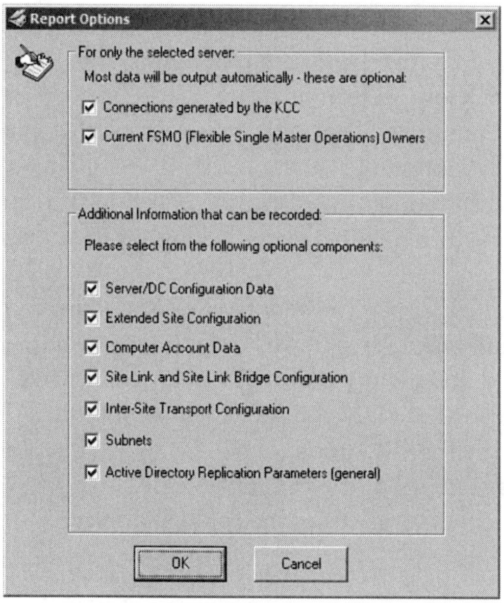

Step 10. The Report Status dialog box tracks progress of report creation and displays a Report Complete message when finished. Click **OK**.

Some of the more important actions you can perform using `replmon` are as follows:

Key Topic

■ **Obtain additional information about the status of replication at a selected server:** Right-click the desired server and select from the following options, which were previously shown in Figure 14-27.

—**Update Status (only for this server):** This option forces an immediate update for the selected server. It also logs and displays the time for this update.

—**Check Replication Topology:** This option forces the Knowledge Consistency Checker (KCC) to recalculate the replication topology for this server.

—**Synchronize Each Directory Partition with All Servers:** This option forces replication for this server's directory partitions with their replication partners.

—**Show Domain Controllers in Domain:** This option displays a dialog box that lists all domain controllers in the domain, together with the name of the site in which each is located and the LDAP distinguished names (DNs) of the associated computer and server objects.

—**Show Replication Topologies:** This option displays a graphical view of all replication partners for every directory partition on the selected server.

—**Show Group Policy Object Status:** This option displays a list of all Group Policy objects (GPOs) on any domain controller in your network. The list includes their Globally Unique Identifiers (GUIDs) and their version numbers in the Group Policy Container (GPC) and Group Policy Template (GPT). It also indicates whether the GPC and GPT versions of the GPO are out of synchronization.

—**Show Current Performance Data:** This option displays System Monitor performance counters that pertain to Active Directory replication. You must first select counters from the **View > Options** menu.

—**Show Global Catalog Servers in Enterprise:** This option displays a list of global catalog servers in this server's forest.

—**Show BridgeHead Servers:** From this option, you can choose to display a list of bridgehead servers in the site to which this server belongs or the entire Active Directory enterprise.

—**Show Trust Relationships:** This option displays a list of trust relationships within the enterprise (including multiple forests) to which this server belongs.

—**Show Attribute Meta-Data for Active Directory Object:** This option displays the attribute metadata for an object whose DN you specify in the Object dialog box that appears when you select this option.

—**Clear Log:** This option clears the contents of the `replmon` log file.

—**Delete:** This option deletes the current server from the `replmon` display.

—**Properties:** This option displays a Properties dialog box for the selected server, including information such as FSMO roles in the server's domain, TCP/IP configuration properties, inbound replication connection data, and so on.

■ **Display pending replication changes:** Changes made to any component of Active Directory are considered pending until replication has propagated them to all other domain controllers. To view any pending replication changes, expand the desired directory partition from the left pane to display the direct replication partners for this partition. Then right-click the desired replication partner, choose **Check Current USN and Un-Replicated Objects**, and then click **OK** to accept the default of **Use Credentials Already Supplied for Server**. The Un-Replicated Objects dialog box then displays a list of pending replication changes.

■ **Perform manual synchronization of directory partitions:** If a domain controller or its network connection has been down for a period of time, you might want to synchronize its data manually. To do so, right-click the desired partition and select **Synchronize This Directory Partition with All Servers**.

Key Topic

repadmin

repadmin is a command-line tool that is installed by default when you install AD DS. It provides most of the same functions as replmon. This includes tasks such as viewing the domain controller's replication topology, forcing replication between domain controllers, and viewing replication metadata. You can also monitor Active Directory for replication problems.

To obtain information about its available parameters, open a command prompt and type **repadmin /?.** Here, we discuss only the parameters you would be most likely to use while using this tool to monitor and troubleshoot Active Directory replication.

To use repadmin, open a command prompt and type **repadmin** together with the desired parameter and any other information as required, and then press **Enter.**

The following sections discuss the most commonly used repadmin parameters.

replicate

The /replicate parameter forces replication between two replication partners. You need to specify the fully qualified domain names (FQDNs) of the two replication partners and the naming context (the distinguished name of the directory partition being replicated). For example, the following command replicates the configuration directory partition from Server1 to Server3 in the que.com domain:

```
Repadmin /replicate server1.que.com server3.que.com
cn=configuration,dc=que,dc=com
```

showmeta

The /showmeta parameter displays the stamp value associated with each update to object attributes in AD DS. The stamp contains identifying information for each replicated attribute. The stamp value contains the updated attribute's USN and determines whether an update needs to be replicated. If the stamp of a replicated value is higher than that of a current value, replication takes place; otherwise, the current value is left alone.

You need to include the DN of the object such as the domain controller for which you want to display the USNs. You can use ADSI Edit to obtain the DN. For example, the following command displays all USNs for the domain controller named Server1 in the que.com domain:

```
Repadmin /showmeta cn=server1,ou="domain controllers",dc=que,dc=com
```

Output to this command contains the following information:

- **Loc.USN:** The local USN value of the update at the domain controller where the update was created.

- **Originating domain controller (DC):** The server at which the update was created, displayed as *site\server*. This object is actually recorded as a GUID value.

- **Org.USN:** The originating USN, which is a value that travels with the updated attribute as it is replicated. This number is assigned at the originating DC.

- **Org.Time/Date:** The date and time of the update, according to the system clock of the DC where the update was created.

- **Ver:** A version number that is incremented each time an attribute is updated. If this value is 1, the attribute has never been overwritten.

- **Attribute:** The name of the updated attribute.

showreps

The /showreps parameter displays the replication partners for each AD DS partition being replicated. It also displays the GUID for the replicated partition, the time and date of the most recent replication attempt, and whether the last attempt was successful. When a failure occurs, it provides a reason for the failure. In addition, it displays the GUID for the server on which it was run and whether this server is a global catalog server. The /showrepl parameter performs the same tasks.

add

The /add parameter manually creates a replication link between domain controllers for the AD DS partition you specify. For example, the following command creates a replication link between server3 and server4 in the que.com domain for the Active Directory configuration partition:

```
Repadmin /add cn=configuration,dc=que,dc=com server3.que.com server4.que.com
```

Note that you can specify the server names either as their GUID or as the DNS FQDN.

sync

The /sync parameter manually forces a replication cycle to occur between domain controllers for the specified Active Directory partition. Using this parameter is tricky because you must specify the originating domain controller by its GUID value and the destination domain controller by its FQDN. For example, the following command forces replication to take place from server2.que.com (which has the indicated GUID) to server3.que.com:

```
Repadmin /sync cn=configuration,dc=que,dc=com server3.que.com
    a68b5cbd-1a6d-448b-9643-22213479d408
```

If replication is successful, you will receive the message Sync from GUID to server completed successfully. You can locate the required GUID by running repadmin /showreps server, where server is the name of the server whose GUID you need (such as server2 in this example).

The following are optional switches that you can use with this parameter:

- **/async**: Starts the replication without waiting for the replication event to be completed.

- **/force**: Overrides the normal schedule of replication.

- **/full**: Forces a full synchronization of all objects from the destination directory database. Ordinarily, only objects that have been changed are replicated.

syncall

The /syncall parameter manually forces replication of the specified Active Directory partition to all replication partners in the domain (for the domain partition), forest (for the configuration or schema partitions), or all partners that contain replicas of an application directory partition. You can specify the FQDN of a domain controller with this parameter to force the specified domain controller to replicate with its partners.

showconn

The /showconn parameter displays information related to intersite replication on the domain controller on which the command is run. You can determine whether the domain controller is replicating with the current bridgehead servers in its site. You can also verify that connections are enabled, the transport protocol is in use, and the time at which connections were completed or changed.

replsummary

The /replsummary (or /replsum) parameter displays a summary table of the most recent replication activities and problems that have occurred. It has several sub-parameters, including the following:

■ **/bysrc**: Displays servers that are replication sources, the last time of outbound replication, and any errors.

■ **/bydest**: Displays servers that are replication destinations, the last time of inbound replication, and any errors.

■ **/sort:delta**: Sorts output according to time since last successful replication, with the longest time displayed first.

NOTE

For more information on using repadmin to troubleshoot AD DS replication problems, refer to "Troubleshooting Active Directory Replication Problems" at http://technet.microsoft.com/en-us/library/cc949120(WS.10).aspx.

TIP

Make sure you know what the most important parameters of repadmin are and how you would use them. Know how you would perform these tasks using either replmon or repadmin. The exam might ask you for two ways of performing a task.

---

dcdiag

Also called the Domain Controller Diagnostic Tool, the dcdiag command-line tool analyzes the condition of domain controllers. The output of this tool informs you of any problems, thereby assisting you in troubleshooting domain controllers. It performs a series of tests that verify different functional areas of the domain controller, including connectivity, replication, topology integrity, trust verification, replication latency, replication of trust objects, and so on. You can select the domain controllers to be checked according to site, domain, enterprise, or single server.

The syntax of the dcdiag tool is as follows:

```
dcdiag.exe /s:Domain Controller [/u:Domain\Username /p:*¦Password¦""]
   [/hqv] [/n:Naming Context] [/f:Log] [/ferr:Errlog] [/skip:Test]
   [/test:Test] [/c]
```
Table 14-3 describes the dcdiag parameters.

Table 14-3 **dcdiag** Command Parameters

Parameter	Description
/s	Specifies the domain controller to be tested.
/u	Specifies the username credential under which the test will be run.
/p	Specifies the password for the username specified with /u.
/h	Displays help information.
/q	Quiet mode, displays error messages only.
/v	Verbose mode, displays comprehensive information.
/n	Identifies the naming context (directory partition) to be tested. You can specify this parameter as a NetBIOS or DNS name or as the distinguished name.
/f:Log	Specifies that all output will be redirected to the specified log file.
/ferr:Errlog	Redirects only the fatal error output to the specified log file.
/skip	Skips the specified tests.
/test	Performs the specified tests.
/c	Comprehensive, runs all available tests except dcpromo and registerindns.

If you do not specify either the /skip or /test parameter, dcdiag runs a default set of tests. You should not use both the /skip and /test parameters at the same time. You can use the /skip and /c parameters together to specify a large number of tests while omitting others. The following are default tests:

- **Replications:** Checks for timely replication between DCs.

- **NCSecDesc:** Checks that the security descriptors on the naming context heads have appropriate permissions for replication.

- **NetLogons:** Checks that the appropriate logon privileges allow replication to proceed.

- **Advertising:** Checks whether each DC is advertising itself and whether it is advertising itself as having the capabilities of a DC.

- **KnowsOfRoleHolders:** Checks whether the DC knows the role holders.

- **RidManager:** Checks whether RID master is accessible and whether it contains the proper information.

- **MachineAccount:** Checks whether the Machine Account has the proper information.

- **Services:** Checks whether appropriate DC services are running.

- **ObjectsReplicated:** Checks for complete replication of the Machine Account and Directory System Agent (DSA) objects.

- **Freesysvol:** Checks that the SYSVOL folder is ready to replicate using FRS.

- **Frsevent:** Checks whether any FRS operation errors have occurred. If replication of the SYSVOL share fails, problems in applying Group Policy can occur.

- **Kccevent:** Checks that the KCC is completing without errors.

- **Systemlog:** Checks that the system is running without errors.

- **VerifyReferences:** Verifies that certain system references are intact for the FRS and replication infrastructure.

NOTE For additional descriptions of available tests, refer to the Windows Support Tools Help and to "Dcdiag" at http://technet.microsoft.com/en-us/library/cc731968(WS.10).aspx.

Troubleshooting the Application of Group Policy Objects

As you have seen in Chapters 11–13, Group Policy is an all-encompassing, powerful tool that enables you to configure a very large number of settings that affect users and computers in your network. Although you might be able to keep up with what Group Policy is doing in a small organization, the application of policy settings tends to quickly become more complicated as the organization grows in size and multiple administrators configure additional policy settings.

Complicated implementations of Group Policy often generate unexpected results. Back in the days of Windows 2000, troubleshooting problems frequently meant printing out settings applied at the various levels, disabling certain GPOs or portions of them, and performing a long series of tests. Since Windows Server 2003, Microsoft has included tools that help you troubleshoot, test, and plan. These include the Resultant Set of Policy snap-in, the Group Policy Modeling Wizard, Group Policy Results, and the Gpresult command.

Resultant Set of Policy

First introduced with Windows Server 2003, Resultant Set of Policy (RSoP) is a powerful tool that queries computers running Windows XP/Vista/7/Server 2003/Server 2008 and informs you of which policies have been applied and in what order. You can run RSoP in either planning mode or logging mode:

- **Planning mode:** Enables you to perform a "what-if" scenario that predicts the effects of a proposed series of policies on a specified user/computer combination. This mode is also known as *Group Policy Modeling*.

- **Logging mode:** Enables you to analyze a specific user/computer combination to obtain information on policy application for this combination. This mode is also known as *Group Policy Results*.

Planning Mode/Group Policy Modeling

Planning mode provides the opportunity to apply GPO settings to an object such as a user or computer to see the net effect a new policy will have. In other words, it performs a "what-if" analysis and reports of the policy settings you would have if you configured the settings you have specified while running RSoP. The following are several situations in which this is useful:

- Simulating the effect of a series of policy settings on a computer or user according to the site, domain, or OU in which the computer or user is located

- After creating a new user or group account in AD DS or making changes to security group membership

- Predicting the effect of moving a computer or user to a different site or OU

- Simulating the effect of a slow network connection

- Simulating a loopback condition

Besides running RSoP for individual users and computers, you can run RSoP planning mode queries for sites, domains, and OUs. Just as you cannot apply policies directly to security groups, you cannot run RSoP queries on security groups. You can run RSoP planning mode from any of the following locations:

- **From Active Directory Users and Computers:** Enables you to simulate the effect of policies applied to a domain or OU. Right-click the required domain or OU and choose **All Tasks > Resultant Set of Policy (Planning)**.

- **From Active Directory Sites and Services:** Enables you to simulate the effect of policies applied to a site. Right-click the required site and choose **All Tasks > Resultant Set of Policy (Planning)**.

- **From Group Policy Management Console:** GPMC includes a Group Policy Modeling node that enables you to simulate the effect of policies applied to a site, domain, or OU. Right-click this node and choose **Group Policy Modeling Wizard**.

- **From its own console:** Enables you to create a customized MMC console that includes the RSoP snap-in. Add the snap-in to an empty console by clicking **File > Add/Remove Snap-in** and then adding Resultant Set of Policy from the list of available snap-ins. After you have done this, you can right-click the

Resultant Set of Policy node and choose **Generate RSoP Data** to start the Resultant Set of Policy Wizard.

Whether the wizard launched is called the Group Policy Modeling Wizard (as it is when started from GPMC) or the Resultant Set of Policy Wizard (as it is when started from any of the other locations), the options provided and the procedure followed are similar, as outlined here:

Step 1.   If you start from the RSoP snap-in, select **Planning mode** and click **Next**.

Step 2.   On the Domain Controller Selection page, select the domain controller from which you want to process the simulation or choose the **Any available domain controller running Windows Server 2003 or later** option. Then click **Next**.

Step 3.   On the User and Computer Selection page shown in Figure 14-29, select a specific user and/or computer to test a planning scenario or accept the information supplied according to the AD DS object you started at. If you started from the Group Policy Planning node of GPMC or from a custom console, you will need to enter information on this page. Make a selection and then click **Next**.

Figure 14-29   Entering user and computer information into the Resultant Set of Policy Wizard.

Resultant Set of Policy Wizard	☒

User and Computer Selection
You can view simulated policy settings for a selected user (or a container with user information) and computer (or a container with computer information).

Example container name: CN=Users,DC=que,DC=com
Example user or computer: QUE\Administrator

Simulate policy settings for the following:

User information
  ⦿ Container: OU=SALES,DC=QUE,DC=COM   [Browse...]
  ○ User: [   ]   [Browse...]

Computer information
  ⦿ Container: OU=SALES,DC=QUE,DC=COM   [Browse...]
  ○ Computer: [   ]   [Browse...]

☐ Skip to the final page of this wizard without collecting additional data

[< Back]   [Next >]   [Cancel]

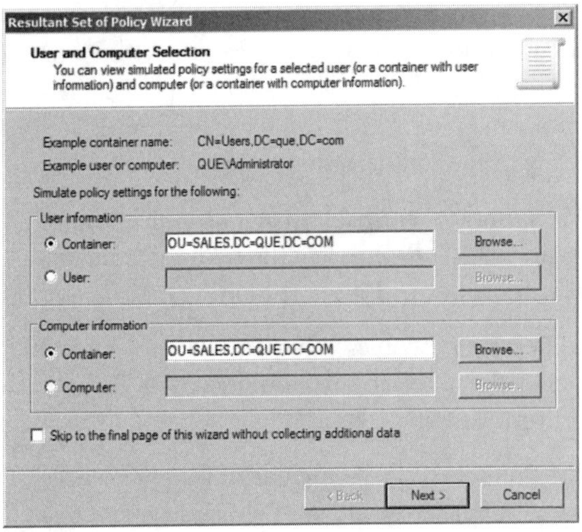

TIP   At most of the pages in this wizard, you can speed up the wizard by selecting the check box labeled **Skip to the final page of this wizard without collecting additional data** if you do not have additional information that you want to enter. This takes you directly to the Summary page.

Step 4.   On the Advanced Simulation Options page shown in Figure 14-30, select any of the following as required and click **Next**:

Figure 14-30   Specifying advanced RSoP simulation options.

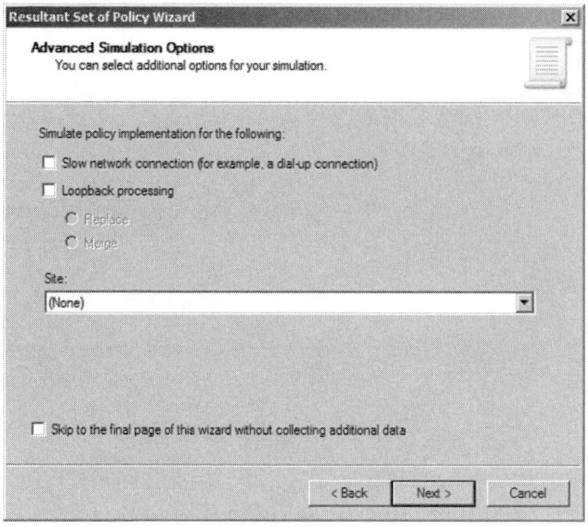

- **Slow network connection:** Ignores any policies configured not to apply across a slow connection.

- **Loopback processing:** Invokes the loopback processing mode described in Chapter 11, "Creating and Applying Group Policy Objects," including the Replace and Merge options.

- **Site:** Enables you to select a site whose policies are to be applied or (None) to not include any sites.

Step 5.   On the User Security Groups page, specify any required changes to the selected user's security groups and then click **Next**.

Step 6.   On the Computer Security Groups page, specify any required changes to the selected computer's security groups and then click **Next**.

Step 7.   On the WMI Filters for Users page, you can include Windows Management Instrumentation (WMI) filters in the simulation. To include selected filters, click the **Only these filters** option and then click **List filters** to locate the filters you want to include (see Figure 14-31). Then click **Next**.

Step 8.   The WMI Filters for Computers page performs the same task for computers as the WMI Filters page does for users. Perform the same tasks as in step 6 and then click **Next**.

Figure 14-31   Specifying WMI filters for users.

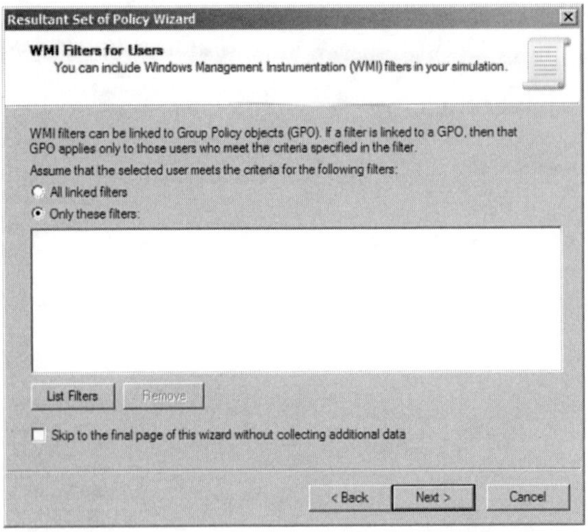

Step 9.   The Summary of Selections page provides a summary of options you have selected while running the wizard (see Figure 14-32). If any of these settings are incorrect, click **Back** to change them. If you do not require extended error information, clear the check box provided. When you're finished, click **Next** to process your selections.

Figure 14-32   The Summary of Selections page summarizes the information you provided to the RSoP Wizard.

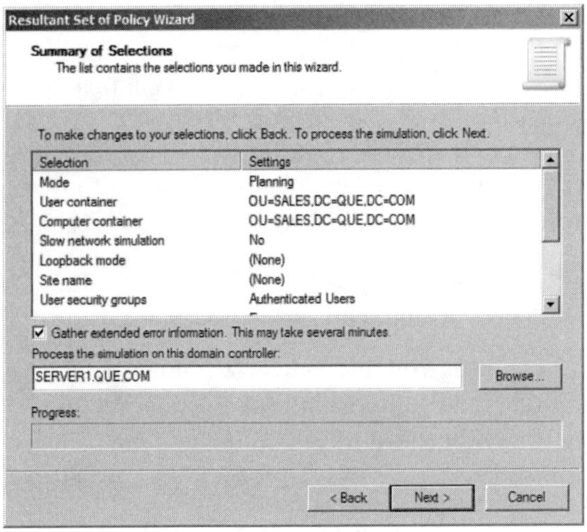

Step 10.   The wizard displays a progress bar as it processes your selections. This process might take a minute or two. When the completion page appears,

click **Finish**. The wizard displays a Resultant Set of Policy snap-in that looks similar to the Group Policy Management Editor snap-in.

Step 11.   To view the effect of applied GPOs, expand the desired node in the console tree. As shown in Figure 14-33, only the subnodes for which policies have been configured appear.

Figure 14-33   The RSoP snap-in displays only those policies for which GPOs are configured.

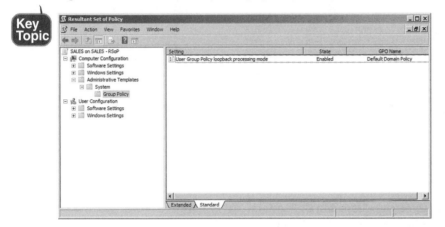

Step 12.   To view the hierarchy of any configured policy, right-click it and choose **Properties**. From the Properties dialog box that appears, select the **Precedence** tab to display the GPOs for which this policy has been configured. As shown in Figure 14-34, these GPOs appear with the priorities ascending from bottom to top. The top policy setting is the one that will apply.

NOTE   If you run RSoP from GPMC, the details pane displays its results with the Settings tab displaying a hierarchical series of applied policy settings similar in appearance to that of Figure 11-3 in Chapter 11.

Logging Mode/Group Policy Results

Logging mode provides the ability to determine which policies are currently being applied to an object. In this mode, you can create a report as well as determine what each of the policies is doing to an object. This is useful for troubleshooting Group Policy problems. You can run logging mode using any of the following methods:

■   **From the Run dialog box:** Log on to the computer at which you want to run RSoP as the appropriate user, click **Start > Run**, type **rsop.msc**, and then press **Enter**. This displays the RSoP snap-in containing only those nodes for which a policy is configured.

Figure 14-34   The Precedence tab displays GPOs for which the policy is configured, with the highest priority setting at the top.

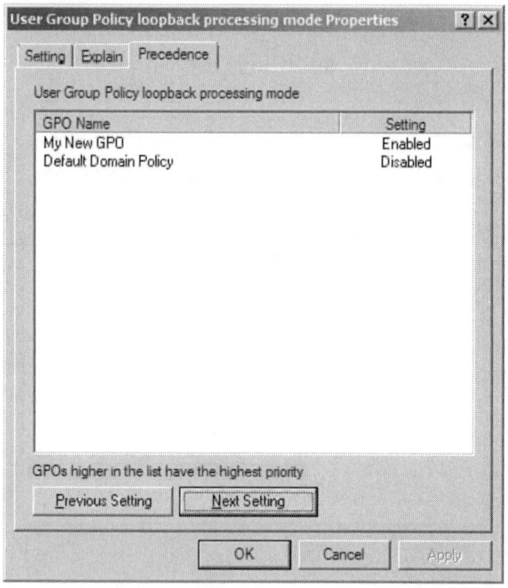

- **From Active Directory Users and Computers:** Navigate to the OU or container where the appropriate user account is located, right-click the account and choose **All Tasks > Resultant Set of Policy (Logging)**. This starts the Resultant Set of Policy Wizard.

- **From Group Policy Management Console:** GPMC includes a Group Policy Results node that enables you to select the required user and computer. Right-click this node and choose **Group Policy Results Wizard**.

- **From its own console:** Enables you to create a customized MMC console that includes the RSoP snap-in, as already described, which enables you to start the Resultant Set of Policy Wizard.

WARNING   For Group Policy Results to work properly, the selected user must have logged on to the selected computer since the applicable GPOs were last configured.

Use the following procedure to run RSoP logging mode from Active Directory Users and Computers (the procedure from the other locations is similar):

Step 1.   Using an administrator account, log on to the domain controller (or to a computer on which the Windows Server 2008 administration tools are installed).

Step 2.   In Active Directory Users and Computers, expand the container in which the user account you want to test is located.

Step 3.   Right-click the user and choose **All Tasks > Resultant Set of Policy (Logging)**, as shown in Figure 14-35.

Figure 14-35   Starting RSoP in logging mode from Active Directory Users and Computers.

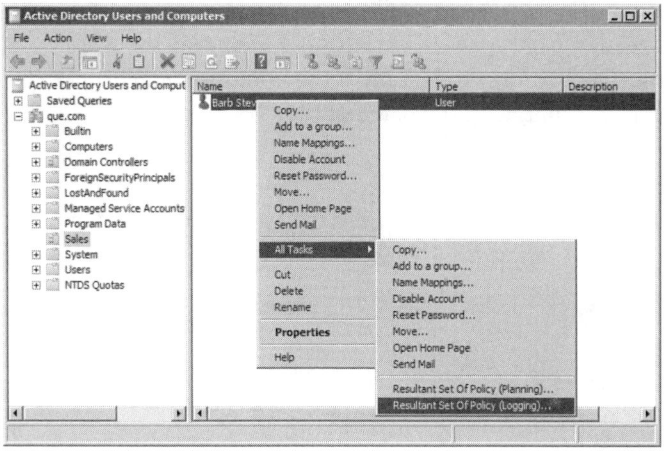

Step 4.   The Resultant Set of Policy Wizard displays a Computer Selection page. To display settings for the user logged on to a client computer, select **Another Computer**, type the name or IP address of the computer in the text box provided (see Figure 14-36), and then click **Next**. If you want to display user policy settings only, select the **Do not display policy settings for the selected computer in the results (display user policy settings only)** check box.

Figure 14-36   Selecting the computer for which RSoP is to process the policy settings.

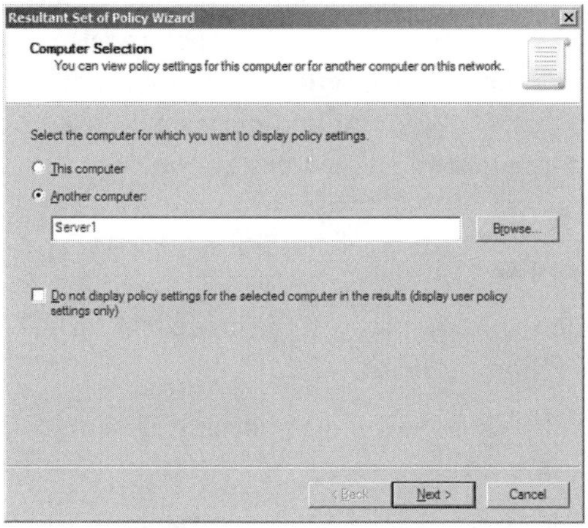

Step 5. The User Selection page confirms the user for which RSoP will be run. Click **Next**.

Step 6. The Summary of Selections page displays the list of selections that you have made. Review these selections and click **Back** to change any settings. Click **Next** to process these settings.

Step 7. When the completion page appears, click **Finish** to display the RSoP console. As with the planning mode, only those nodes for which a policy is applied appear, together, with the name of the GPO being enforced (see Figure 14-37).

Figure 14-37 The RSoP logging mode console shows policies that were applied and their GPO.

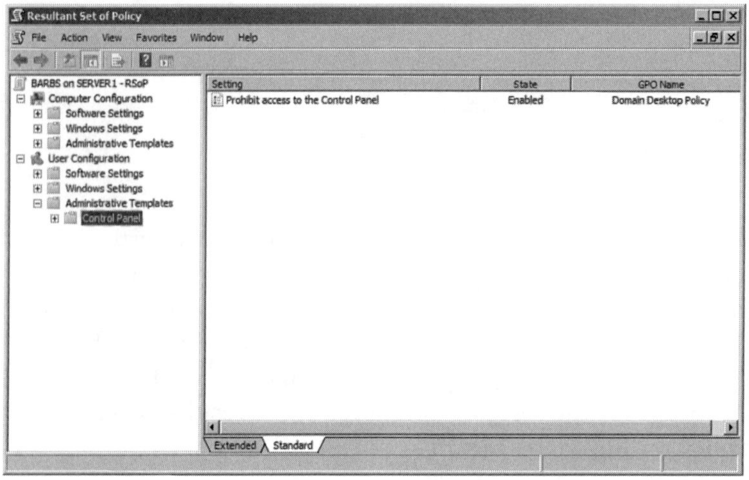

Running RSoP from other locations is similar to that described here for Active Directory Users and Computers. When run from GPMC, you receive a hierarchical view of the results as shown in Figure 14-38. You can also display policy-related events at the targeted computer by selecting the **Policy Events** tab. As shown in Figure 14-39, this displays a list of events that can be useful for policy application troubleshooting. You can obtain more information about an event by double-clicking it.

Analyzing the RSoP Logging Mode Results

Regardless of the procedure used to obtain the RSoP console, the procedure for analyzing the results is the same. Use the following steps:

Step 1. Expand the listings in the console tree to locate the policies you want to examine.

Step 2. In the details pane, right-click the policy name and choose **Properties**.

Figure 14-38   When run from GPMC, RSoP logging mode displays a hierarchical view of the results.

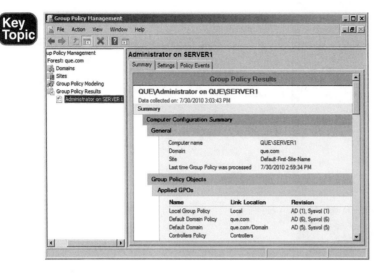

Figure 14-39   The Policy Events tab of Group Policy Results displays policy-related results from the targeted computer.

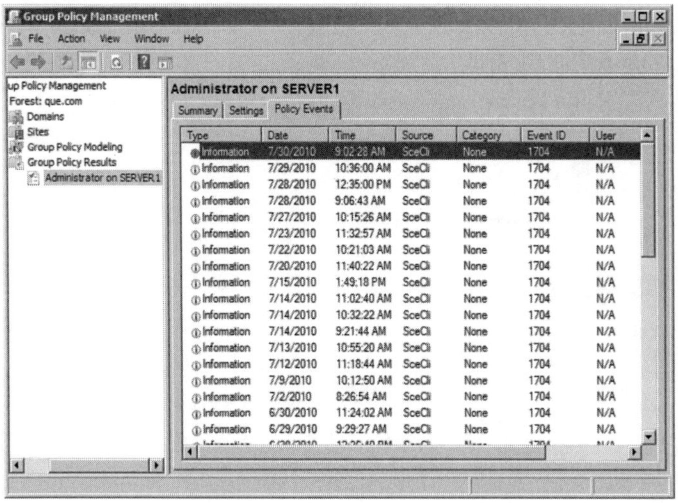

Step 3.   Select the **Precedence** tab. As shown in Figure 14-40, this tab displays the names of the GPOs that apply and their settings.

Step 4.   To display the list of all GPOs applied to the current user, right-click either **Computer Configuration** or **User Configuration** (as needed) and choose **Properties**. This selection displays a Properties dialog box with the following two tabs:

Figure 14-40   Displaying the list of GPOs configured for a given policy.

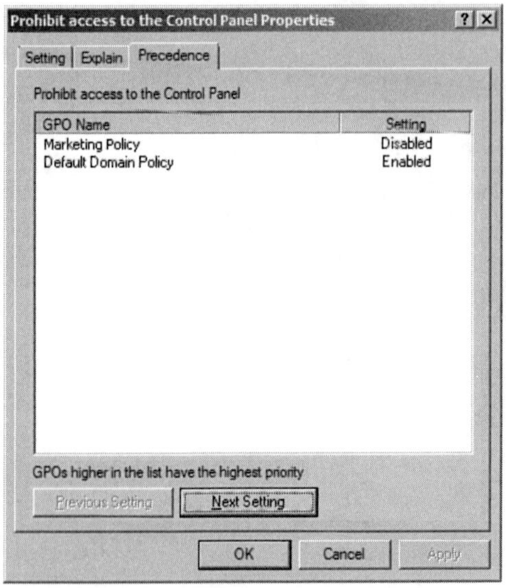

—**General:** Provides the list of GPOs applied, as shown in Figure 14-41. The three check boxes at the bottom control the amount of information displayed. Click **Security** to view permissions information. Click **Edit** to open the Group Policy Object Editor focused on the GPO that is highlighted in the list.

Figure 14-41   Displaying information on all GPOs applied to a user or computer.

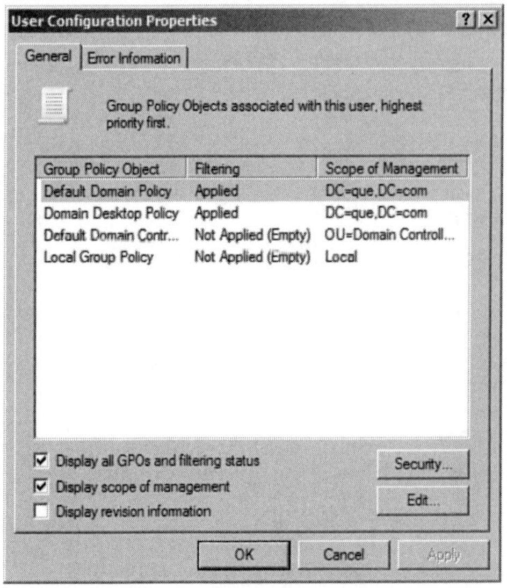

—**Error Information:** Provides information on any GPO components that have failed to apply properly. This information helps to facilitate troubleshooting of policies that have not applied properly. See Figure 14-42.

Figure 14-42   Displaying error information about GPO application.

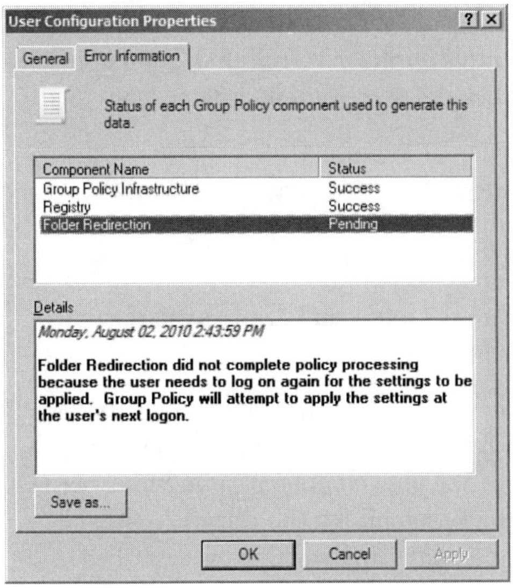

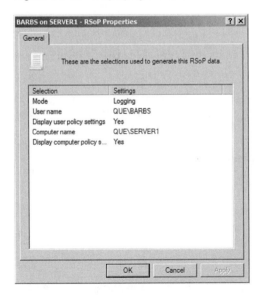

Step 5.   To display the selections used to generate the RSoP data, right-click the user and computer name in the console tree and choose **Properties**. Figure 14-43 shows the list that is displayed.

Figure 14-43   Displaying the selections used to generate the RSoP data.

Step 6.   If you have made changes to GPOs using the Group Policy Object Editor and want to apply these changes to an open RSoP console, right-click the user/computer name and perform the appropriate step described here:

—If you have run RSoP from Active Directory Users and Computers or from its own console, right-click the user/computer name from this location and choose **Refresh Query**.

—If you have run RSoP from Group Policy Management Console, right-click the user/computer name under Group Policy Results and choose **Rerun Query**.

Either of these actions reprocesses the query and displays the refreshed results in the same console.

Step 7.   If you have run RSoP from Active Directory Users and Computers or from its own console and you want to change the user/computer combination being analyzed, right-click the user/computer name and choose **Change Query**. This restarts the Resultant Set of Policy Wizard and enables you to reenter user and computer information, as described earlier in this section.

WARNING   You need to ensure that the latest changes have been applied. Just as a user needs to log off and log back on to receive changes in policies, the user must also log off and log back on so that the RSoP logging mode results reflect changed policies.

Saving RSoP Data

You can save the results of any RSoP query to its own console so that you can easily rerun the query at a later time. Use the following steps:

Step 1.   After running an RSoP query, select the User Account on Computer Account entry near the top of the console tree (such as "BarbS on SERVER1" in Figure 14-37).

Step 2.   Click **View > Archive data in console file**.

Step 3.   Click **File > Save As**, type an appropriate name for the file, and then click **Save**.

Step 4.   You can rerun the same query later by simply double-clicking the file that you have created here.

TIP   When using RSoP in logging mode, the user in question must log on to the computer in question before RSoP will work in logging mode. In an exam question, you might be asked to choose between planning mode and logging mode for a user who has not logged on to that specific computer or to troubleshoot the reasons why RSoP in logging mode does not work for a specific user.

Using the Delegation of Control Wizard

In Chapter 9, "Active Directory User and Group Accounts," the Delegation of Control Wizard was introduced and explained regarding its use for delegating partial administrative control to domains, sites, and OUs. You can also use the Delegation of Control Wizard to delegate the ability to perform the following tasks within Group Policy:

- **Manage Group Policy links:** Enables the ability to apply GPOs to the site, domain, or OU at which the task is delegated, but does not enable the ability to create new GPOs or edit existing ones.

- **Generate Resultant Set of Policy (Planning):** Enables the ability to run the Group Policy Modeling Wizard on the site, domain, or OU at which the task is delegated.

- **Generate Resultant Set of Policy (Logging):** Enables the ability to run the Group Policy Results Wizard on the site, domain, or OU at which the task is delegated.

Gpresult

Gpresult is a command-line version of RSoP that you can use to display logging mode information or create batch files. It is also useful for collecting RSoP data on a Server Core computer.

The syntax for this command is as follows:

```
Gpresult /r [/s computer [/u domain\user /p password]]
    [/user target_user] [/scope {user ¦ computer}] {{/v ¦ /z}]
```

Table 14-4 describes the options that are available with the Gpresult command.

Key Topic

Table 14-4   Options Available with the **Gpresult** Command

Option	Description
/r	Use this option to specify RSoP summary data.
/s computer	Specifies the remote computer to be used. You can use either the computer name or IP address. If absent, the local computer is used.
/user target_user	Specifies the user to be used. If absent, the currently logged-on user is used.

Table 14-4 Options Available with the **Gpresult** Command

Option	Description
`/u domain\user /p password`	Enables you to enter the appropriate username and password to run Gpresult in the context of another user. Include the domain if it is not the same as the current domain.
`/scope {computer ¦ user}`	Limits the display to computer configuration or user configuration data.
`/v`	Displays verbose policy information.
`/z`	Displays all available information about Group Policy—more than is available with the /v option.
`> filename.txt`	Redirects output to the specified file. Because of the large amount of data produced by these options, you should use this option with the /v or /z option.

Figure 14-44 shows a sample of the results obtained by running this tool against the local computer.

Figure 14-44 The results of running **gpresult.exe** against the local computer.

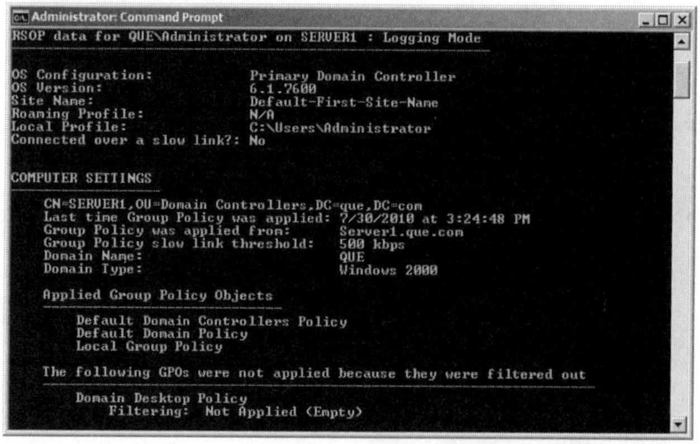

> **NOTE** For more information on Gpresult, refer to "Gpresult" at http://technet.microsoft.com/en-us/library/cc733160(WS.10).aspx.

Gpupdate

First introduced in Windows Server 2003, `Gpupdate` is a tool that refreshes Group Policy settings. Its syntax is as follows:

```
Gpupdate [/target:{computer ¦ user}] [/force] /[wait:value]
    [/logoff] [/boot]
```

Table 14-5 describes the options available with this command.

Table 14-5   Options Available with the **Gpupdate** Command

Option	Description
/target {computer ¦ user}	When specified, only the computer or user settings are processed. Otherwise, both computer and user settings are processed.
/force	Forces the reapplication of all settings.
/wait:value	Number of seconds that policy processing waits to finish. By default, this is 600 seconds. 0 means "no wait" and -1 means "wait indefinitely."
/logoff	Logs off after completion of refresh, to enable processing of client-side extensions such as software installation and folder redirection that require the user to log off and back on.
/boot	Restarts the computer when the refresh completes, to enable processing of client-side extensions such as computer-based software installation policies that require the computer to be rebooted.

TIP   It is helpful to use the `Gpupdate /force` command immediately after creating or editing a GPO so that its settings take effect immediately rather than waiting until the next policy refresh time.

Exam Preparation Tasks

Review All the Key Topics

Review the most important topics in the chapter, noted with the key topics icon in the outer margin of the page. Table 14-6 lists a reference of these key topics and the page numbers on which each is found.

Table 14-6   Key Topics for Chapter 14

Key Topic Element	Description	Page Number
Figure 14-3	Network Monitor displays information on all network traffic that passes across the server's adapter	462
List	Describes the types of actions you can perform using Task Manager	464
Figure 14-5	Event Viewer provides information on several types of events occurring on your computer	466
Figure 14-8	Shows you how to create a customized log in Event Viewer	469
Figure 14-15	Performance Monitor displays a real-time graph of computer performance counters	476
Table 14-2	Describes terminology used with Performance Monitor	477
List	Shows you how to configure Performance Monitor to display a series of counters	477
List	Shows you how to configure data collector sets for logging computer performance	480
Figure 14-23	Configuring data collector sets to display trace action alerts	483
Figure 14-26	Using `replmon` to monitor AD DS replication	488
List	Describes the most significant types of actions you can perform using `replmon`	490
Paragraph	Describes the use of `repadmin`	491
List	Shows you how to run RSoP in planning mode	498
Figure 14-33	Displays the results of an RSoP planning mode query	501
Figure 14-38	Displaying the results of RSoP logging mode as run from the Group Policy Management Console	505
Table 14-4	Describes options used with the `Gpresult` command	509

Complete the Tables and Lists from Memory

Print a copy of Appendix C, "Memory Tables" (found on the CD), or at least the section for this chapter, and complete the tables and lists from memory. Appendix D, "Memory Tables Answer Key," also on the CD, includes completed tables and lists to check your work.

Definitions of Key Terms

Define the following key terms from this chapter, and check your answers in the glossary.

data collector sets, `dcdiag`, Event Viewer, `Gpresult`, `Gpupdate`, Group Policy Modeling, Group Policy Results, instance, Network Monitor, Performance counter, Performance Monitor, Performance object, Reliability Monitor, `repadmin`, `replmon`, Resultant Set of Policy (RSoP), Task Manager, Windows Management Instrumentation (WMI), Windows System Resource Manager (WSRM)

This chapter covers the following subjects:

■ **Backing Up and Recovering Active Directory:** When problems arise with your servers, you must have the ability to recover them to a known good point in time. This section shows you how to back up your server and discusses the various options you have for recovering backed-up data.

■ **Offline Maintenance of Active Directory:** Certain actions can be performed only when your domain controller is taken offline. This section describes the various operational modes of an AD DS domain controller and introduces the actions you can perform only when the domain controller is offline.

CHAPTER 15

Maintaining Active Directory

Chapter 14, "Monitoring Active Directory," showed you how to use the various tools available in Windows Server 2008 R2 to monitor and troubleshoot the functionality of Active Directory Domain Services (AD DS). Now it's time to look at what you must do should AD DS itself become corrupted, deleted, or otherwise damaged. You need to know how to restore Active Directory from a backup—this is often the fastest way to recover from many of these problems. Further, you need to know how to back up Active Directory before you can restore it. In addition, Windows Server 2008 R2 now offers a new feature, the Active Directory Recycle Bin, which simplifies many recovery actions that used to be more cumbersome with older versions of AD DS.

"Do I Know This Already?" Quiz

The "Do I Know This Already?" quiz enables you to assess whether you should read this entire chapter or simply jump to the "Exam Preparation Tasks" section for review. If you are in doubt, read the entire chapter. Table 15-1 outlines the major headings in this chapter and the corresponding "Do I Know This Already?" quiz questions. You can find the answers in Appendix A, "Answers to the 'Do I Know This Already?' Quizzes."

Table 15-1 "Do I Know This Already?" Foundation Topics Section-to-Question Mapping

Foundations Topics Section	Questions Covered in This Section
Backing Up and Recovering Active Directory	1–9
Offline Maintenance of Active Directory	10–12

1. Which of the following are components of system state data on a domain controller running Windows Server 2008 R2? (Choose all that apply.)

   a. System and boot files

   b. AD DS database

    c.   SYSVOL folder

    d.   Installed application files

    e.   COM+ Class Registration database

    f.   System files that are under Windows Resource Protection

2. You have just finished installing Windows Server 2008 R2 on a new computer and have promoted the server to be a domain controller in your company's AD DS domain. You want to configure Windows Server Backup on the domain controller, so you open the Administrative Tools folder to select the backup tool. But you cannot find this tool. What do you need to do?

    a.   Click **Start > Run**, type `compmgmt.msc`, and then press **Enter**. Then select Windows Server Backup from the options in the Computer Management snap-in.

    b.   Click **Start > Run**, type `ntbackup`, and then press **Enter.**

    c.   Open Server Manager and select **Windows Server Backup** from the options in the console tree.

    d.   Open Server Manager and install Windows Server Backup as a server feature.

3. You want to create a script that will be run on all your company's servers to configure backup. Which of the following tools do you need to use to accomplish this task?

    a.   `ntbackup`

    b.   `ntdsutil`

    c.   `wbadmin`

    d.   `esentutl`

4. You are responsible for maintaining backups on a Windows Server 2008 R2 domain controller, so you decide to schedule backups on this server. You have a USB external hard disk that you plan to use for this purpose. The hard disk has two partitions, one of which contains mission-critical documents and another that is available for the backups. What should you do before configuring the backups?

    a.   Copy the mission-critical documents from the first partition to a different hard disk.

    b.   Format the second partition with the NTFS file system.

    c.   Create a folder on the second partition that will hold the backups.

    d.   Convert the disk to dynamic storage.

5. You are the help desk supervisor for your company. The CEO phones and complains that he is unable to log on to his Windows 7 Ultimate computer. Checking with the various technicians, you discover that his user account was accidentally deleted, so you ask the responsible technician to restore his account from backup. Later the CEO reports that he is still unable to log on. What do you need to do to solve this problem?

    a. Restore the user account from last week's backup because the most recent backup must have occurred after the account was deleted.

    b. Use the `repadmin` tool to force replication from the domain controller at which the user account was deleted to other domain controllers in the domain.

    c. Use the `ntdsutil` tool to restore the user account and mark the restoration as authoritative.

    d. Perform a bare-metal recovery of the domain controller closest to the CEO's office.

6. You are responsible for backups of domain controllers in your company's AD DS domain, which runs a mix of Windows Server 2003 and Windows Server 2008 domain controllers. You have added a new domain controller running Windows Server 2008 R2 and are studying the capabilities of the Windows Server Backup utility. Which of the following is a new feature of this tool that was not previously available in previous Windows Server versions?

    a. The capability of restoring AD DS without the need for restarting the computer in Directory Services Restore mode

    b. The capability of performing an authoritative restore of system state data directly from the Recovery Wizard

    c. The capability of restoring system state files to an alternative location

    d. The capability of performing a bare-metal recovery of the server

7. You are responsible for backups of domain controllers in your company's AD DS domain. One domain controller running Windows Server 2008 R2 has suffered a hardware failure, and you need to perform a full server recovery procedure. After replacing the failed components, what should you do next?

    a. Start the server in Safe Mode, log on as a local administrator, open a command prompt, and then use the **wbadmin start systemstaterecovery** command to restore the server's system state.

    b. Start the server in Directory Services Restore Mode, log on as a local administrator, open a command prompt, and then use the **wbadmin start systemstaterecovery** command to restore the server's system state.

    c. Start the server in Directory Services Restore Mode, log on as a local administrator, open a command prompt, and then use the **wbadmin start systemimagerecovery** command to restore the server from the latest system image backup.

    d. Use the Windows Server 2008 R2 DVD-ROM to start the server, select **Repair your computer**, and then select **System Image Recovery**. Then restore the server from the latest system image backup.

8. You are responsible for managing backups and restores in your company's AD DS domain, which is operating at the Windows Server 2003 domain and forest functional level. You have heard about the new Active Directory Recycle Bin in Windows Server 2008 R2 and are anxious to try it out. Which of the following actions must you perform before you can use this feature? (Each correct answer represents part of the solution. Choose two.)

    a. Upgrade the domain and forest functional levels to Windows Server 2008.

    b. Upgrade the domain and forest functional levels to Windows Server 2008 R2.

    c. Use the `Ldp.exe` command-line utility to enable the Active Directory Recycle Bin.

    d. Use the `Ldifde.exe` command-line utility to enable the Active Directory Recycle Bin.

    e. Access the Active Directory Recycle Bin by enabling the **Advanced features** option from the View menu in Active Directory Users and Computers.

9. You want to perform a separate backup of the Group Policy objects (GPOs) in your company's AD DS domain so that you can copy these GPOs to domain controllers in a test lab domain. What tool should you use to perform this backup with the least amount of effort?

    a. `Wbadmin`

    b. Group Policy Management Console (GPMC)

    c. `Ntdsutil`

    d. Windows Server Backup

10. You are responsible for a domain controller in your company's AD DS domain that also acts as a DHCP server and a file server. You need to perform maintenance tasks on this server's directory database file but do not want to disrupt the domain controller's ability to perform DHCP and file services for users. What should you do?

    a. Use the Services snap-in to stop AD DS.

    b. Restart the domain controller in Directory Services Restore Mode.

    c. Copy the database file to a separate computer and work in it from there.

    d. Restart the domain controller in Safe Mode with Networking.

11. Your company has split off operations in one division to a subsidiary company and as a result several OUs, and their contents have been moved to a different domain. Checking the size of the `ntds.dit` file on one of the domain controllers, you notice that it has not decreased in size despite the removal of a large number of objects from the AD DS database. What should you do to reduce the size of this file?

    a. You must wait for 60 days because objects that are deleted from AD DS are not immediately deleted. Rather, they are assigned a tombstone of 60 days. The size of the file will not reduce until after this tombstone period has expired.

    b. You must use the Disk Management utility to defragment the hard disk on which the `ntds.dit` file is located.

    c. You should back up and restore the database. This compresses the file.

    d. You must perform an offline defragmentation of the database because the space consumed by the deleted objects simply remains empty space within the `ntds.dit` file until you do this.

12. During a standard review of the AD DS files on one of the domain controllers in your company's AD DS domain, you notice that the hard drive containing the `ntds.dit` file is running out of space. However, there is plenty of space available on another hard drive in the same server. So, you decide to move the `ntds.dit` file to this hard drive. What should you do to accomplish this task with the least amount of administrative effort?

    a. Restart the server in Directory Services Restore Mode and use the `ntdsutil` utility to move the `ntds.dit` file.

    b. Restart the server in Directory Services Restore Mode and use Windows Explorer to move the `ntds.dit` file.

    c. Use the `net stop ntds` command to stop AD DS and then use the `ntdsutil` utility to move the `ntds.dit` file.

    d. Use the `net stop ntds` command to stop AD DS and then use Windows Explorer to move the `ntds.dit` file.

Foundation Topics

Backing Up and Recovering Active Directory

All computers fail sooner or later. Or perhaps someone (maybe even you) will accidentally delete valuable data. Or a newly released virus could damage the AD DS database, and the damages could be propagated through normal replication. Perhaps an intruder gets in and does a lot of damage before being detected; this occasionally happens despite the best security measures being in place. A good backup and recovery strategy is vital to an organization's continued well-being. Without it, your organization's very existence could be threatened. Backup and recovery is just as important for your AD DS database as it is for your critical production files.

Windows Server 2008 and Windows Server 2008 R2 include a new backup application called Windows Server Backup. This application works somewhat differently from the older backup application included with Windows 2000 and Windows Server 2003. The following are some of the more significant differences:

- Windows Server Backup works by backing up critical volumes. These are the volumes required for recovering AD DS, and include the SYSVOL volume, the system and boot volumes, and the volumes that host the `ntds.dit` database file and the AD DS log files.

- The composition of the system state data depends on the server roles installed on the server and the volumes that host the critical operating system and role files. System state consists of at least the following items and can include more depending upon the installed server roles:
  —Registry
  —COM+ Class Registration database
  —System and boot files
  —AD DS and Active Directory Certificate Services (AD CS) databases
  —SYSVOL folder
  —Cluster service information
  —Internet Information Services (IIS) metadirectory
  —System files that are under Windows Resource Protection

- Windows Server Backup enables you to choose between three recovery modes: full server recovery, system state recovery, and file/folder recovery.

- You can use Windows Server Backup to perform a manual backup or schedule automated backups to a dedicated backup volume physically located on the server itself.

- In addition to local and network-based hard disk volumes, you can use CDs or DVDs as backup media. Magnetic tape volumes are no longer supported.

■ Windows Server Backup does not enable you to back up individual files or folders. You must back up the entire volume that hosts the files or folders to be backed up.

Backup Permissions

Not just anybody has the right to back up and restore data on any files and folders. If this weren't true, anyone could grab data from a computer and make off with it to a competitor's or other unauthorized location. You must have the appropriate permissions and user rights for the data that you want to back up. On a Windows Server 2008 domain controller, this means belonging to the Administrators, Server Operators, or Backup Operators built-in groups by default.

You can modify the default backup rights by using Group Policy. The three groups mentioned here by default have the Backup files and directories and Restore files and directories rights assigned to them. It is good practice to separate these rights so that any one individual does not possess both of them. Some companies remove the Restore files and directories right from the Backup Operators group. They then create a Restore Operators group and assign this group the Restore files and directories right. The assigning of user rights is discussed in Chapter 11, "Creating and Applying Group Policy Objects."

NOTE   Members of the Backup Operators group can perform manual backups but cannot schedule backups by default. You must possess administrative credentials to schedule backups, and you cannot delegate this privilege.

Use of Windows Server Backup

Windows Server Backup enables you to protect against all types of data loss for reasons ranging from hardware or storage media failure to accidental deletion of objects or the entire AD DS database. This section takes a look at installing Windows Server Backup and using it to back up to different types of media, as well as scheduling backups.

Installing Windows Server Backup

Unlike previous versions of Windows, Windows Server Backup is not installed by default; you must install it as a server feature from Server Manager. Use the following procedure to install Windows Server Backup:

Step 1.   Open Server Manager and select the **Features** node.

Step 2.   In the details pane, click **Add Features**.

Step 3.   Scroll the features list to select **Windows Server Backup Features**. If you also want command-line tools for performing backups, expand

Windows Server Backup Features and select this option, as shown in Figure 15-1.

Figure 15-1   You need to install Windows Server Backup Features from the Add Features Wizard of Server Manager.

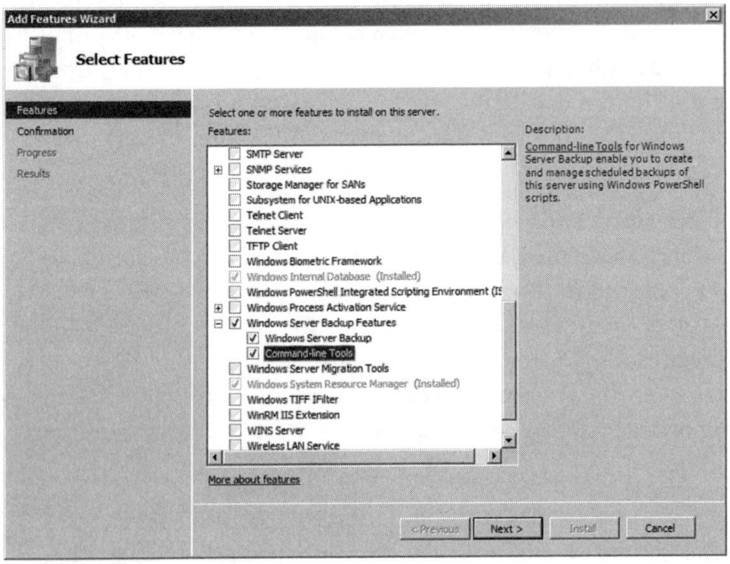

Step 4.   If you receive a message asking to install required features, click **Add Required Features**. Then click **Next**.

Step 5.   Review the information provided by the Confirm Installation Selections page and then click **Install**.

Step 6.   When informed that installation has completed, click **Close**.

Step 7.   If you receive a message requesting that you restart your server, click **Yes**.

TIP   Be aware of the new backup utilities in Windows Server 2008 and the need to install them before use. Windows Server 2008 no longer supports the `ntbackup.exe` utility or the Automated System Recovery (ASR) tool, as an exam question might attempt to trick you on.

Backing Up Critical Volumes of a Domain Controller

Windows Server Backup enables you to back up your domain controller to different types of media, including fixed or removable hard disk volume installed on the server, a network share, or removable media such as CDs or DVDs. To perform this type of backup, you must be a member of the Administrators or Backup Operators group, and an appropriate backup volume must be available. To perform a single backup of critical volumes, proceed as follows:

Step 1.   Open Windows Server Backup by using any of the following methods:

—Click **Start > Administrative Tools > Windows Server Backup**.

—Click **Start** and type `backup` in the Start menu Search field. Then select **Windows Server Backup** from the list that appears.

—Open **Server Manager**, expand **Storage**, and then select **Windows Server Backup** from this location.

Step 2.   From the **Action** menu, select **Backup Once**. This starts the Backup Once Wizard with a Backup Options page, as shown in Figure 15-2.

Figure 15-2   The Backup Options page provides the choice of using previous options if available and configuring different options.

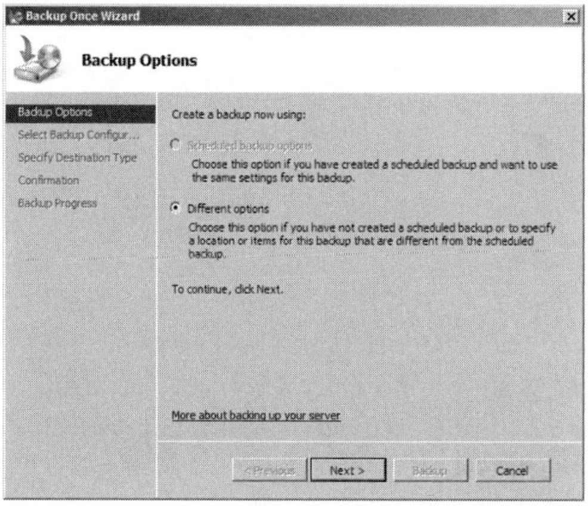

Step 3.   If you have previously scheduled a backup on this server, you can use the **Scheduled backup options** option to perform this backup (in the original version of Windows Server 2008, this option is labeled **The same options that you used in the Backup Schedule Wizard for scheduled backups**). Otherwise, click **Different options** and then click **Next**.

Step 4.   On the Select Backup Configuration page, select **Custom** and then click **Next**.

Step 5. On the Select Items for Backup page, click **Add Items**.

Step 6. On the Add Items dialog box that appears, click **Bare metal recovery**. Selecting this option automatically selects the **System state** option, as well as the boot and system volumes. Click **OK**.

Step 7. You are returned to the Select Items for Backup page, where these items are automatically added, as shown in Figure 15-3.

Figure 15-3   The Select Items for Backup page displays the items you've selected for backup.

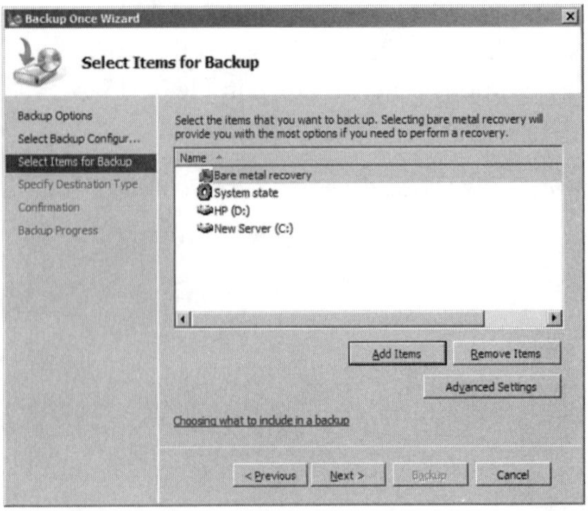

Step 8. To choose the type of Volume Shadow Service (VSS) backup to be created, click **Advanced Settings**. As shown in Figure 15-4, you can also select types of files that are automatically excluded from backup. Select the required option, and then click **OK**.

Step 9. Click **Next** to access the Specify Destination Type page, select either **Local drives** or **Remote shared folder** as required, and then click **Next**.

Step 10. If you choose the **Remote shared folder** option, type the path to the shared folder on the Specify Remote Folder page. If you select the **Local drives** option, select a suitable volume. Then click **Next**.

Step 11. Review the options presented by the Confirmation page and then click **Backup** to perform the backup.

Step 12. The Backup Progress page charts the status of the backup operation. When you are informed that the backup is completed, click **Close** (or to allow the backup to continue in the background, click **Close** at any time). Windows Server Backup displays this backup and its results in the main portion of the application window.

Figure 15-4   The Advanced Settings dialog box presents two options for performing a VSS backup.

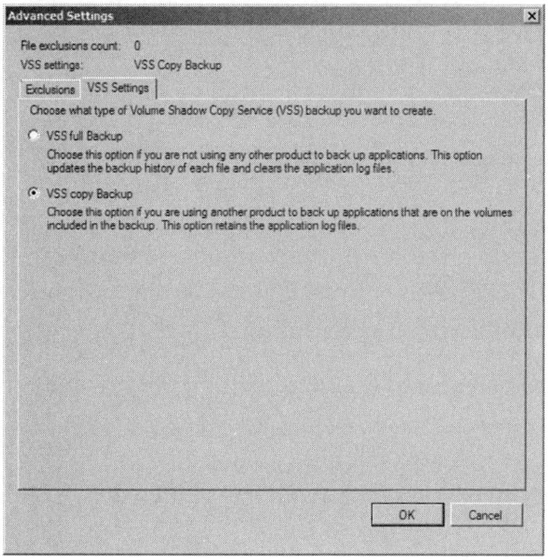

NOTE   For more information on performing domain controller backups, refer to "Performing an Unscheduled Backup of a Domain Controller" at http://technet.microsoft.com/en-us/library/cc731835(WS.10).aspx.

TIP   You can use a similar procedure to back up the entire server. From the Select Backup Configuration page at step 4, select the **Full server (recommended)** option.

The `wbadmin` Command

You can perform backups from the command line with the new `wbadmin` utility, which is installed with the Add Features Wizard when you select the option described earlier to add command-line tools. This tool supports subcommands that enable or disable scheduled backups, run one-time backups, list details of available backups as well as items included in the backups, provide the status of a currently running backup, and perform system state backups and recoveries. The use of this command in running system state recoveries later is discussed in this section.

To obtain information on the available subcommands, type `wbadmin /?` at a command prompt. For example, to back up the system state, you would run the **`wbadmin start systemstatebackup`** command. To obtain information on this and other available subcommands, type **`wbadmin subcommand /?`, where** subcommand is the subcommand you want to obtain information for.

> **NOTE**
>
> For additional information on the wbadmin utility, including examples of the usage of its various subcommands, refer to "Active Directory Backup and Restore in Windows Server 2008" at http://technet.microsoft.com/en-us/magazine/2008.05.adbackup.aspx?pr=blog.

Scheduling a Backup

You can schedule a backup to take place when the server utilization is minimized, such as during the night. Scheduling a backup also ensures that the backup will be performed on a regular basis without administrator intervention.

The procedure for scheduling a backup is similar to that described in the previous section, as the following steps show:

Step 1. From the **Action** menu of the Windows Server Backup application, click **Backup Schedule**.

Step 2. The Backup Schedule Wizard starts with a Getting Started page. Click **Next**.

Step 3. The Select Backup Configuration page displays the same options previously described. Make a selection and then click **Next**.

Step 4. If you have selected the **Custom** option, select the items to be backed up as described in steps 5–8 of the previous procedure and shown in Figure 15-3.

Step 5. From the Specify Backup Time page shown in Figure 15-5, select one or more times a day for the backup to take place and then click **Next**.

Step 6. Select an appropriate backup volume from the choices given in Figure 15-6 and then click **Next**.

Step 7. Select a destination disk from the Select Destination Disk page and then click **Next**.

Step 8. You are warned that the selected disk will be reformatted. Click **Yes** to continue or **No** to select an alternative location. If you click **Yes**, all data on the selected disk (all volumes) will be lost, so ensure that there is no data of value on this disk before you begin this procedure.

Step 9. Click **Finish** to format the disk and create the backup schedule. After the disk is formatted, note the warning on the Summary page of the wizard and click **Close**. Windows Server Backup provides information on the regularly scheduled backup in its main application window.

Figure 15-5 The Backup Schedule Wizard enables you to specify the time at which you want the backup to occur.

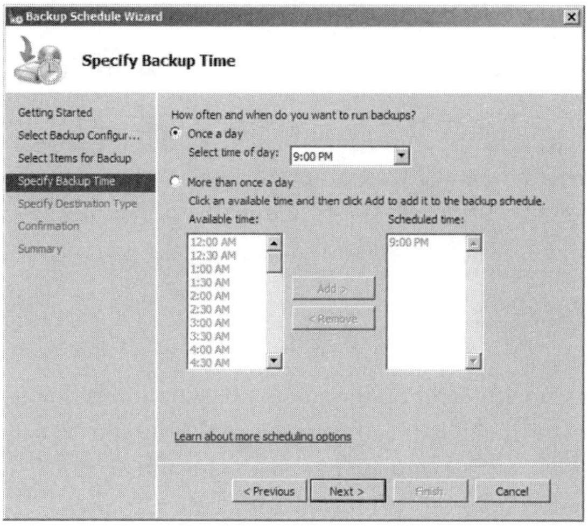

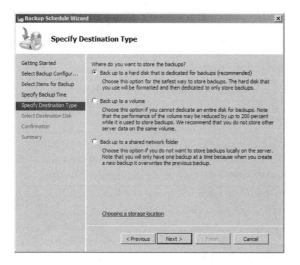

Figure 15-6 The Backup Schedule Wizard provides three choices for backup destination.

After you have scheduled a backup, the option previously shown in Figure 15-2 becomes available so that you can use the options you specified in running the Backup Schedule Wizard to perform an unscheduled backup at any time.

Using Removable Media

You can also perform backups to removable media, including recordable CDs, DVDs, or external hard drives. This is especially convenient for creating an additional backup copy for offsite storage purposes, or for preparing to install a new domain controller using the Install from Media option. The procedure is similar to that described in the previous section. Windows Server Backup will ask for additional media as required.

> **TIP** Windows Server Backup stores backups in Virtual Hard Disk (VHD) format. You can use Microsoft Virtual PC or Virtual Server to mount a backup image as a disk drive on a virtual machine and browse its contents as if it were a normal disk drive.

Recovering Active Directory

The whole idea behind planning, organizing, and undertaking a backup job is that data will be easy to recover in the event of a disaster of some sort. You should be familiar enough with the Windows Server 2008 restore options to be able to restore a single file or an entire volume as required. Windows Server Backup provides three options for restoring data as described in Table 15-2.

Key Topic

Table 15-2 Types of Restore That Windows Server Backup Can Perform

Restore Type	Description
Nonauthoritative restore	A basic restore operation that recovers AD DS to the previous condition that existed at backup time.
Authoritative restore	A restore operation in which restored objects are marked as authoritative so that they will be propagated to other domain controllers and not overwritten at AD DS replication time.
Full server recovery	A restore operation that recovers all components of the operating system, including AD DS and all applications and data from all volumes of the original domain controller.

> **WARNING** You do not want to discover that your backup strategy is not working properly when a failure has occurred and your forest is in shambles. Planning for domain and forest recovery is as important as the backup process, and so is testing of your backups on a periodic basis to ensure that everything is going by design. For more information on planning strategies, refer to "Planning for Active Directory Forest Recovery" at http://technet.microsoft.com/en-us/library/planning-active-directory-forest-recovery(WS.10).aspx.

Directory Services Restore Mode

Directory Services Restore Mode (DSRM) is a special version of Safe Mode that takes the domain controller offline and makes it function as a standalone server, unable to service requests of any kind across the network. This mode is used for all AD DS recovery operations. You also must log on as a local administrator using the Directory Services Restore Mode password that you specified when you first installed the domain controller.

DSRM exposes the domain controller to security risks. Anyone who knows the DSRM password can start the domain controller in this mode and copy, modify, or delete data. Like other passwords, you should change this password regularly. The ntdsutil utility enables you to reset this password. Perform the following procedure:

Step 1.   Click **Start**, type **ntdsutil,** and then select **ntdsutil.exe** from the Programs list.

Step 2.   At the ntdsutil prompt, type **set dsrm password.**

Step 3.   At the Reset DSRM Administrator Password prompt, type **reset password on server null.**

Step 4.   Type and confirm a new password. Note that the password is not displayed on the screen.

Step 5.   Type **quit** twice to exit ntdsutil.

TIP   You can reset the DSRM password on a remote server using this procedure. At step 3, replace the keyword null with the server name.

WARNING   When you boot the server into DSRM, there is no AD DS security. Anyone who uses this mode is free to do whatever she likes. You cannot prevent this except by ensuring the physical security of the domain controller. Furthermore, any administrator can reset the DSRM password by following the preceding procedure when logged in to the domain controller running in normal mode; you do not need to know the current password to perform this procedure. Give domain administrator privileges only to individuals you trust.

Performing a Nonauthoritative Restore

Also called a *normal restore*, the nonauthoritative restore is the simplest form of restore from backup media. Because the data will probably be out-of-date (presumably, some changes have been made to AD DS since the previous backup), normal replication processes will ensure that the database is properly updated. This type of restore is called nonauthoritative because the restored data is subordinate to the "live" AD DS data. In other words, this type of restore results in the restoration of data from other functional domain controller(s) that is in turn overwritten or updated through replication by the "authoritative" data already live from AD DS. Naturally, you would need to have at least one other functioning domain controller to perform this type of restore.

NOTE   You can also use AD DS replication to restore a domain controller simply by reinstalling Active Directory on the server to be restored and then allowing Active Directory replication to take place. However, this process could take a very long time and use considerable network bandwidth in a large domain.

To perform this type of restore, you can use either a backup of critical volumes created as described earlier in this section, or a full server backup. Perform the following procedure:

Step 1.   Restart your computer and press **F8** as the server begins to boot.

Step 2.   After a few seconds, the Advanced Boot Options screen should appear (if it does not, you might need to shut the computer down completely and then restart it). From this screen, use the down arrow to select **Directory Services Restore Mode** as shown in Figure 15-7 and then press **Enter**.

Figure 15-7   Selecting Directory Services Restore Mode.

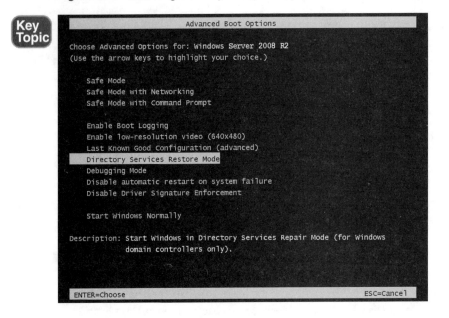

Step 3.   When the logon screen appears, select **Other user**. Type `.\administrator` and then type the DSRM password. This logs you on as the local administrator.

Step 4.   The desktop appears, indicating that you are running in Safe Mode. This occurs because DSRM is a type of Safe Mode in which AD DS is not running and the server is acting as a standalone server.

Step 5.   Open Windows Server Backup using any of the methods described earlier in this chapter.

Step 6.   From the Actions panel, click **Recover**. This opens the Recovery Wizard with a Getting Started page, as shown in Figure 15-8.

Figure 15-8   The Recovery Wizard enables you to restore your server from a local or remote backup.

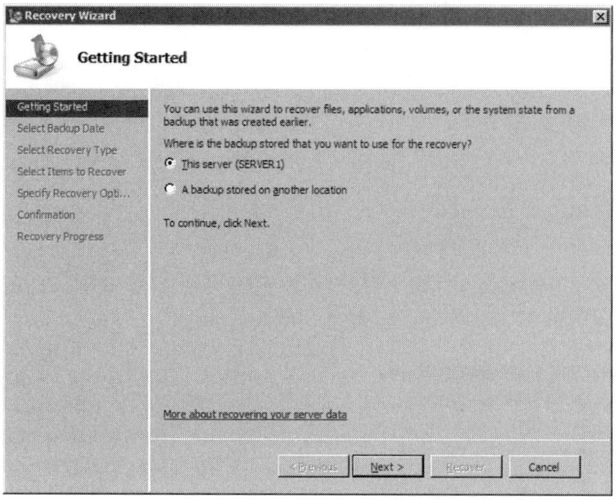

Step 7.   Select the location where your backup is stored and then click **Next**.

Step 8.   The Select Backup Date page displays the date and time of the most recent server backup. If you want to restore from an earlier backup, use the calendar to select the appropriate date and the Time drop-down list to select the appropriate time. Then click **Next**.

Step 9.   The Select Recovery Type page shown in Figure 15-9 offers four recovery options. Select the appropriate option and then click **Next**.

Step 10.   If you select the **Files and folders** option, the Select Items to Recover page displays a tree of available files and folders. Select the desired item(s). If you select the **Volumes** option, select the appropriate volume from the list provided. If you select the **System State** option, refer to the next procedure for recovering system state. When finished, click **Next**.

Step 11.   The Specify Recovery Options page offers several recovery options. If the defaults shown in Figure 15-10 are appropriate, leave these selected. Otherwise, select the desired options and then click **Next**.

Figure 15-9   Selecting the appropriate recovery type.

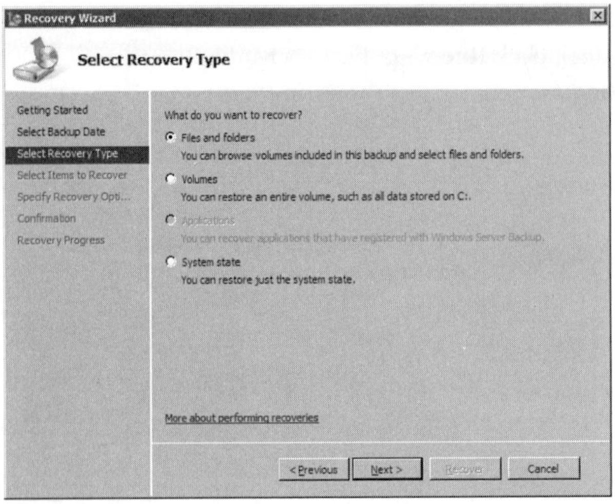

Figure 15-10   Specifying recovery options.

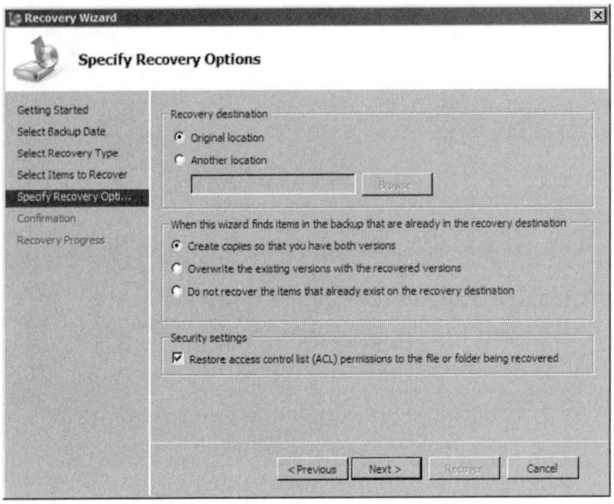

Step 12.   The Confirmation page provides a summary of options that you have selected. If you need to modify these selections, click **Previous** and make the necessary changes. When finished, click **Recover** to proceed.

Step 13.   The Recovery Progress page charts the progress of recovery. When informed that recovery has completed, click **Close**. You can click **Close** at any time to allow recovery to proceed in the background.

Step 14.   Restart your computer in normal mode and log back on as the domain administrator.

Recovering system state is similar but offers a few different options, as follows:

Step 1. Perform steps 1–9 of the previous procedure to restart your computer in DSRM and select the **System state** option from the Select Recovery Type page shown in Figure 15-9.

Step 2. The Select Location for System State Recovery page shown in Figure 15-11 provides options for recovering your Active Directory backup. New to Windows Server 2008 R2 is the option to perform an authoritative restore of Active Directory files from the Recovery Wizard. Make the appropriate selections and then click **Next**.

Figure 15-11 Windows Server 2008 R2 includes an option for performing an authoritative restore from the Recovery Wizard.

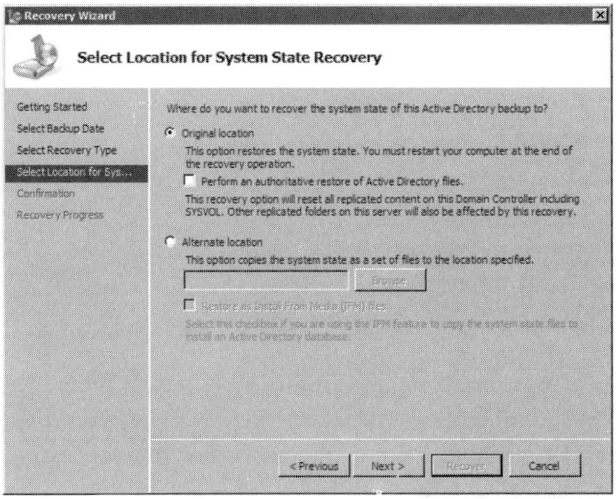

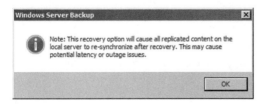

Step 3. You receive the warning shown in Figure 15-12 that all replicated content will be resynchronized after recovery. Click **OK** to proceed.

Figure 15-12 You are warned that all replicated content will be resynchronized.

Windows Server Backup

Note: This recovery option will cause all replicated content on the local server to re-synchronize after recovery. This may cause potential latency or outage issues.

OK

Step 4. Review the information presented on the Confirmation page. If necessary, select **Previous** to make any needed corrections. If you want to reboot the server automatically, select the check box labeled

Automatically reboot the server to complete the recovery process. Then click **Recover** to proceed.

Step 5.   You receive the message box shown in Figure 15-13 informing you that system state recovery cannot be interrupted or cancelled after being started. Click **Yes** to continue.

Figure 15-13   You cannot interrupt system state recovery while it is in progress.

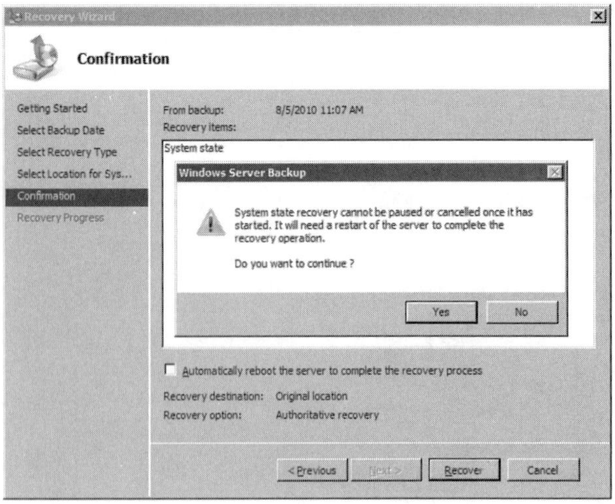

Step 6.   The Recovery Progress page charts the progress of system state recovery. This process takes several minutes; the Recovery Progress page will provide an estimate of the remaining time. You must allow this process to complete before you can click **Close**.

Step 7.   When informed that recovery has completed, the server will reboot automatically if you've selected this option. Otherwise, you receive a message box informing you must restart the computer to complete recovery. Click **Restart**.

Step 8.   Allow the server to reboot into normal mode and log on as the domain administrator.

Step 9.   You receive the message shown in Figure 15-14 informing you that the restore has completed and asking you to reboot once more. Click **Restart Now**.

Using the `wbadmin` Command to Recover Your Server

You learned about the use of the wbadmin command-line tool for backing up your server earlier in this chapter. This command also enables you to perform non-authoritative restore operations. You can use this utility to restore system state from a full server backup, a critical system volumes backup, or a system state backup. Use the following procedure:

Figure 15-14 Completion of system state recovery requires yet an additional reboot.

Step 1. Restart your computer into Directory Services Restore Mode and log on as the local administrator, as described in the previous section.

Step 2. Open a command prompt and type the following command:

```
wbadmin get versions -backuptarget:target_drive:
            -machine:backup_server_name
```

In this command, *target_drive* is the location of the backup to be restored and *backup_server_name* is the name of the server to be restored. This command returns information on the available backup target that you use for the next command.

Step 3. Type the following command:

```
wbadmin start systemstaterecovery -version:MM/DD/YYYY-HH:MM
            -backuptarget:target_drive: -machine:backup_server_name -quiet
```

In this command, *MM/DD/YYYY-HH:MM* is the version of the backup to be restored, **-quiet** runs the command without user prompts, and the other items are as in the previous command.

Step 4. When you are informed that the restore has completed, restart your computer. If you receive a message that other people are logged on to the computer, click **Yes**.

Step 5. If the logon security context displays the DSRM administrator account when the computer restarts, click **Switch user** to log on with a domain account.

NOTE For more information on performing a nonauthoritative restore of AD DS, refer to "Performing a Nonauthoritative Restore of AD DS" at http://technet.microsoft.com/en-us/library/cc730683(WS.10).aspx. This reference also lists several additional considerations that you should be aware of when performing this procedure.

Performing an Authoritative Restore

An *authoritative restore* is a special type of restore that does not replicate changes made to the AD DS database since the last backup. This is useful if an object such as a user, group, or OU has been deleted by mistake. If an administrator has made such an error, the deletion will be replicated to other domain controllers.

If you were to simply restore the deleted objects according to the procedure outlined in the previous section, you would get the deleted objects back—but only temporarily. AD DS replication would replicate the most recent copy back to the restored server, and the restored information would be lost. This situation occurs because each time Active Directory is updated, it increments its update sequence number (USN) by one (this is a number used by AD DS to keep track of replicated updates). The highest value of the USN is always considered the current value. During replication, the USN values are checked, and any server whose USN is not current receives the current value of Active Directory. But when you perform an authoritative restore, the USN of the restored domain controller is increased by 100,000, making it more current than any other versions. This version is then replicated to all other domain controllers.

TIP   You need to know the situations in which you would perform a nonauthoritative or authoritative restore of AD DS. An exam question might test you on this fact.

On a computer running Windows Server 2008 R2, you can perform an authoritative restore by using the procedure already described for recovering system state. Simply select the check box labeled **Perform an authoritative restore of Active Directory files** previously shown in Figure 15-11.

On a server running the original version of Windows Server 2008, you can perform an authoritative restore by using the ntdsutil command immediately after performing a nonauthoritative restore while the server is still running in DSRM. You can also use this procedure on a computer running Windows Server 2008 R2 to selectively mark only certain portions of the AD DS database for authoritative restore. Proceed as follows:

Step 1.   Complete steps 1–4 of the procedure described earlier to start the server in DSRM and perform a nonauthoritative restore of system state, but do not restart your computer. On a Windows Server 2008 R2 computer, do not select the check box labeled **Automatically reboot the server to complete the recovery process**.

Step 2.   At a command prompt, type **ntdsutil** and press **Enter.**

Step 3.   At the `ntdsutil` prompt, type **authoritative restore** and press **Enter**.

Step 4.   At the `authoritative restore` prompt, type **restore subtree** *<DN>*, where *<DN>* is the distinguished name of the object you want to restore (for example, `ou=legal,dc=que,dc=com`).

Step 5.   Click **Yes** on the message box that asks whether you are sure you want to perform the authoritative restore.

Step 6.   When the authoritative restore is completed, you should see the message `Authoritative Restore completed successfully`. Type **quit** to exit the authoritative restore prompt and type **quit** again to exit `ntdsutil`.

Step 7.   Restart the server in normal mode. AD DS replication will propagate the restored objects to the other domain controllers.

WARNING   Take care when performing an authoritative restore. Be careful with this procedure. You will lose all updates to the restored subtree since the time the backup was performed. If you do not specify the subtree properly, you could lose additional updates to AD DS as well.

Recovering Back-Links of Authoritatively Restored Objects

In Chapter 9, "Active Directory User and Group Accounts," you learned how users and groups in one domain can be made members of groups in other domains of the same forest. When this is done, the accounts have what are termed *back-links* in the groups in the second domain. If you have performed an authoritative restore of groups that have these back-links, you must use the `ntdsutil` utility on a domain controller in other domains to recover these back-links. To do this, you must perform the following procedure:

Step 1.   Copy the `.txt` file created by `ntdsutil` during the authoritative restore in the first domain to a domain controller in the second domain.

Step 2.   Restart this domain controller in Directory Services Restore mode, log on as the DSRM local administrator, and restore it from backup media.

Step 3.   While running the second domain controller in Directory Services Restore mode, type **ntdsutil** and press **Enter**.

Step 4.   Type **authoritative restore** and press **Enter**.

Step 5.   Type **create ldif files from** *text_path*, where *text_path* is the path and filename of the `.txt` file created by `ntdsutil` during the first authoritative restore procedure.

Step 6.   Exit `ntdsutil` as previously described, and then restart this domain controller normally.

NOTE   For more information, refer to "Create an LDIF File for Recovering Back-Links for Authoritatively Restored Objects" at http://technet.microsoft.com/en-us/library/cc794865(WS.10).aspx.

Performing a Full Server Recovery of a Domain Controller

If you have a full server backup available, you can also perform a full server recovery of your domain controller. This backup can be located on a separate internal hard drive or on an external hard drive, DVD, or network share. You must also have the Windows Server 2008 installation DVD. The full server recovery procedure restores the operating system, AD DS, and all applications and data from all volumes of the original domain controller.

Use the following procedure to perform a full server recovery of Windows Server 2008 R2. The steps for the original version of Windows Server 2008 are the same, except that some of the wording on the dialog boxes is different:

Step 1.   Insert the Windows Server 2008 R2 DVD-ROM and start your computer.

Step 2.   When prompted, press a key to boot the server from the DVD.

Step 3.   From the Install Windows screen, click **Next** and then click **Repair your computer**.

Step 4.   Ensure that your operating system is highlighted on the System Recovery Options dialog box and then click **Next**.

Step 5.   On the System Recovery Options dialog box shown in Figure 15-15, select **System Image Recovery**.

Figure 15-15   The System Recovery Options dialog box presents options for recovering a computer that will not start normally.

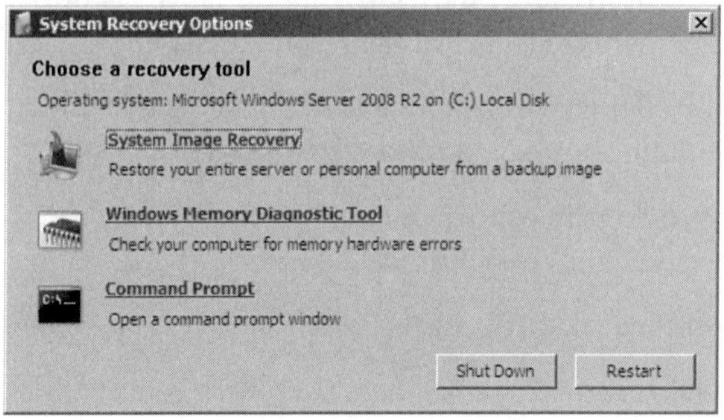

Step 6.   After a few seconds, the Select a system image backup dialog box appears. In most cases, you should leave the default of **Use the latest available system image (recommended)** selected. Click **Next**.

Step 7. The Choose additional restore options page shown in Figure 15-16 provides additional options. Select any of these that are needed and then click **Next**.

Figure 15-16 You can select from these additional restore options.

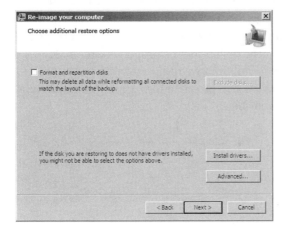

Step 8. You are warned that the System Image Recovery process will erase all data on the selected disks. Click **Yes** to proceed.

Step 9. When the restore is completed, you are informed and your computer is restarted automatically. Click **Restart now** to restart immediately or **Don't restart** to restart your computer later.

Linked-Value Replication and Authoritative Restore of Group Memberships

Linked-value replication is a feature that enables you to replicate changes in group membership more efficiently. This feature replicates only the changes rather than replicating the whole membership when a change occurs. Available when the forest functional level is Windows Server 2003 or higher, this feature improves replication consistency by requiring less network bandwidth and processor usage during replication. It also prevents the loss of updates when administrators are modifying group membership simultaneously at different domain controllers. It is especially useful if you have large groups that contain hundreds, or even thousands, of members. Read-only domain controllers (RODCs) depend on linked value replication to operate properly—this is why you cannot deploy an RODC in a domain where the functional level is Windows 2000.

When you perform an authoritative restore of users or groups in AD DS, the restoration of group memberships is dependent on whether the group was created before or after the implementation of linked-value replication (that is, whether the forest functional level was at Windows 2000 or Windows 2003 at the time the group was created). Membership in a group created after linked-value replication was implemented is always restored properly during an authoritative restore; however, membership in a group created when the forest functional level was still at Windows 2000 might not be properly restored, dependent on the version of `ntdsutil` used to perform the authoritative restore. If you are using the version of `ntdsutil` included with Windows Server 2003 SP1 and later to perform the authoritative restore, group membership is restored regardless of the domain and forest functional levels in effect at the time of the restore. Only if you are using an older version of `ntdsutil` will group memberships not be properly restored. However, `ntdsutil` creates a `.txt` file during authoritative restore that can be used to create an `.ldf` file containing group memberships and in turn can be used with the `Ldifde` utility to re-create group memberships.

> **NOTE**   For more information on using `Ldifde` to create and work with user and group accounts, refer to Chapter 9. For more information on linked-value replication as it applies to authoritative restores, refer to "Performing Authoritative Restore of Active Directory Objects" at http://technet.microsoft.com/en-us/library/cc816878(WS.10).aspx.

The Active Directory Recycle Bin

The Active Directory Recycle Bin is a new feature in Windows Server 2008 R2 that enables you to recover accidentally deleted objects without the need to perform an authoritative restore. The Active Directory Recycle Bin preserves all link-valued and non–link-valued attributes of the deleted AD DS objects (similar to a tombstoned object in Windows Server 2003 and the original Windows Server 2008); when you recover a deleted object, it is restored to the exact same condition that existed immediately prior to its deletion. For example, when you restore a deleted user account from the Active Directory Recycle Bin, all group memberships, rights, and permissions are recovered. Furthermore, you no longer need to reboot your domain controller into DSRM to recover a deleted object; this minimizes disruption to users who might need access to the domain controller while it is offline.

The Active Directory Recycle Bin uses a container named Deleted Objects to hold deleted AD DS objects in a status referred to by Microsoft as *logically deleted*. During its lifetime, you can recover the object either directly or by means of an authoritative restore as already described. When its lifetime has expired, the logically deleted object becomes a recycled object and most of its attributes are removed. This recycled object remains in the Deleted Objects container until its recycled object lifetime expires, at which time the garbage collection process physically removes the object.

The Active Directory Recycle Bin in Windows Server 2008 R2 is not enabled by default. To enable it, your domain must be running at the Windows Server 2008 R2 forest functional level. The following are several actions that you must perform before enabling the Active Directory Recycle Bin:

- Ensure that all domain controllers in the forest are running Windows Server 2008 R2.

- Run the `adprep /forestprep` utility on the schema master to ensure that the schema is updated with the necessary attributes. This utility was discussed in Chapter 3, "Installing Active Directory Domain Services."

- Run the `adprep /domainprep /gpprep` utility on the infrastructure master of each domain in your forest.

- If an RODC is present in the forest, run the `adprep /rodcprep` utility.

- After these preparatory steps have been taken, raise the domain and forest functional levels to Windows Server 2008 R2. This action was also covered in detail in Chapter 3.

NOTE You can also use the Active Directory Recycle Bin to recover deleted objects in an Active Directory Lightweight Directory Services (AD LDS) environment. Requirements for its use are similar to those described here for AD DS.

Enabling the Active Directory Recycle Bin

You can use either the `Enable-ADOptionalFeature` cmdlet in Windows PowerShell or the `Ldp.exe` command-line utility to enable the Active Directory Recycle Bin. To use Windows PowerShell, proceed as follows:

Step 1. Click **Start > Administrative Tools**, right-click **Active Directory Module for Windows PowerShell**, and then choose **Run as administrator**. Accept the UAC prompt if one is presented.

Step 2. To enable the Active Directory Recycle Bin for the `que.com` domain, type the following command (substitute appropriate values for your own domain):

```
Enable-ADOptionalFeature -Identity 'CN=Recycle Bin Feature,CN=Optional
      Features,CN=Directory Service,CN=Windows NT,CN=Services,CN=Configuration,
      DC=que,DC=com' -Scope ForestOrConfigurationSet -Target 'que.com'
```

This command includes the LDAP distinguished name (DN) of the Active Directory Recycle Bin feature.

We introduced the Ldp.exe utility with regard to configuring AD LDS in Chapter 7, "Additional Active Directory Roles." You can use this utility for enabling the Active Directory Recycle Bin by performing the following procedure:

Step 1. Click **Start**, type **ldp.exe** in the Start Menu Search field, and then press **Enter**.

Step 2. From the Connection menu, select **Connect**. Accept the default of localhost or specify the name or IP address of an alternative server and then click **OK**.

Step 3. From the Connection menu, select **Bind**. Select the appropriate credentials (refer back to Chapter 7 for more information on this dialog box) and then click **OK**.

Step 4. From the View menu, select **Tree**. In the Tree View dialog box that appears, select the **Configuration** directory partition as shown in Figure 15-17 and then click **OK**.

Figure 15-17 Selecting the Configuration directory partition from the Tree View dialog box in **ldp.exe**.

Step 5. Expand the Configuration entry in the left pane to reveal its contents, right-click the **Partitions** subnode, and then choose **Modify**.

Step 6. In the Modify dialog box displayed in Figure 15-18, ensure that the DN field is blank and then specify the following items:

—In the Edit Entry Attribute text box, type **enableOptionalFeature**.

—In the Values text box, type **CN=Partitions, CN=Configuration, DC=<domain>,DC=com:766ddcd8-acd0-445e-f3b9-a7f9b6744f2a**. Use the actual name of your domain for *domain*, and replace *com* if necessary. The hexadecimal string in this statement refers to the globally unique identifier (GUID) of the Active Directory Recycle Bin.

—Select the **Add** option under Operation.

Figure 15-18   Using **ldp.exe** to enable the Active Directory Recycle Bin.

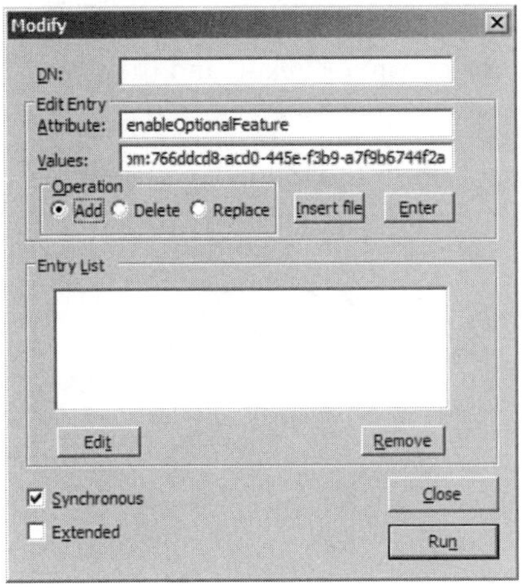

Step 7. After you have performed these actions, click **Enter** and then click **Run**.

Step 8. To verify the enabling of the Active Directory Recycle Bin, locate the `msDS-EnabledFeature` attribute in the right pane of LDP and confirm that its value is set to `CN=Recycle Bin Feature, CN=Optional Features, CN=Directory Service, CN=Windows NT,CN=Services, CN=Configuration, DC=`*domain,* `DC=com`.

Using the Active Directory Recycle Bin to Restore Deleted Objects

As already mentioned, deleted objects are placed in the Deleted Objects container. You first use `ldp.exe` to display this container.

Step 1. Open the `ldp.exe` tool from an administrative command prompt.

Step 2. From the Connection menu, select **Connect**. Type `localhost` or specify the name or IP address of an alternate server if needed, and then click **OK.**

Step 3. From the Connection menu, select **Bind**. Select the appropriate credentials (refer back to Chapter 7 for more information on this dialog box), and then click **OK**.

Step 4. From the Options menu, click **Controls**.

Step 5. In the Controls dialog box, select **Return deleted objects** from the Load Predefined drop-down list and then click **OK**.

Step 6. From the View menu, select **Tree**. In the Tree View dialog box that appears, type the DN of your domain (for example, `DC=que,DC=com`) and then press **Enter**.

Step 7. Expand the entries on the left side of the LDP dialog box and expand the CN=Deleted Objects node.

Step 8. Scroll this node to locate the deleted object, right-click it, and then choose **Modify**.

Step 9. In the Modify dialog box that appears, perform the following actions (see Figures 15-19 and 15-20):

Figure 15-19 Locating the deleted object in the Active Directory Recycle Bin.

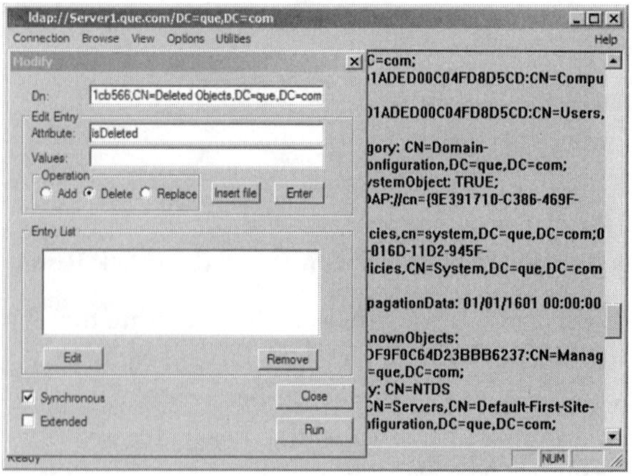

Figure 15-20 Recovering the deleted object from the Active Directory Recycle Bin.

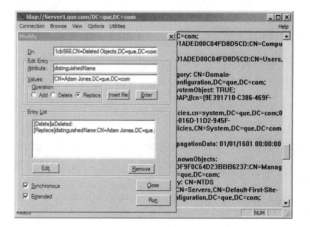

a. In the Edit Entry Attribute text box, type `isDeleted`.
b. Leave the Values text box empty.
c. Under Operation, select **Delete** and then click **Enter**.
d. In the Edit Entry Attribute text box, type `distinguishedName`.

      e. In the Values list box, type the original DN of the deleted object.

      f. Select the **Replace** option under Operation.

      g. Select the **Extended** check box, click **Enter**, and then click **Run**.

Step 10. Repeat step 9 to recover additional objects or click **Close** to close the Modify dialog box.

> **NOTE** For more information on all aspects of using the Active Directory Recycle Bin, refer to "What's New in AD DS: Active Directory Recycle Bin" at http://technet.microsoft.com/en-us/library/dd391916(WS.10).aspx and "Active Directory Recycle Bin Step-by-Step Guide" at http://technet.microsoft.com/en-us/library/dd392261(WS.10).aspx.

Backing Up and Restoring GPOs

Group Policy Management Console (GPMC) provides the capability of backing up and restoring Group Policy objects (GPOs). This procedure copies all data in the GPO to the file system. Included are its GUID and domain, its settings, its discretionary access control list (DACL), links to Windows Management Instrumentation (WMI) filters and IP security settings (but not the filters or settings themselves), a date and time stamp, and a user-supplied description.

Backing Up GPOs

You can back up a single GPO or all GPOs in a domain from GPMC. Use the following procedure:

Step 1. Open the GPMC and expand the console tree to locate the required GPO in the Group Policy Objects node.

Step 2. Right-click the GPO to be backed up and select **Back Up**. Or to back up all GPOs in the domain, right-click the **Group Policy objects** node and select **Back Up All**.

Step 3. On the Back Up Group Policy Object dialog box shown in Figure 15-21, type or browse to the folder in which you want to store the backup. Type an optional description for the backup and then click **Back Up**.

Step 4. A Backup dialog box charts the progress of the backup. When the backup is complete, click **OK**.

Restoring GPOs

If you have deleted a GPO by mistake and want it back, if you have edited it in an undesirable fashion, or it has become corrupted, it is simple to restore the GPO from the GPMC, as the following procedure demonstrates:

Step 1. Right-click the **Group Policy Objects** folder in the console tree of GPMC and choose **Manage Backups**.

Figure 15-21   Backing up a GPO.

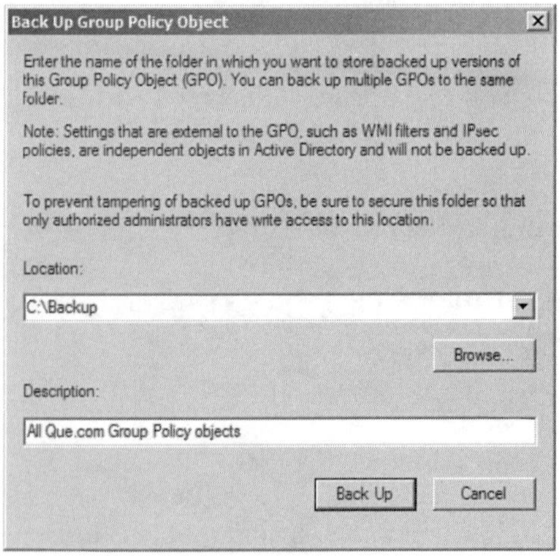

Step 2.   The Manage Backups dialog box shown in Figure 15-22 displays available backups and enables you to perform restores.

Figure 15-22   The Manage Backups dialog box enables you to view, restore, and import GPOs.

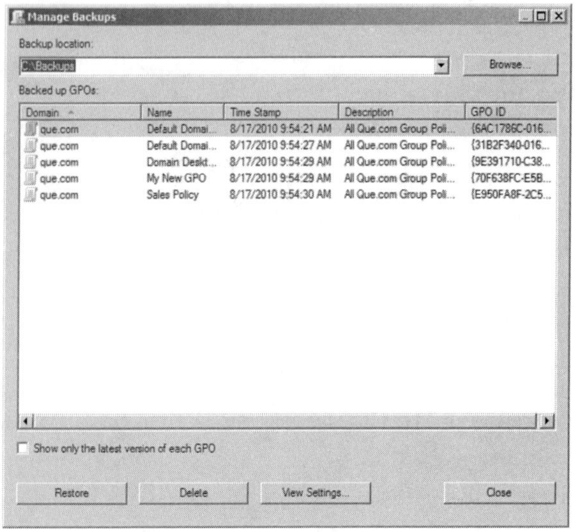

Step 3.   To restore a GPO from this dialog box, select the desired GPO, click **Restore**, and then click **OK** in the message box that displays to perform the restore.

Step 4.   When informed that the restore is completed, click **OK**.

Step 5.   When finished, click **Close** to close the Manage Backups dialog box.

Importing GPOs

From GPMC, you can export GPOs to other domains or import GPOs that you have exported from other domains. To export a GPO, you simply back it up as already described. The import operation is also similar to a restore, except that it is done to a different domain. The Import Settings Wizard assists you in performing the import, as follows:

Step 1.   In the console tree of GPMC, right-click the GPO to be imported and choose **Import Settings**.

Step 2.   The Import Settings Wizard displays a welcome page describing this action. Click **Next**.

Step 3.   The Backup GPO page shown in Figure 15-23 warns you that importing settings permanently deletes existing settings. If you want to back up these settings, click **Backup** or click **Next** to import the GPO without performing a backup.

Figure 15-23   You are warned that importing a GPO will permanently delete the GPO's existing settings.

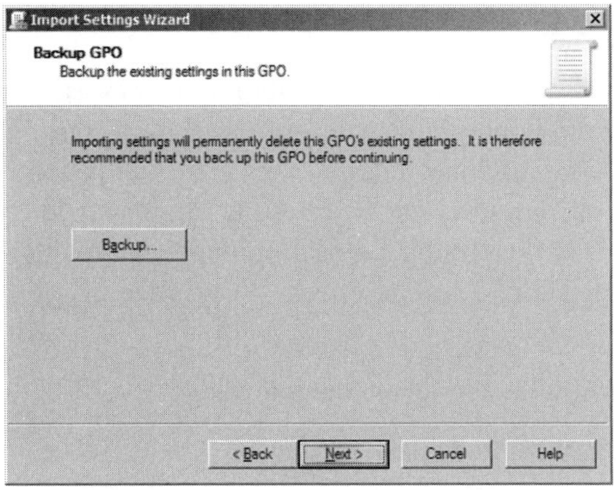

Step 4.   On the Backup Location page, type or browse to the backup folder and then click **Next**.

Step 5.   The Source GPO page shown in Figure 15-24 displays all available backed-up GPOs. If you are in doubt as to the available settings on the desired GPO, click **View Settings** to display a hierarchical list of settings on an Internet Explorer page. When done, select the desired GPO and click **Next**.

Figure 15-24   You can select any of the backed-up GPOs for importing.

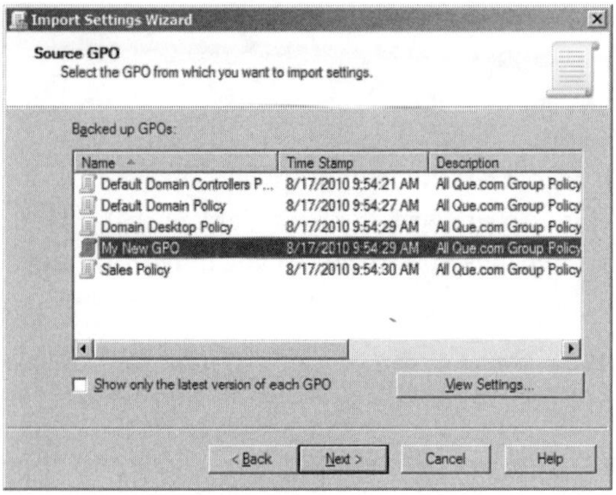

Step 6.   The wizard scans the settings to determine whether any security principals or UNC paths need to be transformed. When finished, click **Next**.

Step 7.   The completion page displays a summary of the settings to be imported. Click **Finish** to perform the import.

Step 8.   An Import dialog box tracks the progress of the import action. When informed that the import is completed, click **OK**.

Using Scripts for Group Policy Backup and Restore

GPMC also provides several Windows Script Host (WSH) script files that assist you in performing deployments of Group Policy at the enterprise level or in configuring Group Policy from a Server Core machine. These scripts also assist you in creating what Microsoft refers to as a *staging environment* for testing the application of GPOs and then porting these GPOs to the production environment after you are assured that they will work properly with no adverse effects. They are found in the Scripts folder of GPMC.

Useful WSH scripts that you should know about include the following:

- **`BackupGPO.wsf`** and **`BackupAllGPOS.wsf`**: Back up GPOs.

- **`RestoreGPO.wsf`** and **`RestoreAllGPOs.wsf`**: Restore GPOs.

- **`CopyGPO.wsf`** and **`CopyAllGPOs.wsf`**: Copy a GPO from one domain to another. You can use this when copying from a staging domain to a production one, or between two domains in the same forest or different forests.

- **`CreateGPO.wsf`**: Create a GPO with the specified name, in the specified domain.

- **`ImportGPO.wsf`**: Import a backup GPO into any domain.

NOTE   For more information on these scripts, refer to "Group Policy Management Console Scripting Samples" at http://msdn.microsoft.com/en-us/library/aa814151(VS.85).aspx.

TIP   You do not need to know the command syntax used by Group Policy scripts for the 70-640 exam, but you should be aware of which script is used for which operation. An exam question could test this fact.

Offline Maintenance of Active Directory

Active Directory requires that certain maintenance operations be performed while AD DS is offline. We have already looked at restoring AD DS when the server is running in DSRM. In this section we look at additional maintenance operations that you will be required to perform from time to time. This includes offline defragmentation and compaction of the AD DS database and database storage allocation.

Restartable Active Directory

New in Windows Server 2008 is the ability to stop or restart AD DS from Microsoft Management Console snap-ins or the `Net.exe` command-line tool. This feature enables you to perform tasks such as offline defragmentation of the AD DS database without the need to restart the domain controller in DSRM. In addition, it reduces the time required to perform these actions.

A domain controller can operate in any of three possible modes:

- **AD DS Started:** This is the normal mode, in which the domain controller can perform authentication requests and all other actions normally performed by a domain controller.

- **AD DS Stopped:** The domain controller acts much like a member server. It cannot service any requests for directory services, but other services that might be running on the domain controller (for example, DHCP or file services) can run normally. Any services that depend on AD DS are also stopped, such as DNS, File Replication Service (FRS), Kerberos Key Distribution Center (KDC), and Intersite Messaging. You can perform many types of maintenance actions in this status.

- **DSRM:** The domain controller is completely offline, acting as a standalone server. It does not service any types of external requests. As already discussed, you use this mode to perform all types of AD DS restore actions.

You can stop AD DS from the Server Manager MMC snap-in, as the following steps show:

Step 1.   In the console tree of Server Manager, expand **Configuration** and select **Services** to display the list of services in the details pane.

Step 2.   Right-click **Active Directory Domain Services** and select **Stop**.

Step 3.   The Stop Other Services dialog box shown in Figure 15-25 displays, informing you of the other services that will also stop. Click **Yes** to stop AD DS and these services.

Figure 15-25   Stopping AD DS also stops these other services.

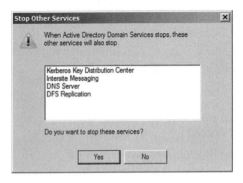

Step 4.   A message box that follows the progress of stopping these services displays.

To restart AD DS, simply right-click **Active Directory Domain Services** and choose **Start**. This restarts the other services automatically as well.

You can also stop and restart AD DS from the command line. Type `net stop ntds` to stop AD DS, and type `net start ntds` to restart AD DS. Confirm your action when requested.

NOTE   For additional information on restartable AD DS, refer to "Restartable AD DS Step-by-Step Guide" at http://technet.microsoft.com/en-us/library/cc732714(WS.10).aspx.

Offline Defragmentation and Compaction

As you work with the AD DS database, performing actions such as creating, modifying, and deleting objects, the database file (`ntds.dit`) can become fragmented just like any other file. Data becomes fragmented and read/write operations take longer to process because the disk head must move back and forth.

AD DS defragmentation can occur in two modes: online and offline. The following sections provide information about these modes.

Online Defragmentation

Online defragmentation takes place automatically while the server is online and able to process directory requests. AD DS performs an online defragmentation every 12 hours on an ongoing basis; however, recovered space is retained within the database and not released to the file system. This process can fully defragment the AD DS database file, but it can never reduce the `ntds.dit` file's size. Even if the quantity of data in the database has reduced (for example, after deleting numerous objects), the empty space remains within the database. You must perform a manual, offline defragmentation to recover this space.

Offline Defragmentation

Offline defragmentation enables you to reduce the `ntds.dit` file size, but it requires that the domain controller be taken offline. Because this process is more vulnerable to corruption by means of issues such as power failures or hardware problems, an offline defragmentation never takes place on the live database file. Instead, a copy of this file is made and this copy is defragmented. When the defragmentation is complete, you must copy the new file back into its original location.

Unlike previous versions of Windows Server, you do not need to restart the server in DSRM. Perform the following procedure to stop AD DS and defragment the database:

Key Topic

Step 1.   Open a command prompt, type the **net stop ntds** command to stop AD DS, and then press **Enter.** You can also use Server Manager as previously described.

Step 2.   Type **ntdsutil** and press **Enter.**

Step 3.   At the ntdsutil prompt, type **activate instance ntds** and press **Enter.**

Step 4.   At the ntdsutil prompt, type **files** and press **Enter.**

Step 5.   At the file maintenance prompt, type **info** and press **Enter.** Note the current path and size of the AD DS database and log files.

Step 6.   At the file maintenance prompt, type **compact to** *drive:\folder*, where *drive:\folder* is the path to the location where the compacted file will be stored. Press **Enter**. When this process is complete, you are informed of the path to the new `ntds.dit` file. See Figure 15-26.

Figure 15-26 `ntdsutil` informs you of the actions you must perform to complete the online compaction process.

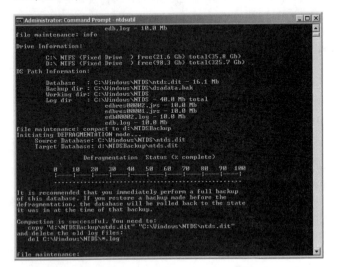

Step 7. Type **quit** twice to exit ntdsutil.

Step 8. As instructed at the end of the compaction process, delete the log files in the log folder, copy the old `ntds.dit` file to an archival location, and then copy the new `ntds.dit` file over the old version.

Step 9. To verify the integrity of the new database file, repeat steps 2–4 to return to the ntdsutil file maintenance prompt. Then type **integrity** and press **Enter.**

Step 10. Type **quit** twice to exit ntdsutil.

Step 11. Type **net start ntds** to restart AD DS.

> **TIP** You can also use this procedure to defragment the AD LDS database. This involves stopping and restarting the AD LDS instance being defragmented. We discussed AD LDS instances in Chapter 7, "Additional Active Directory Roles."

> **TIP** Ensure that you have adequate free disk space available before defragmenting the AD DS database. You must have free space on the current drive that holds at least 15% of the current database size. This space is used for temporary storage during the compaction process.

NOTE   For more information on the offline defragmentation process, refer to "Compact the directory database file (offline defragmentation)" at http://technet.microsoft.com/en-us/library/cc794920(WS.10).aspx.

Active Directory Database Storage Allocation

As your organization's AD DS structure grows in size, you might find that available disk space is dropping to an undesirably low value. If the operating system files and the AD DS database and log files are located on the same physical disk, the disk might become overburdened with requests, resulting in slow performance. Other conditions might also require upgrading or maintenance of the physical disk holding the database or log files.

Any of these situations might require that you move the database and/or log files to a new disk. You must stop AD DS and use the `ntdsutil` utility to perform these tasks. This ensures that the Registry is updated with the new path to these files. Simply copying the files to a new location does not update the Registry and would require that you use the `regedit.exe` command to perform this task.

To move these files to a new location, you should first determine their size and ensure that you have a disk volume of adequate size to accommodate future growth. By default, these files are stored at `%systemroot%\ntds`. Use the `dir` command to determine the current size of the files. Microsoft recommends that the new volume be at least 20% larger than the current size of the files or 500 MB each for the database and log files (minimum total of 1 GB), but best practices suggest that the volume should be considerably larger than this value.

After you have installed a volume of appropriate size, it is best practice to back up the system state using the procedure described earlier in this chapter. This ensures that you can recover should problems occur during the move process. Then perform the following steps:

Step 1.   Open a command prompt, type **net stop ntds** command to stop AD DS, and press **Enter.** You can also use Server Manager as previously described.

Step 2.   Type **ntdsutil** and press **Enter.**

Step 3.   At the `ntdsutil` prompt, type **activate instance ntds** and press **Enter.**

Step 4.   At the `ntdsutil` prompt, type **files** and press **Enter.**

Step 5.   At the `file maintenance` prompt, type **move db to** *drive:\folder*, where *drive:\folder* is the path to new database location. Type **move logs to drive:\folder**, where *drive:\folder* is the path to new log files location. As shown in Figure 15-27, `ntdsutil` informs you of the progress and success of these two actions.

Figure 15-27   `ntdsutil` warns you to back up the new database and log files immediately.

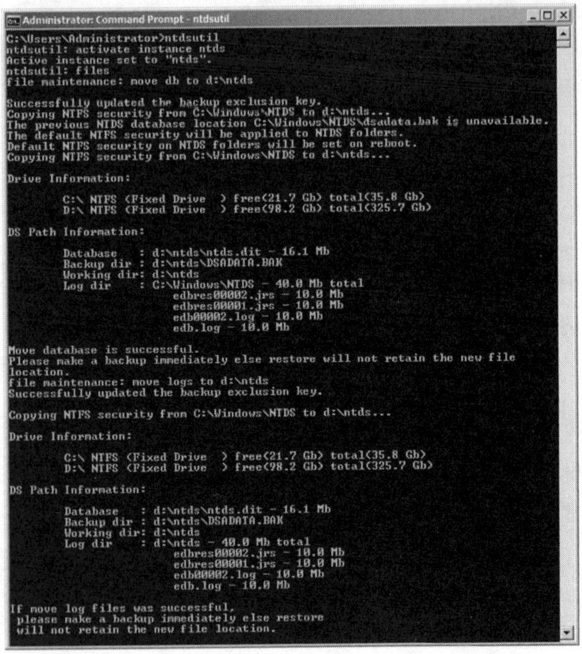

Step 6.   Type **quit** twice to exit ntdsutil.

Step 7.   Type **net start ntds** to restart AD DS.

Exam Preparation Tasks

Review All the Key Topics

Review the most important topics in the chapter, noted with the key topics icon in the outer margin of the page. Table 15-3 lists a reference of these key topics and the page numbers on which each is found.

Table 15-3   Key Topics for Chapter 15

Key Topic Element	Description	Page Number
List	Shows you how to perform a backup of your domain controller	523
Figure 15-3	Selecting items for backup	524
Figure 15-5	Displays options for scheduling a backup	527
Table 15-2	Describes the types of recovery actions possible with Windows Server Backup	528
Figure 15-7	Selecting Directory Services Restore Mode at server startup	530
Figure 15-9	You can perform several different types of server recovery	532
List	Shows how to perform a nonauthoritative restore	533
Figure 15-11	You have several options when performing a system state recovery	533
Paragraph	Explains the importance of the authoritative restore process	536
List	Shows how to perform an authoritative restore	536
Figure 15-15	You have three recovery options when your server is unable to start normally	538
Paragraph	Describes the Windows Server 2008 R2 Active Directory Recycle Bin	540
List	Shows how to back up a GPO	545
List	Shows how to restore a GPO	545
List	Describes the operational modes of an AD DS domain controller	549
List	Shows how to perform an offline defragmentation and compaction of the AD DS database	551

Complete the Tables and Lists from Memory

Print a copy of Appendix C, "Memory Tables," (found on the CD), or at least the section for this chapter, and complete the tables and lists from memory. Appendix D, "Memory Tables Answer Key," also on the CD, includes completed tables and lists to check your work.

Definitions of Key Terms

Define the following key terms from this chapter, and check your answers in the glossary.

Active Directory Recycle Bin, authoritative restore, Directory Services Restore Mode (DSRM), linked value replication, nonauthoritative restore, `ntds.dit`, system state data, `wbadmin.exe`

This chapter covers the following subjects:

■ **What's New with Certificate Services in Windows Server 2008?:** This section introduces the new features available in both the original and R2 versions of Windows Server 2008.

■ **Installing Active Directory Certificate Services:** This section describes the various types and roles of certificate servers and shows you how to install these certificate server roles in Windows Server 2008.

■ **Configuring Certificate Authority Server Settings:** This section describes several actions that you can perform from the Certification Authority snap-in, including the configuration of certificate stores; backing up of certificates, keys, and the entire CA; as well as the assignment of CA administrative roles.

CHAPTER 16

Installing and Configuring Certificate Services

Internet commerce is a burgeoning activity these days, with more and more companies engaging in online selling. At the same time, the bad guys are trying to rip us off with ever-changing tactics. An important line of defense against their actions is that of certifying your websites so that users coming to them are assured that they are legitimate and not imposters that are attempting to steal their identities and more. Windows Server 2008 continues the trend of recent server versions in offering its own certificate services that are integrated with Active Directory. This chapter introduces the concepts of Active Directory Certificate Services (AD CS) and shows you how to install and configure a *public key infrastructure (PKI)*, including various aspects of configuring and managing *certification authorities (CAs)*. You will learn how to configure hierarchies of CA servers, including backup, restore, and archive of certificates and keys and the assignment of CA administration roles.

"Do I Know This Already?" Quiz

The "Do I Know This Already?" quiz enables you to assess whether you should read this entire chapter or simply jump to the "Exam Preparation Tasks" section for review. If you are in doubt, read the entire chapter. Table 16-1 outlines the major headings in this chapter and the corresponding "Do I Know This Already?" quiz questions. You can find the answers in Appendix A, "Answers to the 'Do I Know This Already?' Quizzes."

Table 16-1   "Do I Know This Already?" Foundation Topics Section-to-Question Mapping

Foundations Topics Section	Questions Covered in This Section
What's New with Certificate Services in Windows Server 2008?	1
Installing Active Directory Certificate Services	2–6
Configuring Certificate Authority Server Settings	7–9

1. Which of the following is a new feature of Certificate Services introduced with Windows Server 2008 R2?

    a. Support for cross-forest certificate enrollment

    b. Use of Group Policy for distributing certificates to certificate stores

    c. Use of Online Certificate Status Protocol (OCSP) for checking certificate revocation status

    d. Use of Network Device Enrollment Service (NDES) to enable software on network devices such as routers and switches to enroll for X.509 certificates

2. Which of the following is included in a three-tier PKI hierarchy but not in a two-tier hierarchy?

    a. Enterprise CA

    b. Standalone CA

    c. Root CA

    d. Intermediate CA

    e. Issuing CA

3. You are planning a PKI for your company that will include a multiple-tier hierarchy of CA servers. Which of the following types of CA servers should you plan to keep offline as a safeguard against certificate compromise?

    a. Standalone root

    b. Enterprise root

    c. Intermediate

    d. Issuing

4. When establishing a CA hierarchy, which CA role should you install first?

    a. Enterprise CA

    b. Standalone CA

    c. Root CA

    d. Intermediate CA

    e. Issuing CA

5. When installing an intermediate or issuing CA, which of the following must you have that is not required when installing a root CA?

    a. A certificate revocation list (CRL)

    b. A certificate issued by the parent CA

    c. Internet Information Services (IIS)

    d. Active Directory Domain Services (AD DS)

6. Which of the following types of information are generally included in a certificate practice statement? (Choose all that apply.)

   a. Identifying information for the CA, including its name, server name, and DNS address

   b. Certificate policies implemented by the CA and the types of certificates that it issues

   c. Policies, procedures, and processes for issuing, renewing, and recovering certificates

   d. Available cryptographic algorithms, CSPs, and key lengths

   e. CA security, including physical, network, and procedural components

   f. Certificate revocation policies

   g. The lifetime of each certificate that the CA issues

7. Which of the following best describes the concept of a certificate store?

   a. A text document that specifies which certificates are available to a user, computer, or service

   b. A folder that includes subfolders for various certificate purposes, each of which can include certificates imported to the computer on which it is located

   c. A folder located on the CA server that provides a repository for all certificates issued to users, computer, and services in the domain

   d. A protected area of the Registry on all server and client computers that contains locations for holding certificates for each user, computer, and service

8. You want to create a backup of Certificate Services on your Windows Server 2008 R2 computer, which you have configured as an enterprise subordinate CA. Which of the following procedures can you use? (Choose all that apply.)

   a. Use Wbadmin.exe to back up the Certificate Services folder.

   b. Use Wbadmin.exe to perform a critical volumes backup.

   c. Use Wbadmin.exe to perform a System State backup.

   d. Use the Certificate Export Wizard to perform a backup.

   e. In the Certification Authority snap-in, right-click the certificate server and choose **All Tasks > Back up CA**.

   f. In the Certificates snap-in, right-click the certificate server and choose **All Tasks > Back up CA**.

9. You want to assign the ability to approve certificate enrollment and revocation requests to a junior administrator. This individual should not have excessive administrative capabilities on the CA server. Which administrative role should you assign?

a. CA Administrator

b. Certificate Manager

c. Backup Operator

d. Audit Manager

e. Key Recovery Manager

Foundation Topics

What's New with Certificate Services in Windows Server 2008?

Active Directory Certificate Services (AD CS) in Windows Server 2008 is included as a server role that enables you to perform all certificate management activities without the need for add-on software programs. Included with AD CS are the following role services:

- **Certification Authority:** Enables you to perform all types of certificate management, including the creation, configuration, and revocation of digital certificates for computers, users, and organizations. You can link multiple CAs together to form a PKI.

- **Certification Authority Web Enrollment:** Enables you to configure web-based certificate enrollment including autoenrollment. You can also perform smart card enrollment and create enrollment agents that clients can use for requesting certificates.

- **Online Certificate Status Protocol (OCSP):** Enables clients to use OCSP as a means of determining certificate revocation status.

- **Microsoft Simple Certificate Enrollment Protocol:** Allows routers and other network devices to obtain certificates.

The following are several of the more important new or changed capabilities in Windows Server 2008 Certificate Services:

- Windows Server 2008 introduces a new version 3 (V3) certificate template that supports issuing suite b-compliant certificates, which provide enhanced security without sacrificing performance. Support for the older versions 1 and 2 templates is continued. V3 certificate templates can use the latest cryptographic algorithms and ensure the security of communications between clients and CAs.

- Windows Server 2008 replaces the previous ActiveX enrollment control with a new Component Object Model (COM)-based enrollment control. This provides enhanced support for web-based enrollment pages for enrolling certificates on Windows Vista, Windows 7, and Windows Server 2008 client computers, while providing backward compatibility within limits for Windows 2000/XP/Server 2003 machines. These older clients cannot use web-based enrollment with version 3 certificate templates, but they can use Web-based enrollment with version 1 or 2 templates.

- Group Policy certificate settings enable you to manage certificate settings on all domain computers from a central location. Some examples include management of certificate revocation and renewal of expired certificates. You can also manage several types of certificate stores.

- You can use Group Policy to distribute certificates by placing them in the appropriate certificate stores. Certificate types include trusted root CA certificates, enterprise trust certificates, intermediate CA certificates, trusted publisher certificates, untrusted certificates, and peer trust certificates.

- You can regulate the ability of users to manage their own trusted root certificates and peer trust certificates. You can also specify whether domain users can trust both enterprise root CAs and non-Microsoft CAs or only enterprise root CAs.

- New methods of managing CRLs have been added, including the publication of CRLs and delta CRLs in several locations that enhance the ability of clients to access these lists. You can also use OCSP for checking certificate revocation status. OCSP uses computers configured with the *Online Responder* service to provide revocation status information for certificates issued by one or more CAs within your PKI hierarchy. New Group Policy settings also enhance the management of CRLs and OCSP data.

- Enterprise PKI (PKIView) is a new MMC snap-in included with Windows Server 2008 that facilitates the monitoring and troubleshooting of multiple CAs within your PKI hierarchy. It provides indicators that show the status of various CAs at a glance.

- Network Device Enrollment Service (NDES) enables software on network devices such as routers and switches to enroll for X.509 certificates from a server running AD CS.

New Features of Active Directory Certificate Services in Windows Server 2008 R2

Windows Server 2008 R2 continues to improve on the features included with AD CS by adding the following:

- **Certificate Enrollment Web Service and Certificate Enrollment Policy Web Service:** Enables policy-based certificate enrollment over HTTP with the use of existing methods such as autoenrollment. By acting as a proxy between the client computer requesting a certificate and the CA, the web service eliminates the need for direct communication between the client computer and the CA. This facilitates certificate enrollment via the Internet and between forests.

- **Support for cross-forest certificate enrollment:** Enables the issuance of certificates across forests that are connected with two-way trust relationships. Previously, each forest was required to have its own PKI. The Web Service enrollment feature facilitates this type of certificate enrollment.

- **Improved support for high-volume CAs:** This facilitates the use of Network Access Protection (NAP) with IP Security (IPSec) enforcement and health certificate issuance. When NAP is implemented, health certificates can expire within hours of being issued, and the CA might become inundated with multiple certificate requests from each client computer on a daily basis. When running an enterprise CA, you can choose not to maintain a certificate revocation list (CRL) for these types of certificates, thereby improving the high-volume issuance of health certificates.

This chapter and Chapter 17, "Managing Certificate Templates, Enrollments, and Certificate Revocation," introduce you to the most important procedures for configuring AD CS that you need to know for the 70-640 exam. If you want to perform additional procedures including an advanced lab setup that simulates real-world situations more realistically, refer to the procedures in "Active Directory Certificate Services Step-by-Step Guide," at http://technet.microsoft.com/en-us/library/cc772393(WS.10).aspx. Also refer to the web links found in "Active Directory Certificate Services" at http://technet.microsoft.com/en-us/library/cc732625.aspx.

Installing Active Directory Certificate Services

PKI refers to a technology that includes a series of features relating to authentication and encryption. PKI is based on a system of certificates, which are digitally signed statements that contain a public key and the name of the subject. The certificates are issued by a CA, which can be based either in your own network or operated by an external certificate issuing agency such as VeriSign.

You can install AD CS as a server role from the Add Roles Wizard in Server Manager. Before covering the installation procedure, this section introduces the concepts of certificate authority roles and hierarchies. Best practices dictate that you should not use a single CA but rather a hierarchy of two or more CAs. This provides load balancing and fault tolerance, as well as enabling you to create an offline root CA that can be used to ensure the security of the entire hierarchy.

Configuring Certificate Authority Types and Hierarchies

Table 16-2 introduces the two types of CAs that you can configure in Windows Server 2008.

Key Topic

Table 16-2 Types of Certification Authorities in Windows Server 2008

Certification Authority	Description
Enterprise CA	This type of CA is integrated with Active Directory Domain Services (AD DS). It is installed on a domain controller running Windows Server 2008 Enterprise Edition and stores its certificates within AD DS.

Table 16-2   Types of Certification Authorities in Windows Server 2008

Certification Authority	Description
Standalone CA	This type of CA maintains a separate certificate database that is not integrated with AD DS. It is installed on a member server or stand-alone server.

A PKI can consist of a two-tier or three-tier hierarchy or CA servers, as follows:

- **Two-tier CA hierarchy:** This hierarchy consists of a *root CA* that issues certificates to one or more *subordinate CAs*, whose job is to issue certificates to users and computers on your network. Each subordinate CA can be dedicated to a single type of certificate, such as smart card, Encrypting File System (EFS), and so on, or to a geographical location of a multisite network.

- **Three-tier CA hierarchy:** This hierarchy consists of a root CA that issues certificates to one or more intermediate CAs, which in turn issue certificates to *issuing CAs*. Typically, intermediate CAs are located in different geographical sites, such as cities in which your company does business, and issuing CAs are dedicated to certificate types in a manner similar to those of the lower tier in the two-tier hierarchy.

Within this hierarchy, you can have up to three distinct CA roles as described in Table 16-3.

Key Topic

Table 16-3   Certification Authority Roles in Windows Server 2008

Restore Type	Description
Root CA	This CA is located at the top of every CA hierarchy. It could exist in the form of a root CA operated by your organization, or it could be a CA owned and operated by a third-party issuing authority. In the latter case, you would install the certificate issued by the third-party company on an intermediate or issuing CA server in your own organization.
Intermediate CA	Within a three-tier hierarchy, this CA is directly subordinate to the root CA and issues certificates that validate the issuing CAs. Organizations commonly situate intermediate CA servers in different geographical locations such as cities in which offices are located. Intermediate CAs do not exist in a two-tier CA hierarchy.
Issuing CA	At the bottom of a two- or three-tier hierarchy, the issuing CA issues certificates to users and client computers as needed. Companies often dedicate different issuing CA servers to specific certificate types such as smart cards, EFS, and so on.

TIP   Best practices suggest that when you set up a CA hierarchy, you should use a standalone root CA with enterprise intermediate and issuing CAs. Doing so enables you to keep the standalone CA offline and physically protected in a locked vault. This CA would be brought online only when needed for issuing certificates to CA servers lower in the hierarchy, thereby protecting your PKI from compromise. You should not use an offline enterprise CA because it cannot maintain its integration with AD DS when offline. Consequently it would never be up-to-date.

WARNING   Whatever type of CA hierarchy you use, be aware of one undeniable fact: Only one root CA exists in any hierarchy. You may have any number of intermediate and issuing CAs, but only one root CA. In addition, you must always install the root CA first. In any hierarchy, the root CA is always the most trusted authority.

Installing Root CAs

The procedure for installing a CA depends on its position in the hierarchy. When installing a hierarchy, you begin by installing the root CA, and then intermediate CAs if required, and finally the issuing CAs. Installation of these various types of CAs is similar and proceeds as follows from the Add Roles Wizard in Server Manager:

Step 1.   Ensure that you are logged on as a member of the local Administrators group to install a standalone CA or as a member of the Domain Admins group to install an enterprise CA.

Step 2.   In the Roles node of Server Manager, click **Add Roles**.

Step 3.   On the Select Server Roles page of the Add Roles Wizard, select **Active Directory Certificate Services** and then click **Next**.

Step 4.   The Introduction to Active Directory Certificate Services page provides links to additional information from the server Help and Support files. It is useful to select these links and read the information provided for further understanding of AD CS and its actions. When finished, return to the wizard and click **Next**.

Step 5.   The Select Role Services page shown in Figure 16-1 enables you to install additional role services. Select the required services and then click **Next**. To add the Certification Authority Web Enrollment and Online Responder services, you must add Internet Information Services (IIS) if it is not already installed on the server. Click **Add Requested Role Services**.

Figure 16-1   You can install additional role services from the Select Role Services page when you are installing AD CS.

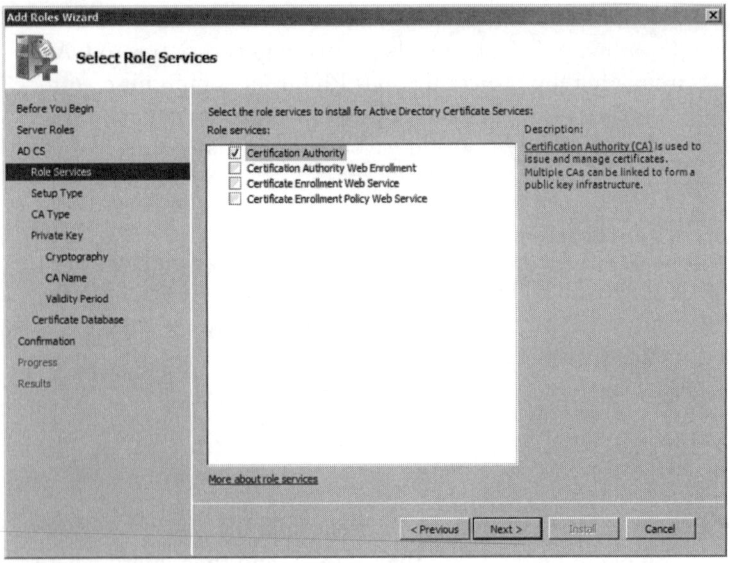

NOTE   You cannot add the Network Device Enrollment Service role service until you have installed and configured AD CS.

Step 6.   On the Specify Setup Type page, select the required type, as shown in Figure 16-2. If installing on a server that is not a domain controller, only the Standalone type will be available. Click **Next**.

Step 7.   On the Specify CA Type page, select **Root CA** for the first CA, and then click **Next**.

Step 8.   The Set Up Private Key page shown in Figure 16-3 provides options for creating a private key. Select an appropriate option and then click **Next**.

Step 9.   If you are using an existing private key, the wizard asks you to select and import the certificate with which the private key is associated. If you are creating a new private key, the wizard presents the options shown in Figure 16-4 for selecting a cryptographic service provider (CSP), hash algorithm, and key length. For learning purposes, it is adequate to accept the defaults provided. Click **Next**.

Step 10.   On the Configure CA Name page, accept the common name provided or type a name of your choosing and then click **Next**.

Step 11.   On the Set Validity Period, accept the default of 5 years or type a different period if desired. Then click **Next**.

Figure 16-2 The wizard asks whether you want to install an enterprise or standalone CA.

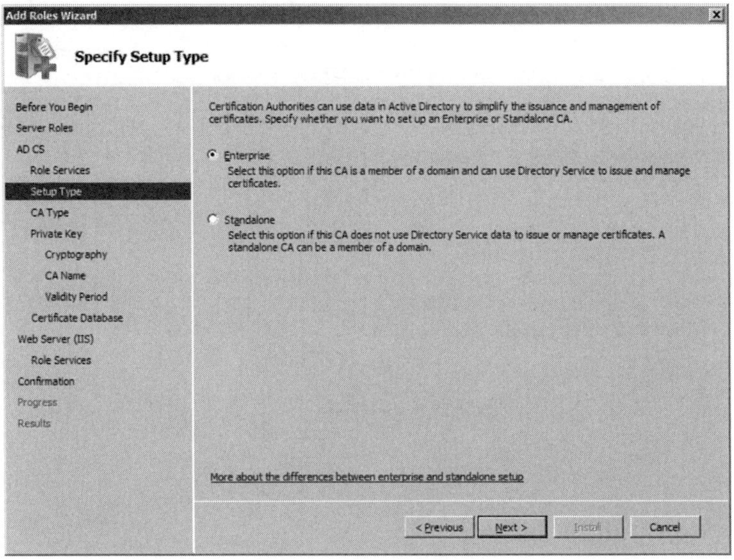

Figure 16-3 You must have a private key to set up a CA. This page provides options for creating a new key or using an existing one.

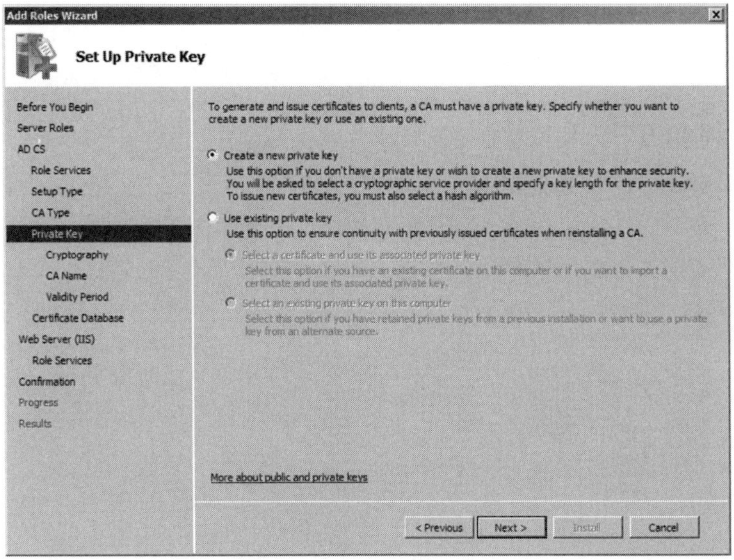

Step 12. On the Configure Certificate Database page, accept the default folder locations or click **Browse** to select an alternative location. Then click **Next**.

Step 13. If installing IIS, you receive the Web Server (IIS) page shown in Figure 16-5. Click the links to additional information if desired and then click **Next**. Then click **Next** again to accept the IIS role services to be installed.

Figure 16-4 The Configure Cryptography for CA page provides options for selecting a cryptographic service provider and hash algorithm.

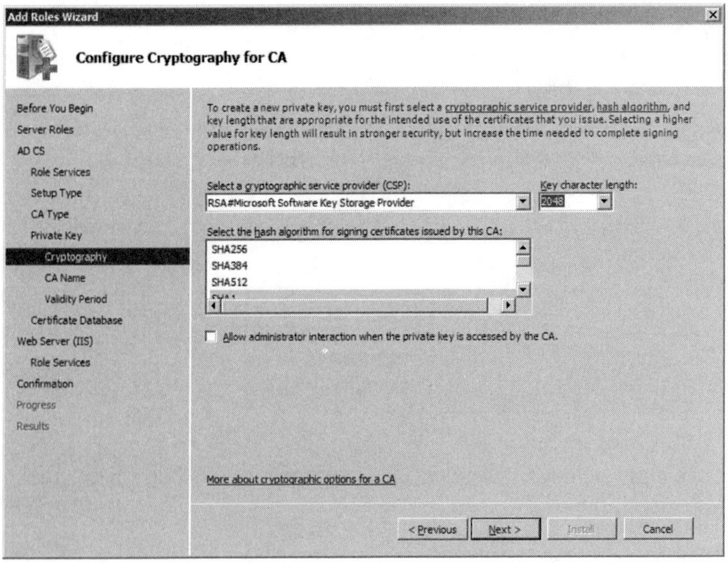

Figure 16-5 When installing IIS, this page provides a large range of role service options for configuring your web server.

Key Topic

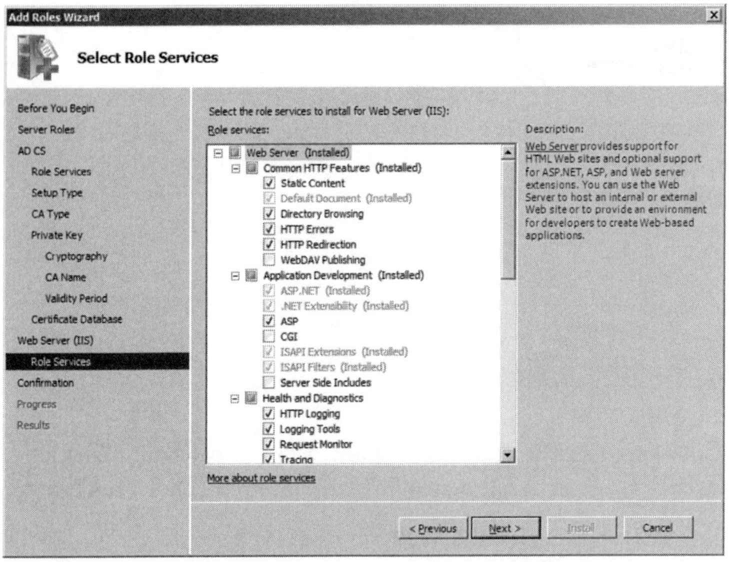

Step 14. On the Confirm Installation Selections page, review the information provided. If you need to change any settings, click **Previous** to return to the appropriate wizard page. When finished, click **Install** to install AD CS with the indicated settings.

Step 15. The Installation Progress page tracks the installation of the roles and role services being installed. When informed that the installation is complete, click **Close**.

When you complete the CA installation, a Certification Authority MMC console is added to the Administrative Tools folder. Tools included in this console are discussed in later sections of this chapter and in Chapter 17. IIS also adds an IIS Manager console to the same folder.

Installing Subordinate CAs

As already mentioned, subordinate CAs can include intermediate CAs in a three-tier PKI hierarchy, as well as issuing CAs in either a two- or three-tier hierarchy. After you have installed the root CA, you can install intermediate CAs if required and then install issuing CAs. Use the following procedure:

Step 1. Follow steps 1–6 of the previous procedure to begin the installation, selecting the **Enterprise** option on the Specify Setup Type page shown in Figure 16-2 when installing AD CS on a domain controller.

Step 2. On the Specify CA Type page, select **Subordinate CA**. Then click **Next**.

Step 3. On the Request Certificate from a Parent CA page shown in Figure 16-6, browse for the parent CA or save a certificate request file to be sent later to the parent CA. To locate a standalone root CA server, you must select the **Computer name** option and then type the name of the root CA server in the Select Computer dialog box that appears. When finished, click **Next**.

Step 4. Complete the installation wizard as described in steps 10–15 of the preceding procedure.

NOTE You can also use a dedicated hardware device known as a *hardware security module* to install a CA. This device is managed separately from the operating system, thereby enhancing the security of the CA hierarchy. For more information, refer to "Set Up a Certification Authority by Using a Hardware Security Module" at http://technet.microsoft.com/en-us/library/cc732052.aspx.

Understanding Certificate Requests

As with previous Windows Server versions, Windows Server 2008 provides web-based certificate enrollment. It enables you to issue and renew certificates for the following:

Figure 16-6   When setting up a subordinate CA, you must have a certificate issued by the parent CA.

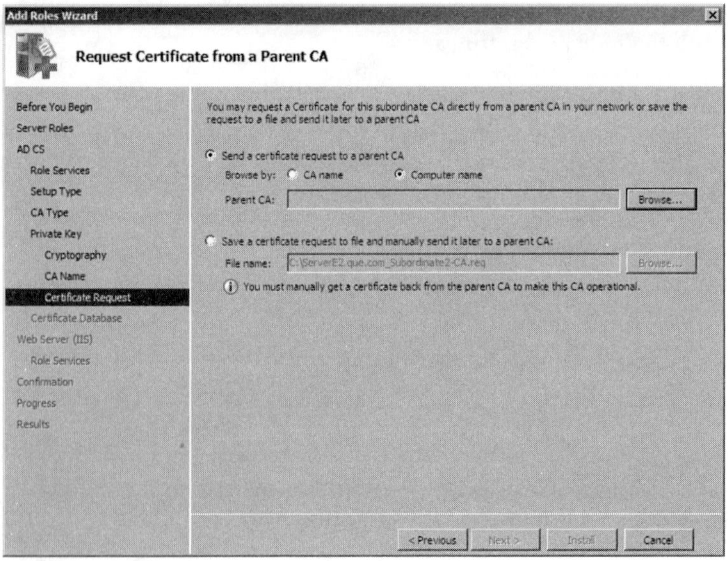

- Domain-based users and computers

- Users and computers outside your domain

- Users and computers not directly connected to your network

- Users with non-Microsoft computers

- Downloading of certificate trust lists

AD CS enables users to request certificates by means of the Certificate Services Web pages, which are automatically installed when you install AD CS. You can also configure autoenrollment of certificates, which enables users and computers to automatically receive certificates and renew expired certificates when required.

Various types of certificate enrollments are discussed in Chapter 17.

Using Certificate Practice Statements

A certificate practice statement is a document that outlines the practices used by IT to manage the certificates that it issues. It describes how the company's certificate policy is interpreted according to the operating procedures and organizational architecture of the company. Included in the certificate practice statement is information of the following types:

- Identifying information for the CA, including its name, server name, and DNS address

- Certificate policies implemented by the CA and the types of certificates that it issues

- Policies, procedures, and processes for issuing, renewing, and recovering certificates

- Available cryptographic algorithms, CSPs, and key lengths

- CA security, including physical, network, and procedural components

- Certificate revocation policies, including conditions under which certificates are revoked, and certificate revocation list (CRL) distribution points and publication intervals

- The lifetime of each certificate that the CA issues, together with a policy for renewing certificates before they expire

Microsoft includes an outline that assists you in creating a certificate practice statement, available for download at http://go.microsoft.com/fwlink/?LinkID=9554. On this page, click the **Download** button opposite the name `Job_Aids_Designing_and_Deploying_Directory_and_Security_Services.zip`. On the File Download page that appears, click either **Open** or **Save**, and then on the folder contents that are downloaded, select the `DSSPKI_2.doc` Word document. Although designed for Windows Server 2003, this Word document is equally applicable for use with Windows Server 2008 and Windows Server 2008 R2. Best practices suggest that you should create a certificate practice statement for each CA in your PKI. This statement can include multiple certificate policies. Note that the certificate practice statement for a subordinate CA can reference common or general information found in the parent CA's certificate practice statement.

Configuring Certificate Authority Server Settings

Several additional settings are available from the Certification Authority console that you should be aware of. These include the configuration of certificate stores, backup and restore of the certificate database, and the assignment of administrative roles for your certificate server.

Installing the Certificates Snap-in

Windows Server 2008 provides the Certificates snap-in, which enables you to manage certificates for a user, computer, or service. This snap-in is not installed in any MMC console by default. Use the following procedure to install the Certificates snap-in:

Step 1.   Click **Start**, type `mmc` in the Start Menu Search programs and files field, and then press **Enter.** This opens a blank MMC console.

Step 2.   Click **File > Add/Remove Snap-in.**

Step 3.   From the Add or Remove Snap-ins dialog box shown in Figure 16-7, select **Certificates** and then click **Add**.

Figure 16-7   Adding the Certificates snap-in to a blank console.

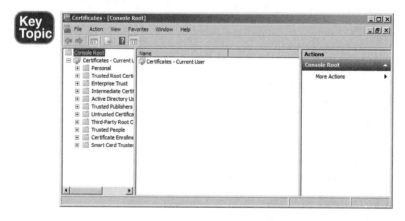

Step 4.   From the Certificates snap-in dialog box that appears, select **My user account**, **Service account**, or **Computer account** as appropriate, and then click **Finish**.

Step 5.   If you select **Computer account** or **Service account**, select the computer to be managed—either the local computer or another computer whose name you can enter from the dialog box provided.

Step 6.   Click **OK**. The snap-in is added to the console as shown in Figure 16-8. Save the console to the desktop with an appropriate name.

Figure 16-8   The Certificates snap-in contains a series of nodes that enable you to manage certificates for a user, computer, or service.

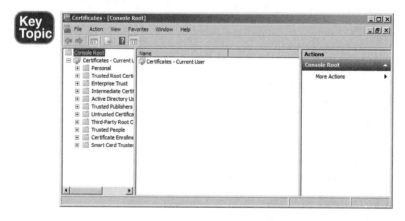

Working with Certificate Stores

Certificates are stored in certificate stores, which are located in a protected area of the Registry on all server and client computers. A series of certificate stores can exist for each user, computer, and service, as previously shown in Figure 16-8. Table 16-4 describes several certificate stores that you can access from the Certificates snap-in.

Table 16-4 Certificate Stores

Certificate Store	What It Contains
Personal	User and computer certificates associated with private keys accessible to the user or computer
Trusted Root Certification Authorities	Certificates for implicitly trusted root CAs, including certificates in the Third-Party store and root certificates from your company and Microsoft
Enterprise Trust	Certificate Trust Lists (CTLs)
Intermediate Certification Authorities	Certificates for subordinate CAs
Trusted Publishers	Certificates from CAs that are trusted by software restriction policies
Untrusted Certificates	Certificates from CAs that are not implicitly trusted
Third-Party Root Certification Authorities	Certificates from commercial CAs such as Equifax and VeriSign
Trusted People	Certificates issued to explicitly trusted people or entities
Certificate Enrollment Requests	Pending or rejected certificate requests
Smart Card Trusted Roots	Certificates installed on smart cards issued to the user or computer

NOTE For more details on certificate stores and their purposes, refer to "Display Certificate Stores" in Windows Server 2008 Help and Support.

Using Group Policy to Import Certificates

You can use Group Policy to make certificates and their associated keys available to all computers covered by a GPO. Doing so enables you to distribute certificates to most of the stores listed in Table 16-4, but not to the Third-Party Root Certification Authorities store. Use the following steps:

Step 1. Open the Group Policy Management Console and select the **Default Domain Policy GPO** or any other appropriate GPO.

Step 2. Right-click this GPO and choose **Edit** to open the Group Policy Management Editor focused on this GPO.

Step 3. Navigate to the **Computer Configuration\Policies\Windows Settings\Security Settings\Public Key Policies** node.

Step 4. As shown in Figure 16-9, you can import certificates to several certificate stores from this node. Right-click the appropriate node and choose **Import**.

Figure 16-9   Group Policy enables you to import certificates to several certificate stores.

Step 5. Follow the steps already outlined in the Certificate Import Wizard to complete the import.

Backing Up Certificates and Keys

You can use the Certificate Export Wizard to back up certificates with their associated private keys. You should do this to ensure that they are available for recovery or to move them to a different computer. Follow this procedure to back up certificates:

Step 1. In the Certificates console for a user, service, or computer account, right-click the certificate to be exported and choose **All Tasks > Export**.

Step 2. Click **Next** to bypass the Welcome page of the Certificate Export Wizard.

Step 3. If a private key is associated with the certificate being exported, the Export Private Key page asks you whether you want to export this key. Click **Yes** or **No** as appropriate and then click **Next**.

Step 4. On the Export File Format page, choose a file format from the following selections and then click **Next**. See Figure 16-10.

Figure 16-10   The Certificate Export Wizard provides a choice of several formats to be used for exporting the certificate.

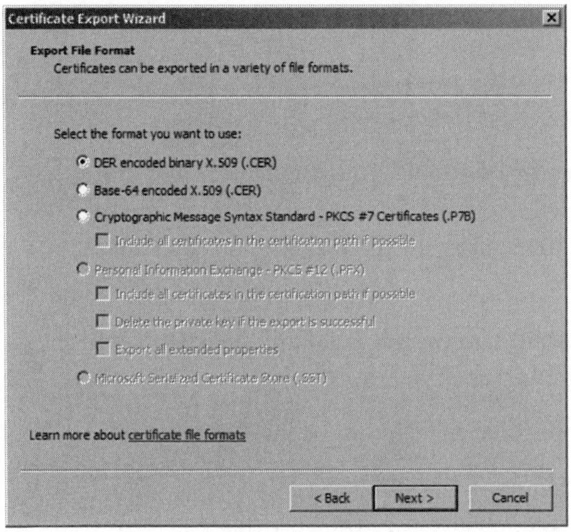

—**DER encoded binary X.509 (CER):** A platform-independent method for encoding certificates for transfer between computers or other devices

—**Base-64 encoded X.509 (CER):** Encodes certificates into ASCII text format for transfer to other computers

—**Cryptographic Message Syntax Standard–PKCS #7 Certificates (.P7B):** For transfer of certificates without private keys between computers or to removable media

—**Personal Information Exchange–PKCS #12 (.PFX):** For transfer of certificates with private keys from one computer to another or to removable media

Step 5.   Specify a filename for the exported file. The file will be saved to the desktop by default; click **Browse** to specify another location.

Step 6.   If exporting the private key, type and confirm a password for the key.

Step 7.   Click **Finish** to export the certificate.

Step 8.   You are informed that the export was successful. Click **OK**.

Restoring Certificates and Keys

You can use the Certificate Import Wizard to restore backed-up certificates or import them to other computers. Follow this procedure to import certificates with their private keys:

Step 1.   In the Certificates console for a user, service, or computer account, right-click the appropriate certificate store and choose **All Tasks > Import**.

Step 2. The Certificate Import Wizard starts. Click **Next**.

Step 3. On the File to Import page, type or browse to the desired file and then click **Next**.

Step 4. If importing a private key, type the password. Also select the following check boxes shown in Figure 16-11 as appropriate:

—**Enable strong private key protection:** Requires prompting before the private key is used. Do not select if a service account or computer uses the key because no means for confirmation exists and the key will fail.

—**Mark this key as exportable:** You should generally select this option so that you can export the key again later.

—**Include all extended properties:** Selected by default, this option ensures that all extended properties of the certificate are imported.

Step 5. On the Certificate Store page, ensure that the certificate is imported to the correct store. Click **Next** and then click **Finish** to import the certificate.

Figure 16-11   When importing a private key, you must enter the password that was supplied at export time. You have three additional options that you can select as required.

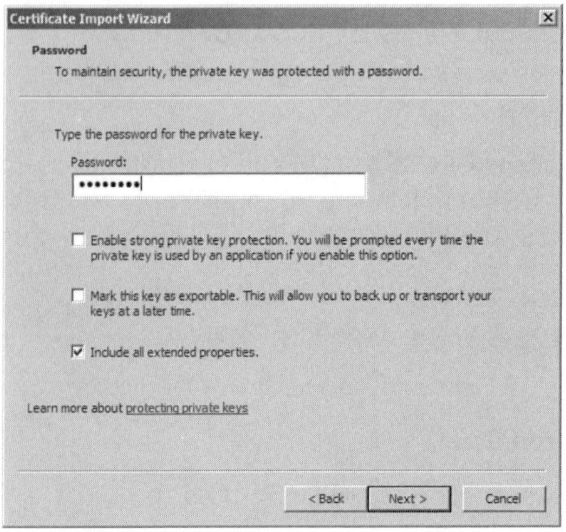

Using Group Policy to Enable Credential Roaming

By enabling credential roaming, you can store X.509 certificates, certificate requests, and private keys specific to a user in AD DS to be stored independently from the user profile and used on any network computer. You can manage these credentials for use on multiple computers and ensure that they are stored securely.

As well as certificates and keys, you can store usernames and passwords using credential roaming policy.

Use the following procedure to enable credential roaming in Group Policy:

Step 1. Open the Group Policy Management Console and select the **Default Domain Policy GPO** or any other appropriate GPO.

Step 2. Right-click this GPO and choose **Edit** to open the Group Policy Management Editor focused on this GPO.

Step 3. Navigate to the **User Configuration\Policies\Windows Settings\Security Settings\Public Key Policies** node.

Step 4. Right-click **Certificate Services Client–Credential Roaming** and choose **Properties**.

Step 5. Enable this policy and specify the additional options shown in Figure 16-12 as required (the values shown are the defaults):

Figure 16-12 The Certificate Services Client–Credential Roaming Properties dialog box enables you to define certificate roaming.

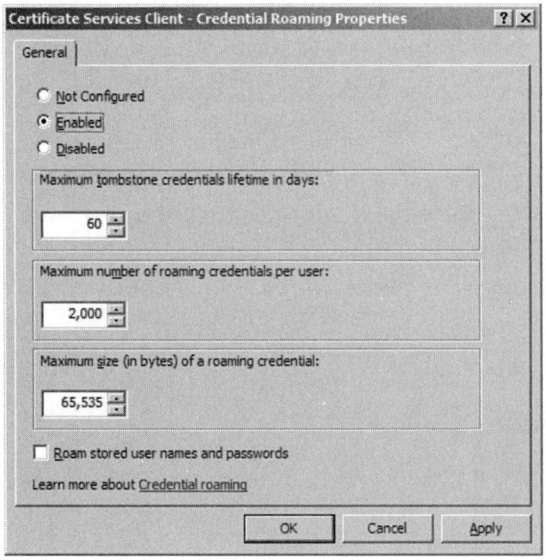

—**Maximum tombstone credentials lifetime in days:** Defines the number of days a roaming credential is retained in AD DS for a locally deleted certificate or key.

—**Maximum number of roaming credentials per user:** Defines the maximum number of certificates and keys used with credential roaming.

—**Maximum size (in bytes) of a roaming credential:** Enables you to limit the size of credentials that are allowed to roam.

—**Roam stored usernames and passwords:** Select this check box to include stored usernames and passwords in the credential roaming policy.

Step 6.   Click **OK**.

Backing Up and Restoring Certificate Databases

Backing up the certificate database is as important as any other backup chore and enables you to recover it should any problems occur. You can use the Wbadmin command to back up system state data as already described in Chapter 15, "Maintaining Active Directory," because the Certificate Services database is part of the system state. At the same time, you should back up IIS because the proper functioning of the certificate server depends on the web enrollment pages. You can also use the Critical Volumes Backup procedure described in the same chapter because this procedure backs up all data on the server.

Certificate Services also enables you to back up its database by itself. To do so, perform the following steps:

Step 1.   In the Certification Authority snap-in, right-click the certificate server and choose **All Tasks > Back up CA**.

Step 2.   Click **Next** to bypass the welcome page of the Certification Authority Backup Wizard.

Step 3.   On the Items to Back Up page of the Certification Authority Backup Wizard shown in Figure 16-13, select the items to be backed up (private key and CA certificate, and certificate database and certificate database log). Also type or browse to an empty folder in which you want to store the backup. Then click **Next**.

Figure 16-13   Backing up the certificate server.

![Certification Authority Backup Wizard dialog box. Items to Back Up page. Select the items you wish to back up: checked "Private key and CA certificate" and "Certificate database and certificate database log"; unchecked "Perform incremental backup". Back up to this location: C:\Backup with Browse button. Note: The backup directory must be empty. Buttons: < Back, Next >, Cancel, Help.]

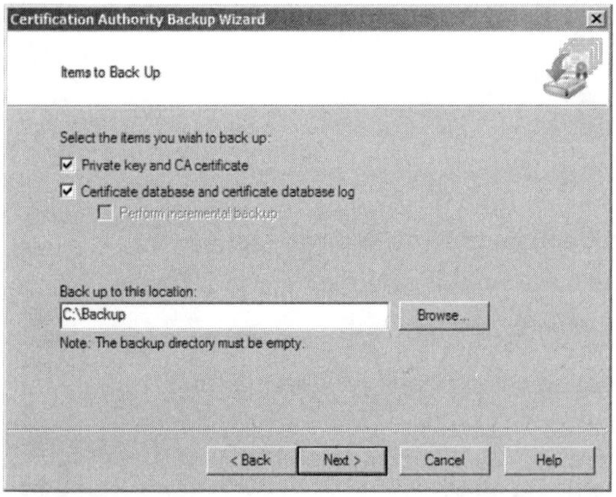

Step 4.   Type and confirm a password for the private key and then click **Next**.

Step 5.   Click **Finish** to perform the backup.

> **TIP**   The folder in which you store the backup must be empty. You can specify a nonexistent folder, and the backup wizard will ask you whether you want to create the folder.

You can restore the Certificate Services database by performing the following steps:

Step 1.   In the Certification Authority snap-in, right-click the certificate server and choose **All Tasks > Restore CA**.

Step 2.   You are informed that you must stop AD CS. Click **OK**.

Step 3.   Click **Next** on the Certification Authority Restore Wizard, select the items to be restored, and type or browse to the location of the backup files. Then click **Next**.

Step 4.   Type the password for the private key that you specified when you performed the backup, click **Next**, and then click **Finish**.

Step 5.   Click **Yes** to restart Certificate Services. If you have additional files to be restored, click **No** and repeat this procedure.

Assigning Administration Roles

AD CS in Windows Server 2008 enables you to implement a system of *role-based administration*, which enables you to assign predefined task-based roles to different individuals. Best practices suggest that you should divide these roles among several individuals to ensure that no single person can compromise your PKI. In addition, you can audit the actions of others.

Table 16-5 describes the available PKI administrative roles.

Table 16-5   PKI Administrative Roles

Administrative Role	What the Role Enables
CA Administrator	Configure and maintain the CA. You can also assign other CA administrative roles and renew the CA certificate.
Certificate Manager	Approve certificate enrollment and revocation requests.
Backup Operator	Back up and recover the CA database, configuration, and database keys.
Audit Manager	Configure auditing, and view and maintain the audit logs.
Key Recovery Manager	Request retrieval of private keys stored by the service.

Besides these roles, the Enrollee nonadministrative role enables users to request certificates from the CA.

By default, members of the local Administrators, Domain Admins, and Enterprise Admins groups are CA administrators on enterprise CA servers and are granted the authority to assign other users to the CA administrative roles described here. On standalone CA servers, members of the local Administrators group (and the Domain Admins group if the server is a member of an AD DS domain) are PKI administrators.

Configuring Certificate Server Permissions

You can assign the PKI administrative roles to the appropriate individuals by creating groups and then assigning these groups the appropriate user rights and permissions. The Security tab of the CA server's Properties dialog box, accessed by right-clicking the CA server in the Certification Authority snap-in and choosing **Properties**, enables you to configure the four permissions shown in Figure 16-14:

Figure 16-14   You can configure four permissions from the Security tab of a CA server's Properties dialog box.

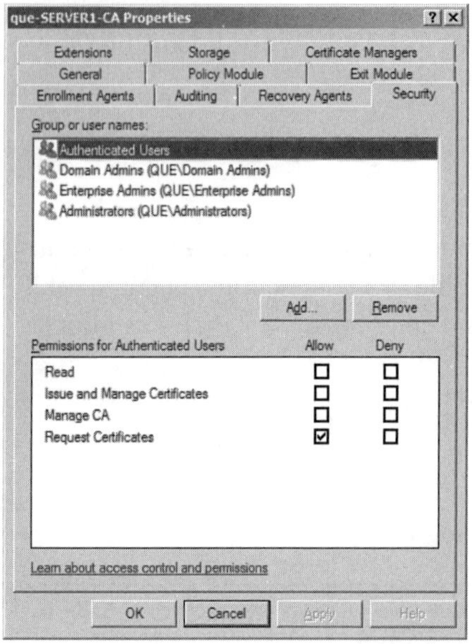

- **Read:** Enables users to read records from the CA's database. This permission is not required for users to obtain certificates; it is normally granted only to those who administer CA servers.

- **Issue and Manage Certificates:** Enables users to approve requests for granting and revoking certificates. Users granted this permission receive the Certificate Manager role.

- **Manage CA:** Enables users to configure and maintain the CA. Users granted this permission receive the CA Administrator role.

- **Request Certificates:** Enables users to request certificates. This is the only permission required for users to request certificates, and is granted to the Authenticated Users group by default.

NOTE   For more information on role-based administration, including a list of the required user rights and permissions, refer to "Implement Role-Based Administration" at http://technet.microsoft.com/en-us/library/cc732590.aspx.

TIP   You might encounter a scenario on an exam question where you must limit the users who can enroll for certificates. To do this, remove the Authenticated Users group from the permissions list and add a group containing the required users with the Request Certificates permission.

Exam Preparation Tasks

Review All the Key Topics

Review the most important topics in the chapter, noted with the key topics icon in the outer margin of the page. Table 16-6 lists a reference of these key topics and the page numbers on which each is found.

Table 16-6   Key Topics for Chapter 16

Key Topic Element	Description	Page Number
Table 16-2	Describes the types of certification authorities available in Windows Server 2008	565
Table 16-3	Describes the certification authority roles that make up a part of a CA hierarchy	566
List	Shows you how to install a root certification authority	567
Figure 16-5	IIS provides a series of role services that are used in setting up web-based certificate enrollment	570
Figure 16-6	When setting up a subordinate CA, you must have a certificate issued by the parent CA	572
Figure 16-8	The Certificates snap-in enables you to manage several properties of certificates	574
Table 16-4	Windows provides a series of certificate stores for each user, computer, or service	575

Complete the Tables and Lists from Memory

Print a copy of Appendix C, "Memory Tables" (found on the CD), or at least the section for this chapter, and complete the tables and lists from memory. Appendix D, "Memory Tables Answer Key," also on the CD, includes completed tables and lists to check your work.

Definitions of Key Terms

Define the following key terms from this chapter, and check your answers in the glossary.

certificate enrollment, certificate, certificate stores, certification authority (CA), enterprise CA, intermediate CA, issuing CA, public and private keys, public key infrastructure (PKI), role-based administration, root CA, standalone CA, subordinate CA

This chapter covers the following subjects:

- **Managing Certificate Templates:** This section introduces the various types of certificate templates used with Windows Server 2008 R2 and shows you how to configure options provided with these templates and enable their use for enrolling certificates from your certificate authority (CA) servers.

- **Managing Certificate Enrollments:** Windows Server 2008 provides several ways in which users can enroll for certificates. This section shows you how to configure autoenrollment, web-based enrollment, and smart card enrollment; it also shows you how you can enforce the use of smart cards on your network.

- **Managing Certificate Revocation:** It might often become necessary to revoke a certificate before its validity period expires for reasons such as compromise. In addition, it is important that applications and devices are able to know if a certificate has been revoked. This section discusses the procedures you must know with regard to certificate revocation.

CHAPTER 17

Managing Certificate Templates, Enrollments, and Certificate Revocation

Chapter 16, "Installing and Configuring Certificate Services," introduced you to the concepts of public key infrastructure (PKI) within Active Directory Certificate Services (AD CS), including the installation and configuration of certification authority (CA) servers and their settings. You learned how to perform maintenance activities including backup and recovery of certificates, keys, and the AD CS database. This chapter continues the discussion of AD CS and shows you how to configure certificate templates and keys, various methods of certificate enrollments, and certificate revocation.

"Do I Know This Already?" Quiz

The "Do I Know This Already?" quiz enables you to assess whether you should read this entire chapter or simply jump to the "Exam Preparation Tasks" section for review. If you are in doubt, read the entire chapter. Table 17-1 outlines the major headings in this chapter and the corresponding "Do I Know This Already?" quiz questions. You can find the answers in Appendix A, "Answers to the 'Do I Know This Already?' Quizzes."

Table 17-1 "Do I Know This Already?" Foundation Topics Section-to-Question Mapping

Foundations Topics Section	Questions Covered in This Section
Managing Certificate Templates	1–5
Managing Certificate Enrollments	6–9
Managing Certificate Revocation	10–12

1. Which certificate template is supported on all computers running Windows 2000 and later?

   a. Version 1

   b. Version 2

   c. Version 3

   d. Version 4

2. You are configuring a certificate template that will be used for smart card certificate enrollment. You want to specify that the user will be prompted to enter her PIN during certificate enrollment. Which tab of the template's Properties dialog box should you select to accomplish this task?

   a. General

   b. Request Handling

   c. Cryptography

   d. Issuance Requirements

   e. Security

3. You are configuring a certificate template that will be used for certificate autoenrollment. Which of the following represent the *minimum* set of permissions that you must allow from the Security tab of the template's Properties dialog box? (Choose all that apply.)

   a. Full Control

   b. Read

   c. Write

   d. Enroll

   e. Autoenroll

4. You are responsible for establishing a smart card autoenrollment policy for users in your company, which operates an AD DS network consisting of a single domain. On accessing the Security tab of the Smartcard User Properties dialog box in the Certificate Templates snap-in, you discover that the Autoenroll permission is not present. What should you do to enable autoenrollment from this template?

   a. Obtain a certificate from a trusted third-party certification authority such as VeriSign and install this certificate on your computer.

   b. Log off and log on as a member of the Enterprise Admins group.

   c. Duplicate the template and configure the duplicate for autoenrollment.

   d. Simply configure the template with the existing Read and Enroll permissions.

5. You want to enroll a certificate with the ability to perform key archival. Which of the following steps should you perform? (Each answer represents part of the solution. Choose three.)

   a. Open the Properties dialog box for the Key Recovery Agent certificate template.

   b. Duplicate an existing template.

    c. From the Request Handling tab of the template's Properties dialog box, select the **Archive subject's encryption private key** option.

    d. From the Recovery Agents tab of the CA's Properties dialog box and ensure that the **Archive the key** option is selected.

    e. Right-click the **Certificate Templates** node in the Certification Authority snap-in, choose **New > Certificate Template to Issue**, select the new template from the Enable Certificate Templates dialog box, and then click **OK**.

6. You want to be able to enroll routers and switches on your network for certificates from AD CS. Your network is configured with a single AD DS domain. What component should you install on your network?

    a. Key recovery agent

    b. Web-based certificate enrollment

    c. OCSP

    d. NDES

7. You are requesting a user certificate by means of web-based certificate enrollment. You would like to use a 4096-bit key size for increased security. What options should you select from the certificate enrollment web pages?

    a. Select the **Advanced certificate request** option from the Request a Certificate page. Select the **Create and submit a request to this CA** option, select the SHA1 hash algorithm, and then select the **Use existing key set** option.

    b. Select the **Advanced certificate request** option from the Request a Certificate page. Select the **Create and submit a request to this CA** option, select the **Create new key set option**, and then choose the required key length.

    c. Select the **Advanced certificate request** option from the Request a Certificate page. Then select the **Submit a certificate request by using a base-64-encoded CMC or PKCS#10 file, or submit a renewal request by using a base-64-encoded PKCS #7 file** option.

    d. Merely select the **User certificate** option from the Request a Certificate page.

8. You want to limit the ability to enroll certificates to users whose AD DS user accounts are members of the Certificate Issuers global group, which you have created for this purpose. What should you do?

    a. Access the **Enrollment Agents** tab of the certificate server's Properties dialog box. In the Enrollment Agents section of this tab, add the Certificate Issuers group and then remove the Everyone group.

    b. Access the **Enrollment Agents** tab of the certificate server's Properties dialog box. In the Enrollment Agents section of this tab, remove the Everyone group and then add the Certificate Issuers group.

    c. Access the **Security** tab of the certificate server's Properties dialog box. Then add the Certificate Issuers group with the Read and Enroll permissions.

    d. Access the **Security** tab of the Properties dialog box for the template to be used for certificate enrollment. Then add the Certificate Issuers group with the Read and Enroll permissions.

9. You want to require that all users in your company's AD DS domain use smart cards for logging on to the domain. What should you do to accomplish this task with the least amount of administrative effort?

    a. Select the user accounts of all required users from Active Directory Users and Computers. Right-click and choose **Properties** and then select the **Smart card is required for interactive log on** option from the dialog box that appears.

    b. Open the Group Policy Management Editor focused on the Default Domain Policy GPO and access the **Computer Configuration\Policies\Windows Settings\Security Settings\Local Policies\Security Options** node. Then enable the **Interactive logon: Require smart card** policy setting.

    c. Open the Group Policy Management Editor focused on the Default Domain Policy GPO and access the **Computer Configuration\Policies\Windows Settings\Security Settings\Account Policies** node. Then enable the **Interactive logon: Require smart card** policy setting.

    d. Create an organizational unit (OU) named Smartcard Users and place the user accounts of the required users in this OU. Then select all the user accounts and enable the **Smart card is required for interactive log on** option.

10. A user in your company's domain is away on maternity leave. You want to re-voke her certificate for the period while she is away and then reenable it after she returns. So, you right-click the certificate and choose **All Tasks > Revoke Certificate**. What should you do next?

    a. Choose the **Unspecified** reason code and click **Yes**.

    b. Choose the **Cease of Operation** reason code and click **Yes**.

    c. Choose the **Certificate Hold** reason code and click **Yes**.

    d. You cannot reenable a revoked certificate. You must proceed with revoking the certificate and then reenroll her for a new certificate when she returns from maternity leave.

11. You want to ensure that applications that check the validity of user certificates can locate the base and delta CRLs without delay. What should you do?

   a. In the Certification Authority console, right-click **Revoked Certificates** and choose **Properties**. Then specify low values of base and delta CRLs from the Revoked Properties dialog box.

   b. In the Certification Authority console, right-click **Revoked Certificates** and choose **Properties**. In the Extensions tab of the Revoked Certificates Properties dialog box, specify the location of the CRL Distribution Point (CDP).

   c. In the Certification Authority console, right-click the CA and choose **Properties**. From the CRL Publishing Parameters tab of the CA's Properties dialog box, specify low values of base and delta CRLs.

   d. In the Certification Authority console, right-click the CA and choose **Properties**. From the Extensions tab of the CA's Properties dialog box, specify the location of the CRL Distribution Point (CDP).

12. Your company operates an AD DS network that includes a PKI consisting of a standalone root CA and two enterprise subordinate CAs on servers running Windows Server 2008 Enterprise Edition. You want to configure the subordinate CAs to support the Online Responder service for keeping track of revoked certificates. Which of the following tasks must you perform? (Each correct answer represents part of the solution. Choose two answers.)

   a. Enable the use of the OCSP Response Signing certificate template from the Certificate Templates snap-in.

   b. Configure the CA servers to publish delta CRLs.

   c. From the Extensions tab of the CA server's Properties dialog box, configure a CRL distribution point on the CA servers.

   d. From the Extensions tab of the CA server's Properties dialog box, select the URL for the online responder and select the check box labeled **Include in the AIA extension of issued certificates**.

   e. From the Extensions tab of the CA server's Properties dialog box, select the URL for the online responder and select the check boxes labeled **Include in the AIA extension of issued certificates** and **Include in the online certificate status protocol (OCSP) extension**.

Foundation Topics

Managing Certificate Templates

A *certificate template* is a file that defines the format and content of certificates issued by the CA. It specifies properties such as the users and computers allowed to enroll for certificates covered by the template and defines the enrollment types permitted. It includes any rules and settings you have specified that are to be applied against actions such as issuance or renewal of certificates. Each certificate template includes a discretionary access control list (DACL) that defines those users and groups permitted to perform actions such as reading and configuring the template, as well as enrolling or autoenrolling certificates based on the template. An enterprise CA stores its certificate templates and their permissions in Active Directory Domain Services (AD DS) on a forestwide basis.

AD CS includes a Certificate Templates snap-in that enables you to configure and manage all types of available certificate templates. Later sections discuss actions you can perform from this snap-in.

Understanding Certificate Template Types

Windows Server 2008 supports the three types of certificate templates described in Table 17-2.

Key Topic

Table 17-2   Types of Certificate Templates

Certificate Template	Description
Version 1 templates	The original templates introduced in Windows 2000. They are read-only and do not support autoenrollment.
Version 2 templates	Introduced in Windows Server 2003, these templates are supported only on computers running Windows XP, Server 2003, or later. They are editable and support autoenrollment. Only servers running Windows Server 2003 or 2008 Enterprise or Datacenter Edition can issue certificates based on these templates.
Version 3 templates	These templates are new to Windows Server 2008 and are supported only on computers running Windows Vista, Windows 7, or Windows Server 2008. They support new features available with Windows Server 2008 including Cryptography API: Next Generation and suite b-compliant certificates, which supports new cryptographic algorithms such as Elliptic Curve Cryptography.

Configuring Certificate Templates

AD CS provides the Certificate Templates snap-in (`Certtmpl.msc`), which provides the following capabilities:

- Creating additional templates by duplicating and modifying existing templates

- Modifying template properties such as validity and renewal periods, crypto-graphic service provider (CSP), key size, and key archival

- Configuring policies applied to certificate enrollment, issuing, and application

- Allowing the autoenrollment of certificates based on versions 2 and 3 templates

- Configuring access control lists (ACLs) on certificate templates

To access the Certificate Templates snap-in, type `certtmpl.msc` at the Run dialog box or in the Start menu Search field. You can also access this snap-in from the Certification Authority snap-in by right-clicking **Certificate Templates** in the console tree and clicking **Manage**. The details pane lists all available certificate templates. You can configure the properties of any certificate template by right-clicking it and choosing **Properties**. From the Properties dialog box, you can configure the following properties:

- **General tab:** Enables you to specify validity and renewal periods and publish certificates in Active Directory.

- **Request Handling tab:** (See Figure 17-1.) Enables you to configure the following certificate template properties for versions 2 and 3 certificate templates:

Figure 17-1 The Request Handling tab of a version 3 certificate template properties dialog box.

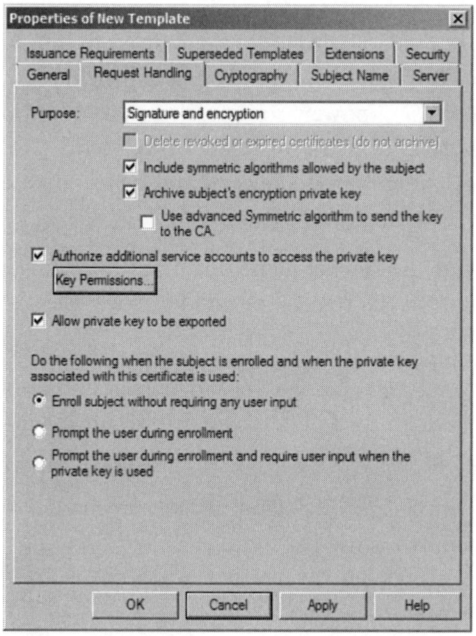

—**Purpose:** Enables you to specify one or more purposes of the template, including encryption, signature, signature and encryption, or signature and smart card logon. You can also enable the inclusion of symmetric algorithms allowed by the subject and the archival of the private encryption key, as well as the deletion of revoked or expired certificates. The **Use advanced Symmetric algorithm to send the key to the CA** option, available when the **Archive subject's encryption private key** option is selected, enables you to use the Advanced Encryption Standard (AES) encryption algorithm for encrypting private keys on transfer to the CA for key archival.

—**Authorize additional service accounts to access the private key:** Available for version 3 computer templates only in Windows Server 2008 R2, this option allows a custom ACL to be specified on the private keys of computer certificates except the root CA, subordinate CA, or cross-CA templates. This option replaces the **Add read permissions to Network Service on the private key** option used in the original version of Windows Server 2008. Default permissions added in Windows Server 2008 R2 include the Read permission for the Online Responder service account and Full Control for the Administrators group and the Local System account.

—**Do the following when the subject is enrolled and when the private key associated with this certificate is used:** Available for user certificate templates only, these settings provide options for the amount of user input required. The default is no user input required during enrollment. For example, you can request that a user enter his PIN when enrolling for a smart card certificate.

- **Cryptography tab:** (See Figure 17-2.) Enables you to define the encryption and hash algorithms and minimum key sizes used. The minimum key size can range from 512 to 16384 bits and is 2048 bits by default. Longer key sizes provide greater security but consume more processing power. You can also choose which cryptographic providers can be used. This tab is present on version 3 templates only. On version 2 templates, the minimum key size and CSP provider are specified on the Request Handling tab.

- **Subject Name tab:** Enables you to define the subject name of a certificate template. You can choose to supply the name in the request or build it from several types of AD DS information.

- **Server tab:** Available in Windows Server 2008 R2 only, this tab provides options to prevent storing certificates and requests in the CA database or prevent the inclusion of revocation information in issued certificates.

- **Issuance Requirements tab:** Enables you to specify default issuance criteria, including the CA certificate manager approval and the number of authorized signatures required.

Figure 17-2   The Cryptography tab of a version 3 certificate template properties dialog box.

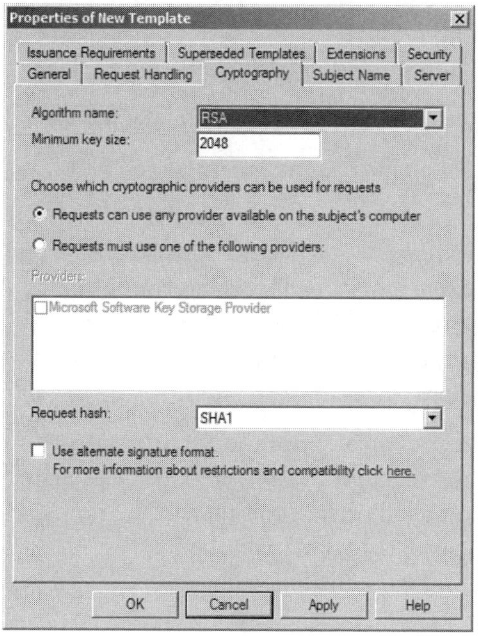

- **Superseded Templates tab:** Enables you to specify any templates that are super-seded by the current template.

- **Extensions tab:** Enables you to define the properties of extensions such as application policies, certificate template information, issuance policies, and key usage.

- **Security tab:** Enables you to define permissions for users and groups on the certificate template. We discuss these permissions next.

TIP   Know the options on the Request Handling tab well. An exam question might present a live version of this tab that requires you to configure multiple options. For more information on this tab, refer to "Request Handling" at http://technet.microsoft.com/en-us/library/cc732007.aspx.

The Properties dialog box of a version 1 template contains only five tabs: General, Request Handling, Subject Name, Extensions, and Security. The available options on most of these tabs are considerably fewer than those on the versions 2 and 3 templates.

Securing Template Permissions

The Security tab of a template's Permissions dialog box enables you to configure the template's ACL and define the security rights for enrollment and use of certificates. The following five permissions are defined from this tab:

Key Topic

- **Full Control:** Grants or denies all of the other four permissions.

- **Read:** Enables the user or computer to enumerate the templates.

- **Write:** Enables you to modify the template's properties or duplicate the template.

- **Enroll:** Enables users and computers to enroll certificates based on the template.

- **Autoenroll:** Enables autoenrollment of user and computer certificates. Not available on version 1 templates.

A user or computer must have both the Read permission and the Enroll permission to enroll a certificate from a selected certificate template. The enterprise CA enforces the Enroll permission when the user requests a certificate using the template. By default, members of the Domain Admins and Enterprise Admins groups have the Read, Write, and Enroll permissions.

To configure a certificate template for autoenrollment, open the **Security** tab of the template's Properties dialog box. Add the required group if not already present and then select the **Read**, **Enroll**, and **Autoenroll** permissions under the Allow column (see Figure 17-3). Also select the appropriate option on the Request Handling tab previously shown in Figure 17-1 from the following:

Figure 17-3 Configuring permissions for autoenrollment.

Key Topic

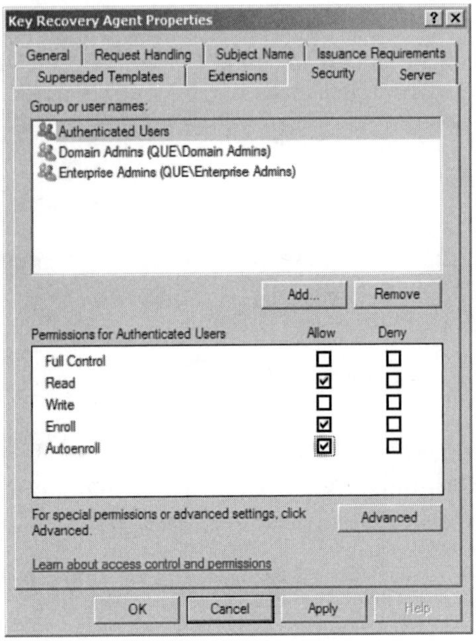

- **Enroll subject without requiring any user input:** Allows "silent" certificate autoenrollment without the need for users to be aware of the certificate usage.

- **Prompt the user during enrollment:** Sends a message to the user during enrollment; for example, to request that a user enter her PIN for a smart card.

- **Prompt the user during enrollment and require user input when the private key is used:** Prompts the user during both enrollment and use of the private key.

Enabling the Use of Templates

By default, AD CS allows certificates to be enrolled from only a very limited number of templates. In the Certification Authority snap-in, select **Certificate Templates** from the console tree to display the list of available templates. To enable the use of a template, add it to this list. Right-click the **Certificate Templates** node and choose **New > Certificate Template to Issue**. From the list in the Enable Certificate Templates dialog box as shown in Figure 17-4, select one or more templates to be enabled and then click **OK**. To disable the use of a template in the list, right-click it and choose **Delete** (or select it and press the **Delete** key). Then click **Yes** in the Disable Certificate Templates message box that appears.

Figure 17-4   Enabling a certificate template.

Managing Different Certificate Template Versions

As already stated, certificate templates come in three versions: 1, 2, and 3. You can tell which version a template is configured for by default, by noting the entry in the Minimum Supported CAs column in the details pane of the Certificate Templates snap-in:

- Version 1 templates: Windows 2000

- Version 2 templates: Windows Server 2003, Enterprise Edition

- Version 3 templates: Windows Server 2008, Enterprise Edition

The extent of configurable properties depends on the template version: Version 1 templates have very few available properties, whereas versions 2 and 3 templates have far more properties, as already described. However, you can create version 2 or 3 templates from version 1 templates by duplicating them.

Duplicating a template also enables you to customize their properties according to the tabs in the template's Properties dialog box as described in the previous section. Use the following steps:

Step 1.   Right-click the duplicate and choose **Duplicate Template**.

Step 2.   In the Duplicate Template dialog box shown in Figure 17-5, select the server type for the duplicated template (**Windows Server 2003 Enterprise** for version 2 and **Windows Server 2008 Enterprise** for version 3), and then click **OK**.

Figure 17-5   When you duplicate a certificate template, you can choose which server the new template is compatible with.

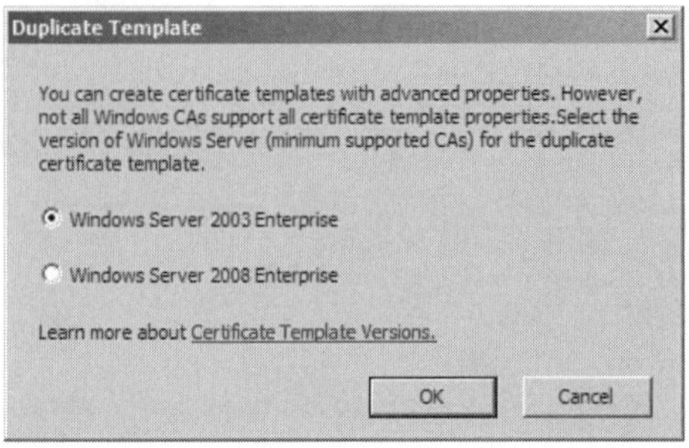

Step 3.   Type a display name for the new template in the General tab of the Properties dialog box that appears and configure any other desired properties on the various tabs of this dialog box.

TIP   Remember the differences between template versions. An exam question might present a scenario in which the autoenrollment options are not available in the template's Properties dialog box. This indicates that you are dealing with a version 1 template. The solution is to duplicate the template and create a version 2 or 3 copy.

Archiving Keys

You can archive the private key of specific certificates when they are issued. Doing so enables the key to be recovered later should it be lost in any way such as by corruption or accidental deletion. An archived key is stored in the CA's database until it is needed for key recovery.

You can create a certificate template that allows key archiving from the Certificate Templates snap-in by performing the following steps:

Step 1. Right-click an appropriate certificate template (for example, the Users template), choose **Duplicate Template**, and then select an appropriate option in the Duplicate Template dialog box previously shown in Figure 17-5.

Step 2. Provide a name such as `Archived User` for this template.

Step 3. Select the **Request Handling** tab of the template's Properties dialog box, and then select the **Archive subject's encryption private key** option (refer back to Figure 17-1). Then click **OK**.

Step 4. To enable this template for certificate enrollment, right-click the **Certificate Templates** node in the Certification Authority snap-in, choose **New > Certificate Template to Issue**, select the new template from the Enable Certificate Templates dialog box, and then click **OK**.

By default, members of the Domain Users group have the Enroll permission for this template. If autoenrollment is required, select the **Autoenroll** permission from the Security tab for the appropriate users or groups. Autoenrollment is discussed later in this chapter.

Configuring Key Recovery Agents

After you have configured a certificate template for archival, certificates created from this template are archived in the CA's database. If a key is lost or corrupted, you can recover the key of a particular subject so that data protected by that key can be accessed. AD CS provides the key recovery agent (KRA) for recovering private keys archived by the CA.

To configure the enrollment of users or groups as key recovery agents, you need to be logged on as a CA administrator, as defined under role-based administration described in Chapter 16. Then proceed as follows:

Step 1. Open the **Security Templates** snap-in, right-click the **Key Recovery Agent** template, and then choose **Properties**.

Step 2.   Access the **Security** tab as described previously and shown in Figure 17-3 and add the required user or group with the **Read** and **Enroll** permissions.

Step 3.   From the Issuance Requirements tab of the same dialog box, clear the check box labeled **CA Certificate Manager Approval** and then click **OK**.

Step 4.   Go to the Certification Authority snap-in and enable the Key Recovery Agent template in the Certificate Templates node of this snap-in, as described earlier in this section.

Step 5.   Create a new MMC console and add the Certificates snap-in, specifying **My user account** when requested. The console tree of the new console contains a Certificates-Current User node. Refer to Chapter 16 if you need more information on this step.

Step 6.   Double-click this node to expand it and display a series of folders in the details pane.

Step 7.   Right-click the **Personal** folder and choose **All Tasks > Request New Certificate**. This starts the Certificate Enrollment Wizard.

Step 8.   Read the notices in the introductory page and then click **Next**.

Step 9.   On the Certificate Enrollment Policy page, leave the default of **Active Directory Enrollment Policy** selected unless you have a policy that you have specifically configured. If so, select the **Add new** option under **Configured by you** and supply the required information on the dialog box that appears. Then click **Next**.

Step 10.   On the Request Certificates page shown in Figure 17-6, select **Key Recovery Agent** and then click **Enroll**.

Figure 17-6   Requesting a key recovery agent certificate.

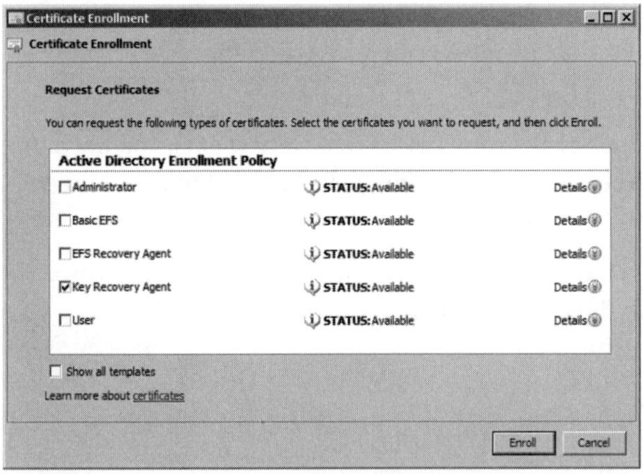

Step 11.   The wizard displays a page while the certificate is created and then informs you that the certificate has been enrolled and installed on the computer. Click **Finish**.

Step 12.   Save the console to a convenient location as `Certificates.msc` and close it.

Step 13.   Back in the console tree of the Certification Authority snap-in, right-click your server name and choose **Properties**.

Step 14.   Select the **Recovery Agents** tab of the CA's Properties dialog box and ensure that the **Archive the key** option is selected. Click **Add**, select your certificate from the Key Recovery Agent Selection dialog box, and then click **OK**. As shown in Figure 17-7, the key recovery agent certificate is listed in the Recovery Agents tab.

Figure 17-7   The key recovery agent certificate is listed in the Recovery Agents tab of the CA's Properties dialog box.

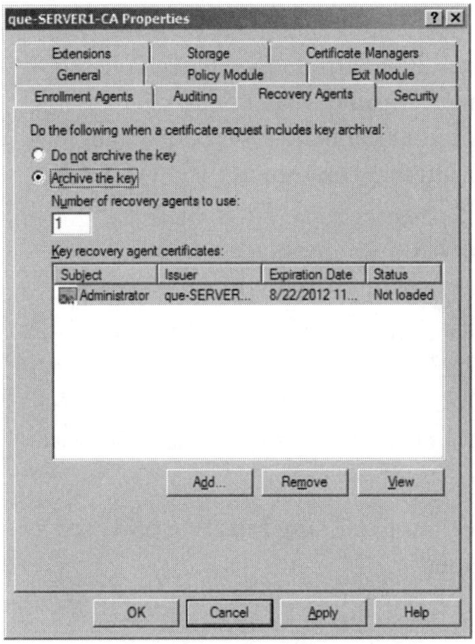

Step 15.   Click **OK** and then click **Yes** to restart AD CS as prompted. After you restart AD CS, the status of the key recovery agent certificate (shown as `Not loaded` in Figure 17-7) should appear as `Valid`, indicating that the key recovery agent is ready to function.

Step 16.   Repeat step 5 to create another new MMC console and add the Certificates snap-in. However, this time, select **Computer** account and then select **Local computer**.

Step 17.   In the console tree of this snap-in, expand **Certificates (Local Computer)**, expand **KRA**, and then select **Certificates**. The key recovery agent certificate should appear in the details pane.

After you have performed this procedure, the user account you employed is now configured to act as a key recovery agent. Any user that is configured as a key recovery agent can use the `Certutil.exe` utility to recover archived keys. This procedure requires that you know the 20-digit hexadecimal serial number of the archived key.

> **NOTE**   For additional details on key recovery agents and their use, refer to "Managing Key Archival and Recovery" at http://technet.microsoft.com/en-us/library/cc730721.aspx and "Enable Key Archival for a CA" at http://technet.microsoft.com/en-us/library/cc753011.aspx.

Managing Certificate Enrollments

As mentioned in Chapter 16, Windows Server 2008 introduces the new role service of Certification Authority Web Enrollment, which enables you to configure web-based certificate enrollment, including autoenrollment. Users can obtain new or renewed certificates across an Internet or intranet connection.

Understanding Network Device Enrollment Services

As introduced in Chapter 16, NDES is an AD CS role service that enables software on network devices such as routers and switches to enroll for X.509 certificates from a server running AD CS. NDES is Microsoft's implementation of the Simple Certificate Enrollment Protocol (SCEP), which enables software on network devices that do not have accounts in AD DS and therefore cannot otherwise be authenticated to the network, to enroll for certificates.

NDES utilizes an Internet Server Application Programming Interface (ISAPI) filter on IIS that performs the following actions:

- Creates one-time enrollment passwords that are provided to administrators
- Receives and processes SCEP enrollment requests for network device software
- Recovers pending requests from the CA

NDES is especially valuable for organizations that are using IPSec with network devices such as switches and routers and want to ensure the security of their communications across such devices.

You cannot install NDES at the same time you install the other AD CS role services. Use the following procedure to install NDES on a server running the original version of Windows Server 2008:

Step 1.   Open Server Manager, expand the **Roles** node, and then select **Active Directory Certificate Services**.

Step 2.   Scroll the details pane to locate the Role Services section and click **Add Role Services**, as shown in Figure 17-8.

Figure 17-8   In the original version of Windows Server 2008, you can install NDES on a server running AD CS from its section in Server Manager.

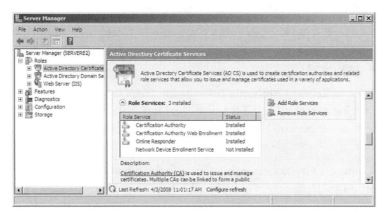

Step 3.   The Add Role Services Wizard will ask you to select a user account to be used by NDES when authorizing certificate requests. You must add this user account to the IIS_IUSRS group before running the Add Role Services Wizard.

Step 4.   Follow the remaining steps in the wizard and click **Install** when the Summary page appears.

NOTE   For additional information pertaining to the original version of Windows Server 2008, refer to "AD CS: Network Device Enrollment Service" at http://technet.microsoft.com/en-us/library/cc753784(WS.10).aspx.

On a server running Windows Server 2008 R2, you must use a separate server from the one that runs AD CS and this server must be running the Enterprise Edition of Windows Server 2008 R2. Proceed as follows:

Step 1.   From Server Manager, click **Add Roles** to start the Add Roles Wizard.

Step 2. From the Select Server Roles page, select **Active Directory Certificate Services** and then click **Next** twice.

Step 3. On the Select Role Services page, clear the **Certification Authority** check box and select the **Network Device Enrollment Service** check box. Then click **Next**.

Step 4. You are prompted to install IIS and Windows Activation Service if these services are not already present. Click **Add Required Role Services** and then click **Next** three times.

Step 5. On the Specify User Account page, click **Select User**, type the username and password for the account to be used by NDES for authorizing certificate requests, click **OK**, and then click **Next**.

Step 6. On the Specify CA page, select either **CA name** or **Computer name**, click **Browse** to locate the CA that will issue the certificates for NDES, and then click **Next**.

Step 7. On the Specify Registry Authority Information page, type the name of the registration authority in the RA name text box. Select that appropriate country or region from the Country/region drop-down list, and then click **Next**.

Step 8. On the Configure Cryptography page, specify the required values for the signature and encryption keys or accept the defaults and then click **Next**.

Step 9. The Confirm Installation Selections page presents a summary of the information you have specified. Click **Install** to proceed.

Step 10. The Installation Progress page tracks the installation of the NDES role service. When informed that the installation is complete, click **Close**.

After you have installed NDES, routers and other network devices can enroll for certificates. Software included with these devices enables you to generate an RSA public/private key pair that enables signing, signature verification, encryption, and decryption. This software also enables you to forward this key pair to the registration authority on the NDES server. At the NDES server, open a browser and access **http://localhost/certsrv/mscep_admin** to receive a random password that you can submit using the device software to the CA. The CA then returns the requested certificate to the device via the NDES server.

NOTE For more information on this process, refer to "Use the Network Device Enrollment Service" at http://technet.microsoft.com/en-us/library/cc755273.aspx and "Configure the Network Device Enrollment Service" at http://technet.microsoft.com/en-us/library/cc770911.aspx.

TIP   An exam question might refer to either the Microsoft Simple Certificate Enrollment Protocol or NDES. Although NDES is a service and MSCEP is a protocol, the exam might use these terms interchangeably.

Enabling Certificate Autoenrollment

The entire purpose of establishing a PKI is to provide users and computers with confidentiality when sending and receiving data across the network. PKI also provides authentication and integrity services. To perform these services, PKI uses a system of certificates that provide clients and servers with the ability to exchange cipher keys used by encryption algorithms. You do not need to know the intricacies of these keys and algorithms for the 70-640 exam, but you do need to be familiar with the process of automatically enrolling users and computers to receive their certificates.

The process of autoenrollment handles all aspects of obtaining and renewing certificates for users and computers. It streamlines the process involved and greatly reduces administrative effort required for these actions. Users need not be aware of these actions unless you explicitly configure certificate templates for user interaction.

Autoenrollment requires an enterprise CA running on Windows Server 2008 Enterprise or Datacenter Edition. Client computers must be running Windows XP or later and be members of the domain. In addition, you must use certificates based on version 2 or 3 certificate templates. Perform the following steps to enable autoenrollment:

Key Topic

Step 1.   Right-click the required template in the Certificate Templates snap-in and choose **Properties**. If the template is version 1, right-click it and choose **Duplicate Template**. In the Duplicate Template dialog box previously shown in Figure 17-5, select **Windows Server 2003, Enterprise** or **Windows Server 2008, Enterprise** as required.

Step 2.   In the Properties of New Template dialog box that appears, provide an appropriate name.

Step 3.   Access the **Security** tab of the template's Properties dialog box and grant the required user or group with the **Read, Enroll,** and **Autoenroll** permissions as previously shown in Figure 17-3.

Step 4.   From the Request Handling tab, specify the appropriate option for prompting the user during autoenrollment. Refer to Figure 17-1.

Step 5.   Go to the Certification Authority snap-in and enable this template in the Certificate Templates node of this snap-in, as described earlier in this chapter.

Step 6.   Configure a Group Policy object (GPO) linked to the appropriate
AD DS container to enroll certificates automatically. To do so, navigate
to the **Computer Configuration\Policies\Windows Settings\
Security Settings\Public Key Policies** node. Right-click **Certificate
Services Client-Auto-Enrollment** and choose **Properties**. From the
dialog box shown in Figure 17-9, enable the policy and configure the
required settings.

Figure 17-9   Configuring autoenrollment settings in Group Policy.

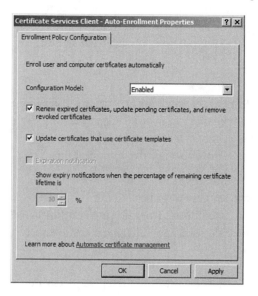

Configuring Web Enrollment

The Certification Authority Web enrollment role service, which was installed with
the CA installation procedure outlined in Chapter 16, enables users to request and
obtain new and renewed certificates across the Internet or a local intranet. This
role service provides web pages that walk users through several tasks associated
with certificate requests.

To request a certificate, proceed as follows:

Step 1.   Open Internet Explorer and type **http://CA_servername/certsrv**. In
this command, *CA_servername* is the name or IP address of the certificate server (not the CA name).

Step 2.   The Microsoft Active Directory Certificate Services Welcome web page
appears, as shown in Figure 17-10. Click **Request a certificate**.

Figure 17-10   The Microsoft Active Directory Certificate Services web pages enable you to request certificates and perform other certificate management activities.

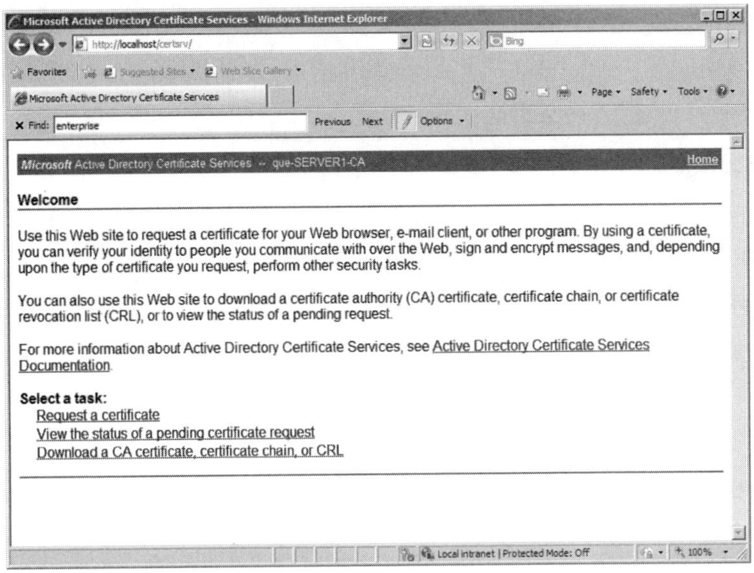

Step 3.   On the Request a Certificate page, select **User certificate** to obtain a user certificate or **Advanced certificate request** to obtain other types of certificates.

Step 4.   If you are requesting a user certificate, no further information is required. Click **Submit** to complete the certificate request. If you select **Advanced certificate request**, you receive the options shown in Figure 17-11. Select the option **Create and submit a request to this CA** to submit a certificate request or select the second option if you have saved a previously created base 64-encoded CMC or PKCS#10 certificate request file.

Step 5.   If you select the **Create and submit a request to this CA** option, you receive the Advanced Certificate Request page shown in Figure 17-12. This page enables you to select the required certificate template, key options, and additional options according to the properties of the template specified. Complete these options and click **Submit**.

Step 6.   If you receive a Web Access Confirmation message box, click **Yes** to proceed.

Step 7.   When informed that the certificate was issued, click **Install this certificate**. You will be informed when the new certificate is installed.

Figure 17-11 You can create other certificate requests or submit a previously created certificate request file.

Key Topic

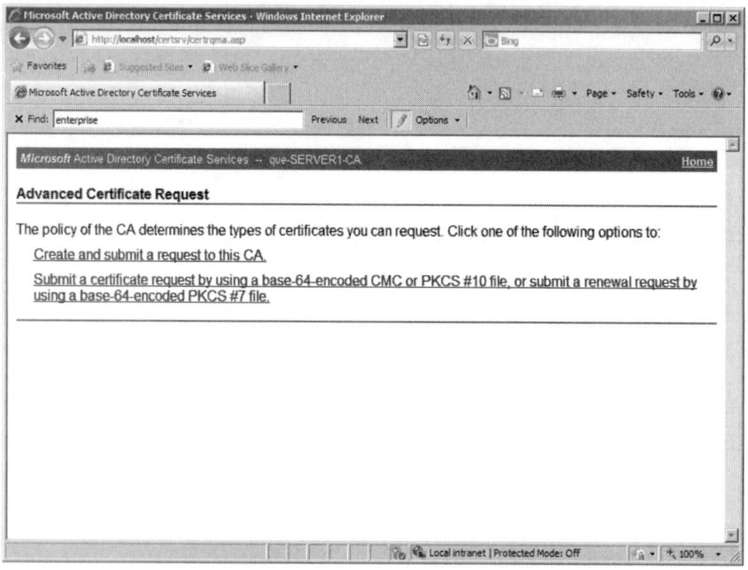

Figure 17-12 The Advanced Certificate Request page enables you to specify additional options related to the desired certificate.

Key Topic

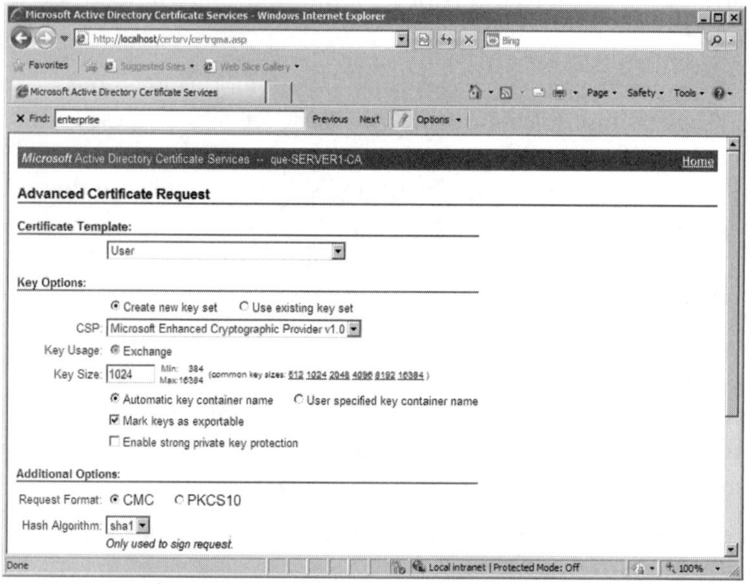

NOTE If you receive a message box stating that `the Web site for the CA must be configured to use HTTPS authentication`, you need to configure HTTPS binding for the Web Server (IIS) role. Open **IIS Manager** from the Administrative

Tools folder, expand the web server node, and then expand the **Sites** subnode. Select the website installed by AD CS and then click **Bindings** from the Actions pane. From the Type list, click **https**. Click **Edit**, select a certificate from the SSL Certificate list, and then click **OK** to save the binding. For more information, refer to "Setting Up Certificate Enrollment Web Services" at http://technet.microsoft.com/en-us/library/dd759243.aspx.

Configuring Smart Card Enrollment

To improve the security of user logons and avoid the hassle of password problems, organizations are turning toward more advanced forms of user authentication. Windows Server 2008 continues the support of smart cards, first introduced in Windows Server 2003. A *smart card* is a credit card–sized electronic device that stores public and private keys, thereby providing for secure, tamperproof identification and authentication. It can be used for secure authentication of clients logging on to an AD DS domain, as well as remote access logons.

This system of authentication uses a smart card reader that attaches to a standard peripheral interface such as a USB port. Many manufacturers produce plug-and-play smart card readers that have been certified by Microsoft for use on computers running Windows XP/Vista/7/Server 2003/Server 2008. Many of the newest portable computers even feature built-in smart card readers. You will also need one or more smart card writers for use during the enrollment process. More information on supported smart cards, readers, and writers is available from the Windows 7 or Windows Server 2008 Help and Support Center.

Smart cards provide a secure means to authenticate clients logging on to an AD DS domain, as well as remote access logon. With the more usual logon name/password combinations, if a malicious individual were to crack the username and password, she could assume the legitimate user's identity and obtain that user's access to domain resources. If that user were an administrator, the malicious user would be able to do considerable damage to the entire network. When smart card authentication is in use, the malicious user would have to obtain the smart card and the user's PIN to gain access. Should the malicious user obtain the card without the PIN and attempt some type of guessing algorithm, the smart card will lock out after several unsuccessful attempts. Also known as *dual-factor authentication*, this combination uses cryptography-based identification, thereby permitting a higher level of secured access to your network.

After you have acquired the required hardware and set up your PKI hierarchy, you are ready to set up smart card authentication for your AD DS domain. You will need to set up a group of smart card issuers (enrollment agents), who are users that are trusted to enroll certificates for general users requiring smart cards. These enrollment agents need to request a signing certificate based on the Enrollment

Agent certificate template. This certificate signs the certificate request for each smart card recipient. Use the following procedure:

Step 1.   Click **Start**, type `certmgr.msc` in the Start menu Search field, and then press **Enter** to start the Certificates console.

Step 2.   Expand the Personal folder and then click **Certificates**. Any issued certificates appear in the details pane.

Step 3.   Right-click **Certificates** and choose **All Tasks > Request New Certificate**. This starts the Certificate Enrollment Wizard.

Step 4.   Click **Next** and on the Select Certificate Enrollment Policy page, leave the default of **Active Directory Enrollment Policy** selected. Then click **Next** again.

Step 5.   On the Request Certificates page, select **Enrollment Agent** (as shown in Figure 17-13) and then click **Enroll**.

Figure 17-13   The Request Certificates page enables you to select a certificate type.

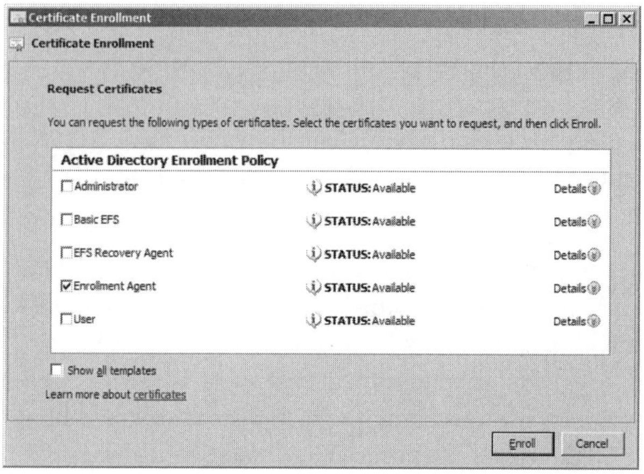

Step 6.   The certificate is created and installed and you are informed of its success (see Figure 17-14). Click **Finish**.

Step 7.   The requested certificate appears in the details pane of the Certificates console.

Creating Enrollment Agents

An *enrollment agent* is a user that is granted the permission to enroll for certificates on behalf of other users. They are typically trusted individuals in secure environments, possibly including senior help desk or IT security employees.

Figure 17-14   The Certificate Enrollment Wizard informs you that the certificate has been issued and installed.

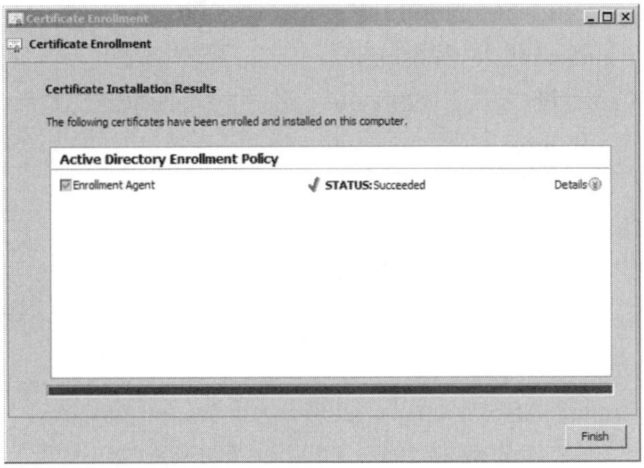

Windows Server 2008 introduces a new restricted enrollment agent functionality that enables limiting the permissions granted to enrollment agents for smart card certificate enrollment so that they can enroll for only certain groups of smart card holders. Previously, enrollment agents were unrestricted—there was no means of limiting the enrollment agent to enrolling only a certain group of users. The new functionality allows the use of an enrollment agent for one or many certificate templates. You can choose which users or security groups the enrollment agent can enroll on behalf of.

> **WARNING**   Always ensure that only trusted employees are granted enrollment agent privileges. Use a security group for designating users as enrollment agents. For additional security, use the Restricted Groups feature in Group Policy to limit the membership of this group. Any user with an Enrollment Agent certificate can enroll for a certificate and generate a smart card on behalf of other users according to the enrollment policy. A malicious user could use the resulting smart card to log on to the network and impersonate the actual user.

To configure restricted enrollment agents, ensure that you are logged on as a CA administrator. First, create security groups for the enrollment agents and for the users that the agents will be permitted to enroll. Then proceed as follows:

Step 1.   Open the Certification Authority snap-in.

Step 2.   Right-click your CA server at the top of the console tree and choose **Properties**.

Step 3.   On the Enrollment Agents tab of the server's Properties dialog box, select **Restrict enrollment agents**.

Step 4.   An Enrollment Agents message box warns you that restrictions on delegated enrollment agents are enforced only on Windows Server 2008 CAs or higher and reminds you to ensure that your enrollment agent policy is appropriate. Click **OK** to proceed.

Step 5.   In the Enrollment Agents list box, Everyone is added by default. You must add the group containing the user accounts of the enrollment agents before removing this group. Click **Add**.

Step 6.   In the Select User, Computer, or Group dialog box, type the name of the group in which the enrollment agents are located and click **OK**.

Step 7.   The group you added appears in the Enrollment Agents list box. Select **Everyone** and click **Remove**.

Step 8.   In the Certificate Templates list box, permission is granted for all templates by default. You must add one or more templates before removing this entry. Click **Add**.

Step 9.   In the Enable Certificate Templates dialog box shown in Figure 17-15, select a template and then click **OK**. Repeat this step to add more templates if necessary (you can add only one template at a time).

Figure 17-15   Enabling certificate templates for smart card enrollment.

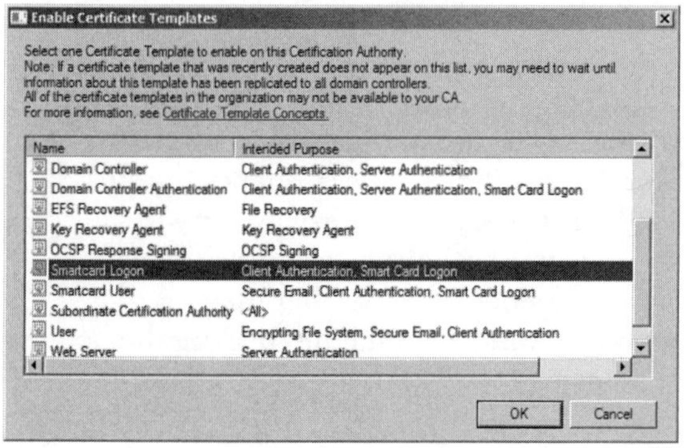

Step 10.   The templates you added appear in the Certificate Templates list box. Select **<All>** and click **Remove**.

Step 11.   In the Permissions list box, Everyone is granted Allow access by default. You must add the required group here before removing this group. Click **Add**.

Step 12.   In the Select User, Computer, or Group dialog box, type the name of the group in which the smart card users are located and click **OK**.

Step 13.   The group you added appears in the Permissions list box. Select
Everyone and click **Remove**.

Step 14.   Click **OK** or **Apply** to apply your selections. The completed Enrollment
Agents tab will appear similar to that shown in Figure 17-16.

Figure 17-16   Configuring restricted enrollment agents policy.

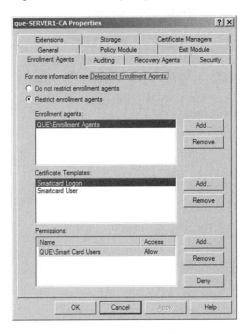

> **TIP**   You can add only one entry in any of the three list boxes in the Enrollment
> Agents tab at a time. To add additional entries, simply click **Add** again.

The enrollment agents must possess an enrollment agent certificate so that they
can enroll users with certificates according to the permissions you have granted
them in the restricted enrollment agent policy. You can autoenroll these agents for
an enrollment agent certificate by following the procedure outlined earlier in this
chapter. When you create the GPO that contains the autoenrollment settings,
grant the group containing the agents the Read and Apply Group Policy permissions and remove any other groups from the GPO's Delegation tab as described in
Chapter 11, "Creating and Applying Group Policy Objects."

> **WARNING**   You cannot limit the users that an enrollment agent can enroll for by
> means of Active Directory containers such as OUs; you must use security groups
> for this purpose. Also note that you must use a CA based on Windows Server 2008

Enterprise or Datacenter Edition; you cannot use Windows Server 2008 Standard Edition.

NOTE   For more information on restricted enrollment agents, refer to "AD CS: Restricted Enrollment Agent" at http://technet.microsoft.com/en-us/library/cc753800(WS.10).aspx and "Establish Restricted Enrollment Agents" at http://technet.microsoft.com/en-us/library/cc754154.aspx.

Using Group Policy to Require Smart Cards for Logon

After you have generated smart cards for all users who require them, you can configure Active Directory to require smart cards for logon. You can specify this requirement for multiple users in a domain or OU at a single time by following the procedure described here:

Step 1.   Open the Active Directory Users and Computers or the Active Directory Administrative Center snap-in.

Step 2.   Select the OU or container in which the user accounts reside to display the accounts in the details pane.

Step 3.   Use the **Ctrl** and **Shift** keys to select multiple users as required, right-click, and then choose **Properties**.

Step 4.   On the Account tab of the Properties on Multiple Objects dialog box in Active Directory Users and Computers or the Account section of the Multiple Users dialog box in Active Directory Administrative Center, select the **Smart card is required for interactive log on** option and then click **OK** (see Figure 17-17).

Step 5.   You are returned to Active Directory Users and Computers or Active Directory Administrative Center. These users now require a smart card and PIN to log on.

If you need to require that all users in a site, domain, or OU use smart cards for logon, you can configure a Group Policy setting. Use the following procedure:

Step 1.   Open the Group Policy Management Editor focused on a GPO linked to the appropriate AD DS container object.

Step 2.   Navigate to **Computer Configuration\Policies\Windows Settings\Security Settings\Local Policies\Security Options**.

Figure 17-17 You can require multiple users to use smart cards from the Multiple Users dialog box in Active Directory Administrative Center.

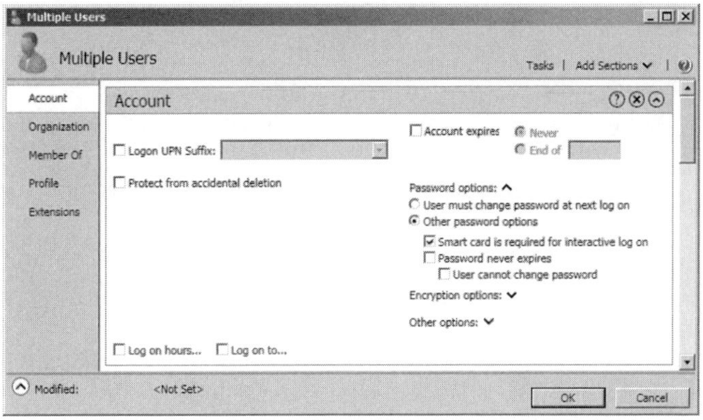

Step 3. Right-click the policy labeled **Interactive logon: Require smart card** and choose **Properties**.

Step 4. On the Interactive logon: Require smart card Properties dialog box, select **Define this policy setting**, select the **Enabled** option, and then click **OK**.

Step 5. Right-click the policy labeled **Smart Card Removal Behavior** and choose **Properties**.

Step 6. Select **Define this policy setting**. As shown in Figure 17-18, this policy provides several options for defining the behavior that occurs if a user removes her smart card:

—**No Action:** The user can continue to work until she logs off.

—**Lock Workstation:** Removal of the smart card locks the computer. The user can unlock the computer by selecting **Log On Interactively** or providing the smart card's PIN.

—**Force Logoff:** Removal of the smart card automatically logs the user off from the computer.

—**Disconnect if a Remote Desktop Services session:** Removal of the smart card automatically logs the user off from the Remote Desktop Services session. The user remains logged on to the computer.

Step 7. Select the appropriate option and click **OK**.

Step 8. Close the Group Policy Management Editor.

Figure 17-18   Group Policy defines four options for action taken when a user removes her smart card.

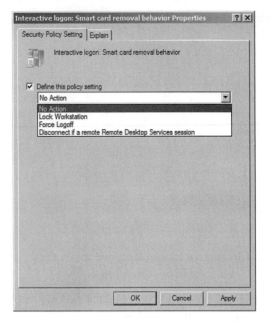

Managing Certificate Revocation

You might need to revoke a certificate before its expiry date for various reasons, such as compromise of the certificate or termination of the user to whom the certificate was issued. When you revoke a certificate, the revoked certificate is published in the certificate revocation list (CRL). Applications requiring certificates check this CRL to ensure that certificates are still valid. Management and maintenance of certificate revocation is an important task in the day-to-day administration of your organization's PKI.

Prior to Windows Vista, the CRL was the only certificate revocation-checking mechanism supported by Microsoft. Introduced to Internet Explorer 7 in Windows Vista and Windows Server 2008 and continued with Internet Explorer 8 in Windows 7 and Windows Server 2008 R2 is the concept of the Online Certificate Status Protocol (OCSP) as a new method of certificate status checking. OCSP includes a client component on each Windows Vista/7 and Server 2008 computer, as well as the server component, which is the online responder. We shall look at the online responder as well as the traditional CRL in this section.

To revoke a certificate, select the **Issued Certificates** node of the Certification Authority snap-in. Right-click the certificate to be revoked and select **All Tasks > Revoke Certificate**. Select a reason code from those displayed in the drop-down list of the Certificate Revocation dialog box (see Figure 17-19) and then click **Yes**. The certificate is removed from the Issued Certificates list and added to the Revoked Certificates list and the CRL.

Figure 17-19 You must select a reason when revoking a certificate.

TIP If you are unsure about the validity of a certificate, you should specify the **Certificate Hold** reason when revoking it. Specifying this reason provides you with an option to unrevoke the certificate later.

Configuring Certificate Revocation Lists

As already mentioned, applications check the CRL to ensure that certificates are still valid. Because CRLs can become long, Windows Server 2008 includes the concept of a *delta CRL*, which is a list of certificates that have been revoked since the last publication of a full CRL. By using delta CRLs, you can publish CRL information more frequently with less replication traffic.

Delta CRLs are published on a differential basis—in other words, each delta CRL includes all revoked certificates since the previous full CRL was published. Figure 17-20 provides an example of CRL publishing. In this example, certificates C1 and C2 were revoked prior to publishing the first base CRL. Certificate C3 was then revoked and appeared in the delta CRL. Certificate C4 was next revoked and the next delta CRL contained both certificates C3 and C4. Finally, a new base CRL was published and contains all revoked certificates. An application that checks CRLs therefore needs to check only the base CRL and the most recent delta CRL to obtain a complete list of revoked certificates.

You can configure the publication intervals of CRLs and delta CRLs by following these steps:

Step 1.   In the Certification Authority console, right-click **Revoked Certificates** and choose **Properties**.

Figure 17-20   An example of base and delta CRL publication.

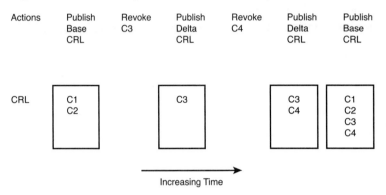

Step 2.   On the CRL Publishing Parameters tab of the Revoked Certificates Properties dialog box shown in Figure 17-21, specify the publication intervals for CRLs and delta CRLs.

Figure 17-21   Specifying publication intervals for CRLs and delta CRLs.

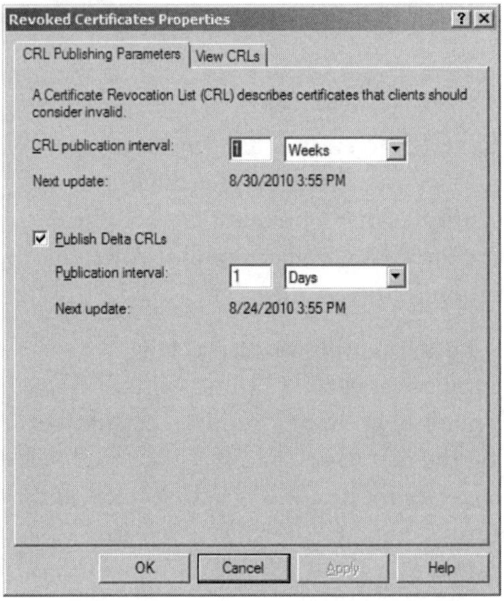

Step 3.   To view current CRLs and delta CRLs, select the **View CRLs** tab and click the appropriate command button.

Before you begin to issue certificates from the CA hierarchy, you should place a copy of the root certificate and the CRL (which is empty to begin with) at the locations specified in the policy module. You can obtain copies of the CA certificate and CRLs (base and delta) from the Certificate Services web pages at **http://*server*/certsrv,** where *server* is the name of the certificate server (refer back to Figure 17-10). On the home page, select the **Download a CA certificate, certificate chain, or CRL** link and then select the appropriate link on the page that appears. On the File Download page that appears, click **Save** and specify the appropriate location for the CRL in the Save As dialog box that appears.

> **WARNING**   Revoking a CA certificate revokes all certificates issued by this CA. Any application that obtains a CRL showing that the parent certificate has been revoked will reject these certificates.

Configuring a CRL Distribution Point

A *CRL distribution point* (*CDP*) is a location on the network from which applications can locate the most recent base and delta CRLs to check for certificate validity. The Extensions tab of the CA's Properties dialog box enables you to add, remove, or modify CDPs in issuing certificates. To do this, right-click the CA server's name in the Certification Authority snap-in and choose **Properties**. Select the **Extensions** tab to display the dialog box shown in Figure 17-22. You can perform the actions described in Table 17-3 from this location:

Figure 17-22   The Extensions tab of the CA server's Properties dialog box enables you to configure the CDP locations.

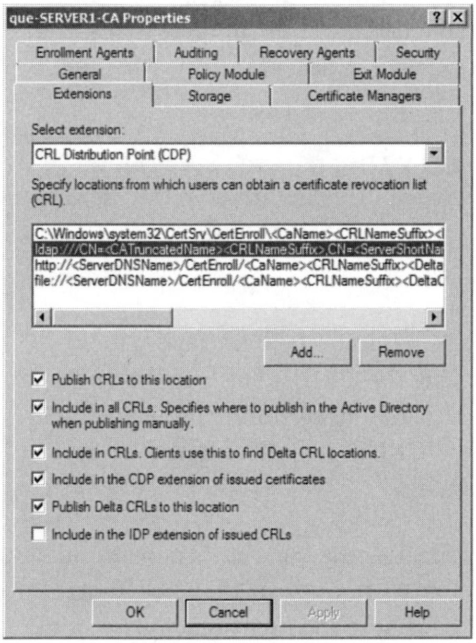

Table 17-3   Configuring a CDP

Available Action	Procedure to Follow
Add a CDP	Click **Add**, type the URL to the new CDP, and then click **OK**.
Remove a CDP	Select the CDP, click **Remove**, and then click **Yes** to confirm its removal.
Specify that a URL will be used as a CDP	Select the CDP and select the **Publish CRLs to this location** check box.
Specify that a URL will be included in all CRLs and published in AD DS	Select the CDP and select the check box labeled **Include in all CRLs. Specifies where to publish in the Active Directory when publishing manually**.
Specify that a URL will be published in CRLs to point clients to a delta CRL	Select the CDP and select the **Include in CRLs. Clients use this to find Delta CRL locations** check box.
Specify that a URL will be used as a delta CRL distribution point	Select the CDP and select the **Publish Delta CRLs to this location** check box.

You can also specify that a URL will not be used for one of these actions by clearing the corresponding check box. After making changes to any of these items, you must stop and restart the Certificate Services service. Click **Yes** when requested.

NOTE   For additional information on configuring CDPs, refer to "Specify CRL Distribution Points" at http://technet.microsoft.com/en-us/library/cc753296.aspx.

Troubleshooting CRLs

Any application that checks CRLs must be able to locate the CRL before it can accept a certificate. If the application cannot locate the CRL, it fails and the certificate holder is not authenticated. When troubleshooting certificate problems, you need to determine whether the issue lies in the CRL. The following are several CRL-related problems that you might encounter:

■   A CRL is valid for a period that is approximately the same as its publication period, which is one week by default. When changes occur to the CRL or delta CRL, they are not reflected in the context of the user or computer until expiry of a cached CRL or delta CRL. Consequently, information on revoked certificates might not be immediately available. Use a short delta CRL publication interval to alleviate this problem.

- Applications that check the CRL must be able to locate the current CRL and delta CRL. Ensure that copies of the CRLs are published to URLs and/or file locations that the applications can access.

- If you are changing the location of a CRL, information on this location is not added to certificates published prior to the change. Change the location of a CRL only when it is absolutely necessary.

- Applications that check the CRL must be able to access all CRLs in the CA hierarchy. If you are employing an offline root CA, you need to ensure that a copy of its CRL is made available at an online location. Configure this online location before any certificates are issued.

Configuring Online Responders

The online responder is an optional role service in AD CS that is new to Windows Server 2008. It is based on OCSP and provides signed responses to clients requesting revocation information for certificates issued by the CA that signed the OCSP signing certificate. Windows Server 2008 provides the OCSP Response Signing certificate template that is used to generate a certificate used by computers configured as online responders. The following are several types of certificates whose certificate validity is often checked using OCSP:

- Smart card logon

- Enterprise Secure Multipurpose Internet Mail Extensions (S/MIME)

- Secure Sockets Layer (SSL)/Transport Layer Security (TLS)

- Extensible Authentication Protocol (EAP)/TLS-based virtual private network (VPN)

The Online Responder role service is available on computers running either the Enterprise or Datacenter edition of Windows Server 2008. You can install this service at the same time as you install AD CS from the Add Roles Wizard in Server Manager as described in Chapter 16. You can also add this service later by using the Add Role Services Wizard in a similar manner to that described for NDES earlier in this chapter. After you have installed this role service, the Online Responder Management snap-in shown in Figure 17-23 is available from the Administrative Tools folder.

We will look at online responder properties, revocation configuration, and array configuration here. Additional information on the online responder role service, including troubleshooting hints, is available in "Online Responder Installation, Configuration, and Troubleshooting Guide" at http://technet.microsoft.com/en-us/library/cc770413(WS.10).aspx.

Figure 17-23   You can configure the online responder from the Online Responder Configuration snap-in.

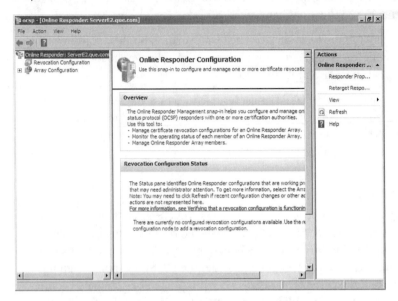

Configuring Responder Properties

Several configurable properties are available that are global to the online responder actions and services. To access these, right-click **Online Responder** in the console tree and choose **Properties**. This opens the Online Responder Properties dialog box shown in Figure 17-24.

Figure 17-24   The Online Responder Properties dialog box.

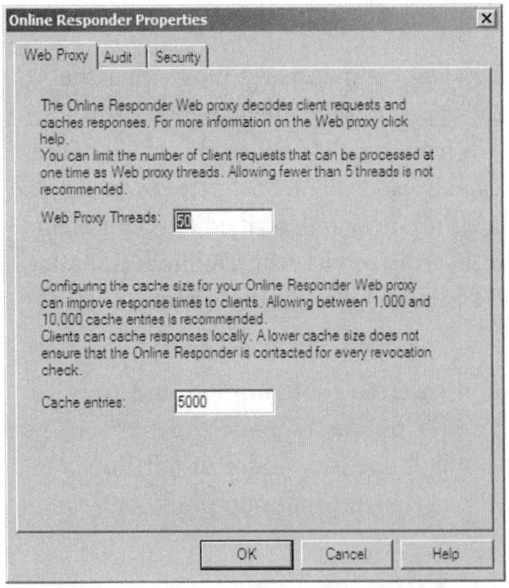

You can manage the following properties from this dialog box:

- **Web Proxy tab:** Enables you to configure the numbers of web proxy threads and cache entries allowed. Increasing these numbers uses more of the server's memory and reducing them reduces the number of clients that can be served.

- **Audit tab:** Enables you to specify that certain actions will be logged to the server's Security log. These include starting or stopping the online responder service, changes to the online responder's configuration or security settings, and logging of requests submitted to the online responder. Note that you must configure auditing of object access in Group Policy as described in Chapter 13, "Account Policies and Audit Policies," for these events to be audited.

- **Security tab:** Enables you to configure permissions for submitting proxy requests for certificate revocation status and for managing the online responder service.

Adding a Revocation Configuration

A revocation configuration includes a series of definitions that enable the online responder to provide a signed OCSP response. Included are the CA certificate, the signing certificate, and the source of the revocation information.

To add a revocation configuration, right-click **Revocation Configuration** and choose **Add Revocation Configuration**. This starts the Add Revocation Configuration Wizard, which takes you through the steps outlined in Figure 17-25 to create your revocation configuration. For detailed information on each of these steps, refer to "Online Responder Installation, Configuration, and Troubleshooting Guide" mentioned in the previous section.

Figure 17-25   Creating a revocation configuration involves four steps.

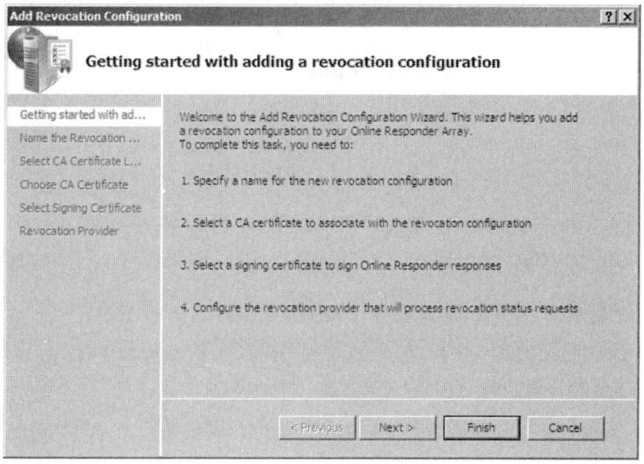

WARNING   Before running the Add Revocation Configuration Wizard, you should enable the CA server to issue a certificate based on the OCSP Response Signing certificate template from the Certification Authority snap-in as described earlier in this chapter.

Configuring Arrays

An *array* is one or more computers on which the online responder service is installed and managed from the Online Responder snap-in. Each computer in an array uses the same global property set and the same revocation configurations. One of these servers is defined as the array controller, resolves any synchronization conflicts, and ensures that updated revocation information is sent to all members of the array.

To add an array member, right-click the **Array Configuration** node and choose **Add Array Member**. Type the distinguished name of the desired computer in the Select Computer dialog box or click **Browse** to locate the computer. Then click **OK**.

Configuring Authority Information Access

Authority Information Access is an extension that can be applied to certificates issued by the CA that points to URLs at which you can retrieve an issuing CA's certificate. This extension is defined in Request for Comments (RFC) 3280 and states how to access CA information and services for the issuer of the certificate that uses this extension. More specifically, for the Online Responder service to work properly, you must include the URL for the online responder in the AIA extension of certificates issued by the CA.

Use the following steps to configure an AIA extensions:

Step 1.   In the Certification Authority snap-in, right-click the server and choose **Properties**.

Step 2.   Select the **Extensions** tab (previously shown in Figure 17-22).

Step 3.   From the Select Extension drop-down list at the top of this tab, select **Authority Information Access (AIA).**

Step 4.   Select an HTTP-based URL in the **Specify locations from which users can obtain the certificate for this CA** list box. If you want to add a URL not shown in this list box, click **Add**.

Step 5.   Select the check boxes labeled **Include in the AIA extension of issued certificates** and **Include in the online certificate status protocol (OCSP) extension** and then click **OK**.

Step 6.   You are informed you must restart AD CS for the changes to take effect. Click **Yes**.

Exam Preparation Tasks

Review All the Key Topics

Review the most important topics in the chapter, noted with the key topics icon in the outer margin of the page. Table 17-4 lists a reference of these key topics and the page numbers on which each is found.

Table 17-4   Key Topics for Chapter 17

Key Topic Element	Description	Page Number
Table 17-2	Describes the certificate templates available in Windows Server 2008	592
Figure 17-1	Configuring the Request Handling tab properties of a new certificate template	593
List	Describes security permissions available with certificate templates	596
Figure 17-3	Shows the security permissions required for certificate autoenrollment	596
Figure 17-4	Shows how to enable a new certificate template	597
Figure 17-5	When duplicating a certificate template, you can choose the required version	598
List	Shows how to configure a key recovery agent	599
Paragraph	Describes Network Device Enrollment Services (NDES)	602
List	Shows how to enable certificate autoenrollment	605
Figures 17-10 to 17-12	Using the web-based certificate enrollment pages to request a certificate	607–608
List	Shows how to configure restricted certificate enrollment agents	611
Paragraph	Describes the purpose of certificate revocation lists (CRLs)	617
Figure 17-22	Shows how to configure a CRL distribution point	619

626   MCTS 70-640 Cert Guide: Windows Server 2008 Active Directory, Configuring

Table 17-4 Key Topics for Chapter 17

Key Topic Element	Description	Page Number
Paragraph	Describes the Online Responder role service	621
Figure 17-24	Shows how to configure the online responder	622

Complete the Tables and Lists from Memory

Print a copy of Appendix C, "Memory Tables" (found on the CD), or at least the section for this chapter, and complete the tables and lists from memory. Appendix D, "Memory Tables Answer Key," also on the CD, includes completed tables and lists to check your work.

Definitions of Key Terms

Define the following key terms from this chapter, and check your answers in the glossary.

Authority Information Access (AIA); autoenrollment; certificate enrollment; certificate revocation list (CRL); certificate template; CRL distribution point (CDP); delta CRL; enrollment agent; key recovery agent (KRA); Network Device Enrollment Services (NDES); Online Certificate Status Protocol (OCSP); online responder; smart card; versions 1, 2, and 3 templates

Practice Exam

1. Brett is the systems administrator for a company that operates an AD DS domain with two sites corresponding to the head office and a suburban branch office. Servers run a mix of Windows Server 2003 R2 and Windows Server 2008 and client computers run a mix of Windows XP Professional, Windows Vista Business, and Windows 7 Professional.

   Brett deploys Active Directory Rights Management Services (AD RMS) on a server in the head office and sets up a rights-enabled application to enable users to create and work with rights-protected files and folders. Users of Windows XP Professional computers report that they are unable to create rights-protected files.

   Brett must enable all users to create rights-protected files. What should he do to accomplish this objective with the least amount of administrative effort?

   a. Install the AD RMS client software on all Windows XP client computers.

   b. Upgrade all Windows XP client computers to Windows Vista or Windows 7.

   c. Upgrade all domain controllers to Windows Server 2008.

   d. Install Active Directory Metadirectory Services (AD MDS) on a Windows Server 2008 computer.

2. Shirley administers the network for a catering company called Thoughtful Food. This firm operates a single domain AD DS network that includes three Windows Server 2008 computers and a mix of Windows XP Professional and Windows 7 Professional clients. Management has notified Shirley that a competitor known as Engorge & Devour has taken a keen interest in her pumpkin soup recipe. Two employees of Thoughtful Food have recently resigned and taken up positions with Engorge & Devour, and management is afraid that they will attempt to steal proprietary formulas and recipes belonging to Thoughtful Food by breaking into the network. Shirley is tasked with improving logon security on Thoughtful Food's

network by limiting the number of failed logon attempts for all users on the network and by establishing an audit policy for tracking failed logon attempts.

Which of the following tasks should she undertake to complete this task? (Each correct answer represents part of the solution. Choose two answers.)

   a.   Edit the Default Domain Policy GPO to enable auditing and account lockout.

   b.   Monitor the security log for failed account management attempts on each domain controller.

   c.   Monitor the security log for failed logon attempts on each domain controller.

   d.   Configure a local security policy on each computer in the domain.

3. Phil is the network administrator for a company that operates an AD DS network consisting of a single domain. DNS is running as an Active Directory–integrated zone on two domain controllers named Server1 and Server2. One morning, several users inform him that they were unable to access a resource by name. In attempting to troubleshoot this problem, he notices that the event logs at Server2 contain several errors with ID 4006 and containing a message that the DNS server was unable to load the records in the specified name found in the Active Directory–integrated zone.

What should Phil do to enable proper name resolution and prevent these errors from occurring in the future?

   a.   Access the **Debug Logging** tab of the server's Properties dialog box and enable logging of incoming and outgoing packets for queries and transfers.

   b.   Access the **Monitoring** tab of the server's Properties dialog box, perform a simple and recursive test, and then check that the `cache.dns` file is present and configured properly.

   c.   Access the **Advanced** tab of the server's Properties dialog box and select the **All names** option in the Name Checking section of this tab.

   d.   Access the **Advanced** tab of the server's Properties dialog box and select the **Strict RFC (ANSI)** option in the Name Checking section of this tab.

4. Edward is the systems administrator for his company, which operates an AD DS forest consisting of a single domain. The network operates at the Windows Server 2003 domain and forest functional level. He has accidentally deleted the Management OU from a domain controller running Windows Server 2008 R2. The deletion has propagated to other domain controllers, and Edward urgently needs to get this OU back before he receives complaints from managers who are unable to log on. He has a system state backup that was created the previous evening. Which of the following steps must he perform to get this OU back? (Each correct answer represents part of the solution. Choose all that apply, and arrange these steps in the order in which Edward must perform them.)

a. At a command prompt, type the **wbadmin get versions** command.

b. Restart the domain controller normally.

c. At a command prompt, type the **net stop ntds** command.

d. Use the ntdsutil utility to mark the restored OU as authoritative.

e. Restart the domain controller using the Windows Server 2008 R2 DVD, and select the **Repair your computer** option.

f. Restart the domain controller in Directory Services Restore Mode.

g. Restore the OU from the Active Directory Recycle Bin.

h. At a command prompt, type the **wbadmin start recovery** command.

i. At a command prompt, type the **wbadmin start systemstaterecovery** command.

j. At a command prompt, type the **net start ntds** command.

5. Mike is the systems administrator for a company that operates an AD DS network consisting of a single domain. The company operates a head office and three branch offices, each of which has been set up with a read-only domain controller (RODC) to handle employee authentication locally.

A technician named Christina regularly travels to the branch offices to ensure that the computer network in each office is working properly. Her job duties require that she perform administrative actions on each RODC, but she does not need to perform such actions on domain controllers located at the head office. She must be ensured that she can log on to each RODC with her domain user account even if the connection to the head office happens to be down.

Which of the following actions should Mike perform so that Christina can perform her duties, without granting her excessive administrative privileges? (Each correct answer represents part of the solution. Choose two answers.)

a. Configure each RODC with a password replication policy that includes Christina's user account in the Denied list.

b. Configure each RODC with a password replication policy that includes Christina's user account in the Allowed list.

c. Add Christina's user account to the Domain Admins global group.

d. Add Christina's user account to the Server Operators global group.

e. Add Christina's user account to each RODC's local Administrators group.

6. Veronica is in charge of Group Policy object (GPO) creation for her company, which operates an AD DS network consisting of six domains and 20 sites. Although Veronica is responsible for creating all GPOs, other administrators are responsible for applying the GPOs to the domains for which they are responsible. Veronica wants to grant these administrators permission to apply the GPOs but not to modify them.

How can Veronica maintain control over the creation of GPOs while permitting other administrators to determine where they will be applied?

a. Right-click the desired domain in the Group Policy Management Console and select **Delegate Control**. In the Delegation of Control Wizard, she should select the **Manage Group Policy links** task.

b. Right-click the desired domain in the Group Policy Management Console and select **Delegate Control**. In the Delegation of Control Wizard, she should specify the required users or groups and then select the **Manage Group Policy links** task.

c. Right-click the desired users or groups in Active Directory Users and Computers and select **Delegate Control**. In the Delegation of Control Wizard, she should select the **Manage Group Policy links** task.

d. Right-click the desired domain in Active Directory Users and Computers and select **Delegate Control**. In the Delegation of Control Wizard, she should specify the required users or groups and then select the **Manage Group Policy links** task.

7. Roy is responsible for maintaining DNS on his company's AD DS network, which consists of a single domain in which all servers run Windows Server 2008 R2. The company operates an office in downtown Denver and a suburban office in Littleton.

After upgrading a member server in the company's suburban office to a domain controller, users at that office report that logon to the domain is slow. On investigating the problem, Roy notices that the service (SRV) resource records for the new domain controller are not registered in the DNS zone for the suburban office. What should he do to re-register these SRV resource records as fast as possible?

a. Restart the DNS Server service.

b. Restart the DNS Client service.

c. Restart the Netlogon service.

d. Reboot the domain controller.

8. Oliver is a systems administrator for a company that operates an Active Directory forest with two domains and eight sites. All servers run either the original or R2 version of Windows Server 2008, and all client computers run either Windows XP Professional or Windows 7 Professional. Administrators at remote sites have informed Oliver that intersite replication is slow at times and he needs to investigate the source of this problem. How should he obtain information regarding the possible causes of this problem? (Choose all that apply.)

    a. Use Event Viewer to check for errors and warnings that relate to replication problems.

    b. Use `dcdiag` to test connectivity and replication at the domain controller.

    c. Use `ntdsutil` to obtain information about replication slowdowns and failures.

    d. Use `repadmin` to obtain information about replication slowdowns and failures.

9. Ellen is the network administrator for a regional hospital complex that operates an AD DS forest containing a root domain and two child domains. All domain controllers in the root domain and one child domain run Windows Server 2003 and the domain controllers in the second child domain run Windows 2000 Server.

Ellen is planning an upgrade of the domain controllers in the root domain to Windows Server 2008. She is also planning to install a read-only domain controller (RODC) in this domain.

Which of the following configuration actions represent the minimum actions that Ellen must perform in order to upgrade the forest to accept Windows Server 2008 domain controllers including the RODC? (Each correct answer represents part of the solution. Choose all that apply.)

    a. Upgrade all domain controllers in the second child domain to Windows Server 2003 or 2008.

    b. Upgrade all domain controllers in the forest to Windows Server 2008.

    c. Upgrade the PDC emulator in the root domain to Windows Server 2008.

    d. Raise the domain and forest functional levels to Windows Server 2003.

    e. Raise the domain and forest functional levels to Windows Server 2008.

    f. Run the `Adprep /forestprep` command at the schema master.

    g. Run the `Adprep /forestprep` command at the domain naming master.

    h. Run the `Adprep /domainprep` command at the RID master in the forest root domain.

    i. Run the `Adprep /domainprep` command at the infrastructure master in the forest root domain.

    j. Run the `Adprep /rodcprep` command at the infrastructure master in the forest root domain.

    k. Run the `Adprep /rodcprep` command at the PDC emulator in the forest root domain.

10. Stephanie is a network administrator for `Certguide.com`, which has just merged with a former competitor named `Que.com`. Customers and business partners of the second company have communicated with the company's employees using their email addresses of the format `user@que.com`. This is a well-established relationship that has existed for a number of years, and managers in both companies want to retain these email addresses.

Stephanie is merging the networks of the two companies under the `certguide.com` AD DS domain, which operates at the Windows Server 2008 domain and forest functional level. Users in the company use their email addresses to log on, and Stephanie needs to incorporate the new users from `que.com` into the network while retaining their existing email address and using these addresses to log on to the `certguide.com` domain.

What should Stephanie do to accomplish this objective with the least amount of administrative effort?

    a. Create a new Active Directory forest named `que.com` and create user accounts for the new users in that forest.

    b. Create a new domain as a separate domain tree named `que.com` and create user accounts for the new users in that domain.

    c. Create user accounts for the new users in the existing domain and assign them user logon names in the format of `user@que.com`.

    d. Create user accounts for the new users in the existing domain and specify an alternative UPN suffix of `que.com`.

11. Scott is responsible for maintaining AD CS on his company's AD DS network, which consists of a single domain. He has used the Certificate Services snap-in to configure a version 2 certificate template that will be used for archiving the subject's encryption private key. Certificates issued with this template will be used for signature purposes. However, Scott discovers that the private keys associated with these certificates are not being archived. What should he do?

    a. On the template's Request Handling tab, select the **Signature and encryption** option and then select **Archive subject's encryption private key**.

   b. On the template's Request Handling tab, select the **Allow private key to be exported** option.

   c. Duplicate the template and select the **Windows Server 2008 Enterprise** option to create a version 3 certificate template.

   d. On the template's Security tab, enable the Autoenroll permission.

12. Donna administers a single AD DS domain called que.com. She has decided against configuring que.com as an Active Directory–integrated zone. Donna has designated her domain controllers as Scorpio01 and Scorpio02. Her DNS servers are called Taurus01, Taurus02, and Taurus03. Taurus01 is the master DNS server. Taurus02 and Taurus03 are secondary DNS servers.

Donna would like only Taurus01 and Taurus02 to be authoritative for the que.com zone, so she specifies these two servers on the Name Servers tab of the que.com Properties dialog box. She accesses the Zone Transfers tab and clicks **Notify** to open the Notify dialog box. How should she configure the options in this dialog box so that all DNS servers are notified of any DNS zone updates? (Each correct answer represents part of the solution. Choose two answers.)

   a. Select the **Automatically notify** check box.

   b. Clear the **Automatically notify** check box.

   c. Select the **Servers listed on the Name Servers tab** option.

   d. Select the option labeled **The following servers** and specify IP address information for Taurus01, Taurus02, and Taurus03.

   e. Select the option labeled **The following servers** and specify IP address information for Taurus01, Scorpio01, and Scorpio02.

   f. Select the option labeled **The following servers** and specify IP address information for Taurus02 and Taurus03.

13. Mark's company has just merged operations with a former competitor. Mark's company operates an AD DS forest with four domains in a single tree and running at the Windows Server 2008 functional level. The other company operates a forest with three domains in a single tree and running at the Windows Server 2003 functional level.

Managers at the other company want to keep their operations as separate as possible; however, employees whose user accounts are in various domains of both forests require access to resources in all domains. What should Mark do to enable access to the other forest with the least amount of effort?

   a. He should create an external trust between child domains of the two forests.

   b. He should create a shortcut trust between child domains of the two forests.

    c. He should create a forest trust between the two forests.

    d. He should inform his manager that the other company's forest should be reconfigured as a second tree in his company's forest.

14. Carolyn is the network administrator for a company that has offices in seven U.S. cities. The company operates an AD DS network with a single domain and sites representing the cities in which offices are located. The offices are connected with WAN links of varying bandwidth and Carolyn has configured site links in Active Directory for the various available links.

Her company operates a small office located in Duluth, which connects to the company's Minneapolis office by a T1 link and to the company's Chicago office by a 56 Kbps dial-up link. The Minneapolis and Chicago offices are also connected by a T1 link.

A junior administrator in Duluth calls Carolyn to inform her that every time administrators in Chicago issue updates to AD DS (which has occurred frequently in recent weeks), a domain controller in Duluth dials the 56 Kbps link despite the rapid T1 link being available. What should Carolyn do to minimize the times the 56 Kbps link is dialed?

    a. Configure the 56 Kbps link to use Simple Mail Transport Protocol (SMTP) replication rather than IP.

    b. Configure the 56 Kbps link to be available outside business hours only.

    c. Create a site link bridge that encompasses the Duluth-to-Minneapolis and Minneapolis-to-Chicago site links and then set the cost of the 56 Kbps link to 300.

    d. Create a site link bridge that encompasses the Duluth-to-Minneapolis and Minneapolis-to-Chicago site links and then set the cost of the site link bridge to 50.

15. Darcy's company operates an AD DS forest consisting of a single tree with an empty root domain and five child domains that represent operational divisions. Darcy is responsible for maintaining the flexible single-master operations (FSMO) roles. In total, how many FSMO roles are present in this tree?

    a. One schema master, one domain naming master, six RID masters, six PDC emulators, and six infrastructure masters.

    b. One schema master, one domain naming master, five RID masters, five PDC emulators, and five infrastructure masters.

c. Six schema masters, six domain naming masters, six RID masters, six PDC emulators, and six infrastructure masters.

d. One schema master, one domain naming master, one RID master, one PDC emulator, and one infrastructure master.

16. Jackie is the domain administrator for her company, which operates an AD DS domain in which all servers run Windows Server 2008 and client computers run either Windows XP Professional or Windows 7 Professional. There is one server configured as an offline standalone root CA and two servers configured as online enterprise subordinate CAs. Another administrator named Len is responsible for all operations of the CA hierarchy. The CIO is concerned that operation of the CA hierarchy would be severely affected should Len's account be compromised.

What should Jackie do to reduce the possibility of this occurrence?

a. Create a special user account for Len that has a 20-character password and limit the privileges of this account to administration of the CA servers.

b. Implement role-based administration in the CA hierarchy.

c. Configure the subordinate CA servers so that certificate enrollment and renewal take place on different servers.

d. Reconfigure the offline standalone root CA as an offline enterprise root CA.

e. Reconfigure the offline standalone root CA as an online enterprise root CA.

17. Justin is configuring a certificate template that will enable autoenrollment of smart cards for users in his company's Windows Server 2008 R2 domain. Justin needs to ensure that a user creating a new smart card is prompted to enter her PIN as part of the enrollment procedure. He opens the Request Handling tab of the certificate template. Which of the following options should he select?

a. **Prompt the user during enrollment**

b. **Prompt the user during enrollment and require user input when the private key is used**

c. **Authorize additional service accounts to access the private key**

d. **Allow private key to be exported**

18. Luke is network administrator for Acme Construction Ltd. The company's network consists of a single AD DS domain called `acmeconstr.com`. Servers in the domain run either Windows Server 2003 or Windows Server 2008, and client computers run either Windows XP Professional or Windows 7 Professional.

Two Windows Server 2008 computers named NS01 and NS02 host DNS zones for the `acmeconstr.com` domain; NS01 hosts a standard primary zone and NS02 hosts a standard secondary DNS zone. Queries that cannot be resolved by these servers are forwarded to Acme Construction's ISP.

Because Acme Construction has put a number of jobs out for tender in the past few months its DNS servers are receiving an exceptionally high number of requests and are becoming bogged down as a result. Luke decides to create a new zone called `bids.acmeconstr.com` to handle the traffic. He decides to configure a new Windows Server 2008 R2 DNS server called NS03 and dedicate it exclusively to servicing DNS requests for the `bids.acmeconstr.com` zone, where all future bids will be directed. In order to do this he needs to delegate control of the `bids.acmeconstr.com` zone to the NS03 server. How should Luke proceed?

a. Manually create an A record for the NS03 server computer.

b. Use the New Delegation Wizard in the DNS console to delegate control of the new zone.

c. Manually create an A record and an NS record for the NS03 server computer.

d. Add the appropriate IP address for NS03 to the Forwarders tab on the NS01 and NS02 server computers

19. Rob is a network administrator for a company that operates a single domain AD DS network. All servers run Windows Server 2008 and all client computers run Windows XP Professional. Both portable and desktop client computers are used on the network. The domain is organized into a series of organizational units (OUs) that reflect the departmental structure of the company.

The CIO has requested that no unattended portable computer be left logged on to the network, unless protected by a password. This requirement is to be enforced on portable computers only because all desktop computers are located in areas that are protected by building security. Rob needs to configure a Group Policy object (GPO) in such a manner that this rule will be properly enforced for portable computers only. How should he accomplish this objective using the least amount of administrative effort and without modifying any other policy settings for these computers?

a. Create a GPO linked to the domain that specifies a password-protected screen saver. Use a Windows Management Instrumentation (WMI) filter to query for the hardware chassis type information so that this GPO applies only to portable computers.

b. Create a global security group and move all computer accounts of portable computers to this group. Create a GPO linked to the domain that specifies a password-protected screen saver. Filter the GPO so that only this group has the Allow-Read and Allow-Apply Group Policy permissions.

c. Create a child OU under each OU in which portable computers are found and move all portable computer accounts to this OU. Create a GPO that specifies a password-protected screen saver. Link this GPO to each child OU containing portable computers.

d. Create one OU and move all portable computer accounts to this OU. Create a GPO linked to this OU that specifies a password-protected screen saver.

20. Debbie is the network administrator for a global manufacturing conglomerate. She has created a large number of universal groups with several hundred users in each group. She has noticed that a large quantity of network traffic has resulted. What is the recommended manner of handling universal groups that Debbie should utilize?

a. Debbie should place the users into universal groups and then place the universal groups into domain local groups.

b. Debbie should place the users into global groups and then place the global groups into universal groups. She should then place the universal groups into domain local groups.

c. Debbie should place the users into local groups and then place the local groups into universal groups. She should then place the universal groups into global groups.

d. The universal groups are configured properly in this scenario; the traffic is being generated from other sources.

21. Lynn has installed and configured a new server running Windows Server 2008 R2 as an additional domain controller on her company's AD DS network, which consists of a single domain with domain controllers and member servers running the original version of Windows Server 2008.

Lynn has heard that Windows Server 2008 R2 offers a new feature called the Active Directory Recycle Bin that enables her to recover accidentally deleted objects without the need for performing an authoritative restore operation. However, she is unable to locate this feature on the new server. What does she need to do to enable the Active Directory Recycle Bin on this server? (Each correct answer represents part of the solution. Choose all that apply.)

a. Upgrade all domain controllers and member servers to Windows Server 2008 R2.

b. Upgrade all domain controllers to Windows Server 2008 R2.

   c. Raise the domain functional level to Windows Server 2008 R2.

   d. Raise the forest functional level to Windows Server 2008 R2.

   e. Use the `Ldifde.exe` command-line utility to enable the Active Directory Recycle Bin.

   f. Use the `Ldp.exe` command-line utility to enable the Active Directory Recycle Bin.

   g. Edit the Registry to enable the Active Directory Recycle Bin.

22. Elaine is responsible for maintaining the user account database for a local school board located in a suburban area just outside a major city. The state has implemented new county school boards that abolish the local boards and join them to the county boards, and Elaine must add several thousand new user accounts to the school board's AD DS domain.

Elaine uses a bulk import tool to import these user accounts, but the process stops after several hundred user accounts have been successfully imported. While troubleshooting the problem, the superintendent asks her to ensure that user accounts for school principals are added as soon as possible, so she opens Active Directory Users and Computers and attempts to create these user accounts. However, this attempt fails.

Which of the following is the most likely cause of this problem?

   a. The infrastructure master for the domain is unavailable.

   b. The RID master for the domain is unavailable.

   c. The `.csv` file Elaine is using is corrupted and she must re-create this file.

   d. Elaine must wait until the user accounts she has added have replicated to all domain controllers in all sites of the domain before she can continue.

23. Tom is the systems administrator for a company that operates an AD DS network consisting of a single domain. The company has formed an alliance with another company that supplies raw materials for manufacturing. Tom has installed a server running Active Directory Federation Services (AD FS) on a Windows Server 2008 R2 computer located on his company's internal network. Now he needs to configure a server on the company's perimeter network so that it can obtain user credentials from clients in the partner company and forward this information to the internal AD FS server.

Tom opens Server Manager on the perimeter network server and starts the Add Roles Wizard. After selecting **Active Directory Federation Services** and clicking **Next**, he receives the dialog box shown in the exhibit. Which option should he select to configure the perimeter network server properly?

a. **Federation Service**

b. **Federation Service Proxy**

c. **AD FS Web Agents**

d. **Claims-aware Agent**

e. **Windows Token-based Agent**

24. Hazel is responsible for monitoring Active Directory functionality on her company's network. She needs to know the update sequence number (USN) of the most recent changes to the AD DS database at a domain controller named DC3. What should she do?

a. Configure a data collector set in Reliability and Performance Monitor with counters for the NTDS performance object.

b. Use the Resource Monitor feature of Windows System Resource Manager.

c. In `replmon`, right-click **DC3** and choose **Update Status (only for this server).**

d. Use the `repadmin` utility with the `/showmeta` option.

25. Richard is the network administrator for a company that operates an AD DS network consisting of a single domain. All users in the Finance department have user accounts in the Finance OU. Richard creates a GPO linked to the Finance OU and configures it to publish Microsoft Excel.

Some of the users in the department report that the application is not available from the Start menu, and other users report that Excel was installed successfully after they double-clicked an Excel spreadsheet. Richard needs to ensure that all users in the Finance OU can run Excel. What should he do?

a. Run the `gpresult` command on each client computer where a user reports a problem.

b. Run the `gpupdate` command on each client computer where a user reports a problem.

c. Access the **Deployment** tab of the software package's Properties dialog box. Change the deployment type from **Assigned** to **Published**. Then instruct users who report a problem to log off and log back on.

d. Access the **Deployment** tab of the software package's Properties dialog box. Change the deployment type from **Published** to **Assigned**. Then instruct users who report a problem to log off and log back on.

26. Brent is a systems administrator for a company that operates a single domain AD DS network. As a result of corporate expansion, the company is opening a new branch office in a neighboring city. Brent installs a new domain controller and several client computers in the new office and sets up a 56 Kbps WAN link between the two offices. He needs to make sure that all changes to Active Directory that are configured on head office domain controllers are replicated to the new office domain controller as soon as possible. He also needs to make sure that network traffic over the WAN is kept minimal and that users in the branch office always authenticate to the domain controller in that office.

What should Brent do to meet these objectives?

a. Create a new OU for the branch office and add all computer accounts for clients and the branch office domain controller to this OU.

b. Designate the branch office as a new Active Directory site. Configure the subnet that includes the computers in this office as belonging to that site and specify the site link cost to be 1.

c. Designate the branch office as a new Active Directory site. Configure the subnet that includes the computers in this office as belonging to that site and specify a 15-minute intersite replication interval.

d. Designate the branch office as a new Active Directory site. Configure the subnet that includes the computers in this office as belonging to that site and specify the replication interval to be 0.

27. Alfredo is a network administrator for a community college. He has installed DNS on a Windows Server 2008 R2 computer called DNS1 that hosts a primary DNS zone for the college's domain. The college network is also home to a UNIX server that has been configured to host the secondary DNS zone. This server, named DNS2, runs BIND 2.4.1. The chief network architect has assigned Alfredo the task of ensuring that DNS2 can receive zone transfers from DNS1.

Which of the following options should Alfredo enable to achieve this result?

a. **Disable recursion (also disables forwarders)**

b. **BIND secondaries**

c. **Fail on load if bad zone data**

d. **Enable round robin**

e. **Enable netmask ordering**

f. **Secure cache against pollution**

28. Maria is the domain administrator for a company that operates an AD DS domain with sites that span 20 cities in the United States, Canada, and Mexico. All client computers run either Windows 7 Professional or Windows 7 Ultimate. She has created ADMX files that define Registry-based policy settings that are to be applied to client computers in all sites of the domain.

Maria needs to create custom ADMX files that support French and Spanish language users in offices where these languages are used. She also needs to ensure that the custom ADMX files are available to all administrators in the domain. What should she do?

a. Create ADMX files and copy them to the `%systemroot%\sysvol\domain\policies\PolicyDefinitions` folder on the domain controller.

b. Create ADMX files and copy them to the `%systemroot%\sysvol\domain\policies\PolicyDefinitions` folder on each client computer.

c. Create ADML files and copy them to the `%systemroot%\sysvol\domain\policies\PolicyDefinitions\[language]` folder on the domain controller.

d. Create ADML files and copy them to the `%systemroot%\sysvol\domain\policies\PolicyDefinitions\[language]` folder on each client computer.

29. Peter has been given the responsibility of configuring Certificate Services for certificate autoenrollment. His company operates a public key infrastructure (PKI) that includes a standalone root certification authority (CA) and an enterprise subordinate CA. The PKI has recently been upgraded from Windows 2000 to Windows Server 2008. He wants to enable autoenrollment of certificates using a template that has been used in the past for web-based enrollment of certificates from the previous Windows 2000–based PKI. Which of the following steps should Peter perform? (Each correct answer represents part of the solution. Choose all that apply.)

    a. Configure an additional Windows Server 2008 computer as an autoenrollment-based subordinate CA.

    b. In the Certificate Templates snap-in, right-click the certificate template and choose **Duplicate Template**.

    c. From the Request Handling tab of the template's Properties dialog box, specify an option for prompting the user during autoenrollment.

    d. From the Security tab of the template's Properties dialog box, grant the required user or group the **Read** and **Enroll** permissions.

    e. From the Security tab of the template's Properties dialog box, grant the required user or group the **Read**, **Enroll**, and **Autoenroll** permissions.

    f. Enable the template from the Certificate Templates node of the Certification Authority snap-in.

    g. Configure a GPO linked to the domain to enroll certificates automatically.

30. Laura is the systems administrator for a company that operates an AD DS domain. The domain and forest functional level are set to Windows Server 2008. She has configured a password policy for users in her company's domain that specifies that passwords must be at least seven characters long. The CIO has informed her that users in the legal department should have highly secure passwords. She configures a password policy in a GPO linked to the Legal OU that specifies that passwords be at least 12 characters long.

A few days later, she receives a call from the CIO asking her why she has not yet implemented the stricter password policy. What must Laura do to implement the policy with the least amount of administrative effort?

    a. She needs to create a global security group, add the required users to this group, and ensure that the group has the Allow–Apply Group Policy permission applied to it.

    b. She needs to create a new domain, place the legal users and their computers in this domain, and then reapply the password policy to this domain.

    c. She needs to create a password settings object containing the required password settings and apply this object to the Legal OU.

    d. She needs to create a global security group and add the required users to this group. She then needs to create a password settings object containing the required password settings and apply this object to the group containing these users.

31. Kathy is the administrator of a state government agency responsible for construction and maintenance of roads and highways. The agency operates a single domain within the government's AD DS forest. The functional level of the domain is Windows Server 2003, and all servers that hold data accessible to outside parties are located on a perimeter network.

    The agency frequently contracts road work to private consultants, who need access to a web-based application that holds specifications and other data required for the work projects. All private consultants operate AD DS networks with either Windows 2000 or Windows Server 2003 domain controllers.

    Kathy is required to provide access for consultant employees without creating or managing user accounts for these employees, and she must keep the internal network secure from external access. Which of the following should she do? (Each correct answer represents part of the solution. Choose all that apply.)

    a. Install an AD RMS server and configure rights-protected documents.

    b. Install AD FS on an internal server and create a federated trust.

    c. Install an AD FS proxy server in the perimeter network.

    d. Install an AD FS web agent.

    e. Install a domain controller on the perimeter network to simplify the authentication of consultant employees.

    f. Install an AD LDS server on the perimeter network to simplify the authentication of consultant employees.

32. Karen is the network administrator for a company that operates an Active Directory domain in which all domain controllers run Windows Server 2003. The company wants to upgrade the domain controllers to Windows Server 2008. Karen's user account is a member of the Domain Admins, Enterprise Admins, and Schema Admins groups in her company's domain.

    Which of the following actions does Karen need to perform before upgrading any of the domain controllers to Windows Server 2008? To answer, select the two required actions from the list that follows in the sequence in which she must execute them.

    a. Run the `Adprep /domainprep` command on the PDC emulator.

    b. Run the `Adprep /forestprep` command on the PDC emulator.

    c. Run the `Adprep /domainprep` command on the infrastructure master.

d. Run the `Adprep /forestprep` command on the domain naming master.

e. Run the `Adprep /domainprep` command on the schema master.

f. Run the `Adprep /forestprep` command on the schema master.

33. Rick is responsible for planning operations master role placements in his company's AD DS forest, which consists of a forest root domain and three child domains. Four domain controllers in the forest root domain are called Server1, Server2, Server3, and Server4. This domain spans two sites, as shown in the exhibit. He needs to determine on which server to place the infrastructure master role. Which of the following represents the best placement of the infrastructure master in the forest root domain?

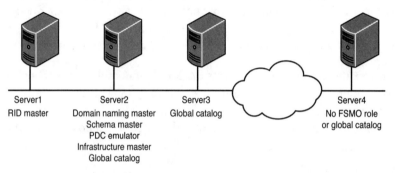

```
Server1          Server2               Server3          Server4
RID master    Domain naming master   Global catalog   No FSMO role
              Schema master                           or global catalog
              PDC emulator
              Infrastructure master
              Global catalog
```

a. On Server1, which hosts the RID master, but not the global catalog. This server has a direct connection to Server2 and Server3.

b. On Server2, which hosts all four other operations master roles plus the global catalog.

c. On Server3, which does not host any other operations master roles, but does host the global catalog.

d. On Server4, which is located across a WAN connection from Server1 and does not host any other operations master roles.

34. Bill is the network administrator for a company that operates a network containing a single AD DS domain. Servers run a mix of Windows Server 2003 and Windows Server 2008, and client computers run a mix of Windows XP Professional and Windows 7 Enterprise. Certificate Services is installed on a Windows Server 2008 R2 domain controller and configured as an Enterprise CA. The company's written security policy stipulates that employees must have user certificates that are to be issued by designated managers. These managers are to be the only individuals authorized to approve, issue, and revoke certificates. Their user accounts are included in the CertMgrs global security group.

What should Bill do to enable the authorized managers to perform these tasks without providing them with excess privileges?

   a. Grant the CertMgrs group the **Allow-Manage** CA permission on the CA server.

   b. Issue each member of the CertMgrs group the Enrollment Agent certificate.

   c. Grant the CertMgrs group the CA Administrator administrative role.

   d. Grant the CertMgrs group the Certificate Manager administrative role.

35. Gerry is the network administrator for a company that operates an AD DS domain named `certguide.com`. Servers run a mix of Windows 2000 Server, Windows Server 2003, and Windows Server 2008. Client computers run either Windows XP Professional or Windows 7 Professional. The company acquires another company named Prep Ltd. Gerry creates a new domain named `prep.certguide.com` to reflect the changes in corporate structure. He must now manage two DNS servers: `dns1.certguide.com` and `dns2.prep.certguide.com`.

    `dns1.certguide.com` is the Start of Authority (SOA) for `certguide.com`, and `dns2.prep.certguide.com` is the SOA for `prep.certguide.com`. Gerry has also configured an intranet server called `trans.prep.certguide.com` that employees from both companies can access for updates on issues relating to the two companies becoming one corporate concern.

    A user of a client computer in `certguide.com` called `client25.certguide.com` reports that she cannot access the intranet server. Gerry discovers that he cannot ping this server by name from the client computer. What can he do to correct this problem? (Each correct answer represents a complete solution to the problem. Choose two answers.)

   a. Add a stub zone for `certguide.com` on dns2.prep.certguide.com.

   b. Add a stub zone for `prep.certguide.com` on dns1.certguide.com.

   c. Add an A resource record for `dns2 prep.certguide.com` on `dns1.certguide.com`.

   d. Add an A resource record for `dns1.certguide.com` on `dns2.prep.certguide.com`.

   e. Configure zone delegation for `prep.certguide.com` on `dns1.certguide.com`.

   f. Add a PTR record for `prep.certguide.com` on `dns1.certguide.com`.

36. Connie works for a company that has just opened a branch office in a neighboring city that is connected to the head office with an ISDN link. Her manager has requested that replication occur at least once daily during the daytime. However, the line is expected to be close to 90% utilized during the day but only about 30% utilized during night hours.

Connie needs to make sure that replication does not use excessive bandwidth during the day, but that at night it will provide adequate bandwidth to complete any synchronization. What should Connie do to complete this request with the least amount of effort?

a. Create one site link, available only at night with the default cost and replication interval. Once a day, force replication manually.

b. Create one site link with the default cost and replication interval. Configure this link to be available from noon to 1 PM and also during the nighttime hours.

c. Create two site links, one available only at night with the default cost and replication interval and one available only during the day with a site link cost of 500.

d. Create two site links, one available only at night with the default replication interval and the other available only from noon to 1 PM also with the default replication interval.

e. Create two site links, one available only at night with the default replication interval and the other available only during the day with a replication interval of 4 hours.

37. Stephanie has installed a standalone root CA and an enterprise subordinate issuing CA for her company's domain. Which of the following additional tasks should she perform before issuing certificates to users on the network? (Each correct answer represents part of the solution. Choose three answers.)

a. Configure certificate templates.

b. Configure the Certificate Services web pages.

c. Configure certificate revocation lists (CRLs) or online responders.

d. Configure key archival and recovery.

38. Shannon is the systems administrator for a company that operates a single domain AD DS network. A user named Steven has created a group named Designers on his computer, which runs Windows 7 Ultimate. He has added the domain user accounts of several colleagues in his work unit to the Designers group and now wants to assign permissions to a shared folder on the work unit's file server to the group. However, when he accesses the shared folder, he is unable to add the Designers group to the folder's ACL.

Steven approaches Shannon for help. What should she do?

a. Create a domain local group named Work Unit and add the domain user accounts of the colleagues to this group. Then create a global group named Designers, add the Work Unit group to this group, and add the Designers domain local group to the folder's ACL.

b. Create a global group named Work Unit and add the domain user accounts of the colleagues to this group. Then create a domain local group named Designers, add the Work Unit group to this group, and add the Designers domain local group to the folder's ACL.

c. Ask Steven to create local user accounts for each of the work colleagues on the file server and add these accounts to the Designers group.

d. Ask Steven to check the network connectivity between his computer and the file server. His action should work if the connectivity is not a problem.

39. Cassandra is in charge of monitoring and maintaining her company's domain controllers. She opens Event Viewer on a domain controller named Server1 and notices that several thousand events, many of which are related to updates delivered via Windows Update, are present. She wants to create a custom log so that she can locate the most important events rapidly, so she opens the Create Custom View dialog box. Which of the following criteria can she use in creating the custom log? (Choose all that apply.)

a. Time interval during which the events were logged

b. Event level such as critical, error, warning, and so on

c. The logs from which she wants to view data

d. Event ID numbers

e. Task categories

f. Users and computers associated with the event

40. Heidi is the network administrator for a financial company, which operates an AD DS network consisting of a single domain. Servers on the network run a mix of Windows Server 2003 and Windows Server 2008. She will be upgrading Windows Server 2003 DNS servers to Windows Server 2008 R2 and needs to obtain information about the configuration of the DNS zones. Which of the following commands should she run?

a. `Dnscmd /enumzones`

b. `Dnscmd /statistics`

c. `Dnscmd /zoneinfo`

d. `Dnscmd /info`

41. Bob is responsible for software deployment and maintenance for his company, which operates an AD DS network consisting of a single domain. The company is planning to upgrade all users from Microsoft Office 2003 to Office 2007, and Bob must ensure that employees are unable to use Office 2003. In addition, he must ensure that users retain their user files such as customized spell check dictionaries after the upgrade.

What should he do to accomplish these objectives? (Each correct answer represents part of the solution. Choose two answers.)

   a. Select the **Advanced** deployment option from the Deploy Software dialog box.

   b. Select the **Required upgrade for existing packages** option from the Add Upgrade Package dialog box.

   c. Select the **Uninstall the existing package, then install the upgrade package** option from the Add Upgrade Package dialog box.

   d. Select the **Package can upgrade over the existing package** option from the Add Upgrade Package dialog box.

   e. Select the **Immediately uninstall the software from users and computers** option from the Remove Software dialog box.

42. Ted is the network administrator for CertGuide Ltd. The company has a subsidiary named Que. The CertGuide network consists of a single AD DS forest containing one domain named `certguide.com`. The domain and forest functional levels are Windows Server 2008. The Que network consists of an AD DS forest containing two domains named `que.com` and `corp.que.com`. These domains operate at the Windows 2000 native forest and domain functional levels.

A file server named Server2 is a member of the `certguide.com` domain. All users in all three domains need to save files on Server2 every day. Ted needs to ensure that the domain administrators of the `que.com` and `corp.que.com` domains cannot grant users in the `certguide.com` domain permissions on servers in the `que.com` and `corp.que.com` domains. What should Ted do to accomplish this objective?

   a. Create two one-way external trust relationships in which the `certguide.com` and `corp.que.com` domains trust the `que.com` domain.

   b. Create two one-way external trust relationships in which the `que.com` and `corp.que.com` domains trust the `certguide.com` domain.

   c. Create a one-way forest trust relationship in which the `certguide.com` domain trusts the `que.com` domain.

   d. Create a one-way forest trust relationship in which the `que.com` domain trusts the `certguide.com` domain.

e. Upgrade the que.com and corp.que.com domains to Windows Server 2008 and make the que.com domain the root domain of a second tree in the existing forest.

43. Rebecca is the network administrator for a clothing manufacturer. The company's network is configured as a single AD DS domain. All domain controllers run Windows Server 2008 R2 and the domain and forest functional levels are set to Windows Server 2008 R2.

The company buys out a competitor. The former competitor also operates a single domain AD DS network that runs at the Windows Server 2008 domain and forest functional levels. Rebecca wants to export the settings of a GPO from her company and import them into the second company. How can she perform this task with the least amount of administrative effort?

a. Use the BackupGPO.wsf script to back up the settings in her domain and then use the RestoreGPO.wsf script to import them in the second domain.

b. Use the BackupGPO.wsf script to back up the settings in her domain and then use the ImportGPO.wsf script to import them in the second domain.

c. Use the Wbadmin command to back up the settings in her domain and then use the Wbadmin command to restore them to the second domain.

d. Create a forest trust between the two companies and then access the required GPO from the Group Policy Management Console and copy it to the second company.

44. Heather is an administrator for a company that operates an AD DS network consisting of a single domain that runs at the Windows 2000 domain functional level. There are three sites corresponding to the company's head office and two small branch offices. Domain controllers on the network run either Windows 2000 Server or Windows Server 2003, but the company has plans of introducing domain controllers running Windows Server 2008 to the network.

Heather has read about all the advantages of using RODCs to authenticate users in her company's branch offices and is planning to set up an RODC in each of the branch offices. Which of the following does she need to do before setting up the RODCs? (Each correct answer represents part of the solution. Choose four answers.)

a. Upgrade all Windows 2000 Server domain controllers to either Windows Server 2003 or Windows Server 2008.

b. Upgrade all Windows 2000 Server and Windows Server 2003 domain controllers to Windows Server 2008.

c. Raise the domain and forest functional levels to Windows Server 2003.

   d. Raise the domain and forest functional levels to Windows Server 2008.

   e. Upgrade the PDC emulator to Windows Server 2003.

   f. Upgrade the PDC emulator to Windows Server 2008.

   g. Run the `Adprep /rodcprep` utility on the schema master.

   h. Run the `Adprep /rodcprep` utility on the infrastructure master.

45. Julian is the network administrator for a company that has operated a UNIX-based network and is switching over to a Windows Server 2008–based AD DS network. He installs Windows Server 2008 R2 on a new computer and runs `dcpromo.exe` to promote this server to the first domain controller in the new domain.

   Julian wants to ensure that AD DS has been properly installed on the new domain controller. Which of the following should he do? (Each correct answer represents part of the solution. Choose three answers.)

   a. Open Active Directory Users and Computers and verify that an organizational unit (OU) named Users is present.

   b. Open Active Directory Users and Computers and verify that an OU named Domain Controllers is present.

   c. In Windows Explorer, navigate to the `%systemroot%` folder and verify the existence of the Active Directory database and shared system volume folders.

   d. In Windows Explorer, navigate to the root of the system drive and verify the existence of the Active Directory database and shared system volume folders.

   e. Open the Domain Name System (DNS) Manager snap-in and verify that two zones containing the domain name are present in the console tree. One of these should be prefixed with `_msdcs`.

   f. Open the DNS Manager snap-in and verify that a reverse lookup zone containing the domain name has been created and is visible in the console tree.

46. Janet is responsible for configuring application directory partitions on the domain controllers in her company's AD DS domain. She has configured a financial application to store its data in an application directory partition on a domain controller named DC1. She now needs to enable fault tolerance for this partition by configuring an appropriate partition on another domain controller named DC2. What should she do?

   a. Use the `ntdsutil` utility to create an application directory partition replica on DC2.

  b. Use the `ntdsutil` utility to create a new application directory partition on DC2 and then specify the application directory partition's reference domain to point to DC1.

  c. Use the `repadmin` utility to specify replication of the application directory partition on DC1 to DC2.

  d. Use the `dnscmd` utility with the `/ZoneChangeDirectoryPartition` parameter to specify an application directory partition on DC2 to which the data on DC1 will be replicated.

47. Managers at Betty's company have requested that she configure all computers used by data entry clerks so that they are unable to access the Internet. However, data entry supervisors need access to the Internet. All computers used by both data entry clerks and supervisors run either Windows Vista Business or Windows 7 Professional.

All members of the data entry team belong to the Data Entry security group and data entry supervisors also belong to the Supervisors security group.

Which of the following should Betty do to accomplish this objective?

  a. Create two Group Policy objects (GPOs): one to disable Internet access and the other to enable Internet access. Grant the Data Entry group the **Read** and **Apply group policy** permissions on the first GPO and grant the Supervisors group the **Read** and **Apply group policy** permissions on the second GPO.

  b. Create one GPO that disables Internet access and grant the Data Entry group the **Read** and **Apply group policy** permissions.

  c. Create one GPO that disables Internet access and grant the Data Entry group the **Read** and **Apply group policy** permissions. Grant the Supervisors group the **Read** permission only on this GPO.

  d. Create one GPO that disables Internet access and grant the Data Entry group the **Read** and **Apply group policy** permissions. Also, deny the Supervisors group the **Apply group policy** permission on this GPO.

48. Wendy is responsible for maintaining certificates in her company's AD DS domain, which operates a two-tier PKI hierarchy consisting of an offline stand-alone root CA and an enterprise subordinate CA. She needs to create an additional copy of the certificate and private key used by the company's CEO for storage at a remote location. What should she do to accomplish this task with the least amount of effort?

  a. Use the Certificate Export Wizard to export the certificate and choose **Yes** when asked whether she wants to export the private key. Browse to a suitable removable disk for the file location and provide a secure password for the key.

    b. Use the Certification Authority Backup Wizard to back the certificate up and choose **Yes** when asked whether she wants to export the private key. Browse to a suitable removable disk for the file location and provide a secure password for the key.

    c. Use the **ntdsutil** command to back up the certificate and private key and use the **password** keyword to provide a secure password for the key.

    d. Use the **wbadmin** command to back up the certificate and private key and use the **password** keyword to provide a secure password for the key.

49. Ester's company is expanding its North American operations to Asia. To accommodate these operations, she needs to add several objects and attributes to the schema. Her boss has added her user account to the Schema Admins group for this purpose. Working from a branch office domain controller, Ester attempts to locate the Active Directory Schema snap-in. She calls the help desk and asks to be given the appropriate permission to access this snap-in but is told that this is not a permissions issue. What does Ester need to do to access this snap-in? (Each correct answer represents part of the solution. Choose two answers.)

    a. She must first register the Schema snap-in by using the `regsvr32` command from the Run dialog box.

    b. She needs to install the Active Directory Schema snap-in to a new MMC console.

    c. She needs to go to the schema master computer to modify the schema. Because the domain controller she is working from does not have this snap-in, it must not be the schema master.

    d. She should contact the help desk manager because she has received incorrect advice from the support technician. She needs to belong to both the Schema Admins and Enterprise Admins groups to access this snap-in.

50. Betsy is responsible for administering her company's PKI. The company has an offline root CA and four enterprise subordinate CAs, each of which issues certificates to users in a major division of the company.

As a result of corporate downsizing and reorganization, one of the four major divisions is being disbanded. Betsy must ensure that resources on the network will not accept certificates from the subordinate CA located in the division that is being disbanded. Which of the following should she do? (Each correct answer represents part of the solution. Choose three answers.)

    a. At the disbanded division's subordinate CA, revoke all the certificates that it has issued.

    b. Uninstall the AD CS role from the disbanded division's subordinate CA.

   c.   Bring the offline root CA online, revoke the disbanded division's subordinate CA's certificate and then take the root CA back offline.

   d.   Publish a new base CRL.

   e.   Publish a new delta CRL.

   f.   Copy the new CRL to the network's CRL distribution point.

   g.   Add the AIA extension to all URLs at which certificates issued by the disbanded division's subordinate CA can be retrieved.

51. Brian is responsible for maintaining AD DS replication on his company's network, which consists of three domains and nine sites. When he uses `replmon` to check the automatically configured replication topology, he notices that connection paths are not established in what he thinks is the optimum manner.

    What can Brian do to manually change the topology?

   a.   Edit the Registry to indicate the appropriate paths.

   b.   Use Active Directory Sites and Services to manually create a site link object connecting the required servers.

   c.   Force the Knowledge Consistency Checker (KCC) to update the replication topology.

   d.   Brian cannot modify the replication paths. The KCC does not permit this type of configuration.

52. Dennis is responsible for managing Active Directory Lightweight Directory Services (AD LDS) on his company's network. He needs to create a replica of an AD LDS instance that he has created in order to provide fault tolerance. Which of the following tools should he use to accomplish this task?

   a.   `Adsiedit.exe`

   b.   `Ldp.exe`

   c.   `Ntdsutil.exe`

   d.   Active Directory Lightweight Directory Services Setup Wizard

53. Marilyn is responsible for security on her company's network. While reviewing the security log one morning, she notices that a hacker has been using brute-force methods to attempt to crack passwords on the network.

    Marilyn's company does not have the financial resources to implement a more secure authentication method such as smart cards at the present time, so she decides to create a policy to strengthen password security. Which of the following should she do? (Each correct answer represents part of the solution. Choose all that apply.)

a. Enable the **Password must meet complexity requirements** setting.

b. Enable the **Store passwords using reversible encryption** setting.

c. Enable the **Users must change password at next logon** setting.

d. Increase the **Minimum password length** setting.

e. Decrease the **Maximum password age** setting.

54. Sheldon is a network administrator for his company, which operates an AD DS network consisting of a single domain operating at the Windows Server 2008 forest and domain functional levels. He is really counting his blessings because his company has gone through a major downsizing in which almost one quarter of all jobs have been eliminated, mostly through layoffs. As a result, he has been cleaning up the company's AD DS network by clearing out a lot of user and group accounts that are no longer needed.

Sheldon has been monitoring the `ntds.dit` file and has been expecting the size of this file to reduce because it now holds much less data. However, he has seen nothing yet. What should he do?

a. He must wait for 24 hours for the deletions to be propagated to other domain controllers.

b. He must wait for 60 days because objects that are deleted from AD DS are not immediately deleted. Rather, they are assigned a tombstone of 60 days. The size of the file will not reduce until after this tombstone period has expired.

c. He should back up and restore the database. This compresses the file.

d. He must perform an offline compaction of the database because the space that was consumed by the deleted objects simply remains empty space within the `ntds.dit` file until he does this.

55. Paul administers the network for a new company whose AD DS root domain will be named `que.com`. He installs Windows Server 2008 R2 on a computer named DC01 and runs `dcpromo.exe` on this computer to create the first domain controller in the new forest. He accepts the option to create a new DNS server.

Paul also sets up a Windows Server 2008 member server running Internet Information Services (IIS) 7.0 and 12 client computers running Windows 7 Professional. He configures all 13 of these computers with static IP addresses and specifies the IP address of DC01 as their preferred DNS server.

Which of the following steps must Paul take to ensure that both the address (A) and pointer (PTR) resource records of the client computers and the IIS server are recorded properly when he adds them to the que.com domain?

a. Create a forward lookup zone for the network and enable it to accept dynamic updates.

b. Create a reverse lookup zone for the network and enable it to accept dynamic updates.

c. Enable DC01 to accept dynamic updates.

d. Configure the client computers to send updates to DC01.

e. Enable the zones for que.com to accept dynamic updates.

56. Alexander is the domain administrator for the que.com domain, which operates at the Windows Server 2008 R2 functional level. He has configured AD CS on a server in the domain. Several users in the legal.que.com domain attempt to enroll for a user certificate, but receive a message that the template was not found. What should Alexander do so that these users can locate this template?

a. Create a duplicate of the User certificate template and specify the **Windows Server 2008** option. Then specify the **Autoenroll** permission for the Authenticated Users group.

b. Place the users in a security group and configure the Security tab of the template's Properties dialog box with the appropriate permissions to the template.

c. Configure the automatic certificate request policy in a GPO linked to the legal.que.com domain.

d. Configure the web enrollment pages to use basic authentication.

57. Rachel is responsible for ensuring that the servers on her company's Windows Server 2008 network can handle all requests sent by users on the network. She wants to display graphs of server performance data in real-time and, at the same time, create resource allocation policies that determine how server resources such as processor and memory are allocated to processes running on the server. Furthermore, she wants the ability to configure events under which the server will automatically modify how server resources are allocated. Which of the following tools enables her to perform all these actions?

a. Network Monitor

b. Task Manager

c. Reliability and Performance Monitor

d. Event Viewer

e. Windows System Resource Manager (WSRM)

58. George is responsible for creating and managing GPOs for a company that operates an AD DS forest with three domains, each of which has 10 or more OUs representing different work groups in the company. All servers run Windows Server 2008 and client computers run Windows XP, Windows Vista, or Windows 7. The functional level of the forest is Windows Server 2008.

George needs to create a series of similar GPOs that will be linked to various OUs in the forest. What should he do to accomplish this task with the least amount of administrative effort?

- **a.** Create a Starter GPO and link it to the required OUs. Then edit this GPO to introduce OU-specific settings.
- **b.** Create a Starter GPO and copy it to each domain. Then use the Starter GPO to create GPOs in the required OUs and edit these GPOs to introduce OU-specific settings.
- **c.** Create one GPO and link it to all OUs that require its settings. Then edit the GPO in each OU to introduce OU-specific settings.
- **d.** Create a new GPO in each OU that contains the required settings for its OU.

59. Wayne is the network administrator for a medical office that operates an AD DS network consisting of a single domain. He suspects that unauthorized users have been attempting to access the DNS server and wants to log packets being sent to and received from a specific range of IP addresses at the DNS server. What should he do?

- **a.** Access the Monitoring tab of the DNS server's Properties dialog box and enable both simple and recursive queries.
- **b.** Access the Event Logging tab of the DNS server's Properties dialog box and enable the **All events** option.
- **c.** Access the Debug Logging tab of the DNS server's Properties dialog box, enable **Log packets for debugging,** and specify the **Filter packets by IP address** option.
- **d.** Configure Network Monitor with a capture filter that enables the capture of frames originating from the required range of IP addresses.

60. Theodore is the network administrator for a company that operates an AD DS network consisting of a single domain. The domain contains OUs that mirror the departmental structure of the company. A user named Jill, who is a member of the Marketing OU, has been delegated permission to reset passwords in that OU. Jill has been transferred to the Design OU and will no longer need the capability of resetting passwords in the Marketing OU.

How should Theodore prevent Jill from resetting passwords in the Marketing OU, with the least amount of administrative effort?

a. Move Jill's user account from the Marketing OU to the Design OU. Her permissions will be reset automatically.

b. Run the Delegation of Control Wizard to revoke Jill's permissions to the Marketing OU.

c. Access the Security tab of the Marketing OU Properties dialog box and remove Jill's permission to reset passwords.

d. Delete Jill's user account and then re-create it in the Marketing OU.

61. John is the network administrator for a company that operates an AD DS network consisting of two domains and two sites. The head office is located in Toronto and a branch office is located in Boston. Each office has two domain controllers and the global catalog, and all operations master roles are hosted on the domain controllers in the Toronto office. Several universal groups are used for assigning permissions to resources in both domains and both offices.

Users in Boston report that logon times are often slow, and John decides to implement universal group membership caching in this office. He opens Active Directory Sites and Services and expands the console tree to obtain the view shown in the exhibit. Which item should John select to implement universal group membership caching?

   a. The Inter-Site Transports folder

   b. The Boston site

   c. The Servers folder beneath the Boston site

   d. SERVER3

   e. The NTDS Settings folder beneath SERVER3

62. David is responsible for software deployment throughout his company, which operates an AD DS domain with eight OUs that represent administrative divisions in the company. Employees are frequently moved between administrative divisions, and their work responsibilities and software needs change when this happens. Furthermore, they should not have access to software that they no longer need after a move.

When employees move, David must ensure that these requirements are met. What should he do?

   a. In the Upgrades tab of the Software Installation Properties dialog box, select the **Required upgrade for existing packages** check box.

   b. In the General tab of the Software Installation Properties dialog box, select the **Display the Deploy Software dialog box** option.

   c. In the Advanced tab of the Software Installation Properties dialog box, select the **Uninstall the applications when they fall out of the scope of management** check box.

   d. In the Delegation tab of the Properties for the associated GPOs, ensure that the **Apply Group Policy** permission is granted to only those security groups that require access to the applications.

63. Evan is the systems administrator for a company that operates an AD DS network consisting of a single domain and five sites, which represent the head office and four branch offices. Each branch office is configured with a read-only domain controller (RODC).

Evan receives a call from a branch office employee named Melissa, who is experiencing extremely long delays in logging on to the network. Evan wants to verify whether Melissa's credentials are cached at the RODC.

What should Evan do? (Each correct answer represents part of the solution. Choose three answers.)

   a. Access the Active Directory Sites and Services snap-in.

   b. Access the Active Directory Users and Computers snap-in.

   c. Access the Properties dialog box for Melissa's user account.

d. Access the Properties dialog box for the RODC in Melissa's branch office.

e. Click **Advanced** and then select the **Accounts whose passwords are stored on this Read-only Domain Controller** option from the drop-down list.

f. Click **Advanced** and then select the **Accounts that have been authenticated to this Read-only Domain Controller** option from the drop-down list.

64. Duncan has configured Certificate Services on his company's domain-based PKI to publish a base CRL every Friday at 8 p.m. and a delta CRL Monday to Thursday at 8 p.m. On Wednesday morning, an accounting application needs to check the CRL to ensure that a user's certificate is valid. Which of the following CRLs does the application check?

a. The base CRL and Tuesday's delta CRL

b. The base CRL and Wednesday's delta CRL

c. The base CRL and both Monday's and Tuesday's delta CRL

d. The base CRL and all of Monday's, Tuesday's, and Wednesday's delta CRLs

e. Tuesday's delta CRL only

f. Wednesday's delta CRL only

65. Karla is the network administrator for a company that operates an AD DS network consisting of a parent domain and two child domains. All DNS servers run Windows Server 2008 or Windows Server 2008 R2, and all DNS zones are configured as Active Directory–integrated zones hosted on domain controllers.

Karla notices that the zone data for one of the child domains contains several entries for unknown computers that are not domain members. What should she do to prevent this from occurring in the future?

a. Select the **Secure only** option on the General tab of the zone's Properties dialog box.

b. Change the zone replication scope to the **All DNS servers in this domain** option.

c. On the Zone Aging/Scavenging Properties dialog box, select the **Scavenge Stale Resource Records** option.

d. Right-click the server in the console tree of DNS Manager and choose **Scavenge Stale Resource Records**.

66. Karen is a network manager for a global musical instrument company that operates a complicated AD DS forest consisting of five domain trees and a total of 32 individual domains. The domain structure includes the following tree root domains:

`mm-corp.us`, `asiamusical.com`, `willywilly.com.au`, `worldwideguitars.com`, and `virtual-realm.com`

Users in `development.california.mm-corp.us` often need to collaborate with their Australian counterparts in `development.willywilly.com.au`, and users in both domains complain that it takes an extremely long time for shared folders to open even though there is excellent connectivity between physical locations.

Which of the following should Karen do to improve this situation?

a. Karen should purchase additional bandwidth to reduce the delay in accessing shared resources.

b. Karen can create a forest trust between the `california.mm-corp.us` and `willywilly.com.au` domain trees.

c. Karen should create a shortcut trust between `development.california.mm-corp.us` and `development.willywilly.com.au`.

d. Karen should move the users from the two domains into a common domain.

67. Hubert is the systems administrator for a clothing manufacturer based in San Francisco. During a standard review of the AD DS files on his domain controller, he notices that the hard drive containing the `ntds.dit` file is running out of space. However, plenty of space is available on the RAID-5 array attached to the server. He decides to move the file to the RAID-5 array. How should he perform this procedure using the least amount of administrative effort?

a. Restart the server in Directory Services Restore Mode and use Windows Explorer to move the file.

b. Restart the server in Directory Services Restore Mode and use the `ntdsutil` utility to move the file.

c. From a command prompt, stop AD DS, use the `ntdsutil` utility to move the file, and then restart AD DS.

d. From a command prompt, stop AD DS, use Windows Explorer to move the file, and then restart AD DS.

e. While the server is running, open a command prompt and use `ntdsutil` to move the file.

f. While the server is running, use Windows Explorer to move the file.

68. Kim is the network administrator for a company that operates an AD DS network consisting of one domain and four sites. She installs a new domain controller and a new member server running Windows Server 2008 R2 in one of the sites but notices several days later that replication is not taking place properly. Investigating this problem, Kim discovers that these servers have been placed in the wrong site. What should she do to correct this problem? (Each correct answer represents part of the solution. Choose two answers.)

    a. Use Active Directory Sites and Services to place the domain controller in the correct site.

    b. Use Active Directory Sites and Services to place the member server in the correct site.

    c. Use Active Directory Administrative Center to place the domain controller in the correct site.

    d. Use Active Directory Administrative Center to place the member server in the correct site.

    e. Reconfigure the domain controller with an IP address corresponding to the subnet specified for the correct site.

    f. Reconfigure the member server with an IP address corresponding to the subnet specified for the correct site.

69. Peter is a network administrator for a company that operates an AD DS forest consisting of two domains in separate trees. The company has offices in New York and Rome, which are connected by a 236 Kbps WAN link. Each office is represented by a separate AD DS site as well as its own domain.

Peter's company stores resource location data in AD DS so that users can perform searches to locate the appropriate resources on their client computers, which run either Windows XP Professional or Windows 7 Professional. However, users in the Rome office report that search times for resources are unacceptably slow.

Which of the following should Peter do to improve search times at the Rome office?

    a. Enable universal group membership caching at the Rome office.

    b. Configure a global catalog server at the Rome office.

    c. Configure a domain controller for the New York domain in the Rome office.

    d. Configure a domain controller for the Rome domain in the New York office.

70. Lenny is responsible for configuring Group Policy in his company's domain. The domain functional level is set to Windows Server 2003. Lenny's manager has requested that he implement an account policy that specifies that all user accounts will be locked out if an incorrect password is entered five times within a one-quarter-hour period. The account is to remain locked out until a support technician unlocks it.

How should Lenny configure the account policy? (Each correct answer represents part of the solution. Choose three answers.)

a. Set the account lockout threshold to 0.

b. Set the account lockout threshold to 1.

c. Set the account lockout threshold to 4.

d. Set the account lockout duration to 0.

e. Set the account lockout duration to 1.

f. Set the reset account lockout counter value to 0.25.

g. Set the reset lockout counter to 15.

h. Set the reset lockout counter to 900.

71. Michelle administers a server named Server3 that has Active Directory Lightweight Directory Services (AD LDS) installed. She installs an instance of AD LDS together with its associated application directory partition that will store data for a directory-enabled engineering design application.

Michelle wants to create a new OU in the AD LDS application directory partition that will organize users that require access to the design application. Which of the following tools can she use for this purpose? (Each correct answer represents a complete solution to the problem. Choose two answers.)

a. Ldp.exe

b. Ntdsutil.exe

c. Dsadd.exe

d. Adsiedit.msc

e. Dssite.msc

72. Stuart is responsible for administering the DNS servers in his company's AD DS network, which contains an Active Directory–integrated zone. A DNS server named Server1 does not appear to be receiving accurate zone transfer information.

Stuart decides to capture information that relates to DNS update data that should be sent and received at Server1, so he enables every debugging option available on the Debug Logging tab of the server's Properties dialog box, as shown in the exhibit. The next day, after noticing that the log has collected a large quantity of data he realizes that he does not need detailed information and that he should clear certain options. Which of the following options should he clear? (Choose all that apply.)

a. **Log packets for debugging**

b. **Queries/Transfers**

c. **Updates**

d. **Notifications**

e. **Details**

f. **Filter packets by IP address**

73. Arlene is responsible for configuring Group Policy in her company's AD DS domain. The domain contains OUs that mirror the company's departmental organization. Another administrator has applied a GPO to the Sales OU that limits user access to their computers. Arlene's manager has noticed that this GPO has reduced the number of help desk calls generated by the users in this department, so he asks Arlene to apply the same policies to the Marketing department. What is the best way to accomplish this task?

a. Create a new GPO containing the required settings and link this GPO to the Marketing OU.

b. Use the GPO linked to the Sales OU as a Starter GPO to create a new GPO linked to the Marketing OU.

    c. Add the group containing the Marketing team members to the Sales OU.

    d. Simply link the current GPO to the Marketing OU.

74. Carm is the senior network administrator for a large investment company that operates an AD DS forest consisting of nine domains in four domain trees. The forest functional level is Windows 2000.

In recent months, a vigorous server upgrade program has been in place throughout the company and all domain controllers and most member servers have been upgraded to Windows Server 2008 R2. Carm verifies that the domain functional level of each of the tree root domains has been set to Windows Server 2008 R2 and is now proceeding to upgrade the forest functional level to Windows Server 2008 R2. However, he is unable to select this functional level. What might be causing this problem? (Choose all that apply.)

    a. Carm must log on using an account that is a member of the Schema Admins group.

    b. Carm must log on using an account that is a member of the Enterprise Admins group.

    c. Some of the child domains might be still at the Windows 2000 or 2003 domain functional level.

    d. Carm must raise the forest functional level to Windows Server 2003 first and let this change propagate throughout the forest before he can raise the forest functional level to Windows Server 2008 R2.

    e. Two of the child domains are connected by a shortcut trust relationship. Carm must remove this trust before he can raise the forest functional level.

75. Teresa is responsible for configuring and maintaining Group Policy in her company's AD DS domain. The domain contains computers running Windows XP Professional, Windows Vista Business, Windows 7 Professional, Windows Server 2003, and Windows Server 2008. There are eight OUs representing company departments, all of which have multiple GPOs linked to them.

Because of an organizational change, Teresa needs to move the Design OU under the Engineering OU. She needs to find out which objects in the Design OU are adversely affected by GPOs linked to the Engineering OU. She must achieve this goal without disruption to users. Which of the following should she do?

    a. Use the Group Policy Modeling Wizard for the Engineering OU. Choose the **Design OU** to simulate policy settings.

    b. Use the Group Policy Results Wizard for the Engineering OU. Choose the **Design OU** to simulate policy settings.

    c. Use the Group Policy Modeling Wizard for the Design OU. Choose the **Engineering OU** to simulate policy settings.

    d. Use the Group Policy Results Wizard for the Design OU. Choose the **Engineering OU** to simulate policy settings.

76. Jennifer is responsible for maintaining the user and group accounts databases in her company's AD DS domain. The company is expanding its operations and will be hiring several hundred new university graduates as soon as they have finished their exams. These graduates will work in several different departments of the company and require access to numerous shared resources in different components of the network.

Human Resources (HR) has prepared an Excel spreadsheet containing all required information on the new hires, such as names, addresses, work departments, locations, and so on. Jennifer must create new user and group accounts for these new hires. What should she do to create the accounts with the least amount of administrative effort?

    a. Export the Excel spreadsheet to a comma-separated text file and use `Csvde` to create the required accounts.

    b. Export the Excel spreadsheet to a LDIF-formatted file and use `Ldifde` to create the required accounts.

    c. Use the `dsadd` command to add the required accounts to the database.

    d. Use the New Object—User and New Object—Group wizards to create the required accounts.

77. Matt has successfully installed and configured an enterprise root CA for his company, which operates an AD DS network consisting of a single domain. Matt has also configured a certificate template for autoenrollment.

What additional tasks must Matt perform to enable autoenrollment of user certificates? (Each correct answer represents part of the solution. Choose two answers.)

    a. Install Internet Information Services (IIS) 7.0 on the CA.

    b. Install an enterprise subordinate CA.

    c. Configure a certificate trust list (CTL).

    d. Configure the CA to issue certificates based on the template he has just configured.

    e. Configure a GPO linked to the domain to enroll certificates automatically.

78. Charles is the administrator for a company whose AD DS domain spans four sites: Pittsburgh, Cincinnati, Cleveland, and Baltimore. He has configured site links to reflect the geography so that replication traffic takes the shortest routes. To that end, Charles configures the site link cost between shorter paths to 200 and the cost between longer paths to 100.

The following week, Charles notices that replication is inconsistent and seems to take longer than it should. What should he check first in troubleshooting this problem?

   a. Charles should use the SMTP transport protocol rather than the IP protocol.

   b. Charles should change bridgehead servers at each site to the most powerful servers available to accommodate the increased traffic burden.

   c. Charles should configure site link bridges to bridge the links on the longer paths.

   d. Charles should reverse the site link costs.

79. Working at one of the six domain controllers in his company's network, Brendan accidentally deleted his company's Executive OU. Realizing that none of the executives would be able to log on the next morning, Brendan knew he must restore this OU as rapidly as possible. Fortunately, a backup of the system state of the domain controller had been created the day before.

Which of the following actions does Brendan need to perform? (Each correct answer represents part of the solution. Choose two answers.)

   a. Use the `net stop ntds` and the `wbadmin start systemstaterecovery` commands to restore System State from backup.

   b. Start the domain controller in Safe Mode and then use the `wbadmin start systemstaterecovery` command to restore System State from backup.

   c. Start the domain controller in Directory Services Restore Mode and then use the `wbadmin start systemstaterecovery` command to restore System State from backup.

   d. Select the **Repair your computer** option.

   e. Use the `ntdsutil` program to mark the restored Executive OU as authoritative by specifying the LDAP DN of the Executive OU.

   f. Select the **System Image Recovery** option.

80. Cindy is a systems administrator for a company that operates a single domain AD DS network. All servers run Windows Server 2008 and all client computers run Windows 7 Professional. Cindy is setting up special user-based options for installation of a custom accounting application provided by a software vendor.

She wants to configure the software options so that users can view the installation process as it takes place on their computers. She creates a GPO linked to the domain and in the Group Policy Management Editor; she creates a software installation policy that assigns the software in the User Configuration\Policies\Software Settings\Software Installation branch. Which of the following should she configure?

   a. Under Installation User Interface Options on the Deployment tab of the package's Properties dialog box, select **Basic**.

   b. Under Installation User Interface Options on the Deployment tab of the package's Properties dialog box, select **Maximum**.

   c. Under Deployment Options on the Deployment tab of the package's Properties dialog box, select **Do not display this package in the Add/Remove Programs control panel** option.

   d. Under Deployment Options on the Deployment tab of the package's Properties dialog box, select **Install this application at logon**.

81. Judy is the systems administrator for a company that operates an AD DS forest containing three domains. There are six sites, each of which represents a city in which the company does business. Each site contains at least two domains and several OUs within each domain, and each site is configured with a proxy server that all users are expected to access the Internet through.

Judy has created GPOs that set the proxy configuration for all computers in the forest, including portable computers that traveling users carry to different offices in the course of their job duties. How should she configure this GPO to ensure that users always access the Internet by means of the proxy server in the office where they are located?

   a. She should link each GPO to its site and specify the **Enforced** option.

   b. She should link each GPO to its site and do nothing else.

   c. She should link each GPO to the OUs located in its site and specify the **Block Inheritance** option.

   d. She should link each GPO to the domains located in its site and specify the **Block Inheritance** option.

   e. She should link each GPO to the domains located in its site and do nothing else.

82. Wilson is the network administrator for a company that operates an AD DS network consisting of a single domain and four sites representing the company's offices, which are located in Dallas, Austin, San Antonio, and Houston. Each site has at least one domain controller that runs DNS and hosts an Active Directory–integrated zone. Domain controllers in the company run a mix of Windows 2000 Server, Windows Server 2003, and Windows Server 2008.

Wilson's company places a contract with a second company in Houston to provide extensive educational materials for company employees. Wilson configures a conditional forwarder on a Houston DNS server to point to a private web server at the second company's network, but employees in the Dallas, Austin, and San Antonio offices report that they are unable to access the private web server.

On contacting administrators in the Dallas, Austin, and San Antonio offices, Wilson discovers that the conditional forwarder setting does not appear in their DNS servers. What should Wilson to?

a. Use Active Directory Sites and Services to force intersite replication.

b. Configure the conditional forwarder with the **All domain controllers in this domain** option.

c. Configure the conditional forwarder with the **All DNS servers in this domain** option.

d. Configure a new zone delegation for each of the Dallas, Austin, and San Antonio sites.

83. Dan is responsible for administering the DNS configuration for his company, which operates an AD DS network consisting of a single domain and sites corresponding to the New York boroughs in which offices are located. The Manhattan office houses a primary standard DNS server named NS01 plus a secondary name server named NS02. The Brooklyn office houses two standard secondary name servers called NS03 and NS04. A facility in Bronx houses two additional standard secondary DNS servers called NS05 and NS06.

Lately, the administrative overhead of looking after these servers and configuring zone transfers has taken up a lot of time. In addition, the zone transfers themselves generate an excessive amount of network traffic. Dan needs to reduce both the administrative time and the network traffic, so he opens the DNS Manager snap-in at NS01 and accesses the Properties dialog box for his zone. From the General tab, he clicks the **Change** button opposite the zone type. Which options should he configure (Each correct answer represents part of the solution. Choose two answers.)

a. He should select **Primary zone**.

b. He should select **Secondary zone**.

c. He should select **Stub zone**.

d. He should select the **Store the zone in Active Directory** option.

e. He should clear the **Store the zone in Active Directory** option.

84. Brenda is the security administrator for a company that operates an AD DS network consisting of a single domain. All servers run Windows Server 2008

and client computers run either Windows XP Professional or Windows 7 Enterprise. The network includes an offline root CA and three enterprise issuing CAs.

In addition to the locally issued certificates, Brenda needs to enable the use by domain clients of several certificates that have been issued by third-party CAs. What does she need to do to ensure that all domain clients will trust certificates issued by the third-party CAs?

- **a.** Install the third-party CA certificates on her company's root CA and place this CA online for sufficient time for the certificates to replicate to other network servers.
- **b.** Install the third-party CA certificates on her company's issuing CAs.
- **c.** Add a copy of each third-party CA certificates to the Trusted Root Certification Authorities node in the Default Domain Policy GPO.
- **d.** Add a copy of each third-party CA certificates to the Trusted Root Certification Authorities certificate store on each client computer.

85. A junior administrator in your company named Sandy has just created a new one-way outgoing trust relationship between your company's domain and a contractor's domain. The purpose of this trust is to enable engineers in your company to send detailed design charts and specifications to the contractor without having to fax them. However, engineers report that they are unable to access the contractor's domain. What should you do to enable access while keeping resources in your company's domain secure?

- **a.** In the trust's Properties dialog box, change the direction of the trust from outgoing to incoming.
- **b.** In the trust's Properties dialog box, change the authentication scope of the trust from selective authentication to domainwide.
- **c.** Remove the trust relationship and create a new two-way trust relationship.
- **d.** Remove the trust relationship and create a new one-way incoming trust relationship.

86. Nolan is a network administrator for a company that operates an Active Directory Domain Services (AD DS) network consisting of two domains. The company has offices in Los Angeles and Tokyo, which are connected by a 128 kbps WAN link. Each office is represented by a separate AD DS site, as well as its own domain.

Nolan's company stores resource location information in AD DS so that users can perform searches to locate the appropriate resources using the Entire

Directory option. However, users in the Tokyo office report that search times for resources are unacceptably slow.

What can Nolan do to improve search times at the Tokyo office?

a. Configure a global catalog server at the Tokyo office.

b. Enable universal group caching at the Tokyo office.

c. Configure a domain controller for the Los Angeles domain in the Tokyo office.

d. Configure a domain controller for the Tokyo domain in the Los Angeles office.

87. Julio is the network administrator for a company that has deployed a new AD DS domain containing Windows Server 2008 domain controllers and member servers and Windows 7 Enterprise client computers.

Julio's boss would like him to keep track of any attempts, authorized or otherwise, to modify the configuration of directory objects in the domain. Julio has configured the system access control lists (SACLs) of these objects to enable auditing. What else must Julio do?

a. In a domain-based GPO, enable auditing of object access attempts.

b. In a domain-based GPO, enable auditing of directory service access attempts.

c. In a domain-based GPO, enable auditing of directory service changes attempts.

d. Use the `auditpol.exe` tool to enable auditing of object access attempts.

e. Use the `auditpol.exe` tool to enable auditing of directory service access attempts.

f. Use the `auditpol.exe` tool to enable auditing of directory service changes attempts.

88. Kent is the network administrator for a company that operates an AD DS network consisting of a single domain. The company has four domain controllers that run either Windows Server 2003 or Windows Server 2008.

Kent has obtained a new computer that he plans to install Windows Server 2008 on and promote to a domain controller. This computer will replace an older domain controller, which holds the RID master and PDC emulator roles and will be recommissioned as a backup file server.

Before demoting this domain controller to member server, Kent must transfer these roles to another domain controller. Which of the following tools can he use for this purpose? (Each correct answer represents a complete solution to the problem. Choose two answers.)

a. Active Directory Domains and Trusts

b. Active Directory Sites and Services

c. Active Directory Users and Computers

d. Active Directory Schema

e. The `Ntdsutil` utility

89. Carol is the network administrator for a company that operates an AD DS network consisting of a single domain. Company executives have signed a long-term partnership agreement with another company that also operates an AD DS network. Users in Carol's company will require access to rights-protected confidential information that is stored on web servers located on the second company's network. Users in the second company will not require access to any documents on Carol's network.

Which two of the following should Carol configure on her network? (Each correct answer represents part of the solution. Choose two answers.)

a. Active Directory Lightweight Directory Services (AD LDS)

b. Active Directory Rights Management Services (AD RMS)

c. Active Directory Federation Services (AD FS)

d. Active Directory Certificate Services (AD CS)

e. A one-way external trust relationship

90. Ruby suspects that an intruder has been attempting to obtain usernames and passwords from her company's Windows Server 2008 R2 domain controller. She would like to capture data transmitted across the network adapter of the domain controller. Which tool should she use?

a. Network Monitor

b. Task Manager

c. Performance Monitor

d. Event Viewer

e. Windows System Resource Manager (WSRM)

91. Lynda is a network administrator for a company that operates an AD DS network containing two domains in a single tree. One of the hard disks on a domain controller failed and had to be replaced. As a result, she had to restore the `ntds.dit` file from backup.

When Lynda restarted the domain controller in Directory Services Restore Mode, she entered her administrator password but was denied access. Which of the following is the most likely reason why she was denied access to Directory Services Restore Mode?

a. Lynda changed her password a few days ago. Because this domain controller had failed beforehand, AD DS did not replicate the password change. She needs to use her old password.

b. A domain-based Group Policy setting denies Lynda the right to log on locally to the domain controller.

c. Lynda is not a member of the Enterprise Administrators group. Only members of the Enterprise Administrators group are allowed access to the Directory Services Restore Mode in a forest that contains more than one domain.

d. Lynda entered the password to the domain rather than the password she specified when installing AD DS.

92. Jim is responsible for maintaining the CRLs in his company. A new user named Brigitte has been hired to work in the Accounting department, and Jim issues a certificate to her. He receives an email from Human Resources informing him that Brigitte has failed a preliminary security evaluation and might be unsuitable for this job, so he revokes her certificate.

The next morning, Human Resources informs Jim that the security evaluation has proven to be successful and Brigitte needs her certificate back. So, he attempts to unrevoke the certificate but receives an error message stating that this attempt failed. Which of the following is the most likely reason why Jim was unable to unrevoke her certificate?

a. Jim should delete the delta CRL containing the revoked certificate before he can unrevoke it.

b. Jim should restore the CRL to the day before he first revoked the certificate.

c. Jim specified the **Unspecified** reason code when he revoked the certificate. He should have used the **Certificate Hold** reason code.

d. Jim should have unrevoked the certificate before it was published to the latest base CRL. After a revoked certificate is published in the base CRL, he cannot unrevoke it.

93. Diane is responsible for maintaining the DNS configuration of her company's AD DS domain. All servers run Windows Server 2008, and client computers run either Windows XP Professional or Windows 7 Enterprise or Ultimate. DNS is configured as an Active Directory–integrated zone on two domain controllers and as a secondary zone on a single external DNS server located on the network's perimeter zone. The external DNS server hosts only the records for her company's web and mail servers.

Diane deploys an additional secondary DNS server on the perimeter network to improve Internet-based name resolution. She uses Reliability and Performance Monitor to monitor the new DNS server and notices that the Transfer Start of Authority (SOA) Requests Sent value is high. She needs to minimize the bandwidth used by the perimeter network DNS servers across the firewall server for zone transfer requests. She must also ensure that only authorized servers can receive copies of this zone file.

Which of the following should she configure on the external DNS server? (Each correct answer represents part of the solution. Choose two answers.)

a. On the Notify list, select **Servers listed on the Name Servers tab**.

b. On the Notify list, select **The following servers** and specify the IP addresses of the perimeter zone secondary DNS servers.

c. Increase the value of the **Refresh** interval.

d. Decrease the value of the **Refresh** interval.

e. Increase the value of the **Retry** interval.

f. Decrease the value of the **Retry** interval.

g. Disable dynamic updates.

94. Stan is responsible for configuring password and account lockout policies for his company's AD DS domain. He has configured the domain password policy as shown in the exhibit.

The network has a Windows Server 2008 R2 computer that is configured as an application server. One application utilizes a domain account named App to log on to the application server. This account is granted the Log On as a Service right on the server.

Several weeks after the application was configured, the help desk starts to receive calls from users complaining that they are unable to access the application. What should Stan do to enable proper user access using the least amount of administrative effort?

   a. In Group Policy Management Editor, change the **Maximum password age** setting to 999.

   b. Use `Adsiedit.msc` to configure a password settings object (PSO) that specifies a maximum password age of 999:00:00:00 and apply the PSO to the App user account.

   c. In Group Policy Management Editor, change the value of **Enforce password history** to 0.

   d. In Active Directory Administrative Center, configure the password for the App user account to never expire.

95. Evelyn is planning a PKI for her company's AD DS network. She needs to install an enterprise root CA on a Windows Server 2008 R2 computer on the network. Which of the following computers can she use for this purpose? (Choose all that apply.)

   a. Windows Server 2008 R2 Web Edition

   b. Windows Server 2008 R2 Foundation Edition, configured as a member server

   c. Windows Server 2008 R2 Foundation Edition, configured as a domain controller

   d. Windows Server 2008 R2 Standard Edition, configured as a member server

   e. Windows Server 2008 R2 Standard Edition, configured as a domain controller

   f. Windows Server 2008 R2 Enterprise Edition, configured as a member server

   g. Windows Server 2008 R2 Enterprise Edition, configured as a domain controller

   h. Windows Server 2008 R2 Datacenter Edition, configured as a member server

   i. Windows Server 2008 R2 Datacenter Edition, configured as a domain controller

96. Ursula's AD DS domain uses a standard DNS zone with a primary DNS server called Alpha and two secondary servers called Beta and Gamma. All three servers are listed as name servers on the Name Servers tab of the DNS zone's Properties dialog box. Their IP addresses are 192.168.1.61, 192.168.1.62, and 192.168.1.63, respectively.

Ursula has configured zone transfer to allow zone transfers only to servers listed on the Name Servers tab. Nevertheless, zone transfers are not taking place across the network in a timely fashion. Ursula clicks the **Notify** button on the Zone Transfers tab and notices that the dialog box is configured as shown in the exhibit. What should she do? (Each correct answer represents part of the solution. Choose all that apply).

a.   Select the **Automatically notify** check box.

b.   Select **The following servers** option.

c.   Add the IP address 192.168.1.63 to the list.

d.   Remove the IP address 192.168.1.62 from the list.

e.   Select the **Servers listed on the Name Servers tab** option.

97. Shelley is a network administrator for a company that operates a single-domain AD DS network. There are three sites that represent offices located in St. Louis, Detroit, and Chicago. These offices are connected with two T1 links, from St. Louis to Chicago and from Chicago to Detroit. No direct physical connection exists between St. Louis and Detroit. The site links are configured as described in the following table:

Site Link	Replication Schedule	Replication Interval	Site Link Cost
St. Louis–Chicago	2:00 AM to 7:00 AM	30 minutes	300
Chicago –Detroit	7:00 PM to 2:00 AM	45 minutes	100

Shelley works in the St. Louis office and configures most of the changes to
AD DS from that office. Users in Detroit complain that changes to AD DS take
more than a day to appear in their office. What should Shelley do to ensure that
changes made in St. Louis appear in Detroit by the start of the following business day?

    a.   Reduce the replication interval of the Chicago–Detroit site link to 30 min-
utes.

    b.   Reduce the cost of the St. Louis–Chicago site link to 100.

    c.   Modify the replication schedule of the St. Louis–Chicago site link to
10:00 PM to 4:00 AM.

    d.   Create a site link bridge that bridges the two site links from St. Louis to
Detroit.

98. Ryan has installed Windows Server 2008 R2 on a new server using the Server
Core option. He would like to install AD DS and promote the server to be a
replica domain controller in his company's single domain network. What should
he do?

    a.   Run Server Manager from the command prompt and select the AD DS
role.

    b.   Run Server Manager from the command prompt and select the `dcpromo`
option.

    c.   Execute the `dcpromo` command from the command prompt and specify the
appropriate answers when prompted.

    d.   Execute the `dcpromo` command from the command prompt and specify an
unattended answer file containing the required information.

99. Joanne is the network administrator for a company that builds outdoor furniture. The company operates an AD DS network consisting of a single domain in
which each department has its own OU. All servers run Windows Server 2008,
and the domain and forest functional levels are set to Windows Server 2008.

Joanne's company purchases another company that manufactures camping and
recreational equipment. All servers on this company's network run Windows
Server 2003, and the domain and forest functional levels are set to Windows
Server 2003. Executives in both companies have agreed that the acquired company network will remain as a separate forest. Joanne needs to create several
similar GPOs in different OUs in her company's network. She also needs to
take the settings from the Financial OU in her company's network and copy
them to the Financial OU in the acquired company's domain. What should she
do to accomplish these tasks with the least amount of administrative effort?
(Each correct answer represents part of the solution. Choose two answers.)

a. In the outdoor furniture company's domain, create a Starter GPO and link this GPO to the appropriate OUs. Then make any necessary changes for each OU.

b. In the outdoor furniture company's domain, create a Starter GPO. Then create GPOs based on the Starter GPO and link them to the appropriate OUs.

c. In the outdoor furniture company's domain, use Group Policy Management Console (GPMC) to back up the GPO linked to the Financial OU. Then import this GPO to the other company's network and link it to the Financial OU in that domain.

d. In the outdoor furniture company's domain, use GPMC to back up the Starter GPO. Then import this GPO to the other company's network and use it to create the appropriate GPO in this network's Financial OU.

100. Jonathan is the systems administrator for his company, which runs a large AD DS network that consists of several domains all contained within two tree structures. The company has operations in both North America and Asia. Jonathan works in the Los Angeles head office, where the root domain is located, including the domain controllers that hold the roles of domain naming master and schema master. One weekend, the domain naming master crashed and the hardware techs discovered that it requires several new parts, including a new SCSI hard drive. The parts will take at least 10 days to be delivered and installed. However, Jonathan urgently needs to create two new domains that will encompass the company's new ventures into Australia. Without a functioning domain naming master, he is unable to create the new domains. He realizes that it is necessary to have another domain controller seize the role of domain naming master.

Which of the following does Jonathan need to do to accomplish this task?

a. Use Active Directory Users and Computers.

b. Use Active Directory Domains and Trusts.

c. Use the `ntdsutil` command-line utility.

d. Install another new computer with Windows Server 2008. Use `dcpromo.exe` to promote it to a domain controller and specify that it is to be a domain naming master.

101. Merle is responsible for securing a new physical printer that her company has purchased especially for printing confidential documents. She installs the printer in a secure office and configures a logical printer for the device on a Windows Server 2008 computer. She also configures the appropriate permissions and enables auditing in a GPO for her company's domain.

After printing several documents to the new printer, she examines the print server's security logs and finds that no entries related to the printer have been recorded. What is the most likely cause for the lack of entries in the security log?

   a. The security log does not record activity by an administrator.

   b. Merle failed to enable auditing in the printer's Properties dialog box.

   c. The events were recorded in a log on the domain controller.

   d. The security log only records attempts by unauthorized users to access the printer.

102. Brandon is the network administrator for a company that operates an AD DS network consisting of a single domain. Servers run a mix of Windows Server 2008 and Windows Server 2008 R2, and client computers run either Windows XP Professional or Windows 7 Professional or Ultimate.

Brandon wants to deploy Active Directory Rights Management Services (AD RMS) to provide rights-enabled protection for sensitive corporate documents. Which of the following additional role services and features must Brandon install when he is installing AD RMS? (Each correct answer represents part of the solution. Choose all that apply.)

   a. Internet Information Services (IIS)

   b. Active Directory Certificate Services (AD CS)

   c. Active Directory Metadirectory Services (AD MDS)

   d. Windows Process Activation Service

   e. Message Queuing Services

103. Andy is the network administrator for a company that runs an AD DS network with a single domain. One of the domain controllers has been running slowly during much of the day, and Andy suspects that he might need to upgrade the processor. Andy has added additional RAM to the computer, but he wants to be informed of potential processor bottlenecks.

Andy decides he wants to have the domain controller inform him when the processor utilization exceeds 85%. What should he do? (Each correct answer represents part of the solution. Choose two answers.)

   a. Configure Windows System Resource Manager to generate an alert when the Processor\%Processor Time counter exceeds 85%.

   b. Configure Performance Monitor to generate an alert when the Processor\%Processor Time counter exceeds 85%.

   c. Configure a data collector set to generate an alert when the Processor\%Processor Time counter exceeds 85%.

   d. In Server Manager, ensure that the Alerter service is configured to start automatically and send a message to his computer. He will then receive a message box on his computer when an alert is created.

   e. View the Application log in Event Viewer to determine whether any alerts have been generated.

   f. View the System log in Event Viewer to determine whether any alerts have been generated.

104. Allison is the network administrator for a company that operates an AD DS network consisting of a single domain. The network includes a standalone root CA and an enterprise subordinate issuing CA.

Allison has configured an autoenrollment certificate template and a GPO that enables users to automatically receive certificates. She needs to provide certificates for routers and switches on the network. How should she proceed?

   a. Install the Simple Certificate Enrollment Protocol (SCEP) on the issuing CA server.

   b. Configure an online responder on the issuing CA server.

   c. Configure a certificate template that includes the Authority Information Access (AIA) extension.

   d. Create a security group that contains the machine accounts for the routers and switches and then grant this group the Autoenroll permission for the required template.

105. Erica is administrator of Acme Construction, which operates an AD DS network consisting of a single domain. Acme is headquartered in Toronto with branch offices in Buffalo, Detroit, and Miami. Erica's companywide domain name will be `acmeconstr.com`. Initially, Erica plans to install a DNS server at headquarters and another in each of the three branch offices. She plans to have the DNS server in Toronto host her company's domain. Additionally, Erica intends to delegate responsibility for maintaining DNS systems and zone information to network administrators located at each of the branch offices.

Which of the following plans will achieve the desired results for Erica?

   a. The DNS server in Toronto will host a standard primary zone for the `acmeconstr.com` domain. Each branch office will host a standard primary zone.

   b. The DNS server in Toronto will host a standard primary zone for the `acmeconstr.com` domain. Branch offices will be configured as subdomains. Each branch office will host a standard secondary zone for its subdomain.

   c. The DNS server in Toronto will host a standard primary zone for the `acmeconstr.com` domain. Branch offices will be configured as subdomains. Each branch office will host a standard primary zone for its subdomain.

    d. The DNS server in Toronto will host a standard primary zone for the `acmeconstr.com` domain. Branch offices will be configured as subdomains. Each branch office will host a stub zone for its subdomain.

106. Trevor is a network administrator for a company that operates an AD DS forest containing two domains in separate trees named `que.com` and `certguide.com`. A junior administrator has accidentally deleted the Financial OU from the `que.com` domain. This domain contains some security groups that have back-links of groups in the `certguide.com` domain as members of these groups.

Trevor authoritatively restores the Financial OU, but users in this OU report that they are unable to access objects in the `certguide.com` domain. He realizes that he should create an LDIF file for recovering the back-links of these groups in the `certguide.com` domain for the authoritatively restored objects in the Financial OU. Which utility should he use to perform this operation?

    a. `Ntdsutil.exe`

    b. `Esentutl.exe`

    c. `Ldifde.exe`

    d. `Wbadmin.exe`

107. Sharon is responsible for configuring BitLocker policies for her company's AD DS domain. More specifically, she needs to ensure that recovery information for the operating system drive in a RODC and located in a branch office is properly backed up to AD DS. She must ensure that the key package used for encrypting the operating system drive is included in the backup. So, she opens up the Group Policy Management Editor focused on the Default Domain Controllers Policy GPO and accesses the **Computer Configuration\Policies\ Administrative Templates\Windows Components\BitLocker Drive Encryption** node. What should she do? (Each answer represents part of the solution. Choose two.)

    a. Enable the **Store BitLocker recovery information in Active Directory Domain Services** policy and select the **Require BitLocker backup to AD DS** check box.

    b. Access the Fixed Data Drives subnode, enable the **Choose how BitLocker protected fixed drives can be recovered** policy, and select the **Require BitLocker backup to AD DS** check box.

    c. Access the Operating System Drives subnode, enable the **Choose how BitLocker protected operating system drives can be recovered** policy, and select the **Require BitLocker backup to AD DS** check box.

    d. Select the **Allow data recovery agent** check box and then select the **Allow 48-digit recovery password** option.

    e. Select the **Store recovery passwords and key packages** option.

    f. Select the **Store recovery passwords only** option.

108. Juan is responsible for configuring certificate autoenrollment for his Windows Server 2008 environment and would like to implement this feature as soon as possible. Juan is considering a third-party solution because he wants to have the most secure environment possible and wants to assign certificates to both users and computers. What should Juan do?

    a. Windows Server 2008 enables Juan to assign certificates to both users and computers. There is no need to use a third-party tool.

    b. Windows Server 2008 offers autoenrollment to users but not to computers. Consequently, he should look for a third-party tool that assigns to computers only.

    c. Juan's instincts are correct. Because Group Policy in Windows Server 2008 can assign certificates to computers only, he should find a third-party tool to do this task.

    d. Certificates are more important for computers. Although in theory it is possible to utilize a third-party tool to assign certificates to users, assigning them to computers gives him better control and is actually more secure.

109. Sandra is the senior administrator of a Windows Server 2003 forest that consists of a single domain, and Ralph is a UNIX administrator who works alongside her. The company's CIO has asked Sandra and Ralph to reduce the total cost of ownership of the two networks by improving the efficiency of user access from one network to the other and reducing the current duplication of resources existing in the Windows and UNIX networks.

Which of the following should Sandra and Ralph do? (Each correct answer represents part of the solution. Choose two answers.)

    a. Create an external trust between the Windows domain and the UNIX realm.

    b. Create a forest trust between the Windows forest and the UNIX realm.

    c. Create a realm trust between the Windows domain and the UNIX realm.

    d. Upgrade the Windows network to Windows Server 2008.

    e. Migrate the UNIX network to Windows Server 2008 AD DS.

110. Kevin is installing a PKI for his company, which operates an AD DS domain in which all servers run Windows Server 2008. He has installed a root CA and is now at the computer that will host an enterprise subordinate CA. However, on the Specify Setup page he discovers that the Enterprise CA option is grayed out and only the Standalone CA option is available. What must Kevin do to install an enterprise subordinate CA on this computer?

   a. Log on to the server as a member of the Enterprise Admins group.

   b. Log on to the server as a member of the Schema Admins group.

   c. Use Server Manager to install AD DS on this server.

   d. Run `dcpromo.exe` to promote the server to a domain controller.

   e. Install a standalone CA on the server and then use the Certification Authority console to promote the server to an enterprise CA.

111. Tricia is a junior administrator for a large enterprise corporation whose Active Directory network contains two domains, seven sites, and 11 OUs, each of which represents a different company department. The IT manager has assigned Tricia the responsibility of administering the Design OU and has provided her with Full Control permission for this OU.

Tricia needs to configure a GPO for deployment of a specialized design application to all employees the Design department of each of the company's offices. These employees should have access to the application at all times, regardless of which department they are accessing the application from. It is not to be available to employees of other departments, even if they are working from computers located in the Design department.

Which of the following steps should Tricia take to deploy this application?

   a. She should create a GPO that is linked to the Design OU. In this GPO, she should add a Windows Installer package for the application under the User Configuration\Policies\Software Settings\Software Installation node. On the Deploy Software dialog box, she should select **Assigned**.

   b. She should create a GPO that is linked to the Design OU. In this GPO, she should add a Windows Installer package for the application under the Computer Configuration\Policies\Software Settings\Software Installation node. On the Deploy Software dialog box, she should select **Assigned**.

   c. She should create a GPO that is linked to the Design OU. In this GPO, she should add a Windows Installer package for the application under the User Configuration\Policies\Software Settings\Software Installation node. On the Deploy Software dialog box, she should select **Published**.

   d. She should create a GPO that is linked to the Design OU. In this GPO, she should add a Windows Installer package for the application under the Computer Configuration\Policies\Software Settings\Software Installation node. On the Deploy Software dialog box, she should select **Published**.

112. Maggie is the network administrator for a company that operates an AD DS forest containing two geographically distinct domains: `que.com` located in

Atlanta and `west.que.com` located in San Jose. Each domain has a single site named by its city and containing three domain controllers. The two sites are connected by an ISDN link.

Maggie is configuring the placement of global catalog servers to optimize user logon and resource access. Which of the following configurations should she use?

a.   Place a single global catalog server at the Atlanta site only.

b.   Place a single global catalog server at each site.

c.   Place two global catalog servers at the Atlanta site only.

d.   Place two global catalog servers at the San Jose site only.

e.   Place two global catalog servers at each site.

113. Sam is a domain administrator for a company that operates a single domain AD DS network. All servers run Windows Server 2008 R2. Sam needs to grant a junior administrator named Julie the ability to create child OUs in the company's Employees OU. She needs to verify the existence of the OUs she creates, but she should not be able to perform other administrative tasks. Sam accesses the Delegation of Control Wizard and specifies Julie's user account. Which of the following should he do?

a.   Select the **Create a custom task to delegate** option, select **Organizational Unit** objects, and then grant Julie the **Read** and **Write** permissions.

b.   Select the **Create a custom task to delegate** option and then select the option labeled **This folder, existing objects in this folder, and creation of new objects in this folder**.

c.   Select the **Delegate the following common tasks** option and then select **Create, delete, and manage OUs**.

d.   Select the **Create a custom task to delegate** option, select **Organizational Unit** objects, and then grant Julie the **Read** and **Create all child objects** permissions.

114. Jane is the network administrator for a company whose AD DS forest includes a domain tree called `que.org` with child domains named `calif.que.org`, `ariz.que.org`, and `texas.que.org`. In the California domain there is an OU named Sales. This OU contains a user named Don Smith. Jane has implemented several GPOs within the domain, including the following:

—Site Group Policy: Wallpaper is set to Green. Task Manager is disabled.

—Domain Group Policy: Display Properties tab is disabled (**Enforced** setting is selected). Task Manager is not disabled.

—OU1 Policy: Wallpaper is set to Red. The Display Properties tab is enabled. (**Block Inheritance** is set to On.)

—OU2 Policy: Wallpaper is set to Blue.

The OU policies are set in the order of OU1 being on top and OU2 on the bottom of the application order list. What is the resultant set of policies?

a. Don logs on and his wallpaper is red. Task Manager is not disabled. Display Properties is disabled.

b. Don logs on and his wallpaper is green. Task Manager is disabled. Display Properties is enabled.

c. Don logs on and his wallpaper is blue. Task Manager is not disabled. Display Properties is disabled.

d. Don logs on and his wallpaper is green. Task Manager is disabled.

115. Nancy is a systems administrator for her company, which has just purchased a new computer running Windows Server 2008 R2. She has installed this computer as a DNS server on the internal network and has assigned it a static IP address of 172.22.1.3. She accesses the Monitoring tab of the server's properties dialog box on the DNS snap-in, selects the simple and recursive query test type, and then runs these tests. However, she receives a `Fail` response in both test columns.

What should Nancy try first to troubleshoot this failure?

a. Determine whether the root hints are correct.

b. Restart the DNS server service.

c. Access the **Debug Logging** tab and specify logging of incoming and outgoing packets with the Queries/Transfers option.

d. Determine whether the server contains the `1.0.0.127.in-addr.arpa` zone.

116. Roy is the network administrator for Que, which operates a single AD DS domain named `que.com`. Servers run a mix of Windows Server 2008 and Windows Server 2008 R2, and client computers run a mix of Windows XP Professional and Windows 7 Enterprise. Que's main office is located in Buffalo and there is a branch office in Rochester. Roy creates a GPO that redirects the Start menu for users in the Rochester office to a shared folder on a file server.

Users in Rochester report that many of the programs they normally use are missing from their Start menus, even though the programs were available on the Start menu the previous day. Logging on to one of the client computers, Roy notices that all the programs in question are present on the Start menu. Roy verifies that users can access the shared folder on the server. He needs to find out why the Start menu changed for the affected users. How can he accomplish this task? (Each correct answer represents a complete solution to the problem. Choose two answers.)

a. On one of the affected computers, run the `gpresult` command.

b. On one of the affected computers, run the `gpupdate` command.

c. In the Group Policy Management Console, right-click the **Group Policy Results** node and choose **Group Policy Results Wizard**.

d. In the Group Policy Management Console, right-click the **Group Policy Modeling** node and choose **Group Policy Modeling Wizard**.

e. In Active Directory Sites and Services, right-click the **Rochester** site and choose **All Tasks > Resultant Set of Policy (Planning)**.

117. Gary is the network administrator for a company that has entered into a partnership relationship with a second company. He has set up an Active Directory Federation Services (AD FS) server to enable users in the second company to access web-based data by means of a single sign-on capability.

Gary wants to test which claims the Federation Service sends in AD FS security tokens. Which of the following should he configure?

a. A Windows token-based agent

b. A Federation Service proxy

c. A trust policy

d. A claims-aware application

118. Ian is the administrator of a company that operates an AD DS network that contains two domains. Both domains operate at the Windows Server 2003 domain and forest functional levels. He has installed a new Windows Server 2008 computer and promoted this server to be an additional domain controller in his domain.

Having heard about the new capability of configuring fine-grained password policies, Ian decides to give it a try and configure a PSO that specifies a minimum of 10 characters. He then associates this PSO with his user account and attempts to change his password to a new one that is 8 characters long.

When this attempt succeeds, Ian wonders why the new PSO was not applied to his account. Which of the following is the reason Ian was able to specify an eight-character password?

a. Ian needs to associate the PSO with a global security group to which his user account belongs before it is applied.

b. Ian needs to associate the PSO with an OU to which his user account belongs before it is applied.

c. Ian needs to upgrade all domain controllers in the domain to Windows Server 2008 or Windows Server 2008 R2 and set the domain functional level to Windows Server 2008 or higher before the PSO is effective.

d. Ian needs to upgrade all domain controllers in both domains of the forest to Windows Server 2008 or Windows Server 2008 R2 and set the domain and forest functional levels to Windows Server 2008 or higher before the PSO is effective.

119. Kas is a systems engineer for a company that operates an AD DS domain with two Windows Server 2003 domain controllers and three Windows Server 2008 domain controllers. She is responsible for assigning the flexible single-master operations (FSMO) roles to specific domain controllers for optimum network functionality.

Kas needs to ensure proper synchronization of the system clocks on all computers on the network. To this end, she wants to have one of the Windows Server 2008 domain controllers look after this requirement. Which of the following roles should she assign to this domain controller?

a. Domain naming master

b. Schema master

c. Infrastructure master

d. PDC emulator

e. RID master

120. Nellie is the network administrator for a financial company that operates a series of branch offices in major North American cities. The company operates an AD DS network consisting of a single domain, in which each office is configured as its own site. To improve the efficiency of intersite replication, Nellie has decided that she needs to create a site link bridge.

Which of the following steps should Nellie perform to accomplish this task? (Each correct answer represents part of the solution. Choose three answers.)

a. In the console tree of Active Directory Sites and Services, right-click the **Inter-Site Transports** folder and choose **New Site Link Bridge**.

b. In the console tree of Active Directory Sites and Services, right-click the **Simple Mail Transport Protocol (SMTP)** folder and choose **New Site Link Bridge**.

c. In the console tree of Active Directory Sites and Services, right-click the **IP** folder and choose **New Site Link Bridge**.

d. In the New Object—Site Link Bridge dialog box, type a name for the site link bridge.

e. In the New Object—Site Link Bridge dialog box, select at least two sites she wants bridged and then click **Add**.

f. In the New Object—Site Link Bridge dialog box, select at least two site links she wants bridged and then click **Add**.

g. In the New Object—Site Link Bridge dialog box, select the check box labeled **Bridge all site links**.

Answers to Practice Exam

1. **A.** Brett should install the AD RMS client software on all Windows XP client computers. In addition, he should ensure that these computers have Service Pack 2 (SP2) or higher installed. This software is available for download from Microsoft and is required to enable users on Windows XP computers to create rights-protected content. Brett could upgrade these computers to Windows Vista, but this would require far more administrative effort and expense, so answer B is incorrect. It is not necessary to upgrade domain controllers to Windows Server 2008 or install AD MDS on a server; neither of these actions would enable users on Windows XP computers to create rights-protected content, so answers C and D are incorrect. For more information, see the section "Installing AD RMS" in Chapter 7.

2. **A, C.** Shirley should edit the Default Domain Policy GPO to specify auditing and account lockout parameters for the domain. She must also monitor each domain controller's security log for failed logon attempts. Auditing enables Shirley to discover when and where any failed logon attempts occur. Account Management includes items such as the creation, change, or deletion of a user or group account, and also the renaming, disabling, or enabling of a user account or change of password. Auditing and monitoring of these events would not meet the requirements of this scenario, so answer B is incorrect. Configuring local security policy on each computer would apply only to these computers and not to the domain controllers that authenticate users on the domain. Therefore answer D is incorrect. For more information, see the section "Use of GPOs to Configure Auditing" in Chapter 13.

3. **C.** The 4006 error means that the DNS name contains characters that are not supported by the default Multibyte (UTFB) name checking setting. Selecting the **All names** option enables the translation of DNS names containing any type of characters. Logging of incoming and outgoing packets would provide Phil with information concerning the type of data passing through the DNS server but would not prevent these errors, so answer A is incorrect. The cache.dns file is not at fault here, so answer B is incorrect. The Strict RFC (ANSI) option would use strict name checking and could

actually make this situation worse and generate more 4006 errors than observed, so answer D is incorrect. For more information, see the section "Advanced Server Options" in Chapter 4.

4. **F, A, I, D, B.** Edward must perform these steps in the specified sequence to perform an authoritative restore of the system state on the domain controller. He must restart the domain controller in Directory Services Restore Mode and log on as the local administrator (not the domain administrator). At a command prompt, he must first use the `wbadmin get versions` command to obtain information on the available backup target that he feeds into the `wbadmin start systemstaterecovery` command. When the restore is complete, he uses `ntdsutil` to mark the restore of the Management OU as authoritative and then restarts the domain controller normally. Note that the exam might present a question of this nature in which you must drag the required tasks to a work area and drop them in the correct sequence and that the answer will be scored as incorrect if the tasks are not in the correct sequence even if the list contains all the correct tasks. Edward cannot perform this task by stopping and restarting AD DS; he must use Directory Services Restore Mode, so answers C and J are incorrect. He would use the **Repair your computer** option only if performing a full server recovery, which is not required here. Therefore, answer E is incorrect. The network must be running at the Windows Server 2008 R2 domain and forest functional levels to enable and use the Active Directory Recycle Bin, so answer G is incorrect. He would use the `wbadmin start recovery` command to recover a specified set of volumes, files, or folders, but not to restore System State as required in this scenario. Therefore, answer H is incorrect. For more information, see the section "Recovering Active Directory" in Chapter 15.

5. **B, E.** Mike should configure each RODC with a password replication policy that includes Christina's user account in the Allowed list. This ensures that her password is stored locally so that she can log on to the RODC even if the connection to the head office is down. Mike should also add Christina's user account to each RODC's local Administrators group. This provides her with administrative rights to the RODC, without granting her domain administrative rights. Placing Christina's user account in the Denied list would prevent her from logging on to the RODC, so answer A is incorrect. Adding her user account to the Domain Admins global group would grant her excessive administrative privileges, so answer C is incorrect. Adding her user account to the Server Operators global group would also grant her excessive administrative privileges and would also not provide complete local administrative capabilities on the RODC, so answer D is incorrect. For more information, see the sections "Administrator Role Separation" and "Replication of Passwords" in Chapter 8.

6. D. The Delegation of Control Wizard enables Veronica to delegate the task of managing Group Policy links, which provides the administrators in the other domains the ability to apply the GPOs but not modify them. She has to do this once for each domain within which she wants to delegate control. The Group Policy Management Console does not offer the ability to delegate administrative control, so answers A and B are incorrect. It is not possible to delegate control of users or groups, only of sites, domains, or OUs, so answer C is incorrect. For more information, see the section "Delegating Administrative Control of Active Directory Objects" in Chapter 9 and "Delegating Control of GPOs" in Chapter 11.

7. C. Roy should restart the Netlogon service at the suburban office domain controller. Doing so re-registers the domain controller's SRV resource records. He can perform this action from the Services branch of Server Manager or by typing **net stop netlogon** followed by **net start netlogon**. Neither the DNS Server service nor the DNS Client service is responsible for re-registering the SRV resource records, so answers A and B are incorrect. He could re-register these records by rebooting the domain controller, but this would take more time, so answer D is incorrect. For more information, see the section "DNS Resource Records" in Chapter 2.

8. A, B, D. Some of the tools Oliver can use include Event Viewer, dcdiag, and repadmin. The Event Viewer logs enable him to view errors and warnings that might indicate the source of a replication problem. dcdiag performs a series of tests that verify different functional areas of the domain controller, including connectivity, replication, topology integrity, trust verification, replication latency, replication of trust objects, and so on. repadmin provides information related to directory replication failures. In particular, its /showreps command displays the replication partners, both inbound and outbound, the time of the last replication attempt and whether or not it was successful. The /showconn command displays the connection objects for the domain controller, the enabled state of the replication, and the transport protocol in use. Oliver can also use the replmon tool to monitor Active Directory replication. He could also use the NTDS object in Reliability and Performance Monitor, which contains a series of counters that monitor functionality within Active Directory, including the Directory Replication Agent. Ntdsutil is an administrative tool that enables Oliver to perform a range of actions including transfer and seizure of operations master roles, authoritative restores, and offline database defragmentation, but it does not provide information on replication problems. Therefore answer C is incorrect. For more information, see the section "Monitoring and Troubleshooting Active Directory Replication" in Chapter 14.

9. A, C, D, F, I, K. To install an RODC in your AD DS forest, your forest must meet the following requirements:

    ■ The domain and forest functional levels must be at least Windows Server 2003. Consequently, all domain controllers in all domains of the forest must run Windows Server 2003 or higher.

    ■ You must run `Adprep/forestprep` on the schema master of the forest before introducing Windows Server 2008 domain controllers.

    ■ You must run `Adprep/domainprep` at the infrastructure master of each domain in which you plan to introduce Windows Server 2008 domain controllers.

    ■ The PDC emulator must be running on a Windows Server 2008 computer in the domain in which you plan to introduce an RODC—in this case, the forest root domain.

    ■ You must run `Adprep/rodcprep` at the PDC emulator of the domain in which you plan to introduce an RODC.

    All these steps are necessary and should be performed in the order given here before you can introduce an RODC. It is not necessary to upgrade all domain controllers in the forest to Windows Server 2008, nor to raise the domain and forest functional levels to Windows Server 2008, so answers B and E are incorrect. You must run the `Adprep /forestprep` command at the schema master and not the domain naming master, so answer G is incorrect. You must run the `Adprep /rodcprep` command at the infrastructure master and not the RID master, so answer H is incorrect. You must run the `Adprep /rodcprep` command at the PDC emulator and not the infrastructure master, so answer J is incorrect. For more information, see the sections "Upgrading a Windows Server 2003 Domain Controller" and "The `Adprep` Utility" in Chapter 3 and "Planning the Use of RODCs" in Chapter 8.

10. D. Stephanie should create user accounts for the new users in the existing domain and specify an alternative UPN suffix of que.com. She can specify this UPN suffix in Active Directory Domains and Trusts, and then it will be available when she creates the user accounts in Active Directory Users and Computers. Creating a new forest or domain tree named que.com would require considerable additional administrative effort and is not required by this scenario, so answers A and B are incorrect. It is not possible to simply assign the user accounts user logon names in the format of user@que.com without first specifying que.com as an alternative UPN suffix, so answer C is incorrect. For more information, see the sections "Alternate User Principal Name (UPN) Suffixes" in Chapter 3 and "Configuring the UPN" in Chapter 9.

11. A. Scott should access the template's Request Handling tab. He should select the **Signature and Encryption** option from the Purpose drop-down list and then select **Archive subject's encryption private key**. This option is not available if he has selected **Signature** from the Purpose drop-down list because the Signature option requires that the key not be recoverable. The **Allow private key to be exported** option only allows users to export keys for backup; it does not provide for key archival, so answer B is incorrect. Scott does not require a version 3 template to enable key archival, so answer C is incorrect. Key archival does not require the ability to autoenroll certificates, so answer D is incorrect. For more information, see the section "Configuring Certificate Templates" in Chapter 17.

12. A, F. Donna should select the **Automatically notify** check box. She should also select **The following servers** and specify IP address information for Taurus02 and Taurus03. This enables these two servers to be kept up-to-date regarding the status of the DNS zone. Clearing the **Automatically notify** check box eliminates the other options found in the dialog box from further consideration, so answer B is incorrect. Specifying the **Servers listed on the Name Servers tab** option would not enable Taurus03 to be notified of updates, so answer C is incorrect. Taurus01 is the master DNS server, and as such, should not be specified in the Notify list, so answer D is incorrect. In this scenario, the domain controllers Scorpio01 and Scorpio02 are not running DNS, so answer E is incorrect. For more information, see the section "Configuring DNS Notify" in Chapter 4.

13. C. By creating a forest trust, Mark can enable transitive trust relationships between all domains of the forests involved. In this scenario, the forest trust is the best option because users require access to more than one domain in the other company's forest. Mark could create external trusts between various child domains. This would take more administrative effort, so answer A is incorrect. A shortcut trust is a shortened path between two child domains in the same forest and not between two different forests, so answer B is incorrect. No need exists for reconfiguring the other company's forest as a second tree in Mark's company's forest, so answer D is incorrect. For more information, see the section "Forest Trusts" in Chapter 10.

14. C. Carolyn should create a site link bridge that encompasses the Duluth-to-Minneapolis and Minneapolis-to-Chicago site links and then set the cost of the 56 Kbps link to 300. The use of a site link bridge enables her to route AD DS replication across a pair of fast links rather than a single, much slower link. The cost of a site link bridge is the sum of the costs of the site links contained within it. In this case, it is 200 (when costs are not provided, you should assume that the cost of each site link is the default value of 100). Consequently, Carolyn must set the cost of the 56 Kbps link to a value greater than the cost of the site link bridge so that replication preferentially follows the two T1 links rather than the slower 56 Kbps link. Simple Mail Transport Protocol (SMTP) replication replicates only the schema and configuration partitions between different domains, so answer A is incorrect. Configuring the 56 Kbps link to be available outside business hours only would prevent daytime replication, but replication would still use this link at other times, so answer B is incorrect. It is not possible to specify a cost for a site link bridge, so answer D is incorrect. For more information, see the section "Site Link Bridges" in Chapter 6.

15. **A.** The schema master and domain naming master are forestwide roles and the other three FSMO roles are domainwide roles. Consequently, there is one schema master and one domain naming master, plus six RID masters, six PDC emulators, and six infrastructure masters in this forest. Even though the root domain is configured as an empty root domain, it has one of each of the domainwide FSMO roles, so answer B is incorrect. Because the schema master and domain naming master are forestwide roles, only one of each is required and answer C is incorrect. Every domain must have its own RID master, PDC emulator, and infrastructure master, so answer D is incorrect. For more information, see the section "Configuring Operations Masters" in Chapter 5.

16. **B.** Jackie should implement role-based administration in the CA hierarchy. This enables her to assign different predefined task-based roles such as PKI Administrator, Certificate Manager, and Key Recovery Manager to different individuals. Doing so reduces the chance that the entire PKI would be compromised should one user account become compromised. Use of a special user account with a strong password and a Password Settings Object (PSO) to enforce a strong password might help to prevent the account's compromise, but it is still preferable to implement role-based administration, so answer A is incorrect. Configuring the subordinate CA servers so that certificate enrollment and renewal take place on different servers would not help here, so answer C is incorrect. Reconfiguring the offline standalone root CA as an offline enterprise root CA would prevent it from being up-to-date and is not recommended, so answer D is incorrect. Placing this machine online would increase the risk of compromising the entire CA hierarchy, so answer E is incorrect. For more information, see the section "Assigning Administration Roles" in Chapter 16.

17. **B.** Justin should select the **Prompt the user during enrollment and require user input when the private key is used** option. This option causes a message box to be displayed asking the user to input her PIN. The **Prompt the user during enrollment** option does not require that the PIN be entered, so answer A is incorrect. The **Authorize additional service accounts to access the private key** option allows a custom ACL to be specified on the private keys of computer certificates except the root CA, subordinate CA, or cross-CA templates. This is not used for user-based certificates, so answer C is incorrect.

Justin might need to select the **Allow private key to be exported** option to enable the export of private keys associated with the smart card certificates as a backup precaution. However, this option does not require input of the PIN, so answer D is incorrect. For more information, see the section "Configuring Certificate Templates" in Chapter 17.

18. B. Luke should use the New Delegation Wizard in the DNS console to delegate control of the new zone to the NS03 server computer. The wizard automatically creates the A and NS resource records required by the NS03 server. Manually creating and configuring these records would require an excessive amount of administrative effort, so answers A and C are incorrect. Aside from the fact that delegation takes precedence over forwarding if Luke added the appropriate IP address for NS03 to the Forwarders tab on the NS01 and NS02 server computers, those computers would still need to handle queries for the new zone in some fashion. Therefore answer D is incorrect. For more information, see the section "Configuring Zone Delegation" in Chapter 4.

19. A. Windows Management Instrumentation (WMI) filters enable Rob to specify a query that filters the effect of a GPO. Rob can configure the WMI filter on the WMI Filters node of the Group Policy Management Console (GPMC). Hardware chassis type–information is a type of information that can be entered into the query. Creating a global group and moving the computer accounts of all portable computers to this group would also take more administrative effort than using a WMI filter, so answer B is incorrect. Rob could accomplish the required task by means of creating child OUs in each department and linking the GPO to these OUs, but this would take far more administrative effort than using a WMI filter, so answer C is incorrect. If he were to create a single OU to hold the portable computer accounts and enforce the restriction on this OU, policies in other GPOs linked to departmental OUs would no longer apply, so answer D is incorrect. For more information, see the section "Windows Management Instrumentation" in Chapter 11.

20. B. Debbie should place the users into global groups and then place the global groups into universal groups. She should then place the universal groups into domain local groups. Because of the manner in which universal group membership changes are replicated as she has configured them here, the user objects are being referenced and creating excess replication. Simply placing the universal groups into domain local groups while still adding the users directly to the universal groups does not reduce replication traffic, so answer A is incorrect. Local groups are local to the machine on which they are created and are not available to the domain, so answer C is incorrect. As already explained, the universal group configuration is creating this large quantity of replication traffic, so answer D is incorrect. For more information, see the section "AGDLP/AGUDLP" in Chapter 9.

21. B, C, D, F. To use the Active Directory Recycle Bin, the domain and forest functional levels must both be raised to Windows Server 2008 R2. This requires that all domain controllers be upgraded to Windows Server 2008 R2. After Lynn has performed these tasks, she can enable the Active Directory Recycle Bin, which she can do by using either the `Enable-ADOptionalFeature` cmdlet in Windows PowerShell or the `Ldp.exe` command-line utility. Lynn does not need to upgrade the member servers to Windows Server 2008 R2 in order to raise the functional levels, so answer A is incorrect. She cannot use either the `Ldifde.exe` command-line utility or the Registry Editor to enable the Active Directory Recycle Bin, so answers E and H are incorrect. For more information, see the sections "The Active Directory Recycle Bin" in Chapter 15 and "Forest and Domain Functional Levels" in Chapter 3.

22. B. The RID master keeps track of all relative identifiers (RIDs) assigned within its domain and issues blocks of 500 RIDs to all other domain controllers in the domain so that administrators can create accounts. If this computer becomes unavailable, Elaine can create new user accounts until the available pool of RIDs is exhausted, after which new account creation will fail until the RID master can issue a new pool of RIDs. The infrastructure master is not involved in user account creation, so answer A is unavailable. If the `.csv` file had become corrupted, Elaine would have been able to manually add the principals' user accounts, so answer C is incorrect. It is not necessary to replicate the user accounts to other domain controllers before continuing to add additional accounts, so answer D is incorrect. For more information, see the section "RID Master" in Chapter 5.

23. B. Tom should select the **Federation Service Proxy** option. This service serves as a proxy to the Federation Service on a perimeter network or demilitarized zone. This service uses WS-Federation Passive Requestor Profile (WS-FPRP) protocols to obtain user credentials from browser clients, and it forwards this information to the Federation Service on their behalf. Tom should not install the Federation Service on a perimeter network server, so answer A is incorrect. The Claims-aware Agent service works with claims-aware applications and the Windows Token-based Agent service supports conversion from an AD FS security token to a Windows NT access token by means of Windows-based authorization mechanisms. Neither of these (which together make up the AD FS Web agent) are needed in this scenario, so answers C, D, and E are all incorrect. Note that on the exam, a question such as this one might be presented as a "hot-spot" item in which you must select the correct option directly from the exhibit as displayed on the interface. For more information, see the section "Installing the AD FS Server Role" in Chapter 7.

24. D. The `repadmin` utility with the `/showmeta` option displays a list of updated attributes in the AD DS database, together with their update sequence numbers (USNs), thereby providing Hazel with the information she needs. Neither the NTDS performance object counters nor the Resource Monitor feature of Windows System Resource Manager provides this information, so answers A and B are incorrect. Hazel could use `replmon`, but she would have to right-click the server and choose **Properties**. The **Update Status (only for this server)** option simply updates the date and time of the most recent replication, so answer C is incorrect. For more information, see the section "Repadmin" in Chapter 14.

25. D. The fact that users were able to run Excel after double-clicking on an Excel spreadsheet but that it was not available from the Start menu indicates that the software was published to the users rather than assigned. Richard can ensure that all users can run Excel by changing its deployment type from **Published** to **Assigned**, which he can do from the Deployment tab of the package's Properties dialog box. The `gpresult` command would show the policy settings that are being applied. However, the problem here is not whether the policy settings were applied, rather it was the deployment type that Richard had selected, so answer A is incorrect. The `Gpupdate` command refreshes the application of policy settings. Again, the problem is not the application of policy settings, so answer B is incorrect. The application should be assigned to users and not published, so answer C is incorrect. For more information, see the sections "Assigning and Publishing Software" and "Software Package Properties" in Chapter 12.

26. C. AD DS uses the concept of sites to include physically distinct portions of a network that are well connected internally but separated from other portions of the network by a slow link such as a WAN connection. By designating the branch office as an Active Directory site, Brent can ensure that users in that office authenticate to the domain controller in the same office. He can also configure the intersite replication interval to balance the conservation of bandwidth with the rapid availability of AD DS changes between the two offices. Creating an OU for the branch office does not cause users to always authenticate to the branch office domain controller, nor does it regulate replication traffic between the two offices; therefore, answer A is incorrect. In a scenario like this one where only one site link exists, the site link cost is immaterial, so answer B is incorrect. It is not possible to specify a zero replication interval; this number is processed as the nearest multiple of 15 minutes from 15 to 10,080 minutes (one week); therefore, answer D is incorrect. For more information, see the section "The Need for Active Directory Sites" in Chapter 6.

27. B. To ensure that DNS2 can receive zone transfers from DNS1, Alfredo should select the **BIND secondaries** option on DNS1. Selection of this option prevents DNS1 from performing fast zone transfers to the secondary DNS server (DNS2). This is needed in this case because older UNIX servers, running versions of BIND earlier than version 4.9.4, cannot handle fast zone transfers. Selecting **Disable recursion** prevents a DNS server from querying other DNS servers for name resolution. Round robin rotates the order of matching resource records in the response list for the web server addresses returned to DNS clients. The **Fail on load if bad zone data** option causes a DNS server to reject zone transfers if errors are discovered in the transfer. The **Enable netmask ordering** option causes the DNS server to reorder the A resource records based on local subnet priority if the request is for a multihomed computer. The **Secure cache against pollution** option prevents unauthorized users from adding resource records from nonauthoritative servers to the DNS cache. None of these options enable DNS2 to receive zone transfers as required for this scenario, so answers A, C, D, E, and F are incorrect. For more information, see the section "Server Options" in Chapter 4.

28. C. Maria should create ADML files and copy them to the `%systemroot%\sysvol\ domain\policies\PolicyDefinitions\[language]` folder on the domain controller. ADML files are language-specific policy definition files that enable administrators to apply the policies in the localized languages. In this case, `[language]` would be `FR-CA` for French-language files and `ES` for Spanish-language files. She would not use ADMX files because these are not language-specific, so answer A is incorrect. She does not need to copy these files to every client computer that requires them because they are distributed from domain controllers, so answers B and D are incorrect. For more information, see the section "ADMX Central Store" in Chapter 11.

29. B, C, E, F, G. Peter needs to perform all these steps to enable autoenrollment of certificates on his Windows Server 2008–based PKI. He must create a duplicate of the template previously used for enrollment in Windows 2000 because Windows 2000–based templates do not support autoenrollment. The option for prompting the user enables the user to provide any required input such as a PIN for a smart card. Users must have the Read, Enroll, and Autoenroll permissions for autoenrollment to succeed. Peter then needs to complete the task by enabling the template in the Certificate Templates node of the Certification Authority snap-in and configuring an appropriate GPO to enroll certificates automatically. Peter does not need to configure another Windows Server 2008 computer to enable autoenrollment, so answer A is incorrect. The Read and Enroll permissions are insufficient to enable autoenrollment; users must have the Autoenroll permission as well, so answer D is incorrect. For more information, see the sections "Managing Certificate Templates" and "Certificate Autoenrollment" in Chapter 17.

30. D. Laura needs to create a global security group and add the required users to this group. She then needs to create a password settings object containing the required password settings and apply this object to the group containing these users. The new fine-grained password policy in Windows Server 2008 enables her to create a password policy that applies only to specified users or groups. Laura cannot link a GPO to a group, so answer A is incorrect. Laura could create a new domain and apply the policy in this manner. This was the method she would have needed to do before Windows Server 2008; however, application of a fine-grained password policy takes far less administrative effort and expense, so answer B is incorrect. It is not possible to apply a fine-grained password policy to an OU, so answer C is incorrect. For more information, see the section "Fine-Grained Password Policies" in Chapter 13.

31. B, C, D. Kathy should install AD FS on an internal server and create a federated trust. She should also install an AD FS proxy on the perimeter network, as well as an AD FS web agent. The proxy enables external users to access the web application and the web agent authenticates these users, managing the security tokens and authentication cookies required by the web server. This scenario does not require rights-protected documents, so she does not need to install an AD RMS server and answer A is incorrect. Use of either an AD LDS server or a domain controller on the perimeter network would require that she administer user accounts for the external users. Use of AD FS eliminates this need, so answers E and F are incorrect. For more information, see the section "Active Directory Federation Services (ADFS)" in Chapter 7.

32. F, C. Karen must run the `Adprep /forestprep` command on the schema master and then she must run the `Adprep /domainprep` command on the infrastructure master. She cannot run the `Adprep /domainprep` command on the PDC emulator or the schema master, so answers A and E are incorrect. She cannot run the `Adprep /forestprep` command on the PDC emulator or the domain naming master, so answers B and D are incorrect.

You should note that in an "ordered list" or "build list and reorder" exam question, you must place the required items in the proper order for the answer to be scored correct. Therefore, specifying the answer to this question as "C, F" is incorrect. A question of this type would appear as a "drag-and-drop" question type on the exam. For more information, see the section "The `Adprep` Utility" in Chapter 3.

33. A. Rick should place the infrastructure master on a domain controller that does not host the global catalog but has a direct connection to a global catalog server. If he places the infrastructure master on a global catalog server, the infrastructure master would be unable to locate any outdated data and therefore it would never update that data. Consequently, answers B and C are incorrect. For the infrastructure master to function properly, it should be located in the same site as a global catalog server, so answer D is incorrect. For more information, see the section "Placement of Operations Masters" in Chapter 5.

34. C. Bill should grant the CertMgrs group the CA Administrator administrative role. He can do this by granting this group the **Allow-Issue and Manage Certificates** permission on the CA server. This is one of several role-based administrative roles available in Windows Server 2008 that enable him to assign predefined task-based roles to users or groups. Granting the CertMgrs group the **Allow-Manage CA** permission on the CA server would assign them the PKI Administrator role, which provides these users with excessive privileges, so answer A is incorrect. Issuing them the Enrollment Agent certificate would enable them to enroll certificates based on other users, but would not grant them the ability to revoke certificates, so answer B is incorrect. As already stated, the PKI Administrator role provides excessive privileges, so answer D is incorrect. For more information, see the section "Assigning Administration Roles" in Chapter 16.

35. B, E. Gerry can solve this problem by adding a stub zone for `prep.certguide.com` on `dns1.certguide.com` or by configuring zone delegation for `prep.certguide.com` on `dns1.certguide.com`. A stub zone is a read-only copy of a zone that stores only those resource records necessary to identify the authoritative DNS servers for that zone. It enables the DNS server hosting a parent zone to be aware of the authoritative DNS servers for the child zone, thereby enabling clients to find the intranet server. Delegation of a zone to a child zone on another DNS server enables the parent to be aware of new authoritative DNS servers for the child zone, also solving this problem. Adding a stub zone for `certguide.com` on `dns2.prep.certguide.com` is in the wrong direction for solving this problem, so answer A is incorrect. Simply adding A records to zone information doesn't let either DNS server know where the start of authority (SOA) for a particular zone resides, so answers C and D are incorrect. DNS uses PTR resource records to resolve IP addresses to their corresponding fully qualified domain names (FQDNs); the scenario does not indicate any problem with this action, so answer F is incorrect. For more information, see the sections "Stub Zones" in Chapter 2 and "Configuring Zone Delegation" in Chapter 4.

36. B. Connie needs to configure one site link only. She should specify that replication be available from noon to 1 PM and also during the nighttime hours. This enables her to meet the requirement of one replication during the day as well as the need for complete overnight synchronization. By allowing the daytime link to replicate between noon and 1 PM only, she has selected a time when traffic would likely be lower. Connie could manually force replication once a day; however, doing so takes daily effort, so answer A is incorrect. Site link costs do not influence the replication interval; they only enable the KCC to select the best link, so answer C is incorrect. Connie could configure two site links with two distinct replication schedules. However, this would take more effort than creating a single link, so answer D is incorrect. If Connie were to set a four-hour daytime replication interval, replication would occur several times during the day. However, she needs only one replication during the day, so answer E is incorrect. For more information, see the section "Site Links, Site Link Bridges, and Bridgehead Servers" in Chapter 6.

37. A, C, D. Stephanie should configure certificate templates, CRLs, or online responders, and key archival and recovery before she begins issuing certificates to users on her network. When she installs Certificate Services together with IIS, the Certificate Services web pages are automatically installed and configured. They need no further configuration, so answer B is incorrect. For more information, see the sections "Managing Certificate Templates" and "Managing Certificate Revocation" in Chapter 17.

38. B. The problem here is that Steven attempted to assign permissions for a resource on one machine to a local group configured on a different machine. In contrast to a domain local group, a local group can be used to configure permissions on resources on its computer only. So, Steven needs to use a domain local group and the recommended solution follows the AGDLP strategy. It is not possible to add a domain local group to a global group, so answer A is incorrect. Creating local user accounts for each user on the file server is not the recommended strategy, so answer C is incorrect. Network connectivity is the problem; he cannot use a local group from one computer on another one, so answer D is incorrect. For more information, see the section "Configuring Group Membership" in Chapter 9.

39. A, B, C, D, E, F. All these criteria are available from which Cassandra can create a custom log that displays the types of events that she wants to monitor. She can also select other criteria such as the source of the event (services, programs, or drivers) and keywords associated with the event such as Audit Success, Audit Failure, and so on. For more information, see the section "Customizing Event Viewer" in Chapter 14.

40. C. Heidi should run the Dnscmd /zoneinfo command. This command displays Registry-based configuration information for the specified DNS zone. She would include the zone name as a parameter in this command and would repeat the command as required to obtain information on additional zones. The Dnscmd /enumzones command displays a list of zones configured on the server. The Dnscmd /statistics command displays or clears statistical data for the server. The Dnscmd /info command displays Registry-based server configuration information. None of these commands provide zone configuration information, so answers A, B, and D are incorrect. For more information, see the section "Command-Line DNS Server Administration" in Chapter 2.

41. B, D. By selecting the **Required upgrade for existing packages** check box on the Upgrades tab of the package's Properties dialog box, Bob ensures that the upgrade is mandatory; in other words, Office 2003 is automatically upgraded to Office 2007 without the users having an option. By selecting the **Package can upgrade over the existing package** option, Bob ensures that the user's application preferences, document type associations, and so on are retained. The **Advanced** deployment option is used for adding modifications to existing packages, not for configuring upgrades, so answer A is incorrect. The **Uninstall the existing package, then install the upgrade package** option totally removes all references to the previous version, including components such as spell check dictionaries, so answer C is incorrect. The **Immediately uninstall the software from users and computers** option would also remove components such as spell check dictionaries, so answer E is incorrect. For more information, see the section "Upgrading Software" in Chapter 12.

42. A. Ted should create two one-way external trust relationships in which the `certguide.com` and `corp.que.com` domains trust the `que.com` domain. In this scenario, permissions need to flow in only one direction, so CertGuide needs to trust Que. If the trust is created such that the `que.com` and `corp.que.com` domains trust the `certguide.com` domain, this is the wrong direction, so answer B is incorrect. It is not possible to create a forest trust relationship with a domain that is operating at the Windows 2000 forest and domain functional level. Therefore, it is necessary to create two separate external trusts to satisfy the objective of this scenario; consequently, answers C and D are incorrect. Because this problem can be solved using external trusts, there is no need to upgrade the `que.com` and `corp.que.com` domains and add them to the existing forest, so answer E is incorrect. For more information, see the section "Creating and Configuring Trust Relationships" in Chapter 10.

43. B. Rebecca should use the `BackupGPO.wsf` script to back up the settings in her domain and then use the `ImportGPO.wsf` script to import them in the second domain. The `RestoreGPO.wsf` script is used to restore backed-up GPOs in the same domain, so answer A is incorrect. She cannot use `Wbadmin` to back up and restore GPOs, so answer C is incorrect. It is not necessary to establish a forest trust between the two domains for the purpose of exporting and importing a GPO, so answer D is incorrect. For more information, see the section "Backing Up and Restoring GPOs" in Chapter 15.

44. A, C, F, G. Heather needs to upgrade all Windows 2000 domain controllers to either Windows Server 2003 or Windows Server 2008 and then raise the domain and forest functional levels to Windows Server 2003. She also needs to upgrade the PDC emulator to Windows Server 2008 and run the `adprep /rodcprep` utility on the schema master. Note that, however, if all domain controllers are running Windows Server 2008, it is not necessary to run the `adprep`

`/domainprep` utility. It is not necessary to upgrade all the domain controllers to Windows Server 2008 or to raise the functional levels to Windows Server 2008, so answers B and D are incorrect. However, it is necessary to upgrade the PDC emulator to Windows Server 2008; upgrading this server to Windows Server 2003 is insufficient, so answer E is incorrect. She must run the `adprep` `/rodcprep` utility on the schema master and not the infrastructure master, so answer H is incorrect. For more information, see the section "Planning the Use of RODCs" in Chapter 8.

45. B, C, E. When Julian created the first domain, an OU named Domain Controllers is automatically created. In addition, DNS is installed and contains two zones with the domain name, one of which is prefixed with _msdcs. Further, the Active Directory database and shared system volume folders are created under the `%systemroot%` folder. Active Directory Users and Computers will contain a folder named Users. This is not an OU, so answer A is incorrect. The Active Directory database and shared system volume folders are created under the `%systemroot%` folder and not in the root of the system drive, so answer D is incorrect. A reverse lookup zone is not created in DNS by default, so answer F is incorrect. For more information, see the section "Verifying the Proper Installation of Active Directory" in Chapter 3.

46. A. Janet should use the `ntdsutil` utility to create an application directory partition replica on DC2. This enables the data in the application directory partition existing on DC1 to be properly replicated to DC2. The application directory partition reference domain is the parent domain of the application directory partition; in other words, it is the domain name as included in the partition's DN. Janet does not need to specify this parameter, so answer B is incorrect. She cannot use `repadmin` to simply replicate the partition without first creating a replica, so answer C is incorrect. The `/ZoneChangeDirectoryPartition` parameter specifies that DNS zone data will be stored in an application directory partition specified in the `<NewPartitionName>` parameter. This does not create an application directory partition replica, so answer D is incorrect. For more information, see the section "Creating Application Directory Partition Replicas" in Chapter 4.

47. D. In this scenario, the data entry supervisors are members of both the Data Entry and Supervisors groups. To enable the data entry supervisors to access the Internet, Betty needs to deny the Supervisors group the **Apply group policy** permission. It might be possible to accomplish this task by creating two Group Policy objects (GPOs) if they are configured so that the supervisors' GPO is applied after the data entry GPO; however, this approach takes more administrative effort and is therefore not the best solution. Consequently, answer A is incorrect. If Betty were to simply grant the Data Entry group the **Read** and **Apply group policy** permissions, the data entry supervisors will be unable to reach the Internet because of their membership in the Data Entry group, so answers B and C are incorrect. For more information, see the section "Security Filtering of GPOs" in Chapter 11.

48. A. Wendy should use the Certificate Export Wizard to export the certificate and choose **Yes** when asked whether she wants to export the private key. Browse to a suitable removable disk for the file location and provide a secure password for the key. The Certification Authority Backup Wizard backs up the entire CA and not just the certificate, so answer B is incorrect. The ntdsutil command is used for managing a large number of items related to AD DS, but certificate backup is not one of them, so answer C is incorrect. She could use the wbadmin command to back up the entire server, but not just the certificate and private key, so answer D is incorrect. For more information, see the section "Backing Up Certificates and Keys" in Chapter 17.

49. A, B. By default, the Active Directory Schema snap-in is not present when a domain controller is installed, so Ester has to install it. First, she needs to register this snap-in by using the regsvr32 command from the Run dialog box. She cannot install this snap-in until she performs this step. Ester does not need to be at the schema master because he can connect to it from another computer, so answer C is incorrect. She does not need to belong to the Enterprise Admins group to access the Schema snap-in, so answer D is incorrect. For more information, see the section "Configuring the Schema" in Chapter 5.

50. C, D, F. Betsy should revoke the certificate of the disbanded division's subordinate CA, publish a new base CRL, and then copy this CRL to the network's CDP. Revoking the certificate of the disbanded division's subordinate CA automatically revokes all certificates issued by this CA, so she does not need to revoke certificates from this CA and answer A is incorrect. She might want to uninstall AD CS from the disbanded division's subordinate CA, but this is not required by this scenario, so answer B is incorrect. She could publish a delta CRL, but it is more expedient to publish a new base CRL that ensures all applications and processes across the network are aware of the large number of certificates that have been revoked in this process. Therefore answer E is incorrect. The AIA extension is used for locating the URL of an online responder. Online responders are not being used in this scenario, so answer G is incorrect. For more information, see the section "Certificate Revocation Lists" in Chapter 17.

51. B. Brian can use Active Directory Sites and Services to manually create a site link object connecting the required servers. He cannot perform this task by editing the Registry, so answer A is incorrect. The Knowledge Consistency Checker (KCC) would probably re-create the same replication topology and not the one that Brian thinks should be present, so answer C is incorrect. Because Brian can use Active Directory Sites and Services to modify the replication topology, answer D is incorrect. For more information, see the section "Configuring Site Links" in Chapter 6.

52. D. The Active Directory Lightweight Directory Services Setup Wizard enables Dennis to create a replica of an AD LDS instance. From the Setup Options page of this wizard, he needs to select the **A replica of an existing instance** option and follow the instructions provided. `Adsiedit.exe` enables him to perform general administrative tasks on an AD LDS instance. `Ldp.exe` enables him to perform general administrative actions on any LDAP directory service, including AD DS and AD LDS. `Ntdsutil.exe` enable him to perform many actions such as authoritative restores. None of these tools enable him to create replicates of AD LDS instances, so answers A, B, and C are incorrect. For more information, see the section "Installing AD LDS Instances" in Chapter 7.

53. A, D, E. Each of these settings helps to increase password security. The **Password must meet complexity requirements** setting requires that users employ three of the four character groups (uppercase letters, lowercase letters, numerals, and special characters). The **Minimum password length** setting specifies the minimum number of characters in the password, and the **Maximum password age** setting defines the maximum number of days a user can employ a password before being required to change it. Storing passwords using reversible encryption actually decreases password security, so answer B is incorrect. If a hacker gains a password, it does not matter whether he has to change it right away, so answer C is incorrect. For more information, see the section "Domain Password Policies" in Chapter 13.

54. D. Sheldon must perform an offline defragmentation of the database to recover the space once used by the deleted objects. Waiting for another 24 hours does not help, so answer A is incorrect. Although tombstoning exists as described, this process does not affect the space used by the database file, so answer B is incorrect. Backing up and restoring data will not change the overall file size, so answer C is incorrect. For more information, see the section "Offline Defragmentation and Compaction" in Chapter 15.

55. B. Paul must create a reverse lookup zone for the network and enable it to accept dynamic updates. This action ensures that the pointer (PTR) resource records are recorded properly. By default, when Paul promoted DC01 to domain controller and installed DNS, the forward lookup zone was created but no reverse lookup zone, so Paul must create this zone. Because the forward lookup zone was created by default, answer A is incorrect. The zones are enabled to accept dynamic update; it is not necessary to enable the server, so answer C is incorrect. The client computers send their updates to DC01 automatically, so answer D is incorrect. Dynamic updates are enabled automatically for the new zone, so answer E is incorrect. For more information, see the section "Reverse Lookup Zones" in Chapter 2.

56. B. Alexander should place the users in a security group and configure the Security tab of the template's Properties dialog box with the appropriate permissions to the template. By default, only members of the Authenticated Users group in the parent domain have permissions on the templates. This scenario does not specify the need for certificate autoenrollment, so answer A is incorrect. Automatic certificate request polices are also used for autoenrollment, so answer C is incorrect. The users were able to authenticate to the web enrollment pages but not the required template, so web authentication was not a problem and answer D is incorrect. For more information, see the section "Securing Template Permissions" in Chapter 17.

57. E. Windows System Resource Manager (WSRM) is a new Windows Server 2008 tool that enables her to control how processor and memory resources are allocated to applications, services, and processes running on the server. Rachel can use this tool to set up resource allocation policies that determine how computer resources such as processor and memory are allocated to processes running on the server. She can specify process matching criteria and conditions under which WSRM can switch to a different matching criterion. She can also use this tool to display performance counters in real-time. Network Monitor captures network traffic across her server's network adapter card but does not perform any of the tasks required here, so answer A is incorrect. Both Task Manager and Reliability and Performance Monitor can display real-time server performance data, but they do not enable her to set up resource allocation policies and control how server resources are allocated, so answers B and C are incorrect. Event Viewer logs data about events occurring on the server, including errors, warnings, and informational events. It does not perform any of the tasks required here, so answer D is incorrect. For more information, see the section "Windows System Resource Manager" in Chapter 14.

58. B. George can use a Starter GPO to create the similar GPOs required by this scenario. This is a set of preconfigured Administrative Template policy settings, including comments, which he can use for ease of creating new GPOs. He would then right-click each OU in turn and choose **New GPO**, and in the New GPO dialog box, specify the Starter GPO as a starting point for creating the required GPO. He cannot link the Starter GPO to the required OUs, so answer A is incorrect. Creating one GPO and linking it to all OUs would result in the same GPO being applied to each OU, so answer C is incorrect. He could create a new GPO in each OU that contains the required settings for its OU, but this would take more administrative effort, so answer D is incorrect. For more information, see the section "Starter GPOs" in Chapter 11.

59. C. Wayne should access the DNS server's Properties dialog box, enable **Log packets for debugging,** and specify the **Filter packets by IP address** option. This option enables him to specify the range of IP addresses within which DNS will collect debug logging information. He would also select both the **Incoming** and **Outgoing** options under Packet Direction on this tab. The simple and recursive queries verify whether DNS can resolve zone data, but these queries do not log incoming or outgoing requests at the DNS server, so answer A is incorrect. The Event Logging option does not log individual queries sent to or from the DNS server, so answer B is incorrect. Wayne could specify a capture filter in Network Monitor, but this would capture much more traffic than that captured by debug logging, so answer D is incorrect. For more information, see the section "Debug Logging" in Chapter 4.

60. C. Theodore should access the Security tab of the Marketing OU Properties dialog box and remove Jill's permission to reset passwords. Moving Jill's user account from one OU to another does not reset any permissions, so answer A is incorrect. The Delegation of Control Wizard does not include the ability to revoke permissions, so answer B is incorrect. If Theodore were to delete and re-create Jill's user account, this would remove her permission to reset passwords, but it would also remove all other permissions and group memberships because the new user account would have a new SID, even though it has the same name as the old account. Therefore answer D is incorrect. For more information, see the section "Delegating Administrative Control of Active Directory Objects" in Chapter 9.

61. B. John needs to select the Boston site. When he does so, the details pane will display several objects including the NTDS Site Settings object. He should right-click this object and choose **Properties**. From the Site Settings tab of the NTDS Site Settings Properties dialog box, he should select the **Enable Universal Group Membership Caching** check box and click **OK** or **Apply**. None of the other locations in this snap-in enable John to enable universal group membership caching, so answers A, C, D, and E are all incorrect. Note that on the exam, a question of this type might appear as a "hot-spot" item in which you must select the proper location from a live version of the dialog box. For more information, see the section "Universal Group Membership Caching" in Chapter 5.

62. C. By selecting the **Uninstall the applications when they fall out of the scope of management** check box, David can ensure that applications are removed when a user is moved from one OU to another one. This check box is found on the Advanced tab of the Software Installation Properties dialog box for all software and also on the Deployment tab of an individual application's Properties dialog box. The **Required upgrade for existing packages** check box is used to ensure that users receive an upgrade of an older software package. It does not remove packages that are no longer required, so answer A is incorrect. The **Display the Deploy Software dialog box** option enables David to select the assigned or published option for individual applications when adding new software packages. It does not remove applications that are no longer required, so answer B is incorrect. The **Apply Group Policy** permission ensures that GPOs are properly applied but does not remove applications that are no longer required, so answer D is incorrect. For more information, see the section "Software Installation Properties" in Chapter 12.

63. B, D, E. Evan should access the Active Directory Users and Computers snap-in. From the Domain Controllers OU, he should right-click the RODC's computer account and choose **Properties**. He should then select the **Password Replication Policy** tab of the RODC's computer account Properties dialog box and select the **Accounts whose passwords are stored on this Read-only Domain Controller** drop-down list entry. If Melissa's user account is included in the password replication policy, it will appear here. If it is not present, Evan can click **Add** and then add her user account. The Active Directory Sites and Services snap-in does not enable Evan to check the status of the password replication policy, so answer A is incorrect. Evan needs to check the properties of the RODC computer account and not Melissa's user account, so answer C is incorrect. The **Accounts that have been authenticated to this Read-only Domain Controller** option displays a list of users who have been authenticated by the RODC, regardless of whether their passwords are cached at the RODC, so answer F is incorrect. For more information, see the section "Administering the RODC's Authentication Lists" in Chapter 8.

64. A. The application will check the base CRL and Tuesday's delta CRL. The application is performing its check before Wednesday's delta CRL has been issued, so answer B is incorrect. The delta CRL contains all certificates revoked since the publication of the most recent base CRL. So it does not need to check previous delta CRLs, and answers C and D are incorrect. The application must check the base CRL as well as the latest delta CRL, so answers E and F are incorrect. For more information, see the section "Certificate Revocation Lists" in Chapter 17.

65. A. Karla should select the **Secure only** option on the General tab of the zone's Properties dialog box. This option prevents computers that are not domain members from registering resource records in DNS. The problem observed here is not caused by an improper zone replication scope, so answer B is incorrect. Scavenging removes resource records from computers that have been disconnected from the network, such as remote access computers that have improperly disconnected and have left invalid (stale) resource records behind. Scavenging would remove the improper resource records but would not prevent them from being added by nondomain computers in the future. Therefore, answers C and D are incorrect. For more information, see the section "Dynamic, Nondynamic, and Secure Dynamic DNS" in Chapter 2.

66. C. The way that Kerberos authentication within complex forests works is that when users in a domain request access to resources in a different domain tree of the same forest, the authentication path passes upward to each successive parent domain in the tree and then down the other tree to the desired domain. Then the access token is passed back across the same path in reverse. A shortcut trust creates a direct authentication path between the two child domains, circumventing this roundabout path. Purchasing additional bandwidth would have minimal improvement and would be quite expensive, so answer A is incorrect. A forest trust is used between two forests and not between domain trees of the same forest, so answer B is incorrect. It is most likely that administrative and organizational reasons would prohibit merging domains in this scenario, so answer D is incorrect. For more information, see the section "Shortcut Trust Relationships" in Chapter 10.

67. C. Hubert should open a command prompt, stop AD DS, use the `ntdsutil` utility to move the file, and then restart AD DS. To move this file, he must use this utility to ensure that the appropriate Registry settings are also modified. The use of Windows Explorer to move this file will not allow the Registry to be automatically modified, so answers A, D, and F are incorrect for this reason. Hubert could restart the server in Directory Services Restore mode and use the `ntdsutil` utility to move the file; this method would work and in fact was the required procedure before Windows Server 2008. However, it takes more administrative effort, so answer B is incorrect. Hubert cannot move this file while it's in use, so answers E and F are incorrect. For more information, see the section "Offline Defragmentation and Compaction" in Chapter 15.

68. A, F. Active Directory Sites and Services enables Kim to specify the site into which a domain controller should be placed. Each site contains a Servers object that contains the domain controllers located within the site. Kim can right-click the incorrectly placed server and choose **Move**, and then in the Move Server dialog box, select the correct site and click **OK**. Kim can use this procedure for domain controllers only and not member servers, so answer B is incorrect. For member servers, she must reconfigure the server with an IP address corresponding to the subnet specified for the correct site; this procedure automatically moves the server to the specified site. Kim cannot use Active Directory Administrative Center (new to Windows Server 2008 R2) to move either the domain controller or the member server, so answers C and D are incorrect. She cannot move the domain controller by specifying an IP address corresponding to the subnet for the correct site, so answer E is incorrect. For more information, see the section "Configuring Sites and Subnets" in Chapter 6.

69. B. Peter should configure a global catalog server at the Rome office. A GC server contains directory information about all objects in the forest, including the location of resources in each domain. Universal group membership caching stores information about universal group membership in the domain controller where it is implemented but does not store information about resources in AD DS, so answer A is incorrect. Installing a domain controller for each domain in the other office would increase replication traffic across the WAN link. This is unnecessary for solving this problem, so answers C and D are incorrect. For more information, see the section "Planning the Placement of Global Catalog Servers" in Chapter 5.

70. C, D, G. Lenny should specify an account lockout threshold of 4 passwords, an account lockout duration of 0, and a reset account lockout counter value of 15 minutes. The account lockout threshold specifies the number of incorrect passwords that can be entered before the account locks out. It can be set from 0 to 999 and a value of 0 means that the account never locks out. The account lockout duration can be set from 0 to 99,999 minutes and a value of 0 means that the account remains locked out until unlocked by an administrator or individual who has been delegated this responsibility. The reset account lockout counter value specifies the number of minutes to wait until the lockout counter resets itself to 0. It can be set to any value between 0 and 99999; a value of 0 means that this counter is never reset. If Lenny set an account lockout threshold to 0, the accounts would never lock out and if he set it to 1, the accounts would lock out after one incorrect password, so answers A and B are incorrect. If he set the account lockout duration to 1, the accounts would lock out for one minute only, so answer E is incorrect. If he set the reset account lockout counter value to 0, the account lockout counter would never reset, so answer F is incorrect. If he set the reset account lockout counter to 900, the counter would not reset until 15 hours have elapsed (the value of this counter is specified in minutes, not seconds). Therefore, answer H is incorrect. For more information, see the section "Configuring Account Policies" in Chapter 13.

71. C, D. Michelle can use `Dsadd.exe` or `Adsiedit.msc` to create an OU within an Active Directory Lightweight Directory Services (AD LDS) application directory partition. `Dsadd` is a command-line tool that enables her to add objects including users, groups, computers, OUs, contacts, and quotas to any directory-enabled database including both AD DS and AD LDS. `Adsiedit.msc` is the Active Directory Services Interface (ADSI) snap-in, which enable her to view, create, modify, or delete any AD LDS object. `Ldp.exe` enables her to perform general administrative actions on any Lightweight Directory Access Protocol (LDAP) directory service, including AD DS and AD LDS, but this does not include creating objects such as OUs, so answer A is incorrect. `Ntdsutil` enables her to perform many administrative actions including transfer and seizure of operations master roles and authoritative restores, but it does not enable her to create objects in the database, so answer B is incorrect. `Dssite.msc` is the Active Directory Sites and Services snap-in, which enables her to connect to an AD LDS instance and administer directory data replication. It also does not enable her to create objects, so answer E is incorrect. For more information, see the section "AD LDS User Accounts and Groups" in Chapter 7.

72. B, D, E, F. The **Queries/Transfers** option is not needed for this scenario, so he can clear this check box. The **Notifications** option is not needed because Stuart is attempting to troubleshoot an update problem, not a notification one. He should clear the **Filter packets by IP address** check box because there is no need here to filter by IP address. Stuart has realized that detailed information is not needed so he should clear the **Details** check box. If he were to clear the **Log packets for debugging** check box, no information would be collected, so answer A is incorrect. He needs to keep **Updates** selected because this is the type of data required according to the scenario, so answer C is incorrect. Note that on the exam, a question like this could be presented as a "hot spot" item, in which you are expected to select the required items from a live version of the dialog box to answer the question. For more information, see the section "Debug Logging" in Chapter 4.

73. D. Because the GPO already exists and it is possible to link the same GPO to more than one AD DS container, the simplest method to accomplish this task is simply to link the current GPO to the Marketing OU. It would be possible to create a new GPO linked to the Marketing OU, but this solution would take more administrative effort, so answer A is incorrect. Arlene cannot use a GPO that is already linked to an OU as a Starter GPO, so answer B is incorrect. Adding the group containing the Marketing team members to the Sales OU might have unexpected results due to other policies being applied, so answer C is incorrect. For more information, see the section "Managing GPO Links" in Chapter 11.

74. B, C. Carm must log on using an account that is a member of the Enterprise Admins group. He must also ensure that all domains in the forest, not just the tree root domains, are at the Windows Server 2008 R2 domain functional level. He does not need to be a member of the Schema Admins group, so answer A is incorrect. He can raise the forest functional level from Windows 2000 to Windows Server 2008 R2 in one step provided that all domains are at the Windows Server 2008 R2 domain functional level, so answer D is incorrect. There is no need to remove any external or shortcut trust relationships, so answer E is incorrect. For more information, see the section "Forest and Domain Functional Levels" in Chapter 3.

75. C. Teresa should use the Group Policy Modeling Wizard for the Design OU. She should choose the **Engineering OU** to simulate policy settings. This wizard processes an RSoP planning mode query, which tests potential policy settings prior to actually putting them into production. Teresa needs to test the

settings for the Design, OU, not the Engineering OU, so answer A is incorrect. She would use the Group Policy Results Wizard to perform an RSoP logging mode query, which tests the application of current policy settings, not to test policy settings that have not yet been applied. Therefore answers B and D are incorrect. For more information, see the section "Planning Mode/Group Policy Modeling" in Chapter 14.

76. A. Jennifer should export the Excel spreadsheet to a comma-separated text file and use `Csvde` to create the required accounts. She can automate the creation of hundreds or even thousands of user, group, or computer accounts in this manner. Excel cannot export to an LDIF-formatted file, so answer B is incorrect. She might be able to use `dsadd` to script the creation of the accounts, but the procedure would not be as simple as using `Csvde`, so answer C is incorrect. It would take far more effort than required to use the New Object-User and New Object-Group dialog boxes to complete this task, so answer D is incorrect. For more information, see the section "Using Bulk Import to Automate Account Creation" in Chapter 9.

77. D, E. These two steps are the minimum necessary requirements for completing the procedure for enabling autoenrollment of user certificates. Matt would need to install Internet Information Services (IIS) only if he needs to use the certificate enrollment web pages, which are not needed during autoenrollment, so answer A is incorrect. Although companies should install an enterprise subordinate CA and take the root CA offline to prevent its compromise, installing the subordinate CA is not necessary, so answer B is incorrect. A certificate trust list (CTL) is a signed list of trusted root CA certificates considered as reputable for purposes such as client authentication or secure email. It is not needed for certificate autoenrollment, so answer C is incorrect. For more information, see the section "Certificate Autoenrollment" in Chapter 17.

78. D. Charles should reverse site link costs. He has configured the longer paths with the shortest costs. Because the shortest cost links are preferred, he has created a topology in which the longer paths are used in preference. Charles would use SMTP only when there is unreliable communication across site links; further, SMTP is used only for replicating the schema and configuration partitions between domains, so answer A is incorrect. The ISTG and KCC look after selecting the most appropriate bridgehead server, so answer B is incorrect. The KCC also looks after bridging site links, so answer C is incorrect. For more information, see the section "Site Link Costs" in Chapter 6.

79. C, E. To restore the Executive OU properly, Brendan needs to do an authoritative restore. He needs to first start the domain controller in Directory Services Restore Mode and restore the System State data from backup. Then he needs to mark the restore of the Executive OU as authoritative, which he can do with the ntdsutil command. In Windows Server 2008 R2, Brendan could also use the Active Directory Recycle Bin in this scenario, but he must enable this option before he can use it. Although stopping AD DS enables him to do several other directory management actions such as defragmenting the database, he cannot perform a restore using this method, so answer A is incorrect. He also cannot do a restore using Safe Mode, so answer B is incorrect. The **Repair your computer** and **System Image Recovery** options are part of performing a full server recovery and not part of the authoritative restore, so answers D and F are incorrect. For more information, see the section "Recovering Active Directory" in Chapter 15.

80. B. Cindy should select **Maximum** from the Installation User Interface Options on the Deployment tab of the package's Properties dialog box. This option provides the entire user interface that is supported by the application during installation. If she were to select the **Basic** option, users would see only progress bars and errors, so answer A is incorrect. The **Do not display this package in the Add/Remove Programs control panel** option removes the package from this location so that users are less able to remove the application; it does not affect the amount of information users see during program installation, so answer C is incorrect. The **Install this application at logon** option fully installs the application using its default options; it also does not affect the amount of information users see during the installation, so answer D is incorrect. For more information, see the section "Software Package Properties" in Chapter 12.

81. A. Judy should link each GPO to its site and specify the **Enforced** option. Linking the GPOs to their sites ensures that they always apply to computers located in that site. She must specify the **Enforced** option or else GPOs linked to domains or OUs could apply conflicting settings that are not desirable; consequently, answer B is incorrect. Linking the GPOs to any other container would produce mixed results because the scenario specifies that every site includes two or more domains and several OUs, so answers C, D, and E are incorrect. For more information, see the section "Configuring GPO Hierarchy and Processing Priority" in Chapter 11.

82. B. Wilson should configure the conditional forwarder with the **All domain controllers in this domain** option. This option enables replication to all domain controllers including those running Windows 2000. The problem in this scenario is not with a directory replication failure, so answer A is incorrect. The **All DNS servers in this domain** option replicates to Windows Server 2003 and Windows Server 2008 domain controllers only. Because Windows 2000 domain controllers are present on the network, conditional forwarding on this zone will not be established on these servers, so answer C is incorrect. Zone delegation is not an issue in this scenario, so answer D is incorrect. For more information, see the section "Conditional Forwarders" in Chapter 4.

83. A, D. Dan should select **Primary zone** (which would already be selected in this scenario). He should also select the **Store the zone in Active Directory** option. By creating an Active Directory–integrated zone, he is employing the security and replication of Active Directory to maintain and distribute the zone data to a series of servers. Because Active Directory replication is multimaster, he can make certain updates to any domain controller. These changes propagate to other domain controllers. In this case, DNS zone information will be synchronized among the multiple master servers. This also serves to reduce administrative effort. A secondary zone receives updates from a master DNS server. It also cannot be integrated with Active Directory. Because this is the master server, he should not select this option, and answer B is incorrect. A stub zone contains only information about its zone's authoritative name servers and obtains this information from another DNS server. He must not choose this option, so answer C is incorrect. He needs to have his zone integrated with Active Directory, so he should not clear the **Store the zone in Active Directory** option, and answer E is incorrect. For more information, see the section "Configuring Zone Types" in Chapter2.

84. C. Brenda should add a copy of each third-party CA certificates to the Trusted Root Certification Authorities node in the Default Domain Policy GPO. This node is found under Computer Configuration\Policies\Windows Settings\Security Settings\Public Key Policies. It enables her to ensure that all domain computers receive a copy of the required certificates. Installing the certificates on the root or issuing CA servers would enable these servers to trust the third-party certificates but would not allow client computers to trust these certificates, so answers A and B are incorrect. Manually placing a copy of each certificate in the Trusted Root Certification Authorities certificate store on each client computer would take far more administrative effort than using Group Policy to accomplish the same task, so answer D is incorrect. For more information, see the section "Certificate Stores" in Chapter 16.

85. D. You should remove the trust relationship and create a new one-way incoming trust relationship. Sandy has created the trust relationship in the wrong direction. It is not possible to reverse the direction of the trust from the trust's Properties dialog box, so answer A is incorrect. Changing the authentication scope of the trust does not solve the problem, so answer B is incorrect. Creating a two-way trust is not necessary; doing so reduces security because employees of the contractor company could then access your domain. Therefore, answer C is incorrect. For more information, see the section "Creating and Configuring Trust Relationships" in Chapter 10.

86. A. Nolan should configure a global catalog server at the Tokyo office. It contains directory information about all objects in the forest, including the location of resources in each domain of the forest. Universal group caching stores information about universal group membership in the domain controller where it is implemented but does not store information about resources in AD DS, so answer B is incorrect. Replicating the entire contents of each domain between domain controllers in the two sites across the WAN link would overload the link and is unnecessary for solving this problem, so answers C and D are incorrect. For more information, see the section "Planning the Placement of Global Catalog Servers" in Chapter 5.

87. F. Julio should use the `auditpol.exe` tool to enable auditing of directory service changes attempts. Directory service changes is a new auditing category in Windows Server 2008 that tracks modifications to directory objects whose SACLs have been configured for auditing. This includes modification of an object's attribute, creation of new objects, moving of objects between AD DS containers, and deletion of objects. Object access auditing tracks access to or modification of system objects such as files, folders, or printers. This is not required by the present scenario, so answers A and D are incorrect. Auditing of directory service access tracks attempts at accessing directory objects but not modifying them, so answers B and E are incorrect. Julio can enable auditing of directory service changes by using `auditpol.exe` only; it is not possible to enable auditing of this category using a GPO, so answer C is incorrect. For more information, see the section "Use of `Auditpol.exe` to Configure Auditing" in Chapter 13.

88. C, E. Kent can use either the Active Directory Users and Computers snap-in or the `Ntdsutil` utility to transfer these roles to the new domain controller. He would use the Active Directory Domains and Trusts utility to transfer the domain naming master role. This role is not involved here, so answer A is incorrect. The Active Directory Sites and Services snap-in is not used for transferring FSMO roles, so answer B is incorrect. He would use the Active Directory Schema snap-in to transfer the schema master role. This role is also not involved here, so answer D is incorrect. For more information, see the section "Transferring Operations Master Roles" in Chapter 5.

89. B, C. Carol should configure AD RMS and AD FS. AD RMS enables her to create and work with rights-protected files and folders and ensure that only authorized users have access to these types of data. AD FS provides a single sign-on capability for authenticating users to multiple web-based applications, such as those holding data on the other company's servers in this scenario. AD LDS provides storage for directory-enabled application data without the need for a full directory service. AD CS provides a centralized certification authority for working with digital certificates. Neither AD LDS nor AD CS is needed in this scenario, so answers A and D are incorrect. Carol can enable access for her users to the web-based data on the other company's network by means of AD FS, so it is not necessary to create a one-way external trust relationship and answer E is incorrect. For more information, see the sections "Active Directory Rights Management Services" and "Active Directory Federation Services" in Chapter 7.

90. A. Network Monitor enables Ruby to capture, view, and analyze frames (packets) as they are transmitted over a network to all network adapter cards on the server. She can configure filters that limit the display to only those frames originating from specified sources or using specified protocols to more rapidly locate those that might indicate suspicious activity. Task Manager provides information about currently running processes and enables her to modify their property or terminate misbehaving applications. Performance Monitor enables her to monitor the performance of her server including the display of real-time performance graphs and logs of performance data. Event Viewer logs data about events occurring on the server, including errors, warnings, and informational events. Windows System Resource Manager (WSRM) enables her to control how processor and memory resources are allocated to applications, services, and processes running on the server. None of these other tools capture information about data transmitted across the network adapter cards, so answers B, C, D, and E are incorrect. For more information, see the section "Network Monitor" in Chapter 14.

91. D. When Lynda first promoted the server to domain controller, she had to enter a Directory Services Restore Mode (DSRM) administrator password. This password is stored locally in the security accounts manager (SAM) and not in Active Directory. When she starts the computer in DSRM, it acts as a stand-alone server and is not connected to Active Directory. Consequently, domain user accounts and password are unavailable. Changes to a password on her domain account are irrelevant because she must use the DSRM password here, so answer A is incorrect. It is possible that a Group Policy setting would deny the Log on Locally right, but this would prevent any administrator from accessing the server, so answer B is incorrect. Lynda does not need to belong to the Enterprise Administrators group to use DSRM. In fact, anyone with access to the DSRM password can access this mode (this is why it is important to protect this password carefully so that an unauthorized user does not get at the database). Consequently, answer C is incorrect. For more information, see the section "Directory Services Restore Mode" in Chapter 15.

92. C. If there is a possibility Jim might want to unrevoke a certificate, he must specify the **Certificate Hold** reason when revoking it. Any certificate that has been revoked using a different reason cannot be unrevoked, and Jim must issue a new certificate in this circumstance. Jim cannot simply delete the delta CRL, so answer A is incorrect. It is not possible to restore a CRL to a previous day, so answer B is incorrect. The ability to unrevoke a certificate is not related to its publication in the base CRL, so answer D is incorrect. For more information, see the section "Managing Certificate Revocation" in Chapter 17.

93. B, C. Diane should access the Zone Transfers tab of the same dialog box, click **Notify**, and then ensure that **The following servers** is selected and that the IP addresses of the perimeter zone secondary DNS servers are specified. Specifying this option on the Notify list will ensure that only the authorized secondary DNS servers receive notifications of zone updates. Diane should also access the Start of Authority (SOA) tab of the zone's Properties dialog box and increase the value of the **Refresh** interval. An increase in the value of this interval reduces the bandwidth required for the zone transfer SOA requests sent by both perimeter network DNS servers. Specifying **Servers listed on the Name Servers tab** would cause additional zone transfers that involve the primary DNS servers in the internal network, so answer A is incorrect. Decreasing the value of the Refresh interval would increase the amount of zone transfer traffic across the firewall server, so answer D is incorrect. The Retry interval specifies how much time will elapse before the secondary server tries again to contact the master server, in the event that the master server does not respond to the initial refresh attempt. Its value is immaterial to the problem specified in this scenario, so answers E and F are incorrect. Dynamic updates are used by the master DNS servers to maintain the Active Directory–integrated zone and are not utilized by the secondary servers on the perimeter zone. She should not modify this setting, so answer G is incorrect. For more information, see the sections "Zone Scavenging" in Chapter 2 and "Configuring DNS Notify" in Chapter 4.

94. D. Stan should configure the password for the App user account to never expire. In this scenario, the App user account is governed by the policies configured in the Default Domain Policy GPO, which specifies a maximum password age of 30 days. After this time interval, the password associated with this account is no longer valid and the account will no longer be able to log on, so the users were no longer able to access the application used by this account. Changing the **Maximum password age** setting to its maximum of 999 would affect all domain users and thereby reduce the domain's security. Furthermore, the domain logon would still expire after this time interval (almost three years) and the problem would recur, so answer A is incorrect. Stan could configure a PSO with a 999-day password age, but this would take more administrative effort and the problem would still recur as mentioned here, so answer B is incorrect. Changing the value of **Enforce password history** to 0 would enable immediate reuse of a password, but the App user account password would still expire after 30 days. Furthermore, all domain users would be able to reuse their passwords immediately, thereby reducing domain security. Therefore answer C is incorrect. For more information, see the sections "Creating User, Computer, and Group Accounts" in Chapter 9 and "Configuring Account Policies" in Chapter 13.

95. C, E, G, I. Evelyn can install an enterprise root CA on a domain controller running any of Windows Server 2008 R2 Foundation Edition, Standard Edition, Enterprise Edition, or Datacenter Edition. Note, however, that some features of AD CS require the Enterprise or Datacenter Edition. It is not possible to install an enterprise root CA on a computer running the Web edition of Windows Server 2008, so answers A is incorrect. The server must be configured as a domain controller and not as a member server, so answers B, D, F, and H are incorrect. For more information, see the section "Certificate Authority Types and Hierarchies" in Chapter 16.

96. A, E. Ursula should select the **Automatically notify** check box. She should then select the **Servers listed on the Name Servers tab** option. The Notify dialog box enables her to configure secondary DNS servers to be automatically notified when changes to the zone data in the primary zone occur. Because all the secondary servers are listed on the Name Servers tab in this scenario, there is no need for her to select **The following servers** or to add or remove items in the list box. Therefore, answers, B, C, and D are incorrect. For more information, see the section "Configuring DNS Notify" in Chapter 4.

97. C. As the site links are configured, replication cannot complete across both site links during one night. Consequently, changes made in St. Louis replicate to Chicago one day later and to Detroit on the second day. Shelley needs to modify the replication schedule to include a common time period so that replication crosses the entire network nightly. Modification of the replication interval or the site link cost will not help in this scenario, so answers A and B are incorrect. Because Active Directory bridges all site links automatically, Shelley does not need to create a site link bridge, so answer D is incorrect. For more information, see the section "Replication Scheduling" in Chapter 6.

98. D. Ryan should execute the `dcpromo` command from the command prompt and specify an unattended answer file containing the required information. Server Core does not contain any GUI, and he must supply all required information in the form of the answer file. He can execute Server Manager using the command line (`ServerManagerCmd.exe`), but he cannot select roles or options in this manner because there is no GUI, so answers A and B are incorrect. Also, `dcpromo` on a Server Core machine cannot run the GUI, so answer C is incorrect. For more information, see the section "Server Core Domain Controllers" in Chapter3.

99. B, C. By using a Starter GPO, Joanne can create multiple GPOs with similar settings linked to the appropriate OUs in her company's network. The Starter GPO is a set of preconfigured Administrative Templates policy settings, including comments, which she can use for ease of creating new GPOs. The Backup function contained within GPMC enables her to export the settings in the GPO linked to the Financial OU and then import them into the other company's domain, where she can link the GPO to that company's Financial OU. It is not possible to link a Starter GPO to any AD DS container; it is used only for ease of creating other GPOs, so answer A is incorrect. Starter GPOs are a new feature of Windows Server 2008 and cannot be used on a Windows Server 2003 network, so answer D is incorrect. For more information, see the sections "Starter GPOs" in Chapter 11 and "Backing Up and Restoring GPOs" in Chapter 15.

100. C. To seize the role of domain naming master, Jonathan needs to use the `ntdsutil` command-line utility. It is appropriate to seize this role in this scenario because the hard disk of the old server has failed and it will have to be re-installed after parts have arrived. Consequently, to AD DS it will be an entirely new domain controller and the old domain controller will never be online again. Role seizure is appropriate under these circumstances. Active Directory Users and Computers can transfer any of the three domainwide operations master roles but cannot seize any of these roles, so answer A is incorrect. Using Active Directory Domains and Trusts, Jonathan can transfer the role of domain naming master to another domain controller but not seize this role, so answer B is incorrect. Jonathan cannot specify the role of domain naming master during the promotion of another server to domain controller, so answer D is incorrect. For more information, see the section "Transferring and Seizing of Operations Master Roles" in Chapter 5.

101. B. Enabling auditing of any type of object access is a two-stage process. In this case, Merle only performed the first part, which was enabling auditing in a GPO applicable to the Active Directory container (site, domain, or OU) in question. She must also enable auditing of each specific object, which she can do from the object's Properties dialog box. The security log records activities performed by all users, administrators, authorized users, unauthorized uses, and so on, so answers A and D are incorrect. The events are recorded on the Security log of the computer at which they occurred, so answer C is incorrect. For more information, see the section "Use of GPOs to Configure Auditing" in Chapter 13.

102. A, D, E. Brandon must install IIS, Windows Process Activation Service, and Message Queuing Services when he installs Active Directory Rights Management Services (AD RMS). If these roles and services are not present, the installation wizard will ask him to install them. AD RMS uses a system of rights account certificates to identify users that are empowered to access and work with protected information from an AD RMS–enabled application, but Brandon does not need to install Active Directory Certificate Services (AD CS) when he is installing AD RMS. Therefore answer B is incorrect. Active Directory Metadirectory Services (AD MDS) provides a view of user information in the AD DS directory database and coordinates information across AD DS along with other components such as Active Directory Lightweight Directory Services (AD LDS) and Microsoft Exchange Server. AD RMS does not require Active Directory Metadirectory Services (AD MDS), so answer C is incorrect. For more information, see the section "Installing AD RMS" in Chapter 7.

103. C, E. Andy needs to create a manually configured data collector set and access the Performance Counter Alert option. When he does this, he can view alerts in the Application log in Event Viewer. Note that he can connect to the domain controller from his desktop computer to view these alerts (right-click **Event Viewer**, choose **Connect to another computer**, and then type the name of the required server). WSRM and Performance Monitor both enable Andy to view performance data in real time; however, neither one is able to create alerts, so answers A and B are incorrect. He cannot configure the Alerter service to display alerts to his desktop, so answer D is incorrect. He needs to look in the Application log and not the System log to find alerts, so answer F is incorrect. For more information, see the section "Data Collector Sets" in Chapter 14.

104. A. Allison should install the Simple Certificate Enrollment Protocol (SCEP) on the issuing CA server. This protocol enables software on network devices that do not have accounts in AD DS, and therefore cannot otherwise be authenticated to the network, to enroll for certificates. Microsoft's implementation of this protocol is known as Network Device Enrollment Services (NDES) and is included as a role service in AD CS. An online responder is a role service that provides signed responses to clients requesting certificate revocation information and is an alternative to the CRL. The Authority Information Access (AIA) extension points to URLs from which issuing CA's certificates can be retrieved. Neither of these options allow for network device certificate enrollment, so answers B and C are incorrect. Although security groups can include computer accounts, routers and switches do not have machine accounts and it is not possible to include these devices in a security group to be granted the Autoenroll permission, so answer D is incorrect. For more information, see the section "Network Device Enrollment Services" in Chapter 17.

105. C. Erica should configure the branch offices as subdomains. Additionally, each branch office should host a standard primary zone for its subdomain. Because the scenario states that the administrators in the branch offices are to be responsible for their specific DNS information and that their DNS servers be configured to host standard primary zones, the branch offices must be configured as subdomains because primary zones require their own domain. This is the only option that enables administrators to control the information stored in their respective DNS zones. If each branch office were to host a standard primary zone, it would not be possible for administrators in each branch office to administer that office's DNS configuration, so answer A is incorrect. Secondary zones are read-only and must receive their information from a primary standard zone;

consequently, local administrators cannot control their zone data and answer B is incorrect. A stub zone contains read-only copies of the SOA record plus NS and A records for authoritative names servers only. It does not allow local administrative control, so answer D is incorrect. For more information, see the section "DNS Zone Types" in Chapter 2.

106. A. Trevor should use the `ntdsutil.exe` utility to perform this task. If an object with back-links in another domain has been authoritatively restored, he needs to run the `create ldif files from <file_path>` command on a domain controller in the other domain (`certguide.com` in this instance). He can run this command from the `authoritative restore` prompt within `ntdsutil`. Before he runs this command, he must copy the `.txt` file created by `ntdsutil` during the authoritative restore to a location on the domain controller in the `certguide.com` domain or an accessible shared folder location and then restore this domain controller from backup. The `Esentutl` tool provides utility functions for the Extensible Storage Engine for Windows. It does not restore back-links, so answer B is incorrect. The `Ldifde` tool enables him to perform several operations on LDIF files but not restoring back-links, so answer C is incorrect. The `Wbadmin` tool enables him to perform backups and restores but does not allow the restoration of back-links, so answer D is incorrect. For more information, see the section "Recovering Back-Links of Authoritatively Restored Objects" in Chapter 15.

107. A, E. The **Store BitLocker recovery information in Active Directory Domain Services** policy is used to enable recovery information for a RODC to be stored in AD DS. When Sharon enables this policy, she can choose from two options for storing recovery passwords and key packages and she should select the **Store recovery passwords and key packages** option to complete the requirements of this scenario. The **Choose how BitLocker protected fixed drives can be recovered** and **Choose how BitLocker protected operating system drives can be recovered** policies are used with Windows 7 client computers only and are not used with servers running either the original or R2 version of Windows Server 2008, so answers B and C are incorrect. The **Allow data recovery agent** check box is not relevant to the requirements of this scenario, so answer D is incorrect. The **Store recovery passwords only** option does not back up the key packages so answer F is incorrect. For more information, see the section "Managing BitLocker" in Chapter 8.

108. A. Windows Server 2008 provides the capability to assign certificates to both users and computers. Because Juan can assign certificates to both users and computers in Windows Server 2008, answers B and C are incorrect. Furthermore, in a fully secure environment, certificates should be assigned to both the computers and the users, so answer D is incorrect. For more information, see the section "Installing Active Directory Certificate Services" in Chapter 16.

109. C, D. Sandra and Ralph should create a realm trust between the Active Directory network and the UNIX realm. They should also upgrade the Active Directory network to Windows Server 2008. The trust enables them to reduce the duplication of resources across the networks and, in addition, Windows Server 2008 features enhanced UNIX interoperability including automatic password synchronization (first introduced in Windows Server 2003 R2). They should not create an external trust because this type of trust can be created only between two Active Directory domains or an Active Directory and Windows NT domains, so answer A is incorrect. They should not create a forest trust because this type of trust can be created only between two Active Directory forests, so answer B is incorrect. It is not necessary—and might not be feasible—to migrate the UNIX realm to Active Directory, so answer E is incorrect. For more information, see the section "External Trusts and Realm Trusts" in Chapter 10.

110. D. Kevin must run dcpromo.exe to promote the server to a domain controller. An enterprise CA can only run on a domain controller, and if Kevin is at a member server, the Enterprise CA option will be unavailable. Kevin does not need to be a member of either the Enterprise Admins or Schema Admins group to install an enterprise CA, so answers A and B are incorrect. Merely using Server Manager to install AD DS without promoting the server to domain controller is insufficient, so answer C is incorrect. The Certification Authority console does not offer an option to promote a standalone CA to an enterprise CA, so answer E is incorrect. For more information, see the section "Installing Subordinate CAs" in Chapter 16.

111. A. Tricia needs to assign the software package to users in the Design OU because of the requirement for it to be available to all employees in this department, regardless of the computer to which they log on, and that it not be available to employees of other departments, even if they log on to computers in the Design department. If she were to assign or publish the software package to computers, it would not be available to Design employees if they logged on to computers in other departments and it would be available to users logging on to computers in the design department. Therefore answers B and C are incorrect. It is not possible to publish software to computers, so answer D is incorrect. For more information, see the section "Deploying Software Using Group Policy" in Chapter 12.

112. B. By placing a single global catalog server at each site, Maggie can achieve the objectives of optimized response time for logon and resource access. If she were to place a single global catalog server at the Atlanta site only, users at the San Jose site would need to send requests over the slow WAN link because the domain controller would need to check universal group membership at the global catalog server on the Atlanta site, so answer A is incorrect. The same would be true if she placed two global catalog servers at the Atlanta site, so answer C is incorrect. This would also be true for users in Atlanta if she placed two global catalog servers in San Jose, so answer D is incorrect. Placing two global catalog servers at each site would achieve load-balancing and fault tolerance but would also generate additional replication traffic across the WAN link, thereby reducing performance. Therefore answer E is incorrect. For more information, see the section "Planning the Placement of Global Catalog Servers" in Chapter 5.

113. D. In the Delegation of Control Wizard, Sam needs to select the **Create a custom task to delegate** option, select **Organizational Unit** objects, and then grant Julie the **Read** and **Create all child objects** permissions. This set of permissions provides Julie with adequate capability to perform the tasks required of her. Granting her the **Read** and **Write** permissions over the same task or using the option labeled **This folder, existing objects in this folder, and creation of new objects in this folder** would both provide her with more capabilities than required to perform her tasks. Consequently, answers A and B are incorrect. The **Delegate the following common tasks** option enables Sam to delegate several common tasks, including **Create, delete, and manage user accounts** and **Create, delete, and manage groups**. However, there is no **Create, delete, and manage OUs** option in this section of the Delegation of Control Wizard, so answer C is incorrect. For more information, see the section "Delegating Administrative Control of Active Directory Objects" in Chapter 9.

114. A. Policies are processed in the local, site, domain, organizational unit (LSDOU) sequence. Consequently, the policies in this scenario are applied in the Site, Domain, OU2, OU1 sequence. On top of this, the Enforced setting prevents policy settings at the domain level from being overwritten by conflicting polices in either the OU2 or OU1 policies. The Block Inheritance setting at OU1 prevents the site or domain GPO policies from applying, except that in this case the Enforced setting in the Domain policy overrides the Block Inheritance setting. Consequently, the wallpaper is red (OU1 policy applies), Task Manager is not disabled (domain policy applies), and Display Properties is disabled (Domain policy). The wallpaper is not green because the lower-level settings override this setting, so answers B and D are incorrect. Display Properties is not enabled because the Enforced setting on the Domain policy overrides the Block Inheritance setting on the OU1 policy, so answer C is incorrect. The Domain policy also causes Task Manager to not be disabled, so answer B is incorrect for this reason also. For more information, see the section "Configuring GPO Hierarchy and Processing Priority" in Chapter 11.

115. D. Nancy should determine whether the server contains the `1.0.0.127.in-addr.arpa` zone. If this zone is absent, the simple test query will fail. In the DNS snap-in, she should expand the entries for the server, select

Reverse Lookup Zones, and then verify that this zone is present. If it is not present, she should add it and retest. The root hints assist servers that are authoritative at low levels of the domain namespace in locating root DNS servers. If they are not present, the recursive test will fail but the simple test will pass. Therefore answer A is incorrect. If they are correct, she should then stop and restart the DNS server service. This is not the first step she should try, so answer B is incorrect. Collecting debug logging data might help if all other troubleshooting steps fail, but it is also not the first step, so answer C is incorrect. For more information, see the section "Monitoring DNS" in Chapter 4.

116. A, C. In a situation such as this one, Roy needs to determine which policy settings are in effect for the users and computers in question. Roy needs to perform a Resultant Set of Policy (RSoP) logging mode analysis. He can do this by right-clicking the **Group Policy Results** node and choose **Group Policy Results Wizard** or by running the gpresult command. The gpupdate command would refresh the application of Group Policy; however, in this scenario, the policy is already working unexpectedly the following day and after users have logged off/on. Such an action causes Group Policy to refresh and it is necessary to determine why it is not applying properly, so answer B is incorrect. Roy would use the Group Policy Modeling Wizard to test the effects of a proposed change affecting the application of Group Policy; this wizard performs an RSoP planning mode analysis. To check the cause of a policy change that has been implemented, Roy needs to use logging mode and not planning mode, so answers D and E are incorrect. For more information, see the section "Resultant Set of Policy" in Chapter 14.

117. D. Gary should configure a claims-aware application. This is a Microsoft Active Server Pages (ASP) .NET application that uses claims that are present in an AD FS security token to perform authorization decisions and personalize applications. The Windows token-based agent is used on a web server that hosts a Windows NT token-based application to support conversion from an AD FS security token to a Windows NT access token. A Federation Service proxy acts as a proxy to the Federation Service on a perimeter network or demilitarized zone. A trust policy enables users to share documents protected in AD RMS across internal or external AD DS forests. None of these can test which claims the Federation Service sends in AD FS security tokens, so answers A, B, and C are incorrect. For more information, see the section "Enabling Applications" in Chapter 7.

118. C. To have a PSO apply properly, the domain functional level must be at the Windows Server 2008 or higher functional level. To achieve this functional level, Ian must upgrade all domain controllers to Windows Server 2008 or Windows Server 2008 R2. He can associate a PSO with a user account, so answer A is incorrect. It is not possible to associate a PSO with an OU, so answer

B is incorrect. It is not necessary to upgrade other domains in the forest to Windows Server 2008 if no PSO is being applied in these domains, so answer D is incorrect. For more information, see the section "Fine-Grained Password Policies" in Chapter 13.

119. D. Besides acting as a primary domain controller for pre-Windows 2000 client computers, the PDC emulator acts as a time server for the domain and ensures that the system clocks on all other computers are synchronized. The PDC emulator connects to an Internet time server to ensure that it has the proper time setting. None of the other FSMO roles are involved in time synchronization, so answers A, B, C, and E are incorrect. For more information, see the section "PDC Emulator" in Chapter 5.

120. C, D, F. Nellie needs to right-click the **IP** folder and choose **New Site Link Bridge**. In the New Object—Site Link bridge dialog box, she should type a name for the site link bridge, select at least two site links to be bridged, and then click **Add**. The Inter-Site Transports folder does not provide the option to create a site link bridge, so answer A is incorrect. The Simple Mail Transport Protocol (SMTP) transport protocol is used only for intersite replication of the configuration and schema partitions in multidomain forests, so answer B is incorrect. Nellie must select two site links and not two sites, so answer E is incorrect. The check box labeled **Bridge all site links** is not found in the New Object—Site Link Bridge dialog box; it is in the Properties dialog box for the intersite transport being configured. Furthermore, she should clear this check box and not select it; therefore, answer G is incorrect. For more information, see the section "Site Link Bridges" in Chapter 6.

Answers to the "Do I Know This Already?" Quizzes

Chapter 2

1. A, B, C, D. The DNS namespace includes root domains, top-level domains, second-level domains, and hostnames. You can even have additional subdomains at levels beneath the second level. However, NetBIOS names are not a component of the DNS namespace.

2. C. When installing a DNS server, you should ensure that it has a static IP address. If it is configured to use DHCP to obtain an IP address automatically, its IP address could change and client computers would be unable to locate the DNS server. The server does not need to be configured as a domain controller or an application server; further, it can function properly with only a single network adapter.

3. A. DNS is a server role in Windows Server 2008 R2, so you use the Add Roles Wizard and not the Add Features Wizard to install it. DNS Manager is used to configure DNS after installation; it is installed when you install DNS. The Control Panel Add or Remove Programs applet was used to install DNS on servers running Windows 2000 Server or Windows Server 2003, but it is no longer used for this purpose.

4. D. A stub zone contains source information about authoritative name servers for its zone only. This zone information is obtained from another server that hosts a primary or secondary copy of the same zone data. Primary zones, secondary zones, and Active Directory–integrated zones all contain complete zone information. There is no such thing as a forwarding zone, only forwarding servers that forward name resolution requests to other DNS servers.

5. B. A secondary zone is a backup copy of DNS zone data hosted on a DNS server that is a secondary source for this zone information. A primary zone is a master copy of DNS zone data and is not used here. A stub zone contains source information about authoritative name servers for its zone only; it does not contain a complete set of zone information. You cannot configure an Active Directory–integrated zone on a server that is not a domain

controller. There is no such thing as a forwarding zone; there are only forwarding servers that forward name resolution requests to other DNS servers.

6.   C. A GlobalNames zone is a special type of Active Directory–integrated zone that enables you to resolve static, global records with single-label names without the need for a WINS server. A primary zone is a master copy of DNS zone data and is not used here. A secondary zone is a backup copy of DNS zone data hosted on a DNS server that is a secondary source for this zone information. A stub zone contains source information about authoritative name servers for its zone only; it does not contain a complete set of zone information.

7.   A. The reverse lookup zone contains octets of the network portion of the IP address in reverse sequence and uses a special domain name ending in `in-addr.arpa`. Thus the correct address is `5.168.192.in-addr.arpa`. You do not use the host portion of the IP address, so `0.5.168.192.in-addr.arpa` is incorrect. The octets must be specified in reverse sequence, so the other two choices are both incorrect.

8.   B. An AAAA resource record is used for mapping the hostname to an IPv6 address. An A resource record is used with IPv4 addresses only. An NS resource record lists the DNS servers that are authoritative in the domain. A PTR resource contains IP address-to-name mappings (reverse lookup; the reverse of what is needed in this question).

9.   D. A CNAME resource record provides aliases (canonical names), which are additional names that point to the same host. This facilitates the action required in this scenario. You would not use duplicated A address records here. An NS resource record specifies the DNS servers that are authoritative in the domain. A PTR resource record specifies reverse IP address-to-name mappings. An MX resource record identifies preferred mail servers on the network.

10.   A. Selecting the **Store the zone in Active Directory** option creates an Active Directory–integrated zone and enables you to select the **Secure only** option, which enables SDDNS, ensuring that only computers with existing domain accounts can update DNS records. If you use the **Nonsecure and secure** option, nondomain computers could update DNS records. If you select the **Primary zone** option, zone data is not stored in Active Directory and the **Secure only** option is not available with this option.

11.   D. The time to live (TTL) value specifies the length of time that a DNS server retains cached information for a zone. Increasing this value enables information to be retained for a longer time, thereby reducing the amount of DNS traffic but with the potential of errors should the IP address configuration of a requested host change within this interval. The refresh interval is used with

secondary DNS servers and is not relevant here. Reducing the TTL value would have the opposite effect and would increase the amount of DNS traffic.

12. B. Reducing the refresh interval enables a secondary server to be more up-to-date, but at the expense of increased network traffic. Increasing the refresh interval would have the opposite effect to what is needed here. The retry interval specifies how much time elapses before the secondary server tries again to contact the master server in the event that the master server does not respond on the first attempt. Its value is not relevant to this situation.

13. A. The **Scavenge Stale Resource Records** option performs an immediate scavenging of all stale resource records without the need to configure scavenging properties first. Selecting the **Scavenge stale resource records** check box or the **Enable automatic scavenging of stale records** option does not enable immediate scavenging as specified by this scenario. If you were to delete the stale resource records from the details pane of the DNS Manager snap-in, they would be re-created by replication from the other DNS servers.

Chapter 3

1. A, B, C, D, E, F. All these are best practices that you should follow and be completely aware of at an early stage of planning your domain structure. You should also ensure that you know everything there is to know about the network.

2. B, C, D, E. You can install AD DS on any of the Foundation, Standard, Enterprise, or Datacenter editions of Windows Server 2008 R2. You cannot install AD DS on the Web edition.

3. A, D. You can use either the Add Roles Wizard or the dcpromo.exe command to install AD DS on a Windows Server 2008 or Windows Server 2008 R2 computer. AD DS is considered a server role and not a server feature, so you cannot use the Add Features Wizard. The Manage Your Server and Configure Your Server tools were used in Windows Server 2003 but are no longer supported.

4. C. You must have a partition formatted with the NTFS file system in order to install AD DS. In fact, you must have NTFS to install Windows Server 2008 in the first place; the Setup Wizard will ask you to format your partition with NTFS before installation starts. You do not need DHCP to install AD DS. Although you need DNS with AD DS, the Active Directory Installation Wizard will install DNS if it is not present on a server somewhere on the network. You can install AD DS using as little as 500 MB of hard disk space, although it is recommended that you have much more space than this.

5. B. Active Directory Administrative Center is a new tool in Windows Server 2008 R2 that consolidates many of the administrative tasks within a single

console. Active Directory Users and Computers, Active Directory Sites and Services, and Active Directory Domains and Trusts have all been available since Windows 2000. User Manager for Domains was used with Windows NT 4.0 and has not been used since that time.

6. D. You must use dcpromo.exe together with an answer file that provides the required parameters to install a domain controller on a Server Core machine. Server Core does not contain any GUI tools or wizards, and it also does not permit you to specify parameters during the installation. Because you can use dcpromo.exe with an answer file, you do not have to reinstall Windows Server 2008 as a full edition server.

7. C. When you run the Active Directory Installation Wizard on a server that is already a domain controller, the domain controller is demoted to a member server. The wizard will not install a new or second copy of AD DS in these circumstances, nor will an error message appear.

8. A. The Windows 2000 mixed functional level, which supported Windows NT 4.0 domain controllers, is no longer supported by either the original or R2 versions of Windows Server 2008. All the other functional levels listed are supported in Windows Server 2008 R2.

9. A. You should run adprep /forestprep and then run adprep /domainprep. These commands prepare the forest and domain for receiving the Windows Server 2008 R2 domain controller. You must run them in this sequence and not in the opposite sequence. You cannot raise either the domain or forest functional level until after you have upgraded or removed all the Windows Server 2003 domain controllers.

10. C. ADMT assists you in migrating objects such as users, groups, and computers between AD DS domains in the same forest or different forests. You might be able to perform this task from Active Directory Users and Computers or Active Directory Administrative Center, but doing so would take more time and administrative effort. You can use USMT to migrate documents and settings to new computers running Windows Vista or 7, but this tool does not migrate user accounts between domains.

11. A. Sharon@sales.que.com is a valid implicit UPN for this user. Sharon@sales would be a valid explicit UPN. The other two options given are possible representations of the user and domain but are not UPN formats.

Chapter 4

1. C. A conditional forwarder forwards requests to another DNS server for name resolution requests for its specified domain only; other name resolution requests

pass to the Internet. A forwarder passes all name resolution requests that it cannot handle to specified DNS servers, which is not what is needed here. Configuring the partner company's DNS server as the conditional forwarder is backward to the result desired here.

2. B. You should check the root hints on the DNS server. These specify the IP addresses of the Internet root servers that contain information for all the top-level Internet domains. If they are incorrect or missing, users will be unable to access external websites. Conditional forwarders direct requests for specific DNS domains to a server that is authoritative for that domain only and do not regulate Internet access. Zone delegation enables the management of DNS zones to other locations on your network. Round robin randomizes access to multiple DNS servers that resolve names on the same zone. None of these provide Internet name resolution.

3. A, C. The New Delegation Wizard creates A (or AAAA) and NS resource records for the zone delegation. The other types of resource records are not needed for defining a zone delegation.

4. A. You should use the dnscmd /recordadd command. This command adds the specified type of resource records and can specify name servers or add zone delegations. The dnscmd /config command performs several configuration tasks including disabling recursion. The dnscmd /zoneresetsecondaries command configures the scope of zone transfers. The dnscmd /zoneadd command adds new forward or reverse lookup zones.

5. C. Debug logging records information on packets sent to and from the DNS server and stores this information in a text file named dns.log. DNS monitoring enables you to run test queries that check your server's configuration but does not create this log file. Event logging determines what type of events are recorded in the Event Viewer log. DNS notify enables a master server to notify secondary servers of changes to its zone but does not perform logging.

6. E. The Trust Anchors tab is new to DNS in Windows Server 2008 R2 and enables you to view and specify trust anchors, which are preconfigured public keys associated with specific zones and are used with the new DNS Security Extensions (DNSSEC) feature. The Event Logging and Debug Logging tabs enable you to configure logging options. The Advanced tab enables you to specify several options but not DNSSEC. The Security tab enables you to specify permissions but does not provide security extensions.

7. C. You should ensure that the **Enable netmask ordering** option is selected. Of the listed options, all of which are found on the Advanced tab of the DNS server's Properties dialog box, this is the only one that achieves the stated result.

8. B. The Monitoring tab of the DNS server's Properties dialog box enables you to perform two types of test queries to check your server's configuration. Of these, you need the recursive query option to satisfy the requirements specified here, although you would generally also select the simple query option (which performs a local query to a zone for which the server is authoritative). The **Disable recursion** option prevents the server from forwarding queries to other servers but does not perform any testing capabilities. The **Automatically notify** option enables the DNS server to notify secondary servers of changes to its zone configuration.

9. C. You should select the **To all domain controllers in this domain** option. Of the possible DNS replication scopes available, this is the only one that will replicate properly to a DNS server running Windows 2000.

10. A. The secondary server checks its history file to determine what updates need to be sent. If this file has been deleted, it is unable to obtain this information and must request a full zone transfer (AXFR). The serial number determines whether a zone transfer should be initiated, not what type of transfer is needed; it is not possible for the secondary server's serial number to be greater than the primary server's serial number. If the secondary server's IP address is not listed on the Name Servers tab at the primary server and the **Only to servers listed on the Name Servers tab** option is selected, zone transfers will not take place.

11. D. When your network uses Active Directory–integrated zones, you do not need to specify the DNS Notify option. If the zones were not integrated with Active Directory, you would need to click **Notify** and select the **Servers listed on the Name Servers tab** option. The Allow Zone Transfers options determine which DNS servers receive zone transfers and are not relevant to this situation.

12. A. Active Directory–integrated zone data is stored in one ForestDnsZones application directory partition plus one DomainDnsZones application directory partition for each domain in the forest, hence four of these partitions in this scenario.

13. C. You should create application directory partition replicas on the domain controllers to which the data is to be replicated. Specifying a reference domain merely changes which domain is the parent of the application directory partition. Creating additional application directory partitions creates separate partitions without any link to the partition you've already created. Application directory partitions have their own separate replication topology. You must configure this to ensure the proper replication.

Chapter 5

1. A. When the forest contains just a single domain, the global catalog server plays only a minor role. The global catalog server is much more important in any situation where there is more than one domain in the forest, regardless of the number of sites or domain controllers.

2. D. You use Active Directory Sites and Services to promote a domain controller to global catalog server. Expand the site in which the desired domain controller is located, expand the folder for the desired server, and access the NTDS Settings Properties dialog box to select the Global Catalog check box. The other Active Directory administration tools do not contain an option for designating a global catalog server.

3. C. It makes the greatest sense to designate universal group membership caching on a domain controller in a small branch office of a multiple domain enterprise where no global catalog server is located and which is connected to the head office by a low-bandwidth WAN. You do not need universal group membership caching at any office where global catalog servers are also located, and you do not need universal group membership caching when only a single domain exists. You must be using a domain controller when enabling universal group membership caching.

4. B. You should designate the branch office domain controller as a global catalog server. This enables users in this office to complete their logons without reference to a head office domain controller, and it also facilitates the location of resources in other domains. Configuring the branch office domain controller for universal group membership caching facilitates user logon but does not expedite the location of resources in other domains. Configuring the head office domain controllers for global catalogs or universal group membership caching does not help.

5. C. There is always just one schema master and one domain naming master per forest, regardless of the number of domains. Each domain has its own RID master, PDC emulator, and infrastructure master, so there are four of each of these operations masters in this scenario; it does not matter that the forest root domain is empty.

6. B. You must register the Active Directory Schema snap-in by typing **regsvr32 schmmgmt.dll** before you can install it. Microsoft has taken this step because modification of the schema is a serious matter that could compromise Active Directory severely if done improperly. The snap-in is not found in Control Panel Add or Remove Programs, nor do you need to download RSAT to obtain

it. The Active Directory Management Center does not include tools for managing the schema.

7. A. It is not possible to delete an attribute in the schema in order to remove it from influencing the functionality of the schema; you can only deactivate it. It is for this reason you must take adding attributes and classes to the schema seriously.

8. D. The PDC emulator acts as a time server for all domain controllers in its domain, and if it is unavailable, time errors of this type could occur, possibly resulting in logon failures. None of the other operations masters act as time servers.

9. A. You should not place the infrastructure master on a domain controller that is configured as a global catalog server unless all domain controllers are configured as global catalog servers. Otherwise, the infrastructure master would be unable to update its references to objects in other domains properly.

10. A, D. The major role of the infrastructure master is to update references to objects in other domains of the forest and to track group memberships that cross domain boundaries. The major role of the domain naming master is to ensure that names of new domains are unique. Neither of these two functions are required if the forest consists of only a single domain with no prospect of adding an additional domain.

11. A. The infrastructure master updates references to objects in other domains of its forest. In its absence, these references will not be updated and users might not be able to access these objects. None of the other operations masters act in this fashion.

12. A, C, D. You can use Active Directory Users and Computers to transfer any of the infrastructure master, RID master, or PDC emulator roles to another domain controller. You must use Active Directory Domains and Trusts to transfer the domain naming master role and Active Directory Schema to transfer the schema master role.

13. B. To get this role up and running immediately, you must seize it; to do this, you must use the ntdsutil tool. It is not possible to transfer the role when the current role holder is unavailable; further, the Active Directory Administrative Center does not offer the capability of either transferring or seizing FSMO roles.

Chapter 6

1.   A, C, D. Configuring branch offices as separate sites enables you to schedule replication, specify branch office-specific group policies, and isolate segments with poor network connectivity. You do not need to use sites when configuring universal group membership caching.

2.   A, B, E. After creating a new site, you need to ensure that the site is linked to other sites, add subnets for the new sites, and install one or more domain controllers at the new site. A licensing server was recommended in Windows Server 2003, but this capability was removed from Active Directory Sites and Services in Windows Server 2008. Active Directory automatically creates site link bridges, and you don't need to specify a site link bridge in most circumstances.

3.   A. You should assign the subnet containing computers located in Louisville to the Louisville site. When you create a new site, by default no subnets are associated with this site, so the computers located in Louisville think that they are in the Indianapolis site. Explicit UPN suffixes are used to simplify logon procedures in a multidomain forest. Universal group membership caching makes universal group membership available to all domain controllers in a multidomain forest. Neither is required in a single-domain scenario. Because this is an issue of traffic unnecessarily routed across the slow link, you do not need to upgrade the link to a faster one such as a T1 link.

4.   D. To use SMTP-based replication, you must install an enterprise CA that will sign the messages sent across the link. Site links and site link bridges are created automatically, and you do not need to create additional ones. Site link costs are specified only when more than one site link is available for connecting between different sites.

5.   B. By default, all site links are configured with a default cost of 100. By increasing this cost to 200 on the dial-up link, you specify that intersite replication should use the T1 link preferentially, thereby reducing long distance costs. Setting this cost to 50 would cause replication to favor this link, which is the opposite of the desired result. It is not necessary to create a site link bridge. You would use SMTP replication only for cross-domain replication when the available links are unreliable.

6.   C. You should create site link bridges that connect the offices according to the available direct connections. By default, all site links are automatically bridged, but this automatic bridging does not always work properly when there are sites that are not well connected. You might need to modify the costs of some site links, but the question indicates some sites are not connected as opposed to being unreliably connected. You do not need to create additional site links in this

scenario. SMTP replication is not needed here; further, it would not replicate domain or application partitions or any AD DS information between domain controllers in the same domain.

7.   D. The ISTG is a single domain controller at each site that is used by the KCC to build the network's intersite replication topology. The process that runs automatically on every domain controller in the forest and builds intersite and intrasite replication topologies is a description of the KCC and not the ISTG. Site link bridges are built automatically and are not included in the function of the ISTG. Each site has its own ISTG; it is not a single domain controller in the forest.

8.   B, D. Intersite replication can be configured and scheduled; intrasite replication occurs automatically at frequent intervals that can be specified as once, twice, or four times per hour. Intrasite replication uses the RPC over IP transport protocol exclusively.

9.   A. Windows Server 2008 R2 uses DFS replication for replicating all AD DS database components, except for replicating the SYSVOL folder on domain controllers in domains that are still using the Windows 2000 or Windows Server 2003 domain functional levels. The original version of Windows Server 2008 used DFS replication for replicating the SYSVOL folder to other domain controllers, provided that the domain is operating at the Windows Server 2008 functional level, and used FRS replication for replicating other AD DS components.

10.   A, D, E. SMTP replication replicates only the schema and configuration partitions (not the domain partition), and SMTP replication replicates these partitions only between different domains in the same forest. Finally, you can use Active Directory Sites and Services to modify the schedule for replicating RPC over IP only.

11.   D. Of the options provided, the one that ensures that replication will take place as desired in this scenario is to configure replication to take place once every 30 minutes and schedule replication to not take place between 8 AM and 12 noon, and again from 1 PM to 5 PM. If you retain the default replication interval, which is every 180 minutes, replication might not occur every lunch hour. If you configure replication to take place once every four hours, replication will occur during business hours when the WAN link is busy. Manually forcing replication to take place during lunch hour would work but would take more effort and is prone to errors.

12.   B. The dialog box that enables you to modify the schedule of intrasite replication is found in the Properties dialog box for the NTDS Settings folder within any of the servers in your site. This setting is not found in the site's Properties

dialog box. The Inter-Site Transports folder does not contain any settings pertaining to intrasite replication. The default interval for intrasite replication is 60 minutes, not 15 minutes.

Chapter 7

1. B. An additional component that supports a Windows Server 2008 role is known as a *role service*. For example, the Active Directory domain controller is considered as a role service in support of the AD DS role. A *feature* is a server component that provides additional functionality to roles or the server itself. Although the terms *extension* and *add-on* have meaning in other fields of computing, they are not used in conjunction with server roles and features.

2. D. You should specify ports 50000 and 50001 rather than the default ports of 389 and 636 from the Ports page of the installation wizard. You can use alternative port numbers if you desire, but you should not use ports 389 and 636, which are used by AD DS for communicating with LDAP and SSL. It is not necessary to install either DNS or the AD DS server role before installing AD LDS. You can select either option from the Application Directory Partition page of the Add Roles Wizard.

3. B, D, F, G. You can use any of Active Directory Sites and Services, Active Directory Schema, Active Directory Services Interface (ADSI), and `Ldp.exe` to manage the AD LDS instance. All these tools perform various types of administrative actions in AD LDS. None of the other tools mentioned perform AD LDS administrative actions.

4. A. You need to bind a user account to the `Ldp.exe` interface. This is usually your currently logged-on user account, but you can specify another user account by providing the proper credentials. AD LDS does not require that you have a certificate. An authentication server is used to authenticate users requesting directory data from AD LDS instances but is not used when working with `Ldp.exe`.

5. C. The `Ldifde` tool is used from an administrative command prompt to import data from a legacy application or file, so that it can be used with AD LDS. The `Ntdsutil` tool manages many properties of AD DS or AD LDS, but it does not import data. The `Csvde` tool imports comma-separated data during actions such as bulk user or group account creation, but it does not import data to AD LDS. You cannot use `Xcopy` to simply copy the data.

6. A. You should configure an AD LDS security principal for Ryan. This is a user account that resides directly in AD LDS and enables authentication of Ryan to use the directory-enabled applications without granting him access to network resources. Configuring a domain user account for Ryan would grant him access

to shared resources, which is not desired. Membership in the Domain Guests group does not give him access to shared resources but also does not give him access to the applications. Ryan must be authenticated to AD LDS before receiving access to the applications, so his local user account does not give him access.

7. C. When installing AD RMS on a member server, you should create a user account that is a member of the Domain Users group only. Only when installing AD RMS on a domain controller do you need to create a user account that is a member of the Domain Admins group. You need to perform all the other actions listed here; in particular, note that the functional levels do not need to be set to Windows Server 2008 or Windows Server 2008 R2.

8. C. This certificate establishes a user's identity when she first attempts to open rights-protected content. It contains the public key of the user, as well as the corresponding private key, which is encrypted with the public key of the activated computer. The CLC is sent to the client computer when connected to the network and enables this computer to publish rights-protected content. The machine certificate is created on the client computer running Windows Vista/7 when an AD RMS-enabled application is used for the first time. It includes the public key of this computer. The CLC and machine certificate are required by the computer, not the user. The user license specifies the rights granted to the authenticated user for the rights-protected content. It is associated with the RAC but cannot be obtained before the user has received the RAC.

9. B. The AD RMS Enterprise Administrators role enables Paul to manage all AD RMS policies and settings. The AD RMS Auditors role would enable the ability to manage audit logs and reports. The AD RMS Template Administrators role enables the ability to manage rights policy templates. Neither of these roles enables the ability to manage policies and settings. There is no such role as AD RMS Server Operators. (The Server Operators group in AD DS enables members to perform several administrative functions on domain controllers but does not extend capabilities to AD RMS administrators.)

10. B. The Federation Service Proxy role service acts as a proxy to the Federation Service on a perimeter network or demilitarized zone. You would not use Federation Service because this service is used on servers installed within the main network. Claims-aware agents and Windows token-based agents do not authenticate users from partner companies.

11. A. To install the Federation Service role service of AD FS, your server must be joined to an AD DS domain. To install AD FS, the server must be running IIS with ASP .NET 2.0 and Microsoft .NET Framework 2.0; however, the Add Roles Wizard will ask you to install these components if they are not already

present on the server. In the original version of Windows Server 2008, the server had to be running either the Enterprise or Datacenter Edition; however, you can install the Federation Service role service on Windows Server 2008 R2 Standard Edition.

12. D. You need to set up a trust policy. This enables uses to share documents protected in AD RMS across internal or external AD DS forests. A group claim specifies a set of incoming group claims to be accepted from the account partner, which is the partner company, and a custom claim contains information about users. *Claims* are statements made by a server about a client in the process of negotiating trusts. They are not applicable in this scenario. An account store stores user accounts that AD FS must authenticate to use your company's federated applications. Although required, the account store does not enable users to share protected documents, so this is not applicable here as well.

13. A. In claim mapping, incoming claims are passed from the account partner to the resource partner, which in turn maps these claims into organization claims sent to the resource application by the resource federation service. They are not passed from the resource partner to the account partner. Although incoming claims are sequenced as indicated, this is not referred to as claim mapping. Account stores are not used in the method described here.

14. A, B, C. UPN, email, and common name claims are collectively known as *organization* or *identity claims*.

15. C, D. To use Hyper-V, the server must have a processor that includes a hardware-assisted virtualization option and it must be equipped with hardware-enforced DEP. You can install Hyper-V on a server that is running Standard Edition, and it is also possible to install Hyper-V on a standalone server that is not joined to an AD DS domain. Although the server must be running a 64-bit edition of Windows Server 2008, the R2 version comes only in 64-bit software, so mentioning R2 precludes the server from running a 32-bit version of Windows Server 2008.

Chapter 8

1. B, D, E. You need to ensure that the PDC emulator role is hosted on a domain controller running Windows Server 2008 or higher. You also need to ensure that a domain controller running Windows Server 2008 or higher is available and has network connectivity to the proposed RODC and run the `Adprep /rodcprep` utility. The forest and domain functional levels should be set to Windows Server 2003 or higher. You generally do not want to install a domain controller running Windows Server 2008 or higher in the same site as the proposed RODC.

2. B, C, E. You can designate the new RODC to be a DNS server and/or a global catalog server during installation. You can also delegate administration of the RODC during installation. An RODC can never be the first domain controller for a new domain. The BitLocker drive encryption and password replication policy settings are configured after you have installed the RODC.

3. A. You would use the `dsmgmt` utility to designate a user or group with administrative access to the RODC. Active Directory Users and Computers enables you to manage users, groups, and computers but does not allow you to delegate administrative control of an RODC. The `ntdsutil` utility performs various management tasks within AD DS. `syskey` enables you to store a system-generated password for starting an RODC. Neither of these tools enables you to delegate administrative access to the RODC.

4. C. Each RODC has a local Administrators group that is stored locally on the SAM. By delegating administrative control of the RODC to Karen, her user account is added to this group, giving her these capabilities without enabling her to perform administrative actions elsewhere in the domain. If you were to add her user account to the Domain Admins or Server Operators group, she would receive excessive privileges. The Power Users group is present only for backward capability with some applications written for Windows Server 2003, Windows XP, and older operating systems, and does not grant her any administrative capabilities.

5. A. You should configure a Group Policy setting that enables the use of a USB flash drive to store the encryption keys and password. Doing so enables you to use BitLocker on a computer that is not equipped with a TPM. You can use `syskey` to specify a password that must be entered at server startup; however, this does not provide any encryption. You need to use the Add Features Wizard to add BitLocker, but you also need to configure the indicated Group Policy setting. Because you can enable BitLocker in Group Policy, the last option is not correct.

6. C. You should add the user accounts of the users to the Allowed list for password replication. This enables caching of their passwords locally on the RODC. Because the AD DS database at the RODC is read-only, you cannot specify new passwords from Active Directory Users and Computers. The Denied list prevents passwords from being cached locally, and users would always need to cross the WAN to be authenticated. Because you can use the Allowed list, you do not need to replace the RODC with a writable domain controller.

7. D. The **Accounts that have been authenticated to this Read-only Domain Controller** option displays user, computer, and group accounts that the RODC has authenticated and provides you with the information you need. The

Accounts whose passwords are stored on this Read-only Domain Controller option displays those accounts whose passwords have been cached but does not indicate which accounts have been authenticated. You must access these options from the partnered writable domain controller and not from the RODC.

Chapter 9

1. C. Sharon should use a global group. All 55 users belong to a single domain, so a global group is most appropriate in this situation. A local group on a member server or client computer provides access to resources on that computer only. A domain local group provides access to resources within its domain only. (Note, however, that Sharon can and should add the global group to domain local groups in each domain for access to the resources.) Sharon does not need a universal group because all users are located in a single domain.

2. B. You would use a template account in creating a large number of domain user accounts that have similar properties and need for resource access. It is simple to copy this account and supply a username and password for each user that requires access.

3. A. The Csvde tool enables you to import data to AD DS from files containing information in the comma-separated (CSV) format. It is easy to export Excel data to a file in this format. It is not as simple to convert this data to a format that would be supported by either Ldifde or Dsadd. Using the Active Directory Administrative Center would take much more time to create these user accounts.

4. C. You should use WSH to run this script. Windows PowerShell is a powerful new scripting tool that provides a large number of subcommands called *cmdlets*; however, it does not accept VBScript commands. JScript is a separate scripting language and not an import tool. A batch file is used with commands such as Dsadd but not with VBScript commands.

5. D. Active Directory Domains and Trusts provides you with the capability of creating a UPN suffix. You would use either Active Directory Administrative Center or Active Directory Users and Computers to specify the UPN suffix that each user will use during logon; however, these tools do not allow you to add a new UPN suffix. Active Directory Sites and Services does not enable any facet of UPN suffix administration.

6. B. You should create contacts for each of these individuals and add these contacts to a distribution group. A *contact* is simply a collection of information about an individual or organization. It can be included in a distribution list

created for sending email messages. User accounts provide them with access to the domain, which is not desired here. Security groups enable permissions to be granted to their members; you cannot include contacts as members of security groups.

7. A, C, D. Of the types of information listed here, these are the most helpful ones. They will enable you to design an OU structure that will best suit the company's needs. Although you will need to consult with company executives throughout the design process, you do not need this information for inclusion in the OU design. Information on partner companies is needed for planning trust relationships but is not needed for designing the company's OU structure.

8. A, B, C, E. You can add user accounts and domain local groups from the same domain, global groups, and universal groups from any domain in the forest to this domain local group. However, you cannot add domain local groups from other domains to this group.

9. A, C, D, E. You can nest the global group into universal and domain local groups in any domain and global groups in the same domain. However, you cannot nest the group into a global group in a different domain (in this case, the parent domain).

10. D. You should add the user accounts to global groups in their respective do-main. Then add these global groups to the universal group and, finally, add the universal group to three domain local groups—one located in each child domain to which the users need access. Then finally grant permissions to the domain lo-cal groups. This strategy follows Microsoft's AGDLP recommended group nesting strategy. Although the other strategies might seem simpler, they can all introduce problems at some time in the future. For example, adding the user ac-counts to the universal group increases replication traffic any time the member-ship in this group changes. Granting permissions to the universal group might expose this group to unnecessary resources and can increase replication traffic should these permissions change.

11. B. A Protected Admin user account is an administrative user account other than the default account created when Windows Server 2008 R2 is installed or the first domain administrator account created when AD DS is installed. When us-ing this account to perform an administrative task, you will be prompted by UAC to confirm your intentions by clicking **Yes** or **Continue** in a message box. When using either of the default administrative accounts mentioned here, you will not receive a UAC prompt. When using an administrative account other than the default accounts, you will not be asked to type your username and pass-word. When using a standard user account, you will be required to type an ad-ministrative password, not merely click **Yes** or **Continue** in a message box.

12. C. You should disable Ryan's account and then rename and reenable it after the new employee is hired. This is the most secure means of deprovisioning an account so that it cannot be used in the interim and so that all its rights and privileges are maintained for later use. It does not make sense to turn the account into a template. You could remove the account from the groups that grant him access to the resources he used in performance of his job; however, Ryan could still log on until you rename the account, and this entire method is more complex and error-prone. If you delete Ryan's account, you will need to re-create all the privileges associated with it when you re-create the account; disabling the account instead leaves these privileges intact but prevents use of the account in the interim.

13. A. The Delegation of Control Wizard enables you to grant the ability to perform various administrative tasks to users or groups. This includes the **Reset user passwords and force password change at next logon** task. You can (and should) use a group account rather than individual user accounts when running this wizard. The Account Operators group would grant the help desk technicians more administrative privileges than required in this scenario.

Chapter 10

1. D. A shortcut trust is used to improve user logon times and resource access between two child domains in the same forest. The other trust types are not configured within a forest; they all are configured to provide access to a domain that is external to the current forest.

2. C. You need to configure an external trust so that users can receive the required access. A forest trust is available only when both forests involved operate at the Windows Server 2003 forest functional level or higher; hence, you cannot have a forest trust here. A realm trust enables access to users in a Kerberos v.5 realm. A shortcut trust is used to improve user logon times and resource access between two child domains in the same forest and not to an external forest.

3. A, B, D. Forest trusts and shortcut trusts are always transitive, whereas you can specify that a realm trust be created as either transitive or nontransitive. An external trust is always nontransitive.

4. A. You should configure a one-way external trust in which the `certguide.com` domain trusts the `que.com` domain. A trust in this direction enables users in the trusted (`que.com`) domain to access resources in the trusting (`certguide.com`) domain. If you configured a one-way external trust in which the `que.com` domain trusts the `certguide.com` domain, users in the `certguide.com` domain would be able to access resources in the `que.com` domain and not the other way

around. You do not use a shortcut trust in this situation; this type of trust is used only between child domains in the same forest.

5. C. You would use the `netdom` command-line tool to create a trust relationship when working at a Server Core computer. Remember that a Server Core computer has no GUI, so graphical tools such as Active Directory Administrative Center and Active Directory Domains and Trusts are not available. The `dsmgmt` command-line tool is used to designate a user or group with administrative access to a read-only domain controller (RODC). It is not used in trust management.

6. C. You should choose the **Selective authentication** option. This option enables you to specify the users and groups from a trusted forest who are permitted to authenticate to servers containing resources in the trusting forest. Forestwide authentication would enable access to all resources in the trusting forest, and domainwide authentication (available with external trusts) would enable access to resources in the trusting domain. There is no such option as one-way authentication.

7. C, D. You can validate a trust relationship from either Active Directory Domains and Trusts or the `netdom trust` command. When using Active Directory Domains and Trusts, it is necessary to select the Trusts tab of your domain's Properties dialog box and then access the Properties dialog box of the other domain from this location. Only then can you access the Validate button to verify the trust. When using the `netdom trust` command with the `/verify` keyword, you specify the trusted domain name, in this case the `que.com` domain, with the `d:` parameter and the trusting domain name, in this case `certguide.com`, without this parameter.

8. B. When working at the `sales.que.com` domain, you can directly access the Trusts tab of its Properties dialog box, and from this location select the `marketing.certguide.com` domain and access the Authentication tab of its Properties dialog box. This enables you to choose the **Selective authentication** option, which provides the desired results. The **Domain-wide authentication** option would permit unrestricted access by any users in the trusted domain to all available shared resources in the trusting domain, according to sharing and security permissions attached to the resources, which is not desired. You cannot configure this option from the Trusts tab of the `marketing.certguide.com` domain without connecting to this domain first.

9. A. The correct syntax is **Netdom trust** *trusting_domain* **/domain:***trusted domain* **/quarantine:Yes**, so you need to specify **que.com** as the trusting domain and **certguide.com** as the trusted domain and not the other way around. If you

specify **/quarantine:No** in this command, you disable SID filtering, which is not the desired result here.

Chapter 11

1. B. GPCs are stored in the domain partition of AD DS and GPTs are stored in the SYSVOL shared folder. Group Policy is specific to each domain in the forest, so the domain partition is used for GPCs. In addition, each domain has a folder hierarchy found in the domain controllers at the shared folder `%systemroot%\SYSVOL\sysvol\<domain_name>\Policies.`

2. A. First introduced in Windows Server 2003 R2, Group Policy Management Console is the tool that enables you to perform all management activities on GPOs including such functions as creating and linking GPOs, modifying their inheritance, disabling or deleting them, and so on. You use the Group Policy Management Editor to edit policy settings within GPOs but not to manage them. Active Directory Users and Computers contained Group Policy management tools in Windows 2000 and Windows Server 2003 before R2 but no longer does so. Active Directory Administrative Center performs many administrative activities in Windows Server 2008 R2 but not with Group Policy.

3. D. The Administrative Templates folder enables you to configure these types of settings on computers and users to which the GPO is applied. The Preferences container includes new Group Policy extensions that control items such as folder options, mapped drives, printers, scheduled tasks, and so on. Software Settings enables you to specify what software is deployed to users and computers. Windows Settings includes scripts and security settings as well as other settings that affect the behavior of the Windows environment.

4. C. You should not delete the GPO. There is no way to recover a deleted GPO if you need its settings back in the future (although you could recover it from a backup if one exists). Performing any of the other actions listed retains the GPO together with its settings but renders it incapable of applying its settings to any container in your domain.

5. A, D. You can grant Ted the required capabilities by using the Delegation tab in GPMC or by using the Delegation of Control Wizard. If you make him a member of the Group Policy Creator Owners group, he would have more capabilities than required here, and if you make him a member of the Server Operators group, he would not have any capabilities for administering GPOs.

6. C. By default, GPOs are applied in the sequence L, S, D, OU. If child OU GPOs are present, they are applied in sequence after top-level OU GPOs have been applied.

7. B. You should configure the GPO with the Enforced setting. This setting prevents policies contained in the GPO where it is specified from being overwritten by other GPOs that are processed later. This includes OU-based policies. Note that you configure a specific GPO and not an AD DS container with this setting. The Block Inheritance setting prevents GPOs that are linked to parent containers from being applied at the lower level; this is not what is desired here. Because OU-based policies override domain-based policies, you must use the Enforced setting.

8. C. By configuring your domain with the Block Inheritance setting, you prevent conflicting site-based GPO settings from applying to your domain. Note that, unlike the Enforced setting, the Block Inheritance setting applies to the container (domain or OU) where it is specified and not to an individual GPO. The Enforced setting prevents policies contained in the GPO where it is specified from being overwritten by other GPOs that are processed later, which would be OU-based policies and not site-based policies.

9. D. By denying the Apply Group Policy permission to the Domain Admins group, you prevent the settings in the GPO from applying to any member of this group regardless of the computer to which they log on. It might be possible to use a WMI filter or a Windows PowerShell script to perform this action, but either of these would be far more complex and error-prone than denying the Apply Group Policy permission. Disabling the link for computers used by members of this group would prevent the GPO from applying to these computers, but it would still be applied elsewhere; further, you would need to place these computers into their own OU to do so.

10. B. You should enable the loopback processing mode with the replace option. This option ensures that the user-based settings that would normally be applied are disregarded. If you were to use the merge option, this would merge both the user and computer settings, resulting in a combined set of policies. Disabling the computer settings would enable library patrons to access restricted information. Disabling the user settings would affect not just the public computers but also those in the staff offices.

11. C. ADMX files work with Windows Vista, Windows 7, and Windows Server 2008 only, so policies applied using this format do not apply to Windows XP computers. WMI filters are processed by Windows XP computers (only Windows 2000 or older computers ignore these filters). This would not be a case of using an incorrect loopback setting or an incorrect subfolder of SYSVOL.

12. B, D, E. Settings in the Desktop, Shared Folders, and Start Menu and Taskbar sections of Administrative Templates apply to users only. Control Panel and

System settings apply to both computers and users, and Printers settings apply to computers only.

13. A. The Restricted Groups setting enables you to limit the membership of any groups, including the local administrators group on client computers. This setting is found in the Computer Configuration node and not in the User Configuration node or the Delegation tab of the GPO's properties. You cannot delegate control of client computers from the Delegation tab.

14. D. You should create a new GPO linked to the child domain and specify the name of the Starter GPO in the New GPO dialog box. The Starter GPO contains settings that can be used for creating new GPOs in this fashion. Note that you cannot link a Starter GPO to any AD DS container. It would be possible to copy settings in the Starter GPO to the Default Domain Policy GPO or another GPO, but this would defeat the purpose of using a Starter GPO in the first place.

Chapter 12

1. D. It is not possible to publish software to computers. This is true because users must manually commence the installation of published software. The other three methods mentioned here are the only ones available for deploying software by means of Group Policy.

2. C, D. When you assign a software package to users, the software is installed when the user reboots her computer. If a component is deleted or becomes corrupted, this component is reinstalled automatically at the next reboot. Because the software is installed at the next reboot, it is not installed when selected from the Start menu; also the user does not need to access Control Panel to install it. The software is available only at computers to which the Group Policy object (GPO) assigning it applies.

3. B, E. When you publish a software package to users, it is not advertised on the Start menu; the user must access Control Panel Add or Remove Programs (Windows XP) or Programs and Features (Windows Vista/7) to install it. Further, it is not installed when the computer is rebooted. When published to a user, the user can access the software at any computer that he might access. Published software is not resilient; if a component is deleted or becomes corrupted, the user must return to Control Panel to reinstall it.

4. C. A `.zap` file is a text file with the `.zap` extension that specifies the path to the setup files associated with the application. This Zero Administration Package file enables you to publish applications that do not come with an `.msi` file. An `.mst` file is a transform file and an `.msp` file is a patch file; neither of these

enables deployment of a software package. An `.exe` file is the package's executable and does not provide deployment capability.

5. A. The **Basic** option, which is available from the General tab of the Software installation Properties dialog box, limits the information displayed during software installation to progress bars and error messages. The **Maximum** option provides more detailed information, which is not desired in this scenario. The Deployment tab is found on the Properties dialog box for a specific software package and not the Software installation Properties dialog box. This tab provides these two options, but they apply only for the specific software package and not for other packages.

6. B. The **Uninstall the applications when they fall out of the scope of management** option, when selected, automatically removes the software should the GPO that installed it no longer be applied to the user or computer. By clearing this option, applications installed on Phil's laptop are retained despite his user account having been transferred to the Design OU. Adding Phil's user account to a group in the Marketing OU that has privileges for the software packages that he requires does not work because applications are deployed from GPOs that apply to OUs and cannot be linked to groups. Granting Phil the **Read** and **Read & Execute** permissions also does not retain the applications if the **Uninstall the applications when they fall out of the scope of management** option is selected. Linking the GPO to the Design OU would provide all users in this OU with access to the application, which is not desired.

7. B. The **Package can upgrade over the existing package** option retains the user's application preferences, document type associations, and so on, when upgrading a software package to a newer version. The **Uninstall the existing package, then install the upgrade package** option would wipe out the preferences and plug-ins, forcing each user to reinstall or re-create them. Clearing the **Required upgrade for existing packages** check box would enable users to continue using Photoshop CS4 but would have no effect on the upgrade to CS5 for users performing this upgrade. It is not necessary to create `.mst` files to meet the objective here.

8. D. Transform files with the `.mst` extension enable you to make changes to an installation database. For example, you can change the language of a user interface by employing a transform file. You cannot use `.zap` or `.msp` files for this purpose. Because you can use transform files in this scenario, you do not need to create multiple GPOs and perform multiple deployments to ensure that all users have local language versions of Microsoft Office.

9. A. You can redeploy the software including these patches and hotfixes by merely selecting the **All Tasks > Redeploy application** option from the application's

right-click menu from the Software Settings\Software installation subnode under either Computer Configuration or User Configuration in the Group Policy
Management Editor. It is not necessary to perform an upgrade of the application in this scenario, so none of the described options from the Upgrades tab of
the application's Properties dialog box are required here.

10. B. The **Allow users to continue to use the software, but prevent new
installations** option is available when removing outdated software and enables
users to be able to use the older package; however, this package is no longer
supported in Group Policy. If you choose the **Immediately uninstall the
software from users and computers** option, users will be unable to continue
using the older package. The **Required upgrade for existing packages** check
box is used only when upgrading older applications and not when removing
them. It would be possible to provide copies of the old CAD package, but the
Allow users to continue to use the software, but prevent new installations
option renders this move unnecessary.

Chapter 13

1. B. The Minimum password age policy enables you to prevent users from cycling
rapidly through passwords and thereby defeating the Enforce password history
policy. When enabled, a user cannot change her password again for the interval
specified by this policy.

2. E. The Store passwords using reversible encryption policy reduces security because it stores passwords in a format that is essentially the same as plain text.
You should enable this policy only if needed for clients that cannot use normal
encryption.

3. A, B, C. All these policies affect user lockouts and help to prevent unauthorized
access by intruders while minimizing inconvenience to legitimate users. By enabling the Account lockout duration policy and specifying a short interval such
as 10 minutes, an intruder attempting a password attack of some type will be
locked out of the account. If a legitimate user is locked out because of entering
her password incorrectly, she only needs to wait this specified interval before
she is able to log on; during this interval, the intruder will likely try elsewhere.
The Account lockout threshold policy setting specifies how many incorrect
passwords can be entered before the account is locked out; keep this value low
enough so that a legitimate user has several attempts should she make typing
mistakes. The Reset account lockout counter after policy specifies the number
of minutes after which the account lockout counter is reset to zero; it prevents
lockouts in the event that a legitimate user makes errors at several different

times. The Password must meet complexity requirements policy prevents use of simple passwords but does not affect account lockout.

4. D. You should specify the password policy settings in a PSO that is linked to a security group in the Legal OU that contains the user accounts of Legal department employees. Password policies specified in a GPO linked to an OU are not enforced by default; only the password policies specified in a GPO linked to the domain are enforced. Neither the Block Inheritance nor the No Override option changes this effect. You cannot link a PSO to an OU; you can link only to a user or group.

5. B, D. You need to use `Adsiedit.msc` to create a PSO containing the fine-grained password policy settings that you want to apply. Then you need to use Active Directory Users and Computers (or in Windows Server 2008 R2, Active Directory Administrative Center) to link the PSO to the group to which it should apply (in this case, the Research group). You would use `Gpedit.msc` (the Group Policy Management Editor) to create domain-based account policy settings and the Group Policy Management Console to access a GPO in which you apply these settings. However, these tools are not used in creating PSOs. Windows PowerShell enables you to perform many Windows- and Active Directory–based management actions, but you cannot configure a PSO.

6. A. When multiple PSOs have been configured, the PSO applied directly to a user's account will override all other PSOs. If multiple PSOs are applied to the same group, the PSO with the lowest Password Settings Precedence value will apply. Any settings defined in PSOs will override the default settings that have been applied to any domain-based GPO.

7. B. The Security Templates tool enables you to save a custom security policy template on a member server. You can then use the Security Configuration and Analysis tool to create a database containing settings in the policy template and apply them to the standalone server. You cannot apply these settings directly to the standalone server by means of Security Configuration and Analysis. The Security Configuration Wizard enables you to check the security settings applied to your servers but not to copy settings from one server to another. You could manually specify all the required settings using the Local Security Policy snap-in at the standalone server; however, this procedure is more tedious and error-prone than using the Security Configuration and Analysis and Security Templates tools.

8. D. You should audit the Detailed Directory Service Replication subcategory of directory service auditing. This subcategory tracks all the actions specified here. To enable this auditing subcategory, use the Advanced Audit Policy Configuration node in the Windows Server 2008 R2 Group Policy Management Console. In

the original version of Windows Server 2008, you must use the `Auditpol.exe` command-line tool to configure this auditing subcategory.

9. **A, D.** The audit account management event includes creation, modification, or deletion of user accounts or groups; renaming or disabling of user accounts; or configuring and changing passwords, and the audit logon events tracks logon or logoff by a user at a member server or client computer. Audit account logon events tracks logon or logoff by a domain user account at a domain controller and not at local computers. Audit object access tracks when a user accesses an object such as a file, folder, Registry key, or printer that has its own system access control list (SACL) specified. This action is not required in this scenario.

10. **C.** Auditing of object access is a two-step process. First, you must enable auditing of object access in the appropriate GPO, as you have done. Second, you must also configure the SACL for each required object. This involves specifying auditing entries for the folder containing the documents to be audited. It is not necessary to enable auditing of logon events to track modifications to documents. Auditing of object access can be enabled at any GPO applicable to the server containing the documents; it is not necessary to enable this in a GPO linked to the Legal OU. Directory service access tracks access to AD DS objects such as user or group accounts or OUs; it does not track access to document files or folders.

11. **D.** The Audit Account Lockout policy enables you to configure auditing of this specific action. It is found only under Logon/Logoff within Advanced Audit Policy Configuration\Audit Policies. The new granular auditing policies found in Windows Server 2008 R2 enable this level of auditing, which is not found in the Computer Configuration\Policies\Windows Settings\Security Settings\Local Policies\Audit Policy subnode and is not available on older Windows Server computers. Further, this setting is not found under Account Logon (which deals with logons and logoffs at domain controllers and not at member servers or client computers).

12. **B.** The `Auditpol.exe` tool enables you to configure auditing from the command line, as is necessary when working at a Server Core computer. `Adsiedit.msc` enables you to configure fine-grained password policies among other tasks. `Gpedit.msc` is the Group Policy Management Editor, which enables you to configure GPOs on computers running the full version of Windows Server 2008. `Scwcmd.exe` is a command-line version of the Security Configuration Wizard, which enables you to maintain security of your servers. None of these tools enables you to configure auditing from the command line.

Chapter 14

1. **A, B, C.** Network Monitor enables you to filter captured traffic using any of these criteria and others. Captured frames do not include information on the operating system used by the originating computer.

2. **A, C, D, E.** You can perform all these actions from Task Manager, but you cannot create performance alerts or monitor a remote computer from Task Manager (the latter actions require the capabilities of Performance Monitor).

3. **B, C.** You can run a program at low priority by starting it from a command prompt with the /low parameter, or by setting its priority to **Low** in Task Manager. Performance Monitor, Windows System Resource Manager, or Server Performance Advisor do not enable you to change the priority of an application.

4. **D.** You can filter any log according to several criteria, one of which is the event level. To do this for events taking place with AD DS, you must perform this action on the Directory Service log because this is the log at which AD DS events are displayed. The System log records events related to the server in general and the Security log records events related to auditing. Neither of these can be filtered to a Directory Service event source. It is not necessary to use the Registry Editor; you would do this only to increase the level of detail that processes are recorded in.

5. **B, D, E.** Task Manager, Performance Monitor, and Windows System Resource Manager can all display graphs of processor and memory usage. Network Monitor displays information about data frames transmitted across the network. Event Viewer displays information about events taking place on the computer, applications running on the computer, or successful or failed accesses to resources. Server Performance Advisor was used in Windows Server 2003 as a tool that gathers information from a series of sources, including performance counters, Registry keys, and Event Tracing for Windows. None of the latter three tools display performance graphs.

6. **C.** Sharon needs to use the Data Collector Sets tool to log data over a period of time in order to obtain a performance baseline for the domain controller. The **Save Image As** option saves an image of the currently visible data but does not save data that is no longer visible. Performance Monitor does not have an Export option for saving performance data. The Resource Manager option in WSRM enables her to view performance data but not save it.

7. **A.** Reliability Monitor provides this type of trend analysis. None of the other tools mentioned here can do this job.

8. C. You should configure a Performance Counter Alert Data Collector Set. This feature logs conditions that you specify, such as a high processor utilization, and alerts you when such conditions occur. An Event Trace Data Collector Set creates trace logs that log data only when a specific activity takes place; however, this type of data collector set does not send messages for specific conditions. An event log is created by Event Viewer and logs a large number of events but not this type of message. A System Diagnostics Data Collector Set creates reports on local hardware resources, system response times, and processes on the computer along with system information and configuration data. It does not provide alerts.

9. B, C, E. You can use `replmon` and `repadmin` to monitor replication and check for problems. You can also use Event Viewer to locate errors in the various Windows logs. Active Directory Sites and Services does not provide replication-related data. `Netdiag` diagnoses network connectivity problems but not replication problems.

10. B. The Generate Status Report option in `replmon` enables you to create and save a replication status report for a monitored domain controller. The Show Replication Topologies option displays a list of domain controllers with which the monitored domain controllers replicates but does not log replication information. The `dcdiag` tool provides a number of tests on domain controller status but not replication status. Event Viewer displays many messages related to AD DS in its Directory Service log but not the desired replication information, although it might provide clues as to why replication is not taking place as desired.

11. A, B, G. You need to perform a planning mode analysis in RSoP to complete the requirements of this task, and you can perform this action from any of Active Directory Users and Computers, Active Directory Sites and Services (for site-based policies), or the Group Policy Management Console. You can also do this by creating a custom MMC console. The `Gpresult` command and the Run dialog box enable you to perform a logging mode RSoP query, but not the planning mode query required in this scenario. The other tools do not have capabilities for performing an RSoP analysis.

12. A, B, C, D, E. All these properties can be included in an RSoP planning mode query.

13. D. If a user has not logged on to a given computer, RSoP in logging mode will not work on that computer for that user. You should run the logging mode query on Fred's computer, not your own. None of the other reasons indicated here would be likely, although this problem could occur if Fred's user account had somehow become disabled since the time he made his complaint to you.

14. A. The `Gpupdate /force` forces the immediate application of Group Policy to all concerned users and computers. There is no `/apply` parameter with this command. The `Gpresult` command performs a logging mode query; it does not force the application of Group Policy and neither the `/force` nor the `/apply` parameter is valid with this command.

Chapter 15

1. A, B, C, E, F. Of the items mentioned here, the only one that is not a component of system state data on a domain controller is the installed application files. When installed, cluster service information and the Internet Information Services (IIS) metadirectory are also components of system state.

2. D. In both the original and R2 versions of Windows Server 2008, Windows Server Backup is not installed by default when you install the operating system. You need to install Windows Server Backup as a server feature from the Features node in Server Manager. Windows Server Backup is not an option found in the console tree of either the Computer Management or Server Manager snap-ins. The `ntbackup` utility was used for performing backups in Windows Server 2003 and older server versions; it has been replaced by Windows Server Backup in Windows Server 2008.

3. C. You use the `wbadmin` tool to configure backups from the command line in Windows Server 2008. This tool includes the capability of scripting backups. The `ntbackup` tool was used in Windows Server 2003 and older versions for this purpose, but its use is no longer supported. The `ntdsutil` tool is used for performing a variety of actions on the domain controller including authoritative restore operations, but it is not used for backups. The `esentutl` tool provides utility functions for the Extensible Storage Engine for Windows; it does not perform backups.

4. A. You need to copy the mission-critical documents from the first partition to a different hard disk. When you run the Backup Schedule Wizard to configure scheduled backups, the entire hard disk will be formatted as a single partition for use as a backup device; consequently, the existing partitions and all data contained within will be erased. It is not necessary to format this partition because the Backup Schedule Wizard formats the disk; nor is it necessary to create a folder to hold the backups. You cannot configure a portable hard disk for dynamic storage.

5. C. You must perform an authoritative restore of the user account to prevent its deletion again when AD DS replication propagates changes to other domain controllers. This will happen because the user account's update sequence number (USN) is lower than the current object's USN that is used to determine

what changes are replicated to other domain controllers. The authoritative restore increases the restored object's USN by 100,000, making it higher than the current object's USN. This is not a case of a newer backup having occurred since the deletion. Forcing a replication will not help because the USN is lower than the current object's USN. It is not necessary to perform a bare-metal recovery of any domain controller.

6.   B. Windows Server 2008 R2 offers a new check box labeled **Perform an authoritative restore of Active Directory files**, found on the Select location for System State Recovery page of the Recovery Wizard. It isn't possible to restore AD DS without the need for restarting the computer in Directory Services Restore Mode. The capabilities of restoring system state files to an alternative location and performing a bare-metal recovery of the server have been present in previous Windows Server versions, and are not new to Windows Server 2008 R2.

7.   D. This scenario requires that you restart the server from the Windows Server 2008 R2 DVD-ROM, select **Repair your computer**, and then select **System Image Recovery**. This enables you to perform a full server recovery of the domain controller. You cannot simply restore the server's system state (which you would do from Directory Services Restore Mode and not from Safe Mode) under these conditions. It is also not possible to perform a full server recovery from Directory Services Restore Mode; the `wbadmin start systemimagerecovery` command is not valid.

8.   B, C. You need to upgrade the domain and forest functional levels to Windows Server 2008 R2. You then need to use `Ldp.exe` to enable the Active Directory Recycle Bin. You cannot use this feature at the Windows Server 2008 domain or forest functional levels. The `Ldifde.exe` utility does not allow you to enable this feature, nor is it accessible from the **Advanced features** option from the View menu in Active Directory Users and Computers.

9.   B. GPMC enables you to back up a single GPO or all the GPOs in the domain. `wbadmin` and Windows Server Backup would back up the GPOs as a component of system state, but it is simpler to perform this backup from GPMC. `Ntdsutil` performs a large number of administrative functions, but backing up GPOs is not one of them.

10. A. You should use the Services snap-in to stop AD DS. You can also open a command prompt and type the `net stop ntds` command to perform this task. Restarting the domain controller in Directory Services Restore mode or in Safe Mode with Networking would stop the domain controller from performing DHCP and file services actions. Copying the database file to a separate computer also would not work.

11. D. You must perform an offline defragmentation of the database to recover the space once used by the deleted objects. Although tombstoning exists as described, this process does not affect the space used by the database file. Simply defragmenting the hard disk does not work because the unused space is still present in the `ntds.dit` file and not as free space on its hard disk. Backing up and restoring data will not change the overall file size.

12. C. You should use the `net stop ntds` command to stop AD DS and then use the `ntdsutil` utility to move the `ntds.dit` file. You must use this utility to make sure that the appropriate Registry settings are also modified. You could restart the server in Directory Services Restore mode and then use `ntdsutil` to move the file. This was the method you would have needed in older Windows versions. It is still valid but takes more administrative effort than simply stopping AD DS; Microsoft is always looking for the simplest way to perform a task in any exam question. You cannot use Windows Explorer to move the file because this method would not automatically modify the Registry.

Chapter 16

1. A. Of the items mentioned, only the support for cross-forest certificate enrollment is new to Windows Server 2008 R2. The other items mentioned are all included in the original version of Windows Server 2008.

2. D. A three-tier PKI hierarchy includes all of root CA, intermediate CA, and issuing CA, whereas a two-tier hierarchy consists of only a root CA and issuing CA. Enterprise and standalone CAs are types of CAs according to whether they are integrated with AD DS.

3. A. You should keep a standalone root CA offline as a safeguard against compromise. You should bring this CA online only to issue certificates to CA servers lower in the CA hierarchy. You should not use an enterprise root CA for this purpose because it would become out of date with respect to other AD DS servers. Intermediate and issuing CAs are involved in active day-to-day issuing of certificates and must not be allowed to go offline.

4. C. You always install the root CA first when setting up your CA hierarchy. Then you would install the intermediate CAs (if you are setting up a three-tier hierarchy) and finally the issuing CAs. The root CA can be either an enterprise or standalone CA, although Microsoft recommends a standalone CA so that it can be kept offline except when needed for generating certificates for other CAs in the hierarchy.

5. B. When installing any subordinate CA, such as an intermediate CA, you must have a certificate issued by the parent CA. A CRL is generated at a later time

after you have set up your CA hierarchy. IIS is installed with either a root or subordinate CA to provide access to the web enrollment pages. You can set up a standalone CA hierarchy that is not integrated with AD DS in any way, so AD DS is not a requirement.

6. A, B, C, D, E, F, G. All of these types of information are valid components of a certificate practice statement.

7. D. The certificate store is a protected area of the Registry on all server and client computers. Within the store is a series of sub-stores that include certificates for various purposes. The certificate store is not a text document nor is it a folder or series of folders.

8. B, C, E. Any of these procedures will back up Certificate Services. There is no specific Certificate Services folder. The Certificate Export Wizard enables you to make a backup of a certificate but does not enable backing up Certificate Services. The Certificates snap-in does not provide an option for backing up Certificate Services.

9. B. The Certificate Manager administrative role enables the role holder to approve certificate enrollment and revocation requests without receiving additional privileges. The CA Administrator role would grant this individual additional administrative capabilities. None of the other roles mentioned here would grant the individual the required capability.

Chapter 17

1. A. Only version 1 certificate templates are supported on computers running Windows 2000. Version 2 templates are supported on computers running Windows XP, Windows Server 2003, and later. Version 3 templates are supported only on computers running Windows Vista, Windows 7, or Windows Server 2008. As of 2010, there is no such thing as Version 4.

2. B. The Request Handling tab contains options that specify the amount of user input required during certificate enrollment, including a **Prompt the user during enrollment** setting that prompts the user to enter her PIN for the smart card. The General tab enables you to specify validity and renewal periods. The Cryptography tab enables you to define the encryption and hash algorithms and minimum key sizes used. The Issuance tab enables you to specify default issuance criteria. The Security tab enables you to specify template permissions, including autoenrollment.

3. B, D, E. To enable a certificate template for autoenrollment, you must allow the Read, Enroll, and Autoenroll permissions. Users do not require the Full Control or Write permissions for autoenrollment.

4.   C. You should duplicate the template and configure the duplicate for auto-enrollment. The Smartcard User template is a version 1 template that was originally supplied with Certificate Services in Windows 2000. It does not support autoenrollment. By duplicating this template, you can create either a version 2 or version 3 template, both of which support autoenrollment. You do not need a certificate from a third-party certification authority. Logging on as a member of the Enterprise Admins group does not provide the Autoenroll permission. The Autoenroll permission is required for certificate autoenrollment to be available; you cannot enable autoenrollment by selecting the existing Read and Enroll permissions.

5.   B, C, E. You need to duplicate an existing template. Then you need to select the **Archive subject's encryption private key** option, which is found on the Request Handling tab of the template's Properties dialog box. Then you need to enable the template for certificate issuance from the Enable Certificate Templates dialog box. The Key Recovery Agent template and the **Archive the key** option are used only for key recovery and not key archival.

6.   D. Network Device Enrollment Service (NDES) enables network devices to enroll for certificates. You do not need key recovery agents or web-based certificate enrollment for this purpose. OCSP is the Online Certificate Status Protocol, which enables rapid certificate status validations. It also does not enroll certificates for network devices.

7.   B. This set of options will enable you to select a 4096-bit key size option from the Key size drop-down list available on the Advanced Certificate Request page of the web-based certificate enrollment pages. The SHA1 hash algorithm is not relevant to the requirements specified here. The **Use existing key set** option would not enable you to choose the required key size. Selecting the **User certificate** option from the Request a Certificate page would use the default 1024-bit key size option.

8.   A. The Enrollment Agents tab of the certificate server's Properties dialog box enables you to define a restricted enrollments agent policy. By default, the Enrollment Agents section of this tab contains the Everyone group, so you must remove this group. However, you must add the Certificate Issuers (or other required) group before you can remove the Everyone group (and not the other way around). The Security tab of either the certificate server's or template's Properties dialog box does not enable you to define restricted enrollment agents.

9.   B. Group Policy enables you to enforce use of smart cards by enabling the **Interactive logon: Require smart card** policy setting. This setting is found in the Security Options subnode and not under Account Policies. You could

choose the **Smart card is required for interactive log on** option; however, in a domain with a large number of users this would take far more administrative effort. It is not necessary to create an OU to enforce use of smart cards, although this might be an option if you want to enforce smart card use for only a specific subset of users in your domain.

10. C. By choosing the **Certificate Hold** reason code, you can unrevoke a certificate later. This is the only reason code that enables this action. Because you can use this reason code, it is not necessary to re-enroll the user for a new certificate when she returns from maternity leave.

11. D. A CDP is a location on the network from which applications can locate the most recent base and delta CRLs to check for certificate validity. The Extensions tab of the CA's Properties dialog box enables you to add, remove, or modify CDPs in issuing certificates. The CDP is specified from the CA's properties dialog box and not from the Revoked Certificates Properties dialog box. The values of base and delta CRLs are not relevant to this situation.

12. A, E. You should enable the use of the OCSP Response Signing certificate template. This enables the installation of an OCSP Response Signing certificate on the computer on which the online responder role service is installed. You also must select the URL for the online responder and select the check boxes labeled **Include in the AIA extension of issued certificates** and **Include in the online certificate status protocol (OCSP) extension**. You should also ensure that IIS is installed on the CA servers. The online responder clients use this URL to check certificates for revocation. You do not need to use CRLs, delta CRLs, and CRL distribution points. If you do not select the **Include in the online certificate status protocol (OCSP) extension** check box, clients will be unable to locate the online responder server.

Installing Windows Server 2008 R2

Before you can even begin to work with Active Directory in Windows Server 2008 R2, you must install a copy of the server software on your computer. This appendix provides you with guidance on the server installation procedure, which is not covered in any current Microsoft server exam but nevertheless is an essential topic that you must master.

Windows Server 2008 R2 Hardware Requirements

As with previous Windows versions, your hardware must meet certain requirements in order that Windows Server 2008 R2 will function properly. First, Windows Server 2008 R2 requires a 64-bit processor; Microsoft has discontinued 32-bit software with this release of Windows Server. Table B-1 outlines the minimum and recommended hardware requirements for Windows Server 2008 R2 as provided by Microsoft:

Table B-1 Windows Server 2008 R2 Hardware Requirements

Component	Minimum Requirement	Microsoft Recommended
Processor	1.4 GHz	2 GHz or faster
Memory	512 MB RAM	2 GB RAM or greater
Available Disk Space	32 GB	40 GB or greater
Optical Drive	DVD-ROM drive	DVD-ROM drive
Display	Super VGA (800 × 600) monitor	XGA (1024 × 768) monitor

In addition, you must have the usual I/O peripherals, including a keyboard and Microsoft Mouse or compatible pointing device, and a wired or wireless network interface card (NIC). If you can connect to a network location on which you have copied the contents of the Windows Server 2008 R2 DVD-ROM, you are not required to have a DVD-ROM drive on your computer. As with any other operating system installation, you will receive improved performance if you have a faster processor and additional memory on your system.

Further, when you install Windows Server 2008 R2 on an Itanium-based computer, you must have an Intel Itanium 2 processor and additional hard disk space. Computers with more than 16 GB RAM require additional disk space for paging, hibernation, and dump files. With disk space at an all-time minimum cost, it is easy to acquire a high-capacity hard disk. You will certainly need plenty of disk space on a server that will be a domain controller in a large domain.

Microsoft recommends that you also perform the following actions before installing Windows Server 2008 R2:

- **Disconnect uninterruptible power supply (UPS) devices:** If you are using a UPS, disconnect its serial or USB cable before installing Windows Server 2008 R2.

- **Back up data:** Perform a complete backup of configuration information for your servers, especially network infrastructure servers such as DHCP servers. The backup should include the boot and system partitions as well as the system state data.

- **Disable antivirus software:** Antivirus software can interfere with operating system installation.

- **Run the Windows Memory Diagnostic tool:** This tool tests your computer's RAM. For more information, refer to the Windows Memory Diagnostic Users Guide at http://oca.microsoft.com/en/windiag.asp.

- **Provide mass storage drivers if needed:** Save the driver file to appropriate media so that you can provide it during setup.

- **Note that Windows Firewall is on by default:** Server applications that require inbound connections will fail until you create inbound firewall rules that allow these connections. For more information, refer to "Windows Firewall" at http://technet.microsoft.com/en-us/network/bb545423.aspx.

- **Prepare your Active Directory environment for the Windows Server 2008 R2 domain controller:** Before adding a Windows Server 2008 R2 domain controller or updating an existing domain controller to Windows Server 2008 R2, prepare the domain and forest by running Adprep.exe. We discussed this tool in Chapter 3, "Installing Active Directory Domain Services."

Manually Installing Windows Server 2008 R2

As with other Microsoft operating systems, you can perform a manual or automated installation of Windows Server 2008 R2. Automated installation of Windows Server 2008 R2 simplifies the task of installing multiple servers and uses a technology such as Sysprep or Windows Deployment Services (WDS). The end of this appendix presents a brief summary of these techniques.

Installing a Complete Server

The procedure for installing Windows Server 2008 R2 is the same whether you're installing directly from a DVD-ROM or a network share, except that you must have some type of network client installed on your computer to access a network share. The following procedure outlines installation from a DVD-ROM:

Step 1.   Insert the Windows Server 2008 R2 DVD-ROM and turn on your computer. You should see a message informing you that Windows is loading files; if not, you should access the BIOS setup program included with your computer and modify the boot sequence so that the computer boots from the DVD.

Step 2.   After a few minutes, you receive the Install Windows screen shown in Figure B-1. Ensure that the options displayed are correct and then click **Next**.

Figure B-1   Starting the installation of Windows Server 2008 R2.

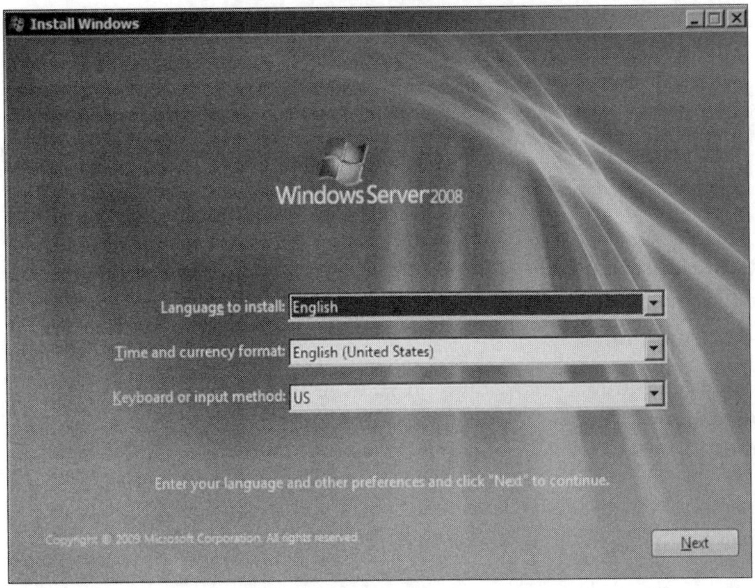

Step 3.   On the next Install Windows screen, click **Install now**.

Step 4.   You receive the options shown in Figure B-2, which enables you to install the complete version of Windows Server 2008 R2 or Windows Server 2008 R2 Core. Select the complete installation and then click **Next**.

Step 5.   Read and accept the licensing terms and then click **Next**.

Step 6.   You receive the option to upgrade or install a clean copy of Windows Server 2008 R2. Select **Custom (advanced)** to install a clean copy of Windows Server 2008 R2. The upgrade option is available only if you have started the installation from within Windows Server 2003 or Windows Server 2008.

Step 7.   Select the disk on which you want to install Windows and then click **Next**.

Figure B-2 This screen enables you to select either the complete installation of Windows Server 2008 R2 or the Server Core option.

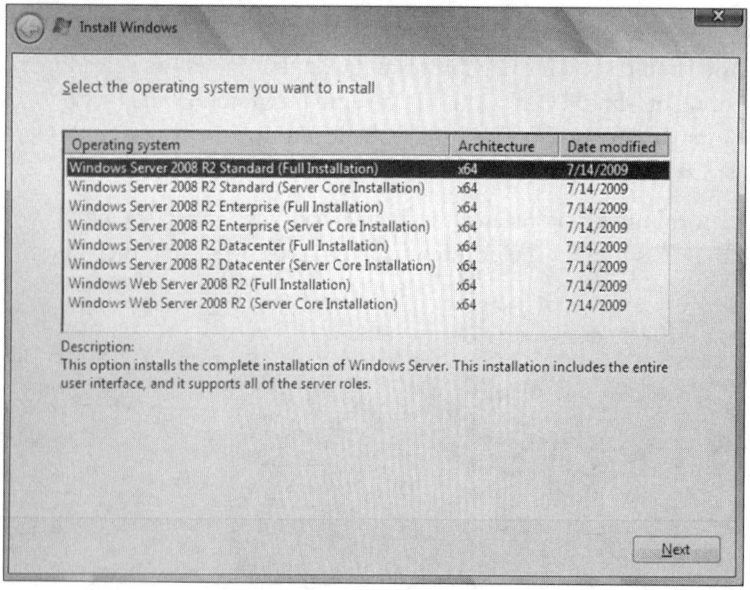

Step 8. Take a coffee break while the installation proceeds. This takes some time (particularly when installing on a virtual machine), and the computer restarts several times.

Step 9. After 30 to 60 minutes (depending on your hardware), Windows restarts a last time and informs you that your password must be changed before logging on for the first time. Click **OK**.

Step 10. Type and confirm a secure password. Windows informs you that your password has been changed. Click **OK**.

Step 11. Windows displays a Welcome message and prepares your desktop. Then the Initial Configuration Tasks screen shown in Figure B-3 appears.

Step 12. Follow the instructions provided by this screen. In particular, ensure that you have configured your network settings, set the correct time zone, and configured the appropriate computer name and domain settings.

After you have performed the initial configuration steps, you will be prompted to press **Ctrl+Alt+Delete** and enter your password when you restart your server.

TIP When you shut a Windows Server 2008 R2 computer down, it displays the Shutdown Event Tracker dialog box, which asks you for a reason for shutting down the server. For learning purposes, it is helpful to disable this item. You can do so by typing `gpedit.msc` to open the Local Group Policy Object Editor. Navigate to

Computer Configuration\Administrative Templates\System, right-click the **Display Shutdown Event Tracker** policy, and click **Properties.** On the dialog box that appears, click **Disabled** and then click **OK.**

Figure B-3   The Initial Configuration Tasks screen enables you to perform a basic set of configuration tasks on your new server.

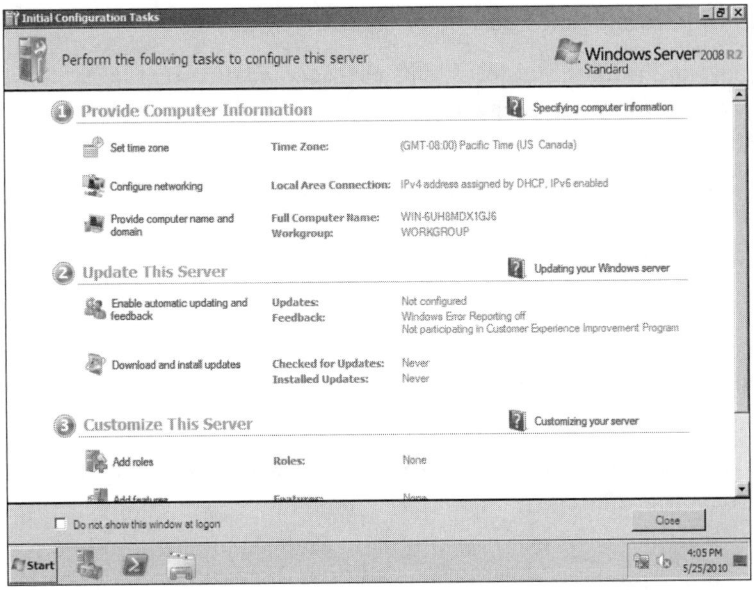

Installing a Windows Server Core Computer

As explained in Chapter 1, "Getting Started with Active Directory," Windows Server Core is a new feature of Windows Server 2008 R2 that installs a minimal version of the server software without the GUI; you perform all configuration tasks from the command prompt. Follow this procedure to install Windows Server Core and perform initial configuration tasks:

Step 1.   Follow the procedure outlined earlier for installing a full version of Windows Server 2008 R2 until you receive the screen previously shown in Figure B-2.

Step 2.   Select the **Windows Server 2008 R2 Standard (Server Core Installation)** option, and then click **Next**.

Step 3.   Complete steps 6–9 of the earlier procedure. Installation will take 20–45 minutes, depending on your hardware.

Step 4.   When installation completes, the computer reboots. As instructed, press **Ctrl+Alt+Delete** to log on and log on as Other User.

Step 5.   Type **administrator** and click the arrow provided to complete the logon. After a minute or so, the desktop appears, containing a command window but no Start menu, taskbar, or desktop icons. This is the standard Windows Server Core interface.

Step 6.   To set the correct time, type **control timedate.cpl.** By default, Server Core sets the time zone to Pacific Time. If you are in a different time zone, you will need to change this. Set the appropriate time zone, change the date and time if necessary, and then click **OK.**

Step 7.   To set an administrator password, type **net user administrator *.** Follow the prompts to type and confirm a secure password for this account.

Step 8.   Windows installs Server Core with a randomly generated computer name. To set a name of your choice, type **netdom renamecomputer %computername% /newname:ServerC1** (where, in this instance, *ServerC1* is the name you're assigning; substitute your desired server name).

Step 9.   Windows warns you that the rename process might have an adverse impact on some services. Type **Y** to proceed and then type **shutdown /r /t 0** to reboot your server.

Step 10.   After the server reboots, press **Ctrl+Alt+Delete** and log on using the password you set in step 7.

Useful Server Core Commands

All configuration, management, and troubleshooting of Windows Server Core is done from the command line. Available utilities enable you to perform almost all regular configuration tasks in this fashion. Table B-2 describes some of the more useful available commands:

Table B-2   Useful Windows Server Core Commands

Command	Meaning
netdom join *computername* /domain:*domainname*	Joins an Active Directory domain. You will be prompted for the username and password of a user with domain administrator privileges.
cscript scregedit.wsf	Enables automatic updates.
oclist	Displays roles currently installed on the server.

Table B-2   Useful Windows Server Core Commands

Command	Meaning
ocsetup	Adds or removes roles.
dcpromo	Installs Active Directory. Refer to Chapter 3 for more information.
ServerManagerCmd	Installs and removes roles, role services, and features. Also lists installed and available roles, role services, and features.
netsh interface IPv4	Includes a series of subcommands that enable you to configure IPv4 networking.
netsh advfirewall	Includes subcommands that enable you to configure the Windows firewall.
Help	Provides a list of all available Windows Server Core commands.

Available commands also include most commands formerly used with MS-DOS and previous Windows versions.

NOTE   For additional information on installing Windows Server Core, as well as any of these commands or other commands available in Windows Server Core, type the command name followed by /? or consult the Server Core Installation Option Getting Started Guide at http://technet.microsoft.com/en-us/library/cc753802(WS.10).aspx.

Upgrading a Windows Server 2003 or 2008 Computer

You can upgrade a computer running Windows Server 2003 with Service Pack 1 (SP1) or later to Windows Server 2008 R2 provided that the computer meets the hardware requirements for Windows Server 2008 R2. You cannot upgrade a Windows 2000 or older computer or a computer running any client version of Windows to Windows Server 2008 R2.

To upgrade to Windows Server 2008 R2, proceed as follows:

Step 1.   While logged on to Windows Server 2003 or Windows Server 2008 as an administrator, insert the Windows Server 2008 R2 DVD-ROM.

Step 2.   When the Install Windows screen appears, click **Install Now**.

Step 3. Select your operating system, either the standard or Windows Core version of Windows Server 2008 R2 and then click **Next**.

Step 4. Accept the licensing terms and then click **Next**.

Step 5. On the Which Type of Installation Do You Want? page, select **Upgrade**.

> **WARNING** When upgrading a Windows Server 2003 or 2008 installation, you must upgrade the same server version. For example, if you have the Enterprise version of Windows Server 2003, you must upgrade to Windows Server 2008 R2 Enterprise. Otherwise, the Upgrade option will be unavailable on the Which Type of Installation Do You Want? page.

Step 6. Windows checks compatibility of your hardware and software and displays a compatibility report that informs you of any potential upgrade problems. Review this report and make any changes you feel are required. When you are ready to proceed, click **Next**.

Step 7. Take a lunch break while the upgrade proceeds. This will take 60 minutes or longer, depending on your hardware configuration or use of virtual computing software. The server will reboot three or four times.

Step 8. After the final reboot, log on using the password previously used in Windows Server 2003 or 2008. Windows prepares your desktop and displays the Initial Configuration Tasks screen previously shown in Figure B-3.

> **NOTE** For additional information on or and upgrading to Windows Server 2008 R2 including a detailed list of supported upgrade paths, refer to "Installing Windows Server 2008 R2" at http://technet.microsoft.com/en-us/library/dd379511(WS.10).aspx.

Automating Windows Server 2008 R2 Installation

If you need to install Windows Server 2008 R2 on a series of computers in your organization, the following methods are available:

■ **Answer files:** This is an XML-based file (`unattend.xml`) that contains the operating system settings required for an unattended installation of Windows

Vista, Windows 7, or Windows Server 2008 R2. If you have prepared the answer file properly, the server installation proceeds without intervention. Windows Server 2008 R2 provides the Windows System Image Manager utility to facilitate the creation of properly formatted answer files.

- **Sysprep:** Sysprep prepares a Windows installation for copying to additional computers. It removes computer-specific information such as the server name. You can use third-party disk imaging software to prepare multiple copies for distribution to new servers. As well as the Windows Server 2008 R2 installation, images can include installations of a common set of software to be used on all servers. For more information, refer to "Sysprep Technical Reference" at http://technet.microsoft.com/en-us/library/dd744263(WS.10).aspx.

- **Microsoft Deployment Toolkit (MDT) 2010:** MDT is a Microsoft Solution Accelerator that is used for deployment of operating systems and applications. A *solution accelerator* is a set of documents, scripts, job aids, and methodologies that assist IT professionals in designing, deploying, and maintaining Microsoft technologies. For more information, refer to "Microsoft Deployment Toolkit" at http://technet.microsoft.com/en-us/library/dd407791.aspx.

- **Windows Deployment Services (WDS):** WDS is an upgrade to Remote Installation Services (RIS), which was used for deploying installations of Windows 2000/XP/Server 2003 in a domain environment. Similar to RIS, you must have an Active Directory domain, a DHCP server, and DNS to use WDS. WDS can deploy images of either Windows 7 or Windows Server 2008 R2. For more information, refer to "Windows Deployment Services Getting Started Guide" at http://technet.microsoft.com/en-us/library/cc771670(WS.10).aspx.

NOTE   For additional information on Windows Server 2008 R2 deployment, refer to any preparation book for Exam 70-646, PRO: Windows Server 2008, Server Administrator, or exam 70-647, PRO: Windows Server 2008, Enterprise Administrator.

Glossary

account lockout

A series of policy settings that locks a user out of an account after a predetermined number of incorrect attempts at entering a password has occurred. This increases security by foiling random dictionary-based or brute-force password hack attempts.

account partner

In AD FS, an organization that has been granted access to a resource partner's web-based application. Users in the account partner can access this application without the need for a separate user account in the resource partner's domain.

account policies

A series of settings in Group Policy that determine the characteristics of an acceptable password as well as account lockout settings and Kerberos settings.

Active Directory Administrative Center

A new Active Directory snap-in in Windows Server 2008 R2 that enables the administration of most Active Directory functions from a single console.

Active Directory Application Mode (ADAM)

A standalone mode of Active Directory that enables organizations to use directory-enabled applications in their own directory, with its own schema, independently of the main corporate Active Directory database.

Active Directory Federation Services (AD FS)

A set of technologies in Windows Server 2008 that enables partner companies to access Active Directory resources across the Internet in a trusted manner, without having to have user accounts in the resource domain.

Active Directory Lightweight Directory Service (AD LDS)

An update to ADAM that provides directory services for directory-enabled applications on Windows networks without the need for deploying additional domains or domain controllers.

Active Directory Migration Tool (ADMT)

A utility that enables you to move objects such as users, groups, and computers between Active Directory domains in the same or different forests.

Active Directory Recycle Bin

A new feature of AD DS in Windows Server 2008 R2 that enables you to recover deleted objects without the need to perform a restore operation.

Active Directory Rights Management Services (AD RMS)

A directory service that uses a certification base to confirm the identity of users of information on the network, thereby enabling you to create and work with rights-protected information, and ensure that only authorized users have access to these items.

Active Directory Service Interfaces (ADSI)

A directory service model implemented as a set of COM interfaces. ADSI allows Windows applications to access Active Directory, often through ActiveX interfaces such as VBScript.

Active Directory–integrated zone

A DNS zone that is hosted on a domain controller and stored in one or more AD DS application directory partitions.

AD LDS instances

A single running copy of the AD LDS directory service, which includes a separate directory data store, a unique service name, and a unique service description.

administrative templates

The section of Group Policy from which administrators can configure settings that are applied to users' desktops, specify programs that users can run, and so on. They apply changes to client computer Registry settings.

ADMX central store

The new storage location in Windows Server 2008 that considerably reduces the quantity of storage space required for GPO maintenance, especially in a large domain with many OUs and many linked GPOs.

Adprep

A utility that prepares a Windows 2000 or Windows Server 2003 forest or domain for receiving domain controllers running Windows Server 2008. It has several parameters, the most important of which are `forestprep`, which prepares the forest, and `domainprep`, which prepares the domain.

ADSI Edit

A utility that enables you to view and edit information about any AD DS or AD LDS object, including schema and configuration data.

AGDLP

An acronym that stands for Microsoft's recommendation of placing Accounts into Global groups, then placing these groups into Domain Local groups, and finally granting Permissions to the domain local groups.

AGUDLP

An acronym that stands for Microsoft's recommendation of placing Accounts into Global groups, then placing these groups into Universal groups, then placing these groups into Domain Local groups, and finally granting Permissions to the domain local groups.

application directory partition

A partitioned section of Active Directory that is replicated only to specified domain controllers. Application data partitions are used by applications (in particular, DNS) to store their application-specific data.

assigned applications

Through the Software Installation utility in Group Policy, administrators can assign applications to users and computers. Assigned applications are always available to the user, even if the user attempts to uninstall them. Applications assigned to a computer will automatically be installed on the next restart.

attribute

The basic unit of an object, an attribute is a single property contained in the schema that through its values defines the object. For example, an attribute of a standard user account is the account name.

auditing

A security process that tracks the usage of selected network resources, typically storing the results in a log file.

Auditpol.exe

A command-line tool that enables you to configure audit policy settings and directory service auditing subcategories.

authentication scope

The range within which AD DS will authenticate a user from another domain. When defining a trust relationship, you can use this option to restrict the level of access external users will have when accessing resources in a trusted domain.

authoritative restore

A type of AD DS restore operation in which restored objects will replace updated objects in the directory. This process increases the restored object's update sequence number (USN) by 100,000, making it higher than the current object's USN.

Authority Information Access (AIA)

A certificate extension that points to URLs at which you can retrieve an issuing CA's certificate.

autoenrollment

The ability to automatically enroll users and computers for certificates, retrieve existing certificates, and renew expired certificates without user intervention.

BitLocker

A feature of Windows Server 2008 and Windows 7 that enables you to encrypt the entire contents of any hard drive partition on your computer. It is useful for protecting sensitive data on computers such as laptops or branch office domain controllers that are susceptible to theft.

block inheritance

A Group Policy setting that prevents a child container from applying GPO settings linked to higher containers. For example, you can use Block Inheritance at the organizational unit (OU) level so that only OU-level policies are applied.

bridgehead server

The contact point for the exchange of directory information between Active Directory sites.

built-in account

A user account that is created by default when Windows is installed on a computer. An example is the local Administrator account.

certificate

A method of granting access to a user based on unique identification. Certificates represent a distinctive way to establish a user's identity and credentials. They originate from a certification authority (CA).

certification authority (CA)

A trusted authority either within a network or a third-party company that manages security credentials such that it guarantees the user object that holds a certificate is who it claims to be.

certificate enrollment

The process by which users and computers can be given permission to make requests for certificates, retrieve existing certificates, and renew expired certificates. Each CA that is installed on a server has web pages that users can access to submit basic and advanced certificate requests.

certificate revocation list (CRL)
A document published by a CA that lists certificates that have been issued but are no longer valid. By default, the CA publishes the CRL on a weekly basis.

certificate stores
Places where certificates are stored, which are located in a protected area of the Registry. A series of certificate stores can exist for each user, computer, and service.

certificate template
Provided by AD CS to simplify the process of requesting and issuing certificates for various purposes. Each template contains the rules and settings that must be in place to create a certificate of a certain type. Certificate templates are available only on enterprise root and subordinate CAs.

claim
In AD FS, a statement made by a server about a client, such as its name, identity, key, group, privilege, or capability. You can enable specific claim types that are accepted by the account partner, and claims that fail to match these types will be rejected. Claim types can include identity claims, group claims, or custom claims, and identity claims can include UPN claims, email claims, and common name claims.

claim mapping
In AD FS, the act of processing incoming claims to the resource application hosted by the resource federation service.

class
A series of attributes associated with each schema object. The attributes associated with each class are defined by a classSchema object in the schema.

conditional forwarding
The relaying of a DNS request for zone information for specific domains from one server to another one, when the first server is unable to process the request.

connection object
An Active Directory object stored on domain controllers that is used to represent inbound replication links. Domain controllers create their own connection objects for intrasite replication through the Knowledge Consistency Checker (KCC), whereas only a single domain controller in a site creates connection objects for intersite replication through the Intersite Topology Generator.

container
An object in Active Directory that is capable of holding other objects. An example of a container would be the Users folder in Active Directory Users and Computers.

credential caching

The storing of a limited set of passwords on an RODC. You can configure credential caching to store only those passwords of users authorized to log on at a given RODC.

CRL distribution point (CDP)

A certificate extension that indicates URL locations where a CRL can be retrieved. Multiple HTTP, FTP, FILE, or LDAP locations can be included.

Csvde

A utility that imports comma-separated text files into the AD DS database. You can use this utility to automate the bulk creation of user or group accounts.

Data collector sets

Binary files that save performance statistics for later viewing and analysis in the Performance Monitor snap-in; you can also export them to spreadsheet or database programs for later analysis.

dcdiag

Also called the Domain Controller Diagnostic Tool, this tool analyzes the condition of domain controllers. The output of this tool informs you of any problems, thereby assisting you in troubleshooting domain controllers.

dcpromo

The command-line utility used to promote a Windows Server 2008 system to a domain controller. dcpromo could also be used to demote a domain controller to a member server.

delta CRL

A CRL that includes the list of certificates revoked since the issuance of the most recent complete (base) CRL. Its use optimizes bandwidth usage in situations where certificates are frequently revoked.

Directory Services Restore Mode (DSRM)

A special version of Safe Mode in which a domain controller is restarted as a standalone server. The directory database is rendered offline so that you can perform operations such as restoring the AD DS database.

Distributed File System (DFS)

A Windows Server 2008 service that allows resources from multiple server locations to be presented through Active Directory as a contiguous set of files and folders, resulting in greater ease of use of network resources for users.

DNS notify

A process in which the master DNS server for a zone notifies secondary servers of changes so that the secondary servers can check to determine whether they need to initiate a zone transfer.

dnscmd

A command-line tool that can perform most of the DNS server administrative tasks in Windows Server 2008.

DNSSEC (Domain Name System Security Extensions)

A suite of DNS extensions that adds security to the DNS protocol by providing origin authority, data integrity, and authenticated denial of existence. It enables DNS servers to use digital signatures to validate responses from other servers and resolvers.

domain controller (DC)

A server that is capable of performing authentication. In Windows Server 2008, a domain controller holds a copy of the Active Directory database.

domain functional level

Windows Server 2008 R2 domains can operate at one of four functional levels: Windows 2000 native, Windows Server 2003 native, Windows Server 2008, or the Windows Server 2008 R2 functional level. Each functional level has different tradeoffs between features and limitations.

domain local group

A domain local group can contain other domain local groups from its own domain as well as global groups from any domain in the forest. A domain local group can be used to assign permissions for resources located in the same domain as the group.

Domain Name System (DNS)

A hierarchical name-resolution system that resolves hostnames into IP addresses, and vice versa. DNS also makes it possible for the distributed Active Directory database to function by allowing clients to query the locations of services in the forest and domain.

domain naming master

One of the two forestwide flexible single master operations (FSMO) roles, the domain naming master's job is to ensure domain name uniqueness within a forest.

domain user account

A user account that is stored in the AD DS database. It permits a user to log on to any computer in the domain in which it is located or a trusted domain.

Dsadd

A command-line tool that enables you to add objects such as users, groups, contacts, or computers to the AD DS database.

dynamic DNS (DDNS)

An extension of DNS that allows Windows 2000 and later computers to automatically register their A records with DNS at the time they obtain an IP address from a DHCP server.

Dynamic Host Configuration Protocol (DHCP)
A service that enables an administrator to specify a range of valid IP addresses to be used on a network, as well as exclusion IP addresses that should not be assigned (for example, if they were already statically assigned elsewhere). These addresses are automatically given out to computers configured to use DHCP as they boot up on the network, thus saving the administrator from having to configure static IP addresses on each individual network device.

enforced
A Group Policy setting available to GPMC that enforces the application of a GPO to all lower-level containers. For example, an enforced domain-level policy is applied to all OUs in the domain regardless of settings in OU-based GPOs.

enrollment agent
A user who has been issued a special certificate that grants the owner of the certificate the authority to enroll users into advanced security and issue certificates on behalf of the users.

enterprise CA
A CA that is integrated with AD DS. Enterprise CAs replicate certificates with AD DS replication and require that users be authenticated.

Event Viewer
A Microsoft Management Console (MMC) snap-in that enables an administrator to view and/or archive event logs on a Windows 2000/XP/2003/Vista/Windows 7/Server 2008 computer. You can monitor information about application, security, system, DNS, and Active Directory events.

external trust
A trust relationship created between a Windows Server 2008 Active Directory domain and a Windows NT 4 domain, or between Active Directory domains in different forests.

federated application
In AD FS, a web-based application that is configured so that users in an organization connected by means of a federation trust can be authenticated to access this application without the need for a separate AD DS user account.

federation trust
In AD FS, a relationship between two organizations that allows for access to web-based applications without establishing an external or forest trust between the organizations' domains.

filtering
A Group Policy option that enables you to limit the effect of a GPO according to definitions such as security group membership or Windows Management Instrumentation (WMI).

fine-grained password policies
A new feature of Windows Server 2008 that enables you to configure password policies that apply only to specific users or groups within a domain.

flat namespace
A namespace that cannot be partitioned to produce additional domains. Windows NT domains were examples of flat namespaces, as opposed to the Windows Server 2008 hierarchical namespace.

flexible single-master operations (FSMO) servers
Five roles required by AD DS in Windows Server 2008 that do not follow the typical multimaster model and instead are hosted on only a single domain controller in each domain, in the case of the infrastructure master, PDC emulator, and RID master, or on only a single domain controller in the forest, in the case of the domain naming master and the schema master.

forest functional level
The four forest functional levels are Windows 2000, Windows Server 2003, Windows Server 2008, and Windows Server 2008 R2. The default forest functional level is Windows Server 2003. When the forest functional level is raised to Windows Server 2008 or Windows Server 2008 R2, advanced forestwide Active Directory features are available according to the level chosen.

forest root
The first domain created in a forest.

forest trust
A trust relationship established between two Active Directory forests.

forward lookup query
A DNS name-resolution process by which a hostname is resolved to an IP address.

forwarding
The relaying of a DNS request from one server to another one when the first server is unable to process the request.

full zone transfer (AXFR)
A zone transfer in which the master server transmits the entire zone database to that zone's secondary servers.

fully qualified domain name (FQDN)
A DNS domain name that unambiguously describes the location of the host within a domain tree. An example of an FQDN would be the computer www.certguide.com.

global catalog (GC)
Contains a partial replica of every Windows Server 2008 domain object within the Active Directory, enabling users to find any object in the directory. The partial replica contains the most commonly used attributes of an object, as well as information on how to locate a complete replica elsewhere in the directory, if needed.

global catalog server
The Windows Server 2008 server that holds the global catalog for the forest.

global group
A global group can contain users from the same domain that the global group is located in, and global groups can be added to domain local groups to control access to network resources.

Gpresult
A command-line utility that displays information about the current effect Group Policy has had on the local computer and logged-in user account.

Gpupdate
A tool that refreshes Group Policy settings so that computers and users receive them more rapidly after you have modified policy settings.

Group Policy
The Windows Server 2008 feature that allows for policy creation, which affects domain users and computers. Policies can be anything from desktop settings to application assignments to security settings and more.

Group Policy Management Console (GPMC)
The MMC snap-in from which you can perform all management activities on GPOs including such functions as creating and linking GPOs, modifying their inheritance, disabling or deleting them, and so on.

Group Policy Management Editor
The Microsoft Management Console (MMC) snap-in that is used to modify the settings of a Group Policy object.

Group Policy Modeling
Also known as *RSoP planning mode*; predicts the effect of applying a set of GPOs to a specified user/computer combination before these GPOs have actually been applied, thereby performing a "what-if" analysis of applying the GPOs.

Group Policy object (GPO)
A collection of policies that apply to a specific target, such as the domain itself (Default Domain Policy) or an organizational unit (OU). GPOs are modified through the Group Policy Management Editor to define policy settings.

Group Policy Results
Also known as *RSoP logging mode*; provides the ability to determine which policies are currently being applied to an object.

Hyper-V
The new virtualization tool included with the 64-bit editions of Windows Server 2008 that enables you to run multiple instances of the operating system on a single server.

incremental zone transfer (IXFR)
A zone transfer in which the master server transmits only the modified portion of each zone file to that zone's secondary servers.

infrastructure master
The FSMO role that is responsible for receiving replicated changes from other domains within the forest and replicating these changes to all domain controllers within its domain. There is one infrastructure master per domain, and it also is responsible for tracking what Active Directory container an object is located in.

inheritance
The process by which an object obtains settings information from a parent object.

instance
Multiple occurrences of a given object being monitored in Performance Monitor. For example, if your computer has two hard disks, two instances of the PhysicalDisk object will be present.

intermediate CA
Found in a three-tier CA hierarchy, this CA is directly subordinate to the root CA and issues certificates that validate the issuing CAs. Organizations commonly situate intermediate CA servers in different geographical locations such as cities in which offices are located.

Intersite Topology Generator (ISTG)
The Windows Server 2008 server that is responsible for evaluating and creating the topology for intersite replication.

issuing CA
A CA server that is involved in the day-to-day issuing of certificates for computers and users on the network.

key recovery agent (KRA)

A user who possesses a certificate for recovering private keys archived by the CA. Employing a KRA helps to ensure that private keys belonging to deleted users will not be permanently lost.

Knowledge Consistency Checker (KCC)

A Windows Server 2008 service that functions to ensure consistent database information is kept across all domain controllers. It attempts to ensure that replication can always take place.

Ldifde

A utility that enables you to import data formatted in the LDAP Data Interchange Format (LDIF) format to the AD DS database. You can use this tool to automate the creation of user, computer, or group accounts.

Ldp.exe

A GUI-based tool that enables you to perform several types of administrative actions on any LDAP directory service, including AD DS and AD LDS.

linked policy

A Group Policy that exists in one object and is linked to another object. Linked policies are used to reduce administrative duplication in applying the same policies to multiple OUs.

linked value replication

A feature that replicates only the changes in group membership of AD DS users rather than replicating the whole membership when a change occurs, thereby enabling you to replicate changes in group membership more efficiently.

local user account

A user account that is stored in the SAM of a member server or client computer. Such an account can be used to log on to that computer only, and does not possess any domain privileges.

loopback processing

A special mode of processing GPOs in which computer settings prevail over user settings, as opposed to the opposite (normal) sequence. It is useful in situations such as kiosks where computers are freely accessible to the public.

mandatory upgrade

An upgrade to an existing software package deploying using Group Policy that is automatically installed to all computers and users to which the software policy applies.

nesting

The act of creating a hierarchy of groups, in order to provide users from different containers (domains, OUs, and so on) access to the resources they require for their jobs.

Network Device Enrollment Services (NDES)
An AD CS role service that enables software on network devices such as routers and switches to enroll for X.509 certificates from a server running AD CS.

Network Monitor
A utility that enables you to capture, view, and analyze frames transmitted across the network to network adapter cards on your computer. It is useful for detecting incursions by unauthorized users and tracing their activity on the network.

nonauthoritative restore
An AD DS restore operation in which restored objects are not marked as authoritative.

non-dynamic DNS (NDDNS)
A type of DNS that does not update automatically; this was the default prior to Windows 2000. At that time, the administrator was required to enter A records manually to keep the DNS database up-to-date.

ntds.dit
The AD DS database file.

Ntdsutil
A command-line utility that provides a number of Active Directory management functions.

object
A distinct entity represented by a series of attributes within Active Directory. An object can be a user, group, computer, folder, file, printer, and so on.

one-way trust
A trust relationship that operates in only a single direction. For example, users in domain A can access resources in domain B, but users in domain B cannot access resources in domain A. You can configure one-way trusts to Active Directory domains, Windows NT domains, or Kerberos realms outside your forest.

Online Certificate Status Protocol (OCSP)
A protocol that enables rapid certificate status validations. AD CS in Windows Server 2008 includes an OCSP Responder role service.

online responder
An optional role service in AD CS that is new to Windows Server 2008. It is based on OCSP and provides signed responses to clients requesting revocation information for certificates issued by the CA that signed the OCSP signing certificate.

operations master
A Windows Server 2008 domain controller that has been assigned one or more of the special Active Directory domain roles, such as schema master, domain naming master, PDC emulator, infrastructure master, and relative identifier (RID) master.

optional removal
A method of removing software in Group Policy that allows users to continue using an outdated software package that is no longer supported.

optional upgrade
An upgrade to a software package deployed using Group Policy that a user is not forced to install.

package
A collection of software compiled into a distributable form, such as a Windows Installer (.msi) package created by the software creator or by using a third-party packaging product such as Veritas WinInstall.

partial attribute set
A schema attribute that tracks the internal replication status of partial replicas, such as those found on GC servers.

password complexity
A rule that can be applied using Group Policy that prevents users from employing simple, easy-to-guess passwords. The default password complexity requires at least three of the following four groups: lowercase letters, uppercase letters, numerals, and special characters.

password policy
Policy settings in a domain-based GPO that specify the requirements for passwords in the domain.

password replication policy
A policy setting that enables you to define which passwords are stored by default on an RODC. You can specify which user accounts and groups are allowed to cache their passwords and which ones are denied this capability.

password settings object (PSO)
An object class defined in the AD DS schema that holds attributes for the fine-grained password and account lockout policy settings.

patch files
Files issued by an application developer that correct a minor bug or provide additional capability to an application already in use.

Performance counter
A statistical measurement associated with a performance object such as %disk time, queue length, and so on.

Performance Monitor

A monitoring tool that provides a comprehensive capability to monitor a large number of metrics that analyze every component of your server's performance.

Performance object

Hardware or software components that the Performance Monitor can use for tracking performance data.

primary domain controller (PDC) emulator

The domain-level FSMO role that serves to replicate data with Windows NT 4 BDCs in a domain, in effect functioning as an NT 4 PDC. This server also functions as a time synchronization master, ensuring that all computers in the domain have the same time configured.

primary zone

A master copy of DNS zone data hosted on a server that is the primary source of information for records found in this zone.

Protected Admin

An administrative user account other than the default domain administrator, which operates normally with ordinary user rights and asks for confirmation of any administrative task by displaying a User Account Control (UAC) prompt.

public and private keys

Used in public key encryption, a public key and private key are generated by a CA, and these keys are returned to the client in the form of digital certificates. The public key is given to those who need to encrypt data and send it to the client. The client then decrypts the data using its private key, which only the client has.

public key infrastructure (PKI)

An industry-standard technology that allows for the establishment of secure communication between hosts based on a public key/private key or certificate-based system.

published applications

Through the Software Installation utility in Group Policy, administrators can publish applications to users. Published applications appear in Add or Remove Programs (XP) or Programs and Features (Vista/7) and can be optionally installed by the user.

read-only domain controller (RODC)

A Windows Server 2008 feature in which the domain controller is installed with a read-only directory database. You cannot perform any directory updates directly from the RODC. It is especially suitable in reduced security environments such as branch offices.

realm trust
A trust relationship in Windows Server 2008 that is created between an Active Directory domain and a UNIX realm.

recursion
The name-resolution technique wherein a DNS server queries other DNS servers on behalf of the requesting client to obtain the required FQDN, which it returns to the client.

redeployment
The process of reinstalling a modified application using Group Policy to computers covered by the Group Policy object (GPO) that originally deployed the application.

relative identifier (RID)
The part of the security identifier (SID) that uniquely identifies an account or group within a domain.

relative identifier (RID) master
The domain-level FSMO role responsible for managing pools of RIDs and ensuring that every object in the domain gets a unique RID.

Reliability Monitor
A monitoring tool that provides a trend analysis of your computer's system stability with time. It shows how events such as hardware or application failures, software installations or removals, and so on affect your computer's stability.

repadmin
Active Directory Replication Administrator, a command-line utility that enables administrators to monitor AD DS replication. You can view the domain controller's replication topology, monitor the status of replication, display replication metadata, force replication between domain controllers, and force the KCC to recalculate replication topologies.

replication
The process of copying data from one Windows Server 2008 domain controller to another. Replication is a process managed by an administrator and typically occurs automatically whenever changes are made to a replica of an object.

replication scope
The subset of DNS servers or domain controllers that actively participate in replication of the specific zone.

replmon

Active Directory Replication Monitor, a GUI-based tool that enables you to monitor AD DS replication. Although still based on Windows Server 2003 R2, this tool functions properly with Windows Server 2008 and Windows Server 2008 R2. You can also use this utility to display and recalculate the replication topology and force replication.

resource partner

In AD FS, an organization that hosts a server containing a web-based application that has been configured for access by users in the trusted organization.

resource records

Standard database record types used in DNS zone database files. Common types of resource records include Address (A or AAAA), Mail Exchanger (MX), Start of Authority (SOA), and Name Server (NS), among others.

Resultant Set of Policy (RSoP)

A Windows Server 2008 Group Policy tool that lets you simulate the effects of group policies without actually implementing them. RSoP has two modes: logging mode and planning mode. Logging mode determines the resultant effect of policy settings that have been applied to an existing user and computer based on a site, a domain, or an organizational unit. Planning mode simulates the resultant effect of policy settings that are applied to a user and computer.

reverse lookup query

A DNS name-resolution process by which an IP address is resolved to a hostname.

role-based administration

The act of assigning predefined task-based PKI administrative roles to different individuals. Best practices suggest that you should divide these roles among several individuals to ensure that no single person can compromise your PKI.

root CA

The topmost CA in a PKI hierarchy, this is the most authoritative certificate server. You should protect this server with the highest level of security possible, such as storing it in a vault. If it is compromised, the entire PKI hierarchy is compromised.

root hints

A list of the names and IP addresses of DNS servers that are authoritative for the Internet root domains. Used by a DNS server to forward queries for Internet domains that it is unable to resolve from its own database.

round robin

A load-balancing mechanism used by DNS servers to distribute name resolution activity among all available DNS servers.

scavenging

The process by which a DNS server searches for and deletes aged (stale) resource records.

schema

In Active Directory, a schema is a database that contains the description of object classes and the attributes that the object classes must possess and can possess.

schema master

The Windows Server 2008 domain controller that has been assigned the operations master role to control all schema updates within a forest.

secondary zone

An additional copy of DNS zone data hosted on a DNS server that is a secondary source for this zone information.

secure dynamic DNS (SDDNS)

An enhancement to DNS that enables you to permit dynamic updates only from authorized client computers in an Active Directory–integrated zone.

secure zone transfer

A method of digitally signing zone transfers that enables secondary DNS servers to verify that zone transfers are being received from a trusted source.

security identifier (SID)

A number that uniquely identifies a user, group, or computer account. Every account is issued one when created, and if the account is later deleted and re-created with the same name, it will have a different SID. After an SID is used in a domain, it can never be used again.

seizing a role

The act of moving an operations master role from one domain controller to another when the original role holder is no longer available on the network. You cannot seize a role if the original role holder is available; you must transfer it instead. After you have seized a role, you cannot bring back the original role holder without reinstalling Active Directory in most cases.

Server Core

A new feature of Windows Server 2008 that enables you to install a minimal version of the server without a GUI, Start menu, taskbar, or many ancillary components. A Server Core computer can hold most of the roles that an ordinary Windows Server 2008 computer holds, but with a smaller network footprint and fewer points of attack.

shortcut trust

A Windows Server 2008 trust relationship between two domains within the same forest. Shortcut trusts are used to reduce the path authentication needs to travel by directly connecting child domains.

SID filtering

A mechanism that validates the SIDs of users in a trusted domain that is attempting to authenticate across a trust relationship to a trusting domain. It enhances security by verifying that the authentication request contains SIDs of security principals in the trusted domain only.

Single Sign-on (SSO)

The ideal of having one username and password that works for everything on a network. Windows Server 2008 features such as Active Directory Federation Services bring this closer to reality than ever before.

site

A physical component of Active Directory. Sites are created for the purpose of balancing logon authentication with replication. They can have zero (in planning), one, or multiple IP subnets. These subnets should be well-connected with fast LAN links.

site link

A connection between sites, a site link is used to join multiple locations together.

site link bridge

A collection of site links that helps Active Directory work out the cost of replicating traffic from one point to another within the network infrastructure that is not directly connected by a single site link. By default, all site links are bridged, but this can be disabled in favor of manually configured site link bridges.

site link cost

A way for AD DS to determine what path to replicate traffic over on a routed network. The lower the cost, the more preferable it is for AD DS to use a particular site link. For example, if you have a T1 and an ISDN site link connecting the same sites, the T1 site link would have a lower cost than the ISDN site link, making it the preferred path for traffic.

smart card

A credit-card–sized device that is used with an access code to enable certificate-based authentication and single sign-on to the enterprise. Smart cards securely store certificates, public and private keys, passwords, and other types of personal information. A smart card reader attached to the computer reads the smartcard.

standalone CA

A CA whose database is stored locally and not integrated with AD DS. Typically, an organization will have a standalone root CA coupled with enterprise subordinate CAs. This practice enables the administrator to keep the standalone root CA offline and secured in a safe location such as a vault. It is brought back online only when required for issuing certificates to subordinate CAs.

Starter GPOs

Sets of preconfigured Administrative Templates policy settings, including comments, which you can use for ease of creating new GPOs. When you use a Starter GPO to create a new GPO, the new GPO includes all settings, their values, comments, and delegation as defined in the Starter GPO.

stub zone

A DNS zone that contains source information about authoritative name servers for its zone only. The DNS server hosting the stub zone obtains its information from another server that hosts a primary or secondary copy of the same zone data.

subordinate CA

A CA whose certificates come from a root CA, whose job is to issue certificates to users and computers on the network. Each subordinate CA can be dedicated to a single type of certificate, such as smart cards, Encrypting File System (EFS), or to a geographical location of a multisite network.

syskey

A locally stored system key that encrypts the SAM database on Windows 2000 and later computers. It is required for computers to start. For added security, you can remove this key and store it on a floppy disk or specify a password to be entered manually on startup.

system state data

Operating system–specific data that is backed up by the Windows Server Backup program as a unit. It contains the Registry, COM+ class registration database, and system and boot files; on domain controllers, it includes the AD DS database and the SYSVOL folder.

Task Manager

An administrative utility that provides data about currently running processes, including their CPU and memory usage, and enables you to modify their priority or shut down misbehaving applications.

template account

A special account created for the sole purpose of copying as needed when creating a large number of user accounts with similar privileges.

time to live (TTL)
The amount of time a packet destined for a host will exist before it is deleted from the network. TTLs are used to prevent networks from becoming congested with packages that cannot reach their destinations.

transferring a role
The act of moving one of the operations masters roles from one domain controller to another when the original role holder is available on the network. You cannot transfer the role if the original holder is not available.

transform files
Modifications to a Windows Installer software package distributed in the form of .mst files. You can use transform files to modify the behavior of a package being deployed using Group Policy—for example, to include foreign languages in Microsoft Office.

transitive trust
An automatically created trust in Windows Server 2008 that exists between domain trees within a forest and domains within a tree. Transitive trusts are two-way trust relationships. Unlike the situation with Windows NT 4, transitive trusts in Windows Server 2008 can flow between domains. This way, if Domain1 trusts Domain2, and Domain2 trusts Domain3, Domain1 automatically trusts Domain3.

two-way trust
A relationship between domains in which the two domains act as both trusting and trusted; in other words, users and groups in either domain can access resources in the other domain. It is merely a combination of trust relationships in opposite directions.

universal group
An Active Directory group that can be used anywhere within a domain tree or forest.

universal principal name (UPN)
An alternative username that is formatted in a manner similar to that of an email address (for example, user@domain.com). Its use enables a user to more easily log on to a domain in the forest other than the domain to which the user belongs.

universal principal name (UPN) suffix
The portion of the UPN following the "@" character. By default, this is the DNS domain name of the domain in which the user account is located. However, you can define an alternative UPN suffix that enables you to conceal the actual domain structure of the forest or match the user's email address domain name.

User Account Control (UAC)
Starting with Windows Vista and continued in Windows 7 and Windows Server 2008, a new feature called User Account Control (UAC) requires users performing administrative tasks to confirm that they actually initiated the task. UAC displays a prompt that requests approval when you want to perform an administrative task. Should malicious software attempt to install itself or perform undesirable actions, you will receive a prompt that you can use to prevent such actions from occurring.

user logon name
The name employed by a user to log on to a domain. AD DS uses this name and its associated password to authenticate the user.

user principal name (UPN)
An alternative username that is formatted in a manner similar to that of an email address (for example, user@domain.com). Its use enables a user to more easily log on to a domain in the forest other than the domain to which the user belongs.

user principal name (UPN) suffix
The portion of the UPN following the @ character. By default, this is the DNS domain name of the domain in which the user account is located. However, you can define an alternative UPN suffix that enables you to conceal the actual domain structure of the forest or match the user's email address domain name.

versions 1, 2, and 3 templates
Certificate templates that support various versions of Windows operating systems and include features compatible with these and later operating systems. Version 1 templates were introduced with Windows 2000. Version 2 templates were introduced with Windows XP and Windows Server 2003. Version 3 templates were introduced with Windows Vista and Windows Server 2008 and are also used with Windows 7 and Windows Server 2008 R2.

wbadmin.exe
A command-line tool that enables you to perform backups and restores. In Windows Server 2008, this is the only tool that you can use to perform system state backups and restores.

Windows Installer
A feature of Active Directory that provides for automated installation and repair of applications across the network. It also provides for cleaner and more efficient removal of old software without leaving unused .dll files or removing those also used by other programs.

Windows Management Instrumentation (WMI)

A Windows Server 2008 management infrastructure for monitoring and controlling system resources.

Windows Server virtualization

The capability of running multiple copies of different operating systems on a single server. The 64-bit edition of Windows Server 2008 and Windows Server 2008 R2 contains a built-in virtualization capability known as Hyper-V. You can use Microsoft Virtual Server 2005 on 32-bit editions of Windows Server 2008 or on older Windows Server versions.

Windows System Resource Manager (WSRM)

A administrative feature that enables you to control how processor and memory resources are allocated to applications, services, and processes running on the server.

zone

A discrete portion of the local or Internet-based DNS namespace, for which a single DNS server is authoritative.

zone delegation

The act of dividing the DNS namespace into a series of zones and delegating their management by creating resource records in other zones that point to the authoritative DNS servers for the zone being delegated.

Index

Browse by Exams ▲ | Browse by Technology ▲ | Browse by Format | Explore ▲ | I'm New Here – Help!

Store | Forums | Safari Books Online

Your Publisher for IT Certification

Pearson IT Certification is the leader in technology certification learning and preparation tools.

Visit **pearsonITcertification.com** today to find

- **CERTIFICATION EXAM** information and guidance for IT certifications, including

  cisco. | CompTIA | **Microsoft**

- **EXAM TIPS AND TRICKS** by reading the latest articles and sample chapters by Pearson IT Certification's expert authors and industry experts, such as
  - Mark Edward Soper and David Prowse – CompTIA
  - Wendell Odom – Cisco
  - Shon Harris – Security
  - Thomas Erl – SOACP

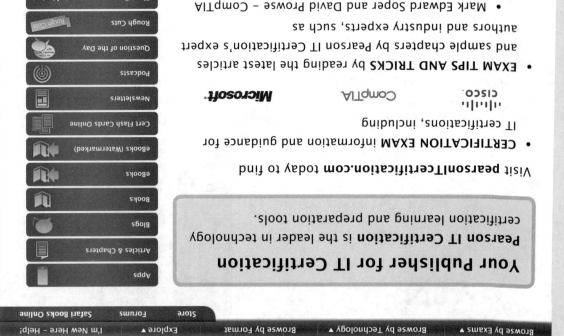

- **SPECIAL OFFERS** (pearsonITcertification.com/promotions)
- **REGISTRATION** for your Pearson IT Certification products to access additional online material and receive a coupon to be used on your next purchase

Be sure to create an account on **pearsonITcertification.com** and receive member's–only offers and benefits.

Pearson IT Certification is a publishing imprint of Pearson

Connect with Pearson IT Certification

pearsonITcertification.com/newsletters

 twitter.com/pearsonITCert

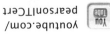 facebook.com/pearsonitcertification

youtube.com/pearsonITCert

pearsonitcertification.com/rss/

Apps
Articles & Chapters
Blogs
Books
eBooks
eBooks (Watermarked)
Cert Flash Cards Online
Newsletters
Podcasts
Question of the Day
Rough Cuts
Short Cuts
Videos